Cybersecurity Measures for Logistics Industry Framework

Noor Zaman Jhanjhi
Taylor's University, Malaysia

Imdad Ali Shah
Taylor's University, Malaysia

A volume in the Advances in Logistics,
Operations, and Management Science (ALOMS)
Book Series

Published in the United States of America by
    IGI Global
    Information Science Reference (an imprint of IGI Global)
    701 E. Chocolate Avenue
    Hershey PA, USA 17033
    Tel: 717-533-8845
    Fax: 717-533-8661
    E-mail: cust@igi-global.com
    Web site: http://www.igi-global.com

Library of Congress Cataloging-in-Publication Data

Names: Jhanjhi, Noor Zaman, 1972- editor. | Shah, Imdad Ali, 1975- editor.
Title: Cybersecurity measures for logistics industry framework / edited by
  Noor Zaman Jhanjhi, and Imdad Ali Shah.
Description: Hershey, PA : Information Science Reference, [2024] | Includes
  bibliographical references and index. | Summary: "Cybersecurity Measures
  for Logistics Industry Framework discusses the environment of the
  logistics industry in the context of new technologies and cybersecurity
  measures. Covering topics such as AI applications, inventory management,
  and sustainable computing, this premier reference source is an excellent
  resource for business leaders, IT managers, security experts, students
  and educators of higher education, librarians, researchers, and
  academicians"-- Provided by publisher.
Identifiers: LCCN 2023004840 (print) | LCCN 2023004841 (ebook) | ISBN
  9781668476253 (hardcover) | ISBN 9781668476260 (paperback) | ISBN
  9781668476277 (ebook)
Subjects: LCSH: Computer security. | Business logistics. | Data protection.
  | Inventory control.
Classification: LCC HF5548.37 .C936 2023 (print) | LCC HF5548.37 (ebook)
  | DDC 658.4/78--dc23/eng/20230209
LC record available at https://lccn.loc.gov/2023004840
LC ebook record available at https://lccn.loc.gov/2023004841

This book is published in the IGI Global book series Advances in Logistics, Operations, and Management Science (ALOMS) (ISSN: 2327-350X; eISSN: 2327-3518)

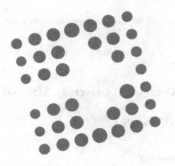

Advances in Logistics, Operations, and Management Science (ALOMS) Book Series

John Wang
Montclair State University, USA

ISSN:2327-350X
EISSN:2327-3518

MISSION

Operations research and management science continue to influence business processes, administration, and management information systems, particularly in covering the application methods for decision-making processes. New case studies and applications on management science, operations management, social sciences, and other behavioral sciences have been incorporated into business and organizations real-world objectives.

The **Advances in Logistics, Operations, and Management Science** (ALOMS) Book Series provides a collection of reference publications on the current trends, applications, theories, and practices in the management science field. Providing relevant and current research, this series and its individual publications would be useful for academics, researchers, scholars, and practitioners interested in improving decision making models and business functions.

COVERAGE

- Risk Management
- Networks
- Finance
- Computing and information technologies
- Marketing engineering
- Organizational Behavior
- Decision analysis and decision support
- Operations Management
- Information Management
- Services management

IGI Global is currently accepting manuscripts for publication within this series. To submit a proposal for a volume in this series, please contact our Acquisition Editors at Acquisitions@igi-global.com or visit: http://www.igi-global.com/publish/.

Titles in this Series

For a list of additional titles in this series, please visit: http://www.igi-global.com/book-series/advances-logistics-operations-management-science/37170

Convergence of Industry 4.0 and Supply Chain Sustainability
Muhammad Rahies Khan (Bahria University Karachi, Pakistan) Naveed R. Khan (UCSI University, Malaysia) and Noor Zaman Jhanjhi (Taylor's University, Malaysia)
Business Science Reference • © 2024 • 320pp • H/C (ISBN: 9798369313633) • US $275.00

Achieving Secure and Transparent Supply Chains With Blockchain Technology
Mustafa Rehman Khan (UCSI University, Malaysia) Naveed Rehman Khan (UCSI University, Malaysia) and Arsalan Mujahid Ghouri (London South Bank University, UK)
Business Science Reference • © 2024 • 345pp • H/C (ISBN: 9798369304822) • US $275.00

Strategies and Approaches of Corporate Social Responsibility Toward Multinational Enterprises
Erum Shaikh (Shaheed Benazir Bhutto University, Sanghar Campus, Pakistan)
Business Science Reference • © 2024 • 400pp • H/C (ISBN: 9798369303634) • US $275.00

Drivers of SME Growth and Sustainability in Emerging Markets
Sumesh Dadwal (Northumbrian University, UK) Pawan Kumar (Lovely Professional University, India) Rajesh Verma (Lovely Professional University, India) and Gursimranjit Singh (Dr.B.R Ambedkar National Institute of Technology, Jalandhar)
Business Science Reference • © 2024 • 330pp • H/C (ISBN: 9798369301111) • US $250.00

Emerging Technologies in Digital Manufacturing and Smart Factories
Ahdi Hassan (Global Institute for Research Education and Scholarship, The Netherlands) Pushan Kumar Dutta (Amity University Kolkata, India) Subir Gupta (Swami Vivekanand University, India) Ebrahim Mattar (College of Engineering, University of Bahrain, Bahrain) and Satya Singh (Sharda University, Uzbekistan)
Business Science Reference • © 2024 • 291pp • H/C (ISBN: 9798369309209) • US $275.00

Implementing Sustainable Development Goals in the Service Sector
Vipin Nadda (University of Sunderland, UK) Pankaj Kumar Tyagi (Chandigarh University, India) Rubina Moniz Vieira (St. Mary's University, London, UK) and Priyanka Tyagi (Chandigarh University, India)
Business Science Reference • © 2024 • 281pp • H/C (ISBN: 9798369320655) • US $275.00

Effective Human Resources Management in the Multigenerational Workplace
Angela M. Even (Purdue University, USA) and Bryan Christiansen (Southern New Hampshire University, USA)
Business Science Reference • © 2024 • 304pp • H/C (ISBN: 9798369321737) • US $325.00

701 East Chocolate Avenue, Hershey, PA 17033, USA
Tel: 717-533-8845 x100 • Fax: 717-533-8661
E-Mail: cust@igi-global.com • www.igi-global.com

Table of Contents

Chapter 11
QR Multilevel Codes to Reduce Cybersecurity Risks in the Logistics of Freight Transport in Ports 322
Gerardo Reyes Ruiz, Center for Higher Naval Studies (CESNAV), Mexico

Detailed Table of Contents

Chapter 1

    Azeem Khan, Sultan Sharif Ali Islamic University, Brunei
    Noor Zaman Jhanjhi, School of Computer Science, SCS, Taylor's University, Subang Jaya,
        Malaysia
    Haji Abdul Hafidz B. Haji Omar, Sultan Sharif Ali Islamic University, Brunei
    Dayang Hajah Tiawa B. Awang Haji Hamid, Sultan Sharif Ali Islamic University, Brunei

Transportation and warehousing are vital components of logistics corporations. Their continuous uninterrupted functioning is of paramount significance for the enterprises involved in the supply chain. As these enterprises are built and rely heavily on digital technologies for their rapid functioning, they are vulnerable to cybersecurity threats and attacks. Hence, to effectively address and promptly respond to these issues organizations need to have proper strategy and planning in place. This chapter endeavors to acquaint readers with these pressing issues. To secure warehousing operations and transportation systems, the methods and tools for assessing the risks and mitigating them are discussed comprehensively.

Chapter 2

    Brendan Ooi Tze Wen, Taylor's University, Malaysia
    Najihah Syahriza, Taylor's University, Malaysia
    Nicholas Chan Wei Xian, Taylor's University, Malaysia
    Nicki Gan Wei, Taylor's University, Malaysia
    Tan Zheng Shen, Taylor's University, Malaysia
    Yap Zhe Hin, Taylor's University, Malaysia
    Siva Raja Sindiramutty, Taylor's University, Malaysia
    Teah Yi Fan Nicole, Taylor's University, Malaysia

This chapter explores the topic of a novel network-based intrusion detection system (NIDPS) that utilises the concept of graph theory to detect and prevent incoming threats. With technology progressing at a rapid rate, the number of cyber threats will also increase accordingly. Thus, the demand for better network security through NIDPS is needed to protect data contained in networks. The primary objective of this chapter is to explore the concept of a novel graph based NIDPS through four different aspects:

data collection, analysis engine, preventive action, and reporting. Besides analysing existing NIDS technologies in the market, various research papers and journals were explored. The authors' solution covers the basic structure of an intrusion detection system, from collecting and processing data to generating alerts and reports. Data collection explores various methods like packet-based, flow-based, and log-based collections in terms of scale and viability.

Chapter 3

Sidra Tahir, UIIT, Pakistan
Anam Zaheer, UIIT, Pakistan

Anomaly detection in IoT-based sleep patterns is crucial for early identification of health issues. This chapter presents a distributed model using federated learning for privacy and data security. The proposed approach involves data collection, preprocessing, model initialization, federated learning server, model distribution, and anomaly detection. Sleep pattern data is preprocessed to extract features, initializing the global anomaly detection model. A federated learning server enables collaborative learning with devices, distributing the updated global model iteratively for synchronized anomaly detection. Precision and accuracy metrics yielded 0.67% precision and 0.84% accuracy, showcasing the effectiveness of the distributed model. Leveraging federated learning ensures privacy, data security, and synchronized anomaly detection across devices, supporting early detection of sleep-related anomalies and health interventions.

Chapter 4

Tayyab Rehman, Air University, Pakistan
Noshina Tariq, Air University, Pakistan
Muhammad Ashraf, Air University, Pakistan
Mamoona Humayun, Jouf University, Saudi Arabia

Network intrusions through jamming and spoofing attacks have become increasingly prevalent. The ability to detect such threats at early stages is necessary for preventing a successful attack from occurring. This survey chapter thoroughly overviews the demand for sophisticated intrusion detection systems (IDS) and how cutting-edge techniques, like federated learning-enabled IDS, can reduce privacy risks and protect confidential data during intrusion detection. It explores numerous mitigation strategies used to defend against these assaults, highlighting the significance of early detection and avoidance. The chapter comprehensively analyzes spoofing and jamming attacks, explores mitigation techniques, highlights challenges in implementing federated learning-based IDS, and compares diverse strategies for their real-world effects on network security. Lastly, it presents an unbiased evaluation of contemporary IDS techniques, assessing their advantages, disadvantages, and overall effect on network security while also discussing future challenges and prospects for academia and industry.

Noshina Tariq, Air University, Pakistan
Tehreem Saboor, Air University, Pakistan
Muhammad Ashraf, Air University, Pakistan
Rawish Butt, Air University, Pakistan
Masooma Anwar, Air University, Pakistan
Mamoona Humayun, Jouf University, Saudi Arabia

The internet of things (IoT) refers to the network of connected devices embedded in everyday objects that enable digital transformation. The rapid proliferation of IoT devices has led to significant advancements in technology and data exchange capabilities. However, the security of user data and IoT systems has become a paramount concern. This chapter focuses on the security challenges and approaches in IoT. Various attacks, such as denial of service, password guessing, replay, and insider attacks, pose significant threats to IoT security. It investigates the state-of-the-art technologies, future challenges and open issues currently facing IoT security. The findings from this chapter serve as a foundation for future work in improving IoT security and protecting user data effectively.

Sidra Tahir, UIIT, Pakistan

Numerous technologies that automate processes and simplify our lives are included in smart homes. These gadgets may be helpful for various things, including temperature, lighting, and security access. Smart homes fundamentally enable remote control of equipment and appliances for homeowners via the internet of things (IoT) platform. Smart houses are able to understand their owners' routines and modify in accordance with their capacity for self-learning. The requirement to identify abnormalities in data created by smart homes arises from the necessity of convenience and cost savings in such a setting, as well as from the involvement of numerous devices. The topic of anomaly detection using deep learning is covered in this chapter. Additionally, the suggested solution is more secure because to the usage of block chain technology. Results show that the suggested strategy has exceptional accuracy and recall.

Siva Raja Sindiramutty, Taylor's University, Malaysia
Noor Zaman Jhanjhi, Taylor's University, Malaysia
Chong Eng Tan, Universiti Malaysia Sarawak, Malaysia
Navid Ali Khan, Taylor's University, Malaysia
Bhavin Shah, Lok Jagruti University, India
Loveleen Gaur, University of South Pacific, Fiji

The digital supply chain has become an integral part of modern business operations, enabling efficient and streamlined processes. However, with the rapid advancement of technology, the supply chain landscape has become increasingly vulnerable to cyber threats and attacks. This chapter explores the critical issue of cybersecurity within the context of the digital supply chain, aiming to equip professionals and practitioners with the knowledge and strategies to safeguard their operations. Lastly, the chapter sheds light on emerging technologies and future trends and concludes with a call to action for securing the digital supply chain. It also highlights the future challenges and directions in cybersecurity for the supply chain, urging professionals to stay vigilant and adapt to evolving strategies and technologies. Overall, this chapter serves as a comprehensive guide for securing the digital supply chain, empowering readers to fortify their operations against cyber threats and ensure the resilience of their supply chain networks.

   Azeem Khan, Sultan Sharif Ali Islamic University, Brunei
   Noor Zaman Jhanjhi, School of Computer Science, SCS, Taylor's University, Subang Jaya,
      Malaysia
   Dayang Hajah Tiawa Binte Awang Haji Hamid, Sultan Sharif Ali Islamic University, Brunei
   Haji Abdul Hafidz B. Haji Omar, Sultan Sharif Ali Islamic University, Brunei

The impact of the internet of things (IoT) on inventory management is explored in this chapter. The chapter discusses comprehensively IoT system components, communication protocols, their architectures, and applications in various sectors. This chapter also investigates how IoT enabled inventory can provide real-time inventory management through timely monitoring, tracking, and optimization of inventories by employing RFID tags and readers. The RFID tags include encoded data in the form of unique IDs, which facilitates effective tracking and monitoring of goods and services pertaining to an organization. RFID readers can detect tags and transmit data encoded in it to the cloud for processing, thereby resulting in well informed data-driven decisions with improved operational efficiency. Furthermore, the chapter explores inventory management processes in the context of IoT-enabled inventories. The chapter also presents a comprehensive comparison of IoT enabled inventories with the traditional inventory management systems.

   Siva Raja Sindiramutty, Taylor's University, Malaysia
   Noor Zaman Jhanjhi, Taylor's University, Malaysia
   Chong Eng Tan, Universiti Malaysia Sarawak, Malaysia
   Navid Ali Khan, Taylor's University, Malaysia
   Abdalla Hassan Gharib, Zanzibar University, Tanzania
   Khor Jia Yun, Tunku Abdul Rahman University of Management and Technology, Malaysia

In this chapter, the authors delve into the utilization of blockchain technology within the realm of supply chain management. The emergence of blockchain technology has heralded substantial progress across diverse sectors, and the domain of supply chain management is undeniably one of them. The decentralized and immutable characteristics of blockchain present a promising resolution to endure hurdles encountered by stakeholders in supply chain management. These challenges encompass issues of transparency, traceability, and efficiency. The abstract commences by acknowledging the transformative essence of blockchain technology, underscoring its profound influence across various sectors. It subsequently narrows its focus to explore the specific applications within the domain of supply chain management. The chapter undertakes an in-depth examination of the multifaceted challenges faced by supply chain stakeholders and elucidates how blockchain technology adeptly tackles these predicaments.

Chapter 10

Supply chains are affected by globalization and digitalization, and organizations face a great challenge in order to stay up-to date and competitive. As a very significant element of the supply chains, inventory management plays a crucial role in supply chain success. Therefore, traditional approaches in inventory management should be altered according to new trends. From this point of view, this study focuses on Internet of Things (IoT) applications in inventory management with a scope of supply chains. The aim of this chapter is to analyze the current studies related to IoT impacts in inventory management by conducting a literature review and a bibliometric analysis, and propose the future research directions that are interrelated with the current trends.

Chapter 11

A country's national security depends on many combined and constantly changing factors. However, one of the most preponderant aspects is the access control of goods and people entering and leaving the country through its customs, as a result of mobility and international trade currently taking place. Throughout the territory of a country, the entry and exit of both merchandise and people of different natures or nationalities, respectively, are carried out by different means of transport. Therefore, it is necessary to establish more efficient control points that manage, supervise, and, where appropriate, tax this activity, because otherwise products, materials, or people that pose a risk to human health may enter the country. In this context, this chapter shows a practical tool, based on multilevel QR codes, to improve the identification and supervision of goods entering a country through its port customs to show a technology that reduces cybersecurity risks in freight transport logistics.

Preface

Dear Readers,

It is with great pleasure that we present to you the edited reference book, *Cybersecurity Measures for Logistics Industry Framework*, edited by Prof. Dr. Noor Zaman Jhanjhi and Imdad Ali Shah. In a world where global supply chains are undergoing a transformative shift towards customer-centricity and sustainability, the role of logistics management technologies becomes increasingly pivotal.

The landscape of logistics is evolving rapidly, driven by innovations that automate procedures, enhance productivity, and foster dynamic relationships among stakeholders. The need for transparency and traceability in the supply chain has never been more pronounced. Against this backdrop, our in-depth study delves into the Top Logistics Industry Trends & Startups, evaluating 901 worldwide startups and scale-ups.

In the last two years, supply chain challenges have taken center stage due to the far-reaching implications of the pandemic on health, travel, and the economy. From shortages of used vehicle parts to workforce deficits, industries across the board have felt the impact. The response to these challenges has been a significant push towards digitization, connecting people globally and streamlining operations. However, as highlighted by Mike Wilson in Forbes, this digital transformation introduces new security concerns that cannot be overlooked.

The Insights Discovery Platform, fueled by Big Data and Artificial Intelligence, has been instrumental in our research, covering over 2 million startups and scale-ups globally. This platform offers an in-depth assessment of industry innovations and early identification of relevant startups and scale-ups.

The primary objective of this publication is to provide a comprehensive understanding of the logistics industry in the context of new technologies. The generic roadmap of this book is designed to cater to a diverse audience, including academics, employees, businessmen, and citizens alike.

The chapters within this book explore a wide range of topics, from the challenges and perspectives of Logistics with the Internet of Things to the impact of Artificial Intelligence on Supply Chain Risk Management. The inclusion of chapters on Advanced Robotics Software, Blockchain Technology in the Supply Chain, and Cyber Risks in Logistics reflects the multidimensional nature of the logistics industry in the contemporary era.

We believe that the insights presented in this book will not only contribute to the academic discourse but also serve as a valuable resource for professionals navigating the evolving landscape of logistics and technology. As we embark on this journey through the pages of *Cybersecurity Measures for Logistics Industry Framework*, we invite you to explore the unfolding trends and transformative technologies shaping the future of the logistics industry.

ORGANIZATION OF THE BOOK

In this edited reference book, we aim to provide a comprehensive overview of cutting-edge topics in cybersecurity and risk management within the logistics industry. Each chapter serves as a valuable contribution, offering insights and strategies to address the evolving challenges faced by professionals and practitioners in the field. Let's delve into a brief overview of each chapter:

Chapter 1: "Risk Management and Cybersecurity in Transportation and Warehousing" by Azeem Khan, Noor Zaman Jhanjhi, Haji Abdul Hafidz Haji Omar, Dayang Hajah Tiawa Awang Haji Hamid explores the vulnerability of logistics corporations to cybersecurity threats. The chapter focuses on the methods and tools for assessing and mitigating risks to secure warehousing operations and transportation systems.

Chapter 2: "Detecting Cyber Threats with a Graph-based NIDPS" by Brendan Ooi Tze Wen, Najihah Syahriza, Nicholas Chan Wei Xian, Nicki Gan Wei, Tan Zheng Shen, Yap Zhe Hin, Siva Raja Sindiramutty, Teah Yi Fan Nicole introduces a novel network-based intrusion detection system (NIDPS) using graph theory to prevent and detect cyber threats. The paper covers data collection, analysis engine, preventive action, and reporting aspects.

Chapter 3: "A distributed model for IoT anomaly detection using federated learning" by Sidra Tahir, Anam Zaheer focuses on early identification of health issues through anomaly detection in IoT-based sleep patterns. The chapter presents a distributed model using federated learning for privacy, data security, and synchronized anomaly detection across devices.

Chapter 4: "Network Intrusion Detection to mitigate jamming and spoofing attack Using Federated Leading, A Comprehensive Survey" by Tayyab Rehman, Noshina Tariq, Muhammad Ashraf, Mamoona Humayun comprehensively surveys the demand for intrusion detection systems (IDS) and explores the use of federated learning-enabled IDS to reduce privacy risks. The paper analyzes spoofing and jamming attacks, mitigation techniques, and evaluates contemporary IDS techniques.

Chapter 5: "IoT Security, Future Challenges and Open Issues" by Noshina Tariq, Tehreem Saboor, Muhammad Ashraf, Rawish Butt, Masooma Anwar, Mamoona Humayun focuses on the security challenges in the Internet of Things (IoT) and investigates state-of-the-art technologies, future challenges, and open issues in IoT security.

Chapter 6: "Enhancing Identification of IoT Anomalies in Smart Homes Using Secure Blockchain Technology" by Sidra Tahir explores anomaly detection in smart homes using deep learning and secure blockchain technology. The chapter emphasizes the need to identify abnormalities in data generated by smart homes for convenience, cost savings, and security.

Chapter 7: "Securing the Digital Supply Chain Cyber Threats and Vulnerabilities" by Siva Raja Sindiramutty, Noor Zaman Jhanjhi, Chong Eng Tan, Navid Ali Khan, Bhavin Shah, Loveleen Gaur addresses cybersecurity in the digital supply chain. The chapter explores strategies to safeguard operations, emerging technologies, and future trends.

Chapter 8: "Internet of Things (IoT) Impact on Inventory Management: A Review" by Azeem Khan, Noor Zaman Jhanjhi, Dayang Hajah Tiawa Awang Haji Hamid, Haji Abdul Hafidz Haji Omar examines the impact of IoT on inventory management. The chapter covers IoT system components, communication protocols, applications, and a comprehensive comparison with traditional inventory management systems.

Chapter 9: "Applications of Blockchain Technology in the Supply Chain Management" by Siva Raja Sindiramutty, Noor Zaman Jhanjhi, Chong Eng Tan, Navid Ali Khan, Abdalla Gharib, Khor Jia Yun explores the use of blockchain technology in supply chain management. The chapter addresses challenges and highlights specific applications within the domain.

Chapter 10: "The Internet of Things (IoT) Applications in Inventory Management through Supply Chain" by Yesim Ozkan-Ozen focuses on the impact of IoT applications in inventory management within supply chains. The chapter conducts a literature review and bibliometric analysis, proposing future research directions aligned with current trends.

Chapter 11: "QR multilevel codes to reduce cybersecurity risks in the logistics of freight transport in ports" by Gerardo Reyes Ruiz introduces a practical tool based on multilevel QR codes to improve the identification and supervision of goods entering a country through its port customs, reducing cybersecurity risks in freight transport logistics.

We trust that the insights provided in these chapters will not only contribute to the academic discourse but also serve as practical guidance for professionals navigating the complexities of cybersecurity and risk management in the logistics industry.

IN SUMMARY

As we conclude this edited reference book on *Cybersecurity Measures for Logistics Industry Framework*, we reflect on the wealth of knowledge and insights shared by our esteemed authors. The diverse chapters collectively form a comprehensive guide addressing the ever-evolving challenges faced by the logistics industry in the digital era.

From risk management and cybersecurity in transportation and warehousing to cutting-edge technologies like federated learning and blockchain, each chapter offers a unique perspective and practical solutions. The authors have delved into the intricacies of cyber threats, detection systems, anomaly identification, and the application of emerging technologies to secure the digital supply chain.

The significance of these contributions extends beyond academic discourse; they serve as a valuable resource for professionals, practitioners, and researchers actively engaged in navigating the intricate landscape of logistics cybersecurity. The exploration of Internet of Things (IoT) security, blockchain applications, and the impact on inventory management provides a roadmap for adapting to the ongoing technological revolution.

We commend the dedication of our authors in dissecting complex topics and presenting them in a manner accessible to a diverse audience. The insights gained from this collection will undoubtedly inform strategic decision-making, enhance operational efficiency, and contribute to the resilience of logistics networks against cyber threats.

In the ever-changing world of logistics and technology, staying abreast of the latest developments is paramount. The chapters in this book not only capture the current state of affairs but also lay the groundwork for future advancements. As we embrace the digital transformation of logistics, the importance of cybersecurity cannot be overstated, and this book serves as a beacon guiding us through the challenges and opportunities.

We express our gratitude to the authors for their scholarly contributions, and to you, the readers, for embarking on this journey with us. May the insights shared within these pages empower you to navigate the dynamic landscape of logistics cybersecurity with confidence and foresight.

Noor Zaman Jhanjhi
Taylor's University, Malaysia

Imdad Ali Shah
Taylor's University, Malaysia

Chapter 1
Risk Management and Cybersecurity in Transportation and Warehousing

Azeem Khan
ⓘD https://orcid.org/0000-0003-2742-8034
Sultan Sharif Ali Islamic University, Brunei

Noor Zaman Jhanjhi
ⓘD https://orcid.org/0000-0001-8116-4733
School of Computer Science, SCS, Taylor's University, Subang Jaya, Malaysia

Haji Abdul Hafidz B. Haji Omar
Sultan Sharif Ali Islamic University, Brunei

Dayang Hajah Tiawa B. Awang Haji Hamid
Sultan Sharif Ali Islamic University, Brunei

ABSTRACT

Transportation and warehousing are vital components of logistics corporations. Their continuous un-interrupted functioning is of paramount significance for the enterprises involved in the supply chain. As these enterprises are built and rely heavily on digital technologies for their rapid functioning, they are vulnerable to cybersecurity threats and attacks. Hence, to effectively address and promptly respond to these issues organizations need to have proper strategy and planning in place. This chapter endeavors to acquaint readers with these pressing issues. To secure warehousing operations and transportation systems, the methods and tools for assessing the risks and mitigating them are discussed comprehensively.

DOI: 10.4018/978-1-6684-7625-3.ch001

INTRODUCTION

An Overview of Transportation and Warehousing in the Supply Chain

As shown in Figure 1, Transportation and warehousing are essential elements of the supply chain that ensures the seamless flow of goods and services from suppliers to consumers. Transportation here, connotes the moving of goods from one place to another using various modes of transportation such as road, train, air, water, and pipelines. Each mode has its own strengths and restrictions, and the selection of these modes depends on factors such as cost, speed, reliability, and the nature of the goods being carried. To optimize efficiency of transportation strategies such as direct shipment or hub-and-spoke models or intermodal transportation are employed(Gyamfi, Ansere, Kamal, Tariq, & Jurcut, 2023; P. M. Kumar et al., 2023; Tashtoush et al., 2022; Yazdinejad, Rabieinejad, Hasani, & Srivastava, 2023).

Warehousing, on the other hand, is concerned with the storage and administration of goods prior to their distribution to customers(Sawal, Ahmad, Muralitharan, Loganathan, & Jhanjhi, 2022). Warehouses are of different types, such as distribution centers, fulfillment centers, and cross-docking facilities, each of them serves specific purposes in the supply chain. Warehouses perform various functions in the supply chain such as receiving goods, storing them in an organized manner, managing inventory levels and fulfilling orders. They also provide value-added services like labeling, package customization, and product inspection. Efficient warehousing operations contribute to effective inventory management and timely order fulfillment(Alkhodair, Mohanty, & Kougianos, 2023; A. Karim, 2022; Ko, Satchidanandan, & Kumar, 2019; Papastergiou, Mouratidis, & Kalogeraki, 2021).

Figure 1. The changing landscape of transportation and warehousing industry (stormshield, 2023)

Within the supply chain, transportation and warehousing are inextricably linked. Transportation relies on warehousing for temporary storage, aggregation of goods, and efficient order picking, whereas warehousing relies on transportation to deliver goods to customers or other distribution sites on time. The flow of information and coordination between transportation and warehousing is critical for seamless operations and meeting customer needs.

In risk management (Amro & Gkioulos, 2023; Mallah, Lopez, & Farooq, 2021)and cybersecurity context, transportation, and warehousing face various challenges, to name a few are thefts, accidents, supply chain disruptions, and cyber threats which significantly impact supply chain operations. Hence, implementing robust risk management strategies and cybersecurity measures becomes crucial for smooth functioning of supply chain operations. In this context, cybersecurity measures constitute protecting information systems, securing data transmission, implementing strict access controls, and conducting regular audits to prevent data breaches and cyber-attacks.

A comprehensive understanding of how transportation and warehousing interact in the supply chain, combined with effective risk management(Humayun, Afsar, Almufareh, Jhanjhi, & AlSuwailem) and cybersecurity practices, is critical for ensuring efficient operations, minimizing disruptions, and protecting the supply chain's integrity and security.

Importance of Risk Management and Cybersecurity in the Transportation and Warehousing Sectors

To handle possible risks, it is significant to have solid risk management processes and cybersecurity safeguards in place in transportation and warehousing industries. In transportation, modern technologies such as GPS tracking, real-time monitoring systems, and telematics are used to relieve risks. In order to protect against cyber threats, secure communication protocols and encryption techniques are used. Automation methods such as barcode scanning and RFID(Pandian, 2019) tagging increase inventory accuracy in warehousing, while access control mechanisms and surveillance systems protect physical assets. Comprehensive cybersecurity measures, such as network firewalls and routine system audits, provide protection against data breaches and cyber-attacks.

There are various benefits to effective risk management(Ebert et al., 2021; supplychain247; Zhao, Abdo, Liao, Barth, & Wu, 2022) in transportation and storage. Organizations may establish contingency plans to avoid interruptions and maximize operations by identifying and analyzing risks. Risk assessments, for instance, allows transportation corporations to identify risky locations and apply safety measures. Robust risk management in warehousing promotes effective inventory management and reduces losses. The combination of risk management and cybersecurity measures improves the overall stability of these systems. The integrity and security of data and information systems are maintained by regular system audits and personnel training on cybersecurity procedures.

Cybersecurity is essential for safeguarding sensitive data, key infrastructure, and guaranteeing smooth transportation and storage operations. Because of the usage of digital technology in transportation, safety measures are required to avoid data breaches, hacking, and unauthorized access. To avoid cybersecurity threats multi-factor authentication(Ahmed & Ahmed, 2019), encryption methods, and intrusion detection systems(Jmila & Khedher, 2022) are used, and they contribute to the security of transportation systems and information systems. The security of customer (Sawal et al., 2022)and operational data is very crucial in supply chain and warehousing management systems hence, cybersecurity mechanisms such as network firewalls, vulnerability assessments, and security awareness trainings should be conducted frequently by the organizations to create awareness among the personnel of an organization thereby, paving a way to reduce the risks of cyber-attacks by this means, ensuring data confidentiality and availability. Experience has shown that by adhering to the policies and principles discussed above, Transportation and warehousing firms can improve operational efficiency thereby, reducing financial losses, preserving physical assets, and maintaining the confidence of supply chain stakeholders by prioritizing risk management through effective and efficient cybersecurity measures(Al-Zahrani, 2022).

Objectives of the Chapter

This book chapter intends to provide a comprehensive overview of the risks and vulnerabilities involved in the transportation and warehousing industries. It highlights the significance of appropriate risk management measures that will mitigate these risks and increase overall operational efficiency. Furthermore, this chapter emphasizes the importance of implementing effective and efficient cybersecurity measures to safeguard organizational information systems infrastructure constituting confidential data from cyber threats and attacks. It has proposed the integration of risk management and cybersecurity measures, highlighting the significance of having a comprehensive plan in place to ensure total protection of transportation and warehousing systems. In addition, this chapter has also provided technical insights, industry best practices, and advanced technology solutions for implementing complete risk management strategy and cybersecurity measures in the transportation and warehousing industries.

Organization of the Chapter

This chapter comprises of twelve sections. Section1 begins with the Introduction providing an overview of the significance of transportation and warehouses in the supply chain. Section 2 delves into the process of identifying and categorizing risks in transportation and warehousing operations. Section 3 explores the specific cyber risks associated with transportation and warehousing sectors. Section 4 sheds light on cybersecurity frameworks and standards pertaining to transportation and warehousing. Section 5 examines cybersecurity strategies for safeguarding various forms of transportation. Section 6 explores cybersecurity issues pertaining to Warehouse Management Systems (WMS). Section 7 describes the topic of analyzing and managing third-party cybersecurity risks. Section 8 examines response plan for interruptions, Section 9 explores cybersecurity awareness programs. Section 10 investigates the influence of new technologies such as IoT, AI, blockchain. Section 11 provides an overview of legislation and standards associated with cybersecurity. Finally, Section 12, summarizes the whole chapter by providing insights and concludes the discussion with future trends and challenges pertaining to the transportation and warehousing industry.

RISK ASSESSMENT IN TRANSPORTATION AND WAREHOUSING

In transportation and warehousing, risk assessment is critical for detecting possible risks, assessing their likelihood, and developing effective solutions to manage and reduce them. This critical role enables firms to improve operational safety, increase efficiency, save costs, and protect workers, assets, and reputation. This complete strategy helps firms to improve their operations, maintain regulatory compliance, and cultivate a safe and secure workplace. The first stage in risk assessment(Humayun, Almufareh, & Khalil) for transportation and warehousing operations is to identify and categorize particular hazards specific to these businesses. This procedure comprises a thorough analysis of potential dangers and threats that may develop during goods transit and material storage. Traffic accidents, equipment failures, supply chain(Ashraf et al., 2023) interruptions, theft or damage to commodities, worker safety concerns, and regulatory compliance challenges are examples of risks. Organizations may acquire a clear awareness of the possible issues they may encounter and build tailored plans to meet them successfully by recognizing and categorizing these risks(Shojae Chaeikar, Jolfaei, & Mohammad, 2023).

Identifying and Classifying Transportation and Warehousing Hazards

Risk assessment in transportation and warehouses includes identifying and categorizing underlying risks. These include road accidents, equipment breakdowns, supply chain disruptions, theft and damage, worker safety hazards, regulatory compliance, environmental risks, and cybersecurity threats as described in Table 1.0. These risks can disrupt operations, create delays, financial losses(Dogra et al., 2021), and affect worker safety and environmental sustainability. Effective risk management solutions are critical for managing these risks and maintaining seamless and secure transportation and warehouse operations(Bhuvana et al., 2023).

Organizations may establish focused risk management strategies by identifying and categorizing these hazards relevant to transportation and storage activities. Safety training programs, equipment maintenance schedules, supply chain diversity, increased security measures(Najmi et al., 2021), regulatory compliance checks, environmental sustainability initiatives, and comprehensive cybersecurity measures to safeguard data and systems are examples of these. Companies may reduce risks and maintain the smooth and secure functioning of their transportation and storage systems by using these strategies(Jayanthi et al., 2023).

Table 1. Key risks in transportation and warehousing: A comprehensive overview

Risk	Description
Traffic Accidents	Primary risk in transportation operations due to potential collisions among vehicles. Factors such as driver error, adverse weather, maintenance issues, and improper loading contribute to accidents.
Equipment Failures	Prevalent risk in transportation and warehousing involving breakdowns or malfunctions of vehicles, forklifts, cranes, and other machinery used for handling goods. Equipment failures disrupt operations, cause delays, and pose safety hazards.
Supply Chain Disruptions	Complex network dependency risk. Natural disasters, labour strikes, and disruptions in the global supply chain impact timely delivery, leading to delays, increased costs, and customer dissatisfaction.
Theft and Damage	Significant risk in transportation and warehousing. Cargo theft, pilferage, and vandalism occur during transit or storage. Inadequate security measures and supply chain vulnerabilities expose companies to financial losses and legal implications.
Worker Safety Hazards	Physical labour and machinery operation risk. Hazards include slips, trips, falls, ergonomic injuries, exposure to hazardous materials, and accidents related to material handling, posing threats to worker safety.
Regulatory Compliance	Legal compliance risk. Failure to adhere to transportation regulations, handling hazardous materials properly, complying with labour laws, and maintaining licensing/permits may result in penalties and reputational damage.
Environmental Risks	Environmental impact risk. Improper disposal of hazardous waste, spills/leaks of harmful substances, and emissions from transportation vehicles contribute to pollution and climate change.
Cybersecurity	Digital security risk. Increasing reliance on digital systems in transportation and warehousing exposes vulnerabilities to cyber threats and data breaches. Hackers targeting transportation management systems, logistics platforms, or customer data can disrupt operations, compromise sensitive information, and cause financial losses.

Methods and Tools for Conducting Risk Assessments

The transportation and warehousing industries are facing a variety of risks that can jeopardize a company's safety, security, and operational continuity. These industries are subject to high cybersecurity risks apart from traditional physical threats such as accidents and infrastructure breakdowns. Therefore, assessing and managing these cybersecurity threats becomes increasingly significant as firms rely more on these networked systems used to store, manage, and maintain data using digital technologies. Thus, this section focuses on the methodologies and tools used in the transportation and warehousing industries to perform risk assessments in the context of risk management and cybersecurity(Humayun, Jhanjhi, Talib, Shah, & Suseendran, 2021). The organizations may successfully manage risks, safeguard key assets, assure integrity and resilience of their operations by identifying possible hazards and vulnerabilities, thereby prioritizing the risks, and applying appropriate controls(Battaglioni, Rafaiani, Chiaraluce, & Baldi, 2022).

Table 2. Cybersecurity risk management methods and tools

Method/Tool	Description
Hazard Identification and Cybersecurity Risks	Analysis of potential hazards in transportation and warehousing, encompassing both physical and cybersecurity risks. Includes consideration of vulnerabilities in IT systems, network infrastructure, IoT devices, cloud services, and data storage.
Risk Assessment Matrix and Cybersecurity	Adaptation of the risk assessment matrix to incorporate cybersecurity parameters. Evaluates and prioritizes risks by assessing the likelihood of cyber-attacks, potential impact on data integrity and confidentiality, and effectiveness of existing cybersecurity measures.
Cybersecurity Frameworks	Overview of established cybersecurity frameworks such as the NIST Cybersecurity Framework and ISO/IEC 27001 standard. These frameworks provide guidelines for risk assessment and management, ensuring a structured approach to identifying, protecting, detecting, responding to, and recovering from cybersecurity incidents.
Vulnerability Assessments and Penetration Testing	Conducting assessments to identify weaknesses in IT systems, networks, and applications. Involves analyzing infrastructure for vulnerabilities, performing controlled attacks to exploit weaknesses, and evaluating the organization's ability to detect and respond to such attacks.
Incident Response Planning	Importance of a robust incident response plan to address cybersecurity threats. Outlines steps during incidents, defines roles, establishes communication channels, and outlines procedures for containment, eradication, and recovery. Regular testing and updating of the plan ensures effectiveness and preparedness.
Security Awareness Training	Regular training sessions to familiarize employees with potential threats and best practices for data protection. Topics include safe browsing habits, strong passwords, and maintaining cybersecurity vigilance. Enhances employees' awareness, cultivates a stronger security culture, and reduces the risk of human error in cyber incidents.
Continuous Monitoring and Threat Intelligence	Implementation of continuous monitoring systems and integration of threat intelligence mechanisms. Proactively identifies and responds to emerging cybersecurity risks by monitoring network traffic, system logs, user activities, and utilizing real-time information on the latest cyber threats and trends.

The transportation and warehousing businesses are vulnerable to a variety of risks, such as cyber-attacks which can corrupt data and disrupt operations. As a result, thorough systematic cybersecurity risk assessments need to be carried out for smooth functioning of these businesses, and they are of utmost significance. These steps can help organizations improve their cybersecurity(Alferidah & Jhanjhi, 2020) posture and resilience. Organizations pertaining to transportation and warehousing industries should adopt a complete approach for risk management by embracing the approaches and technologies as discussed in Table 2.0. In an increasingly interconnected and digitalized world, addressing physical and cyber threats together will improve resilience, protects important assets, and maintains customer and stakeholders' trust(Sánchez et al., 2022).

Risk Prioritization and Mitigation Planning

Risk prioritization and mitigation planning are critical components of effective risk management. Prioritizing risks involves evaluating their likelihood and severity to determine their importance and allocate resources accordingly. By assessing risks and categorizing them based on their priority level, organizations can focus their efforts on addressing the most significant and impactful risks. Once risks are prioritized, mitigation planning comes into play. Mitigation strategies are developed to reduce the likelihood or impact of identified risks. This involves implementing specific actions, controls, and safeguards tailored to each risk. By allocating resources strategically, organizations can ensure the successful implementation of these mitigation measures. Continuous monitoring and regular reviews are essential for evaluating the effectiveness of mitigation strategies(Mpatziakas, Drosou, Papadopoulos, & Tzovaras, 2022).

In summary, risk prioritization allows organizations to focus on the most critical risks, while mitigation planning involves developing tailored strategies to reduce risk likelihood or impact. Continuous monitoring, reviews, and stakeholder engagement ensure the effectiveness and adaptability of mitigation measures. By implementing these practices, organizations can proactively manage risks and enhance their resilience in the face of potential threats(Cowan, 2021; Yousef, Traore, & Briguglio, 2023).

CYBERSECURITY THREATS IN TRANSPORTATION AND WAREHOUSING

As depicted in Fig 2.0, The transportation and warehousing sectors are exposed to a unique set of cyber threats due to the nature of their operations. These sectors heavily rely on interconnected systems, data storage, and digital technologies, making them vulnerable to various types of cyberattacks(G. Li et al., 2019).

Understanding the Unique Cyber Threats Faced by

Table 3. List of common cyberthreats in supply chain

Threats	Definition	causes
Malware	Malicious software designed to infiltrate systems, steal data, disrupt operations, or gain unauthorized control over systems.	Malware can be delivered through various methods, such as phishing emails, malicious attachments, drive-by downloads, or removable media. Malware can also be classified into different types, such as viruses, worms, trojans, spyware, adware, rootkits, etc.
Denial-of-Service (DoS) Attacks	Attacks that aim to overwhelm a system by flooding it with an excessive amount of traffic, rendering it unavailable to legitimate users.	DoS attacks can be performed by a single attacker or a distributed network of compromised devices (botnet). DoS attacks can target different layers of the network stack, such as the application layer, the transport layer, or the network layer.
Ransomware Attacks	Attacks that involve encrypting data and demanding a ransom payment in exchange for restoring access to the affected systems or files.	Ransomware attacks can be executed by exploiting vulnerabilities in systems or applications, or by tricking users into opening malicious attachments or links. Ransomware attacks can cause significant financial losses and operational disruptions for transportation and warehousing companies.
Supply Chain Attacks	Attacks that target third-party vendors or suppliers that provide services to transportation and warehousing companies. These attacks exploit vulnerabilities in the supply chain to gain unauthorized access or compromise systems.	Supply chain attacks can pose a serious risk for transportation and warehousing companies, as they rely on multiple external parties for their operations. Supply chain attacks can compromise the integrity, availability, or confidentiality of data and systems across the supply chain.

Transportation and Warehousing Sectors

To address these risks discussed in Table 3.0, firms in the transportation and warehousing industries should put in place strong cybersecurity safeguards. This involves constantly upgrading and patching software, deploying firewalls and intrusion detection systems, teaching employees on cybersecurity best practices, and developing incident response plans. Proactive monitoring, threat intelligence exchange, and coordination with industry partners are also critical in minimizing cyber threats and maintaining the resilience and security of operations(Benyahya, Collen, Kechagia, & Nijdam, 2022; Mukherjee et al., 2022).

Figure 2. Cyber threats in supply chain(canva)

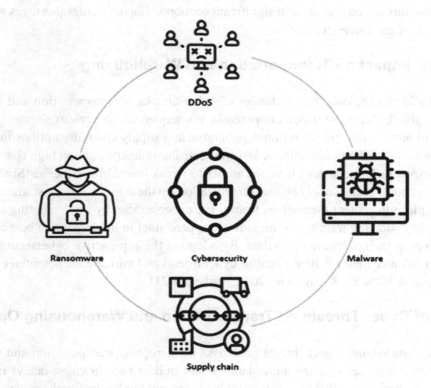

Analysis of Recent Cyber-Attacks and Their Impacts

1.   Attack on the Maersk Shipping Company

The Maersk shipping firm was the victim of a cyber-attack in June 2017. The attack was on Maersk's IT information systems across the world, thereby causing massive interruptions in the corporations' operations. The company's sensitive data, encompassing customer information and entire shipping manifests, was taken over by the hackers. This was a notable occurrence of cyberattack that demonstrated the susceptibility of the transportation and warehousing industries to cyberattacks(Prabakar et al., 2023). The attack was so impactful that it had a substantial economic effect, as it affected the entire organization's operations and caused delays in product delivery thereby incurring great economic and financial losses to the organization(industrialcybersecuritypulse).

2.   The Attack on the Colonial Pipeline

The Colonial Pipeline ransomware attack took place in May 2021. The Colonial Pipeline was another major attack on petroleum pipeline in the United States. The attack was so impactful that it caused the pipeline to be shut down for many days, causing fuel shortages in the country's east. The corporation was obliged to pay the hackers' demanded ransom to save its Information systems infrastructure constituting crucial data of the organization. This disaster was an important chapter in the history of cyberattacks on transportation and warehousing industries that revealed the vulnerability of vital infrastructure to cyber-attacks. Later this tragedy resulted in significant economic impact as fuel shortages were rampant resulting in the rise of gas prices(wikipedia).

Cyber-Attacks' Impact on Transportation and Warehousing

The above two incidents are only two instances of cyber-attacks in transportation and warehousing industries. These attacks have the following potential consequences on various sectors pertaining to an organization, to name a few are operational, economic and supply chain disruptions including data breaches. These attacks on the transportation and warehousing industries are on high rise and growing increasingly widespread. These attacks have the ability to wreak havoc on businesses(Shah, Jhanjhi, & Laraib, 2023), the economy, and supply chains. Organizations in these industries must strategize policies and processes in place to protect themselves from these cyber-attacks by implementing strong cyber-security measures, conducting training for organizations personnel in implementing best cybersecurity practices, and keeping their software up to date. By adopting these proactive cybersecurity measures, organizations can enhance their resilience against cyber threats and mitigate the potential consequences of future attacks(Said, Elloumi, & Khoukhi, 2022; Sarker, 2021).

Implications of Cyber Threats on Transportation and Warehousing Operations

1. Disruption of Operations: Cyber threats pose risks of disrupting transportation and warehousing operations. Attacks can render systems unavailable, result in data loss, or cause delays in shipments. Such disruptions can have cascading effects on supply chains and hinder the timely movement of goods and services(Yeboah-Ofori et al., 2021).

 2. Damage to Reputation: Cyberattacks can severely damage the reputation of transportation and warehousing companies. Exposing sensitive data, causing service disruptions, or being used to propagate malware can erode customer trust and confidence in the organization's ability to secure their information and provide reliable services(Driss, Almomani, e Huma, & Ahmad, 2022).

 3. Financial Losses: As depicted in Fig 3.0, Cyberattacks can lead to substantial financial losses for transportation and warehousing companies. Downtime, data breaches, or ransom payments can all incur significant costs. The expenses associated with recovering from an attack, including system restoration, legal fees, and potential regulatory penalties, can further exacerbate financial losses(Rawat et al., 2022).

Figure 3. Navigating organizational cyber harms: Restoring operations
(Agrafiotis, Nurse, Goldsmith, Creese, & Upton, 2018)

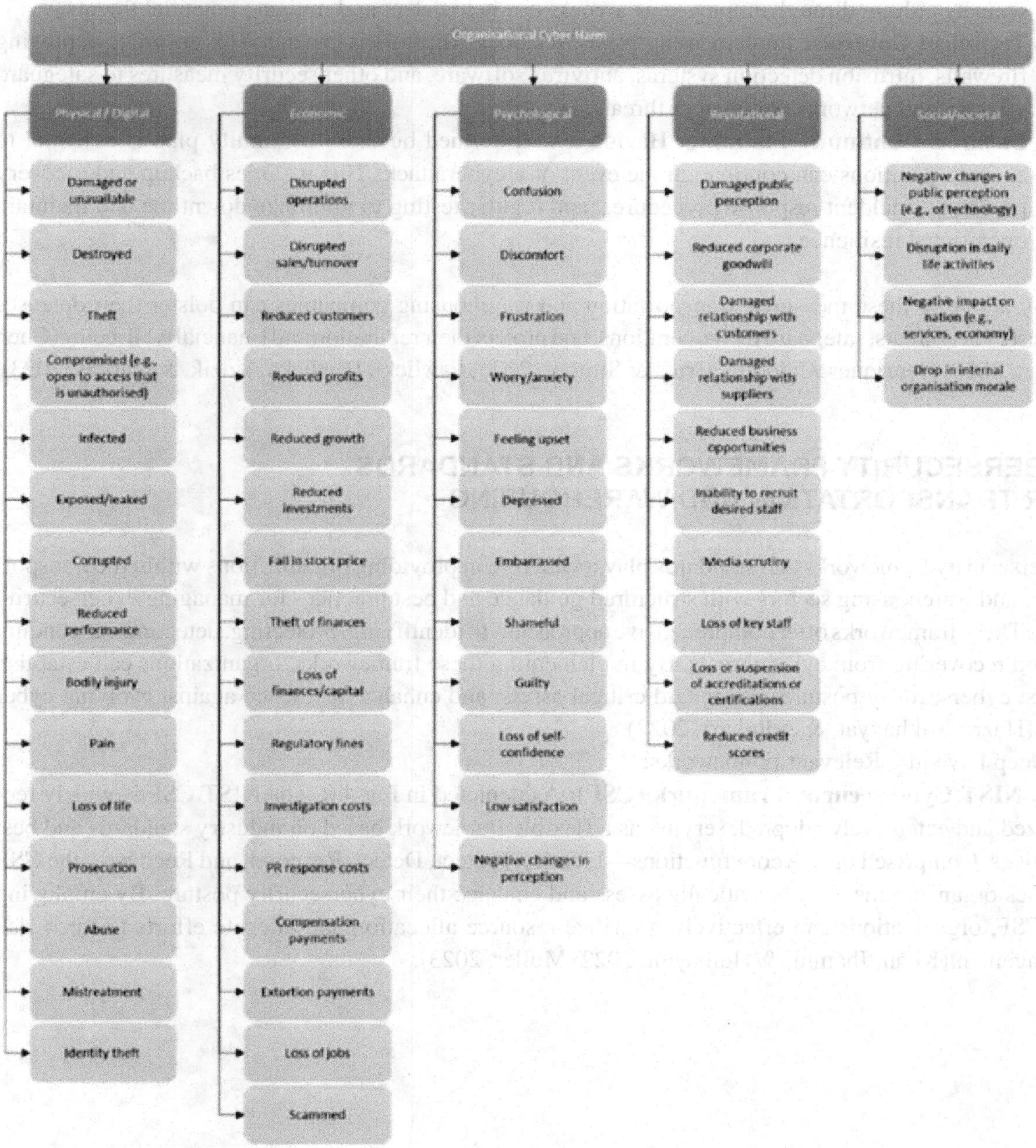

Organisational Cyber Harm				
Physical / Digital	**Economic**	**Psychological**	**Reputational**	**Social/Societal**
Damaged or unavailable	Disrupted operations	Confusion	Damaged public perception	Negative changes in public perception (e.g., of technology)
Destroyed	Disrupted sales/turnover	Discomfort	Reduced corporate goodwill	Disruption in daily life activities
Theft	Reduced customers	Frustration	Damaged relationship with customers	Negative impact on nation (e.g., services, economy)
Compromised (e.g., open to access that is unauthorised)	Reduced profits	Worry/anxiety	Damaged relationship with suppliers	Drop in internal organisation morale
Infected	Reduced growth	Feeling upset	Reduced business opportunities	
Exposed/leaked	Reduced investments	Depressed	Inability to recruit desired staff	
Corrupted	Fall in stock price	Embarrassed	Media scrutiny	
Reduced performance	Theft of finances	Shameful	Loss of key staff	
Bodily injury	Loss of finances/capital	Guilty	Loss or suspension of accreditations or certifications	
Pain	Regulatory fines	Loss of self-confidence	Reduced credit scores	
Loss of life	Investigation costs	Low satisfaction		
Prosecution	PR response costs	Negative changes in perception		
Abuse	Compensation payments			
Mistreatment	Extortion payments			
Identity theft	Loss of jobs			
	Scammed			

Mitigation Measures for Cyber Threats:
To Mitigate the above risks following measures need to be observed by the organizations.

1. **Employee Training:** Transportation and warehousing companies should provide comprehensive training to employees on identifying and reporting suspicious activities. Building a strong cybersecurity culture through employee awareness can help detect and mitigate potential threats.
2. **Technical Controls:** Implementing robust technical controls is crucial. This includes deploying firewalls, intrusion detection systems, antivirus software, and other security measures to safeguard systems and networks from cyber threats.
3. **Business Continuity Planning:** Having a well-defined business continuity plan is essential to ensure operations can continue in the event of a cyberattack. This includes backup and recovery processes, incident response procedures, and regular testing to minimize downtime and maintain operational resilience.

By adopting these measures, transportation and warehousing companies can bolster their defenses against cyber threats, safeguard their operations, and protect their reputation and financial well-being(Chen & Yan, 2023; Henriques, Caldeira, Cruz, & Simões, 2023; Pawlicki, Pawlicka, Kozik, & Choraś, 2023).

CYBERSECURITY FRAMEWORKS AND STANDARDS FOR TRANSPORTATION AND WAREHOUSING

Cybersecurity frameworks and standards play a vital role in providing organizations within the transportation and warehousing sectors with structured guidance and best practices for managing cybersecurity risks. These frameworks offer comprehensive approaches to identifying, protecting, detecting, responding to, and recovering from cyber threats. By implementing these frameworks, organizations can establish robust cybersecurity postures, safeguard critical assets, and enhance resilience against evolving cyber risks(Hazra, Alkhayyat, & Adhikari, 2022).

Deep Dive into Relevant Frameworks:

1. NIST Cybersecurity Framework (CSF): As depicted in Fig 4.0, The NIST CSF is widely recognized and extensively adopted, serving as a flexible framework based on industry standards and best practices. Comprised of five core functions—Identify, Protect, Detect, Respond, and Recover—the CSF enables organizations to systematically assess and enhance their cybersecurity posture. By employing the CSF, organizations can effectively prioritize resource allocation and allocate efforts towards risk management(Khan, Jhanjhi, & Humayun, 2022; Möller, 2023).

Figure 4. NIST cybersecurity framework

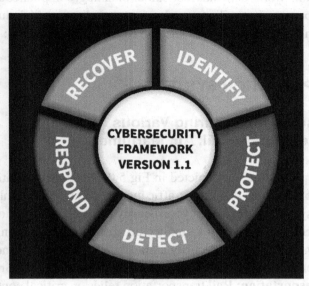

2. ISO/IEC 27001: ISO/IEC 27001 is a globally acknowledged standard for Information Security Management Systems (ISMS). It provides organizations with a comprehensive framework to establish, implement, maintain, and continually improve information security controls. Focusing on risk management and safeguarding the confidentiality, integrity, and availability of information assets, ISO/IEC 27001 assists organizations in defining risk appetite, implementing robust security controls, and undergoing regular audits to ensure compliance(Kitsios, Chatzidimitriou, & Kamariotou, 2023).

3. IEC 62443: Specifically tailored for the industrial automation and control systems (IACS) domain, IEC 62443 offers a series of standards applicable to transportation and warehousing. These standards provide guidance on securing IACS networks and devices, including those utilized within the transportation and warehousing contexts. Emphasizing risk assessment, security by design(Jhanjhi, 2021), network segmentation, access controls, and incident response planning, IEC 62443 addresses the unique cybersecurity challenges associated with critical infrastructure systems, such as SCADA systems and industrial IoT devices(Heluany & Galvão, 2023).

Implementation Considerations and Compliance Requirements:

The implementation of cybersecurity frameworks and standards necessitates careful consideration and planning. Organizations must assess their specific requirements, risks, and regulatory obligations to determine the frameworks that align most effectively with their needs(Saeed, Jhanjhi, Naqvi, & Khan, 2022). Achieving compliance with these frameworks involves establishing policies and procedures, conducting thorough risk assessments, implementing appropriate security controls, monitoring, and auditing systems, and continually improving the cybersecurity posture. Compliance with applicable frameworks and standards not only mitigates risks but also demonstrates the organization's commitment to security, instilling trust among customers, partners, and stakeholders.

In conclusion, cybersecurity frameworks and standards serve as invaluable resources for transportation and warehousing organizations seeking to establish robust cybersecurity practices. The NIST CSF, ISO/IEC 27001, and IEC 62443 are among the frameworks relevant to these sectors. The successful implementation of these frameworks demands meticulous planning, compliance assessments, and ongoing monitoring to enhance cybersecurity resilience and ensure compliance with industry-specific regulations and contractual obligations(Alsmadi, 2023; Khaleefah & Al-Mashhadi, 2023; Shafik, 2023).

SECURING TRANSPORTATION SYSTEMS

Cybersecurity Measures for Securing Various Transportation Modes (Road, Rail, Air, Maritime)

1. Securing Road Transportation: As depicted in Fig 5.0, Road transportation encompasses a wide range of interconnected components, including traffic management systems, toll collection systems, and intelligent transportation systems. Enhancing cybersecurity in road transportation necessitates the implementation of measures such as secure network architectures, encrypted communications, access controls, and intrusion detection systems. Regular security audits, firmware updates, and user training programs can further fortify the overall security posture(Djenouri, Belhadi, Djenouri, Srivastava, & Lin, 2023).

2. Securing Rail Transportation: Rail transportation relies on critical control systems for train operations, signaling, and infrastructure maintenance. To ensure the security of rail transportation, robust access controls, network segmentation, and continuous monitoring are imperative. Employing secure communication protocols, intrusion detection systems, and physical security measures can mitigate cyber threats. Regular vulnerability assessments and incident response planning should be conducted to ensure prompt identification and response to potential security incidents(Hussain, 2023).

3. Securing Air Transportation: Air transportation entails complex networks of airports, air traffic control systems, and aircraft systems. Securing air transportation demands a comprehensive approach. Measures such as strong access controls, encryption of communications, secure data sharing protocols, and continuous monitoring of critical systems aid in preventing unauthorized access and potential cyber-attacks. Rigorous testing, including penetration testing and red team exercises, can identify vulnerabilities and strengthen security measures(M. Liu, Zhang, Chen, Ge, & Zhao, 2023).

Figure 5. Securing transportation: Cyber measures for road, rail, air, and maritime (securehalo)

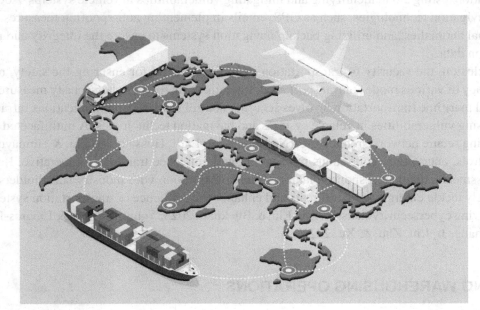

4. Securing Maritime Transportation: Maritime transportation involves interconnected systems, including vessel control systems, port operations, and communication networks. Safeguarding maritime transportation necessitates secure communication channels, network segmentation, and access controls to avert unauthorized access to critical systems. Regular patch management, incident response planning, and employee training are vital to addressing potential cyber threats. Additionally, protecting vessel systems, such as GPS navigation and Automatic Identification Systems (AIS), from tampering or spoofing is essential(Progoulakis et al., 2023).

Securing Control Systems and Communications Infrastructure

Protecting control systems in transportation entails the implementation of defense-in-depth strategies. This includes establishing robust access controls, conducting routine security assessments, and implementing secure remote access protocols. Utilizing intrusion detection and prevention systems (IDS/IPS) and security information and event management (SIEM) systems offers real-time monitoring and threat detection capabilities. Furthermore, segregating control networks from enterprise networks through network segmentation(Humayun, Hamid, Jhanjhi, Suseendran, & Talib, 2021) and employing secure communication protocols such as Virtual Private Networks (VPNs) or Secure Sockets Layer (SSL) safeguards against unauthorized access and data tampering(Srikanth, Geetha, & Prabhu, 2023).

Addressing Vulnerabilities in Vehicle Systems and Navigation Technologies

Vehicle systems, present in cars, trains, aircraft, and ships, are susceptible to cyber threats. Securing these systems requires adherence to secure software development practices, routine vulnerability assessments, and prompt application of security patches and updates. Secure coding practices, code reviews, and penetration testing aid in identifying and mitigating vulnerabilities in vehicle systems. Additionally, securing navigation technologies, such as GPS, entails implementing anti-spoofing measures, monitoring for signal anomalies, and utilizing backup navigation systems to ensure the integrity and reliability of navigation data.

In Conclusion, the security of transportation systems is crucial for ensuring the safety, reliability, and efficiency of various modes of transportation. Implementing robust cybersecurity measures in road, rail, air, and maritime transportation involves securing control systems, communications infrastructure, and addressing vulnerabilities in vehicle systems and navigation technologies. A multifaceted approach encompassing secure network architectures(Nadeem, Amir Latif, Hussain, Jhanjhi, & Humayun, 2022), access controls, encryption, continuous monitoring, and employee training is imperative. Regular security assessments, incident response planning, and collaboration with industry stakeholders are vital to proactively tackle emerging cyber threats and enhance the resilience of transportation systems in the face of evolving cybersecurity risks(W. Liu, Liu, & Bucknall, 2023; Yang, Tan, Lei, & Linares-Barranco, 2023; B. Zhang, Ji, Liu, Zhu, & Xu, 2023).

SECURING WAREHOUSING OPERATIONS

Cybersecurity Considerations for Warehouse Management Systems (WMS)

As depicted in Fig 6.0, When it comes to warehousing operations, Warehouse Management Systems (WMS) assume a pivotal role in ensuring efficiency and effectiveness. To safeguard the security of WMS, several crucial cybersecurity considerations must be addressed. Firstly, the implementation of a secure network architecture featuring appropriate segmentation and firewalls can bolster protection against unauthorized access. Additionally, encrypting data during transmission and at rest can add an additional layer of security, effectively shielding sensitive information stored within the system. Performing regular vulnerability assessments, penetration testing, and security audits is paramount to identifying and rectifying potential vulnerabilities or weaknesses within the WMS. Moreover, keeping software up-to-date, promptly applying security patches, and utilizing robust authentication mechanisms contribute significantly to enhancing the overall security of the WMS(Edirisinghe, 2023; L'Esteve, 2023; Rajakrishnan, 2023).

Figure 6. Fortifying the security of transport and warehousing operations (supplychain247)

Protecting Inventory and Asset Management Systems

Inventory and asset management systems within warehouses house invaluable data pertaining to products, materials, and assets. Safeguarding these systems is essential to mitigate the risks of unauthorized access, theft, or tampering. Implementing access controls based on the principle of least privilege ensures that only authorized personnel can access the inventory and asset management systems. Employing data encryption(Saleh, Abdullah, & Saher, 2022), both during transit and at rest, serves as an additional protective measure for sensitive information. Regular monitoring and auditing of these systems facilitate the identification of anomalies or suspicious activities. Furthermore, establishing backup and recovery mechanisms ensures that data can be restored in the event of a security incident or system failure(Chatziamanetoglou & Rantos, 2023; Truong, Le, & Niyato, 2023).

Ensuring Secure Access Controls and Physical Security in Warehouses

Ensuring secure access controls and maintaining physical security are pivotal aspects of warehouse operations. Implementing robust access controls encompasses measures such as unique user identification, strong passwords, and two-factor authentication(Midha et al., 2023). Employing role-based access control ensures that employees are granted access solely to the systems and areas necessary for their job functions. Regular reviews and revocation of access privileges for former employees or contractors are also imperative. Physical security measures, including surveillance cameras, intruder detection systems, and controlled access to warehouse premises, serve as deterrents against unauthorized entry and theft. The monitoring and logging of access activities contribute to enhanced traceability and accountability of personnel within the warehouse environment(Thantilage, Le-Khac, & Kechadi, 2023).

In conclusion Securing warehousing operations necessitates a comprehensive approach encompassing cybersecurity considerations for Warehouse Management Systems (WMS), the protection of inventory and asset management systems, and ensuring secure access controls and physical security within warehouses. Implementing a secure network architecture, employing data encryption, conducting regular vulnerability assessments, and promptly applying security patches are critical to upholding the security of Warehouse Management Systems (WMS). Protecting inventory and asset management systems entails implementing access controls, data encryption, and regular monitoring. Additionally, secure access controls and physical security measures significantly contribute to the overall security of warehouses. By implementing these measures, warehouses can effectively mitigate the risks associated with cyber threats, unauthorized access, and data breaches, ensuring the integrity, confidentiality, and availability of critical warehouse operations and assets(Borwankar, Pandit, Patel, & Nirmal, 2023; Enache, 2023; Shao, 2023).

THIRD-PARTY RISK MANAGEMENT

Assessing and Managing Cybersecurity Risks Posed by Third-Party Vendors and Partners

The transportation and warehousing industries heavily rely on third-party vendors and partners to provide essential services and support operations. However, this reliance introduces cybersecurity risks that necessitate thorough assessment and effective management. Evaluating cybersecurity risks associated with third-party vendors involves scrutinizing their security practices, vulnerability management processes, incident response capabilities, and data protection measures. This assessment should consider factors such as the sensitivity of shared data, granted access privileges, and the potential ramifications of a third-party breach. Employing a risk-based approach empowers organizations to prioritize high-risk vendors and allocate resources efficiently for due diligence and ongoing monitoring(L. Li, Gong, Wang, & Liu, 2023).

Supplier Evaluation, Due Diligence, and Ongoing Monitoring

A robust approach to managing third-party cybersecurity risks requires comprehensive supplier evaluation, meticulous due diligence, and consistent ongoing monitoring. Supplier evaluation entails appraising security controls, certifications, and past performance to make informed decisions prior to engaging in business relationships. Due diligence activities may include reviewing security policies, conducting on-site visits, and requesting evidence of compliance with relevant cybersecurity standards or frameworks. Ongoing monitoring ensures that vendors maintain their cybersecurity posture and fulfill contractual obligations. This process may encompass periodic security assessments, vulnerability scanning, and continuous monitoring of vendor activities to promptly detect security incidents or anomalies that may impact the organization(Tiwari, Sharma, Choi, & Lim, 2023).

Contractual Agreements and SLAs for Cybersecurity

To effectively control third-party risks, clear and thorough contractual agreements together with definite cybersecurity standards are very crucial in warehousing and transporation industries. These agreements should specifically state expectations for security controls, incident response protocols, data protection measures, and compliance with applicable laws and regulations. Service Level Agreements (SLAs) should include cybersecurity-related performance metrics, such as response times for security issues such as data breach notifications. Furthermore, contractual terms should include responsibility, indemnity, and the organization's right to inspect or analyze the vendor's cybersecurity policies. These agreements must be reviewed and updated on a regular basis to ensure that they are in line with the growing threat landscape and regulatory requirements(Wu, Wang, Wang, & Zhao, 2023).

To summarize, effective management of third-party risks is crucial in the transportation and warehousing industries to protect vital systems, data, and operations. Organizations in the transportation and warehousing sectors may strengthen their cybersecurity resilience and protect their operations against possible cyber threats and vulnerabilities by taking a proactive approach to third-party risk management.

INCIDENT RESPONSE AND BUSINESS CONTINUITY IN TRANSPORTATION AND WAREHOUSING

- Creating an efficient incident response strategy for delays in transportation and warehousing

Developing an effective incident response plan is crucial to mitigate the consequences of disruptions in transportation and warehousing sectors. This effective incident response plan comprises identifying key stakeholders, establishing their roles and responsibilities, and establishing open channels of communication. In addition, to ensure a timely and effective response, the plan includes event classification, escalation protocols, and incident reporting channels. Regular testing, training, and updating of the incident response plan are crucial to align with emerging threats and changes in the operational landscape(Widerholm & Zickerman, 2023).

Incident Detection, Response, and Recovery Strategies

Detecting, responding to, and recovering from incidents constitute essential components of incident response in the transportation and warehousing domains. Employing a robust incident detection framework, comprising intrusion detection systems, log monitoring, and security event correlation, facilitates the timely identification of cybersecurity incidents. Subsequently, orchestrating an effective response becomes pivotal in containing the incident, mitigating its impact, and restoring normal operations. This involves mobilizing the incident response team, conducting forensic investigations, preserving evidence, and implementing remedial measures. Post-incident activities encompass lessons learned sessions, refining incident response processes, and implementing necessary enhancements to prevent future occurrences(Vanichchinchai, 2023).

Business Continuity Planning and Resilience in the Face of Cyber Incidents

Business continuity planning plays a critical role in ensuring operational resilience within transportation and warehousing organizations, particularly in the face of cyber incidents. These plans encompass the formulation of strategies and procedures aimed at maintaining essential functions during and after disruptions. Key aspects include identifying critical processes, establishing backup systems and redundancies, and developing alternative operational modes. Business impact assessments should incorporate scenarios specific to cyber incidents to assess potential consequences and prioritize mitigation efforts. Additionally, setting recovery time objectives (RTOs) and recovery point objectives (RPOs) guides the recovery process and minimizes operational impact. Regular testing, updating, and rehearsal of business continuity plans are vital to validate their effectiveness and uphold organizational resilience(Okuno, 2023).

In conclusion, Within the domain of transportation and warehousing, incident response and business continuity planning play integral roles in risk management and cybersecurity. Establishing an effective incident response plan enables organizations to respond promptly and efficiently to disruptions, thereby minimizing their impact on operations.

TRAINING AND AWARENESS FOR CYBERSECURITY IN TRANSPORTATION AND WAREHOUSING

In the context of Risk Management and Cybersecurity in Transportation and Warehousing, it is essential to consider the importance of training and awareness for cybersecurity. This involves understanding the significance of cybersecurity training for employees, contractors, and partners developing cybersecurity awareness programs and best practices, and addressing the human element in transportation and warehousing cybersecurity(Lombard, 2023).

The Significance of Cybersecurity Training for Workers, Contractors, and Partners

Cybersecurity training is essential for all those working in the transportation and warehousing industries. This includes not only workers but also contractors and partners who may have access to sensitive information or systems. Organizations may enhance their overall cybersecurity posture and lower their risk of cyberattacks(Jhanjhi, Khan, Ahmad, & Hussain, 2022) by offering thorough training on how to recognize and respond to possible cyber threats(Cvahte Ojsteršek, Šinko, & Gajšek, 2023).

Developing Cybersecurity Awareness Initiatives and Best Practices

To successfully manage cybersecurity threats in transportation and warehousing, firms must create strong cybersecurity awareness programs that combine best practices. This might include analyzing current cybersecurity measures, identifying areas for improvement, and developing tools, standards, and guidelines to assist continuing cybersecurity initiatives. Effective communication with internal and external stakeholders is also necessary to ensure that all parties are aware of possible potential risks and how to reduce them(Maharana & Lathabhavan, 2023).

Considering the Human Factor in Transportation and Warehouse Cybersecurity

The human aspect is crucial in transportation and warehouse cybersecurity. Employees, contractors, and partners must be taught to understand and respond to possible cyber risks. This can include instruction on how to detect phishing efforts, create strong passwords, report suspicious behavior, and adhere to other cybersecurity best practices. Organizations may enhance the state of their overall security by addressing the human factor in transportation and warehouse cybersecurity(Fernando, Suhaini, Tseng, Abideen, & Shaharudin, 2023).

To summarize, training and awareness are critical components of good transportation and warehouse cybersecurity. Organizations may strengthen their entire safety framework by offering thorough training to workers, contractors, and partners, implementing effective cybersecurity awareness programs, and addressing the human factor in transportation and warehouse cybersecurity.

EMERGING TECHNOLOGIES AND FUTURE TRENDS

Impact of New Technologies (e.g., IoT, AI, blockchain) on Supply Chain Cybersecurity

As shown in Fig 7.0, the transportation and warehousing industries are gradually embracing emerging technologies such as the Internet of Things (IoT), artificial intelligence (AI), and blockchain(Menon et al., 2023). These technologies have the potential to increase efficiency and production, but they also pose new cybersecurity concerns. A brief discussion on these technologies is given below:

1. Internet of Things (IoT): The Internet of Things (IoT) is a network of things that are linked to the internet. Sensors, actuators, and other devices are examples of such things. The Internet of Things is being utilized in transportation and warehousing for several reasons, including asset tracking, condition monitoring, and device management(Buntak, Kovačić, & Mutavdžija, 2019; D. Kumar, Singh, Mishra, & Wamba, 2022; Song, Yu, Zhou, Yang, & He, 2020).

2. Artificial Intelligence (AI): AI refers to robots' ability to learn and make judgments without being explicitly programmed. AI is being applied in transportation and warehousing for several applications, including route optimization, demand prediction, and anomaly detection(Drissi Elbouzidi et al., 2023).

3. Blockchain: A distributed ledger system that enables safe and transparent transactions. Blockchain is being utilized for several reasons in transportation and storage, including tracking shipments, managing supply chains, and verifying transactions(Ar et al., 2020; Ragab & Altalbe, 2022).

The implementation of these new technologies raises new cybersecurity threats. IoT devices, for example, may be hacked, AI systems can be duped, and blockchain networks can be tampered with. These risks can have serious consequences for logistics and warehouse operations.

Figure 7. Cutting-edge technologies shaping the future of logistics

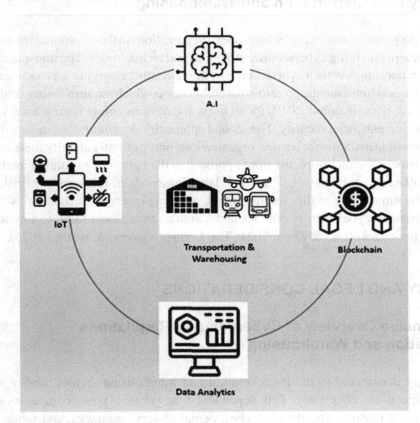

Anticipating Future Cyber Risks and Vulnerabilities

The transportation and warehousing sectors are constantly evolving with the adoption of cutting-edge technologies, but this growth also presents new cyber threats and vulnerabilities that enterprises must anticipate and prevent. The rising usage of cloud computing(Shafiq, Jhanjhi, & Abdullah, 2021) raises security problems such as data breaches and illegal access, needing prioritized data protection. Furthermore, the rising reliance on mobile devices in these businesses creates risks due to inadequate security measures and exposure to public networks, necessitating the deployment of comprehensive mobile device management methods and severe security standards(Ponnusamy, Humayun, Jhanjhi, Yichiet, & Almufareh, 2022). Furthermore, while the widespread use of social media platforms in transportation and warehousing provides benefits, it also exposes firms to hazards such as malware, phishing attempts, and information collection. To combat these risks, caution and reliable security measures such as proactive monitoring, personnel training, and modern cybersecurity solutions, are required. Overall, addressing cybersecurity and staying ahead of new threats is critical for the long-term sustainability and security of logistics and warehouse operations(Chin, Marasini, & Lee, 2023; Chowdhury & Zhu, 2023; Jahani, Jain, & Ivanov, 2023; Rejeb, Rejeb, Simske, & Treiblmaier, 2023).

Evolving Strategies and Technologies for Enhanced Cybersecurity in Transportation and Warehousing

To mitigate the risks posed by emerging technologies, organizations in the transportation and warehousing industry need to adopt emerging cybersecurity strategies and technologies. The transportation and warehousing businesses may improve their cybersecurity by implementing emerging approaches and technology. One of the approaches is Implementing a zero-trust architecture, which requires authentications(joo Fong, Abdullah, Jhanjhi, & Supramaniam, 2019) for all users and devices before having access to information systems, guaranteeing enhanced security. The second approach is by continuous monitoring of information systems for possible malicious activities, organizations may promptly identify these occurrences and respond to them timely. Furthermore, the third approach is the harnessing of threat intelligence, which comprises the collecting and analysis of threat-related information, this assists in risk identification and mitigation. To summarize, in this volatile world, adopting emerging technologies and proactively implementing advanced cybersecurity policies and solutions are critical to protect systems and assets from growing cyber-attacks(Luo & Zhou, 2021; Thi, Luong, Nguyen, & Hoang, 2023).

REGULATORY AND LEGAL CONSIDERATIONS

A Comprehensive Overview of Cybersecurity Regulations in Transportation and Warehousing

Digital technology is essential to the transportation and warehousing sectors' ability to manage and safeguard their operations effectively. This dependency, however, exposes companies to a variety of cyber threats, such as ransomware, data breaches, denial-of-service attacks, and sabotage, which can impair services, jeopardize the integrity of data, harm assets, and tarnish reputation. The industry must abide by cybersecurity laws and standards created to protect transportation systems and the data they manage in order to address these issues(Augello, 2001; Hoffmann & Prause, 2018). The following are some important laws and guidelines:

1. The Transportation Systems Sector Cybersecurity Framework Implementation Guide:

This guide provides transportation system owners and operators with a thorough strategy to reduce cyber risks using the concepts of the National Institute of Standards and Technology (NIST) Cybersecurity

Framework. It was created in collaboration with the Cybersecurity and Infrastructure Security Agency (CISA), the Transportation Systems Sector Coordinating Council (TSSCC), and the Transportation Systems Government Coordinating Council (TSGCC). The manual covers five important tasks: identify, protect, detect, respond, and recover. It also comes with a worksheet to evaluate a company's current cybersecurity posture, spot gaps, set priorities, and interact with stakeholders(Filippova & Voronina, 2021; Zhamshid, Nusratilloevich, Shahida, & Azamat, 2023; J. Zhang, Li, & Wang, 2023).

2.   Analyzing Growing Cyber Threats in Transportation and Logistics:

The Boston Consulting Group (BCG) research, "Navigating Rising Cyber Risks in Transportation and Logistics," evaluates the cybersecurity threats faced by the transportation and logistics (T&L) industry and offers helpful suggestions for raising cybersecurity concerns. The study is divided into four sections: cyber strategy and governance, cyber risk management, cyber resilience, and cyber talent and culture. It also offers a cybersecurity maturity assessment tool that allows T&L enterprises to compare their performance to peers and best practices(Lehto & Pöyhönen; Pöyhönen, Simola, & Lehto, 2023).

3.   The TSA Security Directives for passenger and freight railroad carriers:

These are new cybersecurity requirements issued by the Transportation Security Administration (TSA) in October 2021 for designated passenger and freight railroad carriers. The directives require owners and operators to(Cohen & Shaheen, 2023; Ma, 2023):

1.   Designate a cybersecurity coordinator who is available 24/7 to coordinate with TSA on cyber incidents.
2.   Report any cyber incidents to TSA within 12 hours of discovery.
3.   Conduct a vulnerability assessment of their information technology (IT) and operational technology (OT) systems within 90 days of the directive.
4.   Develop a cybersecurity plan that addresses the identified vulnerabilities within 180 days of the directive.
5.   Implement specific cybersecurity measures to protect IT and OT systems from unauthorized access, such as multi-factor authentication, encryption, segmentation, patching, backup, logging, monitoring, and incident response.

Compliance Requirements and Implications

Compliance with the above-mentioned regulations and standards is not only a legal obligation but also a strategic advantage for transportation and warehousing companies(Grover & Ashraf; Kalubanga & Mbekeka, 2023; Zunarelli, 2023). By following the best practices and recommendations provided by these sources, companies can:

1.   Improve their cybersecurity posture and reduce their exposure to cyber threats.
2.   Enhance their operational efficiency and reliability by minimizing disruptions caused by cyber incidents.
3.   Increase their customer trust and satisfaction by protecting their data privacy and security.

4.   Avoid potential fines, penalties, lawsuits, or reputational damage resulting from non-compliance or cyber breaches.

However, compliance also entails some challenges and costs for transportation and warehousing companies. Some of these are:

1.   The need to allocate sufficient resources, such as budget, time, personnel, technology, and training, to implement the required cybersecurity measures.
2.   The need to coordinate with multiple stakeholders, such as regulators, customers, suppliers, partners, employees, contractors, consultants, auditors, insurers, law enforcement agencies, etc., to ensure compliance across the supply chain.
3.   The need to adapt to changing regulations and standards as new cyber threats emerge, or new technologies evolve.

Legal Aspects and Potential Liabilities Related to Cybersecurity Incidents

Cybersecurity incidents can have serious legal consequences for transportation and warehousing companies (Besiekierska, 2022). Depending on the nature and severity of the incident, companies may face:

1. Civil liability: This refers to the legal responsibility for compensating any damages or losses suffered by third parties as a result of a cyber incident (M. S. Karim, 2022). For example, customers may sue a company for breach of contract or negligence if their personal or financial data is compromised or stolen due to a cyber-attack. If a cyber incident disrupts or negatively affects a company's commercial activities, suppliers or partners may take legal action against the company for breach of contract or other tort claims.

2. Criminal liability: Criminal accountability is the legal term for being held accountable for breaking cybersecurity-related criminal laws or regulations. For instance, if a business does not notify the proper authorities of a cyber incident as required by law, it may be subject to legal action or penalties. Additionally, if a business is discovered to be aiding or participating in any cybercrime, such as hacking, fraud, extortion, sabotage, espionage, or other similar activities, it may face criminal charges or fines (Pravdiuk, 2022).

3. Regulatory liability: Regulatory compliance and cybersecurity standards are both subject to legal compliance obligations. For instance, failing to comply with the cybersecurity requirements established in the TSA Security Directives may result in regulatory fines or enforcement proceedings against a corporation (Kepli, 2023). Similar to this, a company that disobeys data protection laws or regulations, such as the Personal Data Protection Act (PDPA) in Brunei or the General Data Protection Regulation (GDPR) in the European Union, may be subject to disciplinary action or other enforcement actions.

For instance, a company may be subject to regulatory fines or enforcement actions if it doesn't put the cybersecurity safeguards recommended by the TSA Security Directives into place. Similarly, if a firm violates any data protection rules or regulations, such as the General Data Protection Regulation (GDPR) (Lukic, Miller, & Skiera, 2023) in the European Union or the Personal Data Protection Act (PDPA) in Brunei (Slesman & Hoon, 2023), it may face regulatory consequences or enforcement measures.

To reduce these legal risks and liabilities, transportation and warehousing businesses should do the following:

1. Create a strong cybersecurity policy and governance structure that outlines roles, responsibilities, processes, and procedures for managing cyber risks and incidents.
2. Put in place suitable cybersecurity controls and procedures to safeguard their IT and OT systems and data from unauthorized access, modification, disclosure, or destruction.
3. Monitor and audit their cybersecurity performance and compliance on a regular basis and rectify any gaps or vulnerabilities as soon as possible.
4. Maintain openness and accountability by communicating and collaborating with internal and external stakeholders on cybersecurity issues.
5. In the event of a cyber incident or dispute, get legal counsel and support from experienced authorities.

CONCLUSION

Risk management and cybersecurity are major challenges for the transportation and warehousing industries. Organizations in this industry may assist to secure their systems and assets by implementing effective risk management and cybersecurity procedures.

In addition to the methods outlined above, firms in the transportation and warehousing sectors may strengthen their risk management and cybersecurity by doing the following things stated below:

1. **Creating a security culture:** This culture should stress the importance of security as well as the requirement for employees to be aware of cybersecurity dangers.
2. **Investing in training and awareness:** Employees should be educated on cybersecurity best practices as well as how to detect and report suspicious activities.
3. **Regular security audits:** These audits should detect and remediate security threats.
4. **Prompt incident response:** Organizations should have a plan in place for dealing with cyberattacks and other security events.

Organizations in the transportation and warehousing industries may assist to safeguard their systems and assets against cyberattacks by adopting these actions.

Recap of Key Concepts and Insights

1. Transportation and warehousing are key businesses that rely on digital technology more and more.
2. Because of this reliance on digital technology, new cybersecurity concerns such as assaults on IT systems, supply chain disruptions, and data breaches have emerged.
3. In order to secure their systems and assets, organizations in the transportation and warehousing industries must have comprehensive risk management and cybersecurity policies.
   ◦ **Call to action for enhanced risk management and cybersecurity in transportation and warehousing**
     1. Transportation and warehousing companies must emphasize risk management and cybersecurity.
     2. This involves creating and implementing a complete risk management plan, putting in place proper cybersecurity measures, and performing frequent security audits.

3. Organizations should also work with other transportation and warehousing stakeholders to exchange knowledge and best practices.

Future Directions and Challenges in the Field

1. The transportation and warehousing industries are continually developing, and new cybersecurity vulnerabilities emerge all the time.
2. Organizations in this industry need to stay up to date on the latest cybersecurity threats and trends in order to protect their systems and assets.
3. Additionally, organizations need to invest in research and development of new cybersecurity technologies in order to stay ahead of the curve.

REFERENCES

Agrafiotis, I., Nurse, J. R., Goldsmith, M., Creese, S., & Upton, D. (2018). A taxonomy of cyber-harms: Defining the impacts of cyber-attacks and understanding how they propagate. *Journal of Cybersecurity*, *4*(1), tyy006. doi:10.1093/cybsec/tyy006

Ahmed, A. A., & Ahmed, W. A. (2019). An effective multifactor authentication mechanism based on combiners of hash function over internet of things. *Sensors (Basel)*, *19*(17), 3663. doi:10.3390/s19173663 PMID:31443608

Al-Zahrani, A. (2022). Assessing and Proposing Countermeasures for Cyber-Security Attacks. *International Journal of Advanced Computer Science and Applications*, *13*(1), 885–895. doi:10.14569/IJACSA.2022.01301102

Alferidah, D. K., & Jhanjhi, N. (2020). Cybersecurity impact over bigdata and iot growth. *Paper presented at the 2020 International Conference on Computational Intelligence (ICCI)*. IEEE. 10.1109/ICCI51257.2020.9247722

Alkhodair, A., Mohanty, S. P., & Kougianos, E. (2023). FlexiChain 3.0: Distributed Ledger Technology-Based Intelligent Transportation for Vehicular Digital Asset Exchange in Smart Cities. *Sensors (Basel)*, *23*(8), 4114. doi:10.3390/s23084114 PMID:37112453

Alsmadi, I. (2023). *The NICE cyber security framework: Cyber security intelligence and analytics*. Springer Nature. doi:10.1007/978-3-031-21651-0

Amro, A., & Gkioulos, V. (2023). Cyber risk management for autonomous passenger ships using threat-informed defense-in-depth. *International Journal of Information Security*, *22*(1), 249–288. doi:10.1007/s10207-022-00638-y

Ar, I. M., Erol, I., Peker, I., Ozdemir, A. I., Medeni, T. D., & Medeni, I. T. (2020). Evaluating the feasibility of blockchain in logistics operations: A decision framework. *Expert Systems with Applications*, *158*, 113543. doi:10.1016/j.eswa.2020.113543

Ashraf, H., Hanif, M., Ihsan, U., Al-Quayed, F., Humayun, M., & Jhanjhi, N. (2023*). A Secure and Reliable Supply chain management approach integrated with IoT and Blockchain. *Paper presented at the 2023 International Conference on Business Analytics for Technology and Security (ICBATS). IEEE*.10.1109/ICBATS57792.2023.10111371

Augello, W. J. (2001). *Transportation, logistics and the law*.

Battaglioni, M., Rafaiani, G., Chiaraluce, F., & Baldi, M. (2022). MAGIC: A Method for Assessing Cyber Incidents Occurrence. *IEEE Access : Practical Innovations, Open Solutions, 10*, 73458–73473. doi:10.1109/ACCESS.2022.3189777

Benyahya, M., Collen, A., Kechagia, S., & Nijdam, N. A. (2022). Automated city shuttles: Mapping the key challenges in cybersecurity, privacy and standards to future developments. *Computers & Security, 122*, 102904. doi:10.1016/j.cose.2022.102904

Besiekierska, A. (2022). Legal Aspects of the Supply Chain Cybersecurity in the Context of 5G Technology. *Rev. Eur. & Comp. L., 51*(4), 129–147. doi:10.31743/recl.14623

Bhuvana, J., Hashmi, H., Adhvaryu, R., Kashyap, S., Kumari, S., & Wadhwa, D. (2023). Intelligent analytics algorithms in breach detection systems for securing VANETs and data for smart transportation management. *Soft Computing*. doi:10.1007/s00500-023-08399-z

BorwankarJ.PanditS.PatelV.NirmalJ. (2023). IOT-Based Smart Warehouse Monitoring System. *Available at* SSRN 4461490.

Buntak, K., Kovačić, M., & Mutavdžija, M. (2019). Internet of things and smart warehouses as the future of logistics. *Tehnički glasnik, 13*(3), 248-253.

Chatziamanetoglou, D., & Rantos, K. (2023). Blockchain-Based Security Configuration Management for ICT Systems. *Electronics (Basel), 12*(8), 1879. doi:10.3390/electronics12081879

Chen, M., & Yan, M. (2023). How to protect smart and autonomous vehicles from stealth viruses and worms. *ISA Transactions, 141*, 52–58. doi:10.1016/j.isatra.2023.04.019 PMID:37217376

Chin, H., Marasini, D. P., & Lee, D. (2023). Digital transformation trends in service industries. *Service Business, 17*(1), 11–36. doi:10.1007/s11628-022-00516-6

Chowdhury, S., & Zhu, J. (2023). Investigation of critical factors for future-proofed transportation infrastructure planning using topic modeling and association rule mining. *Journal of Computing in Civil Engineering, 37*(1), 04022044. doi:10.1061/(ASCE)CP.1943-5487.0001059

Cohen, A., & Shaheen, S. (2023). *Future of Aviation: Advancing Aerial Mobility through Technology*. Sustainability, and On-Demand Flight.

Cowan, A. (2021). Coming off the tracks: The cyberthreats facing rail operators. *Network Security, 2021*(11), 12–14. doi:10.1016/S1353-4858(21)00131-8

Cvahte Ojsteršek, T., Šinko, S., & Gajšek, B. (2023). Determining Learning Outcomes Relevant for Logistics Higher Education on Sustainability and Industry 4.0. *Tehnički glasnik, 17*(3), 447-454.

Djenouri, Y., Belhadi, A., Djenouri, D., Srivastava, G., & Lin, J. C.-W. (2023). A Secure Intelligent System for Internet of Vehicles: Case Study on Traffic Forecasting. *IEEE Transactions on Intelligent Transportation Systems, 24*(11), 13218–13227. doi:10.1109/TITS.2023.3243542

Dogra, V., Singh, A., & Verma, S., Kavita, Jhanjhi, N., & Talib, M. (2021). Analyzing DistilBERT for sentiment classification of banking financial news. *Paper presented at the Intelligent Computing and Innovation on Data Science: Proceedings of ICTIDS 2021.* Springer. 10.1007/978-981-16-3153-5_53

Driss, M., Almomani, I., Huma, Z., & Ahmad, J. (2022). A federated learning framework for cyberattack detection in vehicular sensor networks. *Complex & Intelligent Systems, 8*(5), 4221–4235. doi:10.1007/s40747-022-00705-w

Drissi Elbouzidi, A., Ait El Cadi, A., Pellerin, R., Lamouri, S., Tobon Valencia, E., & Bélanger, M.-J. (2023). The Role of AI in Warehouse Digital Twins: Literature Review. *Applied Sciences (Basel, Switzerland), 13*(11), 6746. doi:10.3390/app13116746

Ebert, J., Newton, O., O'rear, J., Riley, S., Park, J., & Gupta, M. (2021). Leveraging aviation risk models to combat cybersecurity threats in vehicular networks. *Information (Basel), 12*(10), 390. doi:10.3390/info12100390

Edirisinghe, E. (2023). *Warehouse Management System.* Research Gate.

Enache, G. I. (2023). Logistics Security in the Era of Big Data, Cloud Computing and IoT. Paper presented at the *Proceedings of the International Conference on Business Excellence.* Sciendo. 10.2478/picbe-2023-0021

Fernando, Y., Suhaini, A., Tseng, M.-L., Abideen, A. Z., & Shaharudin, M. S. (2023). A smart warehouse framework, architecture and system aspects under industry 4.0: a bibliometric networks visualisation and analysis. *International Journal of Logistics Research and Applications,* 1-24.

Filippova, T., & Voronina, S. (2021). Organizational and Legal Aspects of Transport Logistics as a Factor of Sustainable Development. Paper presented at the *IOP Conference Series: Earth and Environmental Science.* IOP. 10.1088/1755-1315/670/1/012048

Grover, A. K., & Ashraf, M. H. (2023). *Autonomous and IoT-driven intra-logistics for Industry 4.0 warehouses: A Thematic Analysis of the Literature.* Research Gate.

Gyamfi, E., Ansere, J. A., Kamal, M., Tariq, M., & Jurcut, A. (2023). An Adaptive Network Security System for IoT-Enabled Maritime Transportation. *IEEE Transactions on Intelligent Transportation Systems, 24*(2), 2538–2547. doi:10.1109/TITS.2022.3159450

Hazra, A., Alkhayyat, A., & Adhikari, M. (2022). Blockchain-aided Integrated Edge Framework of Cybersecurity for Internet of Things. *IEEE Consumer Electronics Magazine.* doi:10.1109/MCE.2022.3141068

Heluany, J. B., & Galvão, R. (2023). IEC 62443 Standard for Hydro Power Plants. *Energies, 16*(3), 1452. doi:10.3390/en16031452

Henriques, J., Caldeira, F., Cruz, T., & Simões, P. (2023). A forensics and compliance auditing framework for critical infrastructure protection. *International Journal of Critical Infrastructure Protection, 42*, 100613. doi:10.1016/j.ijcip.2023.100613

Hoffmann, T., & Prause, G. (2018). On the regulatory framework for last-mile delivery robots. *Machines*, *6*(3), 33. doi:10.3390/machines6030033

Humayun, M., Afsar, S., Almufareh, M. F., Jhanjhi, N., & AlSuwailem, M. (2022). Smart Traffic Management System for Metropolitan Cities of Kingdom Using Cutting Edge Technologies. *Journal of Advanced Transportation*.

Humayun, M., Hamid, B., Jhanjhi, N., Suseendran, G., & Talib, M. (2021). 5G network security issues, challenges, opportunities and future directions: A survey. *Paper presented at the Journal of Physics: Conference Series*. IOP Science. 10.1088/1742-6596/1979/1/012037

Humayun, M., Jhanjhi, N., Talib, M., Shah, M. H., & Suseendran, G. (2021). Cybersecurity for Data Science: Issues, Opportunities, and Challenges. *Intelligent Computing and Innovation on Data Science: Proceedings of ICTIDS 2021*, (pp. 435-444). Research Gate.

Hussain, M. N. (2023). Evaluating the impact of air transportation, railway transportation, and trade openness on inbound and outbound tourism in BRI countries.[[industrialcybersecuritypulse. cyber security attack. Retrieved from]. *Journal of Air Transport Management*, *106*, 102307. https://www.industrialcybersecuritypulse.com/threats-vulnerabilities/throwback-attack-how-notpetya-accidentally-took-down-global-shipping-giant-maersk/. doi:10.1016/j.jairtraman.2022.102307

Jahani, H., Jain, R., & Ivanov, D. (2023). Data science and big data analytics: A systematic review of methodologies used in the supply chain and logistics research. *Annals of Operations Research*, 1–58. doi:10.1007/s10479-023-05390-7

Jayanthi, E., Ramesh, T., Kharat, R. S., Veeramanickam, M. R. M., Bharathiraja, N., Venkatesan, R., & Marappan, R. (2023). Cybersecurity enhancement to detect credit card frauds in health care using new machine learning strategies. *Soft Computing*, *27*(11), 7555–7565. doi:10.1007/s00500-023-07954-y

Jhanjhi, N. (2021). A design of IoT-based medicine case for the multi-user medication management using drone in elderly centre. *Journal of Engineering Science and Technology*, *16*(2), 1145–1166.

Jhanjhi, N., Khan, M. A., Ahmad, M., & Hussain, M. (2022). The Impact of Cyber Attacks on E-Governance During the COVID-19 Pandemic. *Cybersecurity Measures for E-Government Frameworks*, 123.

Jmila, H., & Khedher, M. I. (2022). Adversarial machine learning for network intrusion detection: A comparative study. *Computer Networks*, *214*, 109073. doi:10.1016/j.comnet.2022.109073

Joo Fong, T., Abdullah, A., Jhanjhi, N., & Supramaniam, M. (2019). The coin passcode: A shoulder-surfing proof graphical password authentication model for mobile devices. *International Journal of Advanced Computer Science and Applications, 10*(1).

Kalubanga, M., & Mbekeka, W. (2023). Compliance with government and firm's own policy, reverse logistics practices and firm environmental performance. *International Journal of Productivity and Performance Management*. doi:10.1108/IJPPM-09-2022-0463

Karim, A. (2022). Development of secure Internet of Vehicle Things (IoVT) for smart transportation system. *Computers & Electrical Engineering*, *102*, 108101. doi:10.1016/j.compeleceng.2022.108101

Karim, M. S. (2022). Maritime cybersecurity and the IMO legal instruments: Sluggish response to an escalating threat? *Marine Policy*, *143*, 105138. doi:10.1016/j.marpol.2022.105138

Kepli, M. Y. Z. (2023). *Shipping and Logistics in Malaysia: Maritime Institute of Malaysia*. MIMA.

Khaleefah, A. D., & Al-Mashhadi, H. M. (2023). Methodologies, Requirements and Challenges of Cybersecurity Frameworks: A Review. *Int. J. Wirel. Microw. Technol*, *13*, 1–13. doi:10.5815/ijwmt.2023.01.01

Khan, A., Jhanjhi, N. Z., & Humayun, M. (2022). The Role of Cybersecurity in Smart Cities. In *Cyber Security Applications for Industry 4.0* (pp. 195–208). Chapman and Hall/CRC. doi:10.1201/9781003203087-9

Kitsios, F., Chatzidimitriou, E., & Kamariotou, M. (2023). The ISO/IEC 27001 Information Security Management Standard: How to Extract Value from Data in the IT Sector. *Sustainability (Basel)*, *15*(7), 5828. doi:10.3390/su15075828

Ko, W. H., Satchidanandan, B., & Kumar, P. R. (2019). Dynamic watermarking-based defense of transportation cyber-physical systems. *ACM Transactions on Cyber-Physical Systems*, *4*(1), 1–21. Advance online publication. doi:10.1145/3361700

Kumar, D., Singh, R. K., Mishra, R., & Wamba, S. F. (2022). Applications of the internet of things for optimizing warehousing and logistics operations: A systematic literature review and future research directions. *Computers & Industrial Engineering*, *171*, 108455. doi:10.1016/j.cie.2022.108455

Kumar, P. M., Konstantinou, C., Basheer, S., Manogaran, G., Rawal, B. S., & Babu, G. C. (2023). Agreement-Induced Data Verification Model for Securing Vehicular Communication in Intelligent Transportation Systems. *IEEE Transactions on Intelligent Transportation Systems*, *24*(1), 980–989. doi:10.1109/TITS.2022.3191757

L'Esteve, R. C. (2023). Designing a Secure Data Lake. In The Cloud Leader's Handbook: Strategically Innovate, Transform, and Scale Organizations (pp. 183-201): Springer. doi:10.1007/978-1-4842-9526-7_11

Lehto, M., & Pöyhönen, J. (2023). Comprehensive cyber security for port and harbor ecosystems. *Frontiers of Computer Science*, *5*, 1154069.

Li, G., Shen, Y., Zhao, P., Lu, X., Liu, J., Liu, Y., & Hoi, S. C. H. (2019). Detecting cyberattacks in industrial control systems using online learning algorithms. *Neurocomputing*, *364*, 338–348. doi:10.1016/j.neucom.2019.07.031

Li, L., Gong, Y., Wang, Z., & Liu, S. (2023). Big data and big disaster: A mechanism of supply chain risk management in global logistics industry. *International Journal of Operations & Production Management*, *43*(2), 274–307. doi:10.1108/IJOPM-04-2022-0266

Liu, M., Zhang, Z., Chen, Y., Ge, J., & Zhao, N. (2023). Adversarial attack and defense on deep learning for air transportation communication jamming. *IEEE Transactions on Intelligent Transportation Systems*.

Liu, W., Liu, Y., & Bucknall, R. (2023). Filtering based multi-sensor data fusion algorithm for a reliable unmanned surface vehicle navigation. *Journal of Marine Engineering & Technology*, *22*(2), 67–83. doi:10.1080/20464177.2022.2031558

Lombard, C. (2023). Expanding and enhancing incident command system communications support. *Journal of Business Continuity & Emergency Planning*, *16*(4), 304–312. PMID:37170453

LukicK.MillerK. M.SkieraB. (2023). The Impact of the General Data Protection Regulation (GDPR) on Online Tracking. *Available at* SSRN. doi:10.2139/ssrn.4399388

Luo, Y., & Zhou, Q. (2021). Optimization Strategy of Cross-Border E-commerce Logistics Chain from the Perspective of Supply Chain. Paper presented at the *Cyber Security Intelligence and Analytics: 2021 International Conference on Cyber Security Intelligence and Analytics (CSIA2021),* (Volume 2). Springer. 10.1007/978-3-030-69999-4_62

Ma, J. (2023). *Full Steam Ahead: Enhancing Maritime Cybersecurity.*

Maharana, M., & Lathabhavan, R. (2023). Industry 4.0 and its impact on supply chain management: An overview. *International Journal of Services. Economics and Management*, *14*(2), 224–248.

Mallah, R. A., Lopez, D., & Farooq, B. (2021). Cyber-Security Risk Assessment Framework for Blockchains in Smart Mobility. *IEEE Open Journal of Intelligent Transportation Systems*, *2*, 294–311. doi:10.1109/OJITS.2021.3106863

Menon, S., Anand, D., Kavita, Verma, S., Kaur, M., Jhanjhi, N. Z., Ghoniem, R. M., & Ray, S. K. (2023). Blockchain and Machine Learning Inspired Secure Smart Home Communication Network. *Sensors (Basel)*, *23*(13), 6132. doi:10.3390/s23136132 PMID:37447981

Midha, S., Verma, S., Mittal, M., Jhanjhi, N., Masud, M., & AlZain, M. A. (2023). A Secure Multi-factor Authentication Protocol for Healthcare Services Using Cloud-based SDN. *Computers, Materials & Continua*, *74*(2). doi:10.32604/cmc.2023.027992

Möller, D. P. (2023). NIST Cybersecurity Framework and MITRE Cybersecurity Criteria. In Guide to Cybersecurity in Digital Transformation: Trends, Methods, Technologies, Applications and Best Practices (pp. 231-271). Springer. doi:10.1007/978-3-031-26845-8_5

Mpatziakas, A., Drosou, A., Papadopoulos, S., & Tzovaras, D. (2022). IoT threat mitigation engine empowered by artificial intelligence multi-objective optimization. *Journal of Network and Computer Applications*, *203*, 103398. doi:10.1016/j.jnca.2022.103398

Mukherjee, D., Ghosh, S., Pal, S., Akila, D., Jhanjhi, N., Masud, M., & AlZain, M. A. (2022). Optimized Energy Efficient Strategy for Data Reduction Between Edge Devices in Cloud-IoT. *Computers, Materials & Continua*, *72*(1). doi:10.32604/cmc.2022.023611

Nadeem, R., Amir Latif, R. M., Hussain, K., Jhanjhi, N., & Humayun, M. (2022). A flexible framework for requirement management (FFRM) from software architecture toward distributed agile framework. *Open Computer Science*, *12*(1), 364–377. doi:10.1515/comp-2022-0239

Najmi, K. Y., AlZain, M. A., Masud, M., Jhanjhi, N., Al-Amri, J., & Baz, M. (2021). A survey on security threats and countermeasures in IoT to achieve users confidentiality and reliability. *Materials Today: Proceedings.*

Okuno, I. (2023). Introduction of business continuity plan for small and medium-sized local construction companies and restoration activities in Japan in the event of natural disasters. *Paper presented at the IOP Conference Series: Earth and Environmental Science*. IOP Science. 10.1088/1755-1315/1195/1/012047

Pandian, D. A. P. (2019). Artificial intelligence application in smart warehousing environment for automated logistics. *Journal of Artificial Intelligence and Capsule Networks*, *1*(2), 63–72. doi:10.36548/jaicn.2019.2.002

Papastergiou, S., Mouratidis, H., & Kalogeraki, E. M. (2021). Handling of advanced persistent threats and complex incidents in healthcare, transportation and energy ICT infrastructures. *Evolving Systems*, *12*(1), 91–108. doi:10.1007/s12530-020-09335-4

Pawlicki, M., Pawlicka, A., Kozik, R., & Choraś, M. (2023). The survey and meta-analysis of the attacks, transgressions, countermeasures and security aspects common to the Cloud, Edge and IoT. *Neurocomputing*, *551*, 126533. doi:10.1016/j.neucom.2023.126533

Ponnusamy, V., Humayun, M., Jhanjhi, N., Yichiet, A., & Almufareh, M. F. (2022). Intrusion Detection Systems in Internet of Things and Mobile Ad-Hoc Networks. *Computer Systems Science and Engineering*, *40*(3). doi:10.32604/csse.2022.018518

Pöyhönen, J., Simola, J., & Lehto, M. (2023). Basic Elements of Cyber Security for a Smart Terminal Process. *Paper presented at the The Proceedings of the... International Conference on Cyber Warfare and Security*. IOP Science.

Prabakar, D., Sundarrajan, M., Manikandan, R., Jhanjhi, N., Masud, M., & Alqhatani, A. (2023). Energy Analysis-Based Cyber Attack Detection by IoT with Artificial Intelligence in a Sustainable Smart City. *Sustainability (Basel)*, *15*(7), 6031. doi:10.3390/su15076031

Pravdiuk, A. (2022). The state and current issues of legal regulation of cyber security in Ukraine. *European Political and Law Discourse.*, *9*(3), 19–28. doi:10.46340/eppd.2022.9.3.3

Progoulakis, I., Nikitakos, N., Dalaklis, D., Christodoulou, A., Dalaklis, A., & Yaacob, R. (2023). Digitalization and cyber physical security aspects in maritime transportation and port infrastructure. In Smart Ports and Robotic Systems: Navigating the Waves of Techno-Regulation and Governance (pp. 227-248): Springer. doi:10.1007/978-3-031-25296-9_12

Ragab, M., & Altalbe, A. (2022). A Blockchain-Based Architecture for Enabling Cybersecurity in the Internet-of-Critical Infrastructures. *Computers, Materials & Continua*, *72*(1), 1579–1592. doi:10.32604/cmc.2022.025828

Rajakrishnan, M. (2023). *Effectiveness Of Modern Warehousing Technology*. Research Gate.

Rawat, R., Rimal, Y. N., William, P., Dahima, S., Gupta, S., & Sakthidasan Sankaran, K. (2022). Malware Threat Affecting Financial Organization Analysis Using Machine Learning Approach. *International Journal of Information Technology and Web Engineering*, *17*(1), 1–20. doi:10.4018/IJITWE.304051

Rejeb, A., Rejeb, K., Simske, S. J., & Treiblmaier, H. (2023). Drones for supply chain management and logistics: A review and research agenda. *International Journal of Logistics*, *26*(6), 708–731. doi:10.1080/13675567.2021.1981273

Saeed, S., Jhanjhi, N., Naqvi, S. M. R., & Khan, A. (2022). Analytical Approach for Security of Sensitive Business Cloud. *Deep Learning in Data Analytics: Recent Techniques, Practices and Applications*, 257-266.

Said, D., Elloumi, M., & Khoukhi, L. (2022). Cyber-Attack on P2P Energy Transaction between Connected Electric Vehicles: A False Data Injection Detection Based Machine Learning Model. *IEEE Access : Practical Innovations, Open Solutions*, *10*, 63640–63647. doi:10.1109/ACCESS.2022.3182689

Saleh, M., Abdullah, A., & Saher, R. (2022). Message security level integration with iotes: A design dependent encryption selection model for iot devices. *IJCSNS*, *22*(8), 328.

Sánchez, J. M. G., Jörgensen, N., Törngren, M., Inam, R., Berezovskyi, A., Feng, L., Fersman, E., Ramli, M. R., & Tan, K. (2022). Edge Computing for Cyber-physical Systems: A Systematic Mapping Study Emphasizing Trustworthiness. *ACM Transactions on Cyber-Physical Systems*, *6*(3), 1–28. doi:10.1145/3539662

Sarker, I. H. (2021). CyberLearning: Effectiveness analysis of machine learning security modeling to detect cyber-anomalies and multi-attacks. *Internet of Things : Engineering Cyber Physical Human Systems*, *14*, 100393. doi:10.1016/j.iot.2021.100393

Sawal, A. B., Ahmad, M., Muralitharan, M. A., Loganathan, V., & Jhanjhi, N. (2022). Machine Intelligence in Customer Relationship Management in Small and Large Companies. In *Empowering Sustainable Industrial 4.0 Systems With Machine Intelligence* (pp. 132–153). IGI Global. doi:10.4018/978-1-7998-9201-4.ch007

Shafik, W. (2023). A Comprehensive Cybersecurity Framework for Present and Future Global Information Technology Organizations. In *Effective Cybersecurity Operations for Enterprise-Wide Systems* (pp. 56–79). IGI Global. doi:10.4018/978-1-6684-9018-1.ch002

Shafiq, D. A., Jhanjhi, N., & Abdullah, A. (2021). Machine learning approaches for load balancing in cloud computing services. *Paper presented at the 2021 National Computing Colleges Conference (NCCC)*. IEEE. 10.1109/NCCC49330.2021.9428825

Shah, I. A., Jhanjhi, N., & Laraib, A. (2023). Cybersecurity and Blockchain Usage in Contemporary Business. In *Handbook of Research on Cybersecurity Issues and Challenges for Business and FinTech Applications* (pp. 49–64). IGI Global.

Shao, K. (2023). Design and implementation of network security management system based on K-means algorithm. *Paper presented at the Second International Symposium on Computer Applications and Information Systems (ISCAIS 2023)*. SPIE. 10.1117/12.2683547

Shojae Chaeikar, S., Jolfaei, A., & Mohammad, N. (2023). AI-Enabled Cryptographic Key Management Model for Secure Communications in the Internet of Vehicles. *IEEE Transactions on Intelligent Transportation Systems*, *24*(4), 4589–4598. doi:10.1109/TITS.2022.3200250

Slesman, L., & Hoon, C.-Y. (2023). Brunei Darussalam in 2022: Towards Post-COVID-19 Economic Recovery, Diversification and Sustainability. *Southeast Asian Affairs*, *2023*(1), 52–68.

Song, Y., Yu, F. R., Zhou, L., Yang, X., & He, Z. (2020). Applications of the Internet of Things (IoT) in smart logistics: A comprehensive survey. *IEEE Internet of Things Journal, 8*(6), 4250–4274. doi:10.1109/JIOT.2020.3034385

Srikanth, G. U., Geetha, R., & Prabhu, S. (2023). An efficient Key Agreement and Authentication Scheme (KAAS) with enhanced security control for IIoT systems. *International Journal of Information Technology : an Official Journal of Bharati Vidyapeeth's Institute of Computer Applications and Management, 15*(3), 1221–1230. doi:10.1007/s41870-023-01173-2

Stormshield. (2023). *Maritime security and port infrastructure: reconciling modern operational practices and cybersecurity.* Stormshield. https://www.stormshield.com/news/maritime-security-and-port-infrastructure-reconciling-modern-operational-practices-and-cybersecurity/

supplychain247. (2021). *Using Technology to Protect Against Supply Chain Risk.* SupplyChain247. https://www.supplychain247.com/article/using_technology_to_protect_against_supply_chain_risk

Tashtoush, Y. M., Darweesh, D. A., Husari, G., Darwish, O. A., Darwish, Y., Issa, L. B., & Ashqar, H. I. (2022). Agile Approaches for Cybersecurity Systems, IoT and Intelligent Transportation. *IEEE Access : Practical Innovations, Open Solutions, 10*, 1360–1375. doi:10.1109/ACCESS.2021.3136861

Thantilage, R. D., Le-Khac, N.-A., & Kechadi, M.-T. (2023). Healthcare data security and privacy in Data Warehouse architectures. *Informatics in Medicine Unlocked, 39*, 101270. doi:10.1016/j.imu.2023.101270

Thi, T. T. T., Luong, D. T., Nguyen, H. D., & Hoang, T. M. (2023). A Study on Heuristic Algorithms Combined With LR on a DNN-Based IDS Model to Detect IoT Attacks. *Mendel, 29*(1), 62–70. doi:10.13164/mendel.2023.1.062

Tiwari, S., Sharma, P., Choi, T.-M., & Lim, A. (2023). Blockchain and third-party logistics for global supply chain operations: Stakeholders' perspectives and decision roadmap. *Transportation Research Part E, Logistics and Transportation Review, 170*, 103012. doi:10.1016/j.tre.2022.103012

Truong, V. T., Le, L. B., & Niyato, D. (2023). Blockchain meets metaverse and digital asset management: A comprehensive survey. *IEEE Access : Practical Innovations, Open Solutions, 11*, 26258–26288. doi:10.1109/ACCESS.2023.3257029

Vanichchinchai, A. (2023). Links between components of business continuity management: An implementation perspective. *Business Process Management Journal, 29*(2), 339–351. doi:10.1108/BPMJ-07-2022-0309

Widerholm, A., & Zickerman, A. (2023). *Exploring Supply Chain Risk Management & Business Continuity Practices During Disruptive Times: A Case Study on Swedish Firms.* DiVA.

Wu, X., Wang, Q., Wang, L., & Zhao, X. (2023). Customer integration and the performance of third-party logistics firms: A moderated mediation model. *International Journal of Logistics, 26*(6), 615–632. doi:10.1080/13675567.2021.1969349

Yang, S., Tan, J., Lei, T., & Linares-Barranco, B. (2023). Smart traffic navigation system for fault-tolerant edge computing of internet of vehicle in intelligent transportation gateway. *IEEE Transactions on Intelligent Transportation Systems, 24*(11), 13011–13022. doi:10.1109/TITS.2022.3232231

Yazdinejad, A., Rabieinejad, E., Hasani, T., & Srivastava, G. (2023). A BERT-based recommender system for secure blockchain-based cyber physical drug supply chain management. *Cluster Computing*, *26*(6), 3389–3403. doi:10.1007/s10586-023-04088-6

Yeboah-Ofori, A., Islam, S., Lee, S. W., Shamszaman, Z. U., Muhammad, K., Altaf, M., & Al-Rakhami, M. S. (2021). Cyber Threat Predictive Analytics for Improving Cyber Supply Chain Security. *IEEE Access : Practical Innovations, Open Solutions*, *9*, 94318–94337. doi:10.1109/ACCESS.2021.3087109

Yousef, W. A., Traore, I., & Briguglio, W. (2023). Classifier Calibration: With Application to Threat Scores in Cybersecurity. *IEEE Transactions on Dependable and Secure Computing*, *20*(3), 1994–2010. doi:10.1109/TDSC.2022.3170011

Zhamshid, V., Nusratilloevich, Y. A., Shahida, K., & Azamat, K. (2023). Rise of the Machines: The Legal Implications of Robotics and Automation for the Digital Workforce. *International Journal of Cyber Law*, *1*(4).

Zhang, B., Ji, D., Liu, S., Zhu, X., & Xu, W. (2023). Autonomous underwater vehicle navigation: A review. *Ocean Engineering*, *273*, 113861. doi:10.1016/j.oceaneng.2023.113861

Zhang, J., Li, S., & Wang, Y. (2023). Shaping a smart transportation system for sustainable value co-creation. *Information Systems Frontiers*, *25*(1), 365–380. doi:10.1007/s10796-021-10139-3

Zhao, X., Abdo, A., Liao, X., Barth, M. J., & Wu, G. (2022). Evaluating Cybersecurity Risks of Cooperative Ramp Merging in Mixed Traffic Environments. *IEEE Intelligent Transportation Systems Magazine*, *14*(6), 52–65. doi:10.1109/MITS.2022.3151097

Zunarelli, S. (2023). The logistics industry in the digital era: problems and opportunities for the SMEs of the transport sector. *SMEs in the Digital Era: Opportunities and Challenges of the Digital Single Market*, 208. Elger.

Chapter 2
Detecting Cyber Threats With a Graph–Based NIDPS

Brendan Ooi Tze Wen
Taylor's University, Malaysia

Tan Zheng Shen
Taylor's University, Malaysia

Najihah Syahriza
Taylor's University, Malaysia

Yap Zhe Hin
Taylor's University, Malaysia

Nicholas Chan Wei Xian
Taylor's University, Malaysia

Siva Raja Sindiramutty
Taylor's University, Malaysia

Nicki Gan Wei
Taylor's University, Malaysia

Teah Yi Fan Nicole
Taylor's University, Malaysia

ABSTRACT

This chapter explores the topic of a novel network-based intrusion detection system (NIDPS) that utilises the concept of graph theory to detect and prevent incoming threats. With technology progressing at a rapid rate, the number of cyber threats will also increase accordingly. Thus, the demand for better network security through NIDPS is needed to protect data contained in networks. The primary objective of this chapter is to explore the concept of a novel graph based NIDPS through four different aspects: data collection, analysis engine, preventive action, and reporting. Besides analysing existing NIDS technologies in the market, various research papers and journals were explored. The authors' solution covers the basic structure of an intrusion detection system, from collecting and processing data to generating alerts and reports. Data collection explores various methods like packet-based, flow-based, and log-based collections in terms of scale and viability.

DOI: 10.4018/978-1-6684-7625-3.ch002

INTRODUCTION

According to Kumar, Gupta, and Arora (2021) and Sulaiman et. al. (2021), an intrusion detection system abbreviated as IDS, is software that can detect unauthorised traffic or entry into a host or network by detecting unusual behaviours or by examining multiple data streams within the host or network processes. The demand for sophisticated IDSs is necessary in the 21st century due to rapid advancements in the field of Internet of Things (IoT) with more devices than ever being connected to the Internet. Such advancements have also encouraged the wide-spread use of cloud technologies, which may be storing confidential or sensitive user data (Sulaiman et al., 2021). The move to cloud technologies have caused these services to be prone to cyber-attacks from malicious users resulting in data breaches, Distributed Denial of Services (DDoS), compromised communication between senders and receivers among other issues (Kumar, Gupta and Arora, 2021; Ponnusamy, Humayun, et al., 2022). Before the discovery and deployment of the IDS, other steps have been taken to overcome the vulnerabilities such as the implementation of more secure internet protocols. HyperText Transfer Protocol Secure (HTTPS) and Secure Socket Layer (SSL) were among the protocols introduced as well as Firewalls and various cryptography techniques to further secure these spaces. Figure 1.0 provides an overview of the types, detection mechanisms and techniques used in various types of IDS.

Figure 1. Overview of IDS
Source: Aljanabi, Ismail, and Ali (2021)

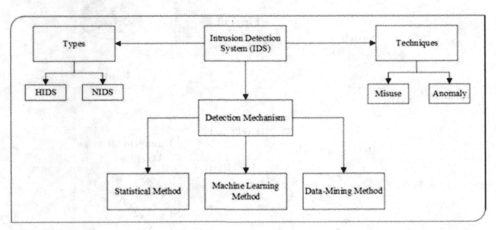

Definition and Importance of IDS and NIDS

Among the common detection mechanisms that are employed on Intrusion Detection Systems are rule-based detection and statistical-based detection (Adnan et. al, 2021). Rule-based detection also known as knowledge-based detection is where an administrator or a super-user would define set parameters also known as rules for normal use. When a user who may be a regular user or intruder performs an action or activity that is not within the defined parameters, an alert will be sounded, and countermeasures will take place. Such systems could also be trained using datasets that contain information on normal activities or actions, an intrusion into the system will then be detected when an action outside of the training model is performed (Aljanabi, Ismail, and Ali, 2021; Ponnusamy, Aun, et al., 2022). Another detection mechanism that is commonly employed is statistical-based detection. Statistical-based detection is where an IDS would compare the traffic of a system with a general model of defined or known normal usage patterns. The IDS would know an attack is taking place when the difference between the reported model and general model is sufficiently large (Adnan et. al., 2021; Annadurai et al., 2022). Another example of how statistical models work would be through the application of multiple mathematical models or techniques and specialist structures to create the profile of a normal user through the analysis of the collected data. An attack profile will be put together for actions that do not match the profile of a normal user. The primary goal of a Network Based IDS or Network Intrusion Detection System (NIDS) is to identify and log information as well as report the abnormality to the network admin (Kumar, Gupta and Arora, 2021; Seong et al., 2021). Figure 2.0 shows the components of a NIDS:

Figure 2. NIDS with its components
Source: Kumar, Gupta, and Arora (2021)

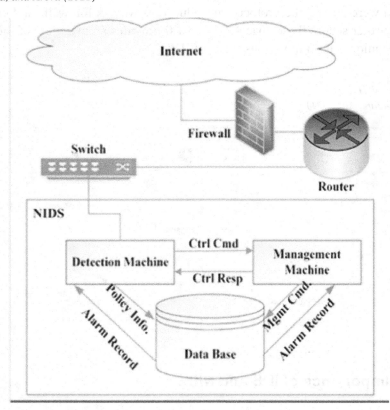

Among the logical components in a NIDS would be a detection machine, management machine and database. The detection machine is responsible for running the detection software which detects abnormalities within the data stream. The management machine is responsible for managing the detection algorithms and strategies. The database component in a NIDS is used for general data logging, to keep track of abnormalities as well as normal data. To maximise the efficiency of the NIDS, it is usually installed at switches and routers within a network to screen data packets and user traffic.

Overview of Proposed Network Intrusion Detection and Prevention System (NIDPS)

This paper aims to propose a viable and feasible Network Intrusion Detection and Prevention System (NIDPS) with the 4 major components of an appropriate IDPS, which are source of data, analysis engine, preventative action and reporting or alarm system, in depth. Each component is compared with real-life examples from existing security service providers such as Snort, Suricata and Zeek. One notable detail is the function of pre-sets ingrained within the system's sourcing of data, which caters to varying types of users with ranging amounts of resources. The presets include 'Individual', 'Small Business' and 'Large organisation'. Each user can select whichever one of the pre-sets according to their number of resources, as well as adjust it to accustom themselves more specifically as additional settings.

The second component of our NIDPS is a graph-based analysis engine, utilising concepts such as Close Centrality (CC) and Eigenvector Centrality (EVC). Information is graphed into a database of graphs, where nodes and edges are used to establish connections throughout the database as well as establish levels of prioritisation in protection of information. The third notable detail of the NIDPS is a preventive action system that utilises community-based prevention and measured centrality-based prevention to complement the analysis engine. Measurements are done through pathways and broadcasting, while communities within the network can be isolated where preventive action can be taken in greater detail.

Importance of Network Intrusion Detection Systems (NIDS) in Contemporary Cybersecurity

According to Nayak and Swapna (2023), the number of IoT devices in the world has been steadily increasing from 5 billion devices in 2015 to an estimated 25 billion devices in 2020. This increase has also demarcated the increasing number of IP addresses. The number of IP addresses used by such IoT devices approaches 1 Trillion in 2022 (Elwary, Awad and Hamed, 2018).The rise of IoT in recent times is mainly due to the seamless connectivity between the device and its surroundings as well as its abilities to wirelessly send data. Technologies such as Bluetooth and IPv6 over Low Power Personal Area Network (6LoWPAN) enables these seamless connections without large power usage which increases the reliability of IoT technologies (Elwary, Awad and Hamed, 2018; Gopi et al., 2021). The main component of an IoT infrastructure includes the sensor which is responsible for collecting data enables such technologies to perform autonomous decisions. The large amount of benefits brought by the IoT paradigm has endorsed both government and non-government sectors to implement these technologies to perform essential functions in sectors such as Agriculture, Finance, Architecture, Healthcare etc (Elwary, Awad and Hamed, 2018; Muzafar et al., 2022).

However, due to the widespread implementation of IoT, such systems and frameworks are also susceptible to security issues which compromises the 3 pillars of information security which are Confidentiality, Integrity and Availability. Among the attacks that pose the biggest threat to the IoT infrastructure is Distributed Denial of Service (DDoS) Attacks (Elwary, Awad and Hamed, 2018; Muzafar & Jhanjhi, 2022). A DDoS attack occurs when a malicious user controls devices lower down the hierarchical order such as sensors to overwhelm the network which causes a disruption of service (Elwary, Awad and

Hamed, 2018). Such attacks pose a threat especially in critical sectors of a country such as finance or healthcare. A DDoS attack which occurred on the 21st of October 2016 which compromised security vulnerabilities within Dyn, a Domain Name Service (DNS) Provider, resulted in major platforms such as Visa, PayPal, Amazon and Netflix losing the ability to provide service to their respective customer bases for 24 Hours. Wireless communication between IoT devices also pose a security concern as they transmit large quantities of private data concerning location, well-being among others. Hence, such systems are prone to eavesdropping or passive attacks where information can be syphoned out by a malicious user.

Therefore, security systems and security mechanisms such as an Intrusion Detection System (IDS) should be in place to overcome the mentioned security vulnerabilities. A Network Intrusion Detection System (NIDS) would be the best line of defence in the context of an IoT ecosystem. According to Nayak and Swapna (2023), large amounts of attacks that occur on IoT systems would occur within the Network Layer of the system. The network layer is responsible for routing data from the application layer to the logic layer which is responsible for storage and processing of the data. The commonly executed attacks within the Network Layer are routing attacks, eavesdropping, DOS attacks and data transit attacks. A security mechanism such as a NIDS would be able to detect and minimise the impact of the attack of an IoT system.

COMPONENTS OF NIDS

Source of Data

According to Shimeall (2018), there are primarily multiple sources of data that may be deployed by a Network Intrusion Detection System to determine if an attack has occurred. One of the streams mentioned is Domain Resolution Data, this type of data is readily available on the network which allows the connection to host from services. Among the streams of data would be the hostname, the result of the connection, the type of request, the date and time, and the collector location. Passive DNS collection is usually employed to collect this data where network traffic monitors are constantly going through requests and incoming responses. The data is then saved and used for analysis and summarisation. Molina-Coronado et al. (2021) mention that networks are typically structured hierarchically, with devices like routers and switches overseeing the traffic flowing to and from the connected devices below them. Higher-level devices, often found at the core of the network, have a comprehensive view of internet-related traffic but a limited perspective on horizontal communications among devices at the same level. Conversely, lower-level devices, such as aggregation and access devices, have a more focused view, capturing traffic from specific network segments. The choice of the capture level significantly impacts a Network Intrusion Detection System (NIDS)'s network coverage, traffic volume for analysis, and the types of cyberattacks it can detect. By collecting data from root network components, we are able to get an insight about the network traffic, making it simpler to identify internet-related attacks targeted at linked devices. Attacks using horizontal traffic that do not reach the root nodes may escape detection by these captures. NIDSs are required for root-level captures to manage enormous data volumes, maintain high levels of efficiency to reduce traffic loss, and decrease detection delays. While analysing traffic from a lower-level device such as a data centre switch offers immunity to noise and disturbances in other network segments, it only covers events that take place in that network segment. The goal of distributed captures is to balance network coverage, performance, and stability by doing partial captures at many network points and collecting the data in one location. Network probes for NIDSs may collect a wide range of information. While some traffic analysers give traffic summaries, often in the form of per-flow data samples, others, which function more like network sniffers, collect entire copies of all data packets. Although it provides a more constrained picture of network traffic, the latter method may be more data volume manageable. Based on individual network monitoring requirements and resource limitations, one should choose amongst various data-gathering techniques.

According to Anjum et al. (2021), packet-based data gathering is more prevalent and commonly used by NIDS. System-level monitoring is possible with the use of statistical data from network traffic, packet headers, and content information. System-level monitoring is where system class traces, process activity, and application logs are taken. The outcome is provided as a binary or multilayer indication based on these characteristics. Binary signalling is used to categorise traffic into two categories: normal and abnormal. According to Molina Coronado et al. (2021), communication networks, which use a variety of network protocols arranged in layers, are crucial for data transmission between nodes. Data units are referred to as frames (at the LAN or link layer), datagrams (at the IP layer), segments (in the TCP/UDP transport layer), or messages (at the application layer) depending on the layer they operate in. These data units are commonly referred to as "packets," and this explanation will presume that IP datagrams are being used. A packet is made up of a payload with the actual data to be transferred and numerous headers with control information. Datagrams are another name for a "packet." Headers and payload are both included in one packet. Headers frequently include information like the TCP header, which indicates the packet is transmitted using the Transmission Control Protocol (TCP), and the IPv4 header, which contains the source and destination addresses, among other headers, that are necessary for the routing and transport of the payload from source to destination. These protocol layers are essential for message transmission over a network. However various apps could use various protocol sets, leading to packets with varied information. Additionally, due to restrictions imposed by link layer protocols like Ethernet's Maximum Transfer Unit (MTU) of 1500 bytes, large messages may be broken into sub-messages. Packet capturing tools such as tcpdump and Gulp are used to capture and store raw network packets, either on a single computer or by configuring a network device to mirror packets to a dedicated port. Capturing raw data can be challenging due to the increasing number of devices and growing network speeds.

Flow-based approaches are perfect for centralised servers managing intensive traffic monitoring since they analyse network traffic over time to derive behaviour characteristics (Farrukh et al., 2022, Almusaylim & Jhanjhi, 2018). They identify anomalies by comparing traffic behaviour to characteristics, however, they rely on professionals to choose the pertinent aspects and frequently use mathematical approaches for data pretreatment. Flow-based techniques, which mainly concentrate on lower-level threats inside the TCP/IP protocol stack, may unintentionally learn about hostile IP addresses and frequently targeted ports. The techniques used to extract and represent data from packets are essential and have a big impact on the results of ML models (Farrukh et al., 2022). Since flow-based techniques examine network traffic over time to determine behavioural characteristics, they are ideal for centralised servers handling intense traffic monitoring (Farrukh et al., 2022). By comparing traffic behaviour to features, they can spot anomalies, but they rely on experts to choose the relevant details, and they typically apply mathematical techniques for data preparation. The TCP/IP protocol stack's lower-level threats are the major focus of flow-based approaches, which may mistakenly learn about hostile IP addresses and commonly targeted ports. The methods used to extract and represent data from packets are crucial and significantly affect the output of ML models (Farrukh et al., 2022; Alferidah & Jhanjhi, 2020). Flow records are exported to collectors for storage, together with the necessary flow information and other variables like start/finish timestamps, byte/packet counts, and observed TCP flags. When compared to raw packet captures, flow records' optional payload field often contains less end-user application data, resulting in more compact captures (Molina-Coronado et al., 2022; Humayun et al., 2020).

According to Zhou et. al. (2018), event logs are a frequent method of data collecting and come in a variety of forms, including web logs, operating system logs, and device logs. It is difficult to categorise these logs definitively because there are no established formats for them. Nevertheless, they have certain common characteristics, such as capturing data such as the date, precise time, operator, and activities taken throughout routine execution. Given that log files are frequently retained continuously, it is an effective tool for data collection. But log files frequently have high memory requirements, little information density, and convoluted formats, making feature extraction and human management difficult. Research from the past has suggested automated and adaptive solutions to these problems. Real-time logs are collected in real-time from probes or files are retrieved from storage by collectors, who then parse the log contents to extract key aspects. Software-Defined Networking (SDN) logs are better organised than conventional network logs, particularly controller logs. These methods also include the collection of statistics and management-related data produced and gathered inside the control plane. Log-based data gathering in SDN assists in identifying protocol characteristics, much as Deep Packet Inspection (DPI) in traditional internet networks. Raw logs acquired from SDN interfaces are filtered by log collectors to remove superfluous information and combine features.

As stated by Snort (2023), it can function as a packet sniffer, or as a packet logger. Thus, it can be deduced that Snort as a network intrusion prevention system would collect its data through packet-based methods. Snort uses rules that define what is malicious and what is not, in order to differentiate between the normal packets and the packets that contain malice and alerts the users of the system accordingly. Zeek also utilises packet-based data collection to monitor data, which is then analysed to search for malicious network activity. Zeek is run by sniffing on one or more network interfaces, which creates logs, insights, and contents of files that have been extracted based on the traffic of the network interfaces (Zeek 2023). With packet-based data collection, Zeek is usually deployed within a home or small office environment, which are best suited for intrusion detection systems that use packet-based data collection.

On the other hand, SolarWinds Security Event Manager makes use of log-based data collection. It collects logs from various sources, and automatically parses it into a readable format for users to investigate and utilise as well as store it for their own uses of the data (SolarWinds n.d.). Compared to packet-based data collection, the Security Event Manager can have its data readily on hand, and well organised. However, these logs often apply complex file formats, have low information density, and also take up a lot of memory (Zhou, D et al. 2018; Muzammal et al., 2020). According to Sagan (2018), Sagan is software that analyses logs in real-time. However, what differentiates Sagan from the rest, is that it was made with speed in mind, thus treating log data similarly to packets, just like Snort and Suricata's packet capture. Sagan's best use case would be for Security Operations Centres, where analysis is required to be fast and without delay.

One more example of an intrusion detection system organisation is Suricata. Suricata uses both packet-based and flow-based data collection, which can be swapped and interchanged. This means that Suricata can capture packets over various threads, or it can also change the capture method to symmetric hash by flow, capturing data in tuples of fives (Suricata 2019). However, an important condition that must be met is that Suricata must be able to access both sides of a flow in the same thread. Normally, during flow-based capture, the flow records are optional, which means that the data is normally compact, and possibly even more compact than captures of raw data (Molina-Coronado, B et al. 2021; Humayun, Jhanjhi, et al., 2020).

However, as innovation calls for it, our NIDPS is aimed towards customisation, giving the software the ability to be suited to all ranges of users from individuals to large organisations. Presets will be provided for the user to select upon installation, according to the size of the user's organisation size. These settings can be changed if the organisation wishes to do so. The first preset is 'Individual'. With the assumption of low computational resources and low memory, the data collection method that would be assigned is packet capture. This is because the individual may not have the memory space for log-based data collection, or the computational resources for flow based. Compared to the other presets, this preset will have slower data collection and thus slower analysis.

The second preset is 'Small Business'. This preset is targeted towards organisations that have yet to be able to afford a lot of computational resources but is required to protect several individuals within the organisation. For this preset, the data collection method assigned is flow-based. This is so that information is more readily analysed and is thus, slightly faster than the 'Individual' preset. The final preset is 'Large organisation'. With this preset chosen, the assumption is that the organisation can afford high computational resources, along with large quantities of memory. Thus, log-based data collection will be assigned to this preset, where a large memory is required for the NIDPS to function. However, in exchange for taking up this high amount of memory, data is readily available for the NIDPS to analyse at any given point, and thus speed is much higher than the other presets. There would also be an option upon installation, allowing for the user to select advanced settings, where settings can be tailored according to the user's computational resources, memory, and space. Data collection methods can also be chosen, as the user would be able to read a short description of each data collection method before selection.

Analysis Engine

As with all intrusion detection prevention systems (IDPS), both host and network-based IDPS' require an analysis engine to detect potential threats to a system. One could argue that analysing and flagging suspicious activity would be the bread and butter of any IDPS, as the analysis engine makes use of raw data collected while allowing the IDPS to act when dealing with suspicious activity. As of 2023, the number of compromised records in 2023 number approximately 4.5 billion (Ford, 2023; Chesti et al., 2020). This shows that the demand for a capable IDS will only increase in time, hence the need for improved analysis engines and threat detection systems.

Currently, there are two detection methods most used: signature-based and anomaly-based systems. The first method, at times referred to as misuse detection, relies on identifying common patterns of cyber-attacks and the signatures produced by said threats. It excels at identifying known threats based on existing internal databases by comparing the signature of data packets with previous attack signatures in the past (Ioulianou et al., 2018; Alkinani et al., 2021). However, it lacks the ability to detect zero-day attacks due to the reliance on existing databases. Popular applications of signature-based IDPS' typically include open-source solutions such as Snort or Suricata.

Figure 3. A flow chart of Snort's intrusion detection system
(Zhang and Wang, 2019).

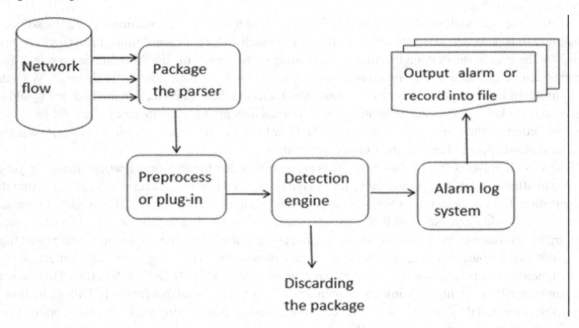

Snort is an open-source NIDPS which works by comparing network traffic with its existing database of rule sets. As seen in Figure 3.0, data is collected and sent through Snort's detection engine. Should a data packet fulfil the conditions of predefined rules, actions can be taken against the packet such as sending alerts to the user (Zhang and Wang, 2019; Jhanjhi et al., 2021). Not only that, Snort also adds an extra layer of personalisation by allowing users to add their own rules and signatures into the rule base in the form of 'snort.conf' files, allowing them to closely monitor incoming traffic and distinguish between normal and suspicious activity (Jain and Anubha, 2021; Fatima-Tuz-Zahra et al., 2020). Zeek (previously known as Bro) is another open-source NIDPS. More specifically, it analyses incoming network traffic to flag any potential threats. Zeek has a wider scope of features in terms of network monitoring, offering its users not only misuse detection capabilities but also those of anomaly detection and protocol analysis (The Zeek Project, 2023; Brohi et al., 2020).

Figure 4. Architecture of Zeek, open source IDPS
(The Zeek Project, 2023).

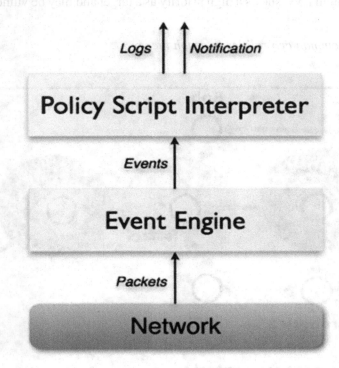

Unlike Snort, Zeek specialises in collecting and analysing traffic data as it is a passive network security monitor. The event engine takes network packets and processes them into events. The policy script interpreter will take, and process said events through either written scripts or default scripts provided by Zeek. In the event of suspicious activity, the system will then alert the user (University of Texas at San Antonio, 2020; Singhal et al., 2020). Figure 4.0 shows Architecture of Zeek, open source IDPS.

The analysis engine used by our NIDPS involves the usage of graph theory. More specifically, the data previously captured by the system will be fed to the analysis engine, producing a graph database which showcases the links between various events in the form of nodes. First, it is crucial to get a basic overview on graph theory and the concepts used in our system. Graph theory starts with graphs that are made up of 'nodes' and 'edges', also commonly referred to as 'vertices' and 'lines' respectively. The nodes function as points in a graph, with one node connected to one or more nodes through edges which show the relationship between two or more linked nodes. The graph can also be directed or undirected, the former being that the edges have direction, and the latter not having any direction for its edges (Chai et al., 2019). The concept of centrality in graph theory will also play a role in threat detection. The first centrality, degree centrality (DC), looks at how many edges are connected to a node or point. A node that has a high degree centrality means it possesses a high activity level in the system, and may have higher authority or access to the system. Next, closeness centrality (CC) will measure the rate at which a node can access all other existing nodes in the system. Lastly, we also have Eigenvector centrality (EVC), which looks at how important a node is based on its connection with other high value nodes (Saqr et al., 2022; Ghosh et al., 2020). Figure 5.0, 6.0, 7.0, 8.0 below shows examples regarding centrality. These concepts are relevant as nodes with high CC will mean that it can reach other related nodes easily and quickly, while having a high EVC shows a high priority as a target and may be vulnerable in the network.

Figure 5. Summary of common centralities in graph theory
(Majeed and Rauf, 2020).

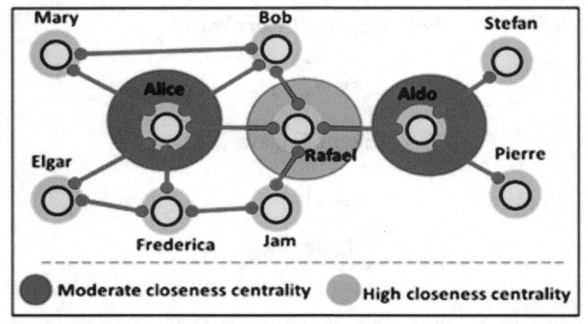

(a) Pictorial overview of the closeness centrality (CC) in a SN.

Figure 6. Summary of common centralities in graph theory
(Majeed and Rauf, 2020).

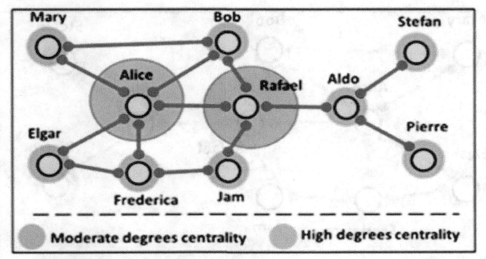

(b) Pictorial overview of the degree centrality (DC) in a SN.

Figure 7. Summary of common centralities in graph theory
(Majeed and Rauf, 2020).

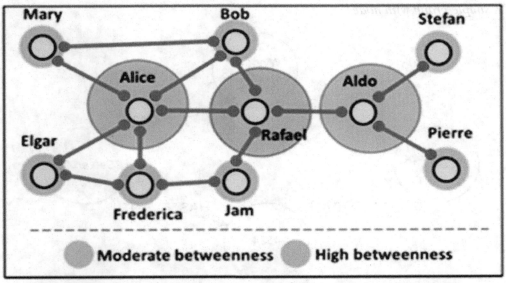

(c) Pictorial overview of the betweenness centrality (BC) in a SN.

Figure 8. Summary of common centralities in graph theory
(Majeed and Rauf, 2020).

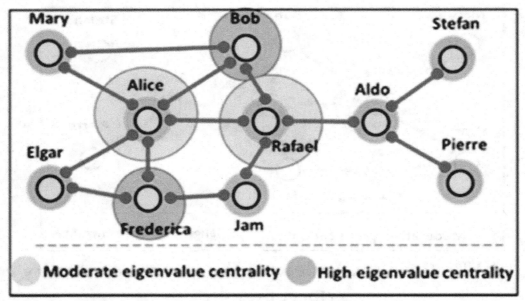

(d) Pictorial overview of the eigenvalue centrality (EVC) in a SN.

Figure 9. A simple graph with nodes

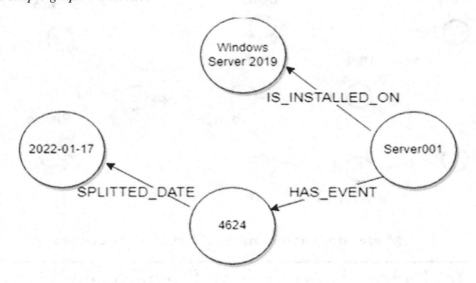

Figure 10. A graph database of a machine's boot process
(Bocquet-Appel, Noyelle and Cattaneo, 2023

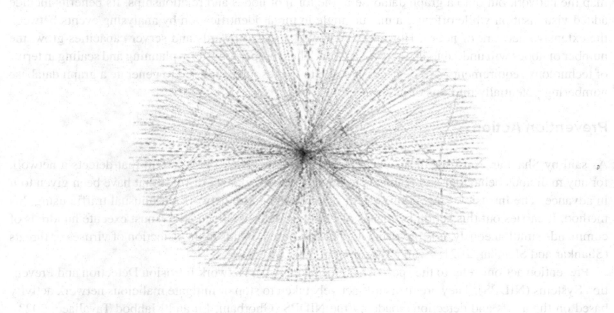

Figure 9 shows A simple graph with nodes Figure 10 shows A graph database of a machine's boot process. Putting together the concepts explained above, the graph based NIDPS would first build up an extensive graph database made up of hundreds of thousands of nodes. These nodes would have different names and can represent various things such as servers, endpoint devices like connected laptops and phones, dates, codes, and so on. The nodes would then produce events ranging from normal activity like user logins and software updates, to any suspicious network activity or threats. Through the graph database, it is also possible to identify potential security risks. As discussed earlier, it is possible to utilise centrality concepts like closeness centrality to figure out which part of the network should be prioritised and safeguarded. A common example would be servers which are connected to many different devices, having a high degree and closeness centrality. Of course, to analyse and process all the existing nodes would be tedious and time consuming. Thus, graph searching algorithms like Dijkstra's algorithm can be utilised to optimise the process by finding the shortest possible paths taken by nodes in the fastest time (Navone, 2020; Azam et al., 2023).

The graph based NIDPS can ward off commonly known threats, as the graph database will have a pattern of events occurring during the attack. Graph database is also useful in predicting novel attacks as the graph tends to have more decentralised nodes with lower degree centrality. System administrators will have a clearer picture visually when dealing with threats both existing and new. To test the NIDPS, four common performance metrics were used: true positive rate, false positive rate, true negative rate, and lastly false negative rate. A true positive is the number of times a threat is correctly identified, while a true negative is correctly identifying the absence of a threat. False positives rates are when the system incorrectly flags normal events as threats, and vice versa for false negatives (Shafi, Jha and Jain, 2022; Azam, Dulloo, et al., 2023). It is important for our system to always minimise false negative rates while maximising true positive rates.

To conclude, the NIDPS' analysis engine follows a graph-based detection system where it is able to map the network out onto a graph database in the form of nodes and relationships. Its benefits include added visualisation while offering a unique angle in threat identification by analysing events between the extensive network of nodes. However, as networks scale upwards and server capacities grow, the number of nodes will undoubtedly increase as well. Thus, proper long-term planning and scaling in terms of technology requirements will be necessary due to the resources needed to generate a graph database numbering potentially millions of nodes.

Prevention Action

As said by Shankar, Network Intrusion Prevention System (NIPS) is a system that detects a network for any malicious behaviour and responds to it using a particular set of rules that have been given to it in advance. The Intrusion Prevention system searches the entire network for unusual traffic using this method. It carries out this action by means of protocol analysis. Since NIPS must execute hundreds of commands simultaneously, it is rapid and application based. It aids in the detection of viruses or threats (Shankar and Shankar, 2021; Azam, Tajwar, et al., 2023).

Prevention actions refer to the specific actions taken by an Network Intrusion Detection and Prevention Systems (NIDPS). They are measures actively taken to stop or mitigate malicious network activity based on the alerts and detections made by the NIDPS (Ghorbani, Lu and Mahbod Tavallaee, 2023). NIDPS prevention actions can be categorised under signature-based, anomaly-based, application layer, firewall integration and response automation. One instance of the prevention action in a NIDPS is blocking traffic from some IP address or range of addresses that are known to conduct malicious activity. By restricting traffic or flagging users from a potentially dangerous IP address, the NIDPS prevents incidents from happening when it takes this action (Redhat.com, 2023). Table below shows a comparison table of possible prevention actions utilised by four well-known network-based Intrusion Detection System (NIDS) solutions: Snort, Suricata, Cisco Firepower Threat Defense, and Zeek/Bro. Figure 11.0 shows NIPS Architecture.

Figure 11. NIPS architecture
(Eleventh Hour CISSP, 2017)

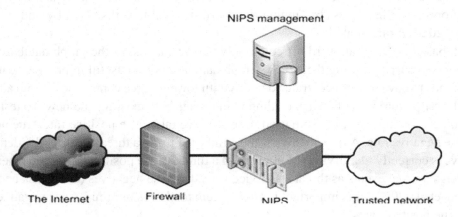

Table 1. Snort, Suricata, Cisco Firepower Threat Defense and Zeek/Bro Prevention Actions Comparison (Source: Aliya Tasneem, Locicero, Cisco & Bou-Harb)

Prevention Action	Snort	Suricata	Cisco Firepower Threat Defense	Zeek/Bro
Signature-Based	Block, Alert, Log	Block, Alert, Log	Block, Alert, Log	Block, Alert, Custom Scripting
Anomaly-Based	Limited with Custom Rules	Thresholds, Alerts, Custom Rules	behavioural Analysis	Custom Scripting and Event Framework
Application Layer	Limited Application Layering	Limited Application Layering	Robust Application Layering	Logs, Alert, Inspect Application-Layer Traffic
Firewall Integration	Iptables and pfSense	Iptables	Cisco Firepower NGFW (Next-Generation Firewall)	It does not integrate with firewall
Response Automation	Limited Response Automation	Robust Response Automation	Robust Response Automation	Custom Scripting

Table 1 shows Snort, Suricata, Cisco Firepower Threat Defense & Zeek/Bro Prevention Actions Comparison. Our NIDPS's efficiency depends on its ability to implement preventive actions based on the insights gained from our analysis engine graph theory. These prevention actions are closely related to our analysis engine's findings, supporting the reasoning behind our approach. As for that, one of the prevention actions for our NIDPS is to implement centrality-based prevention which is crucial in networks. Centrality identified connections between specific network characteristics and an actor's influence. In other words, using ad-hoc formalisation, it determines "the most important actor" or "the most useful entity" in a social network (where a vertex is an actor) (Freeman, 2017; Ananna et al., 2023).

In order to gain a better understanding, consider a directed acyclic graph (DAG), G(V, E), where V stands for the vertices and E for the edges linking them. The data flow depends on the direction of the link while these vertices represent the nodes of a network. As a representation of the network's nodes' link structure, this graph known as a network graph is named that. An edge corresponds to a link that data packets from a node are transported along, which embodies the idea that the link contains important information. In addition, a node's function as an intermediary is crucial in getting this data to its intended location. And, the node's proximity to and connection with the target node are precisely what allow it to achieve that. Therefore, it is possible to conclude that a node's centrality refers to its structural relevance in relation to other nodes in the graph (Rastogi, 2019; Sindiramutty et al., 2024).

There are several ways to measure centrality. The shortest path (geodesic), a path (does not repeat nodes or connections), a trail (does not repeat links), or a walk (can repeat nodes and links) are all options for network traffic. Broadcasting, parallel duplication, serial duplication, or transfer are all possible dissemination strategies. Both parallel and serial duplication, but not transfer, duplicate data to every node (Rastogi, 2019; Azam, Dulloo, Majeed, Wan, Xin, & Sindiramutty, 2023). To correlate with our prevention actions, our NIDPS continually observes network behaviour once the centrality measurements have been calculated to find any outliers. Highly central nodes that are found to be compromised or to be acting strangely are reported as potential security risks. This is because highly central nodes are typically attracting targets for attackers since compromising them may result in extensive control or access to the network (Bloch, Jackson and Tebaldi, 2016). Our NIPDS may occasionally decide to enact tougher access limits for highly central nodes. In order to guarantee that only authorised users may interact with these nodes, our NIDPS will restrict the access to sensitive resources, limit the communication privileges, or add more authentication requirements which result in stricter access control. Another prevention action is isolation where our NIDPS can isolate a highly central node from the network if it is verified to be compromised and poses a security concern. To stop the threat from spreading further, the isolation will break its links with other components and devices. Additionally, our NIDPS may decide to cautiously monitor these nodes rather than taking actions right away in some circumstances. To better grasp the threat, our NIDPS involves close examination of the system behaviour and communication patterns. As for that, our NIDPS minimises potential damage by closely monitoring, isolating, or enforcing stronger controls on these nodes, which lowers the possibility of a successful attack.

Furthermore, our NIDPS implements community-based prevention as one of our prevention actions based on the knowledge obtained from the graph-based analysis. The community-based methods used to graph-based detection systems look for clusters of "close-by" nodes that are densely connected, and they also look for nodes and/or edges that connect communities. In fact, identifying "bridge" nodes or edges that do not directly belong to one particular community can be considered the definition anomalous in this scenario (Akoglu, Tong and Koutra, 2014). The main objective of community-based prevention action is to graph communities or clusters through time and signal an event when there is a structural or contextual change in any of them, as opposed to tracking changes in the entire network.

Here is the thorough explanation on how Community-based prevention is being implemented in our NIDPS. Community-based prevention is supported by its emphasis on pinpointing specific threats (Chakrabarti, Kumar and Tomkins, 2006). It focuses on the discovery of potentially suspicious communities within a network as part of the security measures. Our NIDPS will start taking particular security measures when one of these communities is recognised as suspicious. When a community of devices or users is detected as suspicious, our NIDPS will initiate the prevention action by isolating the potentially suspicious community from the rest of the network. Through this isolation, the community's devices or users are effectively cut off from the rest of the network. Our NIDPS aims to isolate the community in order to stop the spread of the treats and lessen the potential attacks on the network.

As an alternative, our NIPDS may decide to implement communication restrictions within the potentially suspicious community where it involves restricting the communication capabilities of devices or users within the community. To guarantee that only authorised interactions take place within the community, our NIDPS will restrict their access to specific resources, block specific communication channels and impose additional authentication requirements. Our NIDPS will alert and notify the security personnel in addition to situations of isolation or communication restrictions. This enables human operators to respond in real-time and intervene as necessary, giving them the ability to choose the best course of action after being alerted or informed.

As justification for our prevention actions, our NIDPS implements Centrality-based prevention to lessen the possibility of a successful attack and minimise the potential damage by closely monitoring, isolating, and imposing stricter control on these highly central nodes. Our NIDPS aims to protect network integrity and data security by not only identifying threats but also taking preventative measures against them. Furthermore, our NIDPS implements Community-based prevention to identify suspicious behaviours that might not be apparent when analysing individual entities in isolation by classifying devices or users into communities based on their behaviour and communication patterns. By implementing it, our NIDPS lessens the possibility of threats spreading and damage to the network.

Reporting

Whenever the NIDS detects and matches suspicious activity or malicious patterns (signatures), it immediately shuts down the process and raises an alarm to the system administrators so that they can react to the attack appropriately to prevent further damage. These alarms are crucial because they contain information reporting the detected attack and the target and victims of the attack. (Hubballi and Suryanarayanan, 2014) The contents of the alarms can vary significantly from one another and IDPS allows system admins to customise each alert type. Such alerts include pages/ beepers, messages, e-mails, and user-defined programs and scripts. An alert might be generated when some of these scenarios were to occur: a discovery event, a correlation event via violation of policy or access control rule, an intrusion event with a certain impact flag, or a status change for a specific health policy module. (Santos, Panos Kampanakis and Woland, 2016)

There are several types of reporting methodologies a NIDPS can use and it depends on the organisation's objectives, cyber policies, and system capabilities; which ranges from simple log entries of intrusion detection into a console to urgent messages being sent via e-mail messages or SMS. The table 2.0 below shows the comparison of possible alert methodology used by different network-based IDS solutions:

Table 2. Comparison of possible alert methodology used by different network-based IDS solutions

	Snort	Suricata	Cisco Firepower	Zeek/Bro Platform
Reporting methodology used	Snort has the ability to send real-time alerts that are sent to a separate alert file, sent to ● **syslog-ng** (syslog- next generation) ● **swatch** (Simple Watcher) ● **Server Message Block (SMB)** 'WinPopup' (Day, n.d.)	Suricata **logs its output to files** and these logs include alert information, HTTP transaction, etc Suricata generates alerts according to redefined patterns known as rules.	Cisco FMC offers various reporting options such as **logging alerts in server, configuring email alerts, syslog, and SNMP traps.** (Cisco, n.d.)	Reporting of Zeek focuses on the **logging framework in log files** such as DNS, FTP, HTTP, and SSL files. Zeek's logging interface consists of streams, filters & writers. Zeek logs are customizable: extend existing logs with new fields, apply filters to log stream, customise output formats by setting log writer, etc (docs.zeek.org, n.d.)

Snort allows admins to pick and choose specific alerts to be notified in real time, making it highly customizable. You are able to assign individual priority to a rule and include classification of each rule that a priority is attached to. With different priorities attached, you are able to notify different people about different intrusion. Besides that, it allows for different rules to be notified in different techniques as one priority can send you an email or notify you through a pager that an email has been sent. Other methods include swatch or syslog-ng which monitors Snort syslog outputs for predetermined strings; executing a command when a string is found. This will lead to audible alerts or pager applications to be deployed. (Day, n.d.) For Suricata and Snort IDS, there are third-party graphical tools that will help analysts with the process of reading the alert files that the IDSs generate in a simple manner to provide effective analysis power. Snorby and Squil being the two most commonly used free and open source alert management interfaces.

Moving on to the Cisco Firepower, it has a FMC (Cisco Firepower Management Centre) that can configure methods of receiving alerts and external event notifications about certain events so immediate recovery can occur and to help with critical-system monitoring. It allows configuration of external alert responses such as email alerts, logging to a server (syslog), and SNMP traps in order to interact with external servers. It also provides alerts that contain relevant information about the intrusion detected by Firepower and also a predefined report that includes insights into intrusion events and web traffic. Furthermore, the FMC allows incorporation of SIEM (Security Information and Event Management) platforms which is used to correlate Firepower data with other security event sources. (Cisco, n.d.)

SIEM is a collection of software tools for security that includes security information management, log management, and correlation of security incidents. It is used to arrange diverse data and event logs from multiple networked devices to provide visualisation and analysation of data. In an article by Arass and Souissi, they suggest a new SIEM architecture that is tailored to the context of Big Data through Big Data logs and events to produce Smart Data alerts. This new SIEM's seven modules allows for management of a huge amount of logs. It contains data lifecycle (DLC) analysis which includes modules such as a visualisation module that displays the results in a smart manner. The suggested SIEM provides aggregation and normalisation features for log files gathered via many different sources to deliver rich information alerts, all with the help of an efficient and user-friendly SIEM interface. (Arass and Souissi, 2019)

Due to new attack vendors, intrusion alert systems have added sophisticated rule sets and therefore SOC analysts have to face large volumes and a variety of noisy intrusion alerts. The main challenge of an IDS is the high volumes of generated false positive alerts- a phenomenon known as alert fatigue. 99% of alerts produced by NIDS are false positives, repeated warnings, or alert notifications resulting from bogus activities. (Albasheer et al., 2022) Other challenges include high false alarm rates, failure to recognise multi-step attack scenarios, inability to identify the causal relationship between raw alerts, and predictions of attackers next intended targets. Below are some of the actions an IDS can take after an intrusion alert is sent.

An article by Gelman et al suggested a novel alert prioritisation solution known as That Escalated Quickly (TEQ) which is a machine learning framework that reduces alert fatigue by predicting incident-level and alert-level actionability with few modifications to security operation centre workflow. The TEQ has a hands-off featurization system that handles semi-structured input data from random sensors without interfering with downstream tasks. It also consists of an ensemble of models that operates on a greater breadth of alert and it has the ability to identify key information using a single incident. With real-world data, the TEQ can suppress 54% of false positives with 95.1% detection rate, cut down the volume of alerts an analyst needs to review, and save 22.9% of time taken to respond to the relevant occurrence. (Gelman et al., 2023)

Figure 12. The TEQ framework
(*Gelman et al., 2023*)

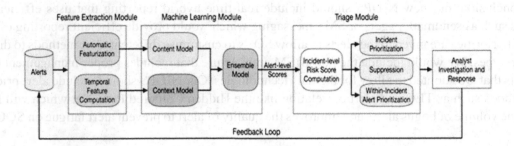

Figure 12 shows the TEQ framework. Another action to be taken after receiving alerts is alert correlation which is a procedure that examines alerts produced by sensors in a network to obtain a broad overview of probable intrusion attempts. By improving the quality of the alert, alert correlation aims to reduce the quantity of generated alerts. One of the proposed alert correlation frameworks by Liu et al suggested a novel alert correlation framework that processes generated alerts in real time and correlates the alerts. Using Bayesian networks, it constructs attack scenarios and forecasts attackers' next goal using the development of attack prediction rules. This framework is used for multi-step attack scenarios detection possessing two modes namely off-line and on-line modes. In the off-line mode, the neural network is trained using known real attack alert logs by processing alert aggregation and associated attack sequences to eliminate erroneous alerts to ultimately produce a Bayesian network attack graph (BAG). Then, a significant number of online alert logs are used in online mode to update neural networks and the BAG. By extracting a range of multi-step attack scenarios from the BAG, we are able to achieve the goal of removing false alerts from redundant NIDS alert logs. (Liu et al., 2019)

Moving on, Yu and Frincke's research proposed the Hidden Coloured Petri-Net (HCPN), which treats alert correlation problem as an inference problem rather than filter problem. This HCPN is a novel approach to alert postprocessing and correlation. The HCPN assigns a probability to each token element (system state) and specifies the relationship between different actions, alarms, and measures done by intruders independently. The HPCN is 'hidden' since it's not seen directly, but can be inferred by going through alerts. This makes it particularly useful for determining an intruders' actions from prospective alerts and predicting their future attacks. With HCPN, we are able to improve the quality of alerts and predict the intruder's next victim. (Yu and Frincke, 2007)

After looking at actions taken by an NIDS to handle alerts that will ensure better intrusion detection, we now look at some of the actions that users or security administrators should take after they receive an intrusion alert. Depending on the analysis and prioritisation of the alerts, security admins will take actions accordingly. Firstly, security admins should verify the validity of the alarm to see whether it is a false positive. When they obtain a verified true positive alert, it is important to isolate the system to prevent propagation or spreading of threat. The security administrator's next step involves blocking the source IP of the perpetrator and undergoing session snipping to reset all existing communication between the intruder and the host. This can be done by sending TCP packets that consist of the rest bit to the intruder's device to break down the TCP connection. Another important action is the analysis of additional information via logs. Security admins should engage in audit logs to search for patterns in the logs or alerts and study the patterns to further improve the NIDS. It is also vital that the security team mitigate the threat and implement new suitable security mechanisms to prevent future incidents.

In conclusion, our new NIDPS should include real-time hybrid reporting that uses efficient alert methods such as sendmail, pagers or SMS messaging which would provide efficient reporting of alerts. Different priorities are given to the alerts to allow SOCs to customise different alert methods to different intrusion types. We would include the new SIEM architecture that includes proper management of logs and alerts that are adopted to allow for big data technologies. Our NIDPS should include alert prioritisation methods such as TEQ and alert correlation like the Hidden Coloured Petri-Net which will help to reduce the volume of bogus alerts and improves the quality of alert to prevent alert fatigue on SOC team.

IMPLEMETATION CONSIDERATION

Hardware vs. Software-Based NIDS

Two predominant approaches to NIDS are hardware-based and software-based solutions. Hardware-based NIDS involve dedicated physical appliances designed specifically for intrusion detection, while software-based NIDS utilize software applications installed on existing network hardware. This report aims to compare the features, advantages, and limitations of hardware and software-based network intrusion detection systems. Hardware-based NIDS often exhibit higher detection accuracy due to their specialized hardware components tailored for packet analysis and filtering. According to Odeh and Taleb (2023), dedicated hardware appliances can process network traffic at higher speeds, ensuring efficient real-time detection of anomalies. Conversely, software-based solutions, might experience performance limitations, especially on high-traffic networks, impacting the detection accuracy and speed.

In terms of scalability, software-based NIDS hold an advantage as they can be easily scaled by upgrading the underlying hardware or by expanding software capabilities without requiring significant changes in the infrastructure (Ahmed et al., 2022; Humayun et al., 2021). Hardware-based solutions, however, might face limitations in scalability due to their reliance on dedicated hardware devices. Cost is a crucial factor influencing the choice between hardware and software-based NIDS. Hardware-based solutions generally involve higher initial costs for purchasing dedicated appliances. Conversely, software-based NIDS are more cost-effective in terms of initial investment, but ongoing maintenance and software updates may add up to the overall expenses over time. Deploying hardware-based NIDS can be simpler since they come as pre-configured appliances, requiring minimal setup. On the contrary, software-based solutions demand more effort for installation and configuration on existing network infrastructure (Möller, 2023; Sankar et al., 2020). Moreover, the management complexity of software-based NIDS increases with network size and diversity. Hardware-based NIDS often boast higher reliability due to their dedicated hardware components, ensuring continuous monitoring and intrusion (Nasser & Nassar, 2023; Adeyemo et al., 2019). However, software-based solutions can achieve redundancy and reliability through virtualization and redundancy mechanisms, albeit requiring careful configuration and management.

In conclusion, both hardware and software-based NIDS have their distinct advantages and limitations. Hardware-based solutions excel in performance, reliability, and simplicity of deployment but can be costly and less scalable. On the other hand, software-based NIDS offer flexibility, scalability, and cost-effectiveness but might suffer from performance limitations and increased management complexity.

Organizations should consider their specific network requirements, budget constraints, and maintenance capabilities to determine the most suitable intrusion detection solution.

Integration With Existing Security Infrastructure

Integrating NIDS with existing security infrastructure enhances the overall defense mechanisms, fortifying networks against sophisticated cyber threats. This report aims to explore the significance of integrating NIDS with existing security frameworks and the benefits it offers in strengthening cybersecurity posture.

Importance of Integration

Integrating NIDS into an organization's existing security infrastructure bolsters threat detection capabilities by complementing other security measures. NIDS monitors network traffic, analyzing patterns and anomalies to identify potential threats. This integration consolidates security efforts, enabling a more comprehensive view of the network's security landscape (Pissanidis & Demertzis, 2023). By combining NIDS with firewalls, antivirus software, and intrusion prevention systems, organizations create a multi-layered defense strategy that enhances the ability to detect and respond to various cyber threats (Azam et al., 2023; Lim et al., 2021). The integration of NIDS with existing security measures augments the capacity to detect diverse types of intrusions. NIDS can identify anomalies such as port scans, denial-of-service attacks, and malicious payloads traversing the network (Bakhsh et al., 2023; (S. J. Hussain et al., 2019). Additionally, correlation of NIDS alerts with data from other security tools provides a more comprehensive understanding of potential threats, reducing false positives and improving incident response times (Nour et al., 2023).

Improved Incident Response

Integrating NIDS with existing security infrastructure streamlines incident response procedures. Real-time detection of potential threats by NIDS enables security teams to promptly address and mitigate security breaches (Topcu et al., 2023; Almusaylim et al., 2018) Furthermore, the integration facilitates the sharing of threat intelligence and correlation of data, empowering security analysts to make informed decisions in mitigating evolving threats (Kayode-Ajala, 2023). By integrating NIDS with existing security measures, organizations bridge potential security gaps that might exist between disparate security tools (Aslan et al., 2023). This cohesion ensures a more comprehensive defense mechanism, minimizing blind spots and enhancing overall operational efficiency. Centralized monitoring and management of security events across different systems further streamline security operations (Bilali et al., 2022)

Integrating Network Intrusion Detection Systems with an organization's existing security infrastructure is imperative in fortifying defenses against a myriad of cyber threats. Through consolidated threat detection, improved incident response, reduced security gaps, and operational efficiency gains, this integration significantly enhances the cybersecurity posture of organizations.

USE CASES AND EXAMPLE

Real-World Examples of Successful NIDS Implementations

Numerous real-world examples highlight the successful implementation of NIDS across diverse sectors, emphasizing their effectiveness in identifying and mitigating potential security breaches.

One notable case study revolves around the implementation of NIDS within financial institutions. Banks such as JP Morgan Chase have leveraged NIDS to fortify their networks against cyber threats, enhancing their overall security posture (Luoma-Aho, 2023). The utilization of NIDS in such institutions has significantly reduced the risk of unauthorized access to sensitive financial data (Nweke, 2023). Similarly, the healthcare industry has witnessed successful NIDS implementation. Hospital networks, like the Mayo Clinic, have integrated advanced NIDS technologies to protect patient data from malicious cyber activities (Jerbi, 2023). The implementation of NIDS here has not only safeguarded confidential medical information but also ensured uninterrupted healthcare services (Sun et al., 2024). Moreover, educational institutions have embraced NIDS to secure their networks against cyberattacks. Universities like Stanford have deployed NIDS to shield their vast interconnected systems from potential threats, thereby safeguarding research data and personal information of students and faculty (Gupta et al., 2023).

Government agencies globally have also benefited from NIDS implementation. The Department of Defense in the United States extensively utilizes NIDS to protect classified information and defend against cyber threats. This implementation has significantly bolstered national security. NIDS have been instrumental in the defense sector as well. Aerospace and defense companies such as Lockheed Martin have employed NIDS to safeguard critical intellectual property and sensitive defense-related information (Bada & Hameed, 2019). This integration has significantly fortified their cybersecurity infrastructure (Wang & Chen, 2021). Moreover, NIDS have played a pivotal role in e-commerce companies' security frameworks. Amazon, for instance, has effectively utilized NIDS to secure its extensive network, ensuring the protection of customer data during transactions (M. Kumar & Singh, 2020). This successful implementation has reinforced customer trust in online transactions (Siampondo & Sumbwanyambe, 2023).

In conclusion, the successful implementation of NIDS across diverse sectors - including finance, healthcare, education, government, defense, and e-commerce - underscores its efficacy in fortifying network security. These real-world examples substantiate the crucial role NIDS play in mitigating cyber threats and maintaining the integrity, confidentiality, and availability of sensitive data.

Case Studies of NIDS Preventing Cyberattacks

Through analyzing a range of data points within network packets, NIDS can effectively identify and thwart potential cyberattacks, offering robust protection to organizations and individuals alike. Several case studies showcase the efficacy of NIDS in preventing cyber breaches across various sectors.

One notable instance involves the deployment of NIDS in a large financial institution, where its implementation significantly mitigated cyber risks. According to Ahmim et al. (2023) the NIDS accurately detected and halted a sophisticated Distributed Denial of Service (DDoS) attack targeting the institution's servers, preventing substantial downtime and potential financial losses. Similarly, in the healthcare sector, a study by Ali et al. (2024) documented how NIDS successfully intercepted malware infiltration attempts into hospital networks, averting potential data breaches and ensuring patient information remained secure.

Furthermore, a case study by Hossain et al. (2023) highlighted the efficacy of NIDS in a multinational corporation by detecting and blocking unauthorized access attempts by external threat actors. The NIDS promptly identified anomalous behaviors, such as unauthorized port scanning and intrusion attempts, fortifying the company's network security posture. Moreover, in a government agency context, Praptodiyono et al. (2023) reported on a successful defense against a ransomware attack facilitated by NIDS.

The system detected the ransomware signatures within the network traffic, enabling swift containment measures to prevent widespread infection and data encryption.

In the educational sector, a study conducted by Rajapaksha et al. (2023) underscored the significance of NIDS in preventing cyber threats within university networks. The system thwarted multiple phishing attacks and malware intrusions, preserving the integrity of academic and administrative data. Similarly, in a retail setting, Jain et al. (2022) illustrated how NIDS played a pivotal role in halting attempts of credit card fraud through the identification of suspicious transactions and network anomalies.

Additionally, in critical infrastructure protection, NIDS proved instrumental in safeguarding industrial control systems. According to Park et al. (2022) the implementation of NIDS within power plants detected and blocked malicious commands aiming to disrupt operational processes, ensuring uninterrupted energy supply. Furthermore, within the transportation sector, Liu et al. (2022) detailed how NIDS prevented cyber threats targeting communication networks in smart transportation systems, safeguarding against potential disruptions and ensuring passenger safety.

In conclusion, the collective evidence from various case studies underscores the crucial role of NIDS in proactively identifying and mitigating cyber threats across diverse sectors. These systems have consistently demonstrated their effectiveness in protecting networks, mitigating potential risks, and preserving the confidentiality, integrity, and availability of critical data and services.

EVALUATION AND PERFORMANCE METRICS

Evaluating the effectiveness of these systems is crucial for ensuring robust security measures. Several criteria are instrumental in determining the efficacy of NIDS, emphasizing its capability to detect, respond to, and prevent cyber threats while maintaining network integrity.

Firstly, the ability to accurately detect and classify various types of attacks is fundamental to NIDS effectiveness (Halbouni et al., 2022). Detection accuracy involves identifying anomalies or patterns deviating from normal network behavior, encompassing signature-based and anomaly-based detection methods (Wang & Zhu, 2022; Azam, Tan, et al., 2023). A proficient NIDS should minimize false positives and negatives while promptly identifying and categorizing known and unknown threats (Mijalkovic & Spognardi, 2022; Sindiramutty et al., 2024a). Timeliness in response is equally critical (Yang et al., 2023). NIDS should react swiftly upon detecting potential threats, ensuring rapid response mechanisms to contain and mitigate the impact of intrusions (Sugumaran et al., 2023). Delayed responses might lead to prolonged exposure, allowing attackers to exploit vulnerabilities, potentially causing severe damage.

Moreover, scalability and resource utilization are pivotal aspects affecting NIDS efficiency (Mishra, 2023). An effective system should operate optimally without significantly burdening network resources, ensuring minimal latency and efficient use of computational power (Prabowo et al., 2023). Scalability is vital to accommodate evolving network infrastructures and increasing data volumes while maintaining performance (Attou et al., 2023). The adaptability and update frequency of NIDS are also crucial. Regular updates to detection mechanisms, incorporating new attack signatures and patterns, are imperative to counter emerging threats effectively (James, 2023). The system's adaptability to changing network dynamics and threat landscapes ensures sustained protection against evolving cyber threats. Additionally, the comprehensiveness of logs and reports generated by NIDS aids in post-incident analysis and forensic investigations (Henriques et al., 2023). Detailed logs facilitate understanding the nature of attacks, enabling security teams to fortify network defenses and develop proactive strategies. Furthermore, usability and user-friendliness are vital for effective NIDS deployment (Jaime et al., 2023). A system with an intuitive interface and clear reporting mechanisms simplifies configuration, monitoring, and management, enhancing the efficiency of security personnel.

In conclusion, the effectiveness of Network Intrusion Detection Systems relies on multifaceted criteria encompassing detection accuracy, timely response, resource efficiency, adaptability, comprehensive logging, and user-friendliness. Evaluating NIDS based on these criteria is pivotal in ensuring robust network security against a continually evolving threat landscape.

REGULATORY COMPLIANCE AND NIDS

In the contemporary landscape governed by stringent data protection regulations, the implementation of NIDS is imperative to ensure the security and integrity of sensitive information (Dixit & Hussain, 2023).

The General Data Protection Regulation (GDPR) enacted in the European Union necessitates robust security measures to protect personal data from unauthorized access and breaches (Carmi et al., 2022). NIDS serve as a crucial component in fulfilling GDPR requirements by actively monitoring network traffic, identifying anomalies, and providing real-time alerts in the event of potential security breaches (Kiac et al., 2023). Moreover, the California Consumer Privacy Act (CCPA) underscores the significance of securing consumer data and mandates organizations to implement stringent security measures (Debbarma, 2023). NIDS aids in compliance with the CCPA by continuously monitoring network traffic patterns and swiftly identifying any deviations or suspicious activities that might compromise consumer data privacy. In addition to regulatory compliance, the utilization of NIDS aligns with industry-specific standards such as the Health Insurance Portability and Accountability Act (HIPAA) in healthcare and the Payment Card Industry Data Security Standard (PCI DSS) in the financial sector (Kunduru, 2023). NIDS implementation assists organizations in these sectors by providing enhanced network visibility, threat detection, and incident response capabilities, thus fortifying the protection of sensitive data (Verma et al., 2022). Furthermore, NIDS contribute to mitigating insider threats, a significant concern for organizations, by monitoring user behavior within the network (Erola et al., 2022; Krishnan et al., 2021). By analyzing network traffic patterns and user activities, NIDS can identify anomalies that may indicate insider threats, aiding in the prevention of data breaches and unauthorized access to confidential information (Mehmood et al., 2023).

In conclusion, Network Intrusion Detection Systems are integral in the landscape of data protection regulations, ensuring compliance with stringent laws and standards while fortifying the security posture of organizations. The continuous monitoring and rapid detection capabilities of NIDS not only aid in compliance with regulations like GDPR and CCPA but also bolster defenses against evolving cyber threats, thus safeguarding sensitive data and enhancing overall cybersecurity resilience.

FUTURE PROSPECT

Advancement of NIDPS and its Potential Impact on Cybersecurity

The increasing presence of technology in our modern society brings with it a new collection of security issues and cyber-attacks. Thus, there exists a constant need for NIDPS to be further developed for the sake of protecting networks from malicious parties.

i.   Application of NIDPS in Internet of Things (IoT) systems

Applications of NIDPS span a wide range of technologies, an example being Internet of Things (IoT) devices. According to Gyamfi and Jurcut (2022), IoT network systems are being increasingly targeted due to its recent emergence in various industries. Some of the common threats faced by IoT networks include spoofing, Man-in-the-Middle attacks, and Sybil attacks. Moving forward, NIDPS systems must be customised to fit the system's needs while still adopting common security standards across different systems. For example, an IoT-based NIDPS can have various implementation methods depending on user requirements as shown in Figure 13.0 below. These features contribute to the safety of IoT networks and devices, bringing increased protection against attacks on the system.

Figure 13. A summary of possible NIDPS implementation features
(Gyamfi and Jurcut, 2022).

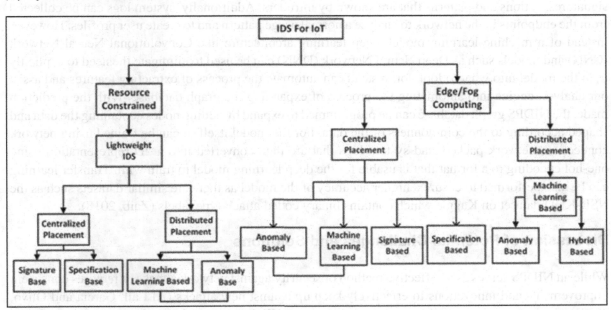

ii.   Implementation of Artificial Intelligence into NIDPS

Implementation of AI technologies such as machine learning, deep learning and neural networks in NIDPS can also bring new possibilities and breakthroughs to current systems. In a signature-based

IDS, one of the major weaknesses is the inability to detect intrusion signatures that have not been hard-coded into the system. However, an anomaly-based IDS can solve the problem by creating a user profile and recognising the usual activities, usage patterns and logs from a user instead of recognising specific signatures themselves. Although this IDS utilises machine learning to learn from the behaviour of users, the number of false positives is high for this system as it immediately alerts the administrator when there is a change of usage in the device or network itself. By implementing AI technologies such as deep learning or even using machine learning in a different approach can help increase the performance of the NIDPS system.

A similar approach can be seen using one of the projects by the authors of this paper, Nicholas and collaboration with Nicole Teah where their project is a Spam Detection machine learning model using Naïve Bayes (Chan and Teah, 2023). According to Petrosyan(2023), the amount of daily spam messages being sent in the United States alone is 8 billion, hence emphasising the importance of this project in cybersecurity as our world is slowly becoming more digitalised every day (Petrosyan, 2023). The model has been trained to perform binary classification using the UC Irvine Machine Learning Repository – SMS Spam Collection dataset which consists of 5574 of ham and spam messages (Almeida and Hidalgo, 2012). In the real world, this trained model can be used to identify spam and ham messages in messaging applications such as email applications and instant messaging applications. By using Naïve Bayes for this model, the algorithm is used to predict probability of the occurrence of an event given the probability of another event and in this case, predicting parts-of-speech, commonly used words and the structure of spam messages.

For our NIDPS, the same approach can be used to read network connections and packets to learn signatures, actions and patterns that are shown by intruders. Additionally, system logs can be collected from the endpoints in the network to analyse a normal usage pattern and to create user profiles. However, instead of a machine-learning model, deep learning architecture like Convolutional Neural Network (CNN) and models such as Deep Neural Network (DNN) can be used to eliminate the need to explicitly train the model into what to look for, instead can automate the process of extracting features and assist our analysis engine into automating the process of expanding the graph database. With the prediction made, the NIDPS graph database can be programmed to expand by adding nodes containing the data and shaped according to the commonness of the data. For the model itself, it can be trained using network connection, network packets and system logs that are then converted into a 2D representation using one-hot encoding to a format that is usable for the deep learning model to train with. Transfer learning can be also performed to ensure a higher accuracy of the model as there are similar datasets such as the NSL-KDD dataset on Kaggle which contains binary coded attack-type labels (Zaib, 2018).

Discussion of Potential Challenges and Solutions

While an NIDPS serves as an effective method of security against network attacks, it requires consistent improvements and innovations to effectively keep up against new attacks (Al Lail, Garcia and Olivo, 2023). There are various challenges present in current NIDPS that are being focused on, namely the detection accuracy of the system and the ever-increasing demand for memory and power.

i.   Detection Accuracy of NIDPS

The accuracy of an NIDPS is crucial in filtering out intrusions while allowing incoming legitimate traffic. Most importantly, it is necessary to increase the true positive rate while simultaneously reducing false positives in the proposed NIDPS (Iglesias Perez and Criado, 2022).

One method of improving the system would be to incorporate deep learning techniques such as CNN, which will increase the detection rate, particularly in large networks while also making the system more robust against zero-day attacks with unknown signatures (Mebawondu et al., 2020). The deep learning model will also produce accuracy scores and analysis such as confusion matrices which can be then used to test the performance of the model and NIDPS. Hence, the model is able to utilise the performance scores by the model to fine-tune the NIDPS to better detect intrusion, reduce false positive and false negative rates.

ii.   Storage, Memory, and Power Usage in NIDPS

As NIDPS technologies focus on analysing network traffic, different methods of data collection will also be utilised. However, as the amount of incoming traffic increases over time, so will the time taken to analyse data for possible threats. To offset this issue, the NIDPS must either be upscaled in storage and memory or utilise more efficient data processing methods.

Current data collection methods involve processing network traffic into sessions, then analysing said session for possible threats. However, storing a whole session and processing it requires a relatively large amount of storage space when handling high network traffic. Hence, new methods aim to reduce storage demand by using partial packet data instead of a whole session packet. This is done by analysing data from the packet header instead, significantly improving load capacity and lowering processing time required (Han and Pak, 2023). Additionally, producing an extensive graph database in our proposed NIDPS solution will also require large amounts of power and storage. To offset these issues, the system could be scaled vertically through hardware upgrades such as a high-performance Graphic Processing Unit (GPU) or reduce the complexity of the graph database via deep learning, feature extraction and feature engineering (Ahmad et al., 2020).

CONCLUSION

From this report, it can be observed that our world is becoming progressively more digitalised, with our daily tasks and processes transitioning onto virtual platforms like the Internet (United Nations, 2020). Hence, there exists a growing need for strong cybersecurity systems which can prevent data breaches and safeguard user information. More specifically, our network intrusion detection prevention system (NIDPS) which aims to monitor, protect, alert and report to the user when threats are detected (Vanin et al., 2022).

To summarise the processes found in the system, the NIDPS will first collect data through either flow-based or log-based methods depending on the user's requirements. Data collected will then be processed and analysed for potential attacks using a graph-based detection system. The NIDPS detects abnormalities in a network by creating nodes and vertices based on common usage patterns and actions in the network. Graph theory also allows the program to identify important nodes in the network such as nodes with many connections, allowing preventive measures to be taken and closely monitoring system nodes that are at high risk of being attacked. In the event of attacks, the NIDPS will take preventive actions such as centrality-based prevention where it prioritises nodes with high importance, monitoring and isolating said nodes should it get compromised. Lastly, the NIDPS will require a reporting system. This includes real-time hybrid reporting that involves effective alert methods such as sendmail, pagers, or SMS messaging that send alert messages to the SOC team when an intrusion is detected. Besides that, we propose a new SIEM architecture that allows for proper management of logs and alerts adaptable for big data technologies. Actions taken by a NIDS are alert prioritisation using TEQ and alert correlation like Hidden Coloured Petri-Net to help reduce volume of false positive alerts which leads to alert fatigue by improving the quality of the alerts.

With the various features presented in our NIDPS, we believe that it can contribute to preventing network attacks while providing a novel perspective in the field of network intrusion detection systems through the use and implementation of graph theory with potential for deep learning features as well.

REFERENCES

Adeyemo, V. E., Abdullah, A., Jhanjhi, N. Z., Supramaniam, M., & Balogun, A. O. (2019). Ensemble and Deep-Learning Methods for Two-Class and Multi-Attack Anomaly Intrusion Detection: An Empirical study. *International Journal of Advanced Computer Science and Applications*, *10*(9). doi:10.14569/ IJACSA.2019.0100969

Adnan, A., Muhammed, A., Abd Ghani, A. A., Abdullah, A., & Hakim, F. (2021). 2021, 'An Intrusion Detection System for the Internet of Things Based on Machine Learning: Review and Challenges'. *Symmetry*, *13*(6), 1011. doi:10.3390/sym13061011

Ahmad, Z., Shahid Khan, A., Wai Shiang, C., Abdullah, J., & Ahmad, F. (2020). Network intrusion detection system: A systematic study of machine learning and deep learning approaches. *Transactions on Emerging Telecommunications Technologies*, *32*(1), e4150. doi:10.1002/ett.4150

AhmedM. R.IslamS.ShatabdaS.IslamA. K. M. M.RobinM. T. I. (2022). Intrusion Detection System in Software-Defined Networks Using Machine Learning and Deep Learning Techniques – A Comprehensive Survey. *Tech Rxiv*. doi:10.36227/techrxiv.17153213.v2

Ahmim, A., Maazouzi, F., Ahmim, M., Namane, S., & Dhaou, I. B. (2023). Distributed denial of service attack detection for the Internet of Things using hybrid deep learning model. *IEEE Access : Practical Innovations, Open Solutions*, *11*, 119862–119875. doi:10.1109/ACCESS.2023.3327620

Akoglu, L., Tong, H. and Koutra, D. (2014). Graph based anomaly detection and description: a survey. *Data Mining and Knowledge Discovery*, *29*(3), 626–688. . doi:10.1007/s10618-014-0365-y

Al Lail, M., Garcia, A. and Olivo, S. (2023). Machine Learning for Network Intrusion Detection—A Comparative Study. *Future Internet*, *15*(7), p.243. . doi:10.3390/fi15070243

Albasheer, H., Md Siraj, M., Mubarakali, A., Elsier Tayfour, O., Salih, S., Hamdan, M., Khan, S., Zainal, A., & Kamarudeen, S. (2022). Cyber-Attack Prediction Based on Network Intrusion Detection Systems for Alert Correlation Techniques: A Survey. *Sensors (Basel)*, *22*(4), 1494. doi:10.3390/s22041494 PMID:35214394

Alferidah, D. K., & Jhanjhi, N. Z. (2020). Cybersecurity Impact over Bigdata and IoT Growth. *2020 International Conference on Computational Intelligence (ICCI)*. IEEE. 10.1109/ICCI51257.2020.9247722

Ali, S., Li, Q., & Yousafzai, A. (2024). Blockchain and federated learning-based intrusion Detection Approaches for edge-enabled industrial IoT networks: A survey. *Ad Hoc Networks*, *152*, 103320. doi:10.1016/j.adhoc.2023.103320

Aljanabi, M., Ismail, M. A., & Ali, A. (2021). Intrusion Detection Systems, Issues, Challenges, and Needs. *International Journal of Computational Intelligence Systems.*, *14*(1), 560. doi:10.2991/ijcis.d.210105.001

Alkinani, M. H., Almazroi, A. A., Jhanjhi, N. Z., & Khan, N. A. (2021). 5G and IoT Based Reporting and Accident Detection (RAD) System to Deliver First Aid Box Using Unmanned Aerial Vehicle. *Sensors (Basel)*, *21*(20), 6905. doi:10.3390/s21206905 PMID:34696118

Almeida, T., & Hidalgo, J. (2012). *UCI Machine Learning Repository*. [online] UC Irvine Machine Learning Repository. https://archive.ics.uci.edu/dataset/228/sms+spam+collection

Almusaylim, Z. A., & Jhanjhi, N. Z. (2018). A review on smart home present state and challenges: Linked to context-awareness internet of things (IoT). *Wireless Networks*, *25*(6), 3193–3204. doi:10.1007/s11276-018-1712-5

Almusaylim, Z. A., Jhanjhi, N. Z., & Jung, L. T. (2018). Proposing A Data Privacy Aware Protocol for Roadside Accident Video Reporting Service Using 5G. In *Vehicular Cloud Networks Environment*. IEEE. doi:10.1109/ICCOINS.2018.8510588

Ananna, F. F., Nowreen, R., Jahwari, S. S. R. A., Costa, E., Angeline, L., & Sindiramutty, S. R. (2023). Analysing Influential factors in student academic achievement: Prediction modelling and insight. *International Journal of Emerging Multidisciplinaries Computer Science & Artificial Intelligence*, *2*(1). doi:10.54938/ijemdcsai.2023.02.1.254

Anjum, N., Latif, Z., Lee, C., Shoukat, I. A., & Iqbal, U. (2021). MIND: A Multi-Source Data Fusion Scheme for Intrusion Detection in Networks. *Sensors (Basel)*, *21*(14), 4941. doi:10.3390/s21144941 PMID:34300681

Annadurai, C., Nelson, I., Devi, K. N., Ramachandran, M., Jhanjhi, N. Z., Masud, M., & Sheikh, A. M. (2022). Biometric Authentication-Based Intrusion Detection using Artificial intelligence internet of things in smart city. *Energies*, *15*(19), 7430. doi:10.3390/en15197430

Arass, M. E., & Souissi, N. (2019). *Smart SIEM: From Big Data logs and events to Smart Data alerts*. ResearchGate. https://www.researchgate.net/publication/333752299_Smart_SIEM_From_Big_Data_logs_and_events_to_Smart_Data_alerts

Aslan, Ö., Aktuğ, S. S., Ozkan-Okay, M., Yılmaz, A. A., & Akin, E. (2023). A comprehensive review of cyber security vulnerabilities, threats, attacks, and solutions. *Electronics (Basel)*, *12*(6), 1333. doi:10.3390/electronics12061333

Attou, H., Mohy-Eddine, M., Guezzaz, A., Benkirane, S., Azrour, M., Alabdulatif, A., & Almusallam, N. (2023). Towards an intelligent intrusion detection system to detect malicious activities in cloud computing. *Applied Sciences (Basel, Switzerland)*, *13*(17), 9588. doi:10.3390/app13179588

Azam, H., Dulloo, M. I., Majeed, M. H., Wan, J. P. H., Xin, L. T., & Sindiramutty, S. R. (2023). Cyber-crime Unmasked: Investigating cases and digital evidence. *International Journal of Emerging Multidisciplinaries Computer Science & Artificial Intelligence*, 2(1). doi:10.54938/ijemdcsai.2023.02.1.255

Azam, H., Dulloo, M. I., Majeed, M. H., Wan, J. P. H., Xin, L. T., Tajwar, M. A., & Sindiramutty, S. R. (2023). Defending the digital Frontier: IDPS and the battle against Cyber threat. *International Journal of Emerging Multidisciplinaries Computer Science & Artificial Intelligence*, 2(1). doi:10.54938/ijemdcsai.2023.02.1.253

Azam, H., Tajwar, M. A., Mayhialagan, S., Davis, A. J., Yik, C. J., Ali, D., & Sindiramutty, S. R. (2023). Innovations in Security: A study of cloud Computing and IoT. *International Journal of Emerging Multidisciplinaries Computer Science & Artificial Intelligence*, 2(1). doi:10.54938/ijemdcsai.2023.02.1.252

AzamH.TanM.PinL. T.SyahmiM. A.QianA. L. W.JingyanH.UddinH.SindiramuttyS. R. (2023). Wireless Technology Security and Privacy: A Comprehensive Study. *Preprint*. doi:10.20944/preprints202311.0664.v1

BadaM.HameedF. (2019). Report on cybersecurity maturity level in Albania. *Social Science Research Network*. doi:10.2139/ssrn.3658345

Bakhsh, S. A., Khan, M. A., Ahmed, F., Alshehri, M., Ali, H., & Ahmad, J. (2023). Enhancing IoT network security through deep learning-powered Intrusion Detection System. *Internet of Things : Engineering Cyber Physical Human Systems*, 24, 100936. doi:10.1016/j.iot.2023.100936

Bilali, V., Kosyvas, D., Theodoropoulos, T., Ouzounoglou, E., Karagiannidis, L., & Amditis, A. (2022). IRIS Advanced Threat Intelligence Orchestrator- a way to manage cybersecurity challenges of IoT ecosystems in smart cities. In Lecture Notes in Computer Science (pp. 315–325). doi:10.1007/978-3-031-20936-9_25

Bloch, F., Jackson, M., & Tebaldi, P. (2016). *Centrality measures in networks*. [online] Social Choice and Welfare. Available at: https://www.semanticscholar.org/paper/Centrality-measures-in-networks-Bloch-Jackson/6bf5a02cd5c9ace5c275416bec0b72a645ce7299.

Bocquet-AppelN.NoyelleM.CattaneoA. (2023). Graph-based Intrusion Detection: A Modern Approach. *figshare.com*. [online] doi:10.6084/m9.figshare.22216987.v1

BrohiS. N.JhanjhiN. Z.BrohiN. N.BrohiM. N. (2020). Key Applications of State-of-the-Art Technologies to Mitigate and Eliminate COVID-19.pdf. Authorea Preprints. doi:10.36227/techrxiv.12115596.v1

Carmi, L., Zohar, M., & Riva, G. M. (2022). The European General Data Protection Regulation (GDPR) in mHealth: Theoretical and practical aspects for practitioners' use. *Medicine, Science, and the Law*, 63(1), 61–68. doi:10.1177/00258024221118411 PMID:35950240

Chai, A., Le, J. P., Lee, A. S., & Lo, S. M. (2019). Applying Graph Theory to Examine the Dynamics of Student Discussions in Small-Group Learning. *CBE Life Sciences Education*, 18(2), ar29. doi:10.1187/cbe.18-11-0222 PMID:31150318

Chan, N. W. X., & Teah, N. Y. F. (2023). *Spam Detection using Naïve Bayes*. CoLab. https://colab.research.google.com/drive/1q3P-3g9SDE5BRIVab1eqFzJyM4hr6IDC?usp=sharing

Chesti, I. A., Humayun, M., Sama, N. U., & Jhanjhi, N. Z. (2020). Evolution, Mitigation, and Prevention of Ransomware. *2020 2nd International Conference on Computer and Information Sciences (ICCIS)*. IEEE. 10.1109/ICCIS49240.2020.9257708

Cisco. (n.d.). *Firepower Management Center Configuration Guide, Version 6.0 - External Alerting with Alert Responses [Cisco ASA 5500-X Series Firewalls]*. Cisco. https://www.cisco.com/c/en/us/td/docs/security/firepower/60/configuration/guide/fpmc-config-guide-v60/Configuring_External_Alerting.html

Clark, C. (2018) 1. What is Sagan? *Sagan User Guide 1.2.2 documentation*. Sagan. https://sagan.readthedocs.io/en/latest/what-is-sagan.html?highlight=data+collection

D., Kumar, R. & Tomkins, A. (2006). *Evolutionary clustering*. ResearchGate. https://www.researchgate.net/publication/221654105_Evolutionary_clustering

Day, B. (n.d.). *Real-Time Alerting with Snort*. LinuxSecurity. https://linuxsecurity.com/features/real-time-alerting-with-snort

Debbarma, R. (2023, September 10). *The changing landscape of privacy laws in the age of big data and surveillance*. Rifanalitica. https://www.rifanalitica.it/index.php/journal/article/view/470

Dixit, S., & Hussain, G. (2023). An effective intrusion detection system in cloud computing environment. In Lecture notes in networks and systems (pp. 671–680). Springer. doi:10.1007/978-981-19-7982-8_56

Elrawy, M., Awad, A., & Hamed, H. (2018). Intrusion detection systems for IoT-based smart environments: A survey. *Journal of Cloud Computing (Heidelberg, Germany)*, 7(1), 21. doi:10.1186/s13677-018-0123-6

Erola, A., Agrafiotis, I., Goldsmith, M., & Creese, S. (2022). Insider-threat detection: Lessons from deploying the CITD tool in three multinational organisations. *Journal of Information Security and Applications*, 67, 103167. doi:10.1016/j.jisa.2022.103167

Farrukh, Y. A., Khan, I., Wali, S., Bierbrauer, D., Pavlik, J., & Bastian, N. (2022). Payload-Byte: A Tool for Extracting and Labeling Packet Capture Files of Modern Network Intrusion Detection Datasets (Version 2). TechRxiv. doi:10.1109/BDCAT56447.2022.00015

Fatima-Tuz-Zahra. Jhanjhi, N. Z., Brohi, S. N., Malik, N. A., & Humayun, M. (2020). Proposing a Hybrid RPL Protocol for Rank and Wormhole Attack Mitigation using Machine Learning. *2020 2nd International Conference on Computer and Information Sciences (ICCIS)*. IEEE. 10.1109/ICCIS49240.2020.9257607

Ford, N. (2023). *List of Data Breaches and Cyber Attacks in 2023*. IT Governance UK. https://www.itgovernance.co.uk/blog/list-of-data-breaches-and-cyber-attacks-in-2023

Freeman, L. (2017). *Centrality in social networks conceptual clarification*. Social Networks. https://www.semanticscholar.org/paper/Centrality-in-social-networks-conceptual-Freeman/5d61ef638fd684facc1e68e654053e9bc065b36f [Accessed 23 Oct. 2023].

Gelman, B., Taoufiq, S., Vörös, T., & Berlin, K. (2023). *That Escalated Quickly: An ML Framework for Alert Prioritisation*. [online] arXiv.org. doi:https://doi.org//arXiv.2302.06648. doi:10.48550

Ghosh, G., Kavita, Verma, S., Jhanjhi, N. Z., & Talib, M. (2020). Secure surveillance system using chaotic image encryption technique. *IOP Conference Series*, 993(1), 012062. 10.1088/1757-899X/993/1/012062

Gopi, R., Sathiyamoorthi, V., Selvakumar, S., Ramesh, M., Chatterjee, P., Jhanjhi, N. Z., & Luhach, A. K. (2021). Enhanced method of ANN based model for detection of DDoS attacks on multimedia internet of things. *Multimedia Tools and Applications*, *81*(19), 26739–26757. doi:10.1007/s11042-021-10640-6

Gupta, M., Akiri, C., Aryal, K., Parker, E., & Praharaj, L. (2023). From ChatGPT to ThreatGPT: Impact of Generative AI in Cybersecurity and Privacy. *IEEE Access : Practical Innovations, Open Solutions*, *11*, 80218–80245. doi:10.1109/ACCESS.2023.3300381

Gyamfi, E. and Jurcut, A. (2022). Intrusion Detection in Internet of Things Systems: A Review on Design Approaches Leveraging Multi-Access Edge Computing, Machine Learning, and Datasets. *Sensors*, *22*(10), 3744. . doi:10.3390/s22103744

Halbouni, A. H., Gunawan, T. S., Habaebi, M. H., Halbouni, M., Kartiwi, M., & Ahmad, R. (2022). CNN-LSTM: Hybrid Deep Neural Network for Network Intrusion Detection System. *IEEE Access : Practical Innovations, Open Solutions*, *10*, 99837–99849. doi:10.1109/ACCESS.2022.3206425

Han, J., & Pak, W. (2023). High Performance Network Intrusion Detection System Using Two-Stage LSTM and Incremental Created Hybrid Features. *Electronics (Basel)*, *12*(4), 956. doi:10.3390/electronics12040956

Harb, E., & Mangino, A. (2019). *ZEEK (BRO) INTRUSION DETECTION SYSTEM (IDS) Training Workshop for Network Engineers and Educators on Tools and Protocols for High-Speed Networks NSF Award 1829698 CyberTraining CIP: Cyberinfrastructure Expertise on High-throughput Networks for Big Science Data Transfers*. CESC. https://ce.sc.edu/cyberinfra/docs/workshop/Bro%20Intrusion%20Detection%20System%20(IDS).pdf

Henriques, J., Caldeira, F., Cruz, T., & Simões, P. (2023). A forensics and compliance auditing framework for critical infrastructure protection. *International Journal of Critical Infrastructure Protection*, *42*, 100613. doi:10.1016/j.ijcip.2023.100613

Hossain, M. A., Hossain, M. S., & Karim, R. (2023). Comprehensive architectural network design based on intrusion detection system. *International Journal of Communication and Information Technology*, *4*(2), 12–19. doi:10.33545/2707661X.2023.v4.i2a.66

Hubballi, N., & Suryanarayanan, V. (2014). False alarm minimization techniques in signature-based intrusion detection systems: A survey. *Computer Communications*, *49*, 1–17. doi:10.1016/j.comcom.2014.04.012

Humayun, M., Jhanjhi, N. Z., Alsayat, A., & Ponnusamy, V. (2021). Internet of things and ransomware: Evolution, mitigation and prevention. *Egyptian Informatics Journal*, *22*(1), 105–117. doi:10.1016/j.eij.2020.05.003

Humayun, M., Jhanjhi, N. Z., Hamid, B., & Ahmed, G. (2020). Emerging smart logistics and transportation using IoT and blockchain. *IEEE Internet of Things Magazine*, *3*(2), 58–62. doi:10.1109/IOTM.0001.1900097

Humayun, M., Niazi, M., Jhanjhi, N. Z., Alshayeb, M., & Mahmood, S. (2020). Cyber Security Threats and Vulnerabilities: A Systematic Mapping study. *Arabian Journal for Science and Engineering*, *45*(4), 3171–3189. doi:10.1007/s13369-019-04319-2

Hussain, S. J., Ahmed, U., Liaquat, H., Mir, S., Jhanjhi, N. Z., & Humayun, M. (2019). *IMIAD: Intelligent Malware Identification for Android Platform*. IEEE. doi:10.1109/ICCISci.2019.8716471

Hussain, S. J., Ahmed, U., Liaquat, H., Mir, S., Jhanjhi, N. Z., & Humayun, M. (2019). *IMIAD: Intelligent Malware Identification for Android Platform*. IEEE. doi:10.1109/ICCISci.2019.8716471

Iglesias Perez, S., & Criado, R. (2022). Increasing the Effectiveness of Network Intrusion Detection Systems (NIDSs) by Using Multiplex Networks and Visibility Graphs. *Mathematics*, *11*(1), 107. doi:10.3390/math11010107

Ioulianou, P., Vassilakis, V., Moscholios, I., & Logothetis, M. (2018). *A Signature-based Intrusion Detection System for the Internet of Things. A Signature-based Intrusion Detection System for the Internet of Things*. White Rose Research Online. https://eprints.whiterose.ac.uk/133312/1/ictf_2018_IoT.pdf

Jaime, F., Muñoz, A., Rodríguez-Gómez, F., & Jeréz-Calero, A. (2023). Strengthening privacy and data security in biomedical microelectromechanical systems by IoT communication security and protection in smart healthcare. *Sensors (Basel)*, *23*(21), 8944. doi:10.3390/s23218944 PMID:37960646

Jain, G., & Anubha. (2021). Application of SNORT and Wireshark in Network Traffic Analysis. *IOP Conference Series. Materials Science and Engineering*, *1119*(1), 012007. doi:10.1088/1757-899X/1119/1/012007

Jain, N., Chaudhary, A., & Kumar, A. (2022). *Credit Card Fraud Detection using Machine Learning Techniques*. IEEE., doi:10.1109/SMART55829.2022.10047360

James, E. (2023, January 9). *Fortifying the IoT landscape: Strategies to Counter security Risks in Connected systems*. Tensor Gate. https://research.tensorgate.org/index.php/tjstidc/article/view/42

Jerbi, D. (2023). Beyond Firewalls: Navigating the Jungle of Emerging Cybersecurity Trends. *J Curr Trends Comp Sci Res*, *2*(2), 191–195.

Jhanjhi, N. Z., Humayun, M., & Almuayqil, S. N. (2021). Cyber security and privacy issues in industrial internet of things. *Computer Systems Science and Engineering*, *37*(3), 361–380. doi:10.32604/csse.2021.015206

Kayode-Ajala, O. (2023, August 4). *Applications of Cyber Threat intelligence (CTI) in financial institutions and challenges in its adoption*. Research Blog. https://researchberg.com/index.php/araic/article/view/159

Kiac, M., Sikora, P., Malina, L., Lokaj, Z., & Srivastava, G. (2023). ADEROS: Artificial Intelligence-Based Detection System of Critical Events for Road Security. *IEEE Systems Journal*, *17*(4), 1–12. doi:10.1109/JSYST.2023.3276644

Krishnan, S., Thangaveloo, R., Rahman, S. B. A., & Sindiramutty, S. R. (2021). Smart Ambulance Traffic Control system. *Trends in Undergraduate Research*, *4*(1), c28–c34. doi:10.33736/tur.2831.2021

Kumar, S., Gupta, S., & Arora, S. (2021). Research Trends in Network-Based Intrusion Detection Systems: A Review. *IEEE Access : Practical Innovations, Open Solutions*, *9*, 157761–157779. doi:10.1109/ACCESS.2021.3129775

Kunduru, A. R. (2023). Cloud Appian BPM (Business Process Management) Usage In health care Industry. *International Journal of Advanced Research in Computer and Communication Engineering*, *12*(6). doi:10.17148/IJARCCE.2023.12658

Lim, M., Abdullah, A., & Jhanjhi, N. Z. (2021). Performance optimization of criminal network hidden link prediction model with deep reinforcement learning. *Journal of King Saud University. Computer and Information Sciences*, *33*(10), 1202–1210. doi:10.1016/j.jksuci.2019.07.010

Liu, J., Liu, B., Zhang, R., & Wang, C. (2019). Multi-step Attack Scenarios Mining Based on Neural Network and Bayesian Network Attack Graph. *Lecture Notes in Computer Science*, *11633*, 62–74. doi:10.1007/978-3-030-24265-7_6

Liu, W., Xu, X., Wu, L., Qi, L., Jolfaei, A., Ding, W., & Khosravi, M. R. (2022). Intrusion detection for maritime transportation systems with batch federated aggregation. *IEEE Transactions on Intelligent Transportation Systems*, 1–12. doi:10.1109/TITS.2022.3181436

Locicero, G. (2020). *Suricata review and attack sceneries*. [online] ResearchGate. https://www.researchgate.net/publication/344292913_Suricata_review_and_attack_sceneries

Luoma-Aho, M. (2023). *Analysis of Modern Malware: obfuscation techniques*. Theseus. https://www.theseus.fi/handle/10024/798038

Majeed, A., & Rauf, I. (2020). Graph Theory: A Comprehensive Survey about Graph Theory Applications in Computer Science and Social Networks. *Inventions (Basel, Switzerland)*, *5*(1), 10. doi:10.3390/inventions5010010

Mebawondu, J. O., Alowolodu, O. D., Mebawondu, J. O., & Adetunmbi, A. O. (2020). Network intrusion detection system using supervised learning paradigm. *Scientific African*, *9*, e00497. doi:10.1016/j.sciaf.2020.e00497

Mehmood, M. T., Amin, R., Muslam, M. M. A., Xie, J., & Aldabbas, H. (2023). Privilege escalation attack detection and mitigation in cloud using machine learning. *IEEE Access : Practical Innovations, Open Solutions*, *11*, 46561–46576. doi:10.1109/ACCESS.2023.3273895

Mijalkovic, J., & Spognardi, A. (2022). Reducing the false negative rate in deep learning based network intrusion detection systems. *Algorithms*, *15*(8), 258. doi:10.3390/a15080258

Mishra, S. (2023). Blockchain and Machine Learning-Based hybrid IDS to protect smart networks and preserve privacy. *Electronics (Basel)*, *12*(16), 3524. doi:10.3390/electronics12163524

Molina-Coronado, B., Mori, U., Mendiburu, A., & Miguel-Alonso, J. (2021). *Survey of Network Intrusion Detection Methods from the Perspective of the Knowledge Discovery in Databases Process*. https://arxiv.org/ftp/arxiv/papers/2001/2001.09697.pdf

Möller, D. P. F. (2023). Intrusion Detection and Prevention. Springer. doi:10.1007/978-3-031-26845-8_3

Muzafar, S., & Jhanjhi, N. Z. (2022). DDoS attacks on software defined Network: Challenges and issues. *2022 International Conference on Business Analytics for Technology and Security (ICBATS)*. IEEE. 10.1109/ICBATS54253.2022.9780662

Muzafar, S., Jhanjhi, N. Z., Khan, N. A., & Ashfaq, F. (2022). DDOS attack detection approaches in on software defined network. *2022 14th International Conference on Mathematics, Actuarial Science, Computer Science and Statistics (MACS)*. IEEE. 10.1109/MACS56771.2022.10022653

Muzammal, S. M., Murugesan, R. K., Jhanjhi, N. Z., & Jung, L. T. (2020). SMTrust: Proposing Trust-Based Secure Routing Protocol for RPL Attacks for IoT Applications. *2020 International Conference on Computational Intelligence (ICCI)*. IEEE. 10.1109/ICCI51257.2020.9247818

N. (2019). *Exploring Information Centrality for Intrusion Detection in Large Networks*. ResearchGate. https://www.researchgate.net/publication/332750935_Exploring_Information_Centrality_for_Intrusion_Detection_in_Large_Networks [.

Nasser, Y., & Nassar, M. (2023). Toward Hardware-Assisted Malware Detection Utilizing Explainable Machine Learning: A survey. *IEEE Access : Practical Innovations, Open Solutions*, *11*, 131273–131288. doi:10.1109/ACCESS.2023.3335187

Navone, E. C. (2020). *Dijkstra's Shortest Path Algorithm - A Detailed and Visual Introduction*. Free Code Camp. https://www.freecodecamp.org/news/dijkstras-shortest-path-algorithm-visual-introduction/

Nayak, P., & Swapna, G. (2023). Security issues in IoT applications using certificateless aggregate signcryption schemes: An overview. *Internet of Things : Engineering Cyber Physical Human Systems*, *21*, 100641. doi:10.1016/j.iot.2022.100641

Nour, B., Pourzandi, M., & Debbabi, M. (2023). A survey on threat hunting in enterprise networks. *IEEE Communications Surveys and Tutorials*, *25*(4), 2299–2324. doi:10.1109/COMST.2023.3299519

Nweke, L. O. (2023). National identification Systems as enablers of Online Identity. In IntechOpen eBooks. doi:10.5772/intechopen.1002294

Odeh, A., & Taleb, A. A. (2023). Ensemble-Based Deep learning models for enhancing IoT intrusion detection. *Applied Sciences (Basel, Switzerland)*, *13*(21), 11985. doi:10.3390/app132111985

Park, W. Y., Kim, S. H., Vu, D., Song, C. H., Jung, H., & Jo, H. (2022). Intrusion Detection System for industrial network. In Lecture notes in networks and systems (pp. 646–658). Springer. doi:10.1007/978-3-031-16075-2_48

Petrosyan, A. (2023). *Daily number of spam emails sent worldwide as of January 2023, by country*. Statista. https://www.statista.com/statistics/1270488/spam-emails-sent-daily-by-country/

PissanidisD. L.DemertzisK. (2023). Integrating AI/ML in Cybersecurity: An Analysis of Open XDR Technology and its Application in Intrusion Detection and System Log Management. *Preprints2023*. doi:10.20944/preprints202312.0205.v1

Ponnusamy, V., Aun, Y., Jhanjhi, N. Z., Humayun, M., & Almufareh, M. F. (2022). IoT wireless intrusion detection and network Traffic Analysis. *Computer Systems Science and Engineering*, *40*(3), 865–879. doi:10.32604/csse.2022.018801

Ponnusamy, V., Humayun, M., Jhanjhi, N. Z., Aun, Y., & Almufareh, M. F. (2022). Intrusion detection systems in internet of things and mobile Ad-Hoc networks. *Computer Systems Science and Engineering*, *40*(3), 1199–1215. doi:10.32604/csse.2022.018518

Prabowo, W. A., Fauziah, K., Nahrowi, A. S., Faiz, M. N., & Muhammad, A. W. (2023). Strengthening Network Security: Evaluation of intrusion detection and prevention systems tools in networking systems. *International Journal of Advanced Computer Science and Applications*, *14*(9). doi:10.14569/IJACSA.2023.0140934

Praptodiyono, S., Firmansyah, T., Anwar, M. N. B., Wicaksana, C. A., Pramudyo, A. S., & Khudher, A. A. (2023). Development of hybrid intrusion detection system based on Suricata with pfSense method for high reduction of DDoS attacks on IPv6 networks. *Eastern-European Journal of Enterprise Technologies*, *5*(9 (125)), 75–84. doi:10.15587/1729-4061.2023.285275

Rajapaksha, S., Kalutarage, H., Al-Kadri, M. O., Petrovski, A., Madzudzo, G., & Cheah, M. (2023). AI-Based Intrusion Detection Systems for In-Vehicle Networks: A survey. *ACM Computing Surveys*, *55*(11), 1–40. doi:10.1145/3570954

Sankar, S., Ramasubbareddy, S., Luhach, A. K., Deverajan, G. G., Alnumay, W. S., Jhanjhi, N. Z., Ghosh, U., & Sharma, P. K. (2020). Energy efficient optimal parent selection based routing protocol for Internet of Things using firefly optimization algorithm. *Transactions on Emerging Telecommunications Technologies*, *32*(8), e4171. doi:10.1002/ett.4171

Saqr, M., Elmoazen, R., Tedre, M., López-Pernas, S., & Hirsto, L. (2022). How well centrality measures capture student achievement in computer-supported collaborative learning? – A systematic review and meta-analysis. *Educational Research Review*, *35*, 100437. doi:10.1016/j.edurev.2022.100437

Seong, T. B., Ponnusamy, V., Jhanjhi, N. Z., Annur, R., & Talib, M. (2021). A comparative analysis on traditional wired datasets and the need for wireless datasets for IoT wireless intrusion detection. *Indonesian Journal of Electrical Engineering and Computer Science*, *22*(2), 1165. doi:10.11591/ijeecs.v22.i2.pp1165-1176

Shafi, M., Jha, R. K., & Jain, S. (2022). LGTBIDS: Layer-wise Graph Theory Based Intrusion Detection System in Beyond 5G. *IEEE Transactions on Network and Service Management*, 1–1. doi:10.1109/TNSM.2022.3197921

Shankar, A. and Shankar, A. (2021). Network Intrusion Detection and Prevention. *International Journal of Applied Engineering Research*, *16*(4), 267–270. doi:https://doi.org/. doi:10.37622/IJAER/16.4.2021.267-270

Shimeall, T. J. (2018). *Four Valuable Data Sources for Network Security Analytics*. Carnegie Mellon University. https://insights.sei.cmu.edu/library/four-valuable-data-sources-for-network-security-analytics-2/

Siampondo, G., & Sumbwanyambe, M. (2023). A Review of the Role of Risk Management in Online Transactions: The Growing Issues of Network and System Security among Zambia's Financial Institutions. *American Journal of Finance*, *8*(2), 1–12. doi:10.47672/ajf.1510

Sindiramutty, S. R., Jhanjhi, N. Z., Ray, S. K., Jazri, H., Khan, N. A., & Gaur, L. (2024). Metaverse: Virtual Meditation. In Metaverse Applications for Intelligent Healthcare (pp. 93–158). IGI Global. doi:10.4018/978-1-6684-9823-1.ch003

Sindiramutty, S. R., Jhanjhi, N. Z., Ray, S. K., Jazri, H., Khan, N. A., Gaur, L., Gharib, A., & Manchuri, A. R. (2024a). Metaverse: Virtual Gyms and Sports. In Metaverse Applications for Intelligent Healthcare (pp. 24–92). IGI Global. doi:10.4018/978-1-6684-9823-1.ch003

Singhal, V., Jain, S. P., Anand, D., Singh, A., Verma, S., Kavita, Rodrigues, J. J. P. C., Jhanjhi, N. Z., Ghosh, U., Jo, O., & Iwendi, C. (2020). Artificial Intelligence Enabled Road Vehicle-Train Collision Risk Assessment Framework for Unmanned railway level crossings. *IEEE Access : Practical Innovations, Open Solutions*, 8, 113790–113806. doi:10.1109/ACCESS.2020.3002416

Snort. (2023). *Network Intrusion Detection & Prevention System*. Snort. https://www.snort.org/

SolarWinds. (n.d.) Security event manager - view event logs remotely. SolarWinds. https://www.solarwinds.com/security-event-manager

Sugumaran, D., John, Y. M. M., C, J. S. M., Joshi, K., Manikandan, G., & Jakka, G. (2023). *Cyber Defence Based on Artificial Intelligence and Neural Network Model in Cybersecurity*. IEEE. doi:10.1109/ICONSTEM56934.2023.10142590

Sulaiman, N. S., Nasir, A., Othman, W. R. W., Abdul Wahab, S. F., Aziz, N. S., Yacob, A., & Samsudin, N. (2021). Intrusion Detection System Techniques: A Review. *Journal of Physics: Conference Series*, 1874(1), 012042. doi:10.1088/1742-6596/1874/1/012042

Sun, Z., An, G., Yang, Y., & Liu, Y. (2024). Optimized machine learning enabled Intrusion Detection 2 System for Internet of Medical Things. *Franklin Open*, 6, 100056. doi:10.1016/j.fraope.2023.100056

Suricata. (2019). *9.2. Packet Capture - Suricata 6.0.1 documentation*. Suricata. https://docs.suricata.io/en/suricata-6.0.1/performance/packet-capture.html

Tasneem, A. Kumar, A. & Sharma, S. (2018). *Intrusion Detection Prevention System using SNORT*. ResearchGate. https://www.researchgate.net/publication/329716671_Intrusion_Detection_Prevention_System_using_SNORT

The Zeek. (2023). *Monitoring With Zeek - Book of Zeek (git/master)*. Zeek. https://docs.zeek.org/en/master/monitoring.html#instrumentation-and-collection

Topcu, A. E., Alzoubi, Y. I., Elbaşi, E., & Çamalan, E. (2023). Social media Zero-Day attack detection using TensorFlow. *Electronics (Basel)*, 12(17), 3554. doi:10.3390/electronics12173554

United Nations. (2020). *The Impact of Digital Technologies*. UN. https://www.un.org/en/un75/impact-digital-technologies

University of Texas at San Antonio. (2020). *Zeek Intrusion Detection Series*. [online] Available at: https://ce.sc.edu/cyberinfra/docs/workshop/Zeek_Lab_Series.pdf

Vanin, P., Newe, T., Dhirani, L.L., O'Connell, E., O'Shea, D., Lee, B. and Rao, M. (2022). A Study of Network Intrusion Detection Systems Using Artificial Intelligence/Machine Learning. *Applied Sciences*, 12(22), 11752. . doi:10.3390/app122211752

Verma, J., Bhandari, A., & Singh, G. (2022). iNIDS: SWOT Analysis and TOWS Inferences of State-of-the-Art NIDS solutions for the development of Intelligent Network Intrusion Detection System. *Computer Communications*, *195*, 227–247. doi:10.1016/j.comcom.2022.08.022

Wang, C., & Zhu, H. (2022). Wrongdoing Monitor: A Graph-Based Behavioral Anomaly Detection in Cyber Security. *IEEE Transactions on Information Forensics and Security*, *17*, 2703–2718. doi:10.1109/TIFS.2022.3191493

Yang, R., He, H., Xu, Y., Xin, B., Wang, Y., Qu, Y., & Zhang, W. (2023). Efficient intrusion detection toward IoT networks using cloud–edge collaboration. *Computer Networks*, *228*, 109724. doi:10.1016/j.comnet.2023.109724

Yu, D., & Frincke, D. (2007). Improving the quality of alerts and predicting intruder's next goal with Hidden Colored Petri-Net. *Computer Networks*, *51*(3), 632–654. doi:10.1016/j.comnet.2006.05.008

Zaib, M. H. (2018). *NSL-KDD Dataset*. Kaggle. https://www.kaggle.com/datasets/hassan06/nslkdd

Zhang, D., & Wang, S. (2019). Optimization of traditional Snort intrusion detection system. *IOP Conference Series. Materials Science and Engineering*, *569*(4), 042041. doi:10.1088/1757-899X/569/4/042041

Zhou, D., Yan, Z., Fu, Y. and Yao, Z. (2018). A survey on network data collection. *Journal of Network and Computer Applications*, *116*, 9–23. . doi:10.1016/j.jnca.2018.05.004

Chapter 3
A Distributed Model for IoT Anomaly Detection Using Federated Learning

Sidra Tahir
UIIT, Pakistan

Anam Zaheer
UIIT, Pakistan

ABSTRACT

Anomaly detection in IoT-based sleep patterns is crucial for early identification of health issues. This chapter presents a distributed model using federated learning for privacy and data security. The proposed approach involves data collection, preprocessing, model initialization, federated learning server, model distribution, and anomaly detection. Sleep pattern data is preprocessed to extract features, initializing the global anomaly detection model. A federated learning server enables collaborative learning with devices, distributing the updated global model iteratively for synchronized anomaly detection. Precision and accuracy metrics yielded 0.67% precision and 0.84% accuracy, showcasing the effectiveness of the distributed model. Leveraging federated learning ensures privacy, data security, and synchronized anomaly detection across devices, supporting early detection of sleep-related anomalies and health interventions.

INTRODUCTION

The technique of discovering and recognizing unusual behavior or occurrences inside an IoT system or network is known as IoT (Internet of Things) anomaly detection. IoT anomaly detection is essential for guaranteeing the safety, dependability, and effective functioning of IoT systems in light of the proliferation of connected devices and sensors. In the IoT, anomaly detection approaches look for departures from anticipated patterns, behaviors, or thresholds. Both malicious and non-malicious incidents, such as equipment breakdowns or sensor failures, can be classified as anomalies. Malicious actions include cyberattacks and unauthorized access attempts. Organizations can proactively address possible risks,

DOI: 10.4018/978-1-6684-7625-3.ch003

save downtime, enhance system efficiency, and guarantee the accuracy of data generated by IoT devices by spotting abnormalities (Al-Amri et al., 2021).

In the context of the Internet of Things, centralized anomaly detection refers to a method in which anomaly detection duties are carried out at a central location or server, generally in the cloud, utilizing information gathered from several IoT devices or sensors. While this strategy has several benefits, there are also a number of drawbacks: Data privacy and security, Network Bandwidth and Latency, Scalability, Dependence on Network Connectivity and regulatory compliances. Distributed anomaly detection distributes the detection process across multiple edge devices or gateways, allowing for localized analysis and faster response times while minimizing data transmission to the central server (Alrashdi et al., 2019).

The detection of anomalies in sleep patterns is of significant importance for early identification of sleep disorders and potential health issues. In this study, we propose a solution for anomaly detection in sleep patterns using federated learning in IoT environments. A distributed method to machine learning known as federated learning allows for the training of models across a number of decentralized devices or edge nodes without the need for centralized data collection. It enables businesses to take use of machine learning's capabilities while safeguarding data privacy, cutting communication costs, and overcoming issues with data centralization. Data is often gathered from numerous sources and centralized on a central server or cloud platform for model training in traditional machine learning techniques. Privacy issues are raised by this centralized data collecting, though, as it's possible for sensitive or private information to be revealed during data transit or storage. This problem is solved by federated learning, which allows model training on data spread across several devices without transferring the raw data.

For the following reasons, federated learning is extremely important for IoT anomaly detection: data privacy, decentralized data, reduced communication costs, Real time anomaly detection, edge intelligence Scalability and adaptability and Collaborative Learning (Al-mashhadi, Anbar, Hasbullah, & Alamiedy, 2021; Hussain, Irfan, Jhanjhi, Hussain, & Humayun, 2021; Tahir, Hafeez, Abbas, Nawaz, & Hamid, 2022).

The proposed solution involves collecting sleep pattern data from IoT devices, wearables, and smart mattresses, and preprocessing the data by normalizing network flow and extracting relevant features. The global anomaly detection model is initialized using the preprocessed data to establish a starting point for learning and adaptation. The federated learning server facilitates collaborative learning by communicating with participating devices, allowing them to perform local updates and fine-tuning based on their unique sleep pattern data. Model updates are aggregated using gradient descent optimization and cluster model aggregation methods to derive a comprehensive global model. The updated model is distributed iteratively to participating devices, enabling consistent and synchronized anomaly detection while preserving data privacy. Anomalies in sleep patterns are identified by comparing local data with the learned patterns within the global model, leading to the early detection of sleep-related anomalies and potential underlying health issues(Humayun, Jhanjhi, & Almotilag, 2022; Humayun, Niazi, Jhanjhi, Alshayeb, & Mahmood, 2020).

To evaluate the performance of the proposed solution, a labeled dataset of sleep sessions is used, with precision and accuracy metrics employed to assess the anomaly detection system. The results demonstrate promising precision and accuracy rates, indicating the effectiveness of the distributed model for anomaly detection in sleep patterns. The study provides valuable insights into leveraging federated learning in IoT environments for early detection of sleep disorders and paves the way for future research to enhance the accuracy and efficiency of anomaly detection and explore applications in other domains beyond sleep pattern analysis.

RELATED WORK

Federated learning offers a promising alternative to centralized, cloud-based methods for enabling IoT cybersecurity. However, when it comes to anomaly detection in the IoT environment, there are still a number of technical challenges that need to be addressed and resolved. It addresses concerns related to data privacy and reduces the significant communication and storage overhead associated with centralized approaches. By leveraging federated learning, which involves distributed training on local devices, they enhanced performance in IoT cybersecurity. To achieve this, the suggested architecture for FedDetect learning (Gao, Cao, Wang, Zhang, & Xu, 2021) incorporates a cross-round learning rate scheduler and a local adaptive optimizer. These components contribute to improved performance and efficiency. To evaluate the performance of the FedIoT platform and the FedDetect algorithm, they conducted experiments using a network of real-world IoT devices (specifically Raspberry Pis). The evaluation focused on both the model and system aspects. The results demonstrate that federated learning efficiently detects a wider range of threat types across multiple devices. Furthermore, the analysis of system efficiency indicates that end-to-end training time and memory costs are realistic and favorable for IoT devices with limited resources (Zhang et al., 2021).

An efficient method for group learning is federated learning (FL), which integrates mobile technology and the Internet of Things (IoT). Nevertheless, there remain several unresolved technical issues that require attention and resolution. The effect of dispersing the training process over several devices on the functionality of Machine Learning (ML) algorithms is one of these difficulties. When compared to centralized learning methods, this distribution frequently results in a considerable decline in prediction accuracy. The fact that each device's local ML model can only access a small percentage of the data it produces restricts its ability to be successful. The performance degradation is significantly influenced by this restriction. Utilizing three IoT datasets that are available to the public, they carried out rigorous testing to address this problem. Using a data augmentation technique, according to our findings, can boost performance by up to 22.9% compared to the baseline (without data augmentation). The strategy utilizing generative adversarial networks took the longest and offered the least performance advantages among the various data augmentation techniques examined. The greatest significant improvements in detection performance, however, were shown with stratified random sampling and uniform random sampling, both of which required only a slight increase in calculation time. (Weinger et al., 2022).

This paper introduces a novel communication-efficient deep anomaly detection system for Industrial Internet of Things (IIoT) time series data sensing. The system leverages federated learning (FL) and addresses the issue of data islands by simultaneously training an anomaly detection model across distributed edge devices. To identify anomalies properly, they proposed a CNN-LSTM model with an attention mechanism (AMCNN-LSTM) (Tang, Chen, & Yang, 2022). This model includes CNN units based on attention mechanisms to collect critical fine-grained data, reduce memory loss, and handle gradient dispersion problems. In addition, the model forecasts time series data using LSTM units. They assessed the proposed model's performance on four real-world datasets and compare it to existing approaches such as LSTM, SVM, CNN-LSTM, SAEs, and GRU. The experimental findings show that the AMCNN-LSTM model performs the best across all four databases. They provided a gradient compression strategy based on Top-k selection to improve communication efficiency. This technique aims to reduce the amount of data transmitted during the FL process. Overall, our proposed FL-based deep anomaly detection system, featuring the AMCNN-LSTM model and gradient compression technique, offers an effective solution for IIoT time series data sensing with improved accuracy and communication efficiency.

Experimental findings show that the gradient can be 300 times compressed with no loss in accuracy. This ground-breaking research is for FL-based deep anomaly detection on devices. (Liu et al., 2021).

IoT devices are being used more often in daily life. However, many gadgets need stronger configuration, implementation, and design, making them vulnerable. As a result, numerous networks with IoT devices are already open to attack. As a result, there is now a new type of malware that solely targets IoT devices. However, due to the enormous scale of the problem in terms of the many device kinds and manufacturers involved, traditional intrusion detection methods are inadequate in identifying hacked IoT devices. This study introduces D-IOT, a distributed autonomous self-learning system designed for locating compromised IoT devices. D-IOT leverages device-type-specific communication profiles to effectively identify abnormal deviations in device communication behavior. These deviations may occur due to malicious actors, without relying on human intervention or labeled data (I. Ullah & Mahmoud, 2021).

The key feature of D-IOT is its ability to autonomously learn and adapt to different IoT device types, enabling accurate detection of compromised devices. By analyzing device communication patterns, D-IOT can identify deviations from expected behavior, signaling potential compromise. Unlike traditional approaches that rely on human input or labeled data, D-IOT operates independently and can continuously update its knowledge base as it encounters new device types and communication patterns. This autonomous learning capability makes D-IOT a robust and scalable solution for identifying compromised IoT devices. Utilizing federated learning, D-IOT effectively aggregates behavior profiles. As a result, D-IOT can handle newly discovered and unanticipated assaults. They carefully and thoroughly assessed more than 30 commercial IoT devices over an extended period, and our results demonstrate that D-IOT exhibits exceptional efficiency, with a remarkable 95.6% detection rate, enabling rapid identification of devices infected with malware, including the notorious Mirai, in a mere 257 milliseconds. When tested in a real-world deployment scenario for smart homes, IOT reported no false alarms (Nguyen et al., 2019).

The Internet of Medical Things (IoMT) is being more widely used in smart hospitals, nursing homes, and residences with in-home care, as well as other medical facilities. It senses patients' vital body indications, monitors their health, and produces multivariate data to provide just-in-time health services using core Internet of Things (IoT) technology, smart medical devices, and cloud computing services. Most of the time, centralized servers analyze this vast volume of data. In a centralized healthcare environment, anomaly detection (AD) is frequently hampered by lengthy reaction times and high-performance overhead. Furthermore, sending patients' confidential health information to a centralized server raises privacy issues, which might pose a number of security vulnerabilities to the AD model, such as data poisoning (A. Ullah et al., 2021). To overcome these issues with centralized AD models, they described a Federated Learning (FL)-based AD model that employs edge cloudlets to execute AD models locally without sharing patient data. In this study, they offered a hierarchical FL that permits aggregation at several levels, enabling multiparty collaboration. The application of FL is constrained since current FL approaches only execute collection on a single server. They described a brand-new disease-based grouping approach that classifies different AD models into different diseases. In order to train the AD model, they also developed a novel Federated Time Distributed (FEDTIMEDIS) Long Short-Term Memory (LSTM) technique. To illustrate our methodology, they provided a Remote Patient Monitoring (RPM) use case and show how it may be implemented utilizing edge cloudlets and the Digital Twin (DT) (D. Gupta, Kayode, Bhatt, Gupta, & Tosun, 2021).

One of the most promising strategies for leveraging distributed resources is federated learning (FL), which allows clients to train a machine learning model while preserving dispersed data collaboratively. As a result of the topic's significant spike in popularity, rapid advancements have been made in a number of crucial areas, including communication efficacy, processing non-IID data, privacy, and security capabilities (Alferidah & Jhanjhi, 2020). The bulk of FL tasks, on the other hand, are solely concerned with supervised jobs and presume that the client training sets are tagged. In this work, they extended the FL paradigm to unsupervised functions by solving the challenge of anomaly detection in decentralized systems and making use of large amounts of unlabeled data on distributed edge devices. Specifically, they suggested a unique approach that divides clients into communities with comparable majority (i.e., inlier) tendencies through a preprocessing stage (Borghesi, Molan, Milano, & Bartolini, 2022). The same anomaly detection model (autoencoders) is then federated and trained across every client community. In order to detect irregularities, the created model is distributed and applied to clients belonging to the same community as the one that entered the related federated process. Experiments demonstrate how accurate our strategy is in detecting communities that adhere to optimal partitioning when known client groups display comparable inlier patterns. Furthermore, the performance is comparable to that of partitioned federated ideal communities' models and substantially better than that of clients training models solely on local data. (Nardi, Valerio, & Passarella, 2022).

Cyberattacks on Internet of Things (IoT) devices are multiplying, getting more advanced, and becoming more targeted. Due to the massive scope of IoT, the variety of hardware and software, and the fact that they are usually utilised in uncontrolled situations, it is challenging to apply standard IT security solutions, such as signature-based IDS/IPS systems (Humayun, Niazi, et al., 2020). Their inability to keep up with the continuously changing IoT threat landscape is also a result of the lengthy gaps between analysis and detection rule publication. Machine learning techniques have demonstrated the ability to respond to new threats more quickly; IoT networks' diversity and heterogeneity (Humayun, Jhanjhi, Hamid, & Ahmed, 2020). This method ensures successful training across various device types while addressing the numerous features of IoT devices. A thorough testbed is used to create and assess the suggested architecture. A variety of simulated IoT/IIoT devices, attackers, and a difficult network architecture are all included in the testbed, which has 100 virtual IoT/IIoT devices, 30 switches, and ten routers (Belenguer, Navaridas, & Pascual, 2022).

Real-world attacks conducted by threat actors are utilized to evaluate the performance of the anomaly detection models on the testbed. The whole lifespan of the Mirai virus, a different botnet that uses the Merlin command and control server, other red-teaming tools doing scanning duties, and more than one attack specifically targeting the emulated devices are just a few examples of the many scenarios covered by these attacks. In summary, this study presents a novel training framework that leverages unsupervised models, FL, and device clustering techniques to address the limitations of traditional model training architectures in IoT environments. The proposed architecture demonstrates its efficacy in detecting anomalies and evaluating robustness against sophisticated attacks using a realistic testbed scenario. (Sáez-de-Cámara, Flores, Arellano, Urbieta, & Zurutuza, 2023).

As the Industrial Internet of Things (IIoT) expands quickly, numerous IoT devices and sensors provide much data through industrial sensing. Massive data may be analyzed using cutting-edge machine-learning techniques to reveal insights that improve decisions and strategic industrial production. However, it is simple to hack weak IoT devices, leading to IoT device failures (i.e., abnormalities) (Humayun, 2020). It is crucial to properly and quickly identify abnormalities since they significantly impact the manufacturing of industrial goods (K. Gupta, Jiwani, & Afreen, 2022). The CNN-LSTM model gathers fine-grained data using CNN units while retaining the benefits of the LSTM unit for time series data prediction. The third goal is to discover anomalies in real time and on the go. To lower communication costs while increasing communication efficacy, the suggested design adopts a gradient compression approach. According to comprehensive experiment findings based on real-world datasets, the suggested framework and technique may detect anomalies efficiently and fast while reducing communication overhead by around 50% when compared to current approaches. (Liu et al., 2020).

The intrusion detection system (IDS) must be capable of keeping up with escalating attack quantities, Internet traffic, and detection speeds. To determine whether network traffic is safe or malicious, flow-based intrusion detection systems (IDSs) use network flow feature (NTF) data as input rather than the time-consuming and labor-intensive packet content inspection processing (Humayun, Jhanjhi, Alsayat, & Ponnusamy, 2020). In order to save computer resources and training time, this study suggests a unique pre-processing technique that groups a preset amount of NTF records into frames and converts those frames into pictures. With federated learning (FL), several users can trade trained models while preserving the confidentiality of their own training data. (Alamri, Jhanjhi, & Humayun, 2019). While maintaining the privacy of their own training data, federated learning (FL) enables multiple users to swap trained models. (Ates, Ozdel, & Anarim, 2019). The BOUN DDoS dataset is used to assess the suggested approaches. The experimental results demonstrate that the FTL and FL training approaches provide effective solutions without requiring data centralization, thus ensuring the privacy of participant data. Moreover, these methods achieve acceptable accuracy in identifying DDoS attacks, with FTL achieving 92.99% accuracy and FL achieving 88.42% accuracy, when compared to the accuracy of Traditional transfer learning (93.95%). In conclusion, this study demonstrates the value of federated transfer learning and federated learning approaches in NIDS and demonstrates how they may safeguard data privacy while attaining acceptable accuracy in detecting DDoS assaults (Toldinas, Venčkauskas, Liutkevičius, & Morkevičius, 2022).

Smart manufacturing (SM) has emerged as a result of the development and increased usage of contemporary sophisticated technologies. One of the key technologies for building smart factories is the Internet of Things (IoT), which connects all industrial assets, such as machinery and control systems, with information systems and business processes. One of the key industries targeted by a number of threats, particularly unknown and uncommon attacks, is industrial control systems of smart IoT-based factories (Omar, A., & Zaman, 2017). Given the widespread distribution of IoT front-end sensing devices in SM, an effective distributed anomaly detection (AD) architecture for IoT-based ICSs should be able to detect anomalies with high sensitivity, learn new data patterns quickly, and be lightweight enough to be installed on platforms with limited resources. The majority of anomaly detection systems to this moment have not met all of these criteria (Humayun et al., 2022). The interpretability of the logic supporting a prediction of an anomalous occurrence is also unimportant. They suggested the FedeX architecture as a remedy for these problems in this study. In the liquid storage data set, FedeX outperforms 14 other established anomaly detection algorithms on every detection criterion. Additionally, it outperforms earlier SWAT data set solutions with a Recall of 1 and an F1-score of 0.9857. They were able to run anomaly detection wor FedeX surpasses 14 other well-known anomaly detection algorithms in the liquid storage data set on every detection criterion. Additionally, with a Recall of 1 and an F1-score of 0.9857, it performs better than prior SWAT data set solutions. Due to FedEx's 14% memory utilisation and rapid training rates, which also demonstrate that it is low-maintenance in terms of hardware requirements, they were able to execute anomaly detection workloads on top of edge computing infrastructure in real-time. kloads on top of edge computing infrastructure in real-time because to FedEx's 14% memory utilization and quick training rates, which also show that it is low-maintenance in terms of hardware needs. Additionally, FedeX is recognized as one of the best frameworks for evaluating anticipated abnormalities using XAI, enabling experts to react fast and have more faith in the model (Huong et al., 2022).

In recent years, the use of smart devices equipped with software, sensors, and other technologies (IoT) has increased. Intending to minimize human intervention in some jobs, they seek to be networked through a network and share data. The data transit via a network has increased due to the development of IoT devices. The interactions and design of these devices have increased the risk of malware assaults, particularly on these devices, which can be used to duplicate additional attacks. As a result, it is important to recognize future attacks. This issue has an AI answer, and the IoT23 data set was utilized for training and testing the model using the Federated Learning approach, a machine learning technique. Federated Averaging was employed as an aggregation method, and a Multi-layer Perceptron was used for the central server and federated members. The outcomes demonstrated the decentralized potential of federated learning, which would benefit each device's internal machine-learning model. On some devices, the model has a 100% accuracy rating. Although this decentralized approach had an accuracy rate of no more than 70%, it generally impacted learning. The data, distribution, and size of each member's dataset impacted the model's performance (Leonel & Prado, 2022).

The Internet of Things (IoT) refers to a network of diverse physical objects that are interconnected and typically operate autonomously while being connected to the Internet. IoT networks serve as a rich source of Personally Identifiable Information (PII) due to the increased automation of everyday tasks, resulting in a substantial amount of user data stored in digital formats. Unfortunately, these data repositories present opportunities for malicious actors to potentially steal, manipulate, and misuse the data for harmful purposes. Machine learning (ML)-assisted IoT security solutions have drawn a lot of interest recently. However, several recent studies make the assumption that abundant training data is readily accessible and can be efficiently transferred to the central server. This presumption is based on the fact that data is generated at the edge by IoT devices and continuously supplied, allowing for a seamless flow of data for training purposes. The traditional approach of storing all data on a single server is considered less favorable in domains where privacy concerns related to user data are prominent. This is why conventional machine learning methods are not the preferred choice in such scenarios. To address this challenge, they proposed a solution by incorporating federated learning (FL) into the system, anomaly detection in IoT networks can be enhanced. Our method utilizes decentralized on-device data to proactively identify intrusions, mitigating the need for centralized data storage and ensuring privacy. Our approach involves utilizing federated training cycles specifically on Gated Recurrent Units (GRUs) models, wherein only the acquired weights are shared with the main server of the federated learning (FL) system. By adopting this strategy, they ensured that the data remains securely stored on the local IoT devices (Hamid, 2023) without being exposed or shared. The ensemble component of the technique also collects updates from several sources to improve the overall accuracy of the ML model. Our experimental findings show that our technique has the highest accuracy rate for detecting attacks and surpasses conventional/centralized machine learning (non-FL) versions in terms of safeguarding user data privacy (Mothukuri et al., 2022).

PROPOSED SOLUTION

Data Collection and Preprocessing

Data collection and preprocessing play vital roles in anomaly detection through federated learning. Various sources, such as IoT devices, wearables, and smart mattresses, are used to gather sleep pattern data, including heart rate, body movement, temperature, and sleep duration. To prepare the data for analysis, it undergoes preprocessing, including network flow data normalization for consistent range. Feature extraction techniques are employed to identify significant attributes like sleep duration, cycles, heart rate variability, and movement patterns. The preprocessed data is securely stored, using robust security measures, to protect against unauthorized access. This ensures the data is ready for the next steps in the anomaly detection process.

Model Initialization

After the data collection and preprocessing stages, the next step is to initialize the global anomaly detection model. This involves setting up a cloud server dedicated to the anomaly detection task. The preprocessed sleep pattern data is used as the input to initialize the global model. Initialization entails configuring the model's architecture, setting initial weights and biases, and defining any necessary hyperparameters. The goal of model initialization is to establish a starting point for the global model to learn and adapt from the distributed data. By initializing the global model with preprocessed data, it is primed to capture patterns and characteristics of normal and abnormal sleep patterns.

Federated Learning Server

The federated learning server receives the initialized global model from the cloud server, which serves as the starting point for the collaborative learning process. It then communicates with the participating devices, such as IoT devices and wearable devices, that hold local data related to sleep patterns, specifically the IoT-23 dataset. During the federated learning process, the server sends the global model to the participating devices, allowing them to perform local updates and fine-tuning using their respective local datasets. These updates typically involve training the model on their local data, refining the model's parameters based on the unique characteristics of their sleep pattern data. Once the participating devices have completed their local updates, the federated learning server aggregates the model updates using gradient descent optimization techniques. The aggregated updates reflect the collective knowledge from the distributed devices and capture the degrees of sleep patterns across the dataset. Furthermore, the server incorporates cluster model aggregation methods to effectively combine the local models and derive a more comprehensive global model. This enables the collaborative learning process to capture a broader range of sleep pattern characteristics and improve the accuracy of anomaly detection.

Model Distribution

After model aggregation, the updated global model is distributed to participating devices. This distribution ensures that devices have access to the refined model, incorporating collective knowledge from collaborative learning. The devices integrate the received model into their local anomaly detection systems, enabling them to apply it to their own sleep pattern data. Model distribution occurs iteratively, periodically sending the updated global model to devices. This iterative process allows devices to continuously benefit from collective learning and adapt their anomaly detection capabilities. By distributing the updated model, the federated learning approach ensures consistent and synchronized anomaly detection while preserving data privacy and security across the distributed network of devices.

Anomaly Detection

After the model distribution phase, the updated global model is utilized to identify anomalies in sleep patterns on each participating device. The devices analyze their local sleep pattern data by comparing it with the learned patterns within the model. Using the model's anomaly detection mechanism, anomalies are determined based on statistical thresholds or machine learning algorithms. Anomalies are classified as abnormal if they exceed the threshold, indicating irregularities or deviations from normal sleep patterns. This process helps identify sleep-related anomalies, such as sleep disorders or unusual patterns, leading to early detection of underlying health issues.

Figure 1. Proposed methodology

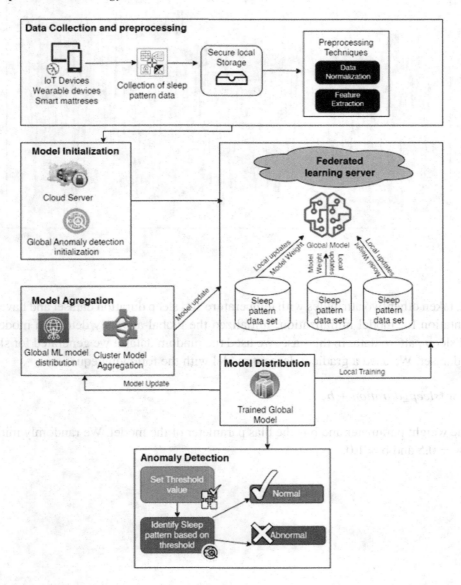

RESULTS AND DISCUSSION

First, we generated a random dataset of sleep pattern data from the iot-23 dataset. We have collected data for 100 sleep sessions, with attributes such as heart rate, body movement, temperature, and sleep duration. Each attribute is represented by a numerical value. First we have taken an IoT- 23 dataset with only two attributes: heart rate and body movement.

Figure 2. Sleep pattern data with attributes heart rate and body movement

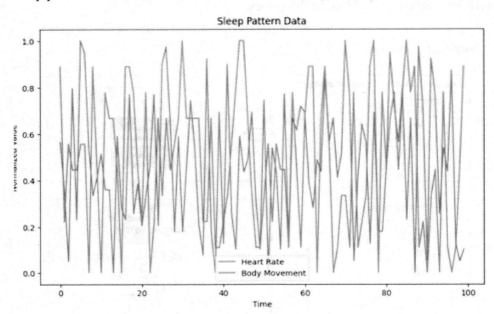

After that, taken other two attributes with temperature and sleep duration dataset and have performed the implementation for model initialization. Initialized the global anomaly detection model using the preprocessed sleep pattern data. In this case, we used the random dataset we generated for sleep pattern from IoT-23 dataset. We used a gradient descent model with the following equation:

$heart\_rate = w*sleep\_duration + b$

where w is the weight parameter and b is the bias parameter of the model. We randomly initialize these parameters, w = 0.5 and b = 1.0.

Figure 3. Sleep pattern data with temperature and sleep duration

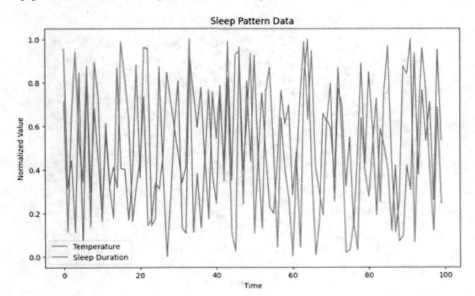

After model initialization, for the federated learning server taken the three participating devices with their local datasets, performed updates and fine-tuning using their respective data

Each device trains its local model using its local dataset. For example, device 1 uses gradient descent optimization to update its local model parameters based on the equation

$heart\_rate = w*sleep\_duration + b$

After local updates, the federated learning server aggregates the model updates. A simple averaging method is used to combine the local models. After that calculated the aggregated model for clustered model and global ML distribution using below equation:

$$Global\ model\ w = \frac{w1 + w2}{2}$$

$$b = \frac{b1 + b2}{2}$$

For calculation of anomaly detection, each participating device applies the updated global model to its own sleep pattern data to detect anomalies. For sleep session for which we want to detect anomalies. Sleep duration 8 hours, actual heart rate 75 beats per minute and set random for other devices. The predicted heart rate and the actual heart rate, anomalies determined using statistical thresholds or machine learning algorithms clustered model.

Figure 4. Clustered model sleep duration with anomalies

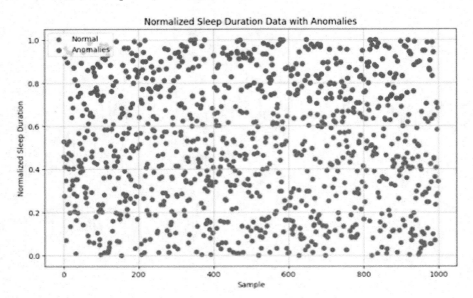

To evaluate the precision and accuracy of the above implementation, we have taken 100 labeled dataset for evaluation purposes. We have a randomly labeled dataset of 100 sleep sessions, where 20 sessions are labeled as anomalies and 80 sessions are labeled as normal. We have applied the anomaly detection model to identify anomalies in sleep patterns. To calculate precision and accuracy, we can use the following formulas:

$$Precision = \frac{True\ Positives}{True\ Positives + False\ Positives}$$

$$Accuracy = \frac{True\ Positives + False\ Positives}{Total}$$

Precision and accuracy are evaluation metrics used to assess the performance of an anomaly detection system. Precision measures the proportion of correctly identified anomalies out of all the instances classified as anomalies(Humayun, 2020). Accuracy measures the overall correctness of the anomaly detection system by calculating the proportion of correctly classified instances (both anomalies and normal instances) out of the total instances.

Figure 5. Precision and accuracy evaluation

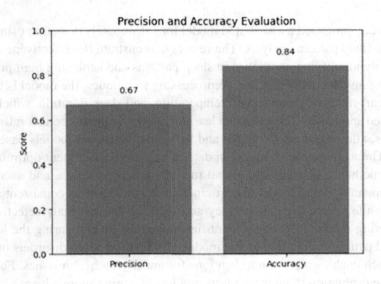

Figure shows that precision and accuracy calculated for anomaly detection. True positive TP as normal anomaly and false positive as abnormal anomaly with labelled dataset. Accuracy calculate 0.84% and precision calculated as 0.67%.

Figure 6. Anomaly detection results

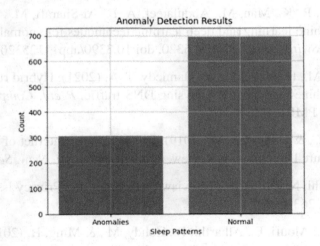

From the figure shows that the green represents as normal anomaly and red represents the abnormal anomalies calculated from the threshold values set and identification based on set threshold value.

CONCLUSION

In conclusion, this study proposed a distributed model for IoT anomaly detection using federated learning in the context of sleep pattern analysis. The results demonstrate the effectiveness of the proposed approach in accurately identifying anomalies in sleep patterns and achieving high precision and accuracy rates. By leveraging data collection and preprocessing techniques, the model is trained on various attributes such as heart rate, body movement, temperature, and sleep duration, which are essential for detecting sleep-related anomalies. The federated learning server facilitates collaborative learning among participating devices, allowing them to update and fine-tune their local models based on their unique sleep pattern data. The aggregation of model updates using gradient descent optimization and cluster model aggregation methods enhances the global model's precision 0.67% and accuracy 0.84%. The distribution of the updated global model to participating devices ensures consistent and synchronized anomaly detection while preserving data privacy and security. The anomaly detection process, based on thresholds clustering model, effectively identifies anomalies by comparing the local sleep pattern data with the learned patterns within the global model. By detecting sleep disorders or unusual patterns early on, this approach enables prompt interventions for underlying health issues. Future work can focus on expanding the evaluation to larger datasets and incorporating more advanced machine learning techniques to further improve the accuracy and efficiency of anomaly detection in IoT environments. Moreover, incorporating real-time monitoring and feedback mechanisms can enable adaptive anomaly detection systems that continuously learn and improve over time.

REFERENCES

Al-Amri, R., Murugesan, R. K., Man, M., Abdulateef, A. F., Al-Sharafi, M. A., & Alkahtani, A. A. (2021). A review of machine learning and deep learning techniques for anomaly detection in iot data. *Applied Sciences (Basel, Switzerland)*, *11*(12), 5320. doi:10.3390/app11125320

Al-mashhadi, S., Anbar, M., Hasbullah, I., & Alamiedy, T. A. (2021). Hybrid rule-based botnet detection approach using machine learning for analysing DNS traffic. *PeerJ. Computer Science*, *7*, 1–34. doi:10.7717/peerj-cs.640 PMID:34458571

Alamri, M., Jhanjhi, N. Z., & Humayun, M. (2019). Blockchain for Internet of Things (IoT) Research Issues Challenges \& Future Directions: A Review. *Int. J. Comput. Sci. Netw. Secur*, *19*, 244–258.

Alferidah, D. K., & Jhanjhi, N. Z. (2020). A Review on Security and Privacy Issues and Challenges in Internet of Things, *20*(4), 263–285.

Alrashdi, I., Alqazzaz, A., Aloufi, E., Alharthi, R., Zohdy, M., & Ming, H. (2019). AD-IoT: Anomaly detection of IoT cyberattacks in smart city using machine learning. *2019 IEEE 9th Annual Computing and Communication Workshop and Conference, CCWC 2019*, (pp. 305–310). IEEE. 10.1109/CCWC.2019.8666450

Ates, C., Ozdel, S., & Anarim, E. (2019). Clustering Based DDoS Attack Detection Using the Relationship between Packet Headers. *Proceedings - 2019 Innovations in Intelligent Systems and Applications Conference, ASYU 2019*. IEEE. 10.1109/ASYU48272.2019.8946331

Belenguer, A., Navaridas, J., & Pascual, J. A. (2022). *A review of Federated Learning in Intrusion Detection Systems for IoT*, 1–13.

Borghesi, A., Molan, M., Milano, M., & Bartolini, A. (2022). Anomaly Detection and Anticipation in High Performance Computing Systems. *IEEE Transactions on Parallel and Distributed Systems*, *33*(4), 739–750. doi:10.1109/TPDS.2021.3082802

Gao, Z., Cao, J., Wang, W., Zhang, H., & Xu, Z. (2021). Online-Semisupervised Neural Anomaly Detector to Identify MQTT-Based Attacks in Real Time. *Security and Communication Networks*, *2021*, 1–11. doi:10.1155/2021/4587862

Gupta, D., Kayode, O., Bhatt, S., Gupta, M., & Tosun, A. S. (2021). Hierarchical Federated Learning based Anomaly Detection using Digital Twins for Smart Healthcare. *Proceedings - 2021 IEEE 7th International Conference on Collaboration and Internet Computing, CIC 2021*, (pp. 16–25). IEEE. 10.1109/CIC52973.2021.00013

Gupta, K., Jiwani, N., & Afreen, N. (2022). Blood Pressure Detection Using CNN-LSTM Model. *Proceedings - 2022 IEEE 11th International Conference on Communication Systems and Network Technologies, CSNT 2022*, (April), (pp. 262–366). IEEE. 10.1109/CSNT54456.2022.9787648

Hamid, B. (2023). A Hybrid Model for Botnet Detection using. *Machine Learning*.

Humayun, M. (2020). IoT-based Secure and Energy Efficient scheme for E-health applications. *Indian Journal of Science and Technology*, *13*(28), 2833–2848. doi:10.17485/IJST/v13i28.861

Humayun, M., Jhanjhi, N. Z., & Almotilag, A. (2022). Real-Time Security Health and Privacy Monitoring for Saudi Highways Using Cutting-Edge Technologies. *Applied Sciences (Basel, Switzerland)*, *12*(4), 2177. doi:10.3390/app12042177

Humayun, M., Jhanjhi, N. Z., Alsayat, A., & Ponnusamy, V. (2020). Internet of things and ransomware : Evolution, mitigation and prevention. *Egyptian Informatics Journal*. doi:10.1016/j.eij.2020.05.003

Humayun, M., Jhanjhi, N. Z., Hamid, B., & Ahmed, G. (2020). *Emerging mart Logistics and Transportation Using IoT and Blockchain*, 58–62. Research Gate.

Humayun, M., Niazi, M., Jhanjhi, N., Alshayeb, M., & Mahmood, S. (2020). Cyber Security Threats and Vulnerabilities: A Systematic Mapping Study. *Arabian Journal for Science and Engineering*, *45*(4), 3171–3189. doi:10.1007/s13369-019-04319-2

Huong, T. T., Bac, T. P., Ha, K. N., Hoang, N. V., Hoang, N. X., Hung, N. T., & Tran, K. P. (2022). Federated Learning-Based Explainable Anomaly Detection for Industrial Control Systems. *IEEE Access : Practical Innovations, Open Solutions*, *10*, 53854–53872. doi:10.1109/ACCESS.2022.3173288

Hussain, S. J., Irfan, M., Jhanjhi, N. Z., Hussain, K., & Humayun, M. (2021). Performance Enhancement in Wireless Body Area Networks with Secure Communication. *Wireless Personal Communications*, *116*(1), 1–22. doi:10.1007/s11277-020-07702-7 PMID:33558792

Leonel, M., & Prado, M. (2022). *Anomaly detection in IoT: Federated Learning approach on the IoT-23 Dataset*. [Thesis, University of Twente].

Liu, Y., Garg, S., Nie, J., Zhang, Y., Xiong, Z., Kang, J., & Hossain, M. S. (2021). Deep Anomaly Detection for Time-Series Data in Industrial IoT: A Communication-Efficient On-Device Federated Learning Approach. *IEEE Internet of Things Journal*, *8*(8), 6348–6358. doi:10.1109/JIOT.2020.3011726

Liu, Y., Kumar, N., Xiong, Z., Lim, W. Y. B., Kang, J., & Niyato, D. (2020). Communication-Efficient Federated Learning for Anomaly Detection in Industrial Internet of Things. *2020 IEEE Global Communications Conference, GLOBECOM 2020 - Proceedings, 2020-Janua*(July). IEEE. 10.1109/GLOBECOM42002.2020.9348249

Mothukuri, V., Khare, P., Parizi, R. M., Pouriyeh, S., Dehghantanha, A., & Srivastava, G. (2022). Federated-Learning-Based Anomaly Detection for IoT Security Attacks. *IEEE Internet of Things Journal*, *9*(4), 2545–2554. doi:10.1109/JIOT.2021.3077803

Nardi, M., Valerio, L., & Passarella, A. (2022). *Anomaly Detection through Unsupervised Federated Learning*. IEEE. doi:10.1109/MSN57253.2022.00085

Nguyen, T. D., Marchal, S., Miettinen, M., Fereidooni, H., Asokan, N., & Sadeghi, A. R. (2019). DÏoT: A federated self-learning anomaly detection system for IoT. *Proceedings - International Conference on Distributed Computing Systems, 2019-July*(Icdcs), (pp. 756–767). IEEE. 10.1109/ICDCS.2019.00080

Omar, M. A. A., & Zaman, N. (2017). Internet of Things (IoT) : Charity Automation. *International Journal of Advanced Computer Science and Applications*, *8*(2), 166–170. doi:10.14569/IJACSA.2017.080222

Sáez-de-Cámara, X., Flores, J. L., Arellano, C., Urbieta, A., & Zurutuza, U. (2023). *Clustered Federated Learning Architecture for Network Anomaly Detection in Large Scale Heterogeneous IoT Networks*. Elesvier. doi:10.1016/j.cose.2023.103299

Tahir, S., Hafeez, Y., Abbas, M. A., Nawaz, A., & Hamid, B. (2022). Smart Learning Objects Retrieval for E-Learning with Contextual Recommendation based on Collaborative Filtering. *Education and Information Technologies*, *27*(6), 1–38. doi:10.1007/s10639-022-10966-0

Tang, M., Chen, W., & Yang, W. (2022). Anomaly detection of industrial state quantity time-Series data based on correlation and long short-term memory. *Connection Science*, *34*(1), 2048–2065. doi:10.1080/09540091.2022.2092594

Toldinas, J., Venčkauskas, A., Liutkevičius, A., & Morkevičius, N. (2022). Framing Network Flow for Anomaly Detection Using Image Recognition and Federated Learning. *Electronics (Basel)*, *11*(19), 3138. doi:10.3390/electronics11193138

Ullah, A., Azeem, M., Ashraf, H., Alaboudi, A. A., Humayun, M., & Jhanjhi, N. Z. (2021). Secure Healthcare Data Aggregation and Transmission in IoT - A Survey. *IEEE Access : Practical Innovations, Open Solutions*, *9*, 16849–16865. doi:10.1109/ACCESS.2021.3052850

Ullah, I., & Mahmoud, Q. H. (2021). A Framework for Anomaly Detection in IoT Networks Using Conditional Generative Adversarial Networks. *IEEE Access : Practical Innovations, Open Solutions*, *9*, 165907–165931. doi:10.1109/ACCESS.2021.3132127

Weinger, B., Kim, J., Sim, A., Nakashima, M., Moustafa, N., & Wu, K. J. (2022). Enhancing IoT anomaly detection performance for federated learning. *Digital Communications and Networks*, 8(3), 314–323. doi:10.1016/j.dcan.2022.02.007

Zhang, T., He, C., Ma, T., Gao, L., Ma, M., & Avestimehr, S. (2021). Federated Learning for Internet of Things. *SenSys 2021 - Proceedings of the 2021 19th ACM Conference on Embedded Networked Sensor Systems*, (pp. 413–419). ACM. 10.1145/3485730.3493444

Chapter 4
Network Intrusion Detection to Mitigate Jamming and Spoofing Attacks Using Federated Leading:
A Comprehensive Survey

Tayyab Rehman
Air University, Pakistan

Muhammad Ashraf
Air University, Pakistan

Noshina Tariq
ⓘ https://orcid.org/0000-0002-9754-253X
Air University, Pakistan

Mamoona Humayun
ⓘ https://orcid.org/0000-0001-6339-2257
Jouf University, Saudi Arabia

ABSTRACT

Network intrusions through jamming and spoofing attacks have become increasingly prevalent. The ability to detect such threats at early stages is necessary for preventing a successful attack from occurring. This survey chapter thoroughly overviews the demand for sophisticated intrusion detection systems (IDS) and how cutting-edge techniques, like federated learning-enabled IDS, can reduce privacy risks and protect confidential data during intrusion detection. It explores numerous mitigation strategies used to defend against these assaults, highlighting the significance of early detection and avoidance. The chapter comprehensively analyzes spoofing and jamming attacks, explores mitigation techniques, highlights challenges in implementing federated learning-based IDS, and compares diverse strategies for their real-world effects on network security. Lastly, it presents an unbiased evaluation of contemporary IDS techniques, assessing their advantages, disadvantages, and overall effect on network security while also discussing future challenges and prospects for academia and industry.

DOI: 10.4018/978-1-6684-7625-3.ch004

INTRODUCTION

The growing prevalence of jamming and spoofing attacks in wireless networks is a cause for concern. The need to develop effective countermeasures has become even more urgent in recent years. Network Intrusion Detection (NID) can be a critical component for protecting against these attacks by detecting malicious activity or events within the network environment (Chaabouni, 2019). However, NID systems have limited effectiveness when faced with complex attack scenarios such as those arising from asymmetric links between multiple Access Points (APs) (Basati, 2023). To address this limitation, novel techniques based on Federated Learning (FL) which utilize data collected from APs across different locations, should be explored. This paper presents an overview of state-of-the-art methods related to NID using federated learning approaches and discusses future directions that researchers should explore in order to create highly secure and resilient network environments against jamming and spoofing attacks (Han, 2022).

Therefore, mitigation goals focus on seeking structured solutions, including security methods such as cryptography-based protection techniques. It may rely on encryption processes explicitly designed to deter Cryptographic Suite Assessment (CSA) against these common types of cyberattacks mentioned above. Detecting suspicious messages before they take proper form within protocols so establishing control mechanisms is vital for anti-jam/spoof detection engines. In addition, isolating any physical attackers by designing efficient countermeasures to avoid existing environmental noise contributed during vulnerable period's demands solutions. Moreover, applying appropriate access controls allows only trusted entities to interact with targeted services or resources and blocks user's authentication by attempting open connections from alleged compromised location(s) (Khan K. M., 2020), (Alloghani, 2019).

Therefore, reducing threats from jamming and spoofing is essential due to their capacity to stop reliable service delivery, as well as financial losses related to assets being exposed often overlooked. It may lead to potentially catastrophic results if no preventive action is taken (Vaishnavi, 2021). Implementation in advance leverages appropriate defences and helps in addressing vulnerabilities that reoccur in the future. It may ultimately harm organizations and raise consequences. Safeguarding also gives the most significant level of assurance for the needed infrastructures' Successful configuration and other benefits, including satisfaction to all parties engaged in the transactions, specified trajectory target operates safely, expects to fulfil compliance rules (YAMAN, 2023). Customer esteem and loyalty, additional growth for the organization, and a positive side scale (Yu, 2022). Multiple difficulties in the execution need good collaboration to protect the investment (Liu, 2022). This survey paper aims to provide a comprehensive review of the research on using federated learning to develop network intrusion detection systems that can mitigate jamming and spoofing attacks (Yin, 2020).The scope of the paper will include an overview of the current state-of-the-art intrusion detection systems, the challenges associated with jamming and spoofing attacks, and the application of federated learning in intrusion detection systems (Kulkarni, 2020), (Belenguer, A review of federated learning in intrusion detection systems for iot. arXiv preprint arXiv:2204.12443., 2022).

In addition to this, the article investigates numerous federated learning algorithms that are used for data manipulation, the protection of privacy, jamming, and spoofing attacks. It also highlights the strengths and weaknesses of federated learning methods, specifically how they are used in network intrusion detection systems (Belenguer, 2022). This survey paper aims to connect intrusion detection systems and federated learning research by comprehensively investigating how federated learning can be used to make intrusion detection systems that protect against jamming and spoofing attacks. The survey paper will also help determine the problems and limits of using federated learning in network intrusion detection systems. It will also suggest possible directions for future research in this field. Overall, the goal of the survey paper is to help improve network intrusion detection systems by showing the pros and cons of using federated learning methods to stop jamming and spoofing attacks. The most important contributions of this study adds are:

1. It provides an in-depth discussion of the need for advanced intrusion detection systems, such as federated learning-enabled IDS.
2. It demonstrates how innovative methods can mitigate privacy hazards and protect sensitive data during intrusion detection.
3. It delivers a comprehensive understanding of spoofing and jamming attacks, their effect on the network, and ways to mitigate them.
4. It provides insight into challenges and considerations in implementing federated learning-based IDS.
5. It analyzes different state-of-the-art and provides their comparative analysis, strengths and weaknesses, and impact on security.
6. Finally, it delivers future challenges and future discussions to help industry and academia.

Section 2 presents traditional network intrusion detection techniques. Sections 3 and 4 provide details on jamming and spoofing attacks, respectively. Federated learning is detailed in Section 5. In Section 6, a comparative analysis of surveyed techniques is presented. Section 7 provides mitigating strategies for jamming and spoofing attacks using federated learning. Future research directions and the conclusion is provided in Sections 8 and 9, respectively.

TRADITIONAL NETWORK INTRUSION DETECTION

Network Intrusion Detection is a process used to prevent malicious activities on computer networks (Hashmi, 2023). It works by monitoring the traffic that passes through a network to detect any suspicious or unauthorized activity, such as attempted hacking attempts or viruses (Ponnusamy, 2022). Network intrusion detection systems analyze and respond to security-related events caused by malicious actors attempting to access the system (Alani, 2021). The goal of these systems is not only to block potential attacks but also to alert security personnel about them to that appropriate action can be taken. It includes logging data for further analysis and preventing attackers from executing their plans within an organization's networks and systems (Chaiban, 2022). In addition, some intrusion detection solutions use algorithms and artificial intelligence models combined with signature-based detection methodologies to identify threats accurately (Zhi, 2020). Jamming and spoofing attacks are malicious activities that pose severe threats to wireless networks. Jamming is the intentional interference of a radio signal, while spoofing involves sending false or faked signals to manipulate or misdirect electronic devices (Sathyamoorthy, 2020). Both attacks can disrupt network operations, steal data, interfere with communications, and cause material damage in specific scenarios. Mitigating jamming and spoofing attacks has become increasingly important as technology continues to advance at an unprecedented rate due to its disruptive nature not only for communication but also for navigation systems such as GPS receivers used in various industries across multiple sector applications like automotive safety services and autonomous machines among others (Alrefaei F. A., 2022). The following are the traditional network intrusion detection techniques:

- **Signature-based detection:** This method uses a set of known attack signatures to identify malicious traffic. Signature-based detection works by analysing network traffic against a database of predefined attack signatures (Soe, 2019). The intrusion is flagged if a match is found, and an alert is generated. The advantage of this approach is its accuracy and low false-positive rate. The disadvantage is that it only detects known attacks (Kwon, 2022).

- **Anomaly-based detection**: In this method, the normal or expected behaviour of the network is established, and any deviation from the normal behaviour is identified as an attack. Network traffic is examined for any odd patterns or activities that deviates from the set baseline in anomaly-based detection techniques (Maseer, 2021). This method has the benefit of being able to identify unidentified attacks. The drawback is that it could lead to a lot of false positives.

- **Stateful protocol analysis:** In order identify malicious actions that signature- or anomaly-based methods might overlook, this technique examines network data. Stateful protocol analysis investigates the state of packets flows to look for unusual activity (Ali, 2023). This method has the advantage of being able to spot sophisticated attacks that other methods might overlook. The drawback may result in significant computational overhead (Gondron, 2021).

- **Hybrid detection**: In this approach, attacks are discovered by combining techniques from signature-based, anomaly-based, and stateful protocol analysis. This method provides a more thorough approach to intrusion detection by combining the advantages of each technique (Gu, 2019). This method has the advantage of identifying known and unidentified attacks while reducing false negatives and false positives. The drawback is that it might need a lot of processing power (Wang G. W., 2020). Figure 1 depicts an illustration of a traditional intrusion detection model.

Figure 1. A traditional intrusion detection mode

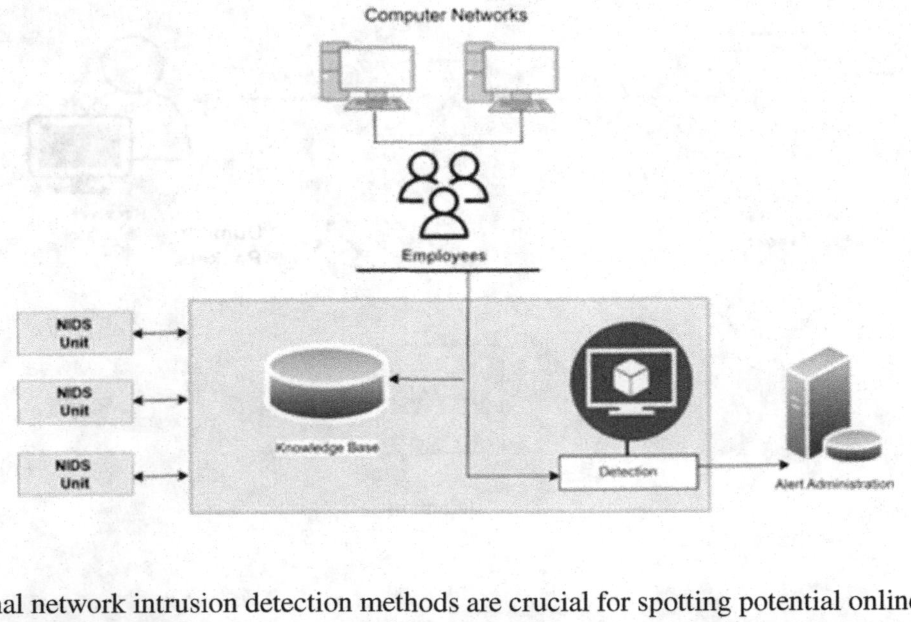

Traditional network intrusion detection methods are crucial for spotting potential online threats and sending real-time security threat alerts (Farooq, 2022). While each technique has advantages and disadvantages, combining these techniques can increase security and accuracy depending on a particular organization's needs and available resources.

JAMMING ATTACKS

Cyberattacks, known as jamming attacks, involve flooding a communication channel with noise or other types of signals in order to obstruct or stop legitimate communication. These attacks try to obstruct data transmission or reception, which can clog networks or even result in total denial of service. Several methods, such as radio frequency jamming, Distributed Denial of Service (DDoS), and Denial of Service (DoS) attacks, can launch jamming attacks (Alrefaei F. A., 2022). Jamming attacks can be divided into two groups: reactive attacks and proactive attacks. Proactive jamming attacks aim to jam all communication channels in a specific area instead of reactive jamming attacks, which aim to interfere with the transmission or reception of specific messages (Spens, 2022). Analyzing multiple indications and traits is necessary to recognize jamming assaults and their parameters in network intrusion detection. Systems for detecting network intrusions make use of algorithms for machine learning as well as signal disruption analysis, frequency analysis, signal power analysis, and other techniques. These systems can assess signal power levels, examine temporal behavior, identify specific frequency bands targeted by jamming attacks, detect anomalous signal patterns, and identify jamming-related patterns using machine learning techniques. These methods allow for the identification and categorization of jamming assaults, offering insightful information for additional study and mitigation. Figure 2 explain the scenario of jamming attack.

Figure 2. A jamming attack scenario

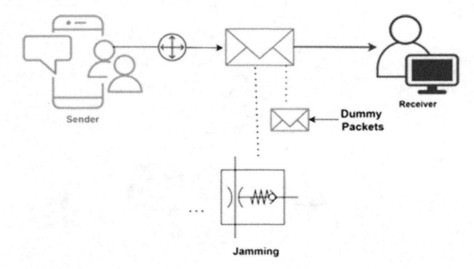

Impact of Jamming Attacks on Network Security

Attacks that disrupt networks significantly, such as jamming attacks, can have a negative impact on network security. Attacks involving jamming can result in data loss, denial of service, and decreased network performance (Gao, 2021). Additionally, the attacker may employ jamming attacks as a component of an Advanced Persistent Threat (APT) or as a strategy to divert network administrators' attention from potential additional cyberattacks (Pey, 2022).

Existing Detection Techniques for Jamming Attacks

In the past, jamming attacks have been detected using signature- or rule-based intrusion detection systems (Tariq, 2018). To recognize known jamming attacks, these systems rely on predefined signatures or rules. These techniques, though, have trouble spotting unheard-of or novel jamming attacks (Rose, 2019).

Machine Learning-Based Detection Techniques

A potential remedy for spotting jamming attacks has emerged: machine learning-based detection techniques. These methods can recognize typical network traffic patterns and spot unusual traffic that might be a sign of a jamming attempt. Popular machine-learning techniques for identifying jamming attacks include supervised, unsupervised, and reinforcement learning (Buettner, 2019).

Limitations of Current Approaches

The methods used to detect jamming attacks still have some drawbacks. For instance, intrusion detection systems based on rules and signatures have difficulty spotting fresh or undiscovered jamming attacks. Large datasets are needed for training machine learning-based techniques, and they may be vulnerable to hostile attacks. Longer detection times may also result from the high computational complexity of machine learning-based techniques (Shu, 2019). Finally, due to the limited range of sensor devices, jamming attacks can be carried out using a wide range of frequencies and can be challenging to detect.

SPOOFING ATTACKS

A cyber-attack known as a spoofing attack when an attacker pretends to be a legitimate user or entity to gain access to private data and privileges or to spread additional attacks. Attacks that use spoofing technique include DNS spoofing, ARP spoofing, IP spoofing, and email spoofing (Fonseca, 2021). Figure 3 provides a detailed view of different types of spoofing attacks in the network environment.

Figure 3. A spoofing attack scenario

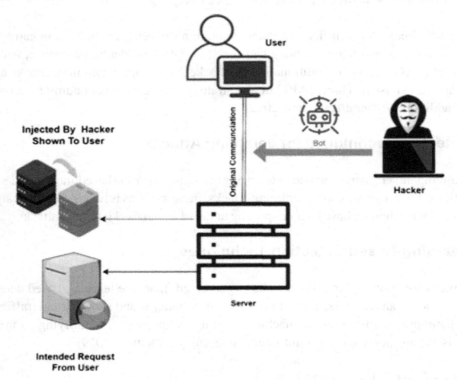

- **IP Spoofing**

In IP spoofing attacks, the attacker falsifies the source IP address of a packet to make it appear as if it is coming from a trusted source (Veeraraghavan, 2020). In order to conceal their identity or pose as a reliable source, attackers using the P spoofing technique alter the source IP address in network packets. Network security must be maintained by the identification and mitigation of IP spoofing attacks in network intrusion detection. Intrusion detection systems (IDS) can spot anomalies related to IP spoofing by inspecting packet headers and traffic patterns. IDS may search for anomalies such packets coming from non-routable or reserved IP addresses, sudden IP address changes during a session, or a large number of source IP addresses linked to a single host. In order to identify and notify administrator of potential IP spoofing operations, intrusion detection systems use algorithms and rule-based processes. This allows administrators to take immediate action to safeguard network resources and maintain secure communication.

- **Email Spoofing**

In email spoofing attacks, the attacker forges the header information of an email to make it appear as if it is coming from a legitimate source (Giorgi, 2020). In email spoofing, the sender's email address is falsified to make it seem as though it came from a different source. In order to deceive recipients into thinking the email is coming from a reliable source, it is frequently employed in phishing attempts.

Examining email headers, confirming the legitimacy of domains, and adopting email authentication protocols like SPF, DKIM, and DMARC are all steps in the detection of email spoofing. Maintaining email security and safeguarding users from fraudulent activity depend on preventing email spoofing.

- **DNS Spoofing**

DNS (Domain Name System) spoofing, commonly referred to as DNS cache poisoning, is a method for interfering with DNS (Domain Name System) resolution. In order to divert users to harmful websites or intercept their communications, it entails faking or manipulating DNS answers. Attacks using DNS spoofing might jeopardize the confidentiality and integrity of network connections. By verifying the integrity and authenticity of DNS data, secure DNS protocols like DNSSEC (DNS Security Extensions) can be used, reducing the hazards associated with DNS spoofing (Kozlenko, 2019).

- **ARP Spoofing**

In ARP spoofing attacks, the attacker sends false address resolution protocol (ARP) messages to associate their MAC address with the IP address of a legitimate user or device on the network (Morsy, 2022).

Table 1. Comparison of spoofing attacks and mitigation techniques

Spoofing Attack	Method	Technique	Reference
IP Spoofing	SAVI (Source Address Validation Improvement)	Machine learning-based traffic analysis	(Sunitha, 2023)
Email Spoofing	SPF (Sender Policy Framework)	DNS-based authentication	(Atlam, 2022)
DNS Spoofing	DNSSEC (Domain Name System Security Extensions)	Cryptographic authentication	(Anuradha Samarakoon, 2022)
ARP Spoofing	ARPWatch	Statistical anomaly detection	(Chai, 2023)

Consequences of Spoofing Attacks on Network Security

Attacks that use spoofing can seriously harm network security. They may lead to denial of service, theft of credentials, and unauthorized access to sensitive data. Attacks like man-in-the-middle or data exfiltration can also be launched using spoofing techniques (Mishra, 2020).

Existing Approaches to Detect and Mitigate Spoofing Attacks

Utilizing IDS and Intrusion Prevention Systems (IPS) is one method for identifying and countering spoofing attacks (Girdler, 2021). These systems can recognize and stop packets with forged IP addresses. Traffic from unauthorized sources can also be stopped using firewalls and Access Control Lists (ACLs) (Abdulqadder, 2020).

Digital Signatures and Certificates

Data integrity and authenticity transmitted across a network can be confirmed using digital signatures and certificates (Lepiane, 2019). Asymmetric key cryptography is used in digital signatures to create a digital signature that the recipient can verify to ensure the data has not been tampered with. Data sender and receiver identities can be confirmed using certificates (Ribeiro, 2021).

Timestamp-Based Verification Techniques

Techniques for timestamp-based verification can be used to confirm the accuracy and veracity of data. These techniques use time stamps to ensure that data has not been tampered with since it was generated. Replay attacks may be discovered using this method (Faisal, 2020).

Drawbacks of Current Spoofing Detection Techniques

The spoofing detection methods used today still have some drawbacks. For instance, network performance may be affected by false positives produced by IDS and IPS-based methods. Both digital signatures and certificate-based methods can be subject to cypher attacks and call for secure key storage (Wang W. A., 2021). Techniques for timestamp-based verification can experience drifting and synchronization problems. Attackers can also employ sophisticated strategies to get around these detection methods and obstruct network administrators' ability to recognize spoofing attacks (Zhu, 2022).

FEDERATED LEARNING

In federated learning, multiple devices train a model without sharing data or a central server. As a result, it is a desirable option for businesses that gather sensitive data because it enables analytics while protecting privacy. Federated learning also makes it possible to train models more effectively because it lets you use decentralized processing power, which can help you save time and money (Nguyen, 2021). As seen in Fig. 4, federated learning is a machine learning technique that enables multiple parties to work together on model training without disclosing their individual data sets. Federated learning's fundamental tenet is that data should be kept local to each device or edge node, and model parameters should only be exchanged during training (Khan A. J., 2020). The communication overhead between devices and servers is reduced, and sensitive data is better protected in terms of privacy and security. In federated learning, the participating devices or nodes use their own data sets and learning algorithms to train their local models (Zhang, 2021). After that, these regional models are transmitted to a central server, which combines them to produce a global model. The updated global model is then distributed back to the devices by the central server for additional training cycles. This procedure is repeated until the final model is accurate enough for each device or node to use for their needs. In industries like healthcare or finance, where data privacy is crucial, federated learning is conducive. Additionally, it allows businesses to work together on training models without divulging confidential information or intellectual property (Zhan, 2021). Figure 4 depicts the overall process flow of an abstract view of the Federated Learning Model with federated client sub models for the intrusion detection system.

Figure 4. An abstract view of the federated learning model

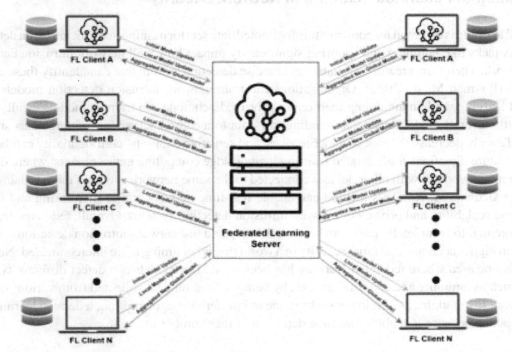

Application of Federated Learning in Network Security

Federated learning is essential for constructing distributed data sets for training network intrusion detection models. Attacks like jamming and spoofing significantly impact how well network intrusion detection systems work. Therefore, creating a reliable and precise detection system that can identify these attacks is crucial (Rahman M. A., 2020). Organizations can train network intrusion detection models using federated learning while maintaining their data's privacy. Each node can train its models locally while updating the overall model rather than sending raw data to a central server for training. This strategy can significantly decrease the risk of data breaches, and sensitive data sets' confidentiality can be safeguarded. Future directions for federated learning include edge computing environments, where devices can share model updates with other devices connected to the same network and train models using local data sets (Aledhari M. R., 2020). This method can enable real-time network traffic monitoring and further increase the scalability and privacy of network intrusion detection systems. Overall, federated learning has the potential to completely transform how we develop and use network intrusion detection systems, resulting in higher accuracy and more security in a world that is becoming more interconnected. Network security is one area where federated learning has been used. The models can detect different types of attacks, such as jamming and spoofing attacks, by being trained on data collected from various devices on a network (Mothukuri, 2021). In networks prone to interference or disruption, federated learning can be constructive because it enables real-time detection of these problems.

Application of Federated Learning in Network Security

Federated learning is essential for constructing distributed data sets for training network intrusion detection models. Attacks like jamming and spoofing significantly impact how well network intrusion detection systems work. Therefore, creating a reliable and precise detection system that can identify these attacks is crucial (Rahman M. A., 2020). Organizations can train network intrusion detection models using federated learning while maintaining their data's privacy. Each node can train its models locally while updating the overall model rather than sending raw data to a central server for training. This strategy can significantly decrease the risk of data breaches, and sensitive data sets' confidentiality can be safeguarded. Future directions for federated learning include edge computing environments, where devices can share model updates with other devices connected to the same network and train models using local data sets (Aledhari M. R.). This method can enable real-time network traffic monitoring and further increase the scalability and privacy of network intrusion detection systems. Overall, federated learning has the potential to completely transform how we develop and use network intrusion detection systems, resulting in higher accuracy and more security in a world that is becoming more interconnected. Network security is one area where federated learning has been used. The models can detect different types of attacks, such as jamming and spoofing attacks, by being trained on data collected from various devices on a network (Mothukuri, 2021). In networks prone to interference or disruption, federated learning can be constructive because it enables real-time detection of these problems.

Federated Learning Architectures for Detecting Jamming and Spoofing Attacks

Network security federated learning can be implemented using a variety of architectures. One common strategy is to employ a federated learning framework, which collects data sets from various networked devices and uses these data sets to create predictive models (Ahmed). A different strategy is to train models on data close to the source using an edge-computing architecture, which speeds up training and improves prediction accuracy (Meftah, 2023).

Challenges and Considerations in Implementing Federated Learning

When federated learning is implemented, several obstacles and factors must be considered. These include managing communication latency and bandwidth, ensuring that the models are trained on a representative sample of data, and mitigating potential biases in the data. As federated learning may be more complicated than conventional centralized machine learning approaches, organizations must also consider the computational infrastructure needed to implement it (Gugueoth, 2023).

Privacy and Security Considerations in Federated Learning

While federated learning enables privacy-preserving analytics, businesses must still take precautions to safeguard the data used to train the models. They must also consider potential model-specific attacks, such as model poisoning attacks, which may lead to inaccurate predictions or malicious behavior. To stop these threats and safeguard their models' integrity, organizations must implement robust security protocols (Mothukuri V. P., 2021).

Federated learning is a machine learning technique that allows multiple devices to work together on model training without sharing their data with other devices or a centralized server. Because of this, it appeals to businesses that need to protect the confidentiality of their data. Federated Learning also allows machine learning models to be trained more quickly and effectively (Das, 2021). Federated learning has found use in network security, where it can be used to identify various attacks like jamming and spoofing. By training models on data gathered from various networked devices, federated learning makes it possible to detect these attacks in real-time (Humayun, 2020). Several architectures, such as Edge Computing architectures that train models on data close to the source and Federated Learning frameworks that record data sets from various devices on a network, can be used for federated learning in network security (Kishor, 2022). However, putting Federated Learning into practice has several drawbacks. It necessitates dealing with communication latency and bandwidth, ensuring that the models are trained on representative data, and mitigating potential biases in the data. Organizations must assess and implement the resources and computational infrastructure needed for federated learning (Jiang, 2022).

Federated Learning must consider privacy and security issues because it deals with sensitive data. Federated Learning permits privacy-preserving analytics, but organizational security protocols and data protection must still be followed. Additionally, organizations must assess and defend against potential model-specific attacks, such as data- and model-poisoning attacks. To prevent harm to the models and maintain their integrity, this necessitates the implementation of solid security protocols (Ben-Itzhak, 2022).

Table 2. State-of-the-Art federated learning network intrusion detection techniques and machine learning comparisons

Technique	Method	Federated Learning	Machine Learning Comparison	References
Federated Intrusion Detection	Collaborative Learning Approach	Enables Training On Decentralized Data	Centralized Models Lack Data Diversity	(Bonawitz et al., 2019)
Deep Neural Networks (Dnns)	Utilizes Multi-Layered Neural Networks	Aggregates Local Model Updates	Limited By Local Data Availability	(Goodfellow et al., 2016)
Transfer Learning	Transfers Knowledge From Related Tasks Or Domains	Incorporates Models From Multiple Sites	Requires Similar Data Distributions	(Pan & Yang, 2010)
Privacy-Preserving Mechanisms	Differential Privacy, Secure Aggregation	Protects Sensitive Data During Training	May Introduce Additional Computational Overhead	(Wang S. L., 2023)
Feature Selection	Selects Relevant Features For Intrusion Detection	Incorporates Feature Selection At Each Site	Enhances Model Efficiency And Reduces Noise	(Thakkar, 2023)
Adversarial Defense Strategies	Adversarial Training	Defends Against Adversarial Attacks	Enhances Model Efficiency And Reduces Noise	(Madry et al., 2018)
Model Aggregation Techniques	Federated Averaging	Combines Local Model Updates	Enhances Model Robustness To Network Threat	(McMahan et al., 2017)

Comparative Analysis of Surveyed Techniques

Each intrusion detection technique has advantages and disadvantages to consider when comparing them. Although rule-based techniques are easy to use and require little computational power, they might miss novel attacks or attacks that do not precisely match the rule (Fung, 2020). Contrarily, machine learning-based techniques can detect novel attacks, but they are computationally intensive and may be subject to overfitting. Anomaly-based techniques can identify unknown attacks but may generate false alarms or fail to recognize frequent or common attacks. While dealing with novel and sophisticated attacks, signature-based techniques are less effective than others in detecting known attacks that match predefined signatures (Yin X. Z., 2021).

Comparative Analysis of Surveyed Techniques

The effectiveness of each technique in detecting network intrusions depends on the type of attack and the data being analyzed. According to a recent research paper by (G. Wang et al. 2021), Machine Learning and Deep Learning-based approaches have shown great promise in detecting network intrusions with high accuracy. However, some of these techniques may require significant computational resources (Wang G. W., 2021). Rule-based techniques are fast and efficient but, as previously noted, may have limitations in detecting novel intrusions or attacks. Anomaly-based approaches are practical when dealing with unknown attacks. However, they could lead to a high rate of false positives if they cannot compare the anomalies to corresponding regular activity. While signature-based techniques are not always effective in detecting novel attacks, they are known to be effective in detecting known threats (Young, 2019).

Identification of Common Challenges and Limitations

Common challenges and limitations exist within each technique. One example of common challenges is that some techniques may require significant amounts of computationally intensive resources to obtain accurate results. Specifics of data and the mathematical model employed is essential since a minor change in input data or model settings can lead to significant differences in detection results (Chaabouni N. M., 2019). Another limitation is that many techniques may produce high rates of false positives, which can dilute the efficacy of the detection. Furthermore, some techniques may not be effective against polymorphic or metamorphic threats, which use obfuscation and mutation techniques to change their structure or signature.

Mitigating Jamming and Spoofing Attacks Using Federated Learning

Jamming and spoofing attacks can be mitigated using Federated Learning, a privacy-preserving, decentralized machine-learning approach, according to a research paper by (X. Yang, 2020). Federated Learning can enable the training of intrusion detection models on data from multiple devices without exposing sensitive data to the network or centralized servers. The research found that this approach can detect jamming and spoofing attacks in wireless networks.

FEDERATED LEARNING MODELS AND ALGORITHMS FOR INTRUSION DETECTION

Various Federated Learning models and algorithms have been proposed for intrusion detection in wireless networks. For example, a research article by (A. Talwadker et al, 2021) proposes a sequential Federated Learning approach for detecting jamming attacks on IoT devices. This approach uses a Random Forest model, achieving high detection accuracy while preserving privacy.

DATA PRIVACY AND SECURITY CONSIDERATIONS IN FEDERATED LEARNING

Data privacy and security considerations are essential in Federated Learning-based solutions for intrusion detection. The necessity for secure multi-party computation (MPC) methods to safeguard sensitive information throughout Federated Learning-based intrusion detection is highlighted in a research study by (A. Parker et al, 2021). The authors suggest a safe Federated Learning system that reliably detects intrusions while protecting participant data privacy.

PERFORMANCE EVALUATION OF FEDERATED LEARNING-BASED SOLUTIONS

Intrusion detection systems based on federated learning have undergone numerous performance tests. (J. Shen et al. 2020) compare the effectiveness of federated learning to typical centralized machine learning systems in order to detect jamming and spoofing attacks on wireless networks. According to the findings, federated learning-based intrusion detection outperforms centralized machine learning while offering better privacy-preserving abilities. Overall, solutions based on federated learning can successfully counteract spoofing and jamming assaults while protecting the confidentiality of sensitive data. These solutions make use of a range of concepts and computations, but data security and privacy issues must continue to be a top priority. Performance assessments of Federated Learning have yielded encouraging results, proving that this strategy may achieve superior accuracy in detection while safeguarding the confidentiality of data.

LEADING FUTURE DIRECTIONS

Each technique has benefits as well as drawbacks when compared to other intrusion detection methods. For instance, rule-based strategies are straightforward to use and need little computer power, but they could miss unique assaults or attacks that don't exactly meet the rule. On the other hand, machine learning-based techniques can detect novel attacks, but they require much computational power and may be prone to overfitting (Wang G. 2021). Another example is anomaly-based techniques that can detect unknown attacks. However, they may produce false alarms or miss common attacks that can occur frequently. Meanwhile, signature-based techniques detect known attacks that match predefined signatures but are less effective when dealing with novel and sophisticated attacks.

Emerging Technologies and Techniques for Countering Jamming and Spoofing Attacks

The effectiveness of each technique in detecting network intrusions depends on the type of attack and the data being analyzed. According to a recent research paper by (G. Wang et al. 2021). Machine Learning and Deep Learning-based approaches have shown great promise in detecting network intrusions with high accuracy, although some of these techniques may require significant computational resources. Rule-based techniques are fast and efficient but, as previously noted, may have limitations in detecting novel intrusions or attacks. Anomaly-based approaches are effective when dealing with unknown attacks. However, they could lead to a high rate of false positives if they cannot compare the anomalies to corresponding normal activity. While signature-based techniques are not always effective in detecting novel attacks, they are known to be effective in detecting known threats.

Integration of Federated Learning With Other Security Mechanisms

Common challenges and limitations exist within each technique. One example of common challenges is that some techniques may require significant amounts of computationally intensive resources to obtain accurate results. Specifics of data and the mathematical model employed is vital since a minor change in input data or model settings can lead to significant differences in detection results. Another limitation is that many techniques may produce high rates of false positives, which can dilute the efficacy of the detection. Furthermore, some techniques may not be effective against polymorphic or metamorphic threats, which use obfuscation and mutation techniques to change their structure or signature.

Potential Applications and Future Trends in Network Intrusion Detection

Network intrusion detection is an important security tool that can help organizations detect and respond to malicious network activity. Network intrusion detection has a variety of possible uses, including the following:

- Identifying attempts at unauthorized entry: When someone tries to enter a system or network without authorization, network intrusion detection systems can identify the attempt. It could involve spotting port scans, brute-force assaults, and other shady behavior.
- Recognizing malware infections and efforts at data espionage: Systems for detecting network intrusions can also be used to determine whether malware has been put on a machine or if any efforts have been made to remove data from the network.
- Keeping an eye out for unusual user conduct or policy infractions: Systems for detecting network intrusions can also monitor user conduct to spot irregularities or rules pointing to malicious intent or insider dangers in a company's network environment.

The accuracy and efficacy of these kinds of solutions are anticipated to be improved by machine learning, according to advances in this field. Additionally, new strategies must be created for these solutions to succeed against new threats as more devices are connected via IoT technologies like 5G networks (Verbraeken, 2020).

Standardization Efforts and Collaborative Research Initiatives

Standardization efforts and collaborative research initiatives are crucial to mitigating attacks using federated learning (FL). These efforts can help ensure that FL systems remain secure, reliable, and effective. The standardization effort is the National Institute of Standards and Technology's (NIST) Special Publication 800-207: Federated Learning Security Considerations. This study provides recommendations for how FL system designs should be made by businesses in order to reduce security issues. Additionally, it describes techniques for ensuring the accuracy of the output from FL models and recommended practices for keeping data securely. In addition to NIST's efforts, a number of cooperative research projects have a goal of enhancing FL system security. For instance, Carnegie Mellon University researchers have released a paper (Murshed, 2021) that describes a method for identifying bad actors in distributed machine-learning networks. The team presented a solution that does not rely on centralized control or trust presumptions about network users to identify rogue nodes by using game theory techniques. Other organizations, like Open Mind, are aiming to produce open-source tools that let programmers use federated learning to design more secure and privacy-preserving systems. Through the use of technology for encryption like homomorphic encryption and differential privacy techniques, they want to establish an environment where users can communicate data securely while maintaining their right to privacy (Humayun M. S., 2022).

Enhancement of Federated Learning Frameworks for Real-Time Detection

A networked machine learning technique called federated learning (FL) enables several parties to train models together without disclosing their data. Due to its capacity to mitigate network attacks and its ability to provide continuous monitoring of network intrusions as well as other harmful activity, it has grown in popularity in recent years (Jin, 2020). The improvement of federated learning framework in Network Intrusion Detection Systems (NIDS) real-time detection is covered in this research. We examine current FL strategies and provide fresh ideas for enhancing accuracy while cutting latency. We contrast our suggested strategy with conventional NIDS systems and give an evaluation mechanism that utilizes simulated attack scenarios. We conclude by urging more investigation into improving FL framework enabling real-time intrusion detection applications (Santhosh Kumar, 2023).

Future Enhancements for AI-Enhanced Network Intrusion Detection

AI has emerged as a viable option for improving network intrusion detection and mitigating jamming and spoofing assaults. Powered by artificial intelligence (IDS) may effectively analyses network traffic patterns, detect anomalies, and detect possible threats in real-time by employing powerful machine learning algorithms and methodologies. This ability to identify and react to intrusions early on is critical for preventing successful assaults and protecting the integrity and confidentiality of personal information.

One potential area for advancement is the creation of powerful AI algorithms designed specifically for identifying and mitigating jamming or spoofing attacks. These systems can analyses network traffic patterns, detect anomalies, and discriminate between legal and malicious activity using machine learning and deep learning methods (Chaithanya, 2022). These AI systems can stay ahead of changing threats by continually acquiring knowledge from new methods of attack and modifying their detection skills.

Furthermore, applying AI to current security infrastructures can lead to the development of automated and adaptive intrusion detection systems (IDS). These systems can identify and respond to jamming and spoofing assaults without the need for human intervention. These IDS can dynamically change their detection levels, alter their attack signatures, and execute proactive countermeasures by continually acquiring knowledge from previous incidents and employing AI algorithms (Das V. C., 2023).The use of AI in NIDS has the potential to significantly reduce jamming and spoofing assaults. AI algorithm improvements, integration with other technologies, and the creation of automated IDS can further boost network security and assure early identification and avoidance of these threats in the future.

CONCLUSION

In order to reduce the issues brought on by jamming and spoofing attacks, this survey paper emphasizes the urgent need for sophisticated intrusion detection systems (IDS). Due to the potential network impact of these attacks, it is essential to have a robust IDS system in place to safeguard sensitive data. A promising strategy to address the privacy issues related to intrusion detection is federated learning-enabled IDS. In addition to discussing the difficulties and factors to be considered when implementing this technology, the paper provides a thorough overview of federated learning-based IDS. The comparative analysis of various state-of-the-art IDS techniques performed in this paper gives researchers a deeper understanding of the advantages and disadvantages of each strategy, enabling them to choose the best technique for a particular situation. In addition, this survey paper offers a direction for additional study and advancement in this field. This paper's challenges and discussions can direct businesses and academia toward creating IDS systems that are more reliable and secure. In future, we intend to create an IDS based on federated learning as part of future work, which will take advantage of this technology's advantages while protecting sensitive data's privacy and security. We are confident that this strategy will significantly increase IDS's attack detection and mitigation capacity, thereby enhancing network security.

REFERNCES

Abdulqadder, I. H., Zhou, S., Zou, D., Aziz, I. T., & Akber, S. M. A. (2020). Multi-layered intrusion detection and prevention in the SDN/NFV enabled cloud of 5G networks using AI-based defense mechanisms. *Computer Networks*, *179*, 107364. doi:10.1016/j.comnet.2020.107364

Ahmed, J., Nguyen, T. N., Ali, B., Javed, M. A., & Mirza, J. (2022). On the physical layer security of federated learning based IoMT networks. *IEEE Journal of Biomedical and Health Informatics*, *27*(2), 691–697. doi:10.1109/JBHI.2022.3173947 PMID:35536821

Alani, M. M. (2021). Big data in cybersecurity: A survey of applications and future trends. *Journal of Reliable Intelligent Environments*, *7*(2), 85–114. doi:10.1007/s40860-020-00120-3

Aledhari, M., Razzak, R., Parizi, R. M., & Saeed, F. (2020). Federated learning: A survey on enabling technologies, protocols, and applications. *IEEE Access : Practical Innovations, Open Solutions*, *8*, 140699–140725. doi:10.1109/ACCESS.2020.3013541 PMID:32999795

Ali, S. E., Tariq, N., Khan, F. A., Ashraf, M., Abdul, W., & Saleem, K. (2023). BFT-IoMT: A Blockchain-Based Trust Mechanism to Mitigate Sybil Attack Using Fuzzy Logic in the Internet of Medical Things. *Sensors (Basel)*, *23*(9), 4265. doi:10.3390/s23094265 PMID:37177468

Alloghani, M., Alani, M. M., Al-Jumeily, D., Baker, T., Mustafina, J., Hussain, A., & Aljaaf, A. J. (2019). A systematic review on the status and progress of homomorphic encryption technologies. *Journal of Information Security and Applications*, *48*, 102362. doi:10.1016/j.jisa.2019.102362

Alrefaei, F., Alzahrani, A., Song, H., & Alrefaei, S. (2022, June). A Survey on the Jamming and Spoofing attacks on the Unmanned Aerial Vehicle Networks. In *2022 IEEE International IOT, Electronics and Mechatronics Conference (IEMTRONICS)* (pp. 1-7). IEEE. 10.1109/IEMTRONICS55184.2022.9795809

Alrefaei, F., Alzahrani, A., Song, H., & Alrefaei, S. (2022, June). A Survey on the Jamming and Spoofing attacks on the Unmanned Aerial Vehicle Networks. In *2022 IEEE International IOT, Electronics and Mechatronics Conference (IEMTRONICS)* (pp. 1-7). IEEE. 10.1109/IEMTRONICS55184.2022.9795809

Anuradha Samarakoon, S. (2022). Bypassing Content-based internet packages with an SSL/TLS Tunnel, SNI Spoofing, and DNS spoofing. *arXiv e-prints*, arXiv-2212.

Atlam, H. F., & Oluwatimilehin, O. (2022). Business Email Compromise Phishing Detection Based on Machine Learning: A Systematic Literature Review. *Electronics (Basel)*, *12*(1), 42. doi:10.3390/electronics12010042

Basati, A., & Faghih, M. M. (2023). APAE: An IoT intrusion detection system using asymmetric parallel auto-encoder. *Neural Computing & Applications*, *35*(7), 4813–4833. doi:10.1007/s00521-021-06011-9

Belenguer, A., Navaridas, J., & Pascual, J. A. (2022). A review of federated learning in intrusion detection systems for iot. arXiv preprint arXiv:2204.12443.

Ben-Itzhak, Y., Möllering, H., Pinkas, B., Schneider, T., Suresh, A., Tkachenko, O., & Yanai, A. (2022). *ScionFL: Secure Quantized Aggregation for Federated Learning*. arXiv preprint arXiv:2210.07376.

Bonawitz, K., Eichner, H., Grieskamp, W., Huba, D., Ingerman, A., Ivanov, V., & Roselander, J. (2019). Towards federated learning at scale: System design. *Proceedings of machine learning and systems, 1*, 374-388.

Buettner, R., & Schunter, M. (2019, October). Efficient machine learning based detection of heart disease. In *2019 IEEE international conference on E-health networking, application & services (HealthCom)* (pp. 1-6). IEEE.

Chaabouni, N., Mosbah, M., Zemmari, A., Sauvignac, C., & Faruki, P. (2019). Network intrusion detection for IoT security based on learning techniques. *IEEE Communications Surveys and Tutorials*, *21*(3), 2671–2701. doi:10.1109/COMST.2019.2896380

Chaabouni, N., Mosbah, M., Zemmari, A., Sauvignac, C., & Faruki, P. (2019). Network intrusion detection for IoT security based on learning techniques. *IEEE Communications Surveys and Tutorials*, *21*(3), 2671–2701. doi:10.1109/COMST.2019.2896380

Chai, T. U., Goh, H. G., Liew, S. Y., & Ponnusamy, V. (2023). Protection Schemes for DDoS, ARP Spoofing, and IP Fragmentation Attacks in Smart Factory. *Systems*, *11*(4), 211. doi:10.3390/systems11040211

Chaiban, A., Sovilj, D., Soliman, H., Salmon, G., & Lin, X. (2022). Investigating the Influence of Feature Sources for Malicious Website Detection. *Applied Sciences (Basel, Switzerland)*, *12*(6), 2806. doi:10.3390/app12062806

Chaithanya, B. N., & Brahmananda, S. H. (2022). AI-enhanced Defense Against Ransomware Within the Organization's Architecture. *Journal of Cyber Security and Mobility*, 621-654.

Das, P., Singh, M., & Roy, D. G. (2021, December). A secure softwarized blockchain-based federated health alliance for next generation IoT networks. In *2021 IEEE Globecom Workshops (GC Wkshps)* (pp. 1-6). IEEE.

Das, V., Cherukuri, A. K., Hu, Q., Kamalov, F., & Jonnalagadda, A. (2023). Proactive AI Enhanced Consensus Algorithm with Fraud Detection in Blockchain. In *Blockchain for Cybersecurity in Cyber-Physical Systems* (pp. 259–274). Springer International Publishing. doi:10.1007/978-3-031-25506-9_13

Faisal, S. M., & Zaidi, T. (2020). Timestamp Based Detection of Sybil Attack in VANET. *International Journal of Network Security*, *22*(3), 397–408.

Farooq, U., Tariq, N., Asim, M., Baker, T., & Al-Shamma'a, A. (2022). Machine learning and the Internet of Things security: Solutions and open challenges. *Journal of Parallel and Distributed Computing*, *162*, 89–104. doi:10.1016/j.jpdc.2022.01.015

Fonseca, O., Cunha, Í., Fazzion, E., Meira, W., da Silva, B. A., Ferreira, R. A., & Katz-Bassett, E. (2021). Identifying networks vulnerable to IP spoofing. *IEEE Transactions on Network and Service Management*, *18*(3), 3170–3183. doi:10.1109/TNSM.2021.3061486

Fung, C., Yoon, C. J., & Beschastnikh, I. (2020, October). The Limitations of Federated Learning in Sybil Settings. In RAID (pp. 301-316).

Gao, D., Wang, S., Liu, Y., Jiang, W., Li, Z., & He, T. (2021). Spoofing-jamming attack based on cross-technology communication for wireless networks. *Computer Communications*, *177*, 86–95. doi:10.1016/j.comcom.2021.06.017

Giorgi, G., Saracino, A., & Martinelli, F. (2020). Email Spoofing Attack Detection through an End to End Authorship Attribution System. In ICISSP (pp. 64-74). ScitePress. doi:10.5220/0008954600640074

Girdler, T., & Vassilakis, V. G. (2021). Implementing an intrusion detection and prevention system using Software-Defined Networking: Defending against ARP spoofing attacks and Blacklisted MAC Addresses. *Computers & Electrical Engineering*, *90*, 106990. doi:10.1016/j.compeleceng.2021.106990

Gondron, S., & Mödersheim, S. (2021, June). Vertical Composition and Sound Payload Abstraction for Stateful Protocols. In *2021 IEEE 34th Computer Security Foundations Symposium (CSF)* (pp. 1-16). IEEE. 10.1109/CSF51468.2021.00038

Goodfellow, I., Bengio, Y., & Courville, A. (2016). *Deep learning*. MIT press.

Gu, Y., Li, K., Guo, Z., & Wang, Y. (2019). Semi-supervised K-means DDoS detection method using hybrid feature selection algorithm. *IEEE Access : Practical Innovations, Open Solutions*, *7*, 64351–64365. doi:10.1109/ACCESS.2019.2917532

Gugueoth, V., Safavat, S., & Shetty, S. (2023). *Security of Internet of Things (IoT) using federated learning and deep learning-Recent advancements, issues and prospects.* ICT Express. doi:10.1016/j.icte.2023.03.006

Han, H., Kim, H., & Kim, Y. (2022). An efficient hyperparameter control method for a network intrusion detection system based on proximal policy optimization. *Symmetry*, *14*(1), 161. doi:10.3390/sym14010161

Hashmi, M. A., & Tariq, N. (2023). An Efficient Substitution Box design with a chaotic logistic map and Linear Congruential Generator for secure communication in Smart cities. *EAI Endorsed Transactions on Smart Cities, 7*(1).

Humayun, M., Jhanjhi, N. Z., Hamid, B., & Ahmed, G. (2020). Emerging smart logistics and transportation using IoT and blockchain. *IEEE Internet of Things Magazine*, *3*(2), 58–62. doi:10.1109/IOTM.0001.1900097

Humayun, M., Sujatha, R., Almuayqil, S. N., & Jhanjhi, N. Z. (2022, June). A transfer learning approach with a convolutional neural network for the classification of lung carcinoma. In Healthcare (Vol. 10, No. 6, p. 1058). MDPI. doi:10.3390/healthcare10061058

Jiang, X., Zhou, X., & Grossklags, J. (2022). Comprehensive Analysis of Privacy Leakage in Vertical Federated Learning During Prediction. *Proceedings on Privacy Enhancing Technologies. Privacy Enhancing Technologies Symposium*, *2022*(2), 263–281. doi:10.2478/popets-2022-0045

Jin, D., Lu, Y., Qin, J., Cheng, Z., & Mao, Z. (2020). SwiftIDS: Real-time intrusion detection system based on LightGBM and parallel intrusion detection mechanism. *Computers & Security*, *97*, 101984. doi:10.1016/j.cose.2020.101984

Khan, A., Jhanjhi, N. Z., Humayun, M., & Ahmad, M. (2020). The role of IoT in digital governance. In *Employing Recent Technologies for Improved Digital Governance* (pp. 128–150). IGI Global. doi:10.4018/978-1-7998-1851-9.ch007

Khan, K., Mehmood, A., Khan, S., Khan, M. A., Iqbal, Z., & Mashwani, W. K. (2020). A survey on intrusion detection and prevention in wireless ad-hoc networks. *Journal of Systems Architecture*, *105*, 101701. doi:10.1016/j.sysarc.2019.101701

Kishor, K. (2022). Communication-efficient federated learning. In *Federated Learning for IoT Applications* (pp. 135–156). Springer International Publishing. doi:10.1007/978-3-030-85559-8_9

Kozlenko, M., & Tkachuk, V. (2019). *Deep learning based detection of DNS spoofing attack.*

Kulkarni, V., Kulkarni, M., & Pant, A. (2020, July). Survey of personalization techniques for federated learning. In *2020 Fourth World Conference on Smart Trends in Systems, Security and Sustainability (WorldS4)* (pp. 794-797). IEEE. 10.1109/WorldS450073.2020.9210355

Kwon, H. Y., Kim, T., & Lee, M. K. (2022). Advanced intrusion detection combining signature-based and behavior-based detection methods. *Electronics (Basel)*, *11*(6), 867. doi:10.3390/electronics11060867

Lepiane, C. D., Pereira, F. L., Pieri, G., Martins, D., Martina, J. E., & Rabelo, M. L. (2019, September). Digital degree certificates for higher education in brazil: A technical policy specification. In *Proceedings of the ACM Symposium on Document Engineering 2019* (pp. 1-10). ACM. 10.1145/3342558.3345398

Liu, J., Huang, J., Zhou, Y., Li, X., Ji, S., Xiong, H., & Dou, D. (2022). From distributed machine learning to federated learning: A survey. *Knowledge and Information Systems*, *64*(4), 885–917. doi:10.1007/s10115-022-01664-x

Maseer, Z. K., Yusof, R., Bahaman, N., Mostafa, S. A., & Foozy, C. F. M. (2021). Benchmarking of machine learning for anomaly based intrusion detection systems in the CICIDS2017 dataset. *IEEE Access : Practical Innovations, Open Solutions*, *9*, 22351–22370. doi:10.1109/ACCESS.2021.3056614

Meftah, A., Do, T. N., Kaddoum, G., Talhi, C., & Singh, S. (2023). Federated Learning-Enabled Jamming Detection and Waveform Classification for Distributed Tactical Wireless Networks. *IEEE Transactions on Network and Service Management*, *20*(4), 5053–5072. doi:10.1109/TNSM.2023.3271578

Mishra, S. K., Mishra, S., Alsayat, A., Jhanjhi, N. Z., Humayun, M., Sahoo, K. S., & Luhach, A. K. (2020). Energy-aware task allocation for multi-cloud networks. *IEEE Access : Practical Innovations, Open Solutions*, *8*, 178825–178834. doi:10.1109/ACCESS.2020.3026875

Morsy, S. M., & Nashat, D. (2022). D-ARP: An Efficient Scheme to Detect and Prevent ARP Spoofing. *IEEE Access : Practical Innovations, Open Solutions*, *10*, 49142–49153. doi:10.1109/ACCESS.2022.3172329

Mothukuri, V., Khare, P., Parizi, R. M., Pouriyeh, S., Dehghantanha, A., & Srivastava, G. (2021). Federated-learning-based anomaly detection for iot security attacks. *IEEE Internet of Things Journal*, *9*(4), 2545–2554. doi:10.1109/JIOT.2021.3077803

Mothukuri, V., Parizi, R. M., Pouriyeh, S., Huang, Y., Dehghantanha, A., & Srivastava, G. (2021). A survey on security and privacy of federated learning. *Future Generation Computer Systems*, *115*, 619–640. doi:10.1016/j.future.2020.10.007

Murshed, M. S., Murphy, C., Hou, D., Khan, N., Ananthanarayanan, G., & Hussain, F. (2021). Machine learning at the network edge: A survey. *ACM Computing Surveys*, *54*(8), 1–37. doi:10.1145/3469029

Nguyen, D. C., Ding, M., Pathirana, P. N., Seneviratne, A., Li, J., & Poor, H. V. (2021). Federated learning for internet of things: A comprehensive survey. *IEEE Communications Surveys and Tutorials*, *23*(3), 1622–1658. doi:10.1109/COMST.2021.3075439

Parker, A., Nithyanand, R., & Juarez, M. (2021). Federated Learning for Private Intrusion Detection. Proceedings of the 2021 Conference on Detection of Intrusions and Malware, and Vulnerability Assessment, (pp. 497-500). Springer. doi: 10.1007/978-3-030-85891-5_24

Pey, J. N. A., Nze, G. D. A., & de Oliveira Albuquerque, R. (2022, June). Analysis of jamming and spoofing cyber-attacks on drones. In *2022 17th Iberian Conference on Information Systems and Technologies (CISTI)* (pp. 1-4). IEEE.

Ponnusamy, V., Yichiet, A., Jhanjhi, N. Z., Humayun, M., & Almufareh, M. F. (2022). IoT wireless intrusion detection and network traffic analysis. *Computer Systems Science and Engineering*, *40*(3), 865–879. doi:10.32604/csse.2022.018801

Rahman, M. A., Hossain, M. S., Islam, M. S., Alrajeh, N. A., & Muhammad, G. (2020). Secure and provenance enhanced internet of health things framework: A blockchain managed federated learning approach. *IEEE Access : Practical Innovations, Open Solutions, 8*, 205071–205087. doi:10.1109/AC-CESS.2020.3037474 PMID:34192116

Ribeiro, R. C., de Almeida, M. G., & Canedo, E. D. (2021). A digital signature model using XAdES standard as a rest service. *Information (Basel), 12*(8), 289. doi:10.3390/info12080289

Rose, S. H., & Jayasree, T. (2019). Detection of jamming attack using timestamp for WSN. *Ad Hoc Networks, 91*, 101874. doi:10.1016/j.adhoc.2019.101874

Santhosh Kumar, S. V. N., Selvi, M., & Kannan, A. (2023). A comprehensive survey on machine learning-based intrusion detection systems for secure communication in internet of things. *Computational Intelligence and Neuroscience, 2023*, 2023. doi:10.1155/2023/8981988

Sathyamoorthy, D., Fitry, Z., Selamat, E., Hassan, S., Firdaus, A., & Zaimy, Z. (2020). Evaluation of the vulnerabilities of unmanned aerial vehicles (uavs) to global positioning system (GPS) jamming and spoofing. *Defence and Technical Bulletin, 13*, 333-343.

Shamshirband, S., Fathi, M., Chronopoulos, A. T., Montieri, A., Palumbo, F., & Pescapè, A. (2020). Computational intelligence intrusion detection techniques in mobile cloud computing environments: Review, taxonomy, and open research issues. *Journal of Information Security and Applications, 55*, 102582. doi:10.1016/j.jisa.2020.102582

Shen, J., Ji, B., Zhang, C., & Feng, H. (2020, October). Federated Learning-based Spoofing and Jamming Detection for Wireless Networks. *IEEE Transactions on Vehicular Technology, 69*(10), 11611–11622. doi:10.1109/TVT.2020.3018239

Shu, J., & Tang, D. (2019). Recent advances in photoelectrochemical sensing: From engineered photoactive materials to sensing devices and detection modes. *Analytical Chemistry, 92*(1), 363–377. doi:10.1021/acs.analchem.9b04199 PMID:31738852

Soe, Y. N., Feng, Y., Santosa, P. I., Hartanto, R., & Sakurai, K. (2019). Rule generation for signature based detection systems of cyber attacks in iot environments. Bulletin of Networking, Computing. *Systems & Software, 8*(2), 93–97.

Spens, N., Lee, D. K., Nedelkov, F., & Akos, D. (2022). Detecting GNSS Jamming and Spoofing on Android Devices. NAVIGATION. *Journal of the Institute of Navigation, 69*(3).

Sunitha, T., Vijayashanthi, V., Navaneethakrishan, M., Mohanaprakash, T. A., Ashwin, S., Harish, T. R., & Stanes, E. A. (2023). Key Observation to Prevent IP Spoofing in DDoS Attack on Cloud Environment. In *Soft Computing: Theories and Applications* [Singapore: Springer Nature Singapore.]. *Proceedings of SoCTA, 2022*, 493–505.

Suwannalai, E., & Polprasert, C. (2020, November). Network intrusion detection systems using adversarial reinforcement learning with deep Q-network. In *2020 18th International Conference on ICT and Knowledge Engineering (ICT&KE)* (pp. 1-7). IEEE.

Talwadker, A., Olabiyi, O., Kosba, A., & Kim, Y. (2021, February). Detecting Jamming Attacks on IoT Devices Using Sequential Federated Learning. *IEEE Internet of Things Journal, 8*(3), 1409–1418. doi:10.1109/JIOT.2020.3048914

Tariq, N., & Khan, F. A. (2018). Match-the-sound captcha. In *Information Technology-New Generations: 14th International Conference on Information Technology* (pp. 803-808). Springer International Publishing.

Thakkar, A., & Lohiya, R. (2023). Fusion of statistical importance for feature selection in Deep Neural Network-based Intrusion Detection System. *Information Fusion, 90*, 353–363. doi:10.1016/j.inffus.2022.09.026

Vaishnavi, K. N., Khorvi, S. D., Kishore, R., & Gurugopinath, S. (2021, June). A survey on jamming techniques in physical layer security and anti-jamming strategies for 6G. In *2021 28th International Conference on Telecommunications (ICT)* (pp. 174-179). IEEE.

Veeraraghavan, P., Hanna, D., & Pardede, E. (2020). NAT++: An efficient micro-nat architecture for solving ip-spoofing attacks in a corporate network. *Electronics (Basel), 9*(9), 1510. doi:10.3390/electronics9091510

Verbraeken, J., Wolting, M., Katzy, J., Kloppenburg, J., Verbelen, T., & Rellermeyer, J. S. (2020). A survey on distributed machine learning. [csur]. *ACM Computing Surveys, 53*(2), 1–33. doi:10.1145/3377454

Wang, G., Wang, X., & Zhao, C. (2020). An iterative hybrid harmonics detection method based on discrete wavelet transform and bartlett–hann window. *Applied Sciences (Basel, Switzerland), 10*(11), 3922. doi:10.3390/app10113922

Wang, G., Wang, Z., Jiang, G., & McLaughlin, K. (2021). Intrusion Detection in Computer Networks: A Review. *IEEE Communications Surveys and Tutorials, 23*(2), 1277–1310.

Wang, G., Wang, Z., Jiang, G., & McLaughlin, K. (2021). Intrusion Detection in Computer Networks: A Review. *IEEE Communications Surveys and Tutorials, 23*(2), 1277–1310.

Wang, S., Luo, X., Qian, Y., Zhu, Y., Chen, K., Chen, Q., Xin, B., & Yang, W. (2023). Shuffle differential private data aggregation for random population. *IEEE Transactions on Parallel and Distributed Systems, 34*(5), 1667–1681. doi:10.1109/TPDS.2023.3247541

Wang, W., Aguilar Sanchez, I., Caparra, G., McKeown, A., Whitworth, T., & Lohan, E. S. (2021). A survey of spoofer detection techniques via radio frequency fingerprinting with focus on the gnss precorrelation sampled data. *Sensors (Basel), 21*(9), 3012. doi:10.3390/s21093012 PMID:33923015

Yadav, N., Pande, S., Khamparia, A., & Gupta, D. (2022). Intrusion detection system on IoT with 5G network using deep learning. *Wireless Communications and Mobile Computing, 2022*, 1–13. doi:10.1155/2022/9304689

Yaman, O., Ayav, T., & Erten, Y. M.YAMAN. (2023). A Lightweight Self-Organized Friendly Jamming. *International Journal of Information Security Science, 12*(1), 13–20. doi:10.55859/ijiss.1194643

Yang, X., Liu, H., Liu, X., & Mao, J. (2020, December). The Detection for Spoofing and Jamming Attacks via Federated Learning in Wireless Networks. *IEEE Transactions on Computational Social Systems*, *7*(6), 1484–1495. doi:10.1109/TCSS.2020.302116

Yin, F., Lin, Z., Kong, Q., Xu, Y., Li, D., Theodoridis, S., & Cui, S. R. (2020). FedLoc: Federated learning framework for data-driven cooperative localization and location data processing. *IEEE Open Journal of Signal Processing*, *1*, 187–215. doi:10.1109/OJSP.2020.3036276

Yin, X., Zhu, Y., & Hu, J. (2021). A comprehensive survey of privacy-preserving federated learning: A taxonomy, review, and future directions. *ACM Computing Surveys*, *54*(6), 1–36. doi:10.1145/3460427

Young, C., Zambreno, J., Olufowobi, H., & Bloom, G. (2019). Survey of automotive controller area network intrusion detection systems. *IEEE Design & Test*, *36*(6), 48–55. doi:10.1109/MDAT.2019.2899062

Yu, Z., Qin, Y., Li, X., Zhao, C., Lei, Z., & Zhao, G. (2022). Deep learning for face anti-spoofing: A survey. *IEEE Transactions on Pattern Analysis and Machine Intelligence*, *45*(5), 5609–5631. doi:10.1109/TPAMI.2022.3215850 PMID:36260579

Zhan, Y., Zhang, J., Hong, Z., Wu, L., Li, P., & Guo, S. (2021). A survey of incentive mechanism design for federated learning. *IEEE Transactions on Emerging Topics in Computing*, *10*(2), 1035–1044. doi:10.1109/TETC.2021.3063517

Zhang, C., Xie, Y., Bai, H., Yu, B., Li, W., & Gao, Y. (2021). A survey on federated learning. *Knowledge-Based Systems*, *216*, 106775. doi:10.1016/j.knosys.2021.106775 PMID:34909232

Zhi, Y., Fu, Z., Sun, X., & Yu, J. (2020). Security and privacy issues of UAV: A survey. *Mobile Networks and Applications*, *25*(1), 95–101. doi:10.1007/s11036-018-1193-x

Zhu, X., Lu, Z., Hua, T., Yang, F., Tu, G., & Chen, X. (2022). A Novel GPS Meaconing Spoofing Detection Technique Based on Improved Ratio Combined with Carrier-to-Noise Moving Variance. *Electronics (Basel)*, *11*(5), 738. doi:10.3390/electronics11050738

Chapter 5
IoT Security, Future Challenges, and Open Issues

Noshina Tariq

iD https://orcid.org/0000-0002-9754-253X

Air University, Pakistan

Tehreem Saboor

Air University, Pakistan

Muhammad Ashraf

Air University, Pakistan

Rawish Butt

Air University, Pakistan

Masooma Anwar

Air University, Pakistan

Mamoona Humayun

iD https://orcid.org/0000-0001-6339-2257

Jouf University, Saudi Arabia

ABSTRACT

The internet of things (IoT) refers to the network of connected devices embedded in everyday objects that enable digital transformation. The rapid proliferation of IoT devices has led to significant advancements in technology and data exchange capabilities. However, the security of user data and IoT systems has become a paramount concern. This chapter focuses on the security challenges and approaches in IoT. Various attacks, such as denial of service, password guessing, replay, and insider attacks, pose significant threats to IoT security. It investigates the state-of-the-art technologies, future challenges and open issues currently facing IoT security. The findings from this chapter serve as a foundation for future work in improving IoT security and protecting user data effectively.

DOI: 10.4018/978-1-6684-7625-3.ch005

INTRODUCTION

The Internet of Things (IoT) is a rapidly growing technology that has the potential to revolutionize many aspects of our lives. It enables us to connect physical objects and systems with each other, allowing for unprecedented levels of automation and control over everyday tasks. However, this increased connectivity also brings new security challenges which must be addressed for IoT devices to remain secure and reliable. This paper provides an overview of the current state-of-the-art in IoT security research, focusing on future challenges and open issues that need to be addressed to ensure the safe deployment of these technologies. The concept behind the Internet of Things (IoT) was first proposed by Kevin Ashton in 1999 (Akhtar, N. 2020). Since then, it has grown into one of the most important emerging technologies today due its ability to enable seamless communication between different types of connected devices such as sensors, actuators, controllers etc., thus enabling various applications ranging from smart homes and cities through industrial automation up until healthcare monitoring systems (Shafiq et al., 2022) As more and more "things" are being connected via networks like Wi-Fi or Bluetooth Low Energy (BLE), there is an increasing demand for robust security solutions that can protect them against malicious actors who might try to gain unauthorized access or disrupt their normal operation. A general representation of IoT is depicted below in Figure 1.

Figure 1. Internet of things

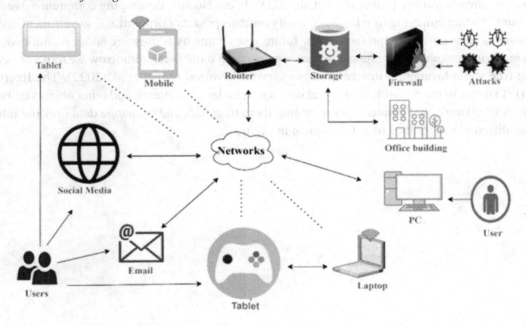

The Internet of Things (IoT) is a rapidly evolving technology that has become an integral part of our daily lives, allowing us to connect and interact with the physical world in ways never before possible. IoT devices are becoming more powerful, interconnected, and ubiquitous every day; however, this also raises significant security concerns surrounding these technologies. As the number and complexity of interconnected systems increase, so do the risks associated with them. For organizations to remain secure while taking advantage of the full potential of IoT-enabled solutions, it will be necessary to address some pressing challenges related to IoT security (Aqeel et al., 2022).

Another important area where improvements can be made is device authentication protocols used when connecting individual smart products together over wireless networks such as Bluetooth Low Energy (BLE) (Inayat et al., 2022). Due to the limited computing power available on many embedded systems found in everyday consumer electronics items like fitness trackers, home automation controllers etc., current authentication methods may not provide adequate protection against sophisticated attacks aimed at gaining control over those devices. For example, if two BLE enabled products were designed using weak encryption algorithms then hackers might target one product as entry point into larger network containing other sensitive personal or business assets (Ssa et al., 2023). To mitigate such threats manufacturers should consider implementing stronger cryptographic solutions during development phase coupled with regular software updates after deployment keep all users safe from cybercriminals looking exploit weaknesses these types of electronic gadgets.

Finally, another issue worth considering regarding future forward thinking around security involves proper handling incidents when occur regardless how small scale large magnitude event may turn out be After all no matter how careful organization goes designing deploying architecture vulnerabilities still exist due nature ever changing technological landscape therefore best way prepare yourself face reality presence attack response plan put action soon detect suspicious activity occurring instead waiting until damage done already too late (Taherdoost et al., 2023). In conclusion, developing comprehensive strategies account existing emerging trends IOT Security remains priority corporations' government agencies alike ensure citizens customers protected now future years come by addressing above mentioned issues actively engaging stakeholders responsible making decisions build better tomorrow we move closer goal realizing true value leveraging internet things everyone involved (Khan et al., 2022). The Internet of Things (IoT) refers to the network of physical devices, vehicles, appliances, and other objects embedded with sensors, software, and connectivity, enabling them to collect and exchange data over the internet. There are different capabilities of IoT as shown in Figure 2.

Figure 2. Definition of IoT

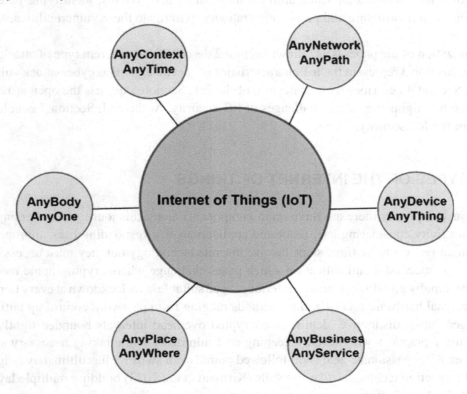

This paper surveys recent developments in IoT security, including new challenges and open issues. In particular, the research is focused on to identify the key security needs related to future application of Internet of Things (IoT), emerging threats causing insecurity or vast opportunities for attackers thereby requiring critical responses for further innovation in design (Ang et al., 2022). Also discussed are risks associated with old age scaling systems regarding physical safety that also increases vulnerabilities toward remote attack since many devices lack secure update mechanisms as well as hardened trusted platforms; reviewing previously mentioned issues will help recognizing immediate solutions needed against invading parties particularly observing benefits from cumulative work by academic literature focusing on interdisciplinary areas within the scope of networked computing environment (Kumar et al., 2022). Additionally, measures such as ensuring secure keys through maintaining digital certificate schemes suggest a balance between privacy & accessibility during creating communication infrastructure based upon public/private key compound protocols intended towards achieving better integrity among data transferred across active wireless point-to-point networks elements whenever connecting two or more distributed contraption points formulates an entirely separate independent system (Sadhu et al., 2022). The major contribution of this paper are as follows:

1. It examines the major attack types targeting IoT devices and networks, providing insights into the vulnerabilities exploited in these attacks.
2. It discusses the security requirements unique to IoT environments, emphasizing the need for robust measures to protect IoT devices, networks, and data from potential threats.

3.   It explores the architectural vulnerabilities inherent in IoT systems, identifying potential weak points in the infrastructure and proposing strategies to mitigate these vulnerabilities.

The organization of the paper is as follow: Section 2 describes the different type of attacks in the IoT environment. Section 3 represent the IoT characteristics in general as well as cyber-attack vulnerabilities perspective. Section 4 describes the architecture of the IoT. Section 5 discuss the open issues of IoT as well Section 6 highlights the future challenges of IoT security. At the end, Section 7 concludes all the discussion for the IoT security.

ATTACK TYPES OF THE INTERNET OF THINGS

Owing into its complexity there are three main components along this journey i) collecting dispersed facts ii) connectivity considering user requested applications iii) Responding back appropriately after processing input request these three steps involve discrete technology but they must access continuous information post successful authentication which poses challenge where cryptographic models would come into play rapidly growing automated interfaces need suitable level lockdown at every tier depending upon their internal hardware securitization methods ranging from password control up until biometric integration generating distinctive identifiers encrypted overhead intervals bounded tightly enforcing standard industry practices while evenly keeping cost minimally while taking necessary steps out of best interest evoking passionate zeal soon followed paired with swift replies ultimately helps developing efficient protection techniques like firewalls (Kirmani et al., 2023) building multiple layers around intra connected subnets differentiating regular packet transmission lines using strong encryption criteria dependent over context chosen objectives thus concluding improvement relative to scalability availability reliability performance latency and monetary coordination principles besides budget allocated amongst society stated variables making global footprint about structure seclusion all together acts principal citation material forming basis behind near observations providing general overview shared purpose aiming without fail compliant laws introducing higher regimes demonstrating concrete changes under leadership when facing catastrophic catastrophes infecting entire sector architecture not reserve defense skills again outside subterfuge attacks (Humayun et al., 2020). One key challenge facing organizations today is ensuring data privacy and security within their connected networks and why it is important. There are various IoT security layers such as network security, cyber security and data security is depicted in Figure 3. Data security layer comprise of data transfer, data acquisition, data privacy, data sharing, and data confidentiality of each layers, discussed below (Tukade et al., 2018):

1.   **Data transfer** is a critical aspect of data security in the context of IoT. When it comes to data transfer, it is essential to ensure that sensitive information is protected throughout its journey from the source device to the intended destination (Gong et al., 2021).
2.   **Data acquisition** refers to the process of collecting and gathering data from various sources within an IoT system. It is an important phase where data is captured from sensors, devices, or other sources for further processing and analysis. Ensuring data security during the data acquisition phase is crucial to maintain the confidentiality, integrity, and availability of the collected data (Abomhara et al., 2014).

3. **Data privacy** is a crucial aspect of data security that focuses on protecting the privacy and confidentiality of personal or sensitive information. It involves implementing measures to ensure that individuals have control over their personal data and that it is handled in accordance with privacy laws and regulations (Razzaq et al., 2023).

4. **Data sharing** is the process of exchanging or providing access to data with other individuals, organizations, or systems. While data sharing is important for collaboration, innovation, and decision-making, it also introduces security risks and challenges. Data security measures should be implemented to ensure that shared data is protected and only accessible by authorized entities (Abbasi et al., 2022).

5. **Data confidentiality** is a fundamental aspect of data security that focuses on protecting sensitive information from unauthorized access or disclosure. It ensures that only authorized individuals or entities have access to the data and that it remains confidential throughout its life cycle (Shafiq et al., 2021).

With more information about individuals being collected by various sensors across multiple locations – both inside and outside corporate boundaries – there's a greater risk for unauthorized access or misuse (Ghazal et al., 2020). Organizations need robust measures in place to protect customer data from malicious actors who may attempt to gain unauthorized access through vulnerable points on an organization's network or via insecure communication channels between different components within its infrastructure. Additionally, they must have effective processes in place for managing user permissions as well as regularly monitoring any changes made throughout their system architectures which could potentially lead backdoors into their networks open new opportunities for attackers.

Figure 3. Internet of things security layers

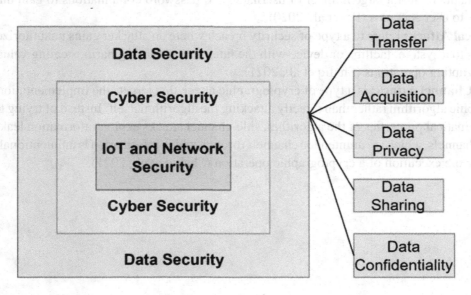

Figure 4 depicts the different types of attacks possible in the IoT Environment with their description and examples. Table 1elaborates the summary of all the attack types as well as their remediation. The details of some important attacks are given below:

1. **Botnet Attack:** Botnets are networks of compromised computers, referred to as bots or zombies, which are under the control of a central command and control (C&C) infrastructure. Botnets are typically formed through the infection of devices with malicious software, such as malware or viruses. The challenge lies in detecting and preventing the initial compromise of devices, as well as disrupting the communication between bots and their C&C servers (Lee et al., 2022).

2. **Distributed Denial of Service (DDoS) Attack:** Botnets are frequently employed to launch DDoS attacks, which overwhelm a target system or network with a massive volume of traffic. DDoS attacks can disrupt services, cause downtime, and result in financial losses. Combating DDoS attacks involves implementing robust network infrastructure, traffic monitoring, and mitigation strategies to detect and block malicious traffic originating from botnets (Riaz et al., 2022).

3. **Malware Attack:** refers to the unauthorized infiltration of malicious software, commonly known as malware, onto a computer system or network. Malware is designed to disrupt, damage, or gain unauthorized access to systems or steal sensitive information (Wani et al., 2020).

4. **Ransomware Attack:** is a type of malicious cyberattack in which an attacker encrypts a victim's files or entire system and demands a ransom payment in exchange for restoring access to the data (Stellios et al., 2021).

5. **Man-in-the-Middle (MitM) Attack:** is a type of cyber-attack where an attacker intercepts and potentially alters communications between two parties who believe they are directly communicating with each other (Zankl et al., 2021).

6. **A Credential Stuffing Attack:** is a type of cyber-attack where an attacker uses automated tools to systematically test a large number of username and password combinations to gain unauthorized access to user accounts (Pal et al., 2020).

7. **Physical Attack:** refers to a type of security breach where an attacker gains unauthorized physical access to a system, facility, or device with the intention of causing harm, stealing valuable assets, or disrupting operations (Shafiq et al., 2021).

8. **Side-Channel Attack:** is a type of cryptographic attack that targets the implementation of a cryptographic algorithm rather than directly attacking the algorithm itself. Instead of trying to break the mathematical properties of the algorithm, side-channel attacks exploit information leaked through side channels, which are unintended channels through which information is unintentionally revealed during the execution of a cryptographic operation (Shahid et al., 2021).

Table 1. A summary of different types of attack and their remediation

Type	Description	Remediation
Botnet Attack	A "boot net attack" is likely a misspelling or misunderstanding of the term "botnet attack." A botnet is a network of compromised computers or devices that are controlled by a malicious actor, known as the botmaster. Botnets are often used to launch various types of cyberattacks, including distributed denial-of-service (DDoS) attacks.	To maintain data confidentiality and prevent unauthorized access, employ symmetric encryption methods that prohibit attackers from retrieving information.
Distributed Denial of Service (DDoS) Attack	A Distributed Denial of Service (DDoS) attack is a malicious attempt to disrupt the normal functioning of a network, website, or online service by overwhelming it with a flood of internet traffic. Unlike a traditional denial-of-service (DoS) attack that originates from a single source, a DDoS attack involves multiple compromised computers or devices, forming a botnet controlled by a botmaster.	To ensure data integrity and maintain the confidentiality of information, it is crucial to implement robust data encryption and seamless data integration. Encryption can effectively protect data from unauthorized access, tampering, or interception during transmission, preventing theft or unauthorized modifications. By applying encryption techniques, the information remains secure and private, safeguarding its integrity throughout the entire data lifecycle.
Malware Attack	A malware attack refers to a malicious attempt to compromise computer systems, networks, or devices by introducing harmful software, known as malware. Malware is designed to disrupt normal operations, steal sensitive information, gain unauthorized access, or cause other harmful effects.	Implement encryption across all communication devices to ensure secure data transmission.
Ransomware Attack	A ransomware attack is a type of malicious cyberattack in which attackers encrypt a victim's data and demand a ransom payment in exchange for restoring access to the encrypted files. It is a form of extortion where the attackers hold the victim's data hostage until the ransom is paid.	To mitigate side-channel attacks, preventive measures such as encryption can be implemented. Additionally, techniques like identity-based methods and message authentication codes can be employed to enhance network security and protect against these types of malicious attacks.
Man-in-the-Middle (MitM) Attack	A Man-in-the-Middle (MitM) attack is a type of cyberattack where an attacker intercepts and alters communication between two parties who believe they are directly communicating with each other. The attacker positions themselves between the legitimate sender and receiver, secretly relaying and possibly modifying the data exchanged.	Implement strong encryption mechanisms, such as SSL/TLS, to secure communications between parties. This ensures that the data transmitted is protected from interception and tampering by attackers.
A Credential Stuffing Attack	A credential stuffing attack is a type of cyberattack where attackers attempt to gain unauthorized access to user accounts by using automated tools to systematically try a large number of username and password combinations. The attack relies on the fact that many users reuse the same username and password across multiple online services.	Implement MFA as an additional layer of security. This requires users to provide multiple forms of authentication, such as a password and a one-time code sent to their mobile device, which makes it more difficult for attackers to gain unauthorized access.
Physical Attack	A physical attack refers to a malicious act or assault carried out physically, targeting individuals, property, or systems. Unlike cyberattacks that occur in the digital realm, physical attacks involve direct physical contact or manipulation.	To mitigate the risks of spoofing and cloning attacks, it is recommended to implement identity-based authentication protocols. Additionally, the use of physically unclonable functions (PUFs) can serve as an effective countermeasure against cloning attacks.
Side-Channel Attack	A side-channel attack is a type of security exploit that targets the unintended side effects or information leaks from a system, rather than directly attacking its cryptographic algorithms or vulnerabilities. Side-channel attacks exploit various physical, electromagnetic, or timing characteristics of a system to extract sensitive information.	Ensure that cryptographic algorithms are implemented securely to minimize side-channel vulnerabilities. Follow industry best practices and guidelines for secure implementation.

Figure 4. Attack types on the internet of things

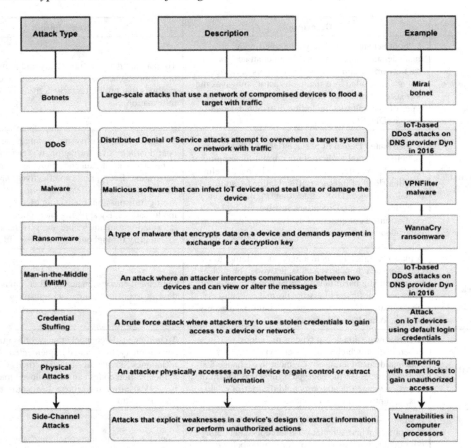

Security Requirements of IoT

There are several security requirements that must be met for the Internet of Things (IoT) to function correctly. These include:

1. Authorization and authentication measures such as secure logins, encryption algorithms and digital certificates.
2. Secure communication protocols, such as Secure Sockets Layer (SSL), Transport Layer Security (TLS) or Message Queuing Telemetry Transport (MQTT).
3. Device hardening techniques involve reducing operating system vulnerabilities through patching and configuration changes (Arshad et al., 2022).. This could also include disabling unused services on devices like routers to reduce attack surfaces significantly by preventing it from being used maliciously or providing avenues of entry into the networked IoT ecosystem.
4. Systematic logging with tools including Wireshark can help detect issues quickly if anomalies occur across different components within an IoT eco-system so they can easily be identified upon review/analysis by personnel responsible for them (Al-Jumeily et al., 2022).

5. Data protection methods (Andersson et al., 2018) should perhaps display higher levels of concern than any other aspect enquired to maintain safety standards within the data homes found throughout various versions IoT implementations due largely to their vulnerability when accessed without authorization exploiting common vulnerable points between local networks and cloud servers allowing hackers access otherwise protected connected products information exchange functionality altering client needs alongside provided product offers effectively rendering both sides liable under consumer law depending on specific regional jurisdiction laws governing private contracts regardless nationhood represented accordingly (Gerodimos et al., 2023).

There are several security requirements that need to be met for the Internet of Things (IoT) to function properly and securely as depicted in Figure 5. This is due to several factors, including the following:

1. **Identity Authentication and Authorization:** Identity authentication and authorization are crucial aspects of IoT security. They play a significant role in ensuring that only authorized individuals or devices can access IoT systems and resources, while also managing the level of access and privileges granted to them. All devices on an IoT network must have secure identity authentication methods in place to ensure only authorized users can access them (Patel et al., 2016).
2. **Secure Communication Protocols and Encryption Standards:** Secure communication protocols and encryption standards are essential components of IoT security. They protect the confidentiality, integrity, and privacy of data exchanged between IoT devices, networks, and cloud services. Communication between IoT devices needs to use industry-standard encryption protocols such as Transport Layer Security (TLS) (Siris et al., 2019).
3. **Intrusion Detection:** Intrusion detection is an important aspect of IoT security that involves monitoring and analyzing network and system activities to identify and respond to potential security breaches or unauthorized access attempts. Mechanisms should be utilized where necessary to detect any malicious activities or threats on the system before they become serious problems for businesses using the platform (Manna et al., 2019).
4. **Data Privacy:** Data privacy is a critical concern in IoT security, as IoT devices collect and process vast amounts of personal and sensitive data. Protecting the privacy of this data is crucial to maintain user trust and comply with privacy regulations. Measures must also be put in place along with data retention policies, so that private information isn't exposed unnecessarily online or stored indefinitely by third parties without permission from its rightful owner (Tariq et al., 2021).

Figure 5. Security requirements of IoT

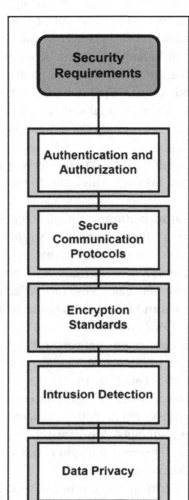

IOT CHARACTERISTICS IN GENERAL

The IoT is a network of physical devices, vehicles, home appliances and other items embedded with electronics software, sensors and connectivity which enables it to connect and exchange data. It has the potential to revolutionize many aspects of our lives, allowing for unprecedented levels of automation in areas ranging from transportation networks and smart city development to agriculture systems. There are several characteristics that are common across IoT solutions:

1. **Connectivity:** The core concept behind IoT solutions is the ability for them to securely communicate with each other over networks such as Bluetooth or Wi-Fi. This communication can occur between two objects but typically occurs on larger scales such as among thousands or millions of connected objects in an ad hoc manner (Tariq et al., 2021).

2. **Sensors:** For an IoT solution to be functional it need a way to sense their environment and act based on real world events occurring around them; thus, they must have some form of sensing technology integrated into their design (e.g., microphones, cameras) (Shafiq et al., 2018). These sensors will then act as triggers so that when certain thresholds are met this information can then be communicated via the immediate local area network (LAN) before being pushed onto the larger internet architecture where analytics tools may interpret the data further adding additional layers value within businesses operations trips above those experienced prior IO introduction (Tariq et al., 2021).

3. **Data Collection and Storage:** For any genuinely useful insights generated by IoT enabled business process all collected sensor data needs storing somewhere – often referred too at big-data frameworks – where analysis algorithm search through billions control event combinations looking correlate associations not previously detectable beforehand. Additionally privacy regulations must also protected deed provide a secure storage location meaning specific records files held both confidently safely preventing against unauthorized access potentially fraud attempt misuse consumer personal identifiable information relevant set law standards applicable jurisdiction question applies safe manner possible minimize risk exposure involved associated processing conduction end user agreement acceptance understanding signed completed project inception stage commencement (Tariq et al., 2021).

4. **Connectivity and Interactivity:** IoT allows for devices to connect with each other and share data, as well as enabling users to interact with them remotely. This network of interconnected devices creates a basis on which new technologies can be developed (Tariq et al., 2021).

5. **Intelligence:** IoT enables machines to make autonomous decisions based on the collected data they receive from connected physical objects in their environments or via cloud-based systems such as analytics platforms, voice recognition software and artificial intelligence (AI) (Cox et al., 2019).

6. **Scalability:** As an open platform, it allows people to develop applications quickly that meet their specific needs without any limitations imposed by hardware constraints or lockouts added by providers. Additionally, scalability helps businesses facilitate digital transformation initiatives that allow organizations to leverage Internet of Things technology infrastructure more efficiently than ever before.

7. **Proactive Behavior:** With sensors providing real time input across multiple distributed locations within a system's architecture, proactive behavior is enabled – allowing processes and activities (triggered automatically) at various levels depending upon changes in environmental conditions around those parts where these structures have been defined accordingly beforehand (Cox et al., 2019).

IoT Characteristics With Regards to Cyber-Attacks Vulnerability

Following are the IoT characteristics with respect to cyber-attacks and their vulnerabilities.

1. **Lack of Security:** The lack of security protocols and the associated vulnerabilities have been identified as one of the primary characteristics that make IoT devices vulnerable to cyber-attacks (Mishra et al., 2018).

2. **Unencrypted Communications:** Many IoT devices do not use encryption when transmitting data, which leaves them open to interception by malicious actors (Tripathi et al., 2021).

3. **Weak Authentication Measures:** Devices can be easily hacked due to weak authentication measures such as default passwords or using unsecure local networks for communication between devices (Khan et al., 2022).

4. **Insufficient Software Updates:** Poorly maintained software updates on an IoT device makes it more prone to exploitation from cyber attackers seeking out known flaws in outdated versions of firmware and applications (Bakshi et al., 2021).

5. **Cloud Services Vulnerabilities:** Cloud-based services used by many IoT systems introduce additional risks since they are often accessible over public networks with limited access control or protection mechanisms in place (Aldowah et al., 2019).

ARCHITECTURAL VULNERABILITIES IN IOT

Internet of Things (IoT) architecture is a complex system that consists of physical devices, networks, and applications. It can be vulnerable to cyber-attacks in many ways, including insecure protocols for communication between the various components of an IoT system, weak authentication methods or lack thereof, inadequate encryption techniques used to secure data transmission from one device to another as well as poor patching practices which make it easier for attackers to exploit known vulnerabilities. In addition, malicious actors may also target the underlying hardware running on these systems by exploiting memory-corruption bugs or other security flaws present within them. The basic architecture for IoT is depicted below in Figure 6. The Internet of Things (IoT) brings numerous benefits and convenience, but it also introduces certain architectural vulnerabilities. Here are some common architectural vulnerabilities found in IoT systems:

1. **Inadequate Authentication and Authorization:** Inadequate authentication and authorization mechanisms pose significant security challenges in the context of IoT. Authentication ensures that only authorized individuals or devices can access IoT systems, while authorization controls the level of access and privileges granted to authenticated entities. Insufficient measures in these areas can lead to unauthorized access, data breaches, and system compromises. IoT devices often lack strong authentication mechanisms, allowing unauthorized access. Also Weak or default credentials can be easily exploited, leading to unauthorized control or data breaches (Patel et al., 2016).

2. **Lack of Secure Communication:** The lack of secure communication is a critical challenge in IoT security. IoT devices often communicate over various networks, including wireless, cellular, or the internet, making them susceptible to interception and unauthorized access. IoT devices may transmit data over unencrypted or insecure communication channels. Also Lack of secure communication protocols exposes sensitive information to interception and manipulation (Patel et al., 2016).

3. **Insufficient Device Management:** Insufficient device management is a significant challenge in IoT security. Managing a large number of diverse IoT devices, including their configuration, updates, and monitoring, can be complex and challenging. Insufficient device management practices can result in vulnerabilities and security gaps that can be exploited by malicious actors. Inadequate device management practices can lead to unpatched vulnerabilities and outdated firmware. Also Without proper monitoring and updates, IoT devices become more susceptible to attacks (Hassan et al., 2021).

4. **Vulnerable Cloud Interfaces:** Vulnerable cloud interfaces pose a significant security challenge in the context of IoT. Many IoT systems leverage cloud services for data storage, processing, and remote management. However, if the interfaces between IoT devices and the cloud are not adequately secured, they can become potential entry points for cyber attackers. Many IoT systems rely on cloud services for data storage and processing. Also Weak authentication, insecure APIs, or misconfigured access control settings can compromise the entire IoT ecosystem (Lee et al., 2022).

5. **Privacy Concerns:** Privacy concerns are a significant challenge in IoT security. The interconnected nature of IoT devices and the vast amount of data they generate raise serious privacy issues that must be addressed to protect the personal information of users. IoT devices collect and process large amounts of personal data, raising privacy concerns. Also Insecure data storage, insufficient data anonymization, or unauthorized data sharing can lead to privacy breaches (Siris et al., 2019).

6. **Lack of Physical Security:** Physical access to IoT devices can lead to compromise. Also inadequate physical security measures, such as weak tamper protection or easily accessible ports, can make devices vulnerable (Siris et al., 2019).

7. **Integration Complexity:** IoT systems often involve the integration of various components and technologies. In addition, incompatibilities, misconfigurations, or insecure interfaces during integration can introduce vulnerabilities (Hassan et al., 2021).

8. **Supply Chain Risks:** IoT devices rely on a complex supply chain involving multiple vendors. Also malicious actors can compromise devices during manufacturing, assembly, or distribution, leading to inherent vulnerabilities (Lee et al., 2022).

9. **Denial-of-Service (DoS) Attacks:** Denial-of-Service (DoS) attacks pose a significant threat to IoT security. These attacks aim to disrupt the availability and functionality of IoT devices, services, or networks, rendering them inaccessible or unresponsive to legitimate users. IoT devices can be harnessed in large-scale botnets to launch DoS attacks. Also inadequate protection against DoS attacks can disrupt IoT services and impact device functionality (Lee et al., 2022).

10. **Lack of Upgradability:** The lack of upgradability is a significant challenge in IoT security. Many IoT devices are designed with limited or no capability to receive software updates or security patches, making them vulnerable to evolving threats and leaving them with outdated and insecure software. Some IoT devices have limited or no capability to receive software updates. Also Without upgradability, vulnerabilities discovered after deployment cannot be easily addressed (Vimal et al., 2022).

Figure 6. Internet of things architecture

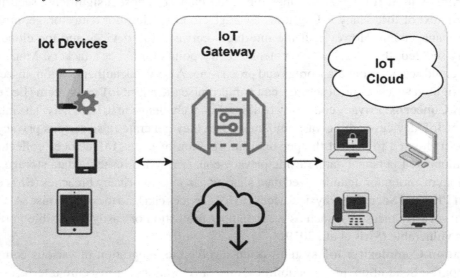

OPEN ISSUES IN IOT SECURITY

There are several open issues in IoT security that continue to pose challenges and require further research and development. Here are five open issues in IoT security as depict in Figure 7:

1. **Lack of Security Standards:** One of the major issues with IoT security is that there are currently no standardized security protocols and measures in place, leaving many devices vulnerable to attack or exploitation (Williams et al., 2022).
2. **Inadequate Authentication Mechanisms:** Many IoT platforms lack secure authentication mechanisms due to cost considerations which leaves them open to potential malicious attackers who can gain unauthorized access (Williams et al., 2022).
3. **Weak Cryptography Algorithms:** Not all Internet-of-Things systems utilize strong encryption algorithms or have adequate key lengths for transmission encoding trustworthiness; this puts any data sent over these networks at risk for interception (Yaacoub et al., 2023).
4. **Unstable Software Updates:** When device manufacturers issue software updates they often contain vulnerabilities because of inadequate testing procedures meaning new threats may be inadvertently introduced into a previously secure system (Yaacoub et al., 2023).
5. **Poorly Secured Sensors & Gateways:** As sensors and gateways become more sophisticated physical security needs to evolve simultaneously if reasonably secure communications links between different components in an architecture are going to stand up against targeted attacks from intruders (Tawalbeh et al., 2020).

Figure 7. Open issues in IoT security

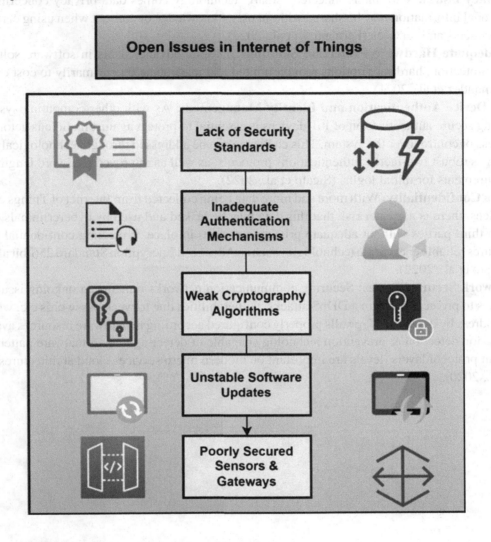

FUTURE CHALLENGES IN IOT SECURITY

As the Internet of Things (IoT) continues to evolve and expand, it brings with it various security challenges that need to be addressed as shown in Figure 8. Here are seven future challenges in IoT security:

1. **Lack of Security Standards:** The Internet of Things (IoT) is composed of a complex network, which makes it difficult to set consistent security standards across all connected devices. This lack of interoperability poses a significant challenge in ensuring the secure operation and deployment of these devices (Sabrina et al., 2022).
2. **Vulnerability to Hackers:** As the number and variety of IoT devices continues to increase, they are becoming increasingly vulnerable to attack from malicious hackers who can easily gain access through weak or nonexistent security measures such as default passwords (Abed et al., 2022).

3. **Privacy Issues:** With interconnected "smart" technology comes data privacy concerns because personal information may be shared without users' knowledge or consent when using certain types of products and services (Fernandez et al., 2022).

4. **Inadequate Hardware Protection Solutions:** Despite advancements in software solutions for IoT protection, hardware options remain limited and inadequate due primarily to cost constraints (Fernandez et al., 2021).

5. **IoT Device Authentication and Identity Management:** As with other computing systems, ensuring secure authentication of IoT devices is essential to protect against malicious actors gaining access or control over the system. This challenge can be addressed through technological solutions such as robust two-factor authentications protocols, as well as improved password length/strength requirements for initial logins (Sicato et al., 2022).

6. **Data Confidentiality:** With more and more data being collected from Internet of Things connected devices, there is a greater risk that this data may be leaked and used by cybercriminals or shared with third parties without adequate privacy measures in place. Protecting confidential user data requires reliable encryption technologies such as Advanced Encryption Standard 256-bit algorithms (Sicato et al., 2022).

7. **Network Security Issues:** Securing communication networks remains an ongoing issue when it comes to protecting Against DDoS attacks, vulnerabilities due to weak passwords etc. which need to address by deploying firewalls properly configured according to hardware resources availability, intrusion detection & prevention technology capable of detecting known malware patterns at different protocol layers' levels are important on modern micro services cloud architectures (Corallo et al., 2020).

Figure 8. Future challenges in IoT security

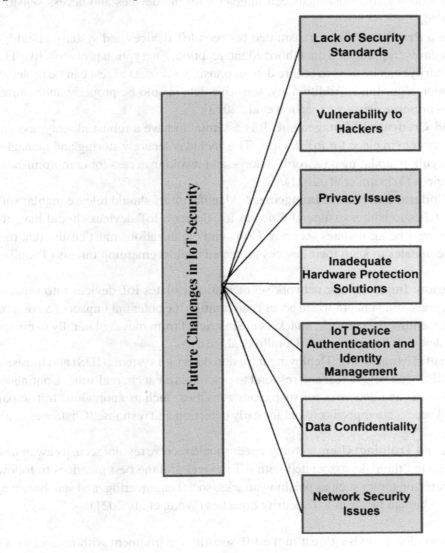

SOLUTIONS TO IOT CYBER THREATS

To address the cybersecurity threats in the IoT landscape, several solutions and best practices can be implemented. Here are some key strategies to mitigate IoT cyberthreats:

1. **Secure Design and Development:** IoT security should be integrated into the design and development process of devices from the beginning. This includes following secure coding practices, conducting threat modeling, and adhering to established security standards (Mishra et al., 2022).
2. **Strong Authentication and Access Control:** Implementing strong authentication mechanisms such as two-factor authentication (2FA) or multi-factor authentication (MFA) can help prevent unauthorized access to IoT devices and systems. Additionally, enforcing strict access control poli-

cies ensures that only authorized individuals can interact with the devices and access sensitive data (Patel et al., 2016).

3. **Encryption and Data Protection:** Data transmitted between IoT devices and systems should be encrypted to prevent eavesdropping and unauthorized interception. Encryption protocols like TLS (Transport Layer Security) can be used to secure data in transit, while data at rest can be protected using strong encryption algorithms. Additionally, sensitive data should be properly anonymized or pseudonymized to preserve privacy (Yaacoub et al., 2023).

4. **Robust Identity and Credential Management:** It is essential to have a robust identity and credential management system in place for IoT devices. This includes securely storing and managing device credentials, regularly updating passwords or keys, and revoking access for compromised or decommissioned devices (Tripathi et al., 2021).

5. **Regular Software Updates and Patch Management:** Manufacturers should release regular software updates and patches to address vulnerabilities in IoT devices. IoT devices should have the capability to receive over-the-air updates securely. Users and organizations must ensure that they promptly apply these updates to keep their devices protected against emerging threats (Tawalbeh et al., 2020).

6. **Network Segmentation:** Implementing network segmentation isolates IoT devices into separate networks or subnets, preventing unauthorized access and limiting the potential impact of a compromised device. By segmenting the network, attackers are restricted from moving laterally to critical systems even if one device is compromised (Corallo et al., 2022).

7. **Intrusion Detection and Monitoring:** Deploying intrusion detection systems (IDS) and intrusion prevention systems (IPS) can help detect and respond to potential threats in real-time. Continuous monitoring of IoT devices and networks for suspicious activities, such as anomalous traffic patterns or unauthorized access attempts, is crucial for early detection and response (Chatterjee et al., 2022).

8. **Security Awareness and Training:** Users and employees should receive regular security awareness and training to understand the risks associated with IoT devices and the best practices to follow. They should be educated on topics such as phishing attacks, social engineering, and safe browsing habits to minimize the human factor in IoT security breaches (Wong et al., 2021).

Following are the solution for the cyber threat in the IoT security environment with respect to AI-based and block chain based solutions:

AI-Based Solutions

AI-based solutions have emerged as powerful tools in combating cyber threats. Here are some AI-based solutions for addressing cyber threats:

1. **Threat Detection and Intelligence:** AI algorithms can analyze vast amounts of data from various sources, including network traffic, system logs, and security feeds, to identify patterns and indicators of cyber threats. By leveraging machine learning and data analytics techniques, AI systems can detect and classify threats in real-time, enabling timely response and mitigation (Zheng et al., 2020).

2. **Anomaly Detection:** AI can learn normal behavior patterns of systems, devices, and users, allowing it to detect anomalies that may indicate potential cyber attacks or intrusions. By continuously monitoring and analyzing data, AI algorithms can identify deviations from normal patterns and raise alerts for further investigation, enabling proactive defense measures (Carnley et al., 2019).

3. **Behavioral Analytics:** AI can analyze user behavior, network traffic, and system activities to identify unusual or suspicious patterns that may indicate a cyber threat. By establishing baseline behaviors and using machine learning algorithms, AI systems can detect anomalies and potential threats based on deviations from expected behavior, enhancing threat detection capabilities (Mollah et al., 2017).

4. **Automated Incident Response:** AI can automate incident response processes, allowing for swift and efficient actions in mitigating cyber threats. AI-powered systems can analyze and correlate threat intelligence, network data, and security events to autonomously respond to detected threats. Automated incident response reduces response times and minimizes human error in critical situations (Alsboui et al., 2021).

Block Chain-Based Solutions

Blockchain-based solutions offer unique advantages in addressing cyber threats due to their decentralized and immutable nature. Here are some blockchain-based solutions for mitigating cyber threats:

1. **Identity and Access Management:** Blockchain can enhance identity and access management by providing a decentralized and secure platform for identity verification and authentication. Blockchain-based identity solutions eliminate the need for centralized identity repositories, reducing the risk of single points of failure and data breaches (Ayoub et al., 2019).

2. **Secure Data Sharing:** Blockchain enables secure and decentralized data sharing among multiple parties without the need for intermediaries. By leveraging smart contracts and cryptographic techniques, blockchain can ensure data confidentiality, integrity, and control, reducing the risk of unauthorized data access or manipulation (Alsboui et al., 2021).

3. **Distributed Threat Intelligence:** Blockchain can facilitate the sharing and distribution of threat intelligence among organizations. By creating a decentralized network of threat intelligence providers, blockchain enables real-time sharing of information about emerging threats, vulnerabilities, and attack patterns, enhancing the collective defense against cyber threats (Zheng et al., 2020).

4. **Decentralized DNS:** Blockchain-based Domain Name Systems (DNS) provide enhanced security and resilience by eliminating the reliance on centralized DNS servers. Decentralized DNS systems leverage blockchain's consensus mechanism to validate and resolve domain name requests, reducing the risk of DNS-related attacks, such as DNS hijacking or DNS spoofing (Alsboui et al., 2021).

CONCLUSION

In conclusion, the Internet of Things holds great potential to revolutionize every field of our life. However, this progress is accompanied by new challenges associated with the security of IoT systems. There are still many open issues that need to be addressed for us to ensure a secure future for our digital world. It is important that we take steps now towards understanding these complexities and developing effective strategies to tackle them effectively before they become more widespread problems. IoT has played a crucial role in the rapid advancement of technology, facilitating the exchange of data. However, ensuring the security of user data is of utmost importance. This study focuses primarily on IoT security, considering the various attacks that IoT systems are susceptible to, including DoS, password guessing, replay, and insider attacks. Among the security services, authentication is paramount, and therefore, we have examined several solution, such as Secure Design and Development, Encryption and Data Protection, Intrusion Detection and Monitoring. After analyzing and comparing these authentication protocols, it becomes evident that many of them rely on encryption cryptography. In our future work, we aim to further enhance the security of IoT environments by proposing secure and efficient IoT authentication schemes. By developing novel authentication methods, we strive to strengthen the security of IoT systems and protect user data effectively.

REFERENCES

Abbasi, M., Plaza-Hernández, M., Prieto, J., & Corchado, J. M. (2022). Security in the Internet of Things Application Layer: Requirements, Threats, and Solutions. *IEEE Access : Practical Innovations, Open Solutions*, *10*, 97197–97216. doi:10.1109/ACCESS.2022.3205351

Abed, A. K., & Anupam, A. (2022). Review of security issues in Internet of Things and artificial intelligence-driven solutions. *Security and Privacy*, 285.

Abomhara, M., & Køien, G. M. (2014, May). Security and privacy in the Internet of Things: Current status and open issues. In 2014 international conference on privacy and security in mobile systems (PRISMS) (pp. 1-8). IEEE.

Akhtar, N. (2020). Security in the internet of Things: a systematic Mapping Study. *Foundation University Journal of Engineering and Applied Sciences (HEC Recognized Y Category, ISSN 2706-7351)*, *1*(2), 31-42.

Al-Jumeily, D., Arshad, D., Tariq, N., Baker, T., Tawfik, H., & Asim, M. (2022). A Lightweight Trust-enabled Routing in RPL-based IoT Networks Against Sybil Attack. *PLoS One*, *17*(7). PMID:35901074

Aldowah, H., Ul Rehman, S., & Umar, I. (2019). Security in internet of things: issues, challenges and solutions. In *Recent Trends in Data Science and Soft Computing: Proceedings of the 3rd International Conference of Reliable Information and Communication Technology (IRICT 2018)* (pp. 396-405). Springer International Publishing. 10.1007/978-3-319-99007-1_38

Alsboui, T., Qin, Y., Hill, R., & Al-Aqrabi, H. (2021). Distributed Intelligence in the Internet of Things: Challenges and Opportunities. *SN Computer Science*, *2*(4), 277. doi:10.1007/s42979-021-00677-7

Andersson, K., You, I., & Palmieri, F. (2018). Security and Privacy for Smart, Connected, and Mobile IoT Devices and Platforms. *Security and Communication Networks*, *2018*, 2018. doi:10.1155/2018/5346596

Ang, K. L. M., Seng, J. K. P., & Ngharamike, E. (2022). Towards crowdsourcing internet of things (crowd-iot): Architectures, security and applications. *Future Internet*, *14*(2), 49. doi:10.3390/fi14020049

Aqeel, M., Ali, F., Iqbal, M. W., Rana, T. A., Arif, M., & Auwul, M. R. (2022). A Review of Security and Privacy Concerns in the Internet of Things (IoT). *Journal of Sensors*, *2022*, 2022. doi:10.1155/2022/5724168

Arshad, D., Asim, M., Tariq, N., Baker, T., Tawfik, H., & Al-Jumeily, O. B. E. (2022). THC-RPL: A lightweight Trust-enabled routing in RPL-based IoT networks against Sybil attack. *PLoS One*, *17*(7), e0271277. doi:10.1371/journal.pone.0271277 PMID:35901074

Ayoub, I., Balakrichenan, S., Khawam, K., & Ampeau, B. (2023). DNS for IoT: A Survey. *Sensors (Basel)*, *23*(9), 4473. doi:10.3390/s23094473 PMID:37177679

Bakshi, G. (2021). IoT Architecture Vulnerabilities and Security Measures. *Security Incidents & Response Against Cyber Attacks*, 199-215.

Carnley, P. R., & Kettani, H. (2019). Identity and access management for the internet of things. *International Journal of Future Computer and Communication*, *8*(4), 129–133. doi:10.18178/ijfcc.2019.8.4.554

Chatterjee, A., & Ahmed, B. S. (2022). IoT anomaly detection methods and applications: A survey. *Internet of Things : Engineering Cyber Physical Human Systems*, *19*, 100568. doi:10.1016/j.iot.2022.100568

Corallo, A., Lazoi, M., Lezzi, M., & Luperto, A. (2022). Cybersecurity awareness in the context of the Industrial Internet of Things: A systematic literature review. *Computers in Industry*, *137*, 103614. doi:10.1016/j.compind.2022.103614

Cox, D. (2019). Five Characteristics That Make IoT Vulnerable To Cyber Attacks.' *Forbes*.

Fernandez, E. B., Washizaki, H., Yoshioka, N., & Okubo, T. (2021). The design of secure IoT applications using patterns: State of the art and directions for research. *Internet of Things : Engineering Cyber Physical Human Systems*, *15*, 100408. doi:10.1016/j.iot.2021.100408

Gerodimos, A., Maglaras, L., Ferrag, M. A., Ayres, N., & Kantzavelou, I. (2023). IOT: Communication protocols and security threats. *Internet of Things and Cyber-Physical Systems*.

Ghazal, T. M., Afifi, M. A. M., & Kalra, D. (2020). Security vulnerabilities, attacks, threats and the proposed countermeasures for the Internet of Things applications. *Solid State Technology*, *63*(1s).

Gong, H., Li, J., Ni, R., Xiao, P., Ouyang, H., Mu, Y., & Tyasi, T. L. (2021). The Data Acquisition and Control System Based on IoT-CAN Bus. *Intelligent Automation & Soft Computing*, *30*(3), 1049–1062. doi:10.32604/iasc.2021.019730

Hasan, M. K., Shafiq, M., Islam, S., Pandey, B., Baker El-Ebiary, Y. A., Nafi, N. S., Ciro Rodriguez, R., & Vargas, D. E. (2021). Lightweight cryptographic algorithms for guessing attack protection in complex internet of things applications. *Complexity*, *2021*, 1–13. doi:10.1155/2021/5540296

Humayun, M., Jhanjhi, N. Z., Hamid, B., & Ahmed, G. (2020). Emerging smart logistics and transportation using IoT and blockchain. *IEEE Internet of Things Magazine*, *3*(2), 58–62. doi:10.1109/IOTM.0001.1900097

Inayat, U., Zia, M. F., Mahmood, S., Khalid, H. M., & Benbouzid, M. (2022). Learning-based methods for cyber attacks detection in IoT systems: A survey on methods, analysis, and future prospects. *Electronics (Basel)*, *11*(9), 1502. doi:10.3390/electronics11091502

Khan, A. A., Laghari, A. A., Shaikh, Z. A., & Dacko-Pikiewicz, Z., & Kot, S. (2022). Internet of Things (IoT) security with blockchain technology: A state-of-the-art review. *IEEE Access : Practical Innovations, Open Solutions*.

Khan, Y., Su'ud, M. B. M., Alam, M. M., Ahmad, S. F., Salim, N. A., & Khan, N. (2022). Architectural Threats to Security and Privacy: A Challenge for Internet of Things (IoT) Applications. *Electronics (Basel)*, *12*(1), 88. doi:10.3390/electronics12010088

Kirmani, S., Mazid, A., Khan, I. A., & Abid, M. (2023). A Survey on IoT-Enabled Smart Grids: Technologies, Architectures, Applications, and Challenges. *Sustainability (Basel)*, *15*(1), 717. doi:10.3390/su15010717

Kumar, P., Bagga, H., Netam, B. S., & Uduthalapally, V. (2022). Sad-iot: Security analysis of ddos attacks in iot networks. *Wireless Personal Communications*, *122*(1), 87–108. doi:10.1007/s11277-021-08890-6

Lee, S. H., Shiue, Y. L., Cheng, C. H., Li, Y. H., & Huang, Y. F. (2022). Detection and Prevention of DDoS Attacks on the IoT. *Applied Sciences (Basel, Switzerland)*, *12*(23), 12407. doi:10.3390/app122312407

Manna, P., & Das, R. K. (2021). Scalability in Internet of Things: Techniques, Challenges and Solutions. *International Journal for Research in Engineering Application & Management (IJREAM)*, 259-261.

Mishra, S., Albarakati, A., & Sharma, S. K. (2022). Cyber Threat Intelligence for IoT Using Machine Learning. *Processes (Basel, Switzerland)*, *10*(12), 2673. doi:10.3390/pr10122673

Mollah, M. B., Azad, M. A. K., & Vasilakos, A. (2017). Secure data sharing and searching at the edge of cloud-assisted internet of things. *IEEE Cloud Computing*, *4*(1), 34–42. doi:10.1109/MCC.2017.9

Pal, S., Hitchens, M., Rabehaja, T., & Mukhopadhyay, S. (2020). Security requirements for the internet of things: A systematic approach. *Sensors (Basel)*, *20*(20), 5897. doi:10.3390/s20205897 PMID:33086542

Patel, K. K., Patel, S. M., & Scholar, P. (2016). Internet of things-IOT: definition, characteristics, architecture, enabling technologies, application & future challenges. *International journal of engineering science and computing, 6*(5).

Razzaq, A., Altamimi, A. B., Alreshidi, A., Ghayyur, S. A. K., Khan, W., & Alsaffar, M. (2023). IoT Data Sharing Platform in Web 3.0 Using Blockchain Technology. *Electronics (Basel)*, *12*(5), 1233. doi:10.3390/electronics12051233

Riaz, S., Latif, S., Usman, S. M., Ullah, S. S., Algarni, A. D., Yasin, A., Anwar, A., Elmannai, H., & Hussain, S. (2022). Malware Detection in Internet of Things (IoT) Devices Using Deep Learning. *Sensors (Basel)*, *22*(23), 9305. doi:10.3390/s22239305 PMID:36502007

Sabrina, F., Li, N., & Sohail, S. (2022). A Blockchain Based Secure IoT System Using Device Identity Management. *Sensors (Basel)*, *22*(19), 7535. doi:10.3390/s22197535 PMID:36236634

Sadhu, P. K., Yanambaka, V. P., & Abdelgawad, A. (2022). Internet of Things: Security and Solutions Survey. *Sensors (Basel)*, *22*(19), 7433. doi:10.3390/s22197433 PMID:36236531

Shafiq, M., Ashraf, H., Ullah, A., Masud, M., Azeem, M., Jhanjhi, N., & Humayun, M. (2021). Robust cluster-based routing protocol for IoT-assisted smart devices in WSN. *Computers, Materials & Continua, 67*(3), 3505–3521. doi:10.32604/cmc.2021.015533

Shafiq, M., Ashraf, H., Ullah, A., Masud, M., Azeem, M., Jhanjhi, N., & Humayun, M. (2021). Robust cluster-based routing protocol for IoT-assisted smart devices in WSN. *Computers, Materials & Continua, 67*(3), 3505–3521. doi:10.32604/cmc.2021.015533

Shafiq, M., Gu, Z., Cheikhrouhou, O., Alhakami, W., & Hamam, H. (2022). The rise of "Internet of Things":review and open research issues related to detection and prevention of IoT-based security attacks. *Wireless Communications and Mobile Computing, 2022*, 1–12. doi:10.1155/2022/8669348

Shahid, H., Ashraf, H., Javed, H., Humayun, M., Jhanjhi, N. Z., & AlZain, M. A. (2021). Energy optimised security against wormhole attack in iot-based wireless sensor networks. *Computers, Materials & Continua, 68*(2), 1967–1981. doi:10.32604/cmc.2021.015259

Sicato, J. C. S., Singh, S. K., Rathore, S., & Park, J. H. (2020). A comprehensive analyses of intrusion detection system for IoT environment. *Journal of Information Processing Systems, 16*(4), 975–990.

Siris, V. A., Fotiou, N., Mertzianis, A., & Polyzos, G. C. (2019). Smart application-aware IoT data collection. *Journal of Reliable Intelligent Environments, 5*(1), 17–28. doi:10.1007/s40860-019-00077-y

Ssa, W., Moustafa, N., Turnbull, B., & Sohrabi, N. (2023). Blockchain-based federated learning for securing internet of things: A comprehensive survey. *ACM Computing Surveys, 55*(9), 1–43. doi:10.1145/3560816

Stellios, I., Kotzanikolaou, P., & Grigoriadis, C. (2021). Assessing IoT enabled cyber-physical attack paths against critical systems. *Computers & Security, 107*, 102316. doi:10.1016/j.cose.2021.102316

Taherdoost, H. (2023). Security and Internet of Things: Benefits, Challenges, and Future Perspectives. *Electronics (Basel), 12*(8), 1901. doi:10.3390/electronics12081901

Tariq, N., Asim, M., Al-Obeidat, F., Zubair Farooqi, M., Baker, T., Hammoudeh, M., & Ghafir, I. (2019). The security of big data in fog-enabled IoT applications including blockchain: A survey. *Sensors (Basel), 19*(8), 1788. doi:10.3390/s19081788 PMID:31013993

Tawalbeh, L. A., Muheidat, F., Tawalbeh, M., & Quwaider, M. (2020). IoT Privacy and security: Challenges and solutions. *Applied Sciences (Basel, Switzerland), 10*(12), 4102. doi:10.3390/app10124102

Tripathi, S. (2021). Secure Architecture For IoTSystems To Counter CyberspaceThreats And Mitigate IntrusionRisk — A Survey Paper. *International Journal Of IntegratedEngineering, 13*(1), 167 -177. availableathttps//ijiedu org accessed 21stMarch 2021

Tukade, T. M., & Banakar, R. (2018). Data transfer protocols in IoT—An overview. *International Journal of Pure and Applied Mathematics, 118*(16), 121–138.

Vimal, V., Muruganantham, R., Prabha, R., Arularasan, A. N., Nandal, P., Chanthirasekaran, K., & Reddy Ranabothu, G. (2022). Enhance Software-Defined Network Security with IoT for Strengthen the Encryption of Information Access Control. *Computational Intelligence and Neuroscience, 2022*, 2022. doi:10.1155/2022/4437507 PMID:36225550

Wani, A., & Revathi, S. (2020). Ransomware protection in IoT using software defined networking. *Iranian Journal of Electrical and Computer Engineering*, *10*(3), 3166–3175.

Williams, P., Dutta, I. K., Daoud, H., & Bayoumi, M. (2022). A survey on security in internet of things with a focus on the impact of emerging technologies. *Internet of Things : Engineering Cyber Physical Human Systems*, *19*, 100564. doi:10.1016/j.iot.2022.100564

Wong, C. M. V., Chan, R. Y. Y., Yum, Y. N., & Wang, K. (2021). Internet of Things (IoT)-Enhanced Applied Behavior Analysis (ABA) for Special Education Needs. *Sensors (Basel)*, *21*(19), 6693. doi:10.3390/s21196693 PMID:34641011

Yaacoub, J. P. A., Noura, H. N., Salman, O., & Chehab, A. (2023). Ethical hacking for IoT: Security issues, challenges, solutions and recommendations. *Internet of Things and Cyber-Physical Systems*.

Zankl, A., Seuschek, H., Irazoqui, G., & Gulmezoglu, B. (2021). Side-channel attacks in the Internet of Things: threats and challenges. In *Research Anthology on Artificial Intelligence Applications in Security* (pp. 2058–2090). IGI Global.

Zheng, Y., Pal, A., Abuadbba, S., Pokhrel, S. R., Nepal, S., & Janicke, H. (2020, October). Towards IoT security automation and orchestration. In *2020 Second IEEE International Conference on Trust, Privacy and Security in Intelligent Systems and Applications (TPS-ISA)* (pp. 55-63). IEEE.

Chapter 6
Enhancing Identification of IoT Anomalies in Smart Homes Using Secure Blockchain Technology

Sidra Tahir
UIIT, Pakistan

ABSTRACT

Numerous technologies that automate processes and simplify our lives are included in smart homes. These gadgets may be helpful for various things, including temperature, lighting, and security access. Smart homes fundamentally enable remote control of equipment and appliances for homeowners via the internet of things (IoT) platform. Smart houses are able to understand their owners' routines and modify in accordance with their capacity for self-learning. The requirement to identify abnormalities in data created by smart homes arises from the necessity of convenience and cost savings in such a setting, as well as from the involvement of numerous devices. The topic of anomaly detection using deep learning is covered in this chapter. Additionally, the suggested solution is more secure because to the usage of block chain technology. Results show that the suggested strategy has exceptional accuracy and recall.

INTRODUCTION

Particular industries, such as intelligent transportation and IoT, have seen significant transformations as a result of the development of new generations of wireless communications and big data technology(Alamri, Jhanjhi, & Humayun, 2019; Humayun, Niazi, Jhanjhi, Alshayeb, & Mahmood, 2020). A prevalent application of the Internet of Things and ubiquitous computing is the Smart Home. In this application, ambient intelligence monitors the home's environment to provide context-aware services and facilitate remote home control (Almusaylim & Zaman, 2019; Zaidan & Zaidan, 2020) may include both wired and wireless communication technologies, and is controlled by a smart terminal, such as a mobile phone or

DOI: 10.4018/978-1-6684-7625-3.ch006

a personal computer, over the Internet. This is one of the distinguishing characteristics of a smart home (Humayun, 2020; Sovacool & Del Rio, 2020; Strengers, Kennedy, Arcari, Nicholls, & Gregg, 2019).

IoT devices contribute ease of use and automation to a smart home, however, there is a potential for data errors to occur(Chow et al., 2020; Humayun, Jhanjhi, Alamri, & Khan, 2020). These dangers are caused by flaws, inconsistencies, and mistakes in the data collected, transported, stored, and processed by the IoT (Alamri et al., 2019)(Ferrag, Shu, Yang, Derhab, & Maglaras, 2020; Saura, Ribeiro-Soriano, & Palacios-Marqués, 2021). Defects in the data can result in information that is inaccurate or deceptive, which has the potential to disrupt the operation of the smart home system and put the users' privacy and safety at risk. The proper identification and resolution of these issues are very necessary to guarantee the dependable and trustworthy functioning of smart homes(Alferidah & Jhanjhi, 2020). The dependability of smart homes is dependent on locating and resolving issues like these.

Deep Learning techniques can play a significant role in mitigating the risks associated with data defects in smart homes. (Churcher et al., 2021; Hussain, Hussain, Hassan, & Hossain, 2020). Machine learning models can detect defects by analyzing IoT data patterns and trends. This allows proactive data cleaning, correction, and re-collection. Additionally, machine learning algorithms can be utilized for predictive maintenance, where they learn from historical data to anticipate potential data defects or device failures, allowing for proactive intervention to prevent disruptions in the smart home environment(N. A. Khan, Jhanjhi, Brohi, Usmani, & Nayyar, 2020; Kishore Kumar, 2021; Soe, Feng, Santosa, Hartanto, & Sakurai, 2020; Xiao, Wan, Lu, Zhang, & Wu, 2018).

By bringing decentralized, irreversible, and transparent data management, blockchain technology plays a significant part in assuring the safety of internet-of-things (IoT) devices that are used in smart homes(Alamri et al., 2019; Shi et al., 2020; Taylor, Dargahi, Dehghantanha, Parizi, & Choo, 2020). Devices in a smart home may eliminate the need for a central authority by utilizing the distributed ledger system provided by blockchain. This allows the devices to record and confirm every transaction and interaction in a safe manner. This decentralized method improves security by eliminating the possibility of a single point of failure and cutting down on the system's susceptibility to cyberattacks. In addition, blockchain technology makes it possible to construct smart contracts, which may automate and regulate the way devices interact with one another according to certain predetermined circumstances. These contracts that carry out their own terms increase safety by lowering the likelihood that they will be tampered with or violated by unauthorized parties (S. Khan, Amin, Azar, & Aslam, 2021). The IoTs gadgets in a smart home may improve overall security and build a more resilient and trustworthy ecosystem by establishing trust with one another and preserving the integrity of their data with the use of blockchain technology.

The data deficiencies of smart homes are essential for a variety of reasons. To begin, the IoT technologies included in smart homes require data that is reliable and precise in order to function properly. Incorrect data can have an effect on the automation and management of smart devices, putting the user's comfort and safety in jeopardy(S. Li, Hao, Ding, & Xu, 2019; W. Liang, Li, Long, Kui, & Zomaya, 2019; Tahir, Hafeez, Abbas, Nawaz, & Hamid, 2022). Privacy and safety are given top priority in smart homes. Data flaws can allow for unauthorized access to sensitive data or the injection of harmful commands, posing a hazard to both users' privacy and their physical safety. Fixing data faults, raising user confidence, and increasing adoption of smart homes are all areas in which machine learning may help the IoT ecosystem retain its integrity and credibility(Benkhelifa, Welsh, & Hamouda, 2018; Ojha, Misra, & Raghuwanshi, 2021; Zaheer, Tahir, Almufareh, & Hamid, 2023).

In the context of smart homes, the primary focus of this study is on the identification of anomalies in the network traffic generated by IoT devices. Typically, smart homes have a gateway that is in charge of collecting and aggregating sensor data as well as the sensors and IoT devices, and network sniffing tools are used to capture the network packets that are being transferred between these components. The study that is being suggested would collect this traffic statistics and make an attempt to categorize the devices into behavioral templates or profiles based on a set of characteristics that have already been established. Devices connected to the IoT need to be categorized immediately for a variety of reasons(Churcher et al., 2021). It may be essential to successfully identify IoT devices in a given situation and environment in order to detect illegitimate devices, unauthorized devices, undesired devices, and devices that do not perform as expected and have the potential to create a security event inside the system. This may be accomplished by successfully identifying IoT devices. In addition, useful device categorization and identification of new and previously undetected devices can enable more effective traffic management as well as the needed network capacity in situations where IoT devices are present. This can be accomplished through the use of useful device identification(Alrashdi et al., 2019).

The remaining parts of this work is divided down into the following sections: the second portion discusses the most recent and relevant research. An explanation of the strategy used to collect data in the third section, a framework and its units that makes use of the deep learning method are shown. The outcomes of the experimental evaluation were broken down, analyzed in section 4, and in the fifth portion of the paper is discussion. The authors summarize their findings and offer suggestions for further research in the concluding section of the article.

RELATED WORK

The deep learning technique utilizes neural networks that are made up of many processing layers for each layer of the framework. This enables automated learning of the fundamental structure present in data sets that are both complicated and huge. Deep learning is utilized extensively in the IoT to carry out activities that are dependent on data that comes from systems that use cutting-edge technology.

Eirini (Anthi, Williams, Javed, & Burnap, 2021) discovered a deep learning-based system designed to enable flexible and effective streamlined detection of assaults in IoT networks, intrusion and anomaly detection. A new attack vector was also developed; that comprised deep learning models, which were exposed to assaults. The proposed models were used to support the judgments made by the intrusion detection system (IDS). Their article provided a rule-based technique for producing attack samples and studied how it may be used to target a variety of classifiers used for detecting and classifying Denial of Service (DOS) attacks in an IoT smart home network. The study investigated which characteristics of DoS packets should be altered and how the use of adversarial samples might contribute to the development of more robust supervised models through the application of adversarial training. When hostile samples were included, the findings showed that the performance of every top-performing classifier was negatively impacted, with the decrease in performance reaching a maximum of 47.2%. The fact that their performance increased after going through adversarial training demonstrates how resistant they are to attacks of this kind.

Rehman (Javed et al., 2021) proposed a cognitive assessment of smart homes to test the capacity of inhabitants of smart homes to carry out simple to complicated activities of daily living by utilizing predefined scores. In addition, their approach utilized supervised classification to evaluate the quality of the tasks that were carried out by the participants. Their work included a temporal feature analysis with the goal of determining whether or not temporal factors contribute to the accurate detection of impaired persons. The purpose of their research was to identify those in the earliest stages of cognitive decline as early as possible. Their work was able to evaluate an individual's state of health by looking at major traits, which also helped to improve the representation of people with dementia—in comparison to the methodologies that were already in use, an improvement in the dependability of their proposed work had an accurate assignment of labels to the residents of the smart home.

Priyadarshini (Priyadarshini, Sahu, Kumar, & Taniar, 2022) completed an overall examination of energy usage in smart houses using machine learning models and presented her findings in a different publication. For forecasting the power consumption of numerous datasets, they relied on machine learning techniques such as Decision Trees (DT), k-Nearest Neighbour (KNN), eXtreme Gradient Boosting (XGBoost), and Random Forest (RF). In addition, they presented an ML-based ensemble model for the purpose of analyzing the consumption and contrasting it with the baseline methods. Statistical measures were utilized as assessment criteria for the investigation. Various datasets were utilized in the research, and the results demonstrated that the suggested DT-RF-XG-based Ensemble Model beat all of the other baseline methods for various datasets, achieving an R2 value of about 0.99.

In another investigation, Meidan (Meidan et al., 2017)used network traffic data and machine learning techniques to identify IoT devices that were connected to a network accurately. In order to train and evaluate the classifier, they collected and tagged network traffic data from nine unique IoT devices, PCs, and mobile phones. Using supervised learning, they trained a multi-stage meta classifier; in the first stage, the classifier distinguished between traffic generated by IoT and non-IoT devices. In the second stage, each IoT device was allotted to a specific IoT device class. The overall IoT categorization accuracy of their model was 99.281%.

Tiankai (T. Liang, Zeng, Liu, Ye, & Zou, 2018) came up with an innovative unsupervised user behavior prediction method. Their work utilized an artificial neural network and introduced a forgetting factor to compensate for the shortcomings of the previous prediction algorithm. Their algorithm possessed a high degree of autonomy and the ability to self-organize through learning. Due to the amnesia feature, the algorithm was also more effective at averting the influence of infrequent and outdated operation records. This was accomplished by storing less information. Using actual end-user operation data revealed that their proposed algorithm demonstrated a higher level of performance than other algorithms in terms of effectiveness.

In another article (Alhajri, Ali, & Shubair, 2018), ML techniques were utilized to categorize indoor environments in (IoT) applications that were still under development. Real-time dimensions of the RF signal in a practical environment served as the foundation for this categorization. A variety of RF data were used to examine a number of various machine learning classification techniques, including as DT, SVM, and KNN. A machine learning approach using the weighted k-nearest neighbor technique that combined the channel transmission function and frequency consistency function performed better than the other methods in classifying the type of smart home with an accuracy of 99.3%, according to the data gathered. The forecast time was found to be less than 10 microseconds, demonstrating that the chosen approach was a strong contender for real-time deployment scenarios.

In another research article (Spanos, Giannoutakis, Votis, & Tzovaras, 2019), Georgios developed a method for ensuring the safety of IoT smart homes that involved the creation of behavioral device templates. The statistical measurements that had been created were processed in order to provide the relevant characteristics, which were then utilized for the construction of clusters of devices. The primary concept was predicated on the observation that, in the case of an aberrant occurrence, the device would be shifted away from the center of the cluster, so producing an alert that could be utilized for the purpose of recommending activities to mitigate the problem. The technique that was used in the suggested solution was described in great depth, and validation was carried out using an actual dataset collected from smart homes.

Bianchi (Bianchi et al., 2019) proposed a novel HAR system that used the possibilities of wearable technology and merged it with the capabilities of deep learning techniques. The wearable sensor that was built had an inertial measurement unit as well as a Wi-Fi portion. This enabled the user to take control of the installation process on their own. The sensor was connected to a convolutional neural network, or CNN, which was programmed to draw conclusions using the least amount of resources feasible. This was performed to maintain the door open for the possibility of its use in low-cost or embedded devices. The idea for the system came from someone wanting to keep track of their daily activities, and it was able to identify nine distinct tasks with an accuracy of 97%.

Francesco (Piccialli, Cuomo, Cola, & Casolla, 2019) pointed the processing of large amounts of data frequently calls for the use of sophisticated mathematical methods and, as a result, necessitates the usage of services for distribution, computation, and digital preservation. Their study presented and explored the implementation of a machine learning strategy on IoT cultural data gathered in the National Archaeological Museum of Naples. Data constituted both a significant problem and a resource for the CH domain. They were able to gather the visit routes of the users in a method that did not interfere with their experience by deploying some Bluetooth sensor boards. The purpose of their study was to conduct an analysis and classification of the visitor behavior data that was collected in order to generate insights that are helpful for cultural stakeholders. The understanding of people's behavior was helpful to museum organizations not only in terms of strategy for the medium to long term but also in terms of choices strictly related to operations.

Bajpai (Bajpai, Sharma, & Chaurasia, 2023) addressed an intrusion prediction and detection mechanism using machine learning technologies that were powerful and more efficient in order to recognize attacks and identify intrusions in advance of the time. In order to create an intrusion detection framework that was used in IoT networks using machine learning, the authors used supervised learning and assessed the overall performance of the method employed. The suggested framework investigated the several performance metrics that are available for every one of the various classifiers. Based on the findings, it was determined that the suggested framework had an attack detection accuracy of f98.68%.

In a further study (Cvitić, Peraković, Periša, & Gupta, 2021), the researchers looked at the possibility of categorizing gadgets without regard to how they work or for what purpose they are being used. For this, a total of 41 IoTdevices were used. A classification model was created, and the concept of supervised machine learning, often known as logitboost, was added to the logistic regression technique. 13 network traffic characteristics produced by IoTdevices were used to build a multiclass classification model. Research classified devices into four separate categories with high levels of performance and accuracy (99.79%) based on the characteristics of the traffic flow of such devices. Accuracy, F-measure, True Positive Ratio, False Positive Ratio, and Kappa coefficient all gave favorable results when taken into account as model performance metrics.

From the above literature, it is concluded that the classification of anomalies from smart home traffic is significant. Defects in the data can result in information that is inaccurate or deceptive, which has the potential to disrupt the operation of the smart home system and put the users' privacy and safety at risk. The proper identification and resolution of these issues are very necessary to guarantee the dependable and trustworthy functioning of smart homes. For this purpose, a framework is proposed that employs blockchain technology to ensure security traffic generated by IoT in smart homes. Moreover, the classification of anomalies will also enable the framework to evolve continuously.

PROPOSED APPROACH

Dataset Collection

In the course of this research, an IoTID20 dataset has been taken into reference(Ullah & Mahmoud, 2020). This dataset brings together IoT devices and the infrastructure that connects them. One example of a typical installation in a smart house was created with the help of a Wi-Fi camera and a locking device. These two IoT devices were linked to a Wi-Fi router designed for use in smart homes. Laptops, tablets, and smartphones are some of the other electronic devices that may be found connected to the smart home network. The IoTID20 dataset includes a total of 80 network characteristics in addition to three label elements. The binary classes for dataset can be seen displayed in Table 1.

Table 1. Details of IoTID20 dataset

Class	Normal	Defected
No of instances	40,496	95,946585,710
Features	80	
Candidate features	10	Active_max, Idel_max, Backward segment average, subflow forward byes, PSH flag count, Packet size, Forward_IAT_max, subflow_forward Packets.

Proposed Framework

In this study, a novel approach is proposed to address the identification of anomalous behavior in IoT devices within a smart home environment. This method categorizes network traffic data by combining the robust security features of blockchain technology with the potent capabilities of deep learning, specifically Convolutional Neural Networks (CNN) (Sabokrou, Fayyaz, Fathy, Moayed, & Klette, 2018). Focusing on characteristics such as Packet Size, Packet/Flow Time, Packet/Flow Number, Packet/Flow Duration, and Number of Unique Communications, the initial phase of the method entails the extraction of dataset information for each connected device. Following the extraction of features, the dataset is preprocessed in preparation for subsequent analysis using intricate smart contract and machine learning algorithms(H. Liang, Sun, Sun, & Gao, 2017).

Integrating blockchain technology (He, Zhang, & Li, 2021; J. Li, Zhang, Zhang, Li, & Yang, 2022) into this architecture adds an additional layer of security to the distributed ledger. By leveraging the decentralized nature of blockchain, the proposed method facilitates the development of a more robust framework and improves information exchange. CNN, as a paradigm of deep learning, offers benefits in terms of accelerating the comprehension of enhanced information and enabling the implementation of a centralized blockchain design. The proposed implementation framework, as depicted in Figure 1, integrates data from multiple sources, such as cameras, smart devices, and IoT systems, which are evaluated within smart applications. These intelligent applications rely heavily on blockchain technology to ensure the integrity and veracity of their data. The proposed framework is applicable for interpreting, analyzing, and predicting data generated by such applications, with the dataset being processed over a blockchain network, thereby effectively mitigating problems associated with data repetition, incorrect values, defects, and noise-related errors.

Figure 1. A secure framework for identification of anomalies in smart home based IoTs

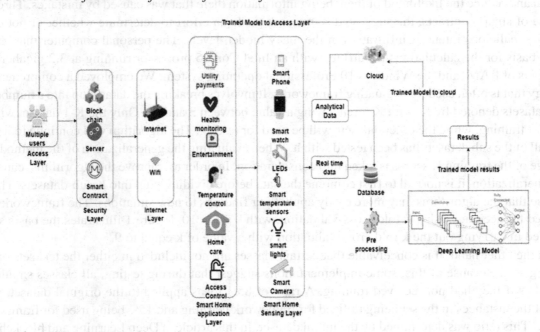

The proposed system's architecture consists of two major components: the blockchain information architecture, which is incorporated at the edge of the IoT architecture, and a sophisticated deep learning framework with multiple hidden layers, hidden neurons, and triggering mechanisms. These design elements are implemented into smart homes to maximize their security and safety. This study's innovative approach to categorizing IoT devices based on their typical network activity is a significant contribution. CNN is utilized in the clustering process, which plays a crucial role in classification due to its simplicity and superior performance compared to other clustering techniques. In order to train the CNN framework, flawed network traffic is identified as independent variables, and the corresponding pooling serves as the classification labels.

In general, the proposed method integrates blockchain technology and deep learning to enable effective categorization of network traffic data in smart homes, thereby enhancing security and enabling more precise identification of unusual device behavior.

Dataset Description and Experimental Evaluation

Experiments are undertaken in this part to determine whether or not the suggested framework is effective. The experiments are based on three genuine data sources, each of which is directly linked to a smart house, and each data source consists of 10 devices that come from a firm that makes smart homes. It's important to recognize that all entries with missing values have been deleted, as that fact has to be recognized. The data were preprocessed in advance in order to remove any inconsistencies in the information and reduce the likelihood of there being information there that was caused by mistakes. Through the use of smart contracts, the suggested framework made an effort to determine whether or not there was any malicious intent or infiltration in the many hidden levels. The personal computer that serves as the basis for the calculations is outfitted with an Intel Core i5 processor running at 3.2 gigahertz, 8 gigabytes of RAM, and the Windows 10 Professional operating system. We employed a comprehensive strategy that is often used for evaluating frameworks. It involves breaking the dataset up into a number of sub-datasets denoted by K, with K often having a value between 3 and 10. Only the K-1 dataset will be used for training, while the other datasets will be used for testing. The algorithm will continue to iterate until all of the sub datasets has been tested with it. When evaluating the generalization of the method, the average of the training K scores is taken into consideration. In order to improve the algorithms' capacity for generalization, it is normal to first combine the data before dividing it up into K sub-datasets. This is done so that the algorithms may more easily apply their findings to new situations. The framework was checked for accuracy using k-fold cross-validation, with k set at 10. Figure 1 illustrates the basic steps involved in carrying out the k-fold cross-validation with a value of k equal to 9.

On the other hand, it is conceivable that certain classes are not included in either the test sets or the training sets. Because of this, some implementations suggest that during testing, all classes should be treated as if they had not received training. A ratio of 85:15 was applied to the original dataset, with 85% of the instances in the set being utilized for framework learning and 15% being used for framework testing. This ratio was determined by the initial dataset. In this article, a Deep Learning and blockchain-based architecture was constructed with input data from three genuine data sources, with a total of ten smart home devices as the focus. The first step in evaluating the algorithms is to split the datasets into two independent portions, one for training and the other for testing. This will allow you to compare the results of the two methods. The data were arbitrarily split into two categories: training, which comprises 85% of the total (135,754 samples), and validation, which comprises 15% of the total (20,364 samples). In addition, the success of a classification framework that is founded on deep learning and blockchain technology has to be communicated through a variety of distinct metrics.

Accuracy is one of these metrics, indicating the proportion of instances correctly classified in the entire set of samples according to equation 1. where TP (true positive examples), TN (true negative examples), FP (false positive examples), and FN (false negative examples). In other words, accuracy represents the proportion of correctly classified examples as explained in Equation 1.

$$Acc = \frac{TP + TN}{TP + TN + FP + FN} \tag{1}$$

According to expression, the F-measure or F1 score represents the harmonic mean of the precision and recall measures (Chicco & Jurman, 2020). According to (Zhang, Liao, & Bellamy, 2020), the harmonic mean is more intuitive than the classical arithmetic mean to calculate the mean of the ratio, as shown in equation 2.

$$F\ measure = \frac{2.(P.R)}{P+R}$$

(2)

Moreover, precision and recall are also calculated as equations 3 and 4, respectively

$$Precision(P) = \frac{Number\ of\ correctly\ Predicted\ anomaly}{Number\ of\ all\ Predicted\ anomlay}$$

(3)

$$Recall(R) = \frac{Number\ of\ relevant\ retrieved\ anomaly}{Number\ of\ Relevant\ anomaly}$$

(4)

RESULTS AND DISCUSSION

With an overall accuracy of 93.7%, the classifier's experimental findings showed impressive performance. This shows that the framework classified occurrences from the dataset correctly, achieving a high degree of prediction accuracy. The accuracy metric acts as a key performance indicator for classifiers, giving a thorough evaluation of their efficiency. The high accuracy in this instance indicates that the classifier was able to correctly anticipate the majority of cases, proving its ability to differentiate between distinct classes successfully, as shown in figure 2.

Figure 2. Results indicating evaluation measures for the proposed framework

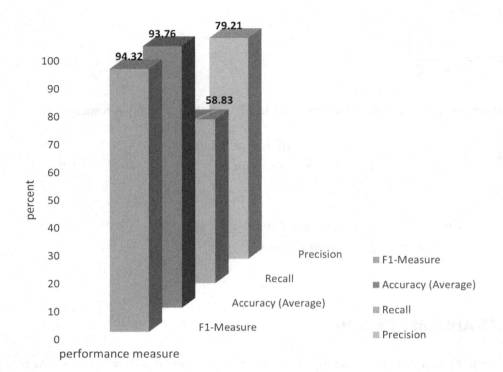

Furthermore, the recall of 58% demonstrates the classifier's capacity to accurately identify positive occurrences among all those that legitimately fall into the positive class. However, the recall metric measures the percentage of true positives that were correctly identified. Its significantly lower value in this situation suggests that the classifier may have overlooked a significant number of positive cases. This can be attributable to the dataset's intrinsic complexity or imbalance, where it might have been particularly difficult to identify certain good examples precisely. It is important to remember, nevertheless, that the classifier's accuracy was 79%. Precision is the capacity to identify positive events among all those that are expected to be positive. The classifier demonstrated a low incidence of false positives, decreasing the occurrence of misclassifications in this respect, as indicated by the considerably higher accuracy score. By enhancing the recall metric, the precision meter offers a more thorough evaluation of the classifier's performance.

The classifier's overall F1 measure of 94% denotes a unified assessment that accounts for both accuracy and recall. When working with unbalanced datasets or situations where accuracy and recall are equally important, the F1 score is extremely helpful. The high F1 score in this instance shows that the classifier successfully struck a good balance between accuracy and recall.

The cross-validation results for various folds of k, spanning from 1 to 10, showed significant changes in the classifier's performance metrics. As the number of folds rose, the recall measure specifically showed a steady rise from 51% to 81%, suggesting an improvement in the classifier's capacity to recognize positive cases accurately. The classifier appears to have benefited from the extra training data that larger folds gave, as seen by the increasing trend, which increases the classifier's ability to accurately capture the traits of positive examples as shown in Figure 3.

Figure 3. Cross-fold validation for proposed framework

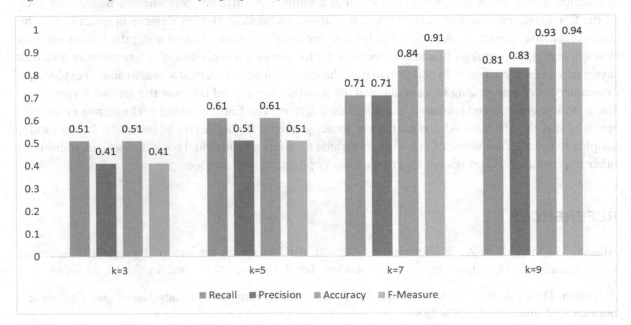

Similar results were shown for accuracy, which significantly improved from 41% to 83% as the number of folds rose. This improvement suggests a lower incidence of false positives, demonstrating the classifier's increased skill in correctly labeling cases as positive. The classifier had a better level of confidence in its positive predictions, as seen by the rising precision values, which led to fewer misclassifications.

Additionally, when the number of folds grew, the accuracy parameter showed an increasing trajectory from 51% to 93%. This finding suggests that adding additional folds to the cross-validation procedure increased the classifier's overall accuracy in predicting the classes of instances. The classifier's accuracy has significantly increased, thus enhancing its dependability and efficiency.

Additionally, as the number of folds rose, the F1 metric showed a substantial improvement, going from 41% to 94%. A balanced trade-off between accuracy and recall is indicated by the F1 score's upward trend, which shows that the classifier successfully struck a balance between accurately detecting positive examples and reducing false positives.

These findings show the importance of the cross-validation method and how it affects the effectiveness of the classifier. The classifier benefits from a bigger training set, resulting in improved discriminating abilities and a greater degree of accuracy when classifying instances, as shown by the steady gains in recall, precision, accuracy, and F1 measure with an increasing number of folds. The results highlight the significance of careful attention when choosing the ideal number of folds in cross-validation, as it can greatly affect the classifier's performance.

CONCLUSION AND FUTURE WORK

In this study, a safe framework for creating an anomaly classification detection framework in IoT networks utilizing blockchain and deep learning was provided. The framework was designed to identify anomalies. The suggested architecture looked at a number of different performance metrics for each of the CNNs and ensured the safety of data transmissions between the IoT devices in smart homes by using blockchain contracts. A substantial level of accuracy has been reached using the framework that was suggested that employs blockchain technology for secure transmission of information in different layers using smart contracts. In addition to this, the study that was presented was also able to explore the consequences of introducing blockchain, and the data that was passed between the various layers of the framework was preserved unaltered in a distributed setting. The findings of the performance evaluation revealed that the CNN-based categorization strategy offered higher levels of accuracy. In the future, we plan to broaden the scope of our work to include a variety of additional huge datasets, in addition to other improved RNN approaches that make use of optimization techniques.

REFERENCES

Alamri, M., Jhanjhi, N. Z., & Humayun, M. (2019). Blockchain for Internet of Things (IoT) Research Issues Challenges \& Future Directions: A Review. *Int. J. Comput. Sci. Netw. Secur*, *19*, 244–258.

Alferidah, D. K., & Jhanjhi, N. Z. (2020). A Review on Security and Privacy Issues and Challenges. *Internet of Things, 20*(4), 263–285.

Alhajri, M. I., Ali, N. T., & Shubair, R. M. (2018). Classification of Indoor Environments for IoT Applications: A Machine Learning Approach. *IEEE Antennas and Wireless Propagation Letters*, *17*(12), 2164–2168. doi:10.1109/LAWP.2018.2869548

Almusaylim, Z. A., & Zaman, N. (2019). A review on smart home present state and challenges: Linked to context-awareness internet of things (IoT). *Wireless Networks*, *25*(6), 3193–3204. doi:10.1007/s11276-018-1712-5

Alrashdi, I., Alqazzaz, A., Aloufi, E., Alharthi, R., Zohdy, M., & Ming, H. (2019). AD-IoT: Anomaly detection of IoT cyberattacks in smart city using machine learning. *2019 IEEE 9th Annual Computing and Communication Workshop and Conference, CCWC 2019*, (pp. 305–310). IEEE. 10.1109/CCWC.2019.8666450

Anthi, E., Williams, L., Javed, A., & Burnap, P. (2021). Hardening machine learning denial of service (DoS) defences against adversarial attacks in IoT smart home networks. *Computers & Security*, *108*, 102352. doi:10.1016/j.cose.2021.102352

Bajpai, S., Sharma, K., & Chaurasia, B. K. (2023). Intrusion Detection Framework in IoT Networks. *SN Computer Science*, *4*(4), 1–17. doi:10.1007/s42979-023-01770-9

Benkhelifa, E., Welsh, T., & Hamouda, W. (2018). A critical review of practices and challenges in intrusion detection systems for IoT: Toward universal and resilient systems. *IEEE Communications Surveys and Tutorials*, *20*(4), 3496–3509. doi:10.1109/COMST.2018.2844742

Bianchi, V., Bassoli, M., Lombardo, G., Fornacciari, P., Mordonini, M., & De Munari, I. (2019). IoT Wearable Sensor and Deep Learning: An Integrated Approach for Personalized Human Activity Recognition in a Smart Home Environment. *IEEE Internet of Things Journal*, *6*(5), 8553–8562. doi:10.1109/JIOT.2019.2920283

Chicco, D., & Jurman, G. (2020). The advantages of the Matthews correlation coefficient (MCC) over F1 score and accuracy in binary classification evaluation. *BMC Genomics*, *21*(1), 1–13. doi:10.1186/s12864-019-6413-7 PMID:31898477

Chow, J. K., Su, Z., Wu, J., Tan, P. S., Mao, X., & Wang, Y. H. (2020). Anomaly detection of defects on concrete structures with the convolutional autoencoder. *Advanced Engineering Informatics*, *45*(December 2019). doi:10.1016/j.aei.2020.101105

Churcher, A., Ullah, R., Ahmad, J., Ur Rehman, S., Masood, F., Gogate, M., Alqahtani, F., Nour, B., & Buchanan, W. J. (2021). An experimental analysis of attack classification using machine learning in IoT networks. *Sensors (Basel)*, *21*(2), 446. doi:10.3390/s21020446 PMID:33435202

Cvitić, I., Peraković, D., Periša, M., & Gupta, B. (2021). Ensemble machine learning approach for classification of IoT devices in smart home. *International Journal of Machine Learning and Cybernetics*, *12*(11), 3179–3202. doi:10.1007/s13042-020-01241-0

Ferrag, M. A., Shu, L., Yang, X., Derhab, A., & Maglaras, L. (2020). Security and privacy for green IoT-based agriculture: Review, blockchain solutions, and challenges. *IEEE Access : Practical Innovations, Open Solutions*, *8*, 32031–32053. doi:10.1109/ACCESS.2020.2973178

He, W., Zhang, Z., & Li, W. (2021). Information technology solutions, challenges, and suggestions for tackling the COVID-19 pandemic. *International Journal of Information Management*, *57*, 102287. doi:10.1016/j.ijinfomgt.2020.102287 PMID:33318721

Humayun, M. (2020). Role of emerging IoT big data and cloud computing for real time application. [IJACSA]. *International Journal of Advanced Computer Science and Applications*, *11*(4). doi:10.14569/IJACSA.2020.0110466

Humayun, M., Jhanjhi, N. Z., Alamri, M. Z., & Khan, A. (2020). Smart cities and digital governance. In *Employing Recent Technologies for Improved Digital Governance* (pp. 87–106). IGI Global. doi:10.4018/978-1-7998-1851-9.ch005

Humayun, M., Niazi, M., Jhanjhi, N., Alshayeb, M., & Mahmood, S. (2020). Cyber Security Threats and Vulnerabilities: A Systematic Mapping Study. *Arabian Journal for Science and Engineering*, *45*(4), 3171–3189. doi:10.1007/s13369-019-04319-2

Hussain, F., Hussain, R., Hassan, S. A., & Hossain, E. (2020). Machine learning in IoT security: Current solutions and future challenges. *IEEE Communications Surveys \& Tutorials*, *22*(3), 1686–1721.

Javed, A. R., Fahad, L. G., Farhan, A. A., Abbas, S., Srivastava, G., Parizi, R. M., & Khan, M. S. (2021). Automated cognitive health assessment in smart homes using machine learning. *Sustainable Cities and Society*, *65*(April 2020), 102572. doi:10.1016/j.scs.2020.102572

Khan, N. A., Jhanjhi, N. Z., Brohi, S. N., Usmani, R. S. A., & Nayyar, A. (2020). Smart traffic monitoring system using unmanned aerial vehicles (UAVs). *Computer Communications*, *157*, 434–443. doi:10.1016/j.comcom.2020.04.049

Khan, S., Amin, M. B., Azar, A. T., & Aslam, S. (2021). Towards interoperable blockchains: A survey on the role of smart contracts in blockchain interoperability. *IEEE Access : Practical Innovations, Open Solutions*, *9*, 116672–116691. doi:10.1109/ACCESS.2021.3106384

Kishore Kumar, K. (2021). IoT-based smart agriculture. Handbook of Research on Innovations and Applications of AI, IoT, and Cognitive Technologies, 5(6), 63–77. doi:10.4018/978-1-7998-6870-5.ch004

Li, J., Zhang, W., Zhang, Z., Li, X., & Yang, X. (2022). Predictive control based on event-triggering mechanism of cyber-physical systems under denial-of-service attacks. *Information Sciences*, *586*, 294–309. doi:10.1016/j.ins.2021.11.082

Li, S., Hao, Z., Ding, L., & Xu, X. (2019). Research on the application of information technology of Big Data in Chinese digital library. *Library Management*, *40*(8/9), 518–531. doi:10.1108/LM-04-2019-0021

Liang, H., Sun, X., Sun, Y., & Gao, Y. (2017). Text feature extraction based on deep learning: A review. *EURASIP Journal on Wireless Communications and Networking*, *2017*(1), 1–12. doi:10.1186/s13638-017-0993-1 PMID:29263717

Liang, T., Zeng, B., Liu, J., Ye, L., & Zou, C. (2018). An unsupervised user behavior prediction algorithm based on machine learning and neural network for smart home. *IEEE Access : Practical Innovations, Open Solutions*, *6*, 49237–49247. doi:10.1109/ACCESS.2018.2868984

Liang, W., Li, K.-C., Long, J., Kui, X., & Zomaya, A. Y. (2019). An industrial network intrusion detection algorithm based on multifeature data clustering optimization model. *IEEE Transactions on Industrial Informatics*, *16*(3), 2063–2071. doi:10.1109/TII.2019.2946791

Meidan, Y., Bohadana, M., Shabtai, A., Guarnizo, J. D., Ochoa, M., Tippenhauer, N. O., & Elovici, Y. (2017). ProfilIoT: A machine learning approach for IoT device identification based on network traffic analysis. *Proceedings of the ACM Symposium on Applied Computing, Part F1280*, (pp. 506–509). ACM. 10.1145/3019612.3019878

Ojha, T., Misra, S., & Raghuwanshi, N. S. (2021). Internet of Things for Agricultural Applications: The State of the Art. *IEEE Internet of Things Journal*, *8*(14), 10973–10997. doi:10.1109/JIOT.2021.3051418

Piccialli, F., Cuomo, S., Cola, V. S., & Casolla, G. (2019). A machine learning approach for IoT cultural data. *Journal of Ambient Intelligence and Humanized Computing*, (0123456789). doi:10.1007/s12652-019-01452-6

Priyadarshini, I., Sahu, S., Kumar, R., & Taniar, D. (2022). A machine-learning ensemble model for predicting energy consumption in smart homes. *Internet of Things : Engineering Cyber Physical Human Systems*, *20*(November), 100636. doi:10.1016/j.iot.2022.100636

Sabokrou, M., Fayyaz, M., Fathy, M., Moayed, Z., & Klette, R. (2018). Deep-anomaly: Fully convolutional neural network for fast anomaly detection in crowded scenes. *Computer Vision and Image Understanding*, *172*(October 2017), 88–97. doi:10.1016/j.cviu.2018.02.006

Saura, J. R., Ribeiro-Soriano, D., & Palacios-Marqués, D. (2021). Setting privacy "by default" in social IoT: Theorizing the challenges and directions in Big Data Research. *Big Data Research*, *25*, 100245. doi:10.1016/j.bdr.2021.100245

Shi, S., He, D., Li, L., Kumar, N., Khan, M. K., & Choo, K.-K. R. (2020). Applications of blockchain in ensuring the security and privacy of electronic health record systems: A survey. *Computers & Security, 97*, 101966.

Soe, Y. N., Feng, Y., Santosa, P. I., Hartanto, R., & Sakurai, K. (2020). Machine learning-based IoT-botnet attack detection with sequential architecture. *Sensors (Basel), 20*(16), 4372. doi:10.3390/s20164372 PMID:32764394

Sovacool, B. K., & Del Rio, D. D. F. (2020). Smart home technologies in Europe: A critical review of concepts, benefits, risks and policies. *Renewable & Sustainable Energy Reviews, 120*, 109663. doi:10.1016/j.rser.2019.109663

Spanos, G., Giannoutakis, K. M., Votis, K., & Tzovaras, D. (2019). Combining statistical and machine learning techniques in IoT anomaly detection for smart homes. *IEEE International Workshop on Computer Aided Modeling and Design of Communication Links and Networks, CAMAD, 2019-Septe*, (pp. 1–6). IEEE. 10.1109/CAMAD.2019.8858490

Strengers, Y., Kennedy, J., Arcari, P., Nicholls, L., & Gregg, M. (2019). Protection, productivity and pleasure in the smart home: Emerging expectations and gendered insights from Australian early adopters. In *Proceedings of the 2019 CHI conference on human factors in computing systems* (pp. 1–13). ACM. 10.1145/3290605.3300875

Tahir, S., Hafeez, Y., Abbas, M. A., Nawaz, A., & Hamid, B. (2022). Smart Learning Objects Retrieval for E-Learning with Contextual Recommendation based on Collaborative Filtering. *Education and Information Technologies, 27*(6), 1–38. doi:10.1007/s10639-022-10966-0

Taylor, P. J., Dargahi, T., Dehghantanha, A., Parizi, R. M., & Choo, K. K. R. (2020). A systematic literature review of blockchain cyber security. *Digital Communications and Networks, 6*(2), 147–156. doi:10.1016/j.dcan.2019.01.005

Ullah, I., & Mahmoud, Q. H. (2020). A scheme for generating a dataset for anomalous activity detection in iot networks. In *Advances in Artificial Intelligence: 33rd Canadian Conference on Artificial Intelligence, Canadian AI 2020, Ottawa, ON, Canada, May 13–15, 2020. Proceedings, 33*, 508–520.

Xiao, L., Wan, X., Lu, X., Zhang, Y., & Wu, D. (2018). IoT security techniques based on machine learning: How do IoT devices use AI to enhance security? *IEEE Signal Processing Magazine, 35*(5), 41–49. doi:10.1109/MSP.2018.2825478

Zaheer, A., Tahir, S., Almufareh, M. F., & Hamid, B. (2023). A Hybrid Model for Botnet Detection using Machine Learning. In *2023 International Conference on Business Analytics for Technology and Security (ICBATS)* (pp. 1–8). IEEE. 10.1109/ICBATS57792.2023.10111161

Zaidan, A. A., & Zaidan, B. B. (2020). A review on intelligent process for smart home applications based on IoT: Coherent taxonomy, motivation, open challenges, and recommendations. *Artificial Intelligence Review, 53*(1), 141–165. doi:10.1007/s10462-018-9648-9

Zhang, Y., Liao, Q. V., & Bellamy, R. K. E. (2020). Effect of confidence and explanation on accuracy and trust calibration in AI-assisted decision making. In *Proceedings of the 2020 conference on fairness, accountability, and transparency* (pp. 295–305). IEEE. 10.1145/3351095.3372852

Chapter 7
Securing the Digital Supply Chain Cyber Threats and Vulnerabilities

Siva Raja Sindiramutty
Taylor's University, Malaysia

Navid Ali Khan
Taylor's University, Malaysia

Noor Zaman Jhanjhi
iD https://orcid.org/0000-0001-8116-4733
Taylor's University, Malaysia

Bhavin Shah
Lok Jagruti University, India

Chong Eng Tan
iD https://orcid.org/0000-0002-3990-3501
Universiti Malaysia Sarawak, Malaysia

Loveleen Gaur
iD https://orcid.org/0000-0002-0885-1550
University of South Pacific, Fiji

ABSTRACT

The digital supply chain has become an integral part of modern business operations, enabling efficient and streamlined processes. However, with the rapid advancement of technology, the supply chain landscape has become increasingly vulnerable to cyber threats and attacks. This chapter explores the critical issue of cybersecurity within the context of the digital supply chain, aiming to equip professionals and practitioners with the knowledge and strategies to safeguard their operations. Lastly, the chapter sheds light on emerging technologies and future trends and concludes with a call to action for securing the digital supply chain. It also highlights the future challenges and directions in cybersecurity for the supply chain, urging professionals to stay vigilant and adapt to evolving strategies and technologies. Overall, this chapter serves as a comprehensive guide for securing the digital supply chain, empowering readers to fortify their operations against cyber threats and ensure the resilience of their supply chain networks.

DOI: 10.4018/978-1-6684-7625-3.ch007

INTRODUCTION

Overview of the Digital Supply Chain

Figure 1. Digital supply chain
(Hitachi, Ltd., 2020)

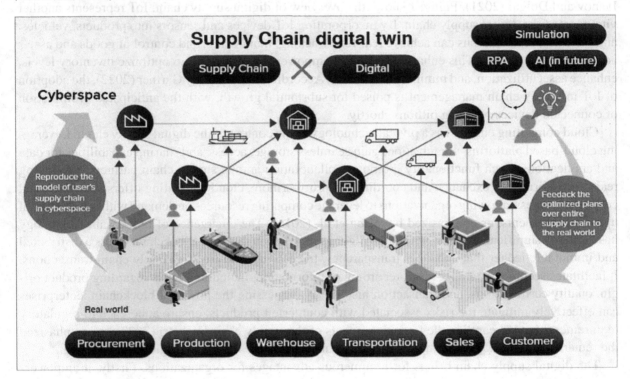

The concept of the digital supply chain has emerged as a transformative force within the field of supply chain management. By leveraging advanced technologies, this approach seeks to improve operational efficiency, visibility, and responsiveness. In response to the rise of digitalization, organizations from various industries are increasingly adopting digital supply chain strategies to gain a competitive advantage in the global marketplace. This section presents a comprehensive overview of the digital supply chain, encompassing its key components, benefits, and challenges. The information is drawn from a synthesis of scholarly research and industry reports. At its core, the digital supply chain involves the integration of various digital technologies into traditional supply chain processes. These technologies include artificial intelligence (AI), big data analytics, the Internet of Things (IoT), cloud computing, and blockchain. By incorporating these advancements, the digital supply chain enables the efficient collection, analysis, and utilization of vast amounts of data. This data-driven approach facilitates real-time decision-making, predictive analytics, and automation, thereby driving improvements in overall supply chain performance (Gaur et al 2022). According to a study conducted by Garay-Rondero et al. (2019), organizations that successfully implement digital supply chain solutions can experience notable enhancements in efficiency, cost reduction, customer satisfaction, and overall performance. Within the digital supply chain framework, data analytics plays a pivotal role as a key component. Through the utilization of big data analytics, organizations can extract valuable insights about customer behaviour, demand patterns, and operational performance. For instance, the application of predictive analytics enables organizations to more accurately forecast demand, thereby facilitating proactive inventory management and mitigating instances of stockouts. Moreover, real-time data analytics empowers organizations to monitor and optimize their supply chain processes, resulting in heightened agility and responsiveness, as highlighted by Ivanov and Dolgui (2021). Figure 1 shows the overview of digital supply chain. IoT represents another vital facet of the digital supply chain. By incorporating IoT devices and sensors into products, vehicles, and facilities, organizations can achieve real-time tracking, monitoring, and control of goods and assets across the supply chain. This enhanced visibility empowers organizations to optimize inventory levels, enhance asset utilization, and minimize lead times. According to a report by Gartner (2022), the adoption of IoT in supply chain management is poised for substantial growth, with the anticipated proliferation of connected devices reaching billions shortly.

Cloud computing emerges as a pivotal technology in the context of the digital supply chain. Leveraging cloud-based platforms, organizations gain seamless storage, access, and sharing capabilities for data and applications. Such functionality promotes collaboration among supply chain partners, facilitating real-time information exchange and coordination. Furthermore, cloud computing offers scalability and cost-effectiveness, allowing organizations to leverage computing resources on demand without substantial upfront investments, as emphasized by Wang et al. (2016). The emergence of blockchain technology has garnered significant interest within the digital supply chain domain. Blockchain offers a distributed and immutable ledger that enhances transparency, traceability, and trust in supply chain transactions. It facilitates secure and tamper-proof recording of information, including details regarding product origin, quality certifications, and transaction history. By harnessing the power of blockchain, enterprises can effectively mitigate the risks associated with counterfeit products, ensure adherence to regulatory requirements, and streamline the financial aspects of the supply chain. Kshetri (2022) has emphasized the remarkable advantages of employing blockchain technology within the digital supply chain.

The digital supply chain brings forth numerous advantages for organizations. Firstly, it empowers organizations to bolster operational efficiency by automating repetitive tasks, optimizing processes, and minimizing manual errors. As a result, organizations can achieve cost savings and enhanced productivity. Secondly, the digital supply chain amplifies visibility throughout the supply chain, allowing organizations to track and monitor inventory levels, shipments, and performance metrics in real-time. This heightened visibility facilitates proactive issue identification and resolution, leading to reduced disruptions and improved customer service (Salikhov et al., 2023; Priyadarshini et al., 2021). Nevertheless, the adoption of digital supply chain strategies comes with its share of challenges. Organizations must tackle concerns surrounding data security and privacy since the heightened connectivity and data sharing associated with digitalization can expose them to cyber threats and breaches. Moreover, enterprises may face opposition to transformation and require significant investments in both infrastructure and workforce enhancement to proficiently execute digital solutions within the supply chain. It is imperative to recognize and tackle these obstacles to guarantee the triumphant assimilation of digital strategies into the supply chain framework. (Korpela et al., 2017). In summary, the digital supply chain signifies a transformative change in the realm of supply chain management, harnessing cutting-edge technologies to bolster efficiency, transparency, and adaptability. By incorporating data analytics, IoT, cloud computing, and blockchain, enterprises can acquire invaluable insights, elevate visibility, and optimize operations across the supply chain. However, alongside its myriad advantages, the digital supply chain necessitates the careful navigation of challenges about data security, privacy, and managing organizational change. Overall, the digital supply chain presents substantial prospects for organizations to secure a competitive edge in today's ever-evolving business landscape.

Importance of Cybersecurity in the Supply Chain Context

In the contemporary era of interconnectivity and digitalization, the supply chain has evolved into a complex web of entities, systems, and processes that bear substantial significance in the global economy. Nevertheless, this heightened interconnectivity and dependence on technology have also rendered supply chains vulnerable to a multitude of cybersecurity risks. Cyber threats directed at the supply chain can disrupt operations, compromise confidential data, and erode trust among partners (Hamid et al., 2019; Humayan et al., 2020). Consequently, it is of utmost importance to acknowledge the significance of cybersecurity within the supply chain domain and adopt resilient measures to fortify defences against cyber threats. The supply chain ecosystem encompasses the intricate exchange of extensive volumes of sensitive information, encompassing trade secrets, financial data, and intellectual property. Unauthorized access or breaches of this data can lead to significant financial ramifications and irreparable harm to a company's standing. Thus, the implementation of cybersecurity measures, including encryption, access controls, and secure communication channels, is paramount to safeguarding the confidentiality and integrity of such critical information (Wong et al., 2022; Schniederjans et al., 2020).

Cyberattacks targeting the supply chain possess the capability to disrupt crucial operations, resulting in production delays, delivery shortcomings, and financial losses. Hence, organizations must establish resilient cybersecurity protocols to proactively detect and effectively mitigate potential threats. Implementing intrusion detection systems, regular vulnerability assessments, and formulating incident response plans are imperative steps in ensuring uninterrupted operations and minimizing the adverse consequences of cyber incidents. (Pournader et al., 2019; Kalogeraki et al., 2018). Contemporary supply chains heavily rely on an extensive network of suppliers, vendors, and contractors. While these external entities bring forth efficiency and specialization, they also introduce inherent cybersecurity vulnerabilities. Cybercriminals may exploit these weaker links within the supply chain to gain unauthorized access to critical systems or introduce malicious software. To mitigate third-party risks and bolster the overall security framework of the supply chain, it is crucial to enforce stringent cybersecurity requirements for third-party vendors, conduct regular audits to assess their compliance, and establish secure communication channels. By implementing these measures, organizations can fortify their defences, minimize the potential for breaches, and enhance the overall security posture of the supply chain. (Hammi et al.,2023; Bandari 2023).

Figure 2. Ten cybersecurity threats
(Doyle, 2020)

Figure 2 shows the top 15 common cybersecurity threats. The regulatory framework about cybersecurity is continuously evolving, as governments and industry organizations enforce stringent requirements to safeguard sensitive data and preserve privacy. Adhering to these regulations, such as the General Data Protection Regulation (GDPR) or the California Consumer Privacy Act (CCPA), is imperative to evade legal ramifications and uphold the confidence of customers and stakeholders. To meet these regulatory obligations, it is vital to implement robust cybersecurity measures, including data encryption, access controls, and incident response plans. These measures not only help organizations meet their legal responsibilities but also contribute to enhancing overall data protection and mitigating potential cybersecurity risks. (Ramgovind et al., 2010; Ali et al., 2017) The trust serves as the cornerstone of fruitful partnerships within the supply chain. A breach of trust resulting from a cyber incident can have profound repercussions, undermining business relationships and tarnishing a brand's reputation. By prioritizing cybersecurity, organizations can showcase their dedication to safeguarding sensitive information, thereby fostering trust among partners and reinforcing the overall resilience of the supply chain ecosystem. Such proactive measures not only instil confidence but also contribute to the long-term sustainability and success of collaborative endeavours within the supply chain (Ahmed et al., 2023; Aljabhan and Obaidat 2023). To summarize, the significance of cybersecurity in the context of the supply chain cannot be emphasized enough. Given the ever-changing threat landscape, organizations must take proactive steps in implementing robust cybersecurity measures. This is crucial to safeguard confidential information, maintain uninterrupted operations, mitigate third-party risks, adhere to regulatory requirements, and preserve trust within the supply chain. By adopting a comprehensive cybersecurity strategy and remaining vigilant to emerging threats, organizations can strengthen their supply chains against cyber risks and retain a competitive advantage in today's interconnected and digital global marketplace.

The key objective of this chapter is to provide a comprehensive understanding of the cyber threats and vulnerabilities that exist within the digital supply chain. It aims to raise awareness about the potential consequences of cyber breaches in the supply chain and highlight the importance of implementing robust cybersecurity measures. The chapter will explore common cyber threats targeting the supply chain through case studies, analyze vulnerabilities in supply chain processes, and emphasize the significance of conducting risk assessments and vulnerability management. Additionally, it will discuss the integration of cybersecurity into supply chain risk management frameworks, outline best practices for securing supplier relationships, information systems, and data, and provide insights into incident response and ensuring supply chain resilience.

UNDERSTANDING THE DIGITAL SUPPLY CHAIN

Components and Stakeholders in the Digital Supply Chain

The traditional supply chain has evolved into a digital supply chain, which leverages digital technologies and data to enhance efficiency, visibility, and collaboration across the supply chain network (Zhao et al., 2023). The digital supply chain consists of various components and involves multiple stakeholders, each playing a crucial role in the seamless flow of goods, information, and services. This section aims to provide an overview of the key components and stakeholders in the digital supply chain.

- **Components of the Digital Supply Chain**

  1. Suppliers and Manufacturer

Suppliers play a vital role in the digital supply chain as they contribute raw materials, components, or finished products that are integral to the manufacturing or distribution process. They serve as a crucial link in the supply chain ecosystem, ensuring the availability of essential resources necessary for the smooth operation of the entire supply chain (Tan et al., 2022). In the digital supply chain realm, suppliers are progressively embracing digital technologies to augment their operational capacities. A notable instance includes the utilization of sophisticated analytics to anticipate demand, monitor inventory levels in real time, and optimize production schedules (Soori et al., 2023). These digital capabilities empower suppliers to promptly and efficiently address customer demands while fostering enhanced collaboration with other participants within the supply chain. Manufacturers, in particular, assume a pivotal position in the digital supply chain, whereby they convert raw materials or components into refined and final goods (Mantravadi & Srai, 2023; Humayan et al., 2020b). In the era defined by digital advancements, manufacturers are embracing a range of cutting-edge technologies, including the IoT, automation, and robotics, to optimize their production processes (Peter et al., 2023). IoT devices play a pivotal role by gathering data from manufacturing equipment, facilitating real-time monitoring, and enabling predictive maintenance (Abusitta et al., 2023; Alferidah., 2020). The integration of automation and robotics within manufacturing operations enhances production efficiency and empowers manufacturers to swiftly adapt to evolving demand patterns (Li et al., 2023). Moreover, manufacturers harness the potential of digital platforms and analytics to obtain valuable insights into their operations, enabling them to make informed decisions based on data and enhance the overall performance of the supply chain (Rathore, 2023).

2. Distributors and Retailers

Distributors and retailers hold a vital position as key stakeholders within the digital supply chain, playing a significant role in facilitating the movement of goods from manufacturers to end consumers (Saranya & Maheswari, 2023). In this digital age, distributors and retailers are actively embracing digital technologies to streamline their operations and enhance the overall customer experience (Tombe & Smuts, 2023). Notably, they leverage e-commerce platforms to effectively market and sell products online, offering customers a seamless ordering and fulfilment process (Pandey & Munjal, 2023). The utilization of advanced analytics and artificial intelligence (AI) algorithms empowers distributors and retailers to optimize inventory levels, personalize marketing campaigns, and enhance the accuracy of demand forecasting (Tang et al., 2023).

3. Logistics and Transportation Providers

Within the digital supply chain, logistics and transportation providers bear the responsibility of physically moving goods, ensuring their timely and accurate delivery to the intended destinations (Xue & Lai, 2023). In the context of the digital era, these providers harness various technologies, including GPS tracking, route optimization software, and real-time visibility tools, to enhance the efficiency of their operations (Kanyepe, 2023). Through the deployment of such digital capabilities, logistics and transportation companies can monitor shipments in real-time, optimize delivery routes, and proactively mitigate potential disruptions (Dzemydienė et al., 2023). By augmenting visibility and facilitating co-ordinated efforts, these providers significantly contribute to the overall agility and responsiveness of the digital supply chain.

4. Technology Providers

Technology providers play a pivotal role in enabling and supporting the digital supply chain, offering a diverse range of digital solutions that enhance and streamline supply chain operations (Vishwakarma et al., 2022). Notably, enterprise resource planning (ERP) systems serve as a prime example by integrating various functions within organizations, encompassing inventory management, production planning, and financial operations (Rahardja, 2023). Supply chain management software further aids in optimizing supply chain processes, tracking inventory, and improving the accuracy of demand forecasting (Yenugula et al., 2023). Moreover, emerging technologies like blockchain and artificial intelligence have the potential to revolutionize supply chain operations by enhancing traceability, transparency, and decision-making capabilities (Aruna et al., 2023). These advancements signify the critical role of technology providers in empowering the digital supply chain ecosystem.

Figure 3. Digital supply chain management
(Team, 2023)

- **Stakeholders in the Digital Supply Chain**

  1. **Customers, Government, and Regulatory Bodies**

Customers play a pivotal role as vital stakeholders within the digital supply chain, as their demand patterns and preferences significantly influence the entire network (Gupta et al., 2023). In the digital era, customers have elevated expectations in terms of product availability, personalized experiences, and prompt delivery (Ta et al., 2023). They engage with various digital touchpoints, such as e-commerce platforms, social media channels, and mobile applications. By effectively capturing and analyzing customer data, companies can gain valuable insights into customer preferences, optimize their product offerings, and provide personalized recommendations (Dwivedi et al., 2022). Engaging with customers and fulfilling their needs are pivotal factors contributing to success within the digital supply chain landscape. Government agencies and regulatory bodies hold a prominent position in shaping and governing the digital supply chain, as they are responsible for establishing and enforcing regulations about trade, safety, security, and data protection (Dubey et al., 2023). Their scope of influence encompasses regulations concerning customs processes, import/export restrictions, and product quality standards. In the digital era, governments are proactively addressing emerging concerns like data privacy and cybersecurity (Afenyo & Caesar, 2023; Humayan et al., 2021). Compliance with government regulations is paramount for supply chain stakeholders, as it ensures the seamless operation of their processes and mitigates potential legal and reputational risks. By adhering to these regulations, stakeholders can safeguard their operations and maintain ethical standards within the digital supply chain ecosystem.

2.   Industry Associations, Standards Organizations, and Financial Institutions

Industry associations and standards organizations play a pivotal role in advancing and implementing best practices within the digital supply chain, fostering collaboration and knowledge sharing among stakeholders (Iranmanesh et al., 2023). These organizations are instrumental in establishing industry standards, guidelines, and certifications that promote consistency and interoperability throughout the supply chain (Bavoria, 2023). For instance, GS1 is renowned for its development and maintenance of global standards for barcodes and product identification. Collaborating with industry associations and adhering to industry standards empowers supply chain stakeholders to enhance efficiency, reduce costs, and improve overall supply chain performance. In the digital supply chain, financial institutions, including banks and payment providers, assume a crucial role. They facilitate financial transactions and offer working capital solutions to support supply chain stakeholders (Hasan et al., 2023). These institutions play a vital role in enabling smooth financial operations within the digital supply chain ecosystem, ensuring timely and secure payment transactions while providing necessary financial resources to sustain the supply chain's functioning. In the digital era, financial institutions are adopting technologies such as blockchain and digital payment platforms to enhance security, transparency, and efficiency in financial transactions (Tsai, 2022). These technologies enable faster and more secure cross-border payments, reduce transaction costs, and improve cash flow management for supply chain participants.

The digital supply chain encompasses a diverse array of components and involves numerous stakeholders, each with a vital role in facilitating the seamless movement of goods, information, and services. Suppliers, manufacturers, distributors, retailers, logistics and transportation providers, technology providers, customers, government and regulatory bodies, industry associations, and financial institutions collectively contribute to the effectiveness and efficiency of the digital supply chain ecosystem. Through the utilization of digital technologies, data analytics, and collaborative platforms, these stakeholders can drive innovation, enhance visibility, elevate customer experiences, and gain a competitive edge within the dynamic and ever-evolving business landscape of today. By embracing the potential of the digital era, stakeholders in the digital supply chain can unlock new possibilities and cultivate a thriving and resilient supply chain network.

Benefits and Challenges of Digitization in Supply Chain Management

This section explores the advantages and obstacles associated with the digitization of supply chain management. In recent times, the introduction of digital technologies has fundamentally transformed the way supply chains function, offering businesses opportunities to streamline operations, boost visibility, and enhance overall efficiency. However, despite the numerous benefits, digitization also presents several challenges that organizations must address to fully leverage its potential. This section highlights the key advantages of digitization in supply chain management, including heightened agility, improved collaboration, enhanced data analytics, and increased customer satisfaction. Additionally, it delves into the challenges that arise, such as cybersecurity risks, concerns over data privacy, technology integration complexities, and the need for skilled talent. By comprehending these benefits and challenges, organizations can navigate the digitization journey more effectively and harness its transformative capabilities within their supply chain operations. Figure 4 shows the important key element in digital supply chain.

Figure 4. Key element in digital supply chain

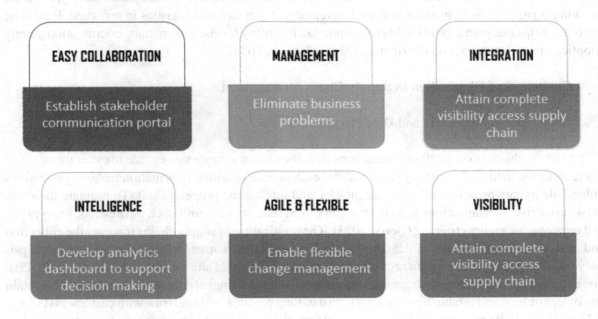

Benefits of Digitization in Supply Chain Management

1. Increased Agility and Improved Collaboration

The digitization of supply chain management empowers organizations to swiftly adapt to changing market conditions and evolving customer demands. Through the implementation of digital technologies, companies can automate processes, enhance the flow of information, and attain real-time visibility into their supply chains. This heightened agility enables organizations to make rapid and informed decisions, accelerate product launches, and effectively respond to disruptions (Raj et al., 2023). Digital platforms facilitate seamless collaboration and the sharing of information among supply chain partners. Cloud-based technologies, for instance, enable real-time data exchange, enabling stakeholders to access and update information simultaneously. Such enhanced collaboration enhances supply chain visibility, fosters trust among partners, and facilitates expedited issue resolution (Tiwari et al., 2023).

2. Enhanced Data Analytics and Improved Customer Satisfaction

The process of digitization generates a vast volume of data, which can be harnessed and analyzed to extract valuable insights. Advanced analytics tools enable organizations to gain a deeper understanding of their supply chains, identify patterns, optimize processes, and make data-driven decisions. By leveraging data analytics, businesses can enhance forecasting accuracy, reduce inventory costs, and improve overall operational efficiency (Aziz, 2023). Digitization also enables organizations to deliver a seamless and personalized customer experience. By integrating digital technologies throughout the supply chain, companies can provide real-time tracking, efficient order management, and personalized communication. These enhancements contribute to improved customer satisfaction, loyalty, and brand reputation (Sharma & Joshi, 2020). Furthermore, digitization provides end-to-end visibility into the supply chain, allowing organizations to monitor and track inventory, shipments, and logistics in real-time. Real-time visibility helps mitigate supply chain risks, optimize inventory levels, and enhance coordination among suppliers, manufacturers, and distributors (Mubarik et al., 2023).

- **Challenges of Digitization in Supply Chain Management**

    1. Cybersecurity Risks and Data Privacy Concerns:

As supply chains undergo digital transformation, they become more susceptible to cyber threats. The interconnected nature of digital systems and the exchange of sensitive information make organizations vulnerable to data breaches, ransomware attacks, and intellectual property theft. To mitigate these cybersecurity risks, organizations need to invest in robust security measures such as firewalls, encryption, and employee awareness training (Berry, 2023). The digitization of supply chains involves the collection and analysis of large volumes of data, including personal and sensitive information. Ensuring data privacy and complying with relevant regulations, such as the General Data Protection Regulation (GDPR), present significant challenges. Organizations must implement stringent data protection measures, obtain customer consent, and establish transparent data handling practices to build trust with customers (George & George, 2023). By prioritizing data privacy and security, organizations can safeguard sensitive information and maintain compliance with regulatory requirements, thereby fostering customer trust and loyalty.

2. Technology Integration and Skilled Talent Requirement

The process of digitization often involves the integration of different digital systems, such as Enterprise Resource Planning (ERP), Customer Relationship Management (CRM), and Transportation Management Systems (TMS). However, integrating these disparate systems can be a complex and time-consuming task, requiring careful planning, resource allocation, and change management efforts (Satriawan, 2023; Ponnusamy et al., 2020). Implementing and managing digital supply chain systems also requires a skilled workforce capable of effectively leveraging emerging technologies. Organizations must invest in talent development programs, recruit professionals with digital expertise, and provide continuous training to keep pace with evolving technologies (Shajek & Hartmann, 2023). By nurturing a skilled workforce, organizations can effectively navigate the challenges of digitization, harness the full potential of digital technologies, and drive innovation within their supply chain operations.

The advent of digitization has brought about significant transformation in supply chain management, offering a multitude of benefits to organizations. Embracing digitization enables increased agility, improved collaboration, enhanced data analytics, heightened customer satisfaction, and improved supply chain visibility. These advantages empower organizations to respond swiftly to market dynamics, streamline operations, and achieve operational excellence. However, organizations must address the challenges that accompany digitization. This includes mitigating cybersecurity risks, ensuring data privacy, managing technology integration complexities, and acquiring and nurturing the necessary talent. By proactively tackling these challenges, organizations can fully leverage the potential of digitization and elevate their supply chain management practices to new heights of success.

Integration of Information Systems and Technologies

The advent of the digital revolution has revolutionized supply chain management, leading to significant changes in traditional practices and paving the way for a more connected and efficient ecosystem. The integration of information systems and technologies holds immense importance in optimizing the digital supply chain, enabling organizations to enhance visibility, streamline processes, and effectively respond to market demands. This report aims to explore the significance of integrating information systems and technologies in the digital supply chain, analyzing key benefits, challenges, and best practices. By drawing insights from various scholarly sources, the report aims to provide a comprehensive understanding of this rapidly evolving field, empowering organizations to leverage the potential of digital supply chain management.

- **Enhanced Visibility and Real-time Data Exchange**

The integration of information systems and technologies in the digital supply chain offers organizations heightened visibility into their operations. Through real-time data exchange across the supply chain network, companies can effectively track and monitor inventory, order status, and logistics. This enhanced visibility empowers organizations to make informed decisions and respond promptly to fluctuations in demand, minimizing stockouts and reducing inventory holding costs (Priyantha, 2023). Furthermore, the integration of information systems enables seamless communication and collaboration among various stakeholders, including suppliers, manufacturers, distributors, and customers (Ghobakhloo et al., 2023; Taj et al., 2022). This interconnectedness fosters improved coordination, facilitates better decision-making processes, and ultimately cultivates a more agile and responsive supply chain. By leveraging integrated information systems, organizations can optimize their supply chain operations, enhance overall efficiency, and gain a competitive edge in the digital era.

Figure 5. Digital supply chain benefits
(Jenkins, 2022)

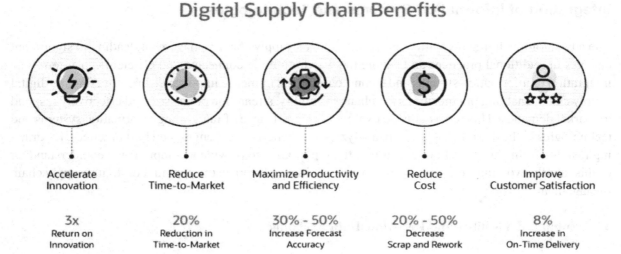

- **Process Streamlining and Efficiency Gains**

The integration of information systems and technologies in the supply chain leads to streamlined processes, resulting in higher levels of operational efficiency. Automation and digitization of manual tasks, as highlighted by Seseli et al. (2023), reduce the likelihood of human errors and improve process accuracy. Technologies such as radio-frequency identification (RFID), barcode scanning, and electronic data interchange (EDI) facilitate the seamless flow of information across various stages of the supply chain (Puica, 2023). This integration minimizes redundancies in data entry, expedites order processing, and enhances overall supply chain efficiency. Moreover, the integration of enterprise resource planning (ERP) systems with other supply chain technologies enables organizations to consolidate and manage data from multiple sources, facilitating better decision-making. Real-time data availability and analytics tools aid organizations in identifying bottlenecks, optimizing inventory levels, and streamlining procurement and production processes (Rathore, 2023b). By streamlining supply chain activities, organizations not only reduce costs but also enhance customer satisfaction through timely delivery and order accuracy. The integration of information systems and technologies thus plays a pivotal role in achieving operational efficiency in the supply chain, enabling organizations to deliver products and services more efficiently and effectively.

- **Improved Collaboration and Communication**

The integration of information systems and technologies in the supply chain fosters improved collaboration and communication among supply chain partners. Through shared access to a centralized database, stakeholders can seamlessly exchange information, leading to reduced communication gaps and enhanced coordination. Shahadat et al. (2023) emphasize that this integration allows supply chain partners to have a common understanding of demand patterns, inventory levels, and customer preferences, enabling them to align their strategies accordingly. Furthermore, emerging technologies such as cloud computing and the IoT provide a platform for real-time collaboration and data sharing (Chaurasiya et al., 2023). Cloud-based platforms enable different stakeholders to access and update information from anywhere, facilitating collaborative decision-making (Mak et al., 2023). IoT devices, including sensors and beacons, enable real-time tracking of products, ensuring visibility throughout the supply chain. By leveraging these technologies, organizations can achieve better coordination, reduce response times, and enhance overall supply chain performance. Overall, the integration of information systems and technologies promotes effective collaboration and communication among supply chain partners, enabling them to work together more efficiently and effectively. This enhanced collaboration leads to improved coordination, better decision-making, and ultimately, enhanced supply chain performance.

CYBER THREAT LANDSCAPE IN THE DIGITAL SUPPLY CHAIN

Overview of Common Cyber Threats Targeting the Supply Chain

In the contemporary interconnected digital environment, the operational efficiency and streamlining of supply chains heavily depend on technology and digital platforms. Nevertheless, this growing dependence on technology also brings forth a multitude of cyber threats that pose significant risks to supply chains. Cybercriminals are continuously refining their techniques to exploit vulnerabilities within supply chains, thereby endangering organizations and their partners. This segment presents a comprehensive outline of prevalent cyber threats that specifically target the supply chain, underscoring the utmost significance of implementing cybersecurity measures to effectively alleviate these risks.

1.   Phishing Attacks, Malware, and Ransomware

Phishing attacks emerge as a prevalent and noteworthy cyber threat encountered within the supply chain domain. These attacks commonly involve the dissemination of deceitful emails, messages, or websites to deceive individuals into revealing sensitive information or unwittingly downloading malware. Cybercriminals often assume the identities of trusted entities operating within the supply chain, enabling them to illicitly access valuable data or compromise essential systems (Möller, 2023). Supply chain operations face substantial risks from malware and ransomware. Malicious software possesses the capacity to infiltrate supply chain networks through infected attachments or compromised websites, leading to detrimental consequences such as data breaches, disruptions in system functionality, and financial losses. Ransomware attacks, specifically, impose a grave threat by encrypting critical supply chain data and subsequently demanding a ransom for its release (Prabucki, 2023).

2.   Third-Party Risks and Insider Threats

The reliance of supply chains on third-party vendors and suppliers introduces an augmented susceptibility to cyber threats. A breach or compromise in any of these third-party systems can trigger a ripple effect throughout the entire supply chain, granting unauthorized access to sensitive information or exploiting security vulnerabilities in partner networks (Friday et al., 2023). Within the realm of the supply chain, insider threats materialize as individuals possessing authorized access to systems and data who intentionally or inadvertently exploit their privileges for malevolent purposes. Such individuals may include employees, contractors, or even business partners who compromise sensitive information or disrupt the smooth functioning of supply chain operations (Marbut & Harms, 2023).

3.   Distributed Denial-of-Service (DDoS) Attacks and Supply Chain Interception

DDoS attacks are orchestrated to overwhelm supply chain systems and networks by inundating them with an immense volume of requests, rendering them inaccessible to legitimate users. The consequences of these attacks are far-reaching and can lead to severe disruptions in critical operations, financial losses, and reputational harm for organizations operating within the supply chain (Ghosh & Bhandari, 2023). Supply chain interception encompasses the act of intercepting physical goods or tampering with components during their transit or storage. Cybercriminals exploit vulnerabilities within the supply chain to introduce counterfeit or compromised products, which can have grave repercussions, including the compromise of customer data or the infiltration of malware into the system (Bi et al., 2023).

4.   Zero-Day Vulnerabilities and Social Engineering Attacks

Zero-day vulnerabilities refer to software vulnerabilities that are unknown to software vendors and lack available patches or defences. Cybercriminals exploit these vulnerabilities to gain unauthorized access to supply chain systems, compromise data, or install malicious software (Leal & Musgrave, 2023). Social engineering attacks exploit human psychology to deceive individuals, thereby compromising the security of the supply chain. These attacks leverage trust, curiosity, or fear to manipulate individuals into bypassing security measures or revealing valuable data (Duman et al., 2023). Figure 6 shows the different between traditional and digital supply chain.

Figure 6. Traditional and digital supply chain
(Read, 2023)

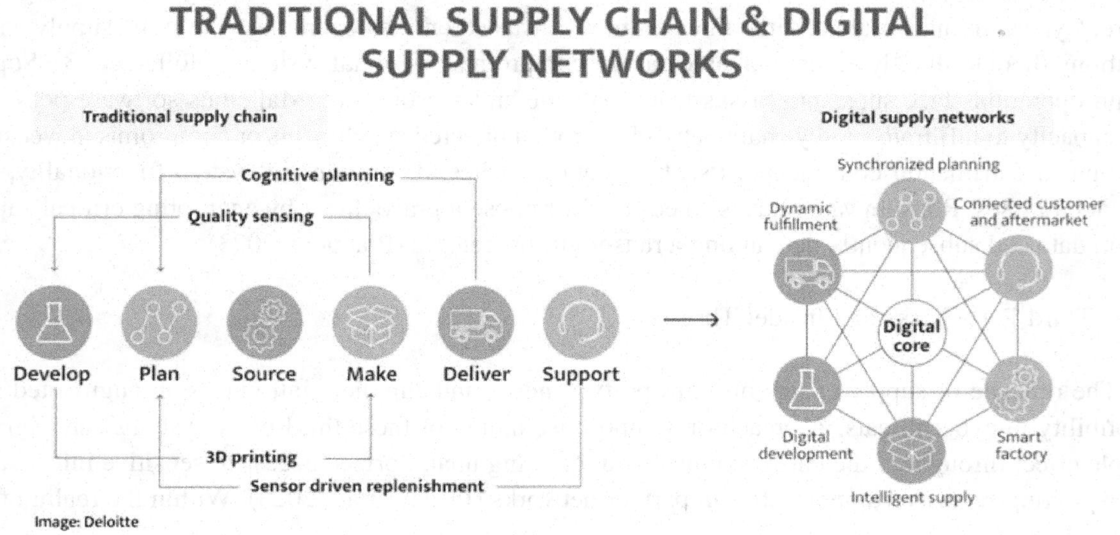

Image: Deloitte

Case Studies Highlighting Major Cyber-Attacks on the Supply Chain

1. Case Study 1: NotPetya Attack on Maersk

In June 2017, a notable cyber-attack named NotPetya wreaked havoc worldwide, with Maersk, the largest shipping company globally, being one of its primary victims. The attack originated from a compromised software update of Ukrainian accounting software known as M.E.Doc, which enjoyed widespread usage in Ukraine. NotPetya, a destructive form of malware, encrypted files and demanded a ransom for their release. The malware swiftly propagated through interconnected systems, affecting organizations on a global scale. Maersk, as a customer of M.E.Doc, encountered severe disruptions in its operations. The attack crippled its IT infrastructure, forcing critical systems used for bookings, container tracking, and documentation into shutdown mode. Maersk had to resort to manual processes, resulting in substantial delays and financial losses. It is estimated that the attack caused approximately $300 million in losses for Maersk (Capano, 2022; Soares, 2023). This case study emphasizes the significance of supply chain visibility and comprehending dependencies on third-party software. It also underscores the crucial nature of implementing effective software patch management procedures and possessing robust incident response capabilities to minimize the adverse impacts of cyber-attacks.

2. Case Study 2: SolarWinds Attack

Unveiled in December 2020, the SolarWinds attack stands out as a remarkably sophisticated cyber-attack targeting the software supply chain (Fourné, 2023). The assailants compromised the software build process of SolarWinds, a widely utilized provider of IT management software. By surreptitiously implanting a malicious backdoor into the Orion software updates, the attackers obtained access to the systems of SolarWinds' customers, including numerous government agencies and large corporations. The SolarWinds attack shed light on the inherent risks associated with compromised software updates, as organizations unwittingly installed the malicious updates, thereby granting unauthorized access to their networks and sensitive data to the attackers (Kerner, 2022). This attack exposed vulnerabilities in supply chain integrity, underscoring the pressing need for robust vendor management practices. Such practices should encompass evaluating the security measures of third-party vendors and implementing mechanisms to verify supply chain integrity.

3. Case Study 3: Notifiable Data Breach in Toll Group

In May 2020, Toll Group, a prominent logistics company based in Australia, encountered a cyber-attack that severely impacted its supply chain operations and led to a significant data breach. The attack took advantage of a vulnerability present in Toll Group's file transfer system, enabling unauthorized access to sensitive customer and employee data. The breach resulted in the exposure of personal information, including names, addresses, and contact details, belonging to thousands of individuals. In response, Toll Group had to temporarily suspend specific systems and services to mitigate the attack and assess the extent of the breach (Barbaschow, 2020). This incident emphasized the paramount importance of implementing robust data protection measures, such as encryption, access controls, and regular vulnerability assessments, to safeguard sensitive information within the supply chain.

4.   Case Study 4: Colonial Pipeline Ransomware Attack

In May 2021, the Colonial Pipeline, which oversees the largest fuel pipeline system in the United States, fell prey to a ransomware attack. The attack specifically targeted the company's IT systems, resulting in a temporary shutdown of the pipeline. Consequently, fuel shortages and disruptions rippled across the East Coast of the United States, causing significant consequences (Shahriar, 2020). The cybercriminal group known as DarkSide was responsible for orchestrating the attack. By exploiting vulnerabilities within Colonial Pipeline's systems, they encrypted critical data and demanded a ransom for its release. This incident shed light on the vulnerabilities inherent in critical infrastructure within the supply chain and underscored the potential ramifications of such attacks (S. M. Kerner, 2022). It emphasized the imperative of implementing robust cybersecurity measures, including regular system updates, well-defined incident response plans, and secure backups. Such measures are vital to ensure operational resilience and mitigate the impact of potential supply chain disruptions.

5.   Case Study 5: JBS Food Company Cyber-Attack

In May 2021, JBS, one of the world's largest meat processing companies, experienced a significant cyber-attack that caused disruptions in its operations across multiple countries. The attack specifically targeted JBS' IT systems and affected various aspects of production and supply chain processes. The responsible party behind the attack was identified as the Russian-based hacking group REvil. As a result of the attack, JBS had to temporarily shut down some of its plants, leading to disruptions in the availability of meat products and subsequent supply chain disruptions. In response, JBS promptly took measures to contain the attack by collaborating with cybersecurity experts and law enforcement agencies (Sheehan, 2023). This case study emphasized the utmost importance of implementing effective supply chain risk management practices, which include conducting thorough vendor security assessments, ensuring secure remote access to systems, and maintaining robust capabilities for detecting and responding to incidents.

These case studies provide compelling evidence of the substantial impact that cyber-attacks can have on the supply chain. They effectively underscore the vulnerabilities faced by organizations and stress the imperative of adopting proactive cybersecurity measures. To safeguard supply chains from the ever-evolving landscape of cyber threats, organizations must place a high priority on achieving supply chain visibility, conducting routine risk assessments, strengthening vendor management practices, implementing mechanisms for verifying supply chain integrity, and formulating comprehensive incident response plans. By undertaking these measures, organizations can effectively mitigate the risks associated with supply chain cyber-attacks, thereby ensuring the resilience and security of their operations.

Figure 7. Type of cyber attacks
(Wallarm, 2023)

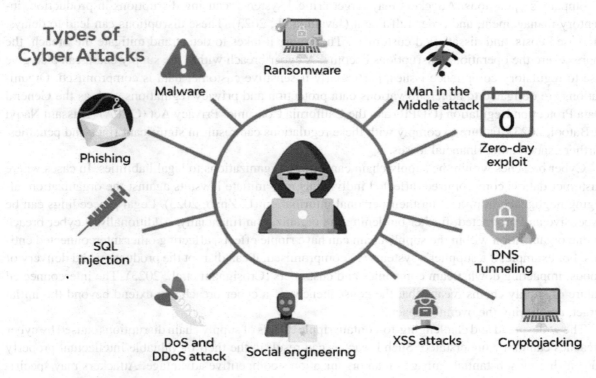

Potential Consequences of Cyber Breaches in the Supply Chain

This section delves into the potential consequences that can arise from cyber breaches within the supply chain and underscores the crucial significance of implementing strong security measures. By examining multiple facets, including financial losses, reputational damage, operational disruptions, regulatory compliance issues, and legal liabilities, this report aims to raise awareness about the essential requirement for proactive cybersecurity strategies in the supply chain industry (Jayakumar et al., 2021; Khan et al., 2022; Khan et al., 2022a). With the growing interconnectivity of the world, supply chains have become increasingly susceptible to cyber threats. A cyber breach within the supply chain can result in far-reaching ramifications that extend beyond a single organization. The subsequent sections delve deeper into the possible outcomes stemming from such breaches. Figure 7 shows the type of cyberattacks.

Cyber breaches can result in significant financial losses for organizations operating within the supply chain. The IMB (2022) conducted a study revealing that the average cost of a data breach amounts to approximately $4.35 million. These expenses encompass various elements, such as incident response, legal services, regulatory fines, and potential lawsuits. Additionally, organizations may experience a decline in revenue due to the detrimental impact on their reputation and loss of customer trust. A cyber breach within the supply chain can inflict severe damage to an organization's reputation. Customers, suppliers, and partners may lose confidence in the affected company's ability to safeguard sensitive information, thereby eroding business relationships (Bandari, 2023). Research has indicated that reputational damage can have enduring consequences, resulting in decreased customer loyalty and a decline in market share (Shahzad, 2023). Cyber breaches within the supply chain can lead to significant disruptions to a company's operations. Attackers may target critical systems, causing disruptions in production, inventory management, and order fulfilment (Javaid et al., 2023). These disruptions can lead to delays, increased costs, and dissatisfied customers. The longer it takes to detect and mitigate the breach, the more severe the operational disruptions become. A cyber breach within the supply chain can also give rise to regulatory compliance issues, particularly if sensitive customer data is compromised. Organizations are obligated to adhere to various data protection and privacy regulations such as the General Data Protection Regulation (GDPR) and the California Consumer Privacy Act (CCPA) (Hussain Naqvi & Batool, 2023). Failure to comply with these regulations can result in significant fines and penalties, further exacerbating financial losses.

Cyber breaches within the supply chain can expose organizations to legal liabilities. In cases where customer data is compromised, affected individuals may initiate lawsuits against the organization, alleging negligence in protecting their personal information (L. Zhao, 2023). Legal proceedings can be expensive and protracted, further burdening the organization financially. Additionally, a cyber breach in one organization within the supply chain can have ripple effects, affecting other interconnected entities. For example, if a supplier's systems are compromised, it can disrupt the production and delivery of goods, impacting downstream companies and customers (Crosignani et al., 2023). The interconnected nature of supply chains means that the consequences of a cyber breach can extend beyond the initial target, amplifying the overall impact.

The widespread and challenging-to-contain ripple effects of supply chain disruptions caused by cyber breaches cannot be understated. Such breaches can result in the theft of valuable intellectual property (IP), inflicting substantial damage on an organization's competitive advantage. Attackers may specifically target proprietary information, trade secrets, or research and development data (Al-Harrasi et al., 2021). The loss of IP can lead to diminished innovation, a weakened market position, and compromised future business prospects. Furthermore, cyber breaches within the supply chain can lead to the loss of business opportunities. Prospective clients and partners may hesitate to engage with organizations that have a history of security incidents. This erosion of trust and credibility can restrict future growth opportunities and hinder the establishment of strategic partnerships (Fernando et al., 2022). Additionally, cyber breaches can have adverse effects on employee morale and productivity within an organization. When employees perceive their workplace as insecure, it can result in increased stress, anxiety, and a decline in job satisfaction (Zhu, 2023). Moreover, employees may be required to redirect their time and efforts towards addressing the breach, disrupting regular work routines and diminishing productivity.

VULNERABILITIES IN THE DIGITAL SUPPLY CHAIN

Identification and Analysis of Vulnerabilities in Supply Chain Processes

The advent of digital transformation has brought forth new vulnerabilities and risks that can jeopardize the integrity, confidentiality, and availability of supply chain operations. To proactively manage and mitigate these risks, organizations must identify and analyze the vulnerabilities inherent in their digital supply chain processes. This section seeks to delve into the diverse vulnerabilities that may exist in digital supply chain processes and offer valuable insights into their analysis. By understanding these vulnerabilities, organizations can implement appropriate security measures to safeguard their digital supply chain operations.

- ## Information Security Vulnerabilities and Third-Party Risks

Information security vulnerabilities are a prominent concern within digital supply chain processes. Insufficient access controls, weak authentication mechanisms, and inadequate encryption protocols are potential sources of these vulnerabilities. Notably, compromised user accounts or weak passwords can lead to unauthorized access to sensitive supply chain data (Jalali, 2023; Kumar et al., 2022). Moreover, attackers can intercept and manipulate data during transmission across interconnected systems, resulting in data breaches and malicious activities (Telo, 2023; Annadurai et al., 2022). Collaborations with multiple third-party vendors and suppliers, although beneficial for efficiency and specialization, introduce additional vulnerabilities. Organizations heavily depend on these external entities, and any security weaknesses or vulnerabilities in their systems can propagate throughout the entire supply chain network (Bandari, 2023). Thus, organizations must evaluate the security practices and capabilities of their partners to ensure a robust and secure digital supply chain ecosystem.

- ## Supply Chain Visibility Gaps and IoT Vulnerabilities

The effectiveness of digital supply chain processes relies heavily on real-time data exchange and visibility, enabling precise demand forecasting, efficient inventory management, and timely deliveries. Nonetheless, the presence of visibility gaps, caused by incomplete or delayed data sharing, poses a significant challenge, leading to inaccurate insights and decision-making (Dobilas, 2023). Exploiting these gaps, malicious actors can manipulate the supply chain, resulting in disruptive events, delays, or the infiltration of counterfeit products into the market. With the proliferation of IoT devices in supply chain operations, automation, tracking, and monitoring capabilities have been significantly enhanced. However, the increased number of connected devices also introduces vulnerabilities that need to be addressed. IoT devices within digital supply chain processes are attractive targets for attackers seeking unauthorized access to the network or aiming to launch distributed denial of service (DDoS) attacks, resulting in disruptive events (Jmal et al., 2023). Furthermore, the limited computational power and security features of IoT devices render them susceptible to exploitation. Social engineering attacks exploit human vulnerabilities to gain unauthorized access to digital supply chain processes. Attackers may assume the identity of authorized personnel, such as suppliers or employees, and manipulate individuals into divulging sensitive information or performing malicious actions (Muhammad et al., 2023). Such attacks can lead to unauthorized access, and data breaches, and compromise the overall integrity of the digital supply chain. Mitigating these security threats is paramount to ensure the secure operation of IoT-enabled digital supply chain processes.

Figure 8. Supply chain security

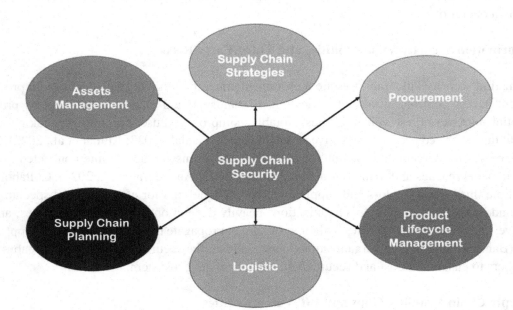

Analysis of Vulnerabilities

- **Technical, Risk Assessments, and Vulnerability Testing**

To effectively analyze vulnerabilities in digital supply chain processes, organizations must adopt a comprehensive approach that integrates technical assessments, risk assessments, and vulnerability testing. This multifaceted analysis enables the identification of potential weaknesses and facilitates the prioritization of mitigation efforts. Technical assessments encompass evaluating the security measures implemented within the digital supply chain processes, including access controls, encryption protocols, firewalls, and intrusion detection systems. To identify weaknesses in systems and applications, penetration testing and vulnerability scanning techniques can be employed (Fatima et al., 2023; Elijah et al., 2019). Adopting this comprehensive approach is vital for organizations to enhance the security of their digital supply chain processes and proactively address potential vulnerabilitiesTo detect and address vulnerabilities in digital supply chain processes, organizations should conduct regular technical assessments, risk assessments, and vulnerability testing. Technical assessments enable the early detection of vulnerabilities, allowing organizations to address them before exploitation occurs. Risk assessments involve a systematic evaluation of potential vulnerabilities by identifying critical assets, assessing threats and vulnerabilities, and quantifying risks (Peng et al., 2023). By prioritizing risks based on their impact and likelihood, organizations can allocate resources effectively for mitigation and develop robust risk management strategies. Vulnerability testing involves targeted assessments to identify specific vulnerabilities within digital supply chain processes, encompassing application security testing, network scanning, and configuration reviews (Suren et al., 2022). Regular vulnerability testing provides valuable insights into potential weaknesses, enabling organizations to implement appropriate patches and security controls to mitigate identified risks. By adopting these proactive measures, organizations can strengthen the security of their digital supply chain processes and safeguard against potential vulnerabilities.

Assessment of Potential Entry Points for Cyber Attacks

This section aims to evaluate possible avenues for cyber attacks within the digital supply chain. By analyzing various stages of the supply chain, encompassing sourcing, manufacturing, transportation, warehousing, and distribution, this report identifies critical vulnerabilities that cybercriminals may exploit. Furthermore, it examines the potential repercussions of these attacks and offers recommendations to mitigate associated risks. The digital supply chain entails the seamless flow of information and goods across multiple stages, including procurement, production, logistics, and distribution (Kurbel et al., 2020; Prabakar et al., 2023). The integration of digital technologies, such as the IoT devices, cloud computing, and data analytics, has revolutionized supply chain management. Nevertheless, these advancements have concurrently introduced new cybersecurity risks (Schmittner & Obaidat, 2021). Targeted cyber attacks on the digital supply chain can lead to substantial financial losses, reputational harm, and disruptions to business operations (Lim & Kim, 2021).

- **Potential Entry Points for Cyber Attacks**

  1. Sourcing and Manufacturing Stage

The sourcing stage encompasses the identification and selection of suppliers, a critical aspect of the supply chain. This phase is susceptible to cyber attacks as malicious individuals may focus their efforts on infiltrating supplier networks and compromising sensitive information, such as pricing data or intellectual property (Yeboah-Ofori & Opoku-Boateng, 2023). To achieve their objectives, threat actors might employ tactics such as phishing attacks or exploit vulnerabilities within supplier management systems to gain unauthorized access to valuable data. Safeguarding this stage is crucial to maintaining the integrity of the digital supply chain. The manufacturing stage involves the actual production of goods and is equally vulnerable to cyber attacks. Disruptions to production processes can have severe consequences, leading to delays and substantial financial losses. Cybercriminals often exploit weaknesses in industrial control systems (ICS) or introduce malware into production networks to disrupt operations (Nelligere et al., n.d.). A notable example is the NotPetya ransomware attack that occurred in 2017, which specifically targeted the manufacturing sector, causing widespread disruptions and significant financial damages (Handfield & Finkenstadt, 2022). Protecting the manufacturing stage from cyber threats is essential to ensure uninterrupted production and minimize potential losses.

  2. Transportation, Warehousing, and Distribution Stage

The transportation stage is responsible for facilitating the movement of goods, both from suppliers to manufacturers and from manufacturers to distributors. However, this stage is susceptible to cyber attacks that exploit vulnerabilities within transportation management systems (TMS) or involve the theft of sensitive shipment data. Adversaries may intercept or manipulate goods during transit, resulting in disruptions to the supply chain and compromising the integrity of the products (Roberts, 2023). Safeguarding this stage is crucial to ensuring the smooth flow of goods and maintaining product authenticity and quality. The warehousing stage involves the storage and management of inventory. Within this stage, cyber attacks can manifest as the theft of inventory data, unauthorized access to warehouse management systems (WMS), or the manipulation of inventory records. Such attacks can lead to inaccuracies in inventory tracking, resulting in stockouts or excess inventory (Islam, 2023). Protecting this stage is essential to maintain efficient inventory management and prevent disruptions to the overall supply chain. The distribution stage encompasses the final delivery of goods to end customers. Cyber attacks targeting this stage may involve the manipulation of order fulfilment processes, leading to delivery delays or incorrect shipments. Attackers may also exploit vulnerabilities in e-commerce platforms or payment systems to carry out fraudulent activities (Lazăra, 2023; R. Sujatha et al 2022). Securing this stage is critical to ensuring timely and accurate delivery, maintaining customer satisfaction, and preventing financial losses due to fraudulent transactions. Cyber attacks within the digital supply chain can have severe consequences for organizations. Financial losses can occur as a result of operational disruptions, intellectual property theft, or ransom payments to regain control of compromised systems (Riggs et al., 2023). Moreover, organizations may face reputational damage, eroding customer trust and reducing market share (Gupta & Seetharaman, 2019; Shah et al., 2022; Shah et al., 2022a). Additionally, supply chain disruptions caused by cyber attacks can have cascading effects on downstream partners and customers, impacting the overall economy (Verma et al., 2022). Organizations must implement robust cybersecurity measures throughout the digital supply chain to mitigate these risks and protect their operations, reputation, and the broader economy.

Importance of Risk Assessments and Vulnerability Management

- **Identifying and Mitigating Potential Risks**

Risk assessments play a vital role in identifying potential vulnerabilities and threats within the digital supply chain. Through comprehensive assessments, organizations can gain valuable insights into weaknesses present in their systems, processes, and infrastructure. This enables the formulation of proactive risk mitigation strategies, including the implementation of suitable security controls and safeguards. As highlighted by Pritika et al. (2023), conducting risk assessments allows organizations to identify critical assets, assess vulnerabilities, and evaluate the potential impact of risks. Ultimately, these assessments facilitate the development of robust risk management frameworks.

- **Protecting Data Integrity and Confidentiality**

Preserving the integrity and confidentiality of sensitive information is crucial within the digital supply chain due to the looming threats of data breaches and cyberattacks. Risk assessments serve as a valuable tool for organizations to identify potential security gaps that could lead to unauthorized access or manipulation of valuable data. To mitigate these risks, implementing effective vulnerability management practices is essential. As suggested by Bandari (2023), organizations can adopt various proactive measures to enhance data security. These include promptly applying security patches, conducting regular system updates, and enforcing robust data encryption measures. By staying up-to-date with security patches and system updates, organizations can address known vulnerabilities and minimize the risk of exploitation by cybercriminals. Data encryption, on the other hand, ensures that sensitive information remains encrypted and inaccessible to unauthorized individuals, even if it is intercepted or compromised.

Implementing these vulnerability management practices helps organizations maintain data integrity and uphold the confidentiality of valuable information within the digital supply chain.

- **Ensuring Business Continuity**

Disruptions within the digital supply chain can have widespread ramifications, affecting not only the organization directly impacted but also its customers and partners. Conducting risk assessments plays a vital role in identifying potential sources of disruption, which may include system failures, vulnerabilities within third-party vendors, or even natural disasters. These assessments enable organizations to develop robust business continuity plans (BCPs) that ensure the prompt recovery and resumption of operations in the face of disruptions. According to the National Institute of Standards and Technology (NIST, 2021), vulnerability management is a critical aspect of effective BCPs. It allows organizations to assess the potential impact of vulnerabilities within their systems and infrastructure. By identifying these vulnerabilities, organizations can implement appropriate safeguards and countermeasures to mitigate the risk of disruptions. This proactive approach to vulnerability management strengthens the overall resilience of the digital supply chain and enhances an organization's ability to maintain operational continuity.

- **Enhancing Compliance with Regulatory Requirements**

The digital supply chain operates within a multifaceted regulatory landscape, where adherence to data privacy and security laws and standards is paramount. Non-compliance with these regulations can result in severe legal and financial consequences. Risk assessments play a crucial role in helping organizations identify potential gaps in compliance, evaluate the effectiveness of existing controls, and align their practices with applicable laws and regulations. For instance, the General Data Protection Regulation (GDPR) mandates that organizations conducting business in the European Union implement risk-based security measures to protect personal data (Lessambo, 2023). Conducting risk assessments allows organizations to assess their current data protection practices and identify areas that require improvement or adjustment to meet GDPR requirements. By demonstrating due diligence through risk assessments, organizations can showcase their commitment to compliance and minimize the risk of penalties associated with non-compliance. Through risk assessments, organizations can ensure that their data privacy and security practices align with relevant regulations, protecting sensitive information and mitigating legal and financial risks.

In the dynamic landscape of the digital supply chain, organizations must prioritize effective risk assessments and vulnerability management to navigate the ever-growing risks and vulnerabilities. Thorough risk assessments enable organizations to identify potential threats, safeguard data integrity, maintain business continuity, and ensure compliance with regulatory requirements. Simultaneously, implementing robust vulnerability management practices empowers organizations to proactively address security gaps, apply timely patches and updates, and defend against emerging threats. By prioritizing risk assessments and vulnerability management, organizations can establish resilient and secure digital supply chains. This approach ensures the smooth flow of operations and helps maintain customer trust in an interconnected world where risks and vulnerabilities continue to evolve.

Figure 9. Supply chain risk management
(Herrera, 2022)

SUPPLY CHAIN RISK MANAGEMENT

STEP 1:
Establishing the proper
governance for the process

STEP 2:
Identifying who your
critical suppliers are

STEP 3:
Assessing risk at your
critical suppliers

STEP 4:
Mitigating risk from
your critical suppliers

SUPPLY CHAIN RISK MANAGEMENT

Introduction to Supply Chain Risk Management (SCRM)

In the modern business landscape, SCRM has emerged as a critical aspect of operations due to the growing complexity and interdependencies within global supply chains. As supply chains span across multiple geographies and involve numerous stakeholders, they are exposed to a wide range of risks that have the potential to disrupt the seamless flow of goods and services. SCRM aims to identify, assess, and mitigate these risks to ensure the continuity of supply chain operations and enhance overall resilience. This section provides an overview of SCRM, highlighting its significance in today's interconnected and globalized business environment. It explores the integration of cybersecurity within the SCRM framework, emphasizing the importance of addressing cyber risks as an integral part of managing supply chain vulnerabilities. Additionally, best practices for identifying, assessing, and mitigating cyber risks in the supply chain are discussed. In the current landscape, supply chains face various risks, including natural disasters, geopolitical disruptions, supplier failures, and cybersecurity threats. These risks can have significant consequences, such as production delays, inventory shortages, customer dissatisfaction, and financial losses (Al-Banna et al., 2023). Hence, organizations must adopt a proactive approach to identify and effectively manage these risks.

Integration of cybersecurity into SCRM Framework

Ensuring effective protection against cyber threats is of utmost importance in securing supply chains. Cybersecurity threats, such as data breaches, ransomware attacks, and unauthorized access to critical systems, pose significant risks. Integrating cybersecurity into SCRM frameworks allows organizations to proactively identify and assess cyber risks within the supply chain. By implementing robust security measures, organizations can detect and respond to potential cyber-attacks at an early stage, minimizing their impact and preventing disruptions to operations (Bhattacharya et al., 2023). Safeguarding sensitive data is crucial in supply chains as they involve the exchange of sensitive and confidential information among partners, including customer data, intellectual property, and trade secrets. Failing to protect this information can lead to severe financial and reputational consequences. Integrating cybersecurity into SCRM frameworks enables organizations to implement data protection measures, such as encryption, access controls, and data loss prevention. These measures ensure the confidentiality, integrity, and availability of critical information throughout the supply chain (Braun et al., 2019). Building and maintaining trust among supply chain partners is essential, and cybersecurity breaches can erode this trust. Integrating cybersecurity into SCRM frameworks demonstrates a commitment to protecting shared information and assets. By implementing strong security practices, organizations can foster trust, strengthen partnerships, and promote effective collaboration in mitigating cyber risks. This collaborative approach facilitates the exchange of threat intelligence, joint incident response, and the implementation of consistent security standards across the supply chain (Sarhan et al., 2022).

Regulatory compliance is a critical aspect for many industries, as they are subject to stringent requirements concerning the protection of sensitive data and the management of cyber risks. By integrating cybersecurity into SCRM frameworks, organizations can ensure compliance with relevant laws and regulations. This includes adhering to industry-specific cybersecurity standards, promptly reporting cyber incidents, and implementing measures to protect personal and sensitive information throughout the supply chain (Pargoo & Ilbeigi, 2023). Maintaining business continuity and resilience is essential in the face of cyber threats. Cyber attacks can significantly disrupt supply chain operations, resulting in financial losses and reputational damage. Integrating cybersecurity into SCRM frameworks helps organizations build resilience by implementing measures to prevent, detect, and recover from cyber incidents. Robust incident response plans, backup and recovery strategies, and redundant systems can minimize the impact of cyber-attacks and ensure the continuity of critical business operations (Parker et al., 2023). By considering regulatory compliance and focusing on business continuity and resilience, organizations can effectively integrate cybersecurity into SCRM frameworks, enhancing their ability to protect sensitive data, maintain operational continuity, and meet industry-specific requirements.

Best Practices for Identifying, Assessing, and Mitigating Cyber Risks in The Supply Chain

Conduct Comprehensive Risk Assessments: Begin by conducting thorough risk assessments to identify and evaluate potential cyber risks within the digital supply chain. This process involves identifying vulnerabilities, assessing threats, and evaluating potential impacts on critical systems and data. Regular risk assessments should be conducted to account for evolving cyber threats and changes within the supply chain environment (Baz et al., 2023). **Establish a Robust Vendor Management Program:** Since the digital supply chain often involves multiple vendors and third-party providers, organizations should implement a comprehensive vendor management program. This program should include due diligence in the vendor selection process, contractual agreements that address cybersecurity requirements, regular audits and assessments of vendors' security practices, and incident response protocols. By ensuring that vendors meet cybersecurity standards, organizations can mitigate risks associated with third-party dependencies (Kähkönen et al., 2023). **Implement Strong Access Controls:** Access controls play a critical role in preventing unauthorized access to sensitive data and systems within the digital supply chain.

Organizations should adopt measures such as multi-factor authentication, strong password policies, and role-based access controls. By enforcing these controls, organizations can ensure that only authorized personnel can access critical systems, reducing the risk of unauthorized data exposure (Nanda et al., 2023)

Regularly Update and Patch Systems: Keeping software and systems up to date is crucial for addressing known vulnerabilities and strengthening defences against emerging threats. Regularly applying updates and patches to all systems within the digital supply chain helps minimize the risk of exploitation (R & T, 2023). **Encrypt Sensitive Data:** Encryption is a fundamental safeguard for protecting sensitive data during transmission and storage within the digital supply chain. Organizations should implement robust encryption mechanisms for all critical data, ensuring that encryption protocols are properly configured and regularly updated. This helps safeguard data confidentiality and integrity (Xia et al., 2023). **Establish Incident Response and Business Continuity Plans:** It is essential to have well-defined incident response and business continuity plans in place to effectively respond to cyber incidents. These plans should outline roles and responsibilities, communication protocols, backup and recovery procedures, and strategies for minimizing the impact of disruptions on the digital supply chain. Regular testing and updating of these plans are critical for their effectiveness (Coutinho et al., 2023). **Conduct Employee Training and Awareness Programs:** Employees play a crucial role in maintaining cybersecurity within the digital supply chain. Organizations should provide comprehensive cybersecurity training and awareness programs to employees, emphasizing the importance of adhering to security policies, recognizing phishing attempts, and promptly reporting suspicious activities. Regular training helps foster a cybersecurity-conscious culture (Mijwil et al., 2023).

Figure 10. Type of supply chain risk
(Kimmy, 2022)

SECURING SUPPLIER RELATIONSHIPS

Importance of Secure Supplier Relationships in the Digital Supply Chain

In the contemporary dynamic and interconnected commercial environment, enterprises heavily depend on the digital supply chain for facilitating the seamless exchange of products and services. With the growing adoption of digitalization by businesses, the establishment of secure relationships with suppliers within the digital supply chain assumes utmost importance. These secure supplier relationships not only contribute to improving operational effectiveness but also play a critical role in safeguarding valuable information, minimizing potential risks, and fostering enduring collaborative partnerships. This section accentuates the significance of secure supplier relationships within the digital supply chain, substantiating the presented arguments with a comprehensive array of authoritative references.

Operational effectiveness holds immense significance within the digital supply chain, where real-time responsiveness and streamlined procedures play a pivotal role. The establishment of secure relationships with suppliers facilitates fruitful collaboration, thereby enhancing operational efficiency (Negar, 2023). By employing secure communication channels and promoting information sharing, organizations can achieve prompt response times, accurate demand forecasting, and optimal inventory management (Kashem et al., 2023). These advantages translate into shorter lead times, heightened customer satisfaction, and overall excellence in operations. As digitalization increasingly pervades supply chain processes, ensuring the security of sensitive information becomes paramount. The digital supply chain is vulnerable to cyber threats and data breaches, necessitating a strong emphasis on information security (Kioskli et al., 2023). Through the establishment of secure supplier relationships, organizations can implement robust security protocols, including encryption, access controls, and secure data exchange mechanisms. These measures effectively mitigate the risks associated with unauthorized access, data leakage, and potential disruptions, thereby safeguarding the integrity and confidentiality of critical information.

The role of secure supplier relationships in the supplier selection and evaluation process is of utmost importance. Organizations must meticulously evaluate suppliers' security practices and capabilities to establish a dependable and secure partnership (Yenugula et al., 2023). By giving priority to security criteria during supplier selection, businesses can identify suppliers that have implemented effective security controls and adhere to industry standards. This approach effectively reduces the likelihood of supply chain disruptions and bolsters the overall resilience of the digital supply chain. Furthermore, secure supplier relationships foster collaboration and innovation within the digital supply chain (Kocabasoglu-Hillmer et al., 2023). When suppliers have confidence in the security of shared information, they are more inclined to engage in transparent communication, exchange valuable knowledge, and collaboratively develop innovative solutions (Sun et al., 2022). This collaborative approach leads to a competitive advantage by enabling the co-creation of novel products, processes, and services. By fostering a culture of trust and information sharing, secure supplier relationships enhance the overall performance and responsiveness of the supply chain.

In the current unpredictable business landscape, supply chain disruptions are an inherent part of operations. Secure supplier relationships play a crucial role in enhancing supply chain resilience by mitigating the impact of such disruptions (Sirisomboonsuk & Burns, 2023). Collaborating with trusted suppliers enables organizations to achieve heightened visibility, transparency, and flexibility within the digital supply chain. This, in turn, empowers businesses to swiftly respond and adapt to unforeseen events like natural disasters, geopolitical challenges, or abrupt shifts in customer demand. Resilient supply chains are better equipped to recover quickly and sustain operations even during challenging circumstances.

Evaluating and Selecting Secure Suppliers

Before engaging with any supplier, conducting a comprehensive risk assessment is imperative to identify potential vulnerabilities and evaluate the supplier's security posture. This assessment should encompass various aspects, including scrutinizing the supplier's data protection policies, security controls, incident response procedures, and compliance with pertinent regulations (Bø et al., 2023). Additionally, evaluating the supplier's security certifications and adherence to industry standards is crucial. Suppliers who have obtained relevant security certifications such as ISO 27001 for information security management or SOC 2 for data protection demonstrate their commitment to maintaining a secure environment (Johnson, 2020). Furthermore, it is essential to assess the supplier's data protection practices, which involve examining aspects like data encryption, access controls, and secure transmission protocols. Validating whether the supplier has implemented measures to safeguard sensitive information from unauthorized access or disclosure is of utmost importance (Z. Li et al., 2023). Take into account the incident response capabilities of the supplier: The supplier's capacity to promptly and efficiently respond to security incidents holds significant importance. Evaluate their incident response plans, which should encompass the identification of potential threats, detection mechanisms, and communication protocols, ensuring alignment with your organization's specific requirements (Shiau et al., 2023). Examine the supplier's physical security measures: Alongside digital security, it is essential to evaluate the physical security measures implemented by the supplier, particularly if they handle sensitive physical assets or have access to critical infrastructure. Assess their facilities, access controls, and surveillance systems to ascertain the robustness of their physical security protocols (Anderson, 2018).

Evaluate the supplier's employee security awareness and training programs: It is crucial to assess the supplier's initiatives for employee security awareness and training. Well-trained and security-conscious employees significantly contribute to establishing a secure supplier relationship. Consider the supplier's financial stability: Assessing the financial stability of potential suppliers is essential to ensure their capability to invest in and maintain robust security measures over time. Financial instability may result in compromises in security investments, posing potential risks (Siraj et al., 2023). Review the supplier's track record and reputation: Investigate the supplier's history and reputation concerning security incidents, data breaches, or any past vulnerabilities. Conduct due diligence by researching industry forums, customer reviews, and news reports to identify any potential concerns (J. Li et al., 2023). Evaluate the supplier's disaster recovery and business continuity plans: Assess the supplier's strategies for disaster recovery and business continuity to ensure they have sufficient measures in place to recover from potential security incidents or disruptions (Russo et al., 2023). Consider the supplier's commitment to continuous improvement: Look for suppliers that display a dedication to continuously enhancing their security practices. This includes conducting regular security audits, and vulnerability assessments, and implementing proactive measures to address emerging threats (Akanmu et al., 2021).

Contractual Considerations for Cybersecurity in Supplier Agreements

The supplier agreement should contain clear and well-defined terms about cybersecurity, establishing the scope of the supplier's obligations. It should explicitly outline the types of data covered, including personally identifiable information (PII), intellectual property, and confidential business information. Additionally, it should incorporate relevant compliance standards, such as the General Data Protection Regulation (GDPR) or the Health Insurance Portability and Accountability Act (HIPAA), to ensure adherence to legal requirements (Syed, 2023). Furthermore, the supplier agreement should provide a comprehensive framework for the cybersecurity controls and practices that the supplier must implement. These controls may encompass encryption mechanisms, access controls, network segmentation, vulnerability management, incident response procedures, and regular security assessments (Wallis & Dorey, 2023). It is crucial to address the use of secure coding practices and the adoption of industry best practices, such as the National Institute of Standards and Technology (NIST) Cybersecurity Framework, to ensure robust security measures (Möller, 2023).

Figure 11. Information security areas

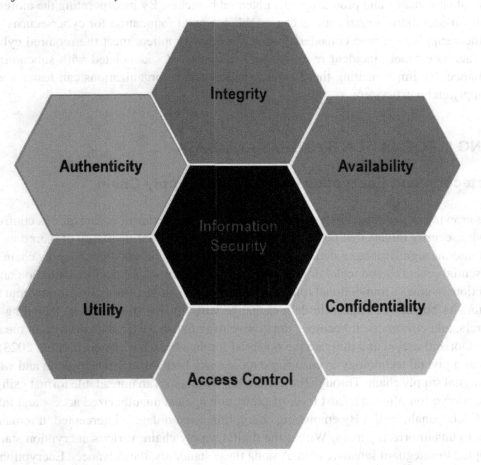

The supplier agreement should incorporate provisions for timely data breach notification and incident response. It should specify the required timeframe within which the supplier must notify the organization of any actual or suspected data breaches (Farid et al., 2023). Additionally, the agreement should outline the supplier's responsibilities in terms of incident response, including containment, investigation, remediation, and cooperation with law enforcement and regulatory authorities. Furthermore, the supplier agreement should address the involvement of subcontractors and third-party vendors in handling the organization's data. It should require the supplier to perform due diligence on subcontractors and ensure that they adhere to the same cybersecurity standards and practices (Romadhona et al., 2023). The agreement should grant the organization the right to audit subcontractors' security controls and impose contractual obligations directly on subcontractors to maintain a consistent level of cybersecurity.

The supplier agreement should include provisions mandating compliance with applicable laws and regulations concerning cybersecurity and data protection. This encompasses requirements related to data privacy, security breach notification, and the protection of personal data (Koukiadaki, 2023). The agreement should clearly define the consequences of non-compliance, such as termination or financial penalties, to incentivize the supplier to maintain a robust security posture. In an era characterized by increasing cyber threats, organizations must prioritize cybersecurity in their supplier agreements to safeguard their valuable assets and protect against potential breaches. By incorporating the aforementioned contractual considerations, organizations can establish a solid foundation for cybersecurity collaboration with their suppliers. These considerations ensure that suppliers meet the required cybersecurity standards, facilitate timely incident response, and mitigate risks associated with subcontractors and non-compliance. By implementing these contractual measures, organizations can foster a secure and resilient supply chain ecosystem.

SECURING INFORMATION SYSTEMS AND DATA

Data Protection and Encryption in the Digital Supply Chain

Amidst the growing dependence on technology and interconnectedness, organizations confront a multitude of cybersecurity threats that pose risks to the integrity and confidentiality of their data. This section delves into the significance of data protection and encryption in the digital supply chain, shedding light on essential practices and technologies employed to ensure secure data transmission and storage. Data protection assumes a foundational role in safeguarding sensitive information throughout the digital supply chain. As businesses engage in data exchange with diverse stakeholders, including suppliers, manufacturers, and customers, it becomes imperative to establish robust data protection measures that thwart unauthorized access and mitigate the potential for data breaches (Queiroz et al., 2023). Encryption stands as a pivotal technology in ensuring data security both during transmission and when at rest within the digital supply chain. Through the conversion of data into an unreadable format using intricate algorithms, encryption offers a robust layer of protection against unauthorized access and interception (Nozari & Edalatpanah, 2023). By employing encryption, even if data is intercepted, it remains incomprehensible to unauthorized parties. Within the digital supply chain, various encryption standards are widely adopted to safeguard sensitive data. Among these standards, the Advanced Encryption Standard (AES) holds recognition for its resilient encryption algorithms (Cui et al., 2023).

AES utilizes symmetric encryption, wherein the same key is used for both the encryption and decryption processes, thereby ensuring secure data transmission. In the digital supply chain, maintaining the integrity and security of encrypted data relies on effective key management practices. Organizations must implement secure key management procedures, encompassing the generation of robust encryption keys, secure storage and distribution of keys, and regular updates and rotation of keys (Dhasarathan et al., 2023). These measures contribute to the overall security and resilience of the digital supply chain ecosystem. By adhering to robust key management practices, organizations can ensure the integrity and confidentiality of encryption keys, thereby safeguarding the data. Securing data during its transmission across different nodes within the digital supply chain is crucial. This is achieved through the use of widely employed protocols such as Secure Socket Layer (SSL) and Transport Layer Security (TLS), which establish secure connections and encrypt data during transmission (Rawat, 2023). These protocols incorporate encryption and authentication mechanisms, effectively preventing unauthorized interception and tampering of data. The advent of cloud computing has brought about significant advancements in the digital supply chain by offering scalable and flexible data storage solutions. However, it also introduces new security challenges. To tackle these challenges, organizations must implement robust security measures, including data encryption, access controls, and strong authentication mechanisms, to protect data stored in the cloud (Liu et al., 2021). These measures ensure the security and confidentiality of data, even in cloud-based environments, and contribute to the overall resilience of the digital supply chain.

Secure Data Sharing and Collaboration Among Supply Chain Partners

The increasing complexity of global supply chains, coupled with the growing importance of data-driven decision-making, necessitates robust mechanisms for secure data sharing and collaboration among supply chain partners. This report explores various strategies, technologies, and best practices for ensuring the confidentiality, integrity, and availability of shared data in supply chain collaborations. Effective collaboration and information sharing are essential for optimizing supply chain operations, reducing costs, improving customer service, and enhancing overall competitiveness. However, sharing data among supply chain partners introduces several security challenges. These challenges include unauthorized access, data breaches, data manipulation, and information leakage (Li et al., 2019). Consequently, supply chain partners must implement comprehensive security measures to safeguard shared data.

a)   Access Control Mechanisms

Access control mechanisms play a fundamental role in ensuring that only authorized individuals can access sensitive data. These mechanisms involve the implementation of robust authentication methods, such as multi-factor authentication and biometrics. Multi-factor authentication requires users to provide multiple pieces of evidence, such as passwords, biometric data, or security tokens, to gain access to shared data (Amft et al., 2023). This approach adds an extra layer of security by requiring multiple forms of verification. Biometrics, on the other hand, leverages unique physical or behavioural attributes, such as fingerprints or facial recognition, for user identification and authentication. By using these distinctive characteristics, biometric authentication provides a high level of security and ensures that only authorized individuals can access the data. Both multi-factor authentication and biometric authentication significantly enhance the security of shared data by preventing unauthorized access and bolstering the overall data protection measures within the digital supply chain

b)   Encryption

Encryption is a robust technique that serves to protect data during both transit and storage. It involves the transformation of data into an unreadable format using encryption algorithms. Two primary types of encryption are commonly used: symmetric encryption and asymmetric encryption. Symmetric encryption employs a single shared key for both the encryption and decryption processes. This key is known to both the sender and the recipient. In contrast, asymmetric encryption, also referred to as public-key encryption, involves the use of a pair of keys: a public key for encryption and a private key for decryption. The public key is shared openly, while the private key remains confidential to the owner. Regardless of the encryption method employed, the main goal is to ensure that even if unauthorized parties gain access to the data, they cannot decipher its contents without the corresponding encryption key (Suganya & Sasipraba, 2023). This robust encryption mechanism contributes significantly to data security within the digital supply chain.

c)   Secure Communication Protocols

Secure communication protocols play a vital role in protecting data exchanged between supply chain partners. Protocols such as Secure Sockets Layer (SSL) and its successor, Transport Layer Security (TLS), are widely used to establish secure and encrypted connections over the internet. These protocols ensure the confidentiality and integrity of data during transmission by encrypting it before sending and decrypting it upon receipt. By implementing SSL or TLS, supply chain partners can mitigate the risk of data interception or tampering during transit. The encryption provided by these protocols ensures that sensitive information remains confidential and cannot be accessed by unauthorized parties. Moreover, the integrity of the data is maintained, as any tampering attempts would result in the decryption process detecting the alterations. The use of SSL and TLS as secure communication protocols within the digital supply chain enhances the overall security posture and instils confidence in the secure exchange of information between supply chain partners (Fadhil et al., 2023).

d)   Blockchain Technology

The advent of blockchain technology has revolutionized the field of secure data sharing and collaboration among supply chain partners. Through the adoption of robust access control mechanisms, encryption techniques, secure communication protocols, and exploration of blockchain's potential, organizations can fortify the security of their shared data and bolster collaborative efforts within the supply chain. Consequently, it is imperative for organizations to thoroughly evaluate their specific requirements and judiciously select the most suitable technological solutions to effectively meet their security objectives. In conclusion, blockchain technology presents a promising foundation for enhancing secure data sharing and collaboration within supply chains. By leveraging its decentralized nature, immutability, and cryptographic underpinnings, organizations can strengthen their collaborative endeavours and mitigate security risks. However, organizations need to assess their unique needs and carefully choose appropriate technological solutions to achieve optimal security outcomes within the supply chain context.

Figure 12. Cloud-based solution for supply chain
(Truong, 2014)

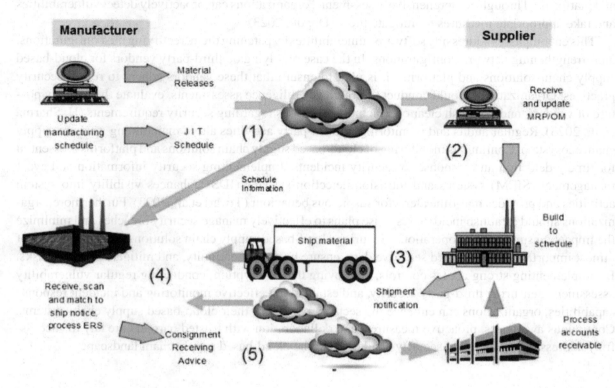

Securing Cloud-Based Supply Chain Solutions and Platforms

The adoption of cloud computing has witnessed a significant rise, prompting many organizations to migrate their supply chain solutions and platforms to the cloud. While leveraging cloud-based supply chain solutions brings forth a plethora of advantages, such as scalability, cost-effectiveness, and improved collaboration, it also introduces a set of security concerns. This section endeavours to emphasize the significance of securing cloud-based supply chain solutions and platforms, while also outlining key measures that organizations should contemplate. Cloud-based supply chain solutions and platforms encounter a range of security challenges that have the potential to jeopardize the confidentiality, integrity, and availability of vital data and operations. These challenges encompass unauthorized access, data breaches, insider threats, risks associated with third-party involvement, and compliance issues (Reece et al., 2023). Insufficient security measures can expose organizations to a range of detrimental consequences, including financial losses, damage to reputation, legal ramifications, and disruptions in supply chain operations. One crucial aspect of securing cloud-based supply chain solutions is the implementation of robust access controls. This entails deploying resilient authentication and authorization mechanisms to ensure that only authorized individuals can access sensitive data and perform specific actions (Chimuco et al., 2023). To mitigate the risk of unauthorized access, effective measures such as multi-factor authentication, role-based access control, and privileged access management solutions prove instrumental (Peterson, 2021). Conducting regular vulnerability assessments and penetration testing is paramount in identifying and addressing security weaknesses within cloud-based supply chain solutions and platforms. Through comprehensive assessments, organizations can proactively detect vulnerabilities and take appropriate measures to mitigate them (Doğdu, 2023).

This encompasses addressing software vulnerabilities by patching them, rectifying misconfigurations, and strengthening network configurations. In the case of relying on third-party vendors for cloud-based supply chain solutions and platforms, it is vital to ensure that these vendors adhere to robust security practices. Organizations should conduct thorough due diligence assessments, evaluate the security posture of vendors, and establish clear contractual obligations regarding security requirements (H. Sharma et al., 2023). Regular audits and monitoring of third-party activities aid in maintaining a secure supply chain ecosystem. Continuous monitoring of cloud-based supply chain solutions and platforms is essential for timely detection and response to security incidents. Implementing security information and event management (SIEM) systems and intrusion detection systems (IDS) enhances visibility into system activities and provides real-time alerts for suspicious behaviour (Tiwari et al., 2023). Furthermore, organizations should establish incident response plans to effectively manage security breaches and minimize the impact on supply chain operations. Securing cloud-based supply chain solutions and platforms is of utmost importance to safeguard sensitive data, ensure business continuity, and mitigate potential risks. By implementing strong access controls, employing data encryption, conducting regular vulnerability assessments, ensuring third-party security, and establishing effective monitoring and incident response capabilities, organizations can enhance the security posture of their cloud-based supply chain systems. Continuous awareness, proactive measures, and collaboration with trusted partners are key to successfully addressing the evolving security challenges in the cloud-based supply chain landscape.

SUPPLY CHAIN AUTHENTICATION AND IDENTITY MANAGEMENT

Importance of Supply Chain Authentication and Identity Management

Supply chain authentication and identity management play a pivotal role in upholding the integrity, security, and efficiency of global supply chains. Given the escalating complexity and globalization of supply chains, robust authentication and identity management systems are increasingly necessary to mitigate risks, combat counterfeiting, enhance traceability, and safeguard sensitive information. This section delves into the significance of supply chain authentication and identity management, as well as its impact on the various stakeholders engaged in the supply chain ecosystem. Supply chains are intricate networks encompassing numerous entities, including manufacturers, suppliers, distributors, retailers, and consumers. The modern supply chain's complexity and scale render it susceptible to various threats, including counterfeit products, unauthorized access, data breaches, and fraudulent activities. In this context, supply chain authentication and identity management serve as critical components for establishing trust, preserving data integrity, and ensuring accountability throughout the entire supply chain process.

a)   Enhanced Risk Mitigation

To mitigate risks within the supply chain, the implementation of reliable supply chain authentication and identity management systems is crucial. These systems enable organizations to employ robust authentication mechanisms, thereby verifying the authenticity of suppliers, products, and associated documentation. By ensuring that only authorized entities are involved in the supply chain process, unauthorized access is prevented, and the likelihood of counterfeiting, fraudulent activities, and data breaches is reduced (Gruchmann et al., 2023). The capability to authenticate and validate each entity within the supply chain enhances risk mitigation efforts and bolsters the overall integrity of the supply chain ecosystem.

b) Prevention of Counterfeiting

The presence of counterfeit products presents substantial risks to both organizations and consumers, ranging from financial losses for businesses to potential harm to consumer health and safety. Supply chain authentication and identity management solutions play a vital role in countering counterfeiting activities. They achieve this by implementing unique identifiers, such as serialized barcodes or RFID tags, that can be authenticated at various stages of the supply chain. These distinctive identifiers enable organizations to effectively track and verify the origin of products, allowing for the identification and removal of counterfeit items from circulation (K. Tiwari et al., n.d.). By ensuring the authenticity of products, organizations can safeguard their brand reputation and cultivate consumer trust.

c) Improved Traceability and Transparency

Traceability plays a vital role in effective supply chain management as it enables organizations to monitor and trace the movement of goods from their origin to the final destination. Supply chain authentication and identity management systems play a pivotal role in establishing end-to-end traceability by assigning unique identities and implementing tracking mechanisms for each entity involved. This comprehensive traceability capability allows for swift and accurate identification of any issues or bottlenecks that may arise within the supply chain, such as delays, quality control problems, or compliance issues (Khanna et al., 2023). Improved traceability brings about enhanced transparency by providing visibility into the supply chain's operations, enabling organizations to promptly address problems, enhance overall efficiency, and meet regulatory requirements. Moreover, heightened transparency fosters trust among stakeholders and contributes to improved customer satisfaction.

d) Safeguarding Sensitive Information

The exchange of sensitive information within supply chains, such as trade secrets, financial data, and customer information, necessitates robust authentication and identity management solutions to safeguard against unauthorized access and data breaches. Through the implementation of effective measures like strong access controls, encryption techniques, and secure communication channels, organizations can ensure that only authorized individuals have access to sensitive data. These security measures significantly reduce the risk of data leakage, intellectual property theft, and financial fraud (Yenugula et al., 2023). By protecting sensitive information, organizations can uphold confidentiality, integrity, and compliance with data protection regulations. Safeguarding sensitive data within the supply chain enhances overall security and minimizes potential legal and reputational risks.

e) Strengthening Collaboration and Accountability

Supply chain authentication and identity management systems play a pivotal role in fostering collaboration and accountability among supply chain partners. Through the establishment of distinct identities and clear roles for each participant, organizations can ensure that responsibilities are appropriately assigned and executed. This fosters a sense of trust and facilitates efficient coordination, thereby reducing the potential for fraud or malicious activities within the supply chain ecosystem. Moreover, authentication and identity management systems provide an auditable trail of activities, enabling organizations to hold individuals accountable for their actions and ensuring compliance with industry standards and regulations (Chandan et al., 2023). By strengthening collaboration and accountability, these systems contribute to overall supply chain efficiency and integrity. The transparent and accountable nature of the supply chain helps build trust among partners, improves decision-making, and facilitates smoother operations.

In the current interconnected and intricate supply chain landscape, supply chain authentication and identity management have become essential for organizations to uphold trust, mitigate risks, and safeguard their brand reputation. Through the implementation of robust authentication mechanisms, organizations can effectively combat counterfeiting, enhance traceability, protect sensitive information, and reinforce collaboration and accountability. As supply chains continue to evolve, the significance of authentication and identity management will only grow, emphasizing the need for organizations to prioritize the adoption of these systems to ensure the integrity and security of their supply chain operations. By doing so, organizations can confidently navigate the evolving supply chain landscape and maintain a competitive edge in the market.

Figure 13. Multifactor authentication mechanism
(Microcosm, n.d.)

Implementing Secure Access Controls and User Authentication Mechanisms

Ensuring secure access controls is paramount to restrict access to sensitive data and systems within the supply chain, permitting only authorized individuals to gain entry. By implementing robust access controls, organizations can effectively prevent unauthorized access attempts and potential security breaches. Access controls encompass various mechanisms, including user identification, authentication, and authorization. User authentication serves as a foundational element of secure access controls, as it verifies the identity of users seeking access to the supply chain system. Multiple authentication mechanisms are available, such as passwords, biometrics, tokens, and multi-factor authentication (MFA). Each mechanism possesses its strengths and weaknesses, requiring organizations to choose the most suitable method based on their specific requirements and risk profile. Passwords stand as the most commonly employed authentication mechanism. However, they can be vulnerable to brute force attacks and password guessing. Therefore, it is crucial to enforce strong password policies that encompass complexity requirements, regular password changes, and password hashing techniques (Jianzhou et al., 2023).

Biometric authentication, such as fingerprint or facial recognition, offers a higher level of security by relying on unique physical characteristics that are difficult to replicate or steal, thereby enhancing the overall security of the supply chain system (Islam, 2023b). Tokens, such as smart cards or USB tokens, serve as an effective means of two-factor authentication. They provide an additional layer of security by requiring physical possession of the token in addition to knowledge of a password or PIN (Albazar et al., 2023). Multi-factor authentication (MFA) combines two or more authentication factors, such as something the user knows (e.g., password), something the user has (e.g., token), or something the user is (e.g., biometric). MFA significantly strengthens the authentication process and reduces the risk of unauthorized access (Rani et al., 2023). The implementation of secure access controls and user authentication mechanisms in the supply chain offers several benefits. Firstly, it helps prevent unauthorized access and protects sensitive data, thereby reducing the risk of data breaches and intellectual property theft (Kumar & Reddy, 2023). Secondly, it enhances the overall security posture of the supply chain, instilling greater confidence among stakeholders in the system's reliability and integrity (Yontar, 2023). Lastly, secure access controls and authentication mechanisms enable organizations to comply with industry regulations and standards, such as the General Data Protection Regulation (GDPR) and ISO 27001, by ensuring the confidentiality, integrity, and availability of data (Yang et al., 2023).

Role of Digital Certificates and Cryptographic Protocols in Identity Management

Identity management plays a crucial role in the supply chain by verifying and validating the identities of different entities involved, including manufacturers, distributors, retailers, and customers. This process aims to establish trust and facilitate secure transactions within the supply chain ecosystem. Digital certificates, based on public-key infrastructure (PKI), are extensively utilized to authenticate the identities of these entities. PKI relies on cryptographic techniques to generate and manage digital certificates, which serve as electronic credentials that verify the legitimacy and authenticity of individuals or organizations. By employing digital certificates, supply chain entities can establish secure communication channels, ensuring that interactions and transactions are conducted with trusted parties (Hoang, 2023). The utilization of PKI-based digital certificates enhances the overall security and integrity of the supply chain by validating the identities of participating entities. This strengthens trust among stakeholders and reduces the risk of unauthorized access, fraud, or malicious activities within the supply chain ecosystem.

- **Authentication, Authorization and Non-repudiation**

Digital certificates serve as essential digital credentials that verify the identity of entities within the supply chain. They provide a trusted third-party validation of an entity's identity, enabling other participants to authenticate and authorize interactions accordingly (Islam, 2023). To enhance authentication, cryptographic protocols like Transport Layer Security (TLS) and Secure Shell (SSH) are employed. These protocols establish secure connections and encrypt sensitive information, further bolstering the security of the authentication process (Mehdi Rizvi & Kushwaha, 2023). Non-repudiation is a critical aspect of identity management in the supply chain, ensuring that parties cannot deny their actions or transactions. Digital certificates, in conjunction with cryptographic protocols like digital signatures and timestamping, provide evidence of the origin and integrity of messages or transactions, minimizing disputes and enhancing accountability (Murimi et al., 2023). Preserving the integrity and confidentiality of data within the supply chain is paramount to prevent unauthorized access and tampering. Digital certificates and cryptographic protocols play vital roles in ensuring data integrity through the use of digital signatures and message authentication codes (MACs) (Suryavanshi et al., 2023). Encryption algorithms, such as the Advanced Encryption Standard (AES), are utilized to protect sensitive information, restricting access solely to authorized parties (Miao et al., 2023). By employing digital certificates and cryptographic protocols, organizations can establish a secure and trustworthy environment within the supply chain, safeguarding identities, data integrity, and confidential information.

- **Benefits and Challenges**

The utilization of digital certificates and cryptographic protocols in identity management within the supply chain offers numerous advantages, including heightened security, reduced fraud, increased trust among stakeholders, and streamlined transactions. However, to effectively implement these mechanisms, challenges such as standardization, scalability, and interoperability between different systems and stakeholders must be addressed. As supply chains continue to grow in complexity and interconnectedness, the role of digital certificates and cryptographic protocols in identity management will continue to evolve. Emerging technologies like blockchain provide decentralized and tamper-proof identity verification mechanisms that complement existing PKI-based systems (N et al., 2023). Furthermore, advancements in quantum-resistant cryptographic algorithms are being explored to ensure long-term security against potential threats posed by quantum computing (Farooq et al., 2023). In summary, digital certificates and cryptographic protocols play a critical role in identity management within the supply chain by providing authentication, integrity, confidentiality, and non-repudiation. Despite challenges, the benefits of implementing these mechanisms outweigh the drawbacks. As technology advances, future developments will further strengthen identity management in the supply chain, ensuring its resilience in an increasingly interconnected world.

Figure 14. Digital certificate mechanism in blockchain
(Alam, 2021)

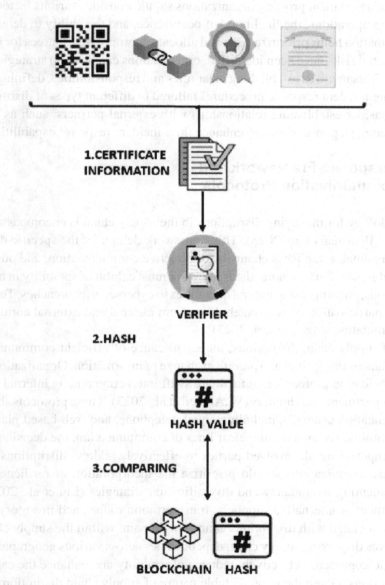

INCIDENT RESPONSE AND CYBERSECURITY INCIDENT MANAGEMENT

Establishing an Effective Incident Response Plan for Supply Chain Disruptions

To create an effective incident response plan, organizations should start by gaining a comprehensive understanding of their supply chain, including all stakeholders, processes, and dependencies. This understanding enables organizations to identify critical nodes and vulnerabilities within the supply chain (Sirisomboonsuk & Burns, 2023). By mapping out the supply chain and conducting risk assessments, organizations can proactively identify potential sources of disruptions and develop strategies to address them. During the risk assessment process, organizations should consider various factors such as the impact of disruptions on operations, the likelihood of occurrence, and the ability to detect and respond to incidents. This information helps prioritize risks and allocate appropriate resources for incident response planning. Once potential risks have been identified, organizations can develop strategies to mitigate and respond to incidents. This involves establishing clear roles and responsibilities, defining communication channels, and creating incident response procedures tailored to different types of disruptions. Organizations should also consider establishing relationships with external partners, such as law enforcement agencies and emergency response teams, to enhance their incident response capabilities.

Developing a Response Framework and Establishing Communication Protocols

A structured methodology for managing disruptions in the supply chain is encompassed by an incident response framework (Bearman et al., 2023). This framework delineates the specific duties and obligations of essential personnel, establishes channels for effective communication, and outlines procedures for escalating critical issues. Furthermore, the framework must exhibit adaptability in addressing a wide spectrum of disruptions, encompassing natural calamities to cybersecurity breaches. To foster a cohesive response, the active participation of key stakeholders from internal and external entities is vital during the framework's formulation stage (Assibi, 2023).

In the context of supply chain disruptions, the significance of efficient communication cannot be overstated, as it guarantees the prompt and precise exchange of information. Organizations must establish well-defined communication protocols that facilitate swift interaction among internal teams, suppliers, customers, and other pertinent stakeholders (W. Ahmed et al., 2023). These protocols should incorporate a variety of communication channels, including email, telephone, and web-based platforms, to ensure redundancy and flexibility. By maintaining clear lines of communication, the decision-making process can be expedited, empowering all involved parties to effectively address disruptions. To mitigate the effects of disruptions, organizations should prioritize the incorporation of resilience into their supply chains by implementing redundancy and diversification strategies (Liu et al., 2023). Redundancy entails the establishment of alternative suppliers, transportation routes, and inventory buffers, thereby mitigating the risk associated with disruptions at any single point within the supply chain. Conversely, diversification involves dispersing supply chain dependencies across various geographic regions or suppliers. These strategic approaches effectively reduce vulnerability and enhance the capacity for a swift recovery from disruptions. Given the unpredictable nature of supply chain disruptions, it is imperative to emphasize the importance of ongoing monitoring and evaluation in maintaining an efficient incident response plan (Mahmood et al., 2023). Organizations should regularly assess the efficacy of their response strategies and incorporate lessons learned from past disruptions. This involves monitoring key performance indicators, conducting comprehensive risk assessments, and actively seeking feedback from relevant stakeholders. By actively monitoring the supply chain and conducting thorough evaluations of the incident response plan, organizations can pinpoint areas that require improvement and bolster their resilience to future disruptions.

In today's interconnected and dynamic business landscape, organizations must give utmost importance to the development of a comprehensive incident response plan to address supply chain disruptions. By comprehending the intricacies of their supply chain, creating a well-defined response framework, establishing effective communication protocols, fostering resilience, and continuously monitoring and evaluating the plan, organizations can effectively minimize the impact of disruptions and ensure uninterrupted business operations. Implementing these strategies necessitates close collaboration and coordination among internal teams, suppliers, and customers. Organizations that invest in robust incident response plans are better positioned to adapt to unforeseen disruptions, thereby maintaining their competitive advantage in the marketplace

Incident Detection, Containment, and Recovery in the Digital Supply Chain

The process of incident detection entails the identification and timely response to anomalous events or security breaches occurring within the digital supply chain. By implementing robust mechanisms for incident detection, organizations can promptly identify and mitigate cyber threats. Advanced threat intelligence platforms, such as Security Information and Event Management (SIEM) systems, leverage real-time monitoring, log analysis, and correlation techniques to identify suspicious activities (Henriques et al., 2023). Additionally, Intrusion Detection Systems (IDS) and Intrusion Prevention Systems (IPS) play a vital role in detecting and alerting organizations about potential attacks (Jeldi & Kumar, 2022). These sophisticated tools and technologies contribute to enhancing the overall incident detection capabilities of organizations in safeguarding their digital supply chains.

- **Containment**

Upon the detection of an incident, it is crucial to promptly implement containment measures to mitigate further harm and restrict the propagation of the attack. An essential strategy for containment is network segmentation, which entails isolating compromised segments to minimize the lateral movement of threats within the digital supply chain (Bandari, 2023). Furthermore, the deployment of endpoint security solutions, such as advanced antivirus software and host-based firewalls, plays a significant role in containing incidents by thwarting the proliferation of malware (Koduru et al., 2023). Additionally, the implementation of robust access controls and identity and access management (IAM) solutions can effectively restrict unauthorized access to critical systems and data (Rahaman et al., 2023).

- **Recovery**

In the context of the digital supply chain, recovery entails the restoration of systems, data, and operations to their normal state following an incident. To facilitate prompt recovery processes, organizations should establish dedicated incident response teams and develop comprehensive response plans (Behie et al., 2023). It is crucial to maintain regular backups of critical data and systems, ensuring that efficient recovery can be achieved in the event of a cyber incident (Logeshwaran, 2023). Additionally, leveraging forensic techniques to analyze the incident and ascertain its underlying causes can aid in implementing preventive measures and mitigating the risk of future incidents (Padovan et al., 2022).

In summary, the effective implementation of incident detection, containment, and recovery measures plays a critical role in establishing a robust cybersecurity strategy within the digital supply chain. Employing proactive measures, such as advanced threat detection systems, network segmentation, and dedicated incident response teams, is essential for promptly identifying, containing, and recovering from cyber incidents. It is also important to conduct regular training and awareness programs to educate employees about potential threats and empower them with the necessary skills to respond effectively. By prioritizing incident management and adopting a comprehensive cybersecurity approach, organizations can minimize the impact of incidents, ensure uninterrupted business operations, and safeguard the integrity of their digital supply chains Figure15 shows six steps of indicent response plan.

Figure 15. Six steps of incident response plan

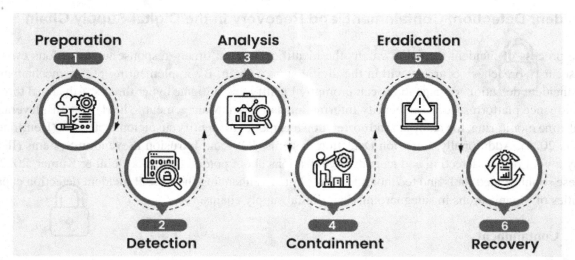

Collaborative Incident Response With Supply Chain Partners

Collaborative incident response with supply chain partners holds significant importance in modern business operations, especially considering the prevalent global interconnectedness and reliance on complex supply chains. Incidents such as natural disasters, cyberattacks, or quality issues can disrupt supply chain operations and lead to far-reaching consequences. Hence, effective collaboration and coordinated response among supply chain partners are imperative to mitigate the impact of such incidents and ensure uninterrupted business continuity. This section aims to delve into the significance of collaborative incident response with supply chain partners, examining the benefits derived from its successful implementation. By working together, supply chain partners can swiftly identify incidents and facilitate containment efforts. Collaborative efforts enable the timely identification of the incident source and its nature, facilitating a targeted and efficient response (Agbede, 2023). Collaborative incident response plays a pivotal role in strengthening supply chain resilience by facilitating effective recovery strategies. Through the sharing of resources, knowledge, and expertise, supply chain partners can collectively develop resilient contingency plans to minimize downtime and achieve swift recovery (N. Zhao et al., 2023). Additionally, collaborative incident response fosters information sharing and joint risk assessment, enabling proactive measures for risk mitigation. By pooling their risk management expertise, partners can identify vulnerabilities within the supply chain and implement more effective strategies to reduce risks (Sánchez & De Batista, 2023). The practice of collaborative incident response with supply chain partners is indispensable for managing and mitigating the impact of incidents within complex supply chains. The benefits derived from collaborative incident response include rapid identification and containment of incidents, enhanced supply chain resilience, and improved risk mitigation strategies.

ENSURING SUPPLY CHAIN RESILIENCE

Building Resilience in the Digital Supply Chain

Enhancing the resilience of the digital supply chain holds immense importance in guaranteeing continuous operations and minimizing the adverse effects of unforeseen circumstances. This section delves into essential strategies and exemplary practices that contribute to bolstering resilience within the digital supply chain, with a specific focus on cybersecurity, data management, collaboration, and agility. Safeguarding against cyber threats is of paramount significance in shielding digital assets and upholding uninterrupted supply chain processes. Organizations must implement robust cybersecurity measures that effectively mitigate the risks associated with cyberattacks and data breaches (Kang, 2023). Such measures include the deployment of firewalls, intrusion detection systems, encryption protocols, and regular security audits. Moreover, the management of data assumes a pivotal role in fortifying resilience within the digital supply chain. To ensure the integrity, availability, and confidentiality of critical information, organizations must establish comprehensive frameworks for data governance (Zakzouk et al., 2023).

The implementation of data backup and recovery mechanisms, along with the utilization of cloud-based storage solutions, can significantly enhance the resilience of data. To effectively address disruptions, collaboration among supply chain partners is essential. Organizations should prioritize the cultivation of robust relationships with suppliers, logistics providers, and customers, fostering enhanced communication and information sharing (Mohamed et al., 2023). The utilization of collaborative platforms and technologies facilitates real-time visibility and transparency throughout the supply chain, enabling proactive risk management (Tripathi et al., 2023). Additionally, the establishment of agility within the digital supply chain is paramount for resilience. Organizations should embrace flexible processes and technologies that enable rapid responses to disruptions and ever-changing market conditions (He et al., 2023). This entails the implementation of advanced analytics and predictive modelling to anticipate risks and optimize decision-making. Excessive dependence on a single supplier can have a substantial impact on the resilience of the digital supply chain. To mitigate the risks associated with supplier disruptions, organizations should embrace a diversified sourcing strategy, engaging multiple suppliers and regions (Mohezar et al., 2023). By evaluating supplier capabilities, conducting regular assessments, and fostering alternative sourcing options, the resilience of the supply chain can be enhanced. It is crucial to prioritize regular risk assessments and engage in scenario planning exercises to identify vulnerabilities and develop effective contingency plans (Kaur et al., 2023). These proactive measures contribute to strengthening the overall resilience of the digital supply chain.

Organizations should conduct a thorough analysis of potential disruptions, assess their potential impact on the digital supply chain, and develop effective mitigation strategies. This proactive approach enables organizations to respond promptly and efficiently to unexpected events. The establishment of resilience within the digital supply chain is of utmost importance for organizations to thrive in the constantly evolving business environment of today. By emphasizing key aspects such as cybersecurity, robust data management, collaboration, agility, supplier diversification, and risk assessment, organizations can fortify their supply chains against disruptive forces. It is vital to maintain a continuous monitoring process and adapt strategies to align with emerging technologies and evolving threats. This ensures the long-term resilience and sustainability of the digital supply chain. Figure 16 shows six strategies for a more resilient supply chain

EMERGING TECHNOLOGIES AND FUTURE TRENDS

Impact of Emerging Technologies (e.g., Blockchain, IoT) on Securing the Digital Supply Chain

Amid the ongoing evolution of the digital landscape, the emergence of groundbreaking technologies like blockchain and the IoT has garnered attention as promising solutions for fortifying the security and efficiency of the digital supply chain. This report delves into the impact of these technologies on enhancing security, transparency, and operational efficiency within supply chain operations. Through an extensive examination of existing literature and insightful case studies, this report sheds light on the potential benefits and challenges associated with the adoption of blockchain and IoT in securing the digital supply chain. The findings underscore the transformative potential of these technologies in revolutionizing supply chain management. They offer robust security measures, real-time monitoring capabilities, and improved traceability, thereby paving the way for enhanced supply chain resilience and effectiveness. The digital supply chain serves as a vital component by connecting numerous stakeholders and enabling the seamless flow of goods, services, and information. However, as supply chain networks become more intricate and interconnected, security concerns have emerged as a significant challenge. To tackle these concerns, emerging technologies like blockchain and the IoT offer innovative solutions that enhance the security of the digital supply chain. This report focuses on evaluating the impact of these technologies in securing the digital supply chain, with a particular emphasis on their potential benefits and challenges. By leveraging blockchain and IoT, organizations can address security vulnerabilities and fortify the resilience of their supply chains in an increasingly interconnected environment.

Figure 16. Six strategies for a more resilient supply chain
(Hippold, 2020)

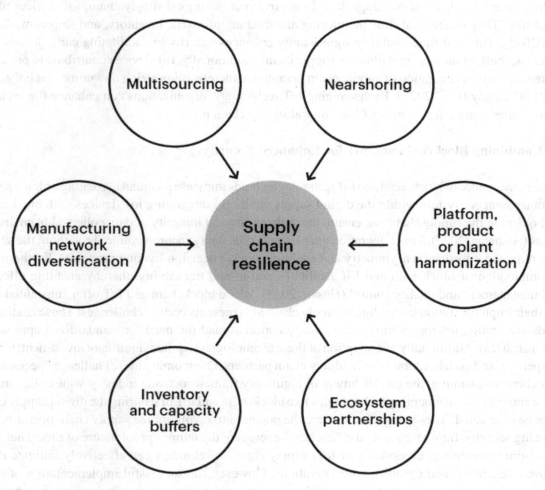

- **Impact of Blockchain on Securing the Digital Supply Chain**

Blockchain, a distributed ledger technology, has garnered considerable attention due to its capacity to provide transparency, immutability, and security to transactions. Within the digital supply chain context, blockchain offers several notable advantages. Firstly, it enables the secure and tamper-proof recording and verification of transactions, thereby ensuring data integrity throughout the entire supply chain (Sharma & Meena, 2023). Secondly, the decentralized nature of blockchain eliminates the need for intermediaries, reducing the risks associated with fraud, counterfeiting, and unauthorized access (Manzoor, 2023). Lastly, the utilization of smart contracts in blockchain facilitates the automated and secure execution of supply chain agreements, effectively minimizing disputes and delays (Çelik et al., 2023). By harnessing the potential of blockchain technology, organizations can enhance the security, trustworthiness, and efficiency of their digital supply chain operations.

- **Impact of IoT on Securing the Digital Supply Chain**

The IoT encompasses a network of physical devices equipped with sensors, software, and connectivity, enabling them to gather and exchange data. In the realm of the digital supply chain, IoT devices play a pivotal role. They enable real-time monitoring and tracking of assets, inventory, and shipments (Soori et al., 2023). This real-time visibility significantly enhances security by facilitating early detection of anomalies, theft, or tampering within the supply chain. Additionally, IoT devices contribute to proactive maintenance and optimization of supply chain operations, thereby minimizing downtime and bolstering overall efficiency (Das, 2023). By leveraging IoT technology, organizations can enhance the security, responsiveness, and effectiveness of their digital supply chain processes.

- **Combining Blockchain and IoT for Enhanced Security**

The convergence of blockchain and IoT technologies holds immense potential in creating a highly secure and transparent ecosystem within the digital supply chain. By integrating IoT devices with blockchain, stakeholders in the supply chain can ensure the authenticity and integrity of data collected from diverse sources (Alshehri, 2023). This integration enables real-time data synchronization throughout the supply chain, reducing information asymmetry and enabling quicker decision-making processes. Furthermore, the combination of blockchain and IoT facilitates end-to-end traceability, thereby enabling effective recall management and quality control (Hasan, 2023). While blockchain and IoT offer substantial benefits, their implementation in the digital supply chain also presents certain challenges. These challenges include scalability, interoperability, data privacy concerns, and the need for standardized approaches (Alshehri, 2023). Additionally, the adoption of these technologies requires significant investment, technical expertise, and collaboration among supply chain partners. Overcoming these challenges necessitates comprehensive planning, the establishment of regulatory frameworks, and industry-wide collaboration

The significance of emerging technologies like blockchain and IoT in securing the digital supply chain cannot be overstated. These technologies have the potential to revolutionize supply chain operations by enhancing security, transparency, and efficiency. Leveraging the tamper-proof nature of blockchain and the real-time monitoring capabilities of IoT, supply chain stakeholders can effectively mitigate risks, improve traceability, and optimize their operations. However, the successful implementation of these technologies requires addressing various challenges, including technical complexities, operational considerations, and regulatory compliance. It is crucial to foster collaboration among stakeholders and invest in research and development to fully unlock the potential of blockchain and IoT in securing the digital supply chain. As these technologies continue to evolve, industry-wide initiatives and ongoing innovation are necessary to maximize their impact and drive transformative changes in supply chain security.

Anticipating Future Cyber Threats and Vulnerabilities

- **Advanced Persistent Threats (APTs) and Insider Threats**

Advanced Persistent Threats (APTs) are highly sophisticated cyber threats that employ persistent attacks to infiltrate systems and steal sensitive data. APTs utilize stealthy techniques to remain undetected for extended periods, enabling attackers to gather intelligence and maintain access to compromised systems. These threats often involve social engineering tactics, exploit zero-day vulnerabilities, and employ customized malware to bypass security measures (Sharma et al., 2023). APTs pose a significant risk to the digital supply chain as they have the potential to compromise critical data, disrupt operations, and inflict financial and reputational damage on organizations. Organizations need to implement robust security measures and stay vigilant against APTs to safeguard their digital supply chain infrastructure and protect sensitive information from unauthorized access. Insider threats continue to pose a persistent risk within the digital supply chain. These threats arise from individuals with authorized access, including employees, contractors, or trusted partners, who misuse their privileges for malicious purposes. Insider threats can manifest in various forms, such as disgruntled employees seeking revenge, individuals coerced by external actors, or unintentional negligence or errors (Möller, 2023). Insiders leverage their knowledge of the supply chain's vulnerabilities and security controls to carry out activities such as data breaches, theft, sabotage, or unauthorized modifications. Effectively detecting and mitigating insider threats requires the implementation of a combination of technical controls, user training, and continuous monitoring to identify suspicious activities and behaviours. Organizations should prioritize proactive measures to mitigate the risk of insider threats and foster a culture of security awareness among employees and partners involved in the digital supply chain.

- **IoT Exploitation and Supply Chain Interdependencies**

The integration of IoT devices within the digital supply chain has witnessed a significant increase in recent years. However, this integration has also brought forth a new set of vulnerabilities that require careful consideration. IoT devices, in many cases, lack robust security controls, rendering them attractive targets for cybercriminals. Common issues include weak default passwords, unpatched vulnerabilities, and inadequate encryption mechanisms, all of which contribute to their susceptibility to exploitation. Consequently, compromising IoT devices within the supply chain enables attackers to gain unauthorized access to critical systems, manipulate data, or disrupt operations (Srihith et al., 2023). Instances of such malicious activities have the potential to cause significant disturbances in the supply chain, jeopardize the integrity of data, and lead to substantial financial losses. The digital supply chain operates within a complex and interconnected framework, relying heavily on the smooth functioning of its various components. By targeting vulnerabilities within any segment of the supply chain, the repercussions can extend throughout the entire system, affecting interconnected subsystems and stakeholders. For instance, a breach in the logistics management system can have far-reaching consequences, disrupting the flow of goods and impacting crucial aspects such as inventory management, production schedules, and customer deliveries. Adversaries exploit the interdependencies within the supply chain to gain unauthorized access, manipulate data, or create disruptions (Barnett et al., 2023The assurance of security and resilience across the entire supply chain is of utmost importance in mitigating the aforementioned risks. Organizations can enhance the security of their digital supply chain, safeguard sensitive data, and uphold the uninterrupted functionality of critical supply chain operations by comprehending and addressing these emerging threats and vulnerabilities. Effective mitigation of these evolving risks entails the implementation of robust cybersecurity measures, periodic evaluation of risks, and the cultivation of a security-conscious culture within the organization.

Evolving Strategies and Technologies for Enhanced Supply Chain Security

The establishment of trust and transparency within the supply chain necessitates the implementation of robust supplier verification and auditing processes. Organizations should engage in thorough background checks and assess the security practices of potential suppliers (Shimels & Lessa, 2023). Regular audits should be conducted to ensure adherence to security standards, such as ISO 28000, which specifically addresses the security management of the supply chain (Marquez-Tejon et al., 2023). The timely and accurate sharing of information plays a vital role in effective supply chain security. Collaborative platforms and technologies enable stakeholders to engage in real-time communication, enabling swift responses to security incidents. Initiatives like the Customs-Trade Partnership Against Terrorism (C-TPAT) facilitate the exchange of information between government agencies and businesses, aiming to identify and mitigate security risks (CBP, n.d.). The advent of advanced tracking and traceability technologies, notably radio frequency identification (RFID) and blockchain is revolutionizing the field of supply chain security. RFID tags enable real-time monitoring of goods, mitigating the risk of theft or tampering (Decker & Zoghi, 2023). Blockchain technology offers an immutable and transparent ledger for recording and validating transactions, thereby enhancing supply chain visibility and establishing trust (Wei, 2023).

Transportation and warehousing stages are particularly susceptible to security threats. The implementation of secure transportation practices, such as the use of tamper-evident seals and GPS tracking, plays a crucial role in preserving the integrity of goods during transit (Xu et al., 2023). Furthermore, employing secure warehousing techniques, including access controls, surveillance systems, and robust inventory management, effectively reduces the likelihood of unauthorized access or theft. The augmentation of supply chain security necessitates the implementation of a comprehensive approach that encompasses risk assessment, supplier verification, information sharing, advanced tracking technologies, secure transportation and warehousing practices, as well as cybersecurity measures. Through the adoption of these evolving strategies and technologies, organizations can effectively mitigate risks, protect their supply chains, and uphold the seamless flow of goods and information. Vigilant and ongoing monitoring, evaluation, and adaptation to emerging threats are essential in maintaining a resilient and secure supply chain ecosystem within the dynamic and ever-changing global landscape.

CONCLUSION

Within this chapter, we have extensively explored the pivotal subject matter of fortifying the digital supply chain, with particular emphasis on the realm of cyber threats and vulnerabilities. Through our discourse, several significant concepts and discernments have emerged. Firstly, we have duly established the indispensability of cybersecurity within the supply chain milieu. Given the escalating digitization of supply chain processes, it has become imperative to proactively address the attendant risks and challenges. Subsequently, we have embarked upon a comprehensive examination of the constituents and stakeholders inherent to the digital supply chain, duly accentuating the advantages and hurdles intrinsic to supply chain management digitization. We have underscored the integrative role of information systems and technologies as an integral facet of the digital supply chain framework. To comprehend the landscape of cyber threats, we have meticulously analyzed prevalent malevolent activities targeting the supply chain, accompanied by illuminating case studies of significant cyber assaults. Furthermore, we have delved into the potential repercussions stemming from cyber breaches within the supply chain, thereby underscoring the imperativeness of adopting proactive measures.

A pivotal facet elucidated within our discourse pertained to the identification and meticulous analysis of vulnerabilities inherent to supply chain processes. We expounded upon plausible ingress points for cyber assaults and underscored the utmost significance of conducting comprehensive risk assessments and implementing robust vulnerability management protocols. Supply chain risk management

(SCRM) emerged as a pivotal strategy indispensably employed to fortify the digital supply chain. We thoroughly explored the assimilation of cybersecurity principles into SCRM frameworks and shed light upon exemplary practices for the identification, assessment, and mitigation of cyber risks. Moreover, we scrutinized the profound importance of cultivating secure supplier relationships within the digital supply chain domain. Our deliberations encompassed the meticulous evaluation and selection of secure suppliers, as well as the contractual considerations germane to incorporating cybersecurity provisions within supplier agreements. Notably, we embarked upon an in-depth exploration of data protection, secure data sharing practices, and the imperative of securing cloud-based supply chain solutions within the purview of safeguarding information systems and data.

The significance of supply chain authentication and identity management as pivotal factors in fortifying supply chain security was diligently underscored. We placed paramount emphasis on the implementation of impregnable access controls, user authentication mechanisms, and the instrumental role played by digital certificates and cryptographic protocols. Furthermore, we embarked upon an exploratory journey elucidating the establishment of efficacious incident response plans and the indispensable need for collaborative incident response with supply chain partners to effectively address supply chain disruptions and cyber incidents. The assurance of supply chain resilience through astute business continuity planning, well-crafted disaster recovery strategies, proactive supply chain monitoring, heightened visibility, and real-time threat intelligence was unequivocally recognized as critical constituents in the systematic mitigation of risks. Moreover, we thoughtfully delved into the reverberations of emerging technologies, such as blockchain and the IoT, upon the securing of the digital supply chain. In doing so, we expounded upon the anticipation of future cyber threats and vulnerabilities, while simultaneously highlighting the ever-evolving strategies and technologies that hold the potential to fortify supply chain security to unprecedented levels. As a comprehensive whole, this scholarly endeavour illuminates the multifaceted nature of securing the digital supply chain, proffering invaluable insights and astute recommendations that stand to empower organizations in their pursuit to safeguard their supply chain processes from the perils of cyber threats and vulnerabilities.

REFERENCES

Abusitta, A., De Carvalho, G. H., Wahab, O. A., Halabi, T., Fung, B. C., & Mamoori, S. A. (2023). Deep learning-enabled anomaly detection for IoT systems. *Internet of Things : Engineering Cyber Physical Human Systems*, *21*, 100656. doi:10.1016/j.iot.2022.100656

Afenyo, M., & Caesar, L. D. (2023). Maritime cybersecurity threats: Gaps and directions for future research. *Ocean and Coastal Management*, *236*, 106493. doi:10.1016/j.ocecoaman.2023.106493

Agbede, O. M. (2023). *Incident Handling and Response Process in Security Operations*. Theseus. https://www.theseus.fi/handle/10024/795764

Ahmed, T., Karmaker, C. L., Nasir, S. B., Moktadir, M. A., & Paul, S. K. (2023). Modeling the artificial intelligence-based imperatives of industry 5.0 towards resilient supply chains: A post-COVID-19 pandemic perspective. *Computers & Industrial Engineering*, *177*, 109055. doi:10.1016/j.cie.2023.109055 PMID:36741206

Ahmed, W., Khan, M. A., Najmi, A., & Khan, S. A. (2023). Strategizing risk information sharing framework among supply chain partners for financial performance. *Supply Chain Forum*, 1–18. Taylor & Francis. 10.1080/16258312.2022.2162321

Akanmu, M. D., Hassan, M. G., Mohamad, B., & Nordin, N. (2021). Sustainability through TQM practices in the food and beverages industry. *International Journal of Quality & Reliability Management*, *40*(2), 335–364. doi:10.1108/IJQRM-05-2021-0143

Al-Banna, A., Yaqot, M., & Menezes, B. C. (2023). Roadmap to digital supply chain resilience under investment constraints. *Production & Manufacturing Research*, *11*(1), 2194943. doi:10.1080/2169327 7.2023.2194943

Al-Harrasi, A. S., Shaikh, A. R., & Al-Badi, A. H. (2021). Towards protecting organisations' data by preventing data theft by malicious insiders. *The International Journal of Organizational Analysis*. Advance online publication. doi:10.1108/IJOA-01-2021-2598

Alam, S. (2021). A Blockchain-based framework for secure Educational Credentials. [TURCOMAT]. *Turkish Journal of Computer and Mathematics Education*, *12*(10), 5157–5167. doi:10.17762/turcomat. v12i10.5298

Albazar, H., Abdel-Wahab, A., Alshar'e, M., & Abualkishik, A. (2023). An Adaptive Two-Factor Authentication Scheme Based on the Usage of Schnorr Signcryption Algorithm. *Informatica (Vilnius)*, *47*(5). doi:10.31449/inf.v47i5.4627

Alferidah, D. K., & Zaman, N. (2020). *Cybersecurity Impact over Bigdata and IoT Growth*. IEEE. doi:10.1109/ICCI51257.2020.9247722

Ali, A. M., Mahfouz, A., & Arisha, A. (2017). Analysing supply chain resilience: Integrating the constructs in a concept mapping framework via a systematic literature review. *Supply Chain Management*, *22*(1), 16–39. doi:10.1108/SCM-06-2016-0197

Aljabhan, B., & Obaidat, M. A. (2023). Privacy-Preserving Blockchain Framework for Supply Chain Management: Perceptive Craving Game Search Optimization (PCGSO). *Sustainability (Basel)*, *15*(8), 6905. doi:10.3390/su15086905

Alshehri, M. (2023). Blockchain-assisted internet of things framework in smart livestock farming. *Internet of Things : Engineering Cyber Physical Human Systems*, *22*, 100739. doi:10.1016/j.iot.2023.100739

Amft, S., Höltervennhoff, S., Huaman, N., Krause, A., Simko, L., Acar, Y., & Fahl, S. (2023). Lost and not Found: An Investigation of Recovery Methods for Multi-Factor Authentication. *arXiv (Cornell University)*. https://doi.org//arxiv.2306.09708 doi:10.48550

Anderson, T. (2018). Evaluating Third-Party Vendors and Suppliers. *Security Magazine*, *62*(9), 52–56.

Annadurai, C., Nelson, I., Devi, K., Manikandan, R., Zaman, N., Masud, M., & Sheikh, A. (2022). Biometric Authentication-Based Intrusion Detection Using Artificial Intelligence Internet of Things in Smart City. *Energies*, *15*(19), 7430. doi:10.3390/en15197430

Aruna, S., Priya, S. M., Reshmeetha, K., Sudhayini, E. S., & Narayanan, A. A. (2023). *Blockchain Integration with Artificial Intelligence and Internet of Things Technologies*. IEEE. doi:10.1109/ICICCS56967.2023.10142527

Assibi, A. T. (2023). Literature Review on Building Cyber Resilience Capabilities to Counter Future Cyber Threats: The Role of Enterprise Risk Management (ERM) and Business Continuity (BC). *OAlib*, *10*(04), 1–15. doi:10.4236/oalib.1109882

Aziz, F. (2023). *Beyond the Ledger: Enhancing Global Sustainability through Data-Driven Accounting Frameworks*. Farooq Aziz.

Bandari, V. (2023, January 20). *Enterprise Data Security Measures: A Comparative Review of Effectiveness and Risks Across Different Industries and Organization Types*. Tensor Gate. https://research.tensorgate.org/index.php/IJBIBDA/article/view/3

Barbaschow, A. (2020, February 3). Toll Group shuts down IT systems in response to "cybersecurity incident." *ZDNET*. https://www.zdnet.com/article/toll-group-shuts-down-it-systems-in-response-to-cybersecurity-incident/

Barnett, M., Samori, I., Griffin, B., Palmer, X., & Potter, L. (2023). A Commentary and Exploration of Maritime Applications of Biosecurity and Cybersecurity Intersections. *Proceedings of the 22nd European Conference on Cyber Warfare and Security*, *22*(1), 65–72. 10.34190/eccws.22.1.1283

Bavoria, R. K. (2023, May 1). *A Study On Enablers And Barriers Of Additive Manufacturing Adoption In Industry 4.0: An Ahp Approach*. D-Space. http://www.dspace.dtu.ac.in:8080/jspui/handle/repository/19859

Baz, J. E., Cherrafi, A., Benabdellah, A. C., Zekhnini, K., Nguema, J. B. B., & Derrouiche, R. (2023). Environmental Supply Chain Risk Management for Industry 4.0: A Data Mining Framework and Research Agenda. *Systems*, *11*(1), 46. doi:10.3390/systems11010046

Behie, S. W., Pasman, H. J., Khan, F. I., Shell, K., Alarfaj, A., El-Kady, A. H., & Hernandez, M. (2023). Leadership 4.0: The changing landscape of industry management in the smart digital era. *Process Safety and Environmental Protection*, *172*, 317–328. doi:10.1016/j.psep.2023.02.014

Berry, H. S. (2023). *The Importance of Cybersecurity in Supply Chain*. IEEE. doi:10.1109/ISDFS58141.2023.10131834

Bhattacharya, S., Maurya, B., Talukdar, D., Asokan, A., & N, M. (2023). Challenges Faced in Countering Cyber Crimes in Political Science and Management: a Critical Study. *EcB*, *12*(7).

Bi, Y., Fan, K., Zhang, K., Yuhan, B., Li, H., & Yang, Y. (2023). A secure and efficient two-party protocol enabling ownership transfer of RFID objects. *IEEE Internet of Things Journal*, *1*(18), 16225–16237. doi:10.1109/JIOT.2023.3267501

Bø, E., Hovi, I. B., & Pinchasik, D. R. (2023). COVID-19 disruptions and Norwegian food and pharmaceutical supply chains: Insights into supply chain risk management, resilience, and reliability. *Sustainable Futures : An Applied Journal of Technology, Environment and Society*, *5*, 100102. doi:10.1016/j.sftr.2022.100102 PMID:36530767

Capano, D. E. (2022). Throwback Attack: How NotPetya accidentally took down global shipping giant Maersk. *Industrial Cybersecurity Pulse*. https://www.industrialcybersecuritypulse.com/threats-vulnerabilities/throwback-attack-how-notpetya-accidentally-took-down-global-shipping-giant-maersk/

Çelik, Y., Petri, I., & Rezgui, Y. (2023). Integrating BIM and Blockchain across construction lifecycle and supply chains. *Computers in Industry, 148*, 103886. doi:10.1016/j.compind.2023.103886

Chandan, A., Rosano, M., & Potdar, V. (2023). Achieving UN SDGs in Food Supply Chain Using Blockchain Technology. *Sustainability (Basel), 15*(3), 2109. doi:10.3390/su15032109

Chaurasiya, S. K., Biswas, A., Nayyar, A., Jhanjhi, N. Z., & Banerjee, R. (2023). DEICA: A differential evolution-based improved clustering algorithm for IoT-based heterogeneous wireless sensor networks. *International Journal of Communication Systems, 36*(5), e5420. Advance online publication. doi:10.1002/dac.5420

Chimuco, F. T., Sequeiros, J. B. F., Lopes, C. G., Simões, T. M. C., Freire, M. M., & Inácio, P. R. M. (2023). Secure cloud-based mobile apps: Attack taxonomy, requirements, mechanisms, tests and automation. *International Journal of Information Security, 22*(4), 833–867. Advance online publication. doi:10.1007/s10207-023-00669-z

Coutinho, B., Ferreira, J. C., Yevseyeva, I., & Basto-Fernandes, V. (2023). Integrated cybersecurity methodology and supporting tools for healthcare operational information systems. *Elsevier, 129*, 103189. doi:10.1016/j.cose.2023.103189

Crosignani, M., Macchiavelli, M., & Silva, A. F. (2023). Pirates without borders: The propagation of cyberattacks through firms' supply chains. *Journal of Financial Economics, 147*(2), 432–448. doi:10.1016/j.jfineco.2022.12.002

Cui, J., Xiao, J., & Wang, Q. (2023). *Research on Data Protection Scheme for Road Maintenance System Based on Hybrid Encryption*. European Union Digital Library. doi:10.4108/eai.24-2-2023.2330677

DasS. (2023). Digital Twin Technology: Enhancing Efficiency and Decision-Making in Industry 4.0. *Social Science Research Network*. doi:10.2139/ssrn.4459204

Decker, L., & Zoghi, B. (2023). The Case for RFID-Enabled Traceability in Cash Movements. *FinTech, 2*(2), 344–373. doi:10.3390/fintech2020020

Dhasarathan, C., Hasan, M. K., Islam, S., Abdullah, S., Khapre, S., Singh, D., Alsulami, A. A., & Alqahtani, A. (2023). User privacy prevention model using supervised federated learning-based block chain approach for internet of Medical Things. *CAAI Transactions on Intelligence Technology*, cit2.12218. Advance online publication. doi:10.1049/cit2.12218

Dobilas, R. (2023). *Improving Supply Chain Performance by Means of Information Sharing: The Case of a Logistics Service Company* [MA Thesis, Kaunas University of Technology].

Doğdu, E. (2023, May 1). *Virtual networking cybersecurity and vulnerabilities in cloud computing applications: a systematic review*. TDL. https://asu-ir.tdl.org/handle/2346.1/39593

Doyle, D. (2020). CyberScotland Bulletin November 2020 — CyberScotland Week. *CyberScotland Week*. https://cyberscotlandweek.com/news-database/bulletinnovember2020

Dubey, R., Bryde, D. J., Dwivedi, Y. K., Graham, G., Foropon, C., & Papadopoulos, T. (2023). Dynamic digital capabilities and supply chain resilience: The role of government effectiveness. *International Journal of Production Economics*, *258*, 108790. doi:10.1016/j.ijpe.2023.108790

Duman, Ş. A., Hayran, R., & Sogukpınar, İ. (2023). *Impact Analysis and Performance Model of Social Engineering Techniques*. IEEE. doi:10.1109/ISDFS58141.2023.10131771

Dwivedi, Y. K., Hughes, L., Wang, Y., Alalwan, A. A., Ahn, S. J., Balakrishnan, J., Barta, S., Belk, R. W., Buhalis, D., Dutot, V., Felix, R., Filieri, R., Flavián, C., Gustafsson, A., Hinsch, C., Hollensen, S., Jain, V., Kim, J., Krishen, A. S., & Wirtz, J. (2022). Metaverse marketing: How the metaverse will shape the future of consumer research and practice. *Psychology and Marketing*, *40*(4), 750–776. doi:10.1002/mar.21767

Dzemydienė, D., Burinskienė, A., Čižiūnienė, K., & Miliauskas, A. (2023). Development of E-Service Provision System Architecture Based on IoT and WSNs for Monitoring and Management of Freight Intermodal Transportation. *Sensors (Basel)*, *23*(5), 2831. doi:10.3390/s23052831 PMID:36905034

Elijah, A. V., Abdullah, A., Zaman, N., Supramaniam, M., & Abdullateef, B. N. (2019). Ensemble and Deep-Learning Methods for Two-Class and Multi-Attack Anomaly Intrusion Detection: An Empirical Study. *International Journal of Advanced Computer Science and Applications*, *10*(9). doi:10.14569/IJACSA.2019.0100969

FadhilI. S. M.NizarN. B. M.RostamR. J. (2023). Security and Privacy Issues in Cloud Computing. *Tech Riv*. doi:10.36227/techrxiv.23506905.v1

Farid, G., Warraich, N. F., & Iftikhar, S. (2023). Digital information security management policy in academic libraries: A systematic review (2010–2022). *Journal of Information Science*, *016555152311600*. doi:10.1177/01655515231160026

Farooq, S., Altaf, A., Iqbal, F., Thompson, E. B., Vargas, D. L. R., De La Torre Díez, I., & Ashraf, I. (2023). Resilience Optimization of Post-Quantum Cryptography Key Encapsulation Algorithms. *Sensors (Basel)*, *23*(12), 5379. doi:10.3390/s23125379 PMID:37420546

Fatima, A., Khan, T. A., Abdellatif, T. M., Zulfiqar, S., Asif, M., Safi, W., Hamadi, H. A., & Al-Kassem, A. H. (2023). *Impact and Research Challenges of Penetrating Testing and Vulnerability Assessment on Network Threat*. doi:10.1109/ICBATS57792.2023.10111168

Fernando, Y., Tseng, M., Wahyuni-Td, I. S., De Sousa Jabbour, A. B. L., Jabbour, C. J. C., & Foropon, C. (2022). Cyber supply chain risk management and performance in industry 4.0 era: Information system security practices in Malaysia. *Journal of Industrial and Production Engineering*, *40*(2), 102–116. doi:10.1080/21681015.2022.2116495

Fourné, M. (2023, May 1). *It's like flossing your teeth: On the Importance and Challenges of Reproducible Builds for Software Supply Chain Security*. TeamUSEC. https://teamusec.de/publications/conf-oakland-fourne23/

Friday, D., Ryan, S., Melnyk, S. A., & Proulx, D. (2023). Supply Chain Deep Uncertainties and Risks: The 'New Normal.' In *Flexible systems management* (pp. 51–72). Springer Nature. doi:10.1007/978-981-99-2629-9_3

Garay-Rondero, C. L., Martínez-Flores, J., Smith, N., Morales, S. C., & Aldrette-Malacara, A. (2019). Digital supply chain model in Industry 4.0. *Journal of Manufacturing Technology Management*, *31*(5), 887–933. doi:10.1108/JMTM-08-2018-0280

Gartner. (2022). *Top 8 Supply Chain Technology Trends for 2023*. Gartner. https://www.gartner.com/en/documents/4117858/top-8-supply-chain-technology-trends-for-2023

Gaur, L., Zaman, N., Bakshi, S., & Gupta, P. (2022). Analyzing Consequences of Artificial Intelligence on Jobs using Topic Modeling and Keyword Extraction. In *2022 2nd International Conference on Innovative Practices in Technology and Management (ICIPTM)*. IEEE. 10.1109/ICIPTM54933.2022.9754064

George, D., & George, A. (2023). Revolutionizing Manufacturing: Exploring the Promises and Challenges of Industry 5.0. Zenodo *(CERN European Organization for Nuclear Research)*. doi:10.5281/zenodo.7852124

Ghobakhloo, M., Iranmanesh, M., Tseng, M., Grybauskas, A., Stefanini, A., & Amran, A. (2023). Behind the definition of Industry 5.0: a systematic review of technologies, principles, components, and values. *Journal of Industrial and Production Engineering*, 1–16. doi:10.1080/21681015.2023.2216701

Ghosh, G., & Bhandari, P. (2023). Supply Chain Related Cyber Attacks. *International Conference on Industrial Engineering and Operations Management Manila*.

Gruchmann, T., Elgazzar, S., & Ali, A. H. (2023). Blockchain technology in pharmaceutical supply chains: a transaction cost perspective. *Modern Supply Chain Research and Applications*. doi:10.1108/MSCRA-10-2022-0023

Gupta, M. K., & Seetharaman, A. (2019). Reputation Risk Management: A New Framework and Its Application in Cybersecurity. *Journal of Risk and Financial Management*, *12*(2), 102.

Gupta, N., Soni, G., Mittal, S., Mukherjee, I., Ramtiyal, B., & Kumar, D. (2023). Evaluating Traceability Technology Adoption in Food Supply Chain: A Game Theoretic Approach. *Sustainability (Basel)*, *15*(2), 898. doi:10.3390/su15020898

Hamid, B., Jhanjhi, N. Z., Humayun, M., Khan, A., & Alsayat, A. (2019, December). Cyber security issues and challenges for smart cities: A survey. In *2019 13th International Conference on Mathematics, Actuarial Science, Computer Science and Statistics (MACS)* (pp. 1-7). IEEE. 10.1109/MACS48846.2019.9024768

Hammi, B., Zeadally, S., & Nebhen, J. (2023). Security threats, countermeasures, and challenges of digital supply chains. *ACM Computing Surveys*, *55*(14s), 1–40. doi:10.1145/3588999

Handfield, R., & Finkenstadt, D. J. (2022). Major Supply Chain Events of 2020 Beyond COVID. In Springer eBooks (pp. 87–102). doi:10.1007/978-3-031-19344-6_8

Hasan, I. (2023, February 16). *Blockchain Database and IoT: A Technology driven Agri-Food Supply Chain*. https://isctj.com/index.php/isctj/article/view/269

Hasan, I., Habib, M., Mohamed, Z., & Tewari, V. (2023). Integrated Agri-Food Supply Chain Model: An Application of IoT and Blockchain. *American Journal of Industrial and Business Management*, *13*(02), 29–45. doi:10.4236/ajibm.2023.132003

He, X., Hu, W., Li, W., & Hu, R. (2023). Digital transformation, technological innovation, and operational resilience of port firms in case of supply chain disruption. *Marine Pollution Bulletin*, *190*, 114811. doi:10.1016/j.marpolbul.2023.114811 PMID:36963261

Henriques, J. F., Caldeira, F., Cruz, T., & Simões, P. (2023). A forensics and compliance auditing framework for critical infrastructure protection. *International Journal of Critical Infrastructure Protection*, *100613*, 100613. doi:10.1016/j.ijcip.2023.100613

Herrera, M. (2022, August 25). *Never Break the Chain: Supply Chain Risk Management*. BCMMETRICS. https://bcmmetrics.com/supply-chain-risk-management/

Hippold, S. (2020). *6 Strategies for a More Resilient Supply Chain*. Gartner. https://www.gartner.com/smarterwithgartner/6-strategies-for-a-more-resilient-supply-chain

Hitachi, Ltd. (2020). Digital Supply Chain: Reimagining the Supply Chain of Tomorrow. *Social Innovation*. https://social-innovation.hitachi/en-in/knowledge-hub/collaborate/digital-supply-chain

Hoang, K. (2023). *Post Quantum Cryptography for Public Key Infrastructure*. Theseus. https://www.theseus.fi/handle/10024/802390

Humayun, M., Niazi, M., Zaman, N., Alshayeb, M., & Mahmood, S. (2020). Cyber Security Threats and Vulnerabilities: A Systematic Mapping Study. *Arabian Journal for Science and Engineering*, *45*(4), 3171–3189. doi:10.1007/s13369-019-04319-2

Humayun, M., Zaman, N., Hamid, B., & Ahmed, G. (2020b). Emerging Smart Logistics and Transportation Using IoT and Blockchain. *IEEE Internet of Things Magazine*, *3*(2), 58–62. doi:10.1109/IOTM.0001.1900097

Humayun, M., Zaman, N., Talib, M. N., Shah, M. H., & Suseendran, G. (2021). Cybersecurity for Data Science: Issues, Opportunities, and Challenges. In Lecture notes in networks and systems (pp. 435–444). Springer International Publishing. doi:10.1007/978-981-16-3153-5_46

Hussain Naqvi, S. K., & Batool, K. (2023). A comparative analysis between General Data Protection Regulations and California Consumer Privacy Act. *Journal of Computer Science. Information Technology and Telecommunication Engineering*, *4*(1). doi:10.30596/jcositte.v4i1.13330

IMB. (2022). *Cost of a Data Breach Report 2022*. IBM. https://www.ibm.com/downloads/cas/3R8N1DZJ

Iranmanesh, M., Maroufkhani, P., Asadi, S., Ghobakhloo, M., Dwivedi, P. K., & Tseng, M. (2023). Effects of supply chain transparency, alignment, adaptability, and agility on blockchain adoption in supply chain among SMEs. *Computers & Industrial Engineering*, *176*, 108931. doi:10.1016/j.cie.2022.108931

Islam, M. D. (2023). A survey on the use of blockchains to achieve supply chain security. *Information Systems*, *117*, 102232. doi:10.1016/j.is.2023.102232

Islam, M. D. (2023b). A survey on the use of blockchains to achieve supply chain security. *Information Systems*, *117*, 102232. doi:10.1016/j.is.2023.102232

Ivanov, D., & Dolgui, A. (2021). A digital supply chain twin for managing the disruption risks and resilience in the era of Industry 4.0. *Production Planning and Control, 32*(9), 775–788. doi:10.1080/09537287.2020.1768450

Jalali, A. (2023). *Password Management : A Study about Current Challenges with Password Management.* DIVA. https://www.diva-portal.org/smash/record.jsf?pid=diva2%3A1765652&dswid=-2613

Javaid, M., Haleem, A., Singh, R. P., & Suman, R. (2023). Towards insighting Cybersecurity for Healthcare domains: A comprehensive review of recent practices and trends. *Science Direct, 1,* 100016. doi:10.1016/j.csa.2023.100016

JayakumarP.BrohiS. N.ZamanN. (2021). Artificial Intelligence and Military Applications: Innovations, Cybersecurity Challenges & Open Research Areas. *Preprint.org.* doi:10.20944/preprints202108.0047.v1

Jeldi, S. B., & Kumar, A. (2022). Data Acquisition And Pre-Processing Using Kf Model For An Intrusion Detection System In Web Mining. *ECB.* https://www.eurchembull.com/uploads/paper/1239d617b696cf0c069cc81a23fa5e72.pdf

Jenkins, A. (2022). Digital Supply Chain Explained. *Oracle NetSuite.* https://www.netsuite.com/portal/resource/articles/erp/digital-supply-chain.shtml

Jmal, R., Ghabri, W., Guesmi, R., Alshammari, B. M., Alshammari, A. S., & Alsaif, H. (2023). Distributed Blockchain-SDN Secure IoT System Based on ANN to Mitigate DDoS Attacks. *Applied Sciences (Basel, Switzerland), 13*(8), 4953. doi:10.3390/app13084953

Johnson, R. (2020). Evaluating the Security Practices of Potential Vendors. *Journal of Information Privacy & Security, 16*(3), 98–104.

Kähkönen, A., Marttinen, K., Kontio, A., & Lintukangas, K. (2023). Practices and strategies for sustainability-related risk management in multi-tier supply chains. *Journal of Purchasing and Supply Management, 29*(3), 100848. doi:10.1016/j.pursup.2023.100848

Kalogeraki, E., Papastergiou, S., Mouratidis, H., & Polemi, N. (2018). A Novel Risk Assessment Methodology for SCADA Maritime Logistics Environments. *Applied Sciences (Basel, Switzerland), 8*(9), 1477. doi:10.3390/app8091477

Kang, Y. (2023). Development of Large-Scale Farming Based on Explainable Machine Learning for a Sustainable Rural Economy: The Case of Cyber Risk Analysis to Prevent Costly Data Breaches. *Applied Artificial Intelligence, 37*(1), 2223862. doi:10.1080/08839514.2023.2223862

Kanyepe, J. (2023). Transport management practices and performance of diamond mining companies in Zimbabwe. *Cogent Business & Management, 10*(2), 2216429. doi:10.1080/23311975.2023.2216429

Kashem, M. A., Shamsuddoha, M., Nasir, T., & Chowdhury, A. A. (2023). Supply Chain Disruption versus Optimization: A Review on Artificial Intelligence and Blockchain. *Knowledge (Beverly Hills, Calif.), 3*(1), 80–96. doi:10.3390/knowledge3010007

Kaur, R., Gabrijelčič, D., & Klobučar, T. (2023). Artificial intelligence for cybersecurity: Literature review and future research directions. *Information Fusion, 97,* 101804. doi:10.1016/j.inffus.2023.101804

Kerner, S. M. (2022). Colonial Pipeline hack explained: Everything you need to know. *WhatIs.com*. https://www.techtarget.com/whatis/feature/Colonial-Pipeline-hack-explained-Everything-you-need-to-know

Kerner, S. O. S. M. (2022). SolarWinds hack explained: Everything you need to know. *WhatIs.com*. https://www.techtarget.com/whatis/feature/SolarWinds-hack-explained-Everything-you-need-to-know

Khan, A., Jhanjhi, N. Z., & Humayun, M. (2022). The Role of Cybersecurity in Smart Cities. In *Cyber Security Applications for Industry 4.0* (pp. 195–208). Chapman and Hall/CRC. doi:10.1201/9781003203087-9

Khan, A., Jhanjhi, N. Z., & Sujatha, R. (2022a). Emerging Industry Revolution IR 4.0 Issues and Challenges. In Cyber Security Applications for Industry 4.0 (pp. 151-169). Chapman and Hall/CRC.

Khanna, T., Nand, P., & Bali, V. (2023). FruitBlock: A layered approach to implement blockchain-based traceability system for agri-supply chain. *International Journal of Business Information Systems*, *43*(1), 107. doi:10.1504/IJBIS.2023.131088

Kimmy. (2022). *What Is Supply Chain Risk Management?* Kyin Bridges. https://www.kyinbridges.com/what-is-supply-chain-risk-management-2/

Kioskli, K., Fotis, T., Mavrogiorgou, A., & Mouratidis, H. (2023). The Importance of Conceptualising the Human-Centric Approach in Maintaining and Promoting Cybersecurity-Hygiene in Healthcare 4.0. *Applied Sciences (Basel, Switzerland)*, *13*(6), 3410. doi:10.3390/app13063410

Kocabasoglu-Hillmer, C., Roden, S., Vanpoucke, E., Son, B., & Lewis, M. W. (2023). Radical innovations as supply chain disruptions? A paradox between change and stability. *The Journal of Supply Chain Management*, *59*(3), 3–19. doi:10.1111/jscm.12299

Koduru, S. S., Machina, V. S. P., & Madichetty, S. (2023). Cyber Attacks in Cyber-Physical Microgrid Systems: A Comprehensive Review. *Energies*, *16*(12), 4573. doi:10.3390/en16124573

Korpela, K., Hallikas, J., & Dahlberg, T. (2017). Digital Supply Chain Transformation toward Blockchain Integration. In *Proceedings of the . . . Annual Hawaii International Conference on System Sciences*. IEEE. 10.24251/HICSS.2017.506

Koukiadaki, A. (2023). Global Supply Chains and Labour Standards: From a Patchwork of Rules to a Web of Rules? In Emerald Publishing Limited eBooks (pp. 127–140). doi:10.1108/978-1-80071-248-520221016

Kshetri, N. (2022). Supply chain management. Edward Elgar Publishing eBooks. doi:10.4337/9781802208177.00013

KumarU. V.ReddyE. (2023). Preventing Unauthorized Users from Accessing Cloud Data. *Social Science Research Network*. doi:10.2139/ssrn.4448543

Kumar, V., Malik, N., Singla, J., Zaman, N., Amsaad, F., & Razaque, A. (2022). Light Weight Authentication Scheme for Smart Home IoT Devices. *Cryptography*, *6*(3), 37. doi:10.3390/cryptography6030037

Lazăra, A. (2023, January 1). *Security Testing for E-Commerce Applications*. Questa Soft. https://www.ceeol.com/search/chapter-detail?id=1123486

Leal, M., & Musgrave, P. (2023). Backwards from zero: How the U.S. public evaluates the use of zero-day vulnerabilities in cybersecurity. *Contemporary Security Policy*, *44*(3), 437–461. doi:10.1080/1352 3260.2023.2216112

Lessambo, F. I. (2023). AML/CFT and Cybersecurity Laws in the European Union (pp. 79–90). Springer. doi:10.1007/978-3-031-23484-2_6

Li, C., Zheng, P., Yin, Y., Wang, B., & Wang, L. (2023). Deep reinforcement learning in smart manufacturing: A review and prospects. *CIRP Journal of Manufacturing Science and Technology*, *40*, 75–101. doi:10.1016/j.cirpj.2022.11.003

Li, J., Xiao, W., & Zhang, C. (2023). Data security crisis in universities: Identification of key factors affecting data breach incidents. *Humanities & Social Sciences Communications*, *10*(1), 270. doi:10.1057/s41599-023-01757-0 PMID:37273415

Li, Z., Liang, F., & Hu, H. (2023). Blockchain-Based and Value-Driven Enterprise Data Governance: A Collaborative Framework. *Sustainability (Basel)*, *15*(11), 8578. doi:10.3390/su15118578

Liu, J., Wu, J., & Gong, Y. (2023). A Resilient Maritime Supply Chain in the Post COVID-19 Era. *Computers & Industrial Engineering*, *109366*. doi:10.1016/j.cie.2023.109366

Liu, Q., Zhou, J., & Liang, H. (2021). Security and privacy in cloud computing. In *Handbook of Research on Cloud Computing and Big Data Applications in IoT* (pp. 174–192). IGI Global.

Logeshwaran, J. (2023, February 8). *A Secured Database Monitoring Method to Improve Data Backup and Recovery Operations in Cloud Computing*. Bohrpub. https://journals.bohrpub.com/index.php/bijcs/article/view/131

Mahmood, Y., Afrin, T., Huang, Y., & Yodo, N. (2023). Sustainable Development for Oil and Gas Infrastructure from Risk, Reliability, and Resilience Perspectives. *Sustainability (Basel)*, *15*(6), 4953. doi:10.3390/su15064953

Mak, W. J., Aziz, M. L. A., Hamid, M. R., & Hashim, M. M. H. M. (2023). *Improving Accessibility of Technical Drilling Applications via Wells on Cloud-based Platform*. IEEE. doi:10.2118/214541-MS

Mantravadi, S., & Srai, J. S. (2023). How Important are Digital Technologies for Urban Food Security? A Framework for Supply Chain Integration using IoT. *Procedia Computer Science*, *217*, 1678–1687. doi:10.1016/j.procs.2022.12.368

Manzoor, U. (2023, May 16). *Blockchain Technology in Marketing: Potential Applications and Implications*. ASMARA Publications. http://asmarapublications.com/journals/index.php/PMS/article/view/8

Marbut, A. R., & Harms, P. D. (2023). Fiends and Fools: A Narrative Review and Neo-socioanalytic Perspective on Personality and Insider Threats. *Journal of Business and Psychology*. doi:10.1007/s10869-023-09885-9

Marquez-Tejon, J., Partearroyo, M. J., & Benito-Osorio, D. (2023). Integrated security management model: A proposal applied to organisational resilience. *Security Journal*. doi:10.1057/s41284-023-00381-6

Mehdi Rizvi, Q., & Kushwaha, R. S. (2023). EXPLORING MODERN CRYPTOGRAPHY: A COMPREHENSIVE GUIDE TO TECHNIQUES AND APPLICATIONS. *International Research Journal of Modernization in Engineering Technology and Science, 05*(05), 2582–5208. doi:10.56726/IRJMETS40247

Miao, Y., Li, F., Li, X., Liu, Z., Ning, J., Li, H., Choo, K. R., & Deng, R. H. (2023). Time-Controllable Keyword Search Scheme with Efficient Revocation in Mobile E-health Cloud. *IEEE Transactions on Mobile Computing*, 1–15. doi:10.1109/TMC.2023.3277702

Microcosm. (n.d.). *User Access Control | Prevent Unauthorized Access to Systems and Applications.* Microcosm. https://www.microcosm.com/solutions/user-access-control

Mijwil, M., Salem, I. E., & M. Ismaeel, M. (2023). The Significance of Machine Learning and Deep Learning Techniques in Cybersecurity: A Comprehensive Review. *Iraqi Journal for Computer Science and Mathematics*, 87–101. doi:10.52866/ijcsm.2023.01.01.008

Mohamed, S. K., Haddad, S., Barakat, M., & Rosi, B. (2023). Blockchain Technology Adoption for Improved Environmental Supply Chain Performance: The Mediation Effect of Supply Chain Resilience, Customer Integration, and Green Customer Information Sharing. *Sustainability (Basel), 15*(10), 7909. doi:10.3390/su15107909

Mohezar, S., Mohamad, M. N., & Nor, M. N. M. (2023). Supply chain risk and SME business continuity strategies in the food industry during COVID-19 pandemic. *Continuity & Resilience Review.* doi:10.1108/CRR-09-2022-0021

Möller, D. P. F. (2023). NIST Cybersecurity Framework and MITRE Cybersecurity Criteria. Springer. doi:10.1007/978-3-031-26845-8_5

Möller, D. P. F. (2023). Ransomware Attacks and Scenarios: Cost Factors and Loss of Reputation. Springer. doi:10.1007/978-3-031-26845-8_6

Mubarik, M. S., Khan, S. A., Kusi-Sarpong, S., & Mubarik, M. (2023). Supply chain sustainability in VUCA: Role of BCT-driven SC mapping and 'Visiceability.'. *International Journal of Logistics*, 1–19. doi:10.1080/13675567.2023.2222660

Muhammad, Z., Anwar, Z., Javed, A. R., Saleem, B., Abbas, S., & Gadekallu, T. R. (2023). Smartphone Security and Privacy: A Survey on APTs, Sensor-Based Attacks, Side-Channel Attacks, Google Play Attacks, and Defenses. *Technologies, 11*(3), 76. doi:10.3390/technologies11030076

Murimi, R., Bell, G., Rasheed, A. A., & Beldona, S. (2023). Blockchains: A Review and Research Agenda for International Business. *Research in International Business and Finance, 66*, 102018. doi:10.1016/j.ribaf.2023.102018

N, S., Vivekananda, B. K., Rajarajan, M., & Das, A. K. (2023). A New Scalable and Secure Access Control Scheme using Blockchain Technology for IoT. *IEEE Transactions on Network and Service Management*, 1. IEEE. doi:10.1109/TNSM.2023.3246120

Nanda, S. K., Panda, S. K., & Dash, M. (2023). Medical supply chain integrated with blockchain and IoT to track the logistics of medical products. *Multimedia Tools and Applications, 82*(21), 32917–32939. doi:10.1007/s11042-023-14846-8 PMID:37362711

National Institute of Standards and Technology (NIST). (2021). *Computer Security Incident Handling Guide* (NIST Special Publication 800-61 Revision 2). NIST. doi:10.6028/NIST.SP.800-61r2

Negar, J. J. (2023, January 1). *Evaluating the Effect of Supply Chain Management Practice on Implementation of Halal Agroindustry and Competitive Advantage for Small and Medium Enterprises.* SSRN. https://papers.ssrn.com/sol3/papers.cfm?abstract_id=4348136

Nelligere, L., Swamy, T., & Mubashir Ahmed, A. (n.d.). Vulnerability Assessment and Analysis of SCADA and Foundation Fieldbus on Industrial Control System (ICS) Networks: A Literature Revie. *Journal of Computer Sciences, 17*(2), 34–65. https://search.ebscohost.com/login.aspx?direct=true&profile=ehost&scope=site&authtype=crawler&jrnl=09739904&AN=163472952&h=RIfIAHCsUQBAX7WEHsAZJ2psL9s%2FaeGPwAn6wgfCB7jHTDV216xabNXSyiX7SyekzAsXaiiUoSNh0yHd56IzXg%3D%3D&crl=c&casa_token=vQeuhcveouAAAAAA:2nRq7od2LEIedxhtbARWgHIiIowH_-NVZA1aGE0dnJ4RZLijyvOOC-T8uUIydu-s8f10b6n_PO_Qa6Ip

Nozari, H., & Edalatpanah, S. A. (2023). Smart Systems Risk Management in IoT-Based Supply Chain. In *Industrial and applied mathematics* (pp. 251–268). Springer Nature. doi:10.1007/978-981-19-9909-3_11

Padovan, P. A., Martins, C., & Reed, C. (2022). Black is the new orange: How to determine AI liability. *Artificial Intelligence and Law, 31*(1), 133–167. doi:10.1007/s10506-022-09308-9

Pandey, S., & Munjal, D. (2023). E-Commerce Website In The Pandemic Situation. *International Research Journal, 20*(5).

Pargoo, N. S., & Ilbeigi, M. (2023). A Scoping Review for Cybersecurity in the Construction Industry. *Journal of Management Engineering, 39*(2), 03122003. doi:10.1061/JMENEA.MEENG-5034

Parker, S., Wu, Z., & Christofides, P. D. (2023). *Cybersecurity in process control, operations, and supply chain.* Elsevier. doi:10.1016/j.compchemeng.2023.108169

Peng, Y., Welden, N. A., & Renaud, F. G. (2023). A framework for integrating ecosystem services indicators into vulnerability and risk assessments of deltaic social-ecological systems. *Journal of Environmental Management, 326*, 116682. doi:10.1016/j.jenvman.2022.116682 PMID:36375428

Peter, O., Pradhan, A., & Mbohwa, C. (2023). Industrial internet of things (IIoT): Opportunities, challenges, and requirements in manufacturing businesses in emerging economies. *Procedia Computer Science, 217*, 856–865. doi:10.1016/j.procs.2022.12.282

Peterson, E. (2021). Achieving Visibility and Control in OT Systems: Remote Maintenance, Securing Remote Access, and the Zero-Trust Approach. *Idaho National Library*. https://www.cisa.gov/sites/default/files/2023-05/Achieving%20Visibility%20and%20Control%20in%20OT%20Systems%20Remote%20Maintenace%2C%20Securing%20Remote%20Access%2C%20and%20the%20Zero-Trust%20Approach_508c.pdf

Ponnusamy, V., Zaman, N., & Humayun, M. (2020). Fostering Public-Private Partnership. In *Advances in electronic government, digital divide, and regional development book series* (pp. 237–255). IGI Global. doi:10.4018/978-1-7998-1851-9.ch012

Pournader, M., Shi, Y., Seuring, S., & Koh, S. L. (2019). Blockchain applications in supply chains, transport and logistics: A systematic review of the literature. *International Journal of Production Research*, *58*(7), 2063–2081. doi:10.1080/00207543.2019.1650976

Prabakar, D., Sundarrajan, M., Manikandan, R., Zaman, N., Masud, M., & Alqhatani, A. (2023). Energy Analysis-Based Cyber Attack Detection by IoT with Artificial Intelligence in a Sustainable Smart City. *Sustainability (Basel)*, *15*(7), 6031. doi:10.3390/su15076031

PrabuckiR. (2023). The Analysis of the NIS 2 Directive, Preamble 54 in Terms of Sectors Related to Manufacturing. *Social Science Research Network*. doi:10.2139/ssrn.4408587

Pritika, N., Shanmugam, B., & Azam, S. (2023). Risk Assessment of Heterogeneous IoMT Devices: A Review. *Technologies*, *11*(1), 31. doi:10.3390/technologies11010031

Priyadarshini, I., Chatterjee, J. M., Sujatha, R., Zaman, N., Karime, A., & Masud, M. (2021). Exploring Internet Meme Activity during COVID-19 Lockdown Using Artificial Intelligence Techniques. *Applied Artificial Intelligence*, *36*(1), 2014218. doi:10.1080/08839514.2021.2014218

Priyantha. (2023). *Logistic Conference*. Naval and Maritime Academy. https://nma.navy.lk/wp-content/uploads/2023/04/E-Journal-LLMC.pdf#page=98

Puica, E. (2023). Improving Supply Chain Management by Integrating RFID with IoT Shared Database: Proposing a System Architecture. In IFIP advances in information and communication technology (pp. 159–170). Springer Science+Business Media. doi:10.1007/978-3-031-34107-6_13

Queiroz, M. M., Wamba, S. F., Pereira, S. C. F., & Jabbour, C. J. C. (2023). The metaverse as a breakthrough for operations and supply chain management: Implications and call for action. *International Journal of Operations & Production Management*, *43*(10), 1539–1553. doi:10.1108/IJOPM-01-2023-0006

R, S. (2023). Immutable Secure Online Electoral Voting System Using Blockchain Technology. SSRN. doi:10.2139/ssrn.4456808

(1758–1761). R, S. T., & T, S. K. (2023). A Review on Major Cyber Threats and Recommended Counter Measures. *International Journal for Research in Applied Science and Engineering Technology*, *11*(3). Advance online publication. doi:10.22214/ijraset.2023.49764

Rahaman, M. S., Tisha, S. N., Song, E., & Cerny, T. (2023). Access Control Design Practice and Solutions in Cloud-Native Architecture: A Systematic Mapping Study. *Sensors (Basel)*, *23*(7), 3413. doi:10.3390/s23073413 PMID:37050474

Rahardja, U. (2023). Implementation of Enterprise Resource Planning (ERP) in Indonesia to Increase the Significant Impact of Management Control Systems. *APTISI Transaction on Management*, *7*(2), 152–159. Advance online publication. doi:10.33050/atm.v7i2.1881

Raj, A., Sharma, V., Shukla, D. M., & Sharma, P. (2023). Advancing supply chain management from agility to hyperagility: A dynamic capability view. *Annals of Operations Research*. doi:10.1007/s10479-022-05158-5 PMID:36619697

Ramgovind, S., Eloff, M. M., & Smith, E. J. (2010). *The management of security in Cloud computing*. IEEE. doi:10.1109/ISSA.2010.5588290

Rani, S., Bhambri, P., Kataria, A., Khang, A., & Sivaraman, A. K. (2023). *Big Data, Cloud Computing and IoT: Tools and Applications*. CRC Press. doi:10.1201/9781003298335

Rathore, B. (2023, January 19). Digital Transformation 4.0: Integration of Artificial Intelligence & Metaverse in Marketing. *EduZone Journal*. https://www.eduzonejournal.com/index.php/eiprmj/article/view/248

Rathore, B. (2023b, January 30). *Integration of Artificial Intelligence & It's Practices in Apparel Industry*. IJNMS. https://ijnms.com/index.php/ijnms/article/view/40

Rawat, A. (2023, May 15). *Smart Contract Based Approach for Fixed Deposit in Blockchain Networks with Remix IDE*. SSRN. https://papers.ssrn.com/sol3/papers.cfm?abstract_id=4451822

Read, T. (2023, February 4). *What Is Supply Chain 4.0 and Where Does It Drive Value?* Blog - Agistix. https://www.agistix.com/blog/what-is-supply-chain-4-0-and-where-does-it-drive-value/

Reece, M., Edward, L. J. T., Stoffolano, M., Sampson, A., Dykstra, J., Mittal, S., & Rastogi, N. (2023). Systemic Risk and Vulnerability Analysis of Multi-cloud Environments. *arXiv (Cornell University)*. https://doi.org//arxiv.2306.01862 doi:10.48550

Riggs, H., Tufail, S., Parvez, I., Tariq, M., Khan, M. A., Amir, A., Vuda, K. V., & Sarwat, A. I. (2023). Impact, Vulnerabilities, and Mitigation Strategies for Cyber-Secure Critical Infrastructure. *Sensors (Basel)*, *23*(8), 4060. doi:10.3390/s23084060 PMID:37112400

Roberts, L. (2023). *Countermeasures for Preventing Malicious Infiltration on the Information Technology Supply Chain* [Doctor of Technology]. Purdue Polytechnic Institute.

Romadhona, P. F., Ismail, M. L., & Ruldeviyani, Y. (2023). Evaluation of information security management in crisis response using KAMI index: The case of company XYZ. In AIP Conference Proceedings. American Institute of Physics. doi:10.1063/5.0115555

Russo, N., Reis, L., Silveira, C., & Mamede, J. H. P. S. (2023). Towards a Comprehensive Framework for the Multidisciplinary Evaluation of Organizational Maturity on Business Continuity Program Management: A Systematic Literature Review. *Information Security Journal: A Global Perspective*, 1–19. doi:10.1080/19393555.2023.2195577

Salikhov, J., Hayrutdinov, S., & Muminov, T. K. (2023). Blockchain-Enabled Sustainable Supply Chain under Information Sharing and Recovery Quality Efforts. *Sustainability (Basel)*, *15*(5), 3929. doi:10.3390/su15053929

Sánchez, M. A., & De Batista, M. (2023). Business continuity for times of vulnerability: Empirical evidence. *Journal of Contingencies and Crisis Management*, *31*(3), 431–440. doi:10.1111/1468-5973.12449

Saranya, P., & Maheswari, R. (2023). Proof of Transaction (PoTx) Based Traceability System for an Agriculture Supply Chain. *IEEE Access : Practical Innovations, Open Solutions*, *11*, 10623–10638. doi:10.1109/ACCESS.2023.3240772

Sarhan, M., Layeghy, S., Moustafa, N., & Portmann, M. (2022). Cyber Threat Intelligence Sharing Scheme Based on Federated Learning for Network Intrusion Detection. *Journal of Network and Systems Management*, *31*(1), 3. doi:10.1007/s10922-022-09691-3

Satriawan, N. (2023). *Proposed Customer Knowledge Management (CKM) in the Truku Logistics Application Feature PT Biru Samudera Selatan*. research.e-siber.org. https://doi.org/ doi:10.31935/sjtl.v1i1.39

Schniederjans, D. G., Curado, C., & Khalajhedayati, M. (2020). Supply chain digitisation trends: An integration of knowledge management. *International Journal of Production Economics, 220*, 107439. doi:10.1016/j.ijpe.2019.07.012

Seseli, E. M. I., Risakotta, K. A., & Bawono, A. (2023). The Role of Accounting Digitization in Entrepreneurial Success in West Java : Quantitative Study of Efficiency, Accuracy, Cost Reduction, Customer Satisfaction, and Data Security. *The Es Accounting and Finance, 1*(02), 82–94. doi:10.58812/esaf.v1i02.65

Shah, I. A., Jhanjhi, N. Z., Amsaad, F., & Razaque, A. (2022). The Role of Cutting-Edge Technologies in Industry 4.0. In *Cyber Security Applications for Industry 4.0* (pp. 97–109). Chapman and Hall/CRC. doi:10.1201/9781003203087-4

Shah, I. A., Zaman, N., & Laraib, A. (2022a). Cybersecurity and Blockchain Usage in Contemporary Business. In *Advances in information security, privacy, and ethics book series* (pp. 49–64). IGI Global. doi:10.4018/978-1-6684-5284-4.ch003

Shahadat, M. M. H., Chowdhury, A. H. M. Y., Nathan, R. J., & Fekete-Farkas, M. (2023). Digital Technologies for Firms' Competitive Advantage and Improved Supply Chain Performance. *Journal of Risk and Financial Management, 16*(2), 94. doi:10.3390/jrfm16020094

Shahriar, H. (2020). Ransomware: Evaluation of Mitigation and Prevention Techniques. *Symposium of Student Scholar*. https://digitalcommons.kennesaw.edu/undergradsymposiumksu/spring2023/presentations/301/

Shahzad, K. (2023). *The Role of Marketing Ethics in Ensuring Clients' Satisfaction*. doi:10.54183/jssr.v3i2.325

Shajek, A., & Hartmann, E. A. (2023). *New Digital Work: Digital Sovereignty at the Workplace*. Springer Nature. doi:10.1007/978-3-031-26490-0

Sharma, A., Gupta, B. B., Singh, A. K., & Saraswat, V. K. (2023). Advanced Persistent Threats (APT): Evolution, anatomy, attribution and countermeasures. *Journal of Ambient Intelligence and Humanized Computing, 14*(7), 9355–9381. doi:10.1007/s12652-023-04603-y

Sharma, H., Garg, R., Sewani, H., & Kashef, R. (2023). Towards A Sustainable and Ethical Supply Chain Management: The Potential of IoT Solutions. *arXiv (Cornell University)*. https://doi.org//arxiv.2303.18135 doi:10.48550

Sharma, M., & Joshi, S. (2020). Digital supplier selection reinforcing supply chain quality management systems to enhance firm's performance. *The TQM Journal, 35*(1), 102–130. doi:10.1108/TQM-07-2020-0160

Sharma, V., & Meena, K. K. (2023). Dentistry in the Digital Age: Embracing Blockchain Technology. *Cureus*. doi:10.7759/cureus.39710 PMID:37398809

Sheehan, J. (2023). 4 Beyond lip-service: Content clouds, 10-K filings, cyber risk and the electric grid. In De Gruyter eBooks (pp. 51–72). doi:10.1515/9783110731217-004

Shiau, W., Wang, X., & Zheng, F. (2023). What are the trend and core knowledge of information security? A citation and co-citation analysis. *Elsevier, 60*(3), 103774. doi:10.1016/j.im.2023.103774

Shimels, T., & Lessa, L. (2023). Maturity of information systems' security in Ethiopian banks: Case of selected private banks. *International Journal of Industrial Engineering and Operations Management, 5*(2), 86–103. doi:10.1108/IJIEOM-10-2021-0014

Siraj, M. T., Debnath, B., Kumar, A., Bari, A. M., Samadhiya, A., & Payel, S. B. (2023). Evaluating barriers to sustainable boiler operation in the apparel manufacturing industry: Implications for mitigating operational hazards in the emerging economies. *PLoS One, 18*(4), e0284423. doi:10.1371/journal.pone.0284423 PMID:37058513

Sirisomboonsuk, P., & Burns, J. (2023). Sustainability in Supply Chains through Rapid Capacity Increases and Minimized Disruptions. *Sustainability (Basel), 15*(7), 5629. doi:10.3390/su15075629

Soares, L. (2023). The evolution of cyber threats and its future landscape. *ResearchGate*. https://www.researchgate.net/publication/369010694_The_evolution_of_cyber_threats_and_its_future_landscape

Soori, M., Arezoo, B., & Dastres, R. (2023). Internet of things for smart factories in industry 4.0, a review. *Science Direct, 3*, 192–204. doi:10.1016/j.iotcps.2023.04.006

Srihith, N. I. D., Donald, N. D., Srinivas, N. T. S., Anjali, N. D., & Chandana, N. A. (2023). Firmware Attacks: The Silent Threat to Your IoT Connected Devices. *International Journal of Advanced Research in Science. Tongxin Jishu*, 145–154. doi:10.48175/IJARSCT-9104

Suganya, M., & Sasipraba, T. (2023). Stochastic Gradient Descent long short-term memory based secure encryption algorithm for cloud data storage and retrieval in cloud computing environment. *Journal of Cloud Computing (Heidelberg, Germany), 12*(1), 74. doi:10.1186/s13677-023-00442-6

Sujatha, R., & Prakash, G. (2022). Cyber Security Applications for Industry 4.0, Chapman and Hall/CRC Cyber-Physical Systems Series. CRC Press.

Sun, J., Tekleab, A. G., Cheung, M. F., & Wu, W. (2022). The contingent roles of market turbulence and organizational innovativeness on the relationships among interfirm trust, formal contracts, interfirm knowledge sharing and firm performance. *Journal of Knowledge Management, 27*(5), 1436–1457. doi:10.1108/JKM-04-2022-0289

Suren, E., Heiding, F., Olegård, J., & Lagerström, R. (2022). PatrIoT: Practical and agile threat research for IoT. *International Journal of Information Security, 22*(1), 213–233. doi:10.1007/s10207-022-00633-3

Suryavanshi, A., G, A., N, M. B. T., M, R., & N, A. H. (2023). *The integration of Blockchain and AI for Web 3.0: A security Perspective*. IEEE. doi:10.1109/ICITIIT57246.2023.10068672

Syed. (2023). Evaluating the Effectiveness of Cyber Security Regulations. All Student Theses. 138.

Ta, H., Esper, T. L., Hofer, A. R., & Sodero, A. C. (2023). Crowdsourced delivery and customer assessments of e-Logistics Service Quality: An appraisal theory perspective. *Journal of Business Logistics, 44*(3), 345–368. doi:10.1111/jbl.12327

Taj, I., & Zaman, N. (2022). Towards Industrial Revolution 5.0 and Explainable Artificial Intelligence: Challenges and Opportunities. *International Journal of Computing and Digital Systems*, *12*(1), 285–310. doi:10.12785/ijcds/120124

Tan, C. L., Tei, Z., Yeo, S. F., Lai, K., Kumar, A., & Chung, L. (2022). Nexus among blockchain visibility, supply chain integration and supply chain performance in the digital transformation era. *Industrial Management & Data Systems*, *123*(1), 229–252. doi:10.1108/IMDS-12-2021-0784

Tang, Y. M., Chau, K. Y., Lau, Y., & Zheng, Z. (2023). Data-Intensive Inventory Forecasting with Artificial Intelligence Models for Cross-Border E-Commerce Service Automation. *Applied Sciences (Basel, Switzerland)*, *13*(5), 3051. doi:10.3390/app13053051

Team, X. (2023, June 22). *Maintaining an integrated Supply Chain : Key Solutions*. Xcelpros. https://xcelpros.com/maintaining-an-integrated-supply-chain-key-solutions/

Telo, J. (2023, February 27). *Smart City Security Threats and Countermeasures in the Context of Emerging Technologies*. https://research.tensorgate.org/index.php/IJIAC/article/view/18

Tiwari, K., Patil, N., Gupta, A., Sabale, A., & Lomte, V. (n.d.). Fake Product Detection Using Blockchain Technology. *International Research Journal of Modernization in Engineering Technology and Science, 05*(05), 2582–5208. https://www.irjmets.com/uploadedfiles/paper/issue_5_may_2023/41058/final/fin_irjmets1685631927.pdf

Tiwari, S., Sharma, P., Choi, T., & Lim, A. (2023). Blockchain and third-party logistics for global supply chain operations: Stakeholders' perspectives and decision roadmap. *Elsevier, 170*, 103012. doi:10.1016/j.tre.2022.103012

Tombe, R., & Smuts, H. (2023). Society 5.0-Inspired Digitalization Framework for Resilient and Sustainable Agriculture. In EPiC series in computing. doi:10.29007/xc5q

Tripathi, P. K., Deshmukh, A. K., & Nath, T. (2023). Emergent Technologies for Supply Chain Risk and Disruption Management. In *Flexible systems management* (pp. 73–94). Springer Nature., doi:10.1007/978-981-99-2629-9_4

Truong, D. (2014). *Cloud-based solutions for supply chain management: a post-adoption study*. Semantic Scholar. https://www.semanticscholar.org/paper/CLOUD-BASED-SOLUTIONS-FOR-SUPPLY-CHAIN-MANAGEMENT%3A-Truong/716e4240a4f5733464bfee9b0c3a43ab08938479

Tsai, C. (2022). Supply chain financing scheme based on blockchain technology from a business application perspective. *Annals of Operations Research*, *320*(1), 441–472. doi:10.1007/s10479-022-05033-3 PMID:34092839

Verma, P., Ahluwalia, P., & Sharma, V. (2022). Cyber Supply Chain Risk Management Framework for the Internet of Things. *Computers & Electrical Engineering*, *97*, 107491.

Vishwakarma, A., Dangayach, G. S., Meena, M. L., Gupta, S., & Luthra, S. (2022). Adoption of blockchain technology enabled healthcare sustainable supply chain to improve healthcare supply chain performance. *Management of Environmental Quality*, *34*(4), 1111–1128. doi:10.1108/MEQ-02-2022-0025

Wallarm. (2023, April 17). *Cyber Attacks*. Wallarm. https://www.wallarm.com/what/what-is-a-cyber-attack

Wallis, T., & Dorey, P. (2023). Implementing Partnerships in Energy Supply Chain Cybersecurity Resilience. *Energies*, *16*(4), 1868. doi:10.3390/en16041868

Wang, S., Wan, J., Li, D. M., & Zhang, C. (2016). Implementing Smart Factory of Industrie 4.0: An Outlook. *International Journal of Distributed Sensor Networks*, *12*(1), 3159805. doi:10.1155/2016/3159805

Wei, G. (2023). The Impact of Blockchain Technology on Integrated Green Supply Chain Management in China: A Conceptual Study. *Dream Journal*, *2*(02), 58–65. doi:10.56982/dream.v2i02.112

Wong, L., Lee, V., Tan, G. W., Ooi, K., & Sohal, A. S. (2022). The role of cybersecurity and policy awareness in shifting employee compliance attitudes: Building supply chain capabilities. *International Journal of Information Management*, *66*, 102520. doi:10.1016/j.ijinfomgt.2022.102520

Xia, J., Li, H., & He, Z. (2023). The Effect of Blockchain Technology on Supply Chain Collaboration: A Case Study of Lenovo. *Systems*, *11*(6), 299. doi:10.3390/systems11060299

Xu, J., Lou, J., Lu, W., Wu, L., & Chen, C. (2023). Ensuring construction material provenance using Internet of Things and blockchain: Learning from the food industry. *Journal of Industrial Information Integration*, *33*, 100455. doi:10.1016/j.jii.2023.100455

Xue, Y., & Lai, K. (2023). Responsible shipping for sustainable development: Adoption and performance value. *Transport Policy*, *130*, 89–99. doi:10.1016/j.tranpol.2022.11.007

Yang, M., Chen, X., Tan, L., Lan, X., & Luo, Y. (2023). Listen carefully to experts when you classify data: A generic data classification ontology encoded from regulations. *Elsevier*, *60*(2), 103186. doi:10.1016/j.ipm.2022.103186

Yeboah-Ofori, A., & Opoku-Boateng, F. A. (2023). *Mitigating cybercrimes in an evolving organizational landscape*. Continuity & Resilience Review. doi:10.1108/CRR-09-2022-0017

Yenugula, M., Sahoo, S. K., & Goswami, S. S. (2023). Cloud computing in supply chain management: Exploring the relationship. *Management Science Letters*, *13*(3), 193–210. doi:10.5267/j.msl.2023.4.003

Yontar, E. (2023). The role of blockchain technology in the sustainability of supply chain management: Gray based dematel implementation. *Cleaner Logistics and Supply Chain*, *8*, 100113. doi:10.1016/j.clscn.2023.100113

You, J., Liu, B., Wang, Y., & Jiang, L. (2023). Tracking the prevalence of compromised passwords using long-term honeypot data. *Proc. SPIE 12700, International Conference on Electronic Information Engineering and Data Processing*. Spie. https://www.spiedigitallibrary.org/conference-proceedings-of-spie/12700/127000K/Tracking-the-prevalence-of-compromised-passwords-using-long-term-honeypot/10.1117/12.2682267.short?SSO=1

Zakzouk, A., El-Sayed, A., & Hemdan, E. E. (2023). A blockchain-based electronic medical records management framework in smart healthcare infrastructure. *Multimedia Tools and Applications*, *82*(23), 35419–35437. doi:10.1007/s11042-023-15152-z

Zhao, L. (2023, June 7). *A Study on the Protection of Consumer Rights and Interests in Online Shopping*. Pioneer Publisher. https://www.pioneerpublisher.com/slj/article/view/329

Zhao, N., Hong, J., & Lau, K. H. (2023). Impact of supply chain digitalization on supply chain resilience and performance: A multi-mediation model. *International Journal of Production Economics*, *259*, 108817. doi:10.1016/j.ijpe.2023.108817 PMID:36852136

Zhu, Q. (2023, February 26). *The Doctrine of Cyber Effect: An Ethics Framework for Defensive Cyber Deception*. arXiv.org. https://arxiv.org/abs/2302.13362

Chapter 8
Internet of Things (IoT) Impact on Inventory Management:
A Review

Azeem Khan
https://orcid.org/0000-0003-2742-8034
Sultan Sharif Ali Islamic University, Brunei

Noor Zaman Jhanjhi
https://orcid.org/0000-0001-8116-4733
School of Computer Science, SCS, Taylor's University, Subang Jaya, Malaysia

Dayang Hajah Tiawa Binte Awang Haji Hamid
Sultan Sharif Ali Islamic University, Brunei

Haji Abdul Hafidz B. Haji Omar
Sultan Sharif Ali Islamic University, Brunei

ABSTRACT

The impact of the internet of things (IoT) on inventory management is explored in this chapter. The chapter discusses comprehensively IoT system components, communication protocols, their architectures, and applications in various sectors. This chapter also investigates how IoT enabled inventory can provide real-time inventory management through timely monitoring, tracking, and optimization of inventories by employing RFID tags and readers. The RFID tags include encoded data in the form of unique IDs, which facilitates effective tracking and monitoring of goods and services pertaining to an organization. RFID readers can detect tags and transmit data encoded in it to the cloud for processing, thereby resulting in well informed data-driven decisions with improved operational efficiency. Furthermore, the chapter explores inventory management processes in the context of IoT-enabled inventories. The chapter also presents a comprehensive comparison of IoT enabled inventories with the traditional inventory management systems.

DOI: 10.4018/978-1-6684-7625-3.ch008

INTRODUCTION

Inventory management is critical in supply chain management because it addresses both production and price problems. Its primary purpose is to lower inventory costs while improving customer service levels through the use of efficient restocking methods. Because it comprises raw materials, work-in-process components, and finished commodities, inventory is a vital component of the supply chain. Figure 1.0 demonstrates the recent rapid development in the deployment and use of IoT devices across a variety of industries, including logistics, healthcare, retail, and manufacturing, to name a few. The Internet of Things (IoT) is a network of interconnected devices that comprise sensors, software, and communication capabilities for data collection and sharing. This technology has revolutionized inventory management by allowing for real-time visibility, automation, and better decision-making. This book chapter examines the impact of IoT on inventory management. This chapter is divided into eight sections. The first section provides background information on IoT in inventory management, as well as the objectives, scope, methodology, and review structure of the study. The second section introduces inventory management, including its definition, purpose, typical inventory management techniques, and related difficulties. Section 3 discusses the notion of IoT in inventory management, covering IoT understanding, definition, core principles, major components of IoT systems, communication protocols, standards, and architectures. Section 4 investigates several Internet of Things inventory management solutions such as real-time tracking, automated inventory replenishment, procurement, predictive maintenance, quality control, supply chain visibility, optimization, demand forecasting, and customer analytics. Section 5 investigates IoT-enabled Inventory Management Systems, covering RFID, sensor networks, data collection, cloud computing, big data analytics, and the integration of IoT with existing inventory management systems. Section 6 investigates the benefits and challenges of IoT in inventory management, such as improved inventory tracking accuracy and efficiency, reduced stockouts and overstocks, improved supply chain visibility and collaboration, cost savings, operational optimization, and security and privacy concerns. Section 7 contains case studies and examples of real-world uses of IoT in inventory management across various sectors, as well as success stories and lessons gained from using IoT in inventory management. Finally, Section 8 examines the future trends and implications of IoT in inventory management with an emphasis on emerging technologies, advancements, potential impacts on inventory management practices, industry trends, policy, and regulatory concerns for IoT-enabled inventory systems.

Figure 1. Emerging trend: Widespread IoT Device installations(statista)

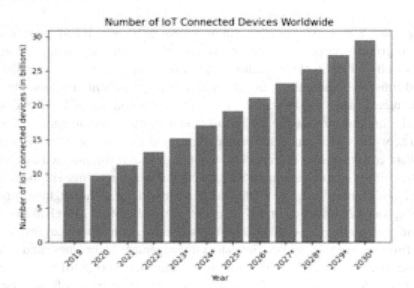

- **Background and significance of IoT in inventory management**

IoT stands for Internet of Things, and it refers to the process of connecting any device having an on/off switch to the Internet. Sensors in IoT devices monitor and report on environmental variables such as location, temperature, light, humidity, movement, and handling speed. The IoT has a substantial influence on inventory management, which is the monitoring of multiple procedures starting form ordering, storing, utilizing, transferring, and selling the firm's goods. IoT devices provide assistance with inventory management by providing real-time data insights, reducing human labor, increasing precision and efficacy, ensuring quality management, and meeting consumer demand and expectations. IoT devices, on the other hand, provide several challenges, including high prices, security and privacy risks, integration and compatibility concerns, and scalability and reliability issues. These challenges may be overcome by using best practices such as selecting the appropriate IoT devices and platforms, implementing strong security measures, utilizing cloud-based services and edge computing, and applying data analytics and artificial intelligence.

OBJECTIVES OF THE RESEARCH AND SCOPE

The book chapter "IoT Impact on Inventory Management" aims to thoroughly analyze the influence of IoT on inventory management approaches. The purpose of this chapter is to offer a thorough understanding of inventory management, including its components and associated expenses. It also intends to investigate the concept of IoT, studying its applications in inventory management and exhibiting real-world examples to demonstrate the benefits it offers. Furthermore, the chapter plans to investigate IoT-enabled inventory management systems, evaluating their functionalities and resolving the challenges connected with employing IoT in this context. Finally, the study's objectives are to shed light on the exciting prospects of IoT in optimizing inventory management methods. This chapter thoroughly examines the impact of the IoT on inventory management. It provides a comprehensive overview of inventory management, emphasizing its significance within the broader context of supply chain management. The chapter delves deeper into the concept of IoT, encompassing its definition, principles, and its practical application in the realm of inventory management. It explores various instances where IoT has been employed in inventory management, accompanied by real-world case studies and examples that illustrate the disruptive potential of this technology. Additionally, the chapter investigates inventory management systems that leverage IoT capabilities, considering both the advantages they offer, and the challenges associated with their implementation. Lastly, the chapter explores future trends and implications, proposing promising areas for further research and advancement.

REVIEW METHODOLOGY AND STRUCTURAL FRAMEWORK

Figure 2.0 depicts the methodological structure used for drafting the book chapter "IoT Impact on Inventory Management," which reflects a scholarly approach to examining the relevant material. The first stage required doing a thorough search on the Copilot platform using the precise phrase "IoT and Inventory Management," which yielded a large collection of 4,731 publications. A variety of filters were utilized to achieve a targeted selection, including the inclusion of journal papers, conference proceedings, and book chapters. This painstaking screening method successfully reduced the corpus to 3,062 articles. To emphasize the study's relevance today, an extra filter was used, limiting the publication timeframe to the last five years, resulting in a revised dataset of 1,215 publications. Following a thorough examination of these papers, their relevance to the research aims and scope of the book chapter was rigorously evaluated. A reasonable selection of 200 very relevant journals was carefully picked, serving as the basic ground for the chapter's detailed analysis and summary.

Figure 2. Selection criteria

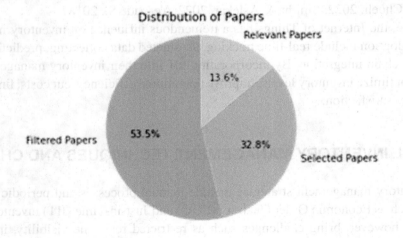

In essence, the methodology used in this book chapter assures an organized and rigorous selection procedure, resulting in a thorough examination of the influence of IoT on inventory management. The systematic presentation of the selected article findings and ideas adds to the academic discourse on IoT-enabled inventory management, making it a significant resource for scholars, practitioners, and stakeholders in this field.

OVERVIEW OF INVENTORY MANAGEMENT

- **Definition and purpose of inventory management**

The process of supervising and maintaining a company's inventory, which includes raw materials, components, and completed goods, is referred to as inventory management. It is an important part of supply chain management that involves regulating the movement of products from producers through warehouses and, eventually, to the point of sale. Inventory management's major goal is to enable organizations to properly handle inventory buying, stocking, storage, and use while reducing costs and enhancing customer satisfaction.(Hameed, Khan, & Hameed, 2019; Jabeen et al., 2023; Kaur, Kaur, & Singh, 2020)

The rise of the Internet of Things (IoT) has transformed commercial inventory management strategies. Sensors provided by the Internet of Things give real-time visibility into inventory location, status, and condition, allowing for more precise monitoring and lowering the risk of stockouts. Automated data collecting via IoT devices reduces errors and speeds up the inventory management process. IoT also enables predictive analytics and demand forecasting, allowing firms to make precise estimates and adjust inventory levels accordingly. Automation powered by IoT simplifies replenishment and order management, assuring prompt replenishment and reducing stockouts or surplus inventory. Furthermore, IoT encourages seamless integration and collaboration throughout the supply chain, improving coordination and just-in-time inventory management. IoT devices monitor equipment performance, optimize asset use, and proactively plan maintenance operations with enhanced asset utilization and maintenance. IoT devices' enhanced security features aid in preventing inventory loss and ensuring overall inventory security.(Kao & Chueh, 2022; Smitha & Aslekar, 2022; Yerpude S., 2018)

To summarize, the Internet of Things has a tremendous influence on inventory management. The benefits of IoT adoption include real-time tracking, automated data collecting, predictive analytics, and increased supply chain integration. By incorporating IoT into their inventory management techniques, businesses may optimize inventory levels, improve operational efficiency, cut costs, limit stockouts, and increase customer satisfaction.

TRADITIONAL INVENTORY MANAGEMENT TECHNIQUES AND CHALLENGES

Traditional inventory management strategies include manual processes and periodic reviews, as well as approaches such as Economic Order Quantity (EOQ) and Just-in-Time (JIT) inventory management. These solutions, however, bring challenges such as restricted real-time visibility, inconsistencies in inventory tracking, and difficulty responding to demand variations. Traditional approaches may fail to manage complicated supply chain networks and time-sensitive inventories, causing inefficiency in management. To solve these issues, innovative alternatives, such as the use of IoT technology, are required to improve inventory management processes and address the limitations of traditional approaches. (Chaurasiya, Biswas, Nayyar, Zaman Jhanjhi, & Banerjee, 2023; Mashayekhy, Babaei, Yuan, & Xue, 2022; Prabakar et al., 2023)

- **Exploring the idea of IoT in inventory management**

The limits of standard inventory management systems highlight the significance of researching creative solutions. The Internet of Things (IoT) gives a tremendous opportunity for organizations to transform their inventory management procedures. IoT helps organizations to better manage inventory levels, optimize supply chains, and increase operational efficiency by using real-time visibility, increased accuracy, and data-driven decision-making capabilities. Organizations may capture and analyze massive volumes of data by using IoT-enabled devices and sensors, allowing for enhanced demand forecasting, effective coordination across supply chain networks, and optimal management of perishable inventory. Incorporating IoT into inventory management operations not only helps solve the obstacles associated with traditional systems, but also opens up the exciting prospects of real-time data interchange and automation in inventory management.(Druehl, Carrillo, & Hsuan, 2018; Hamdy, Al-Awamry, & Mostafa, 2022; Yuan & Xue, 2023)

UNDERSTANDING THE INTERNET OF THINGS (IoT)

- **Definition and basic principles of IoT**

The Internet of Things (IoT) is characterized by a collection of core ideas that dictate its key functionality and operation. In essence, IoT is the connection of gadgets to the internet, allowing them to communicate and exchange data. This connectivity enables the collection and analysis of data created by these devices, laying the groundwork for informed decision-making and insights. IoT is built on the use of sensors and other technologies to remotely monitor and manage physical systems, delivering real-time data and allowing effective administration. Furthermore, integration with other technologies and platforms is crucial for the smooth interaction and interoperability of IoT devices and systems.(Srivatsa, Bharadwaj, Alamuri, Shanif, & Shreenidhi, 2021; Waseem, 2015)

IoT is used in inventory management to connect physical inventory assets and systems to the internet, allowing for easy communication and data exchange. This connectivity allows for the collection and analysis of real-time data from inventory devices and sensors, providing valuable insights into inventory levels, demand trends, and supply chain activities. The integration of Internet of Things devices and systems with existing inventory management technologies and platforms enhances operational efficiency, allowing businesses to make data-driven decisions and optimize inventory control.

- **Essential elements of IoT systems**

Inventory management in the context of the Internet of Things (IoT) encompasses several components that improve inventory monitoring, control, and optimization. When these components are integrated into the inventory management system, they result in enhanced efficiency, cost savings, and better decision-making. The table below outlines the critical components of IoT in inventory management and provides a summary of each:

Table 1. Key components of IoT in inventory management

Components	Description
Sensors and Devices	Utilize sensors such as RFID tags, temperature sensors, moisture sensors, weight sensors, and GPS trackers to collect real-time data on inventory location, status, and condition. Enable precise monitoring and tracking, minimizing stockouts and excess inventory.
RFID Tags and Barcode Labels	RFID tags or barcode labels are affixed to inventory items to facilitate data collection. These tags/labels contain unique identifiers and can store additional information such as expiration dates, stock levels, and other product details. They enable automated scanning and tracking of inventory items throughout the supply chain.
Data Collection	IoT-enabled devices, such as RFID readers or scanners, collect comprehensive inventory data. This includes real-time information on item locations, forecasted demand, temperature readings, and potential damage indicators. The data collected is transmitted to the cloud or inventory management system for further processing and analysis.
Connectivity	IoT devices require connectivity to transfer data. They can utilize various network options, including Wi-Fi, cellular networks, or Low Power Wide Area Networks (LPWAN), to establish a connection with the inventory management system. Connectivity options are chosen based on factors such as range, power consumption, and data requirements.
Cloud Infrastructure	Cloud infrastructure comprises servers, storage systems, and computing resources that enable the secure storage, processing, and analysis of inventory data. Cloud platforms offer scalability, reliability, and accessibility, allowing businesses to efficiently manage large volumes of inventory-related information.
GPS Integration	Integration of GPS technology enhances inventory tracking capabilities by providing precise location information. Each item is equipped with an integrated GPS module, allowing real-time monitoring and accurate identification of its whereabouts. This enables businesses to optimize logistics, reduce search time, and improve overall inventory visibility.
Data Analytics	Advanced data analytics algorithms and techniques are employed to analyze the collected inventory data. These analytics processes identify patterns, trends, and anomalies in the inventory information, enabling businesses to make data-driven decisions regarding demand forecasting, inventory optimization, and supply chain management.
Real-Time Tracking	IoT-enabled inventory management systems facilitate real-time tracking of items. The continuous monitoring and tracking capabilities provide up-to-date information on inventory levels, item movements, and stock availability. Real-time tracking helps businesses reduce storage costs, prevent stockouts, improve order fulfillment, and enhance overall operational efficiency.
Alerts and Notifications	The IoT system generates alerts and notifications based on predefined rules or exceptions. These alerts can include low stock alerts, expiration date reminders, temperature deviations, or unauthorized movement of inventory items. Alerts and notifications enable proactive inventory management actions, ensuring timely responses to critical events and reducing the risk of stockouts or product losses.
Integration with ERP Systems	Integration of IoT data with enterprise resource planning (ERP) systems allows for seamless data flow and automation of inventory management processes. IoT data, including real-time inventory updates and analytics insights, is integrated into the ERP system, enabling automated actions such as stock replenishment, order processing, and supply chain optimization. Integration enhances overall operational efficiency and streamlines inventory-related workflows.

- **IoT communication protocols and standards**

IoT communication protocols and standards are critical in facilitating connectivity and data sharing among IoT networks. These protocols provide criteria for data transmission, assuring device compatibility and interoperability. By adhering to these standards, developers may construct scalable and interoperable IoT systems that seamlessly connect devices and allow for efficient data sharing. Each protocol targets a unique necessity, such as low-power or long-distance communication. Adopting IoT communication protocols and standards is critical for unlocking the full potential of the IoT ecosystem and fostering effective communication across varied components. Table 2.0 provides a detailed overview of various protocols and standards.

Table 2. IoT communication protocols and standards

Protocol/Standard	Description	Use Cases
MQTT (Message Queuing Telemetry Transport)	A lightweight messaging protocol designed for efficient communication between IoT devices and the server. It follows a publish-subscribe model, making it ideal for low-power and low-bandwidth environments.	Industrial IoT monitoring, smart energy management, remote telemetry, asset tracking
CoAP (Constrained Application Protocol)	A specialized protocol designed for resource constrained IoT devices. It is lightweight, supports request-response communication, and operates over UDP, making it suitable for constrained networks and devices with limited processing power and memory.	Smart agriculture, wearable devices, home automation, environmental monitoring
HTTP (Hypertext Transfer Protocol)	A widely used protocol for communication between web browsers and servers. In IoT, HTTP can be used to facilitate communication between IoT devices, gateways, and cloud platforms using RESTful APIs.	IoT data ingestion, cloud-based services integration, web-based dashboards, and control interfaces
AMQP (Advanced Message Queuing Protocol)	A robust and flexible messaging protocol that supports message-oriented communication. It provides reliable and secure message delivery, making it suitable for complex IoT architectures and scenarios requiring advanced queuing capabilities.	Industrial automation, supply chain management, asset tracking, remote monitoring, and control
Zigbee	A wireless protocol designed for low-power, short-range communication in IoT networks. It operates on the IEEE 802.15.4 standard and is widely used in applications like home automation, smart lighting, and sensor networks.	Smart home automation, lighting control, home security systems, building automation
Z-Wave	A wireless protocol designed for home automation applications. It operates in the sub-GHz frequency band, providing reliable and low-power communication. Z-Wave is known for its interoperability and is widely used in smart home systems.	Smart home devices, home energy management, home security and safety systems
Bluetooth	A widely adopted wireless communication standard for short-range IoT applications. It provides connectivity between devices, such as smartphones, wearables, and IoT sensors, and supports low-energy consumption through Bluetooth Low Energy (BLE).	Wearable devices, health monitoring, asset tracking, beacon-based proximity systems
LoRaWAN (Long Range Wide Area Network)	A low-power wide-area network protocol designed for long-range communication in IoT deployments. It operates on the LoRa modulation scheme, allowing for long-distance communication and enabling battery powered IoT devices with extended battery life.	Smart city applications, environmental monitoring, agriculture and livestock management, utility metering
NB-IoT (Narrowband IoT)	A cellular communication standard optimized for IoT devices with low data rate requirements and long battery life. NB-IoT operates in licensed spectrum, offering better network coverage and security compared to other IoT cellular technologies.	Smart metering, asset tracking, industrial monitoring, smart city infrastructure
Wi-Fi	A popular wireless communication standard that provides high-speed connectivity over local area networks. It is widely used in IoT applications that require fast and reliable data transmission.	Smart homes, connected appliances, video surveillance, healthcare monitoring

- **IoT architectures and deployment models**

This section examines the layers of IoT architecture for inventory management, specifically the physical layer/perception layer, network layer, service layer, and application layer. The goal is to optimize inventory management by enabling real-time monitoring, enhanced control, and streamlined processes. As depicted in Figure 3.0, the IoT architecture consists of four layers. At the bottom is the physical layer, also known as the perception layer, following it we have a network layer, then we have a service layer and lastly, at the top from the bottom we have the application layer. Let's explore them in detail(Ashraf et al., 2023; Pal et al., 2023; Pal et al.).

Figure 3. Internet of things layered model
(Ramachandran et al., 2022)

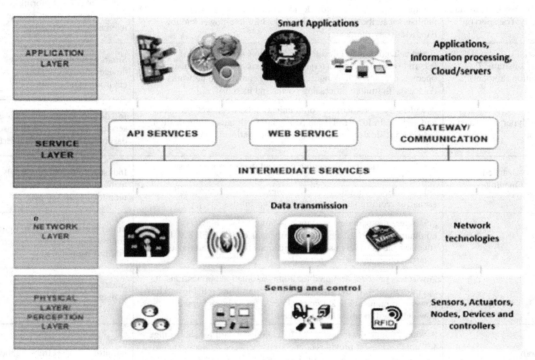

1. Physical Layer/Perception Layer:

The physical layer, also known as the perception layer, forms the foundation of IoT architecture. It encompasses the deployment of sensors and actuators that interact with the physical world. Sensors collect data from the environment, capturing parameters such as temperature, humidity, or motion, while actuators enable control actions based on the collected data. In the context of inventory management, the physical layer enables real-time information gathering about inventory conditions, facilitating proactive decision-making.

2. Network Layer

The network layer, situated above the physical layer, serves as the backbone of IoT architecture. Also referred to as the data management layer, it establishes connectivity between various devices, servers, and things within the IoT application. The network layer facilitates seamless communication and data exchange among different components of the IoT system, ensuring efficient data flow, aggregation, and preprocessing. In the realm of inventory management, the network layer enables the transmission of inventory-related information across the network reliably and securely.

3.   Service Layer

The service layer is an important component of the IoT architecture. It provides key services that improve the functionality and efficiency of IoT applications by being located between the network layer and the application layer. The service layer categorizes data depending on unique needs and applications, including visualization, security, storage, communication services, and analytics. It serves as a link between the network and application levels, allowing for the development, maintenance, and identification of services required for productive inventory management.

4.   Application Layer

The application layer, at the top of the IoT architecture, offers end users application-specific services and capabilities. The application layer provides customized services meant to optimize retail operations in the context of inventory management. Real-time inventory monitoring, demand forecasting, stock optimization, and automatic restocking are examples of these services. The application layer delivers actionable insights that enable effective inventory management and informed decision-making by leveraging data acquired from sensors and processed in the network and service layers.

In conclusion, IoT architecture in inventory management holds immense potential, by leveraging the layers of physical layer/perception layer, network layer, service layer, and application layer, retailers can achieve real-time monitoring, enhanced control, and streamlined processes in inventory management. Understanding the collaborative functioning of these layers is essential for harnessing the full potential of IoT in inventory management, leading to improved profitability, customer satisfaction, and operational performance in the retail industry.

IoT APPLICATIONS IN INVENTORY MANAGEMENT

Inventory management revolves around effectively managing the movement of goods from their origin to their intended destinations. It encompasses activities such as inventory tracking, proper storage, timely restocking, and cost optimization. As an integral part of supply chain management, inventory management directly impacts a company's profitability, customer satisfaction, and competitive position. The Internet of Things (IoT) emerges as a valuable tool for inventory management by offering real-time data, enhanced visibility, and control throughout the supply chain(Bhoi et al., 2022; Saleh, Jhanjhi, Abdullah, & Saher; Sing et al., 2022). The following are key applications of IoT in inventory management:

1.   **Real-time tracking and monitoring systems:** IoT devices like RFID tags, GPS trackers, sensors, and cameras provide constant updates on inventory item locations, conditions, and movements. This minimizes errors, theft, loss, and damage while improving traceability, security, and quality control.

2. **Automated data collection with RFID tags:** RFID tags are small electronic devices that store and transmit data using radio waves. By attaching them to inventory items and utilizing RFID readers for scanning, data collection becomes automated, reducing errors, labor costs, and time, while enhancing accuracy, speed, and efficiency.

3. **Efficient warehouse and logistics management:** IoT devices optimize warehouse and logistics operations through smart storage, picking, packing, and shipping of inventory items. For instance, IoT devices monitor environmental conditions in warehouses, such as temperature, humidity, and light, enabling adjustments to preserve inventory item quality. Moreover, automation using robots, drones, and conveyor belts streamlines tasks like sorting, labelling, and loading.

4. **Performance enhancement with predictive maintenance:** IoT devices enhance inventory management systems by facilitating predictive maintenance of equipment and machinery. Through sensors on IoT devices, equipment health(Aadil et al., 2021) and performance can be monitored, allowing maintenance staff to receive alerts before breakdowns or malfunctions occur. This reduces downtime, repair costs, and risks while improving reliability, productivity, and safety.

5. **Optimized fleet inventory management system:** IoT devices optimize fleet inventory management by enabling real-time communication and coordination among vehicles, drivers, and managers. Real-time traffic information, route optimization, fuel consumption monitoring, and driver behaviour analysis enhance transportation efficiency and safety.

6. **Higher accuracy in forecasting lead times:** IoT devices improve the accuracy of lead time forecasting by providing real-time data on customer demand patterns, market trends, and inventory levels. This reduces issues of overstocking or understocking, resulting in improved customer satisfaction and loyalty.

7. **Smooth Augmented Reality (AR) and Robotics integrations:** IoT devices facilitate the integration of AR and Robotics technologies into inventory management systems, enhancing user experience and performance. For instance, AR glasses provide visual guidance to warehouse workers, offering 3D images for locating, picking, and packing inventory items. Robots can assist or replace humans in repetitive or hazardous tasks.

8. **Reduced loss and equipment damage in the supply chain:** IoT devices minimize loss and equipment damage by issuing real-time alerts for potential issues or risks during transit or storage. Through sensors, shocks, vibrations, or impacts that may harm inventory items or equipment can be detected, prompting relevant parties to take preventive measures.

In conclusion, IoT significantly impacts inventory management by delivering benefits such as real-time data, visibility, control, automation, efficiency, accuracy, and performance enhancement. By leveraging IoT, businesses can optimize inventory levels, reduce costs, improve customer service, and gain a competitive advantage(Anandan, Gopalakrishnan, Pal, & Zaman, 2022; Mukherjee et al.).

IoT-ENABLED INVENTORY MANAGEMENT SYSTEMS

As depicted in Fig 4.0, IoT-enabled inventory systems use various technologies, such as RFID, sensor networks, cloud computing, and big data analytics, to transform how businesses monitor and manage their inventory. This section will explore how RFID technology facilitates IoT-based inventory tracking, how sensor networks collect data from the inventory environment, how cloud computing and big data analytics optimize inventory decisions, and how IoT integrates with existing inventory management systems. By learning these concepts, businesses can leverage the power of IoT to improve their inventory management practices, increase efficiency, and achieve optimal outcomes.

- **RFID (Radio-Frequency Identification) technology and its role in IoT-based inventory management**

RFID, or Radio-Frequency Identification, employs radio waves to identify and track objects. RFID tags, which are tiny electronic devices capable of storing and transferring data, are used, as are RFID readers, which scan and extract data from the tags. Data may be obtained without human involvement by attaching RFID tags to inventory objects. RFID technology is significant in IoT-based inventory management because of its capacity to give real-time and precise information on inventory products across the supply chain. RFID tags can store and communicate a variety of data points, such as model numbers, batch numbers, expiration dates, inventory position and condition. RFID readers read the tags and transmit the information to the cloud for processing and analysis. This technology lowers the number of mistakes, thefts, losses, and damages while boosting traceability, security, and quality control.(A. Mishra & Mohapatro, 2020; N. Mishra & Keshri, 2021; Tan & Sidhu, 2022).

- **Sensor networks and data collection in inventory management**

Sensor networks are made up of devices equipped with sensors that detect and monitor physical or environmental properties such as temperature, humidity, light, motion, vibration, and sound. Wireless communication technologies such as Wi-Fi, Bluetooth, and ZigBee are used by these networks to collect and transport data. Sensor networks play a crucial role in data collection for inventory management by providing real-time and complete information on inventory goods and their surroundings. Sensor networks, for example, may monitor warehouse variables like temperature, humidity, and light and make changes to keep inventory items in good condition. They may also detect shocks, vibrations, or accidents that may cause inventory or equipment damage and promptly alert the necessary parties so that preventative actions may be taken.(Alkinani, Almazroi, Jhanjhi, & Khan, 2021).

- **Cloud computing and big data analytics for inventory optimization**

Over the internet, cloud computing provides on-demand access to pooled computing resources such as servers, storage, databases, software, and applications. Businesses benefit from this technology's scalability, adaptability, dependability, and cost-effectiveness. The analysis of massive and complex datasets using advanced tools and techniques such as machine learning, artificial intelligence, and data mining is known as big data analytics. It provides business insights, patterns, trends, and projections. By processing and analyzing data acquired from RFID tags and sensor networks, cloud computing and big data analytics help in inventory optimization. They can give practical inventory management information and suggestions, such as ideal inventory levels, restocking strategies, demand forecasts, delivery times, warehouse layout, logistics routes, and maintenance forecasts.

Figure 4. Harnessing the power of IoT for optimal inventory management (trackany.live, 2020)

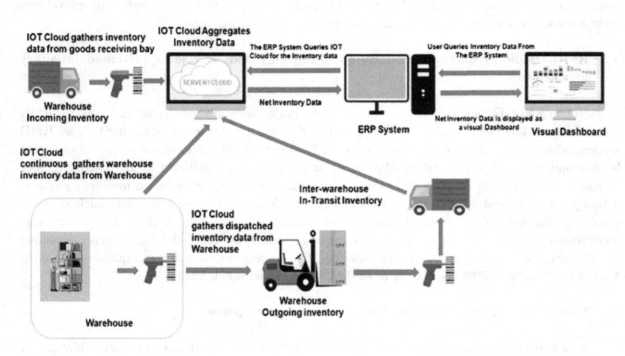

- **Integration of IoT with existing inventory management systems**

Integration of Internet of Things-enabled inventory management systems with current inventory management systems, such as ERP, is critical for improving operations and expediting data interchange. Businesses may keep accurate and up-to-date inventory records across both platforms by syncing data in real-time. This consolidated control and visibility gives a comprehensive picture of inventory levels, locations, and other relevant facts, allowing for more informed decision-making and effective inventory management. Furthermore, integration allows process automation by connecting IoT data with current system operations. By automatically activating activities such as issuing purchase orders or sending notifications when inventory levels are low, this automation lowers manual involvement and improves operational efficiency. Employees may focus on critical activities with increased efficiency and accuracy, thereby enhancing overall productivity and customer satisfaction.

Integration also enables the use of IoT-generated data within the existing inventory management system's analytics and reporting capabilities. Businesses may obtain important insights into inventory trends, demand patterns, and performance indicators by merging IoT data with other relevant data sources. These insights help firms make data-driven decisions, allowing them to optimize inventory planning, procurement, and strategic business plans to satisfy client expectations successfully.

Finally, connecting IoT-enabled inventory management solutions with current systems such as ERP allows for a unified and seamless approach to inventory management. It enables organizations to exploit the benefits of IoT technology while optimizing the value of their existing inventory management systems through real-time data synchronization, process automation, improved decision-making, and scalability.

BENEFITS AND CHALLENGES OF IoT IN INVENTORY MANAGEMENT

IoT is the network of devices, sensors, and software that can collect, transmit, and analyse data in real time. IoT has many applications in inventory management, which is the process of monitoring and controlling the quantity, location, and condition of raw materials, finished goods, and spare parts in a manufacturing facility. In this section, we will examine the advantages and disadvantages of using IoT for inventory management.

- **Improved accuracy and efficiency in inventory tracking**

One of the advantages of IoT for inventory management is that it can provide precise and timely data on the availability, demand, and quality of inventory items. For instance, IoT sensors can measure the temperature, humidity, and vibration of perishable or fragile goods, and notify the managers if they are deteriorated or expired. IoT devices can also automate the replenishment and ordering of inventory items and prevent excess or shortage of inventory. This can reduce waste, improve customer satisfaction, and optimize inventory turnover(Ullah, Ishaq, et al., 2021).

- **Reduction in stockouts and overstocks**

Another advantage of IoT for inventory management is that it can help reduce the risk of stockouts and overstocks. Stockouts occur when there is insufficient inventory to meet customer demand, resulting in lost sales and customer dissatisfaction. Overstocks occur when there is surplus inventory than required, resulting in increased storage costs and obsolescence. IoT devices can track the demand patterns and trends of customers and adjust the inventory levels accordingly. IoT devices can also communicate with each other and with suppliers to coordinate the supply chain and ensure timely delivery. This can increase sales, reduce costs, and enhance customer loyalty.

- **Enhanced supply chain visibility and collaboration**

A third advantage of IoT for inventory management is that it can improve the visibility and collaboration of the supply chain. The supply chain is the network of suppliers, manufacturers, distributors, retailers, and customers involved in producing and delivering goods. IoT devices can track the location, speed, and condition of vehicles, containers, and pallets, and provide updates on the status and ETA of shipments. IoT devices can also collect and analyse data on traffic, weather, fuel consumption, and driver behaviour, and recommend the optimal routes, schedules, and modes of transportation. This can improve the efficiency, reliability, and sustainability of the supply chain.

- **Cost savings and operational optimization**

A fourth advantage of IoT for inventory management is that it can generate cost savings and operational optimization. By using IoT devices to monitor and control inventory items, managers can reduce manual labor, errors, and delays. By using IoT devices to optimize inventory levels and supply chain operations, managers can reduce storage costs, transportation costs, and inventory costs. By using IoT devices to collect and analyse data on inventory performance, managers can identify bottlenecks, inefficiencies, and opportunities for improvement. This can increase productivity, profitability, and competitiveness.

- **Security and privacy concerns in IoT-enabled inventory systems**

Despite the many advantages of IoT for inventory management, there are also some challenges that need to be addressed. One of the main challenges is security and privacy. IoT devices generate and transmit large amounts of sensitive data that can be vulnerable to cyberattacks, theft, or misuse. Therefore, encryption systems must be implemented to protect the data and comply with relevant regulations. Additionally, data integration and analysis is also required to produce meaningful insights from diverse and complex data. This requires appropriate software, hardware, and skills to store, process, and interpret the data from different sources and formats. Furthermore, data reliability and quality must be ensured by calibrating, maintaining, and updating IoT devices regularly to detect any errors or anomalies in the data(Lee, Abdullah, Jhanjhi, & Kok, 2021; Najmi et al., 2021; Seong, Ponnusamy, Jhanjhi, Annur, & Talib, 2021).

CASE STUDIES AND EXAMPLES

IoT has been applied to inventory management across various industries, such as manufacturing, retail, healthcare, and logistics. In this section, we will present some real-world applications of IoT in inventory management and some success stories and lessons learned from implementing IoT in inventory management(El Jaouhari, El Bhilat, & Arif, 2023; Piramuthu, 2022).

- **Real-world applications of IoT in inventory management across various industries**
    1. **Manufacturing:** The Internet of Things may assist manufacturers in monitoring and controlling the inventory of raw materials, components, and final goods in their facilities. Bosch, for example, use RFID tags and readers to track the movement and placement of components and equipment on its manufacturing lines. This reduces errors, delays, and expenses while increasing quality and efficiency. Another example is GE Appliances, which monitors inventory levels and estimates demand for its goods using IoT sensors and cloud computing. This allows the organization to improve its production planning and scheduling while also reducing inventory waste.
    2. **Retail:** IoT may assist businesses in tracking and managing inventories in their storefronts and warehouses. Walmart, for example, employs IoT sensors and cameras to check product stock levels and expiration dates on its shelves. This minimizes waste, stockouts, and theft while improving customer satisfaction and sales. Zara, for example, employs RFID tags and scanners to manage clothing inventories in its stores and warehouses. This enables the organization to modify inventory levels based on consumer preferences and demand trends, lowering inventory expenses.
    3. **Healthcare:** The Internet of Things can assist healthcare professionals in tracking and managing the inventory of medical supplies, equipment, and pharmaceuticals in their facilities. Cardinal Health, for example, monitors the temperature, humidity, and location of medications in its distribution facilities using IoT sensors and cloud computing. This guarantees that

pharmaceuticals are safe, of high quality, and readily available to patients. Another example is Medtronic, which tracks the source and validity of medical items in its supply chain using IoT devices and blockchain technology. This prevents fake goods from accessing the market and causing harm to people.(Jacob et al., 2021; Ullah, Azeem, et al., 2021).

4. **Logistics:** IoT may assist logistics firms in tracking and managing inventory of products in transit and delivery. DHL, for example, tracks the position, speed, and condition of trucks, containers, and pallets in its supply chain using IoT devices and GPS. This enhances cargo visibility, dependability, and sustainability. Another example is UPS, which collects and analyzes data on traffic, weather, fuel usage, and driver behavior using IoT devices and big data analytics to improve routes, timetables, and modes of transportation. This minimizes package delivery time, cost, and carbon impact.(Humayun, Jhanjhi, Hamid, & Ahmed, 2020).

- **Success stories and lessons learned from implementing IoT in inventory management**

   1. **Amazon:** Amazon was a pioneer in the use of IoT for inventory management. Amazon employs drones to scan barcodes and update its inventory system at its facilities. Robots are also used by Amazon to transport things throughout its warehouses and maximize space use. According to Amazon, these technologies have enhanced inventory accuracy by 50% and lowered operational expenses by 20%.

   2. **Zara:** Zara is a renowned apparel store that employs IoT for inventory management. Zara tracks clothing inventory in its stores and warehouses using RFID tags and readers. Zara also collects data on client preferences and demand trends using IoT devices. Zara believes that these technologies have raised sales by 10% while lowering inventory expenses by 15%.

   3. **Coca-Cola:** Coca-Cola is one of the major beverage corporations that employs IoT to control inventories. Coca-Cola monitors the stock levels and consumption trends of its goods in vending machines using IoT sensors and cloud computing. Coca-Cola also collects data on customer comments and satisfaction via IoT devices. Coca-Cola believes that these technologies raised income by 12% while decreasing maintenance expenses by 18%.

   4. **IKEA:** IKEA is a renowned furniture company that uses IoT to manage inventories. RFID tags and readers are used by IKEA to track the inventory of furniture goods in its shops and warehouses. IKEA also collects data on consumer behavior, preferences, and satisfaction via IoT devices. According to IKEA, these technologies have increased customer service by 15% while decreasing inventory expenses by 10%.

Overall, IoT is a potent technology that may improve inventory management in a variety of businesses. Businesses may obtain various benefits by deploying IoT devices to monitor, control, and optimize inventory products and processes, such as enhanced accuracy, efficiency, visibility, cooperation, cost savings, operational optimization, customer happiness, sales, profitability, and competitiveness. However, there are some difficulties (Almusaylim & Zaman, 2019) and issues that must be addressed among them to name a few are data security (Shahid et al.), privacy, integration, analysis, reliability, and quality. As a result, firms must establish proper strategies, methods, and capabilities to utilize IoT efficiently and securely in inventory management.

FUTURE TRENDS AND IMPLICATIONS

The IoT is a fast-emerging technology with the potential to alter inventory management in the future. In this section, we will address some of the emerging technologies and improvements in IoT for inventory management and their possible influence on inventory management practices, industry trends, and policy and regulatory issues for IoT-enabled inventory systems.

EMERGING TECHNOLOGIES AND ADVANCEMENTS IN IoT FOR INVENTORY MANAGEMENT

The following are some of the new technologies and developments in IoT for inventory management:

1. **Edge computing and 5G:** 5G is the next generation of wireless communication technology that outperforms 4G in terms of speed, latency, bandwidth, and dependability. Edge computing is the technique of executing data processing and analysis at the network's edge, closer to the data source. Together, 5G and edge computing can allow real-time data transmission and processing for IoT devices, enhancing the responsiveness, scalability, and security of inventory management systems devices, improving the responsiveness, scalability, and security of inventory management systems. (Douch, Abid, Zine-Dine, Bouzidi, & Benhaddou, 2022).

2. **Blockchain and smart contracts:** Blockchain is a distributed ledger technology that records transactions in a secure, transparent, and immutable way. Smart contracts are self-executing agreements that are encoded on the blockchain and executed automatically when certain conditions are met. Blockchain and smart contracts can enhance the traceability, accountability, and automation of inventory management systems, reducing fraud, errors, and disputes(Aljemy, Alanazi, Alsofiry, & Baig, 2019; Kaushik & Pillai, 2021).

3. **Artificial intelligence and machine learning:** Artificial intelligence (AI) is the ability of machines to perform tasks that normally require human intelligence, such as reasoning, learning, decision making, and problem solving. Machine learning (ML) is a subset of AI that enables machines to learn from data and improve their performance without explicit programming. AI and ML can augment the data analysis and optimization capabilities of inventory management systems, enabling predictive analytics, demand forecasting, inventory planning, replenishment optimization, anomaly detection, and recommendation systems(Botari, Izbicki, & de Carvalho, 2020; Lele & Lele, 2019; Simon, Jhanjhi, Goh, & Sukumaran, 2022).

4. **Augmented reality and virtual reality:** Augmented reality (AR) is the technology that overlays digital information or images on the physical world, enhancing the user's perception of reality. Virtual reality (VR) is the technology that creates a simulated environment that immerses the user in a virtual world. AR and VR can improve the user experience and efficiency of inventory management systems, enabling interactive visualization, navigation, guidance, training, and collaboration(Sahu & Balfour, 2022).
   ◦ **Potential impact on inventory management practices and industry trends**

Some of the potential impact of IoT on inventory management practices and industry trends include:

1. **Leaner and greener inventory management:** IoT can help businesses achieve leaner and greener inventory management by reducing waste, emissions, energy consumption, and costs associated with inventory holding, transportation, and disposal. IoT can also help businesses adopt circular economy principles, such as reuse, recycle, and repair, by facilitating the tracking and recovery of products and materials throughout their lifecycle(Smith, 2012).

2. **Smarter and more agile inventory management:** IoT can help businesses achieve smarter and more agile inventory management by enhancing their visibility, control, and flexibility over their inventory items and processes. IoT can also help businesses adapt to changing customer expectations, market conditions, and competitive pressures by enabling real-time data-driven decisions, dynamic pricing, personalization, and customization(Saeed & Shoukat, 2023).

3. **Collaborative and integrated inventory management:** IoT can help businesses achieve collaborative and integrated inventory management by improving their communication, coordination, and cooperation with their supply chain partners, such as suppliers, manufacturers, distributors, retailers, and customers. IoT can also help businesses leverage the power of network effects, sharing economy, and platform economy by enabling the exchange of data, information, resources, and services among multiple stakeholders.

   ◦ **Policy and regulatory considerations for IoT-enabled inventory systems**

Some of the policy and regulatory considerations for IoT-enabled inventory systems include:

1. **Data protection and privacy:** IoT-enabled inventory systems collect and process large amounts of personal and sensitive data that may pose risks to the data subjects' rights and interests. Therefore, businesses need to comply with relevant data protection and privacy laws and regulations, such as the General Data Protection Regulation (GDPR) in the European Union or the California Consumer Privacy Act (CCPA) in the United States. Businesses also need to adopt appropriate data governance measures, such as data minimization, anonymization, encryption, consent, notification, access control, and audit trail(Humayun, Jhanjhi, Alruwaili, et al., 2020; Shah, Jhanjhi, & Laraib, 2023).

2. **Cybersecurity:** IoT-enabled inventory systems are exposed to various cyber threats that may compromise their confidentiality, integrity, availability, or safety. Therefore, businesses need to comply with relevant cybersecurity laws and regulations, such as the Network and Information Systems Directive (NISD) in the European Union or the Cybersecurity and Infrastructure Security Agency (CISA) in the United States. Businesses also need to adopt appropriate cybersecurity measures, such as risk assessment, vulnerability scanning, patch management, firewall, antivirus, intrusion detection and prevention, incident response(Jhanjhi, Humayun, & Almuayqil, 2021; Kotsias, Ahmad, & Scheepers, 2023).

3. **Ethical and social:** IoT-enabled inventory systems may raise ethical and social issues that may affect the trust, acceptance, and adoption of the technology by the stakeholders. Therefore, businesses need to comply with relevant ethical and social principles and guidelines, such as the Ethical Framework for a Good AI Society by the European Commission or the Principles for Artificial Intelligence by the Organization for Economic Co-operation and Development (OECD). Businesses also need to adopt appropriate ethical and social measures, such as transparency, accountability, fairness, inclusiveness, human dignity, human oversight, human values(Lo Piano, 2020; Sreedevi, Nitya Harshitha, Sugumaran, & Shankar, 2022; Vice & Khan, 2022).

CONCLUSION

This section gives a succinct summary of the study's important results and contributions on IoT-enabled inventory management. It explores implications for research and practice, as well as future work in this industry (Moore, Nugent, Zhang, & Cleland, 2020).

- Key findings and contributions presented

The following significant findings and contributions have emerged from the investigation of IoT applications in inventory management:

1. IoT technologies, such as RFID tags, sensors, and cloud computing, enhance inventory management by improving accuracy, efficiency, visibility, collaboration, cost savings, customer satisfaction, sales, profitability, and competitiveness.
2. Real-world case studies, including industry leaders such as Amazon, Coca-Cola, Zara, and IKEA, demonstrate the tangible benefits of IoT in achieving inventory management excellence.
3. Successful IoT implementations enable organizations to optimize inventory levels, prevent stockouts and overstocks, enhance supply chain visibility, and reduce operational costs.
4. IoT integration in inventory management offers benefits such as improved accuracy, efficiency, collaboration, and cost savings.
5. Key applications of IoT in inventory management include real-time tracking, automated replenishment, predictive maintenance, supply chain visibility, and demand forecasting.
6. IoT-enabled inventory management systems utilize RFID technology, sensor networks, cloud computing, and integration with existing systems.
7. Challenges in IoT-enabled inventory systems include security and privacy concerns that need to be addressed.
8. Protecting sensitive inventory data and adhering to security measures are crucial considerations.
9. Policy and regulatory compliance play a vital role in ensuring responsible and ethical use of IoT in inventory management.
10. Emerging technology, advancements and policy issues are all part of the future of IoT in inventory management.
11. Future advances in IoT technology may result in improved automation, customized client experiences, and improved sustainability.
12. Organizations should keep themselves on developing trends and think about the ethical implications of IoT in inventory management.
   ◦ **Investigations and practical implications**

The following are the implications of integrating IoT into inventory management:

1. Future research should focus on processes and techniques for successful IoT integration in various industry scenarios.
2. More research is needed to understand the long-term benefits of IoT on inventory management performance as well as the obstacles encountered during adoption.

Practice:

1. Organizations should realize IoT's disruptive potential in inventory management and view it as a strategic project.
2. Businesses may use the lessons learnt from successful deployments to create customized strategies for maximizing IoT advantages.
3. It is critical to prioritize privacy and security of data safeguards to avoid potential risks associated with IoT-enabled inventory systems.

RECOMMENDATIONS FOR FUTURE WORK IN THE FIELD OF IOT-ENABLED INVENTORY MANAGEMENT

The following recommendations are made to develop the area of IoT-enabled inventory management:

1. Conduct more research to investigate the influence of IoT on numerous aspects of inventory management, including demand forecasting, supplier collaboration, and warehouse optimization.
2. Explore the possibilities of inventory management using new technologies such as artificial intelligence and blockchain together with IoT.
3. Address data security, privacy, integration, analysis, dependability, and quality issues in IoT-enabled inventory systems.

REFERENCES

Aadil, F., Mehmood, B., Hasan, N. U., Lim, S., Ejaz, S., & Zaman, N. (2021). Remote health monitoring using IoT-based smart wireless body area network. *Computers, Materials & Continua*, 68(2), 2499–2513. doi:10.32604/cmc.2021.014647

Aljemy, K., Alanazi, M., Alsofiry, M., & Baig, A. (2019). Improving IoT security using blockchain. *Paper presented at the 2019 IEEE 10th GCC Conference and Exhibition, GCC 2019*. IEEE. 10.1109/GCC45510.2019.1570521015

Alkinani, M. H., Almazroi, A. A., Jhanjhi, N., & Khan, N. A. (2021). 5G and IoT based reporting and accident detection (RAD) system to deliver first aid box using unmanned aerial vehicle. *Sensors (Basel)*, 21(20), 6905. doi:10.3390/s21206905 PMID:34696118

Almusaylim, Z. A., & Zaman, N. (2019). A review on smart home present state and challenges: Linked to context-awareness internet of things (IoT). *Wireless Networks*, 25(6), 3193–3204. doi:10.1007/s11276-018-1712-5

Anandan, R., Gopalakrishnan, S., Pal, S., & Zaman, N. (2022). *Industrial Internet of Things (IIoT): Intelligent Analytics for Predictive Maintenance*. John Wiley & Sons. doi:10.1002/9781119769026

Ashraf, H., Hanif, M., Ihsan, U., Al-Quayed, F., Humayun, M., & Jhanjhi, N. (2023). A Secure and Reliable Supply chain management approach integrated with IoT and Blockchain. *Paper presented at the 2023 International Conference on Business Analytics for Technology and Security (ICBATS).* IEEE. 10.1109/ICBATS57792.2023.10111371

Bhoi, S. K., Panda, S. K., Jena, K. K., Sahoo, K. S., Jhanjhi, N., Masud, M., & Aljahdali, S. (2022). IoT-EMS: An Internet of Things Based Environment Monitoring System in Volunteer Computing Environment. *Intelligent Automation & Soft Computing, 32*(3).

Botari, T., Izbicki, R., & de Carvalho, A. C. P. L. F. (2020). Local interpretation methods to machine learning using the domain of the feature space. *Paper presented at the Communications in Computer and Information Science.* Springer. 10.1007/978-3-030-43823-4_21

Chaurasiya, S. K., Biswas, A., Nayyar, A., Zaman Jhanjhi, N., & Banerjee, R. (2023). DEICA: A differential evolution-based improved clustering algorithm for IoT-based heterogeneous wireless sensor networks. *International Journal of Communication Systems, 36*(5), e5420. doi:10.1002/dac.5420

Douch, S., Abid, M. R., Zine-Dine, K., Bouzidi, D., & Benhaddou, D. (2022). Edge Computing Technology Enablers: A Systematic Lecture Study. *IEEE Access : Practical Innovations, Open Solutions, 10*, 69264–69302. doi:10.1109/ACCESS.2022.3183634

Druehl, C., Carrillo, J., & Hsuan, J. (2018) Technological innovations: Impacts on supply chains. In. *Contributions to Management Science* (pp. 259-281).

El Jaouhari, A., El Bhilat, E. M., & Arif, J. (2023). Scrutinizing IoT applicability in green warehouse inventory management system based on Mamdani fuzzy inference system: A case study of an automotive semiconductors industrial firm. *Journal of Industrial and Production Engineering, 40*(2), 87–101. doi:10.1080/21681015.2022.2142303

Hamdy, W., Al-Awamry, A., & Mostafa, N. (2022). Warehousing 4.0: A proposed system of using node-red for applying internet of things in warehousing. *Sustainable Futures : An Applied Journal of Technology, Environment and Society, 4*, 100069. doi:10.1016/j.sftr.2022.100069

Hameed, S., Khan, F. I., & Hameed, B. (2019). Understanding Security Requirements and Challenges in Internet of Things (IoT): A Review. *Journal of Computer Networks and Communications, 2019*, 1–14. doi:10.1155/2019/9629381

Humayun, M., Jhanjhi, N., Alruwaili, M., Amalathas, S. S., Balasubramanian, V., & Selvaraj, B. (2020). Privacy protection and energy optimization for 5G-aided industrial Internet of Things. *IEEE Access : Practical Innovations, Open Solutions, 8*, 183665–183677. doi:10.1109/ACCESS.2020.3028764

Humayun, M., Jhanjhi, N., Hamid, B., & Ahmed, G. (2020). Emerging smart logistics and transportation using IoT and blockchain. *IEEE Internet of Things Magazine, 3*(2), 58–62. doi:10.1109/IOTM.0001.1900097

Jabeen, T., Jabeen, I., Ashraf, H., Jhanjhi, N., Yassine, A., & Hossain, M. S. (2023). An Intelligent Healthcare System Using IoT in Wireless Sensor Network. *Sensors (Basel), 23*(11), 5055. doi:10.3390/s23115055 PMID:37299782

Jacob, S., Alagirisamy, M., Xi, C., Balasubramanian, V., Srinivasan, R., Parvathi, R., & Islam, S. M. (2021). AI and IoT-enabled smart exoskeleton system for rehabilitation of paralyzed people in connected communities. *IEEE Access : Practical Innovations, Open Solutions*, *9*, 80340–80350. doi:10.1109/ACCESS.2021.3083093

Jhanjhi, N., Humayun, M., & Almuayqil, S. N. (2021). Cyber Security and Privacy Issues in Industrial Internet of Things. *Computer Systems Science and Engineering*, *37*(3), 361–380. doi:10.32604/csse.2021.015206

Kao, C.-Y., & Chueh, H.-E. (2022). A Vendor-Managed Inventory Mechanism Based on SCADA of Internet of Things Framework. *Electronics (Basel)*, *11*(6), 881. doi:10.3390/electronics11060881

Kaur, M., Kaur, H., & Singh, A. (2020). Smart transportation system using Internet of Things (IoT): A review. *Int. J. Adv. Sci. Technol.*, *29*, 2293–2298.

Kaushik, A., & Pillai, A. S. (2021). Blockchain and IoT based inventory monitoring system. Paper presented at the *Proceedings of the 2nd International Conference on Electronics and Sustainable Communication Systems, ICESC 2021*. IEEE. 10.1109/ICESC51422.2021.9532876

Kotsias, J., Ahmad, A., & Scheepers, R. (2023). Adopting and integrating cyber-threat intelligence in a commercial organisation. *European Journal of Information Systems*, *32*(1), 35–51. doi:10.1080/0960085X.2022.2088414

Lee, S., Abdullah, A., Jhanjhi, N., & Kok, S. (2021). Classification of botnet attacks in IoT smart factory using honeypot combined with machine learning. *PeerJ. Computer Science*, *7*, e350. doi:10.7717/peerj-cs.350 PMID:33817000

Lele, A., & Lele, A. (2019). Artificial intelligence (AI). *Disruptive technologies for the militaries and security*, 139-154.

Lo Piano, S. (2020). Ethical principles in machine learning and artificial intelligence: Cases from the field and possible ways forward. *Humanities & Social Sciences Communications*, *7*(1), 1–7. doi:10.1057/s41599-020-0501-9

Mashayekhy, Y., Babaei, A., Yuan, X.-M., & Xue, A. (2022). Impact of Internet of Things (IoT) on Inventory Management: A Literature Survey. *Logistics*, *6*(2), 33. doi:10.3390/logistics6020033

Mishra, A., & Mohapatro, M. (2020). Real-time RFID-based item tracking using IoT efficient inventory management using Machine Learning. Paper presented at the *4th IEEE Conference on Information and Communication Technology, CICT 2020*. IEEE. 10.1109/CICT51604.2020.9312074

Mishra, N., & Keshri, A. K. (2021) Smart Racking and Retailing Using IOT. Lecture Notes in Electrical Engineering (pp. 645-653). doi:10.1007/978-981-15-5546-6_54

Moore, S. J., Nugent, C. D., Zhang, S., & Cleland, I. (2020). IoT reliability: A review leading to 5 key research directions. *CCF Transactions on Pervasive Computing and Interaction*, *2*(3), 147–163. doi:10.1007/s42486-020-00037-z

Mukherjee, D., Ghosh, S., Pal, S., Akila, D., Jhanjhi, N., Masud, M., & AlZain, M. A. *Optimized energy efficient strategy for data reduction between edge devices in cloud-iot.*

Najmi, K. Y., AlZain, M. A., Masud, M., Jhanjhi, N., Al-Amri, J., & Baz, M. (2021). A survey on security threats and countermeasures in IoT to achieve users confidentiality and reliability. *Materials Today: Proceedings*.

Pal, S., Jhanjhi, N., Abdulbaqi, A. S., Akila, D., Alsubaei, F. S., & Almazroi, A. A. (2023). An Intelligent Task Scheduling Model for Hybrid Internet of Things and Cloud Environment for Big Data Applications. *Sustainability (Basel)*, *15*(6), 5104. doi:10.3390/su15065104

Piramuthu, S. (2022). Drone-Based Warehouse Inventory Management with IoT for Perishables. In Smart Services Summit: Smart Services Supporting the New Normal (pp. 13-21): Springer. doi:10.1007/978-3-030-97042-0_2

Prabakar, D., Sundarrajan, M., Manikandan, R., Jhanjhi, N., Masud, M., & Alqhatani, A. (2023). Energy Analysis-Based Cyber Attack Detection by IoT with Artificial Intelligence in a Sustainable Smart City. *Sustainability (Basel)*, *15*(7), 6031. doi:10.3390/su15076031

Ramachandran, V., Ramalakshmi, R., Kavin, B. P., Hussain, I., Almaliki, A. H., Almaliki, A. A., Elnaggar, A., & Hussein, E. E. (2022). Exploiting IoT and Its Enabled Technologies for Irrigation Needs in Agriculture. *Water (Basel)*, *14*(5), 719. doi:10.3390/w14050719

Saeed, A., & Shoukat, R. (2023). Lean, Green, and Agile Supply Chain Practices. In *Emerging Trends in Sustainable Supply Chain Management and Green Logistics* (pp. 121–142). IGI Global. doi:10.4018/978-1-6684-6663-6.ch006

Sahu, P., & Balfour, D. (2022). *Smart Manufacturing with Augmented Reality*. Paper presented at the SAE Technical Papers. SAE. 10.4271/2022-26-0026

Seong, T. B., Ponnusamy, V., Jhanjhi, N., Annur, R., & Talib, M. (2021). A comparative analysis on traditional wired datasets and the need for wireless datasets for IoT wireless intrusion detection. *Indonesian Journal of Electrical Engineering and Computer Science*, *22*(2), 1165–1176. doi:10.11591/ijeecs.v22.i2.pp1165-1176

Shah, I. A., Jhanjhi, N., & Laraib, A. (2023). Cybersecurity and Blockchain Usage in Contemporary Business. In Handbook of Research on Cybersecurity Issues and Challenges for Business and FinTech Applications (pp. 49-64): IGI Global.

Simon, C. G. K., Jhanjhi, N. Z., Goh, W. W., & Sukumaran, S. (2022). Applications of Machine Learning in Knowledge Management System: A Comprehensive Review. *Journal of Information & Knowledge Management*, *21*(02), 2250017. doi:10.1142/S0219649222500174

Sing, R., Bhoi, S. K., Panigrahi, N., Sahoo, K. S., Jhanjhi, N., & AlZain, M. A. (2022). A Whale Optimization Algorithm Based Resource Allocation Scheme for Cloud-Fog Based IoT Applications. *Electronics (Basel)*, *11*(19), 3207. doi:10.3390/electronics11193207

Smith, A. D. (2012). Green supply chain management and consumer sensitivity to greener and leaner options in the automotive industry. *International Journal of Logistics Systems and Management*, *12*(1), 1–31. doi:10.1504/IJLSM.2012.047056

Smitha, & Aslekar, A. (2022). *IoT in Inventory Management.* Paper presented at the 2022 International Conference on Decision Aid Sciences and Applications, DASA.

Sreedevi, A. G., Nitya Harshitha, T., Sugumaran, V., & Shankar, P. (2022). Application of cognitive computing in healthcare, cybersecurity, big data and IoT: A literature review. *Information Processing & Management*, *59*(2), 102888. Advance online publication. doi:10.1016/j.ipm.2022.102888

Srivatsa, S. G., Bharadwaj, K. R. M., Alamuri, S. L., Shanif, M. M. C., & Shreenidhi, H. S. (2021). Smart Cold Storage and Inventory Monitoring System. *Paper presented at the 2021 6th International Conference on Recent Trends on Electronics, Information, Communication and Technology, RTEICT 2021.* Statista. https://www.statista.com/statistics/1183457/iot-connected-devices-worldwide/

Tan, W. C., & Sidhu, M. S. (2022). Review of RFID and IoT integration in supply chain management. *Operations Research Perspectives*, *9*, 100229. doi:10.1016/j.orp.2022.100229

Ullah, A., Azeem, M., Ashraf, H., Alaboudi, A. A., Humayun, M., & Jhanjhi, N. (2021). Secure healthcare data aggregation and transmission in IoT—A survey. *IEEE Access : Practical Innovations, Open Solutions*, *9*, 16849–16865. doi:10.1109/ACCESS.2021.3052850

Ullah, A., Ishaq, N., Azeem, M., Ashraf, H., Jhanjhi, N., Humayun, M., Tabbakh, T. A., & Almusaylim, Z. A. (2021). A survey on continuous object tracking and boundary detection schemes in IoT assisted wireless sensor networks. *IEEE Access : Practical Innovations, Open Solutions*, *9*, 126324–126336. doi:10.1109/ACCESS.2021.3110203

Vice, J., & Khan, M. M. (2022). Toward Accountable and Explainable Artificial Intelligence Part Two: The Framework Implementation. *IEEE Access : Practical Innovations, Open Solutions*, *10*, 36091–36105. doi:10.1109/ACCESS.2022.3163523

Yerpude S., e. a. (2018). *SMART Warehouse with Internet of Things supported Inventory Management System.* Research Gate.

Yuan, X.-M., & Xue, A. (2023). Supply Chain 4.0: New Generation of Supply Chain Management. *Logistics*, *7*(1), 9. doi:10.3390/logistics7010009

Chapter 9
Applications of Blockchain Technology in Supply Chain Management

Siva Raja Sindiramutty
Taylor's University, Malaysia

Navid Ali Khan
Taylor's University, Malaysia

Noor Zaman Jhanjhi
https://orcid.org/0000-0001-8116-4733
Taylor's University, Malaysia

Abdalla Hassan Gharib
Zanzibar University, Tanzania

Chong Eng Tan
https://orcid.org/0000-0002-3990-3501
Universiti Malaysia Sarawak, Malaysia

Khor Jia Yun
Tunku Abdul Rahman University of Management and Technology, Malaysia

ABSTRACT

In this chapter, the authors delve into the utilization of blockchain technology within the realm of supply chain management. The emergence of blockchain technology has heralded substantial progress across diverse sectors, and the domain of supply chain management is undeniably one of them. The decentralized and immutable characteristics of blockchain present a promising resolution to endure hurdles encountered by stakeholders in supply chain management. These challenges encompass issues of transparency, traceability, and efficiency. The abstract commences by acknowledging the transformative essence of blockchain technology, underscoring its profound influence across various sectors. It subsequently narrows its focus to explore the specific applications within the domain of supply chain management. The chapter undertakes an in-depth examination of the multifaceted challenges faced by supply chain stakeholders and elucidates how blockchain technology adeptly tackles these predicaments.

DOI: 10.4018/978-1-6684-7625-3.ch009

INTRODUCTION

Background and Significance of Blockchain Technology in Supply Chain Management

The emergence of blockchain technology has brought significant advancements and transformative potential across various industries, including supply chain management. This report explores the background and significance of blockchain technology in revolutionizing supply chain processes. This study investigates the fundamental principles of blockchain technology, highlighting its essential characteristics and its utilization in augmenting transparency, security, and efficiency within supply chains. Additionally, the present chapter delves into the prospective hurdles and forthcoming ramifications associated with the integration of blockchain technology in supply chain management. Historically, the realm of supply chain management has encountered obstacles like inadequate transparency, suboptimal documentation practices, counterfeiting, and restricted trust among involved parties. The challenges mentioned above can be effectively tackled through the implementation of blockchain technology, which is characterized by its decentralized nature and unalterable ledger (Tapscott & Tapscott, 2016; Ashraf et al., 2023). Blockchain, as a distributed ledger technology, enables participants to transparently and securely record and authenticate transactions (Squarepants, 2008). Operating within a network of interconnected nodes, blockchain grants each participant access to a duplicate copy of the ledger. Transactions are organized into blocks, which are sequentially and permanently appended to the chain. The decentralized structure of blockchain eliminates the necessity for intermediaries, thereby bolstering the security and dependability of transactions (Swan, 2015). By leveraging blockchain technology, transparency within the supply chain is significantly enhanced through the establishment of a shared and unalterable record of transactions. Every participant is granted access to the blockchain, enabling them to validate the legitimacy of transactions, thereby fostering trust and mitigating the potential for fraudulent practices (Iansiti & Lakhani, 2017). Furthermore, the integration of Internet of Things (IoT) devices and sensors with blockchain empowers real-time tracking and traceability of goods, enabling stakeholders to monitor the location and state of products at every stage of the supply chain (Dorri et al., 2019; Saeed et al., 2022; Ramzan et al., 2022).

Figure 1. Blockchain in supply chain
(Singh, 2022)

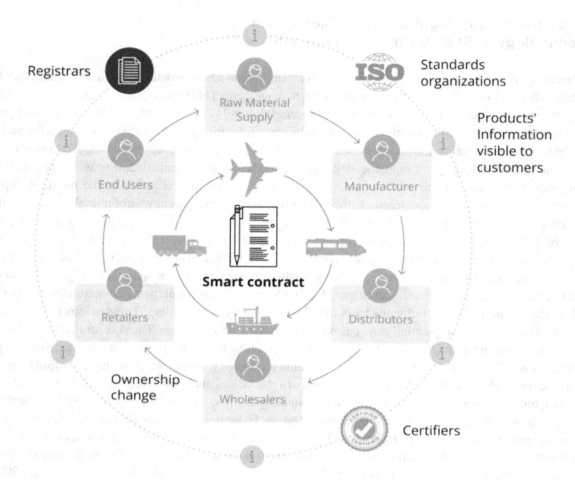

The presence of counterfeit products within supply chains has been an enduring obstacle, resulting in substantial financial losses and reputational harm. However, blockchain technology offers a viable solution by providing an unchangeable record detailing the origin, manufacturing procedures, and ownership history of each product (Crosby et al., 2016). This enhanced transparency equips stakeholders with the ability to detect and mitigate the risks associated with counterfeit goods, thereby augmenting consumer trust and safeguarding brand reputation. Supply chain operations often involve numerous intermediaries, leading to intricate and time-consuming processes. Nevertheless, blockchain technology streamlines these operations by facilitating direct peer-to-peer interactions and automating the execution of smart contracts (Zheng et al., 2017). Smart contracts are self-executing agreements that initiate actions automatically upon meeting predetermined conditions. By eliminating intermediaries and automating contractual processes, blockchain technology holds the potential to substantially decrease costs, reduce delays, and enhance overall efficiency within supply chains. However, the extensive implementation of blockchain technology in supply chain management encounters various challenges. These include scalability limitations, ensuring interoperability among different blockchain platforms, addressing regulatory considerations, and necessitating collaborative efforts among stakeholders (Iansiti & Lakhani, 2017). Surmounting these challenges necessitates meticulous strategizing, technological advancements, and widespread cooperation across the industry. The importance of blockchain technology in supply chain management is projected to experience rapid growth in the forthcoming years. As the technology continues to mature and scalability issues are effectively tackled, blockchain holds the potential to revolutionize the entire landscape of the supply chain ecosystem (David et al., 2017). Its capacity to augment transparency, security, and efficiency can yield streamlined operations, cost reductions, and heightened customer satisfaction. Nevertheless, achieving successful implementation mandates a comprehensive comprehension of the technology, collaborative efforts among stakeholders, and the adoption of effective change management strategies.

In summary, the utilization of blockchain technology holds immense potential for revolutionizing supply chain management. By harnessing its fundamental attributes of transparency, security, and efficiency, organizations can elevate trust levels, mitigate fraudulent activities, and optimize operational processes. Nevertheless, the successful implementation of blockchain necessitates a thorough understanding and mitigation of challenges, as well as active collaboration among stakeholders. As technology continues to advance, its transformative impact on supply chains is expected to be profound.

Research Objective Scope, Methodology, and Structure of the Review

The principal aim of this study is to investigate and analyze the utilization of blockchain technology within the realm of supply chain management. The research endeavours to offer a comprehensive comprehension of how blockchain can effectively tackle fundamental challenges and operational inefficiencies prevalent in conventional supply chain management systems. The research ambit encompasses diverse facets of blockchain technology and its potential ramifications on supply chain management. The primary emphasis will be on scrutinizing the advantages and characteristics of blockchain, examining its applications across various domains of the supply chain, and elucidating the prevailing blockchain-enabled platforms and consortia operating within the industry. The present study aims to identify and analyze the obstacles and constraints linked to the implementation of blockchain technology in the context of supply chain management. To achieve this objective, a methodical examination of scholarly journals, conference proceedings, industry reports, and other reliable sources will be conducted, employing a systematic literature review approach. A thorough search strategy will be devised to locate pertinent articles and publications about the subject matter. In this research, we aim to comprehensively investigate and address the challenges and constraints associated with the integration of blockchain technology in the context of supply chain management. To guarantee the inclusion of the most recent advancements in blockchain technology, this review will encompass publications from the past decade. Through extensive analysis and synthesis of the gathered literature, we aim to extract crucial insights, conceptual frameworks, and pertinent case studies that pertain to the utilization of blockchain in the domain of supply chain management. The analysis shall adhere to the prescribed chapters, ensuring coherent dissemination of information. The study shall further integrate tangible illustrations and empirical instances to furnish pragmatic perspectives on efficacious blockchain implementations within supply chain networks.

The review shall adhere to the prescribed chapters, ensuring a coherent and systematic elucidation of the research findings. Each chapter shall be dedicated to a distinct facet of blockchain technology in supply chain management, encompassing the specified objectives and scope, thereby facilitating a well-structured and comprehensive presentation. The introductory chapter will establish the context by emphasizing the paramount importance of blockchain technology within supply chains. It shall furnish an encompassing portrayal of supply chain management, elucidating its inherent challenges and the transformative potential of blockchain to mitigate them. The subsequent chapters will delve into a comprehensive comprehension of blockchain technology, encompassing its fundamental principles, distributed ledger technology, consensus mechanisms, and the pivotal role of smart contracts in optimizing supply chain management processes. The review will encompass a comprehensive discussion of the advantages and characteristics of blockchain technology in the domain of supply chain management. It will meticulously explore the manifold benefits, including transparency, traceability, heightened visibility, accountability, trust, fraud reduction, streamlined transactions, cost savings, and enhanced efficiency. Additionally, the study will delve into diverse applications of blockchain in supply chain management, encompassing pivotal areas such as product provenance and traceability, inventory management and tracking, supplier management and verification, quality control and compliance, as well as demand forecasting and analytics. The review shall incorporate illustrative case studies and exemplify triumphant instances of blockchain implementations within supply chain networks. Moreover, it will meticulously scrutinize the prevailing blockchain-enabled supply chain platforms, collaborative networks, and consortia. Real-world examples of these platforms will be showcased, accompanied by an insightful analysis of their profound influence on supply chain practices. Additionally, the study will conscientiously address the hurdles and constraints of blockchain adoption in supply chain management. This will encompass a comprehensive examination of scalability and performance issues, challenges related to interoperability and standardization, concerns regarding data privacy and security, as well as the barriers and resistance to change that impede widespread adoption. Lastly, the review will underscore the future trends and implications of blockchain technology in supply chain management, taking into account burgeoning advancements, emerging developments, and their potential impacts on the industry. Furthermore, the study will deliberate upon policy and regulatory considerations pertinent to blockchain-enabled supply chains. The review will culminate with a concise recapitulation of the key findings and contributions, elucidating their implications for both research and practice. Additionally, it will offer valuable recommendations for prospective endeavours in the realm of blockchain in supply chain management, thereby fostering further exploration and advancement in this field.

OVERVIEW OF SUPPLY CHAIN MANAGEMENT

Figure 2. Benefits of blockchain in supply chain
(GEP, n.d.)

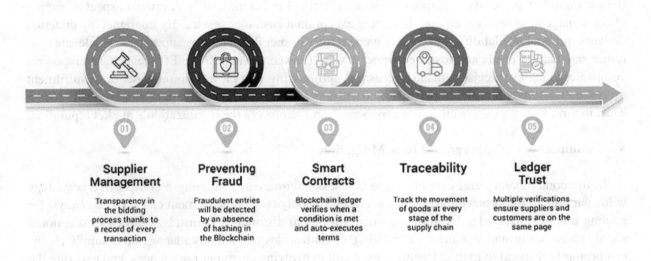

Implementing Blockchain in Supply Chain

Supplier Management	Preventing Fraud	Smart Contracts	Traceability	Ledger Trust
Transparency in the bidding process thanks to a record of every transaction	Fraudulent entries will be detected by an absence of hashing in the Blockchain	Blockchain ledger verifies when a condition is met and auto-executes terms	Track the movement of goods at every stage of the supply chain	Multiple verifications ensure suppliers and customers are on the same page

Definition and Importance of Supply Chain Management

Supply chain management (SCM) assumes a pivotal role in the contemporary global business landscape. It encompasses a series of endeavours aimed at enabling the smooth and efficient movement of goods, services, and information from their source to their ultimate destination. As Christopher (2016) posits, SCM entails the harmonization and consolidation of diverse operations such as procurement, production, transportation, warehousing, and distribution, all of which collectively contribute to the generation of value for both customers and stakeholders. This chapter endeavours to offer a thorough comprehension of the definition and significance of supply chain management, emphasizing its contribution to augmenting organizational performance and competitive advantage. Supply chain management can be delineated as the process of "designing, planning, executing, controlling, and monitoring supply chain activities to generate net value, establishing a competitive infrastructure, capitalizing on global logistics, synchronizing supply with demand, and gauging performance on a global scale" (Council of Supply Chain Management Professionals [CSCMP], 2021, p. 5). SCM encompasses the oversight of material, information, and financial flow throughout every stage of the supply chain, spanning from suppliers to manufacturers, distributors, retailers, and customers (Chopra & Meindl, 2016). The primary objective of SCM is to optimize the overall performance of the supply chain by minimizing expenses, shortening lead times, improving operational efficiency, and heightening customer satisfaction.

- **Cost Reduction and Enhanced Customer Service**

Cost reduction stands as a significant advantage derived from proficient supply chain management. Through the implementation of streamlined supply chain practices, organizations can effectively curtail expenses associated with procurement, production, and transportation (Mentzer et al., 2015). For instance, companies can achieve cost savings by engaging in strategic sourcing and collaborating with suppliers to secure more favourable prices and terms through negotiations. Moreover, SCM empowers organizations to optimize their inventory management procedures, thereby diminishing carrying costs and mitigating the likelihood of stockouts or surplus inventory (Simchi-Levi et al., 2017). A crucial aspect of supply chain management revolves around delivering exceptional customer service. By guaranteeing punctual delivery, product availability, and responsiveness to customer demands, organizations can elevate customer satisfaction levels and foster customer loyalty (Fawcett et al., 2015). Efficient SCM empowers companies to achieve precise demand forecasting, optimize inventory levels, and enhance order fulfilment processes, consequently resulting in expedited and dependable customer deliveries (Mentzer et al., 2016). This, in turn, fosters positive customer experiences and reinforces the organization's market reputation.

- **Competitive Advantage and Risk Mitigation**

In the contemporary and ever-changing business environment, attaining a competitive advantage holds paramount importance for long-term success. Supply chain management can act as a catalyst for gaining a competitive edge by allowing organizations to distinguish themselves through exceptional supply chain performance (Christopher, 2016). Organizations that adeptly manage their supply chains can promptly respond to market fluctuations, adapt to evolving customer preferences, and expedite the introduction of new products or services ahead of their competitors (Fernie & Sparks, 2014). The agility and responsiveness offered by effective supply chain management confer a notable advantage in the market and contribute to the sustainable growth of businesses. Supply chain disruptions stemming from natural disasters, geopolitical issues, or supplier bankruptcy can exert a profound impact on organizations. Nonetheless, proficient supply chain management serves as a crucial tool in mitigating such risks (CSCMP, 2021). Through the development of robust risk management strategies, organizations can identify potential vulnerabilities, establish contingency plans, and fortify the resilience of their supply chains (Wieland & Wallenburg, 2013). Adopting this proactive approach empowers companies to mitigate the adverse effects of disruptions and uphold business continuity, thereby safeguarding their operations and reputation. The effectiveness of supply chain management hinges on collaboration and integration among diverse stakeholders operating within the supply chain network (Lambert & Cooper, 2020; Ali et al., 2022). By fostering information sharing, engaging in joint decision-making, and nurturing mutually beneficial relationships, organizations can augment supply chain visibility, minimize lead times, and enhance overall performance (Chopra & Meindl, 2016). Collaboration facilitates seamless coordination among suppliers, manufacturers, and distributors, yielding streamlined processes, cost reduction, and heightened efficiency (Mentzer et al., 2015; Humayun, 2021).

In conclusion, supply chain management is a pivotal discipline that encompasses the harmonization and integration of diverse processes to optimize the efficient flow of goods, services, and information. The significance of effective supply chain management cannot be emphasized enough, as it empowers organizations to attain cost reductions, elevate customer service standards, gain a competitive advantage, mitigate risks, and foster collaboration and integration. By embracing sound supply chain practices, organizations can enhance their operational efficiency, achieve improved financial performance, and solidify their market position.

Key Challenges and Inefficiencies in Traditional Supply Chain Management

The effectiveness of organizations heavily relies on the role played by supply chain management, as it facilitates the seamless movement of goods, information, and services from suppliers to customers. Nevertheless, conventional approaches to supply chain management frequently face numerous obstacles and inefficiencies, impeding the overall performance and competitiveness of businesses. This section presents a comprehensive introduction to the research topic, highlighting the importance of addressing these challenges. Effective decision-making and coordination among stakeholders within the supply chain heavily rely on the fundamental aspect of information sharing. It enables the flow of crucial knowledge and data necessary for efficient operations. However, a significant challenge arises in the form of information asymmetry, where one party possesses a greater amount of knowledge or information compared to others. This imbalance leads to distorted decision-making processes and suboptimal outcomes. Notably, researchers Dyer and Singh (2018) have shed light on the harmful impacts of information asymmetry on supply chain performance and have stressed the importance of implementing enhanced mechanisms for sharing information.

Efficient supply chain management relies on the vital elements of coordination and collaboration, where multiple entities join forces to meet customer demands. Unfortunately, conventional supply chains frequently encounter coordination issues, leading to delays, excessive inventory, and elevated costs. Recognizing this problem, studies conducted by Mentzer et al. (2015) have emphasized the significance of implementing coordination mechanisms, such as collaborative planning, forecasting, and replenishment (CPFR), to tackle this challenge and improve overall supply chain efficiency. Supply chain visibility encompasses the tracking and monitoring of the flow of goods, information, and funds throughout the supply chain network. When visibility is limited, it becomes challenging to identify bottlenecks, foresees disruptions, and respond efficiently to fluctuations in demand or supply. In light of this issue, researchers, as highlighted by Raza (2021), have underscored the significance of incorporating technologies such as radio frequency identification (RFID) and blockchain to enhance supply chain visibility and traceability. By leveraging these technologies, inefficiencies can be reduced, and the overall responsiveness of the supply chain can be improved. Conventional supply chains often exhibit a lack of adaptability and resilience, rendering them vulnerable to disruptions stemming from unexpected occurrences like natural disasters, supplier insolvencies, or geopolitical concerns. This section examines the obstacles associated with rigid and fragile supply chains and underscores the significance of embracing agile and resilient strategies, as emphasized by Christopher and Peck (2012). By doing so, organizations can mitigate risks, safeguard operations, and maintain uninterrupted business continuity in the face of unforeseen challenges.

Figure 3. Traditional supply chain management
(Riadi, 2021)

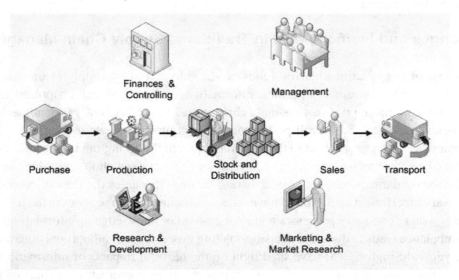

Inventory management holds a pivotal role in supply chain management as it has a direct impact on customer service levels, costs, and cash flow. Ineffectual inventory management practices, such as excessive or inadequate stock levels, can result in stock-outs, escalated holding costs, and missed sales opportunities. To address this issue, researchers Srinivasan and Mukhopadhyay (2019) have recommended the implementation of advanced inventory optimization techniques like just-in-time (JIT) and vendor-managed inventory (VMI). These approaches aim to enhance inventory management efficiency, leading to cost reduction and improved overall performance. The transportation and logistics segment of the supply chain poses unique challenges and inefficiencies. Problems like delays, capacity limitations, inefficient routing, and limited visibility can have a substantial impact on supply chain performance. Scholars Hastig and Sodhi (2020) have emphasized the importance of implementing effective transportation management systems (TMS) and leveraging advanced analytics to optimize routing, reduce costs, and enhance overall logistics operations. By utilizing these strategies, organizations can address transportation-related challenges and improve the efficiency of their supply chain activities. In recent times, there has been a growing acknowledgement among organizations regarding the significance of integrating environmental sustainability and social responsibility into their supply chain practices. This section delves into the challenges associated with incorporating sustainability practices and ethical considerations into conventional supply chains. It emphasizes the importance of responsible sourcing, green logistics, and circular economy initiatives as crucial steps in this integration process, as highlighted by Theeraworawit et al. (2022). By implementing these initiatives, organizations can strive towards more responsible and environmentally-friendly supply chain operations.

Introduction to the Concept of Blockchain Technology in Supply Chains

The emergence of blockchain technology has garnered considerable interest in contemporary times as a prospective means of augmenting supply chain operations. Initially conceived as the foundational framework for cryptocurrencies such as Bitcoin, blockchain serves as a decentralized and distributed ledger, facilitating secure and transparent documentation. As posited by Tapscott and Tapscott (2016), blockchain empowers participants to authenticate and log transactions sans intermediaries, thereby curbing expenses and fostering trust. With the ability to tackle key hurdles like transparency deficiencies, inefficiencies, and information imbalances (Huynh-The et al., 2023), this technology harbours the capability to revolutionize supply chains. Blockchain, a decentralized ledger system, comprises a chain of blocks wherein each block encompasses a collection of transactions. Through a consensus mechanism, every transaction is validated and appended to the chain, rendering it impervious to tampering and unalterable (Swan, 2015; M. S. Kumar et al., 2021). The decentralized characteristics of blockchain guarantee the absence of centralized authority, thereby bolstering security and fortitude (Drescher, 2017; Humayun et al., 2022). By leveraging cryptographic methodologies, blockchain technology safeguards data integrity and confidentiality, heightening its appropriateness for implementation within supply chain domains (Zhang et al., 2021; Sujatha et al., 2022). The amalgamation of blockchain technology into supply chains yields a plethora of advantages, including heightened transparency, traceability, and efficiency. Through the utilization of blockchain, stakeholders within the supply chain ecosystem can establish a communal and unalterable register of transactions, facilitating instantaneous monitoring of the flow of goods, information, and payments (Iansiti & Lakhani, 2017). Such heightened visibility empowers stakeholders to meticulously track and trace products throughout the entirety of the supply chain, thereby mitigating the perils associated with counterfeiting, fraudulent activities, and unauthorized substitutions (Dai et al., 2019; Humayun et al., 2020).

The implementation of blockchain technology in supply chains yields numerous benefits. Firstly, blockchain fosters trust among supply chain collaborators by furnishing a secure and transparent medium for data exchange (Kouhizadeh & Sarkis, 2018). The decentralized characteristics of blockchain obviate the necessity for intermediaries, facilitating direct peer-to-peer engagements and curbing administrative expenses (Viswanadham & Jayavel, 2023). Furthermore, the immutability of the blockchain guarantees the preservation of data integrity, effectively thwarting unauthorized alterations or deletions (Yli-Huumo et al., 2016). Such attributes foster trust, collaboration, and operational efficiency within supply chain endeavours. However, despite its considerable potential, the integration of blockchain technology into supply chains is not exempt from encountering certain challenges. One notable apprehension pertains to scalability, as blockchain networks necessitate substantial computational resources and may encounter performance issues when confronted with a high volume of transactions (Zhang et al., 2019). Moreover, successful implementation requires due consideration of regulatory and legal aspects, as well as the attainment of interoperability and standardization (Aste et al., 2020). These factors represent crucial considerations that must be effectively addressed. Organizations contemplating the adoption of blockchain technology should meticulously evaluate these challenges and devise suitable strategies accordingly.

In conclusion, the potential of blockchain technology to revolutionize supply chain operations through improved transparency, traceability, and efficiency is substantial. The decentralized and immutable attributes of blockchain facilitate secure and trustworthy transactions, resulting in cost reduction and enhanced collaboration among supply chain stakeholders. Nevertheless, it is crucial to effectively address challenges such as scalability and regulatory considerations. Future research endeavours and industry initiatives will play a pivotal role in further exploring the applications and potential of blockchain within the realm of supply chains.

UNDERSTANDING BLOCKCHAIN TECHNOLOGY

Definition and Basic Principles of Blockchain

The emergence of blockchain technology represents a groundbreaking innovation that possesses the capability to revolutionize diverse sectors such as finance, supply chain management, healthcare, and others. The primary objective of this study is to gain a comprehensive understanding of the blockchain by delving into its definition and fundamental principles. By conducting a thorough review of pertinent literature, this report endeavours to elucidate the core concepts that underpin blockchain technology and shed light on its prospective applications. In addition, this chapter will emphasize the noteworthy characteristics and advantages of blockchain, while providing a critical evaluation of its constraints and obstacles. Blockchain can be characterized as a decentralized and distributed ledger technology, enabling multiple stakeholders to securely and transparently uphold a collective and unalterable log of transactions (Naraindath et al., 2023). Frequently referred to as a digital ledger, blockchain is recognized for its ability to record transactions or other data across numerous computers or nodes, obviating the necessity for a central governing body. The blockchain ledger comprises a series of interconnected blocks, wherein each block contains a collection of transactions or data.

Figure 4. Overview of blockchain technology
(*Choudhary, 2023*)

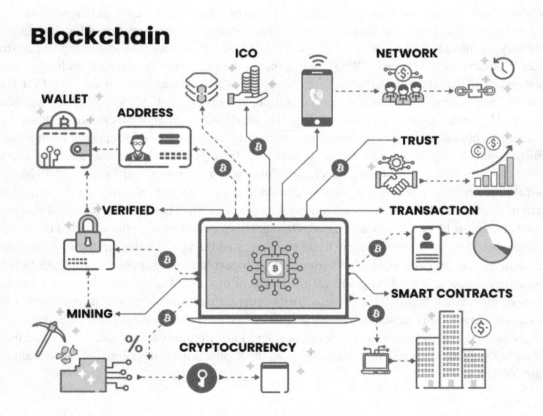

Decentralization stands as a fundamental principle within the realm of blockchain technology. Diverging from the conventional centralized systems, blockchain functions through a peer-to-peer network wherein multiple participants, referred to as nodes, collectively administer and authenticate the ledger. This emphasis on decentralization ensures that no solitary entity possesses absolute authority over the network, thereby bolstering security measures and fostering trust among participants (Deng et al., 2022; A. Khan et al., 2022). Deng et al. (2022) assert that the implementation of decentralization in blockchain networks engenders a more robust and resilient system, characterized by the absence of a single point of failure. As a result, it effectively mitigates the potential risks associated with centralized systems, such as susceptibility to data breaches or manipulation by a central governing body. Distributed consensus represents a vital aspect of the blockchain paradigm, as it entails the establishment of agreement among network participants regarding the legitimacy of transactions and the precise sequence in which they become incorporated into the ledger. By leveraging consensus mechanisms, blockchain ensures that a majority of participants converge upon a consensus regarding the state of the blockchain, thereby engendering formidable resistance against potential manipulations orchestrated by malicious entities (Nawab & Sadoghi, 2023; Xu et al., 2023). The Proof of Work (PoW) consensus mechanism, initially introduced by Nakamoto (2008) in the seminal Bitcoin white paper, has emerged as a widely employed solution. Within the PoW framework, network participants—known as miners—are tasked with solving computationally intensive puzzles to validate transactions and subsequently append them to the blockchain (Soria et al., 2022; Baniata & Kertesz, 2023). Alternatively, the Proof of Stake (PoS) consensus mechanism operates based on participants staking their cryptocurrency holdings, thereby enabling them to authenticate transactions proportionate to their stake in the network (Li et al., 2022; Wendl et al., 2023).

The immutability of the blockchain ledger stands as a pivotal characteristic, bestowing upon it a myriad of advantageous attributes. Once a transaction finds its place within a block and becomes appended to the blockchain, any attempts to modify or expunge it without attaining consensus from the network become exceedingly implausible, if not virtually unattainable (BelMannoubi et al., 2023; Ravi et al., 2021). This immutability feature confers a heightened sense of security and integrity to the blockchain ledger, as it ensures the preservation of historical records, impervious to tampering. Khan et al. (2023) underscore that the immutable nature of the blockchain ledger serves to reinforce trust, rendering intermediary verification of transactions superfluous. Moreover, it holds substantial promise in various domains, notably supply chain management, where the capacity to trace and validate the origin and genuineness of products plays a pivotal role. Cryptographic security serves as a cornerstone of blockchain technology, employing robust cryptographic techniques to safeguard the data and transactions residing within the network. Public-key cryptography, a prevalent approach, guarantees that solely the designated recipients possess the ability to access and decrypt the information transmitted (Review et al., 2019; Ohood M et al., 2021)). Each participant within the network maintains a unique cryptographic key pair, encompassing a public key for encryption purposes and a private key exclusively utilized for decryption functions. Furthermore, blockchain harnesses the potency of cryptographic hash functions to generate distinct digital fingerprints or hashes for every block within the chain. These hashes serve as an assurance of the integrity of the data encapsulated within the respective block, rendering them exceptionally resistant to any attempts of manipulation or unauthorized alterations (Review et al., 2019; Julie et al., 2020).

Transparency and auditability constitute vital attributes facilitated by blockchain technology, stemming from the access granted to all participants, enabling them to peruse the comprehensive transaction history contained within the public ledger. This transparency engenders heightened levels of trust among stakeholders, as it affords them the capacity to independently verify the authenticity and fidelity of transactions, as well as the overall status of the ledger (Dias & Meratnia, 2023). Assiri and Humayun (2023) assert that the transparency inherent to blockchain records facilitates efficient auditing procedures and aids in verifying compliance. Notably, in industries such as finance and supply chain management, where accountability and traceability represent paramount concerns, blockchain's transparency possesses the potential to revolutionize existing processes and substantially mitigate instances of fraudulent activities. Incorporating smart contracts is a common practice in blockchain technology, wherein these contracts are regarded as self-executing agreements that come with predetermined rules and conditions. The blockchain network automatically enforces and executes these contracts, thereby eliminating the requirement for intermediaries and bolstering the efficiency of diverse processes (Taherdoost, 2023). By facilitating automated and trustless transactions, smart contracts can execute the contractual terms once specific prearranged conditions are met (Kordestani et al., 2023; A. P. Singh et al., 2021). This particular characteristic holds profound implications for domains such as supply chain management, financial services, and the safeguarding of intellectual property rights.

Delegated Proof of Stake (DPoS) represents a consensus mechanism that amalgamates the merits of PoW and PoS while addressing the limitations associated with them. DPoS networks employ a selection process wherein a restricted number of delegates are chosen to validate transactions and generate blocks. This approach enhances scalability and throughput while preserving the principle of decentralization. These elected delegates, also referred to as block producers, are determined through voting by token holders (Zhao, 2023). Within the DPoS framework, token holders possess the ability to exercise their voting rights to elect trustworthy delegates who will actively engage in the production of blocks and the validation of transactions. To ensure efficiency, the number of delegates in DPoS is usually capped at a predetermined value. Each delegate is allocated a specific turn to generate blocks, which is determined either by a pre-established schedule or a round-robin algorithm (Yadav et al., 2023). This design facilitates rapid confirmation of transactions and optimal allocation of resources. An exemplary illustration of DPoS in practical implementation is observed in the blockchain platform Steem (now Hive), wherein DPoS is employed to identify block producers and distribute rewards among participants. The widespread adoption of DPoS has led to its incorporation in various platforms such as EOS and Tron, each presenting its variations of this mechanism. While DPoS offers several advantages, it has also faced criticisms. Detractors contend that the reliance on elected delegates somewhat compromises decentralization since voting power tends to be concentrated among a select group of token holders. Concerns regarding potential collusion or corruption among elected delegates have also been raised. Nonetheless, proponents of DPoS argue that the elected delegates possess a vested interest in upholding the network's integrity and, with proper safeguards and accountability measures in place, can effectively carry out transaction validation.

Practical Byzantine Fault Tolerance (PBFT) represents a consensus mechanism designed to attain a consensus within distributed systems, even when confronted with Byzantine faults or the presence of malicious actors. The introduction of PBFT can be attributed to Castro and Liskov in 1999, who presented it as a resolution to the Byzantine Generals' Problem. This problem deals with the intricacy of reaching an agreement within a network wherein certain nodes may exhibit arbitrary or malicious behaviour. PBFT operates on a voting-based algorithm, wherein a client initiates a request that undergoes processing by a series of replicas or nodes within the network. The replicas collaborate to establish agreement on the order and validity of transactions. PBFT ensures fault tolerance and Byzantine agreement among nodes by implementing a two-step process: the pre-prepare phase, during which the primary replica proposes a sequence of requests, and the prepare phase, wherein replicas verify the proposed sequence (Suliyanti, 2023; Wang, Liu, et al., 2023). Once a specific threshold of replicas confirms the sequence, the system achieves consensus and proceeds with committing the transactions. PBFT has found extensive application in permissioned blockchain networks like Hyperledger Fabric, offering numerous advantages such as high throughput, low latency, and resilience against Byzantine faults. However, PBFT is not without limitations. The consensus process necessitates a substantial number of message exchanges between replicas, resulting in augmented network communication overhead. Furthermore, PBFT operates under the assumption that the number of faulty replicas is both limited and predetermined, which renders it less suitable for networks characterized by a significant presence of Byzantine faults (Wang et al., 2023).

Figure 5. Mind map of blockchain applications
(Casino et al., 2019)

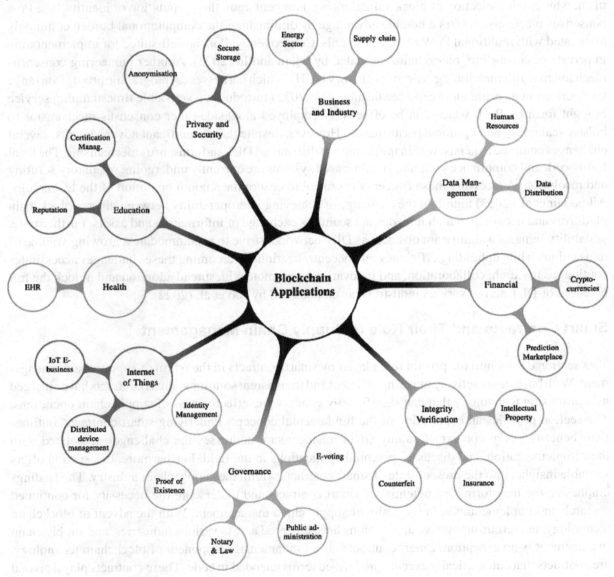

In recent years, remarkable progress and innovation have been witnessed in the field of distributed ledger technology (DLT) and consensus mechanisms. Researchers and practitioners continuously strive to discover novel approaches that address existing challenges and augment the capabilities of DLT networks. A notable area of advancement entails the exploration of hybrid consensus mechanisms, which amalgamate the strengths of diverse algorithms. For instance, certain projects have proposed the combination of PoW and PoS to achieve a delicate equilibrium between security and energy efficiency. These hybrid mechanisms aim to surmount the limitations inherent in individual consensus algorithms and provide heightened scalability, security, and decentralization (Gilbert et al., 2022).

An additional recent advancement pertains to the emergence of alternative consensus mechanisms, which seek to tackle specific challenges. One notable example is the Proof of Authority (PoA) mechanism, wherein the selection of block validators is contingent upon their reputation or identity. The PoA consensus mechanism offers a notable advantage by diminishing the computational burden commonly associated with traditional PoW or PoS protocols. Consequently, PoA is well-suited for implementation in private or consortium blockchains, as stated by Islam and In (2023). Another pioneering consensus mechanism worth mentioning is Proof of History (PoH), which harnesses cryptographic proofs to arrange transactions in a secure and verifiable fashion. Do (2023) introduces a verifiable timestamping service brought forth by PoH, which can be effectively employed alongside other consensus mechanisms to bolster scalability and optimize performance. However, despite these significant advancements, several challenges continue to persist within the domain of distributed DLT and consensus mechanisms. The legal framework and compliance with blockchain-based systems are currently undergoing regulatory scrutiny and resolution. Addressing these concerns is crucial to ensure the smooth operation of the technology. Alkhodair et al. (2023) highlight the challenge of achieving interoperability between diverse blockchain platforms and networks, which impedes the seamless exchange of information and assets. Furthermore, scalability remains a significant obstacle as DLT networks strive to accommodate a growing volume of transactions while upholding efficiency and decentralization. Overcoming these challenges necessitates continuous research, collaboration, and innovation to promote widespread adoption and unlock the full potential of DLT across various industries, as emphasized by Joo et al. (2022).

Smart Contracts and Their Role in Supply Chain Management

This section delves into the pivotal role played by smart contracts in the realm of supply chain management. With businesses actively pursuing efficient and transparent solutions, smart contracts have emerged as a promising technology that can significantly enhance the effectiveness of supply chain operations. The section provides an exploration of the fundamental concepts underlying smart contracts, outlines their benefits in the context of supply chain management, addresses the challenges associated with their implementation, and discusses potential applications in the field. Furthermore, this section offers valuable insights into the present state of smart contracts within the supply chain industry. The findings emphasize the transformative potential of smart contracts and underscore the necessity for continued research and implementation in the realm of supply chain management. With the advent of blockchain technology, numerous innovative applications have emerged across various industries, and supply chain management is no exception. Smart contracts, as a fundamental component of blockchain technology, are contracts that automatically execute predefined terms encoded in code. These contracts play a pivotal role in enabling secure, automated, and decentralized transactions, thereby introducing a heightened level of trust, transparency, and efficiency in supply chain processes. The work of Namasudra and Akkaya (2023) as well as Escobar et al. (2023) provides insights into the significance of smart contracts in this context. This chapter extensively explores the role of smart contracts in supply chain management, delving into their associated benefits, challenges, and potential applications.

An essential benefit of employing smart contracts in supply chain management, as emphasized by Gazzola et al. (2023), is the heightened transparency and traceability they bring forth. Smart contracts enable the seamless monitoring and recording of transactions in real time, allowing for comprehensive product tracking and tracing at every stage of the supply chain, as outlined by Chandan et al. (2023). The enhanced transparency facilitated by smart contracts in supply chain management not only serves as a deterrent against fraudulent activities but also fosters improved accountability among participants, as highlighted by Alamsyah et al. (2023). By automating processes and eliminating the requirement for intermediaries, smart contracts streamline supply chain operations, as noted by Sarfaraz et al. (2022). This streamlined approach enhances efficiency and reduces costs within the supply chain ecosystem. By leveraging predefined rules and conditions, smart contracts facilitate the automatic execution of transactions, thereby minimizing the need for manual intervention and reducing the likelihood of human errors, as highlighted by Jum'a (2023). This automation leads to notable advantages such as enhanced efficiency, decreased administrative costs, and faster settlement of transactions, as indicated by Tan et al. (2022).

Smart contracts leverage the inherent security and immutability offered by blockchain technology, as highlighted by D. Li et al. (2022). By employing cryptographic algorithms, smart contracts guarantee that transactional data stored within the blockchain remains secure and resistant to tampering. The data can only be modified or altered with the consensus of network participants, as emphasized by Turki et al. (2023). This cryptographic foundation ensures the integrity and trustworthiness of the stored data within smart contracts. This characteristic amplifies data integrity and security, which holds significant importance in the realm of supply chain management, where the utmost value is placed on data precision and reliability. Conventional contracts frequently necessitate manual involvement, leaving room for human interpretation and enforcement. Smart contracts, in contrast, facilitate the automation of contractual agreements and optimize the process of contract management (Agrawal et al., 2022). The inherent self-executing nature of smart contracts eliminates the necessity of intermediaries, mitigates the potential for disputes, and guarantees the punctual fulfilment of contractual obligations (Igbekele et al., 2023).

The application potential of smart contracts in supply chain management is extensive. They offer opportunities to automate and optimize various processes within the supply chain, including inventory management, order fulfilment, and payment settlements (Zhang & Chen, 2021). Furthermore, smart contracts can play a significant role in facilitating supply chain financing by automating transaction verification and enabling secure, real-time payment transfers (Lacity, Yan, & Willcocks, 2022). Moreover, smart contracts can enable instantaneous tracking of product provenance, effectively addressing the issue of counterfeiting and safeguarding product authenticity (Bhardwaj et al., 2021). The application of smart contracts in supply chain management holds great promise in revolutionizing the field, as it significantly enhances transparency, efficiency, and security. The capability of smart contracts to automate and optimize processes can yield noteworthy cost reductions and enhance operational efficiency. Nevertheless, for widespread adoption, certain challenges need to be addressed, including legal and regulatory frameworks, standardization, and seamless integration with existing systems. With the growing recognition of the advantages associated with smart contracts, it becomes imperative to conduct additional research and development in this domain to fully unleash their transformative potential in supply chain management.

Figure 6. Private vs. public blockchain
(Iredale, 2023)

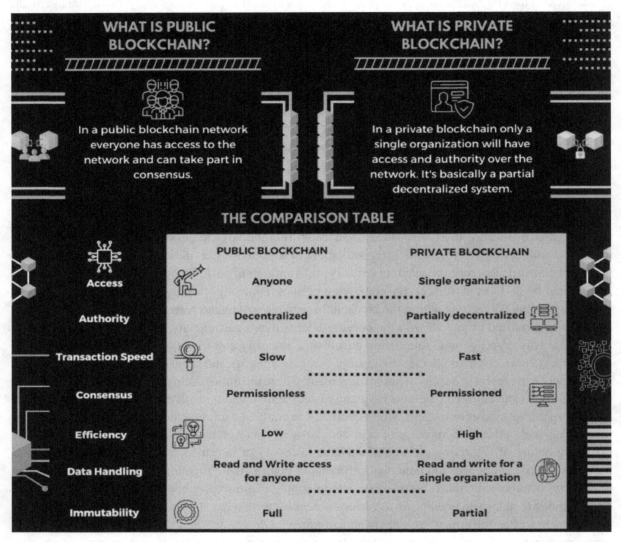

Public vs. Private Blockchain

The objective of this section is to deliver a comprehensive analysis of public and private blockchains, emphasizing their essential characteristics, use cases, advantages, and challenges. The chapter undertakes a thorough examination of the fundamental distinctions between these two blockchain types and investigates their potential ramifications across diverse industries. By leveraging recent research and industry case studies, this chapter provides an impartial evaluation of the strengths and weaknesses of public and private blockchains, thereby providing valuable insights into their appropriateness for various applications. Public blockchains are distinguished by their decentralized structure, enabling participation by any individual as a network node (Murray-Rust et al., 2022). Public blockchains provide transparency, immutability, and consensus mechanisms that safeguard the integrity of the ledger. These blockchains have demonstrated applicability in diverse industries, including cryptocurrencies (e.g., Bitcoin), decentralized finance (DeFi) platforms (e.g., Ethereum), supply chain management, and voting systems. Public blockchains offer a range of advantages, including heightened security through decentralization, resistance to censorship, and transparent transaction records that foster trust. Additionally, they enable community governance and open participation. Nevertheless, the widespread adoption of public blockchains faces challenges such as scalability limitations, high energy consumption (in proof-of-work systems), and regulatory concerns regarding privacy and compliance, which may impede their implementation (Sargent & Breese, 2023; Jebamikyous et al., 2023).

Private blockchains, referred to as permission blockchains, limit access exclusively to authorized participants. These blockchains provide controlled access, enabling organizations to preserve privacy and regulate participants. They are widely employed in industries such as healthcare, finance, and government, where data confidentiality, compliance, and specific governance requirements are of utmost importance (M. Wang, Zhu, et al., 2023; Al-Sumaidaee et al., 2023). Private blockchains offer advantages such as improved privacy, heightened efficiency through faster transaction processing, and the capacity to adhere to industry regulations. They also provide more scalability options and have lower energy consumption compared to public blockchains (Hossain, 2023). However, challenges associated with private blockchains include reliance on trusted entities, potential risks of centralization, and limited transparency, which can influence the level of trust among participants (Liu et al., 2023). Public blockchains exhibit strengths in decentralization, transparency, and strong security, although scalability can be a challenge. On the other hand, private blockchains prioritize privacy, regulatory compliance, and scalability but may compromise certain aspects of decentralization and transparency. The selection between public and private blockchains is contingent upon specific use cases, requirements, and trade-offs (Seth, 2022). Table 1 provides a summary of the principal distinctions between public and private blockchains, emphasizing their contrasting attributes and applications.

Both public and private blockchains find applications in various sectors. Public blockchains are commonly used for cryptocurrency transactions, decentralized finance (DeFi), and voting systems, where transparency and community participation are crucial (Swan, 2015). Private blockchains, on the other hand, are adopted by financial institutions for interbank transfers, supply chain management, and health records, where privacy and regulatory compliance are vital (Kosba et al., 2016). Public and private blockchains offer distinct advantages and cater to different requirements in the rapidly evolving landscape of blockchain technology. Public blockchains excel in promoting transparency, decentralization, and community involvement, while private blockchains prioritize privacy, scalability, and controlled access. The choice between public and private blockchains depends on the specific use case, organizational needs, and regulatory considerations. By understanding the contrasting characteristics and applications of public and private blockchains, stakeholders can make informed decisions when implementing blockchain technology. It is crucial to consider factors such as data privacy, scalability requirements, and the desired level of decentralization to maximize the potential benefits of blockchain in various industries.

Table 1. Comparison of public and private blockchains

Aspect	Public Blockchain	Private Blockchain
Accessibility	Open to anyone	Restricted access
Consensus Mechanism I	Proof of Work (PoW)	Practical Byzantine Fault Tolerance (PBFT), Proof of Authority (PoA), etc
Transaction Privacy	High transparency	Enhanced privacy
Scalability	Limited	Higher transaction throughput
Immutability	Immutable	Controlled by trusted entities

BENEFITS AND FEATURES OF BLOCKCHAIN IN SUPPLY CHAIN MANAGEMENT

Transparency and Traceability of Products

This section delves into the advantages and characteristics of leveraging blockchain technology in supply chain management to enhance product transparency and traceability. Given the escalating intricacies of global supply chains and the growing demand for heightened accountability, blockchain presents a promising solution to tackle these challenges. This section conducts a comprehensive review of recent literature on the subject, focusing on analyzing the primary benefits and functionalities of blockchain in enhancing transparency and traceability across the supply chain. The findings underscore the transformative potential of blockchain in revolutionizing supply chain management practices, fostering increased trust, and driving enhanced efficiency in product tracking and authentication. The efficient flow of goods and services from producers to end consumers relies heavily on effective supply chain management. Nevertheless, conventional supply chain systems frequently encounter difficulties concerning transparency and traceability, resulting in problems like counterfeiting, fraud, and suboptimal inventory management. The advent of blockchain technology presents a promising solution to tackle these challenges by furnishing a transparent and traceable platform for supply chain management (Schäfer, 2022). Within the scope of supply chain management, transparency denotes the capacity to access and validate information about the origin, movement, and handling of products across the supply chain. Blockchain technology facilitates transparency by establishing a decentralized and immutable ledger, where transactions and information are recorded and shared among participants (L. Li et al., 2023).

Figure 7. End to end supply chain with blockchain
(Solistica, n.d.)

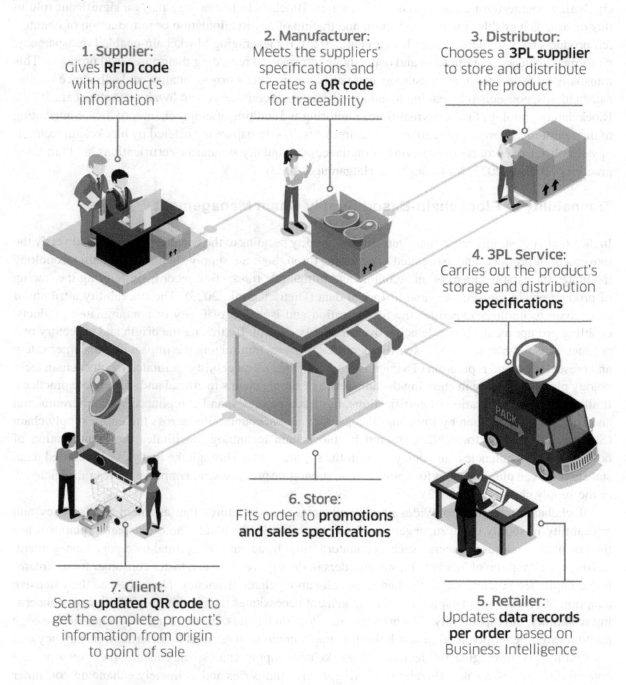

1. Supplier:
Gives **RFID code**
with product's
information

2. Manufacturer:
Meets the suppliers'
specifications and
creates a **QR code**
for traceability

3. Distributor:
Chooses a **3PL supplier**
to store and distribute
the product

4. 3PL Service:
Carries out the product's
storage and distribution
specifications

6. Store:
Fits order to **promotions
and sales specifications**

7. Client:
Scans **updated QR code** to
get the complete product's
information from origin
to point of sale

5. Retailer:
Updates **data records
per order** based on
Business Intelligence

Transparency in Blockchain-Based Supply Chain Management

The transparency aspect of blockchain empowers participants to track and authenticate products at every stage of the supply chain. The ability to identify and trace the origin of counterfeit goods is crucial in combating counterfeiting and fraudulent activities. Blockchain technology plays a significant role in this regard, as it enables the easy detection and tracing of any manipulation or introduction of counterfeit products back to their source (Tanvir et al., 2023). By leveraging blockchain-enabled transparency, consumers gain access to precise and dependable information regarding their purchased products. This transparency fosters trust, as consumers can verify the product's origin, quality, and adherence to ethical standards, consequently leading to enhanced consumer confidence and loyalty (Akella et al., 2023). Blockchain technology facilitates real-time monitoring and auditing of supply chain activities, contributing to the seamless adherence to regulatory requirements. The transparency offered by blockchain technology simplifies the process of verifying compliance with quality standards, certifications, and fair trade practices (Thakur, 2023; Munasinghe & Halgamuge, 2023).

Traceability in Blockchain-Based Supply Chain Management

In the context of supply chain management, traceability pertains to the capability to track and verify the movement of products and associated information throughout the supply chain. Blockchain technology facilitates the establishment of an auditable and immutable transaction record, simplifying the tracing of product origin, provenance, and historical data (Dietrich et al., 2023). The traceability attribute of blockchain technology expedites the identification and isolation of faulty or contaminated products, enabling prompt recalls and enhancing overall quality control. By tracing the origin and trajectory of a product, affected batches can be swiftly identified, thereby minimizing the impact on consumer safety and preserving brand reputation (Thangamayan et al., 2023). Traceability facilitated by blockchain technology plays a vital role in ensuring the adherence of supply chains to ethical and sustainable practices. It allows for the verification of certifications, fair trade practices, and compliance with environmental and social standards, thereby fostering transparency and accountability across the entire supply chain (Sharma, 2023). The traceability offered by blockchain technology facilitates the identification of bottlenecks, inefficiencies, and delays within the supply chain. Through the analysis of recorded data, stakeholders can pinpoint areas for optimization, streamline processes, and improve the overall efficiency of the supply chain (Negi, 2022).

Blockchain technology provides notable advantages and features that augment transparency and traceability in supply chain management. Its decentralized, immutable, and transparent platform has the potential to address concerns such as counterfeiting, fraud, and suboptimal inventory management. Through the adoption of blockchain, stakeholders in the supply chain can foster consumer trust, streamline compliance procedures, and enhance overall supply chain efficiency. Nevertheless, the extensive adoption of blockchain in supply chain management necessitates the resolution of challenges concerning scalability, interoperability, data privacy, and adoption barriers. In summary, blockchain technology harbours significant potential to revolutionize supply chain management by offering transparency and traceability. By leveraging the features of blockchain, supply chains can enhance their security, accountability, and efficiency, thereby benefiting diverse industries and ultimately enhancing consumer confidence in the products they utilize.

Figure 8. Blockchain in supply chain management
(Kumar, n.d.)

BLOCKCHAIN APPLICATIONS IN SUPPLY CHAIN MANAGEMENT

Product Provenance and Traceability

The global supply chain industry encounters a multitude of challenges, encompassing issues of product provenance, traceability, and transparency. These challenges frequently lead to inefficiencies, counterfeit goods, and complexities in identifying the origin and flow of products. Blockchain technology presents promising solutions to tackle these issues by establishing a decentralized, transparent, and immutable ledger for recording and validating transactions. This section delves into the utilization of blockchain in supply chain management, with a particular emphasis on its applications in product provenance and traceability. Product provenance involves the capacity to trace and authenticate the origin and genuineness of a product, encompassing its constituents, materials, and manufacturing procedures. The process of traceability entails the meticulous monitoring of product flow throughout the supply chain, commencing from its origin and concluding with the end consumer. Pertinent data points encompassing aspects such as location, temperature, handling, and quality assurance are recorded during this monitoring process (Xu, Lou, et al., 2023).

Blockchain technology facilitates instantaneous access to the movement of goods, enabling stakeholders to efficiently track and supervise products at each phase of the supply chain. The enhanced visibility offered by blockchain technology assists in the identification of bottlenecks, the alleviation of delays, and the overall enhancement of operational efficiency (Al-Khatib, 2022). By recording the distinctive identifiers of products, such as serial numbers or RFID tags, on the blockchain, the process of verifying their authenticity and identifying counterfeit goods becomes more streamlined. Consumers, enabling them to ensure the legitimacy of their purchases (Naoum-Sawaya et al., 2023), can also access this information. Blockchain technology offers a secure and incorruptible framework for the storage of regulatory and compliance-related information, such as certifications, permits, and records about quality assurance. This utilization of blockchain guarantees adherence to standards and simplifies the process of conducting audits (Bhatt, 2023a). Additionally, blockchain can record and monitor crucial quality assurance data, encompassing factors such as temperature, humidity, and handling conditions, throughout the entirety of the supply chain.

This data facilitates the identification of potential concerns, minimizes wastage, and augments the safety of the product (Tao et al., 2022). Utilizing blockchain technology allows for comprehensive tracking, and documenting the progression of products and related information throughout every stage. The ability to ensure traceability is of utmost importance in sectors such as pharmaceuticals, food, and luxury goods, as it plays a pivotal role in guaranteeing safety, adhering to regulatory standards, and promoting ethical sourcing (Wu et al., 2023). The utilization of blockchain technology presents a promising opportunity to augment the verification of product origin and traceability within the realm of supply chain management. By harnessing the decentralized, transparent, and immutable attributes of blockchain technology, enterprises can attain heightened visibility, authenticity, and operational efficiency across the entirety of their supply chains. Nevertheless, to fully unlock the transformative capabilities of blockchain and foster enhanced customer trust in product authenticity, meticulous planning, collaborative efforts, and thoughtful consideration of the challenges at hand are imperative.

Inventory Management and Tracking

This report primarily concentrates on elucidating the various applications of blockchain technology in the realm of inventory management and tracking within the context of supply chains. By capitalizing on the decentralized and immutable characteristics inherent in blockchain, organizations can elevate their inventory management procedures, optimize operations, and mitigate inefficiencies effectively. This report delves into a comprehensive analysis of the significant benefits associated with utilizing blockchain technology in inventory management and tracking. Specifically, inventory management and tracking using blockchain in the supply chain entails leveraging blockchain technology to augment the transparency, traceability, and efficiency of inventory management processes within a supply chain. The essence of inventory management revolves around vigilant monitoring and effective control of the movement of goods and materials throughout an organization. The scope of inventory management encompasses various activities, including procurement, storage, distribution, and replenishment of inventory. Conventional inventory management systems typically rely on centralized databases or manual procedures, which can result in inefficiencies, discrepancies in data, and a deficiency of trust among participants within the supply chain. In contrast, blockchain technology is characterized by its decentralized and distributed ledger system, which facilitates secure and transparent transaction record-keeping. It offers a shared database that allows multiple participants to access and validate data, thereby eliminating the necessity for intermediaries and mitigating the risks associated with fraud or manipulation (X. Li, 2023).

In the realm of inventory management and tracking, the utilization of blockchain technology can yield numerous advantages. One notable benefit is the augmentation of transparency. By employing blockchain, one can attain immediate and ongoing insight into inventory quantities, whereabouts, and transitions throughout the entire supply chain. This shared access to information among all stakeholders diminishes information disparities and facilitates more informed decision-making. Enhanced traceability represents another noteworthy advantage. Every inventory transaction is meticulously documented as a block on the blockchain, forming an unalterable audit trail. This characteristic enables comprehensive product traceability, empowering stakeholders to validate the source, legitimacy, and journey of goods across the entire supply chain.

Improved Efficiency: Through the implementation of smart contracts, blockchain technology automates inventory management processes, effectively reducing the dependence on manual reconciliations, paperwork, and intermediaries. This optimization leads to streamlined operations, minimizing errors and expediting the overall supply chain cycle time. Enhanced Security: Utilizing cryptographic algorithms, blockchain ensures the utmost security for data and transactions. By doing so, it establishes tamper-resistant inventory records that are shielded from unauthorized access, thereby mitigating the risks associated with counterfeiting or theft. Trusted Collaboration: Blockchain's decentralized nature and consensus mechanisms foster a sense of trust and collaboration among participants within the supply chain. This enables stakeholders, including suppliers, manufacturers, distributors, and retailers, to securely share inventory information without relying on a centralized authority (M. I. Khan et al., 2023).

In the realm of supply chain management, incorporating blockchain technology for inventory management and tracking offers a multitude of benefits, including heightened efficiency, enhanced visibility, cost reduction, and strengthened trust among participants. By leveraging blockchain, traditional inventory management systems can undergo a transformative evolution, introducing an unprecedented level of transparency and security to the process.

Demand Forecasting and Analytics

The incorporation of blockchain technology into demand forecasting and analytics processes within the realm of supply chain management holds immense significance, as it empowers organizations to make well-informed and strategic choices regarding production, inventory management, and logistics. This integration brings forth a multitude of advantages. The utilization of blockchain in demand forecasting and analytics offers various opportunities for improvement. One notable advantage is the enhanced accuracy and trustworthiness of data. Blockchain technology employs a decentralized and immutable ledger, which records and secures all transactions and data exchanges. By leveraging blockchain, stakeholders within the supply chain can guarantee the precision and integrity of demand-related data, including sales records, customer orders, and inventory levels. The transparency and trust established through blockchain technology can subsequently enhance the accuracy of demand forecasting models (Hu et al., 2023). Another key benefit of implementing blockchain technology in demand forecasting and analytics is the secure sharing of data among supply chain participants. In conventional supply chains, data often remains isolated in silos, hindering the ability to obtain a holistic perspective on demand throughout the entire network. However, through the utilization of blockchain, stakeholders can securely share demand-related data while upholding privacy and data ownership rights. This collaborative sharing of data facilitates the generation of more precise forecasts and insights for analytics purposes (Chen, 2023). The integration of blockchain into supply chain solutions offers the advantage of real-time visibility into demand data. By leveraging blockchain technology, transactions and events related to customer orders, inventory levels, and product movements are recorded and readily accessible to stakeholders. This real-time visibility empowers organizations to promptly respond to shifts in demand, allowing for timely adjustments to forecasting and production plans (Kashem et al., 2023).

The utilization of blockchain introduces the capability of employing smart contracts, which are self-executing agreements with predetermined rules and conditions. Smart contracts offer automation possibilities for various processes within demand forecasting and analytics, including data validation, aggregation, and the execution of analytics models. For instance, smart contracts can be programmed to automatically adjust production levels or initiate procurement orders when specific predefined demand thresholds are met. This automation enhances efficiency and accuracy in decision-making (Allenbrand, 2023). The inherent feature of blockchain to establish an immutable and auditable record of transactions renders it highly advantageous for supply chain traceability. Through the integration of demand data with other pertinent information within the supply chain, such as product origin, manufacturing details, and logistics data, organizations can obtain valuable insights into the factors that impact demand. This holistic approach enables the identification of patterns or correlations that contribute to enhanced accuracy in demand forecasting (Tokkozhina et al., 2023). The implementation of blockchain-based systems facilitates the introduction of incentive mechanisms and tokenization, which can incentivize accurate demand reporting and forecasting. Participants who contribute precise demand data can be rewarded with tokens, establishing a system where stakeholders are motivated to provide high-quality data. This incentivization framework fosters a collaborative environment and ultimately leads to more accurate outcomes in analytics and forecasting (Valdivia, 2023).

BLOCKCHAIN-ENABLED SUPPLY CHAIN PLATFORMS AND CONSORTIA

Figure 9. Blockchain enabled supply chain
(Jabbar et al., 2021)

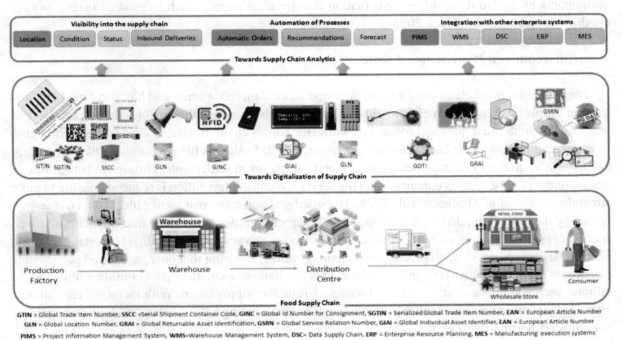

GTIN = Global Trade Item Number, SSCC =Serial Shipment Container Code, GINC = Global Id Number for Consignment, SGTIN = Serialized Global Trade Item Number, EAN = European Article Number
GLN = Global Location Number, GRAI = Global Returnable Asset Identification, GSRN = Global Service Relation Number, GIAI = Global Individual Asset Identifier, EAN = European Article Number
PIMS = Project Information Management System, WMS=Warehouse Management System, DSC= Data Supply Chain, ERP = Enterprise Resource Planning, MES = Manufacturing execution systems

Existing Blockchain-Based Platforms for Supply Chain Management

This section offers a comprehensive overview of the current blockchain-based platforms that are employed in supply chain management. The emergence of blockchain technology has brought about remarkable progress in terms of transparency, traceability, and efficiency within the supply chain industry. Leveraging the distributed ledger technology of blockchain, organizations can benefit from a decentralized, immutable, and secure framework for effectively managing their supply chain processes. The information presented here aims to provide businesses and decision-makers with valuable insights into the capabilities and opportunities that blockchain brings to revolutionize supply chain management.

- **IBM Blockchain and VeChain**

IBM offers the IBM Blockchain Platform as a robust solution specifically designed for supply chain management. This platform harnesses the power of blockchain technology to elevate visibility, traceability, and efficiency within supply chain operations. By leveraging this platform, businesses can effectively track and record every transaction and movement of goods throughout the entire supply chain. This capability ensures the establishment of a secure and unchangeable audit trail, thereby enhancing accountability and transparency (IBM Blockchain - Enterprise Blockchain Solutions and Services, n.d.). VeChain is a specialized blockchain platform explicitly tailored for supply chain management and product authentication. By seamlessly integrating blockchain technology with IoT devices and RFID tags, VeChain enables comprehensive tracking and authentication of products across the entire supply chain. This unique combination empowers businesses to verify the authenticity and quality of their goods. VeChain's platform facilitates the establishment of trust and transparency among supply chain participants by providing real-time information about crucial aspects such as product origin, storage conditions, and logistics (Silva, 2023).

- **Ethereum and Hyperledger Fabric**

The Ethereum blockchain platform has garnered significant recognition and has also found applications in supply chain management. Notably, its smart contract functionality enables the automation and execution of predefined rules and conditions within the supply chain. Businesses can leverage Ethereum to create and deploy smart contracts on its network, which facilitates the streamlining of various processes such as inventory management, procurement, and payment settlements. Through the utilization of smart contracts, efficiency is enhanced, and the need for manual intervention is reduced, leading to more streamlined operations (Pacheco et al., 2023). Hyperledger Fabric, an open-source blockchain framework hosted by the Linux Foundation, is well-suited for enterprise-grade supply chain management solutions. It boasts essential features such as permissioned networks, privacy, and scalability. Hyperledger Fabric enables businesses to establish private blockchain networks, ensuring that only authorized participants can access and contribute to the shared ledger. This mechanism guarantees data confidentiality and facilitates secure collaboration among stakeholders within the supply chain. With its robust capabilities, Hyperledger Fabric provides a reliable foundation for implementing advanced supply chain management solutions (Peregrina-Pérez et al., 2023).

- **Waltonchain, Modum and OriginTrail**

Waltonchain is a specialized blockchain-based platform that prioritizes the integration of RFID (Radio Frequency Identification) technology with blockchain to enhance supply chain management practices. Through the incorporation of RFID tags into products and assets, Waltonchain enables real-time tracking and tracing capabilities throughout the entire supply chain. The collected data is securely stored on the blockchain, ensuring transparency and safeguarding against counterfeiting or tampering. The overarching objective of Waltonchain is to augment operational efficiency, minimize costs, and foster trust among participants within the supply chain (X. Xu, Tian, et al., 2023). Modum provides a dedicated blockchain platform that caters to supply chain compliance and temperature monitoring, with a particular emphasis on industries such as pharmaceuticals. This platform addresses the crucial need for maintaining appropriate temperature conditions during the transportation and storage of sensitive goods. Modum achieves this by seamlessly integrating IoT sensors with blockchain technology, enabling real-time monitoring of temperature and humidity levels. The collected data is securely stored on the blockchain, creating an immutable record of compliance and ensuring the integrity of valuable goods (Uma, 2023). OriginTrail is a decentralized platform that harnesses the power of blockchain technology to facilitate secure data sharing and ensure data integrity within supply chains. It effectively addresses the common challenge of fragmented supply chain data by establishing a unified protocol for data exchange. Through OriginTrail, businesses can securely share and verify supply chain data among multiple stakeholders, fostering transparency, reliability, and trust. The platform also supports interoperability, enabling seamless integration with various systems and technologies already in place within the existing supply chain infrastructure (Tavana et al., 2023).

- **Provenance, Ambrosus and ShipChain**

Provenance, a blockchain-based platform, emphasizes the aspects of traceability and transparency within supply chains. Its primary objective is to enable businesses to effectively monitor and authenticate the source, legitimacy, and ethical benchmarks associated with their products. By leveraging Provenance, consumers gain access to comprehensive insights regarding the journey of a product throughout the supply chain, consequently nurturing confidence and endorsing sustainable and equitable trade principles (Cyrus, 2023). Ambrosus, an innovative blockchain-powered platform, focuses on enhancing supply chain visibility and ensuring quality assurance. By seamlessly integrating blockchain technology with IoT sensors, Ambrosus diligently tracks and documents crucial aspects of products as they traverse the supply chain. This includes real-time monitoring of factors such as temperature, humidity, and location, effectively safeguarding product integrity and mitigating the potential risks associated with spoilage or counterfeiting (Modak, 2023). ShipChain is an advanced blockchain platform specifically engineered to optimize and fortify the worldwide shipping and logistics sector. Through the implementation of blockchain technology, ShipChain establishes a decentralized ecosystem that seamlessly integrates carriers, shippers, and various other key stakeholders. This innovative solution offers comprehensive visibility throughout the entire supply chain, automates documentation and payment procedures, and significantly augments transparency and operational efficiency in the realm of logistics (Alqarni et al., 2023).

- **Blockverify, Wabi and Chronicled**

Blockverify is a purpose-built blockchain platform that places significant emphasis on countering counterfeit practices and verifying the authenticity of products within supply chains. By leveraging Blockverify, businesses gain the capability to meticulously track and validate their products, thereby guaranteeing their legitimacy and safeguarding against counterfeit goods. The platform utilizes the power of blockchain technology to securely store immutable records, enabling efficient detection and prevention of fraudulent activities across supply chains (Khedekar et al., 2022). Wabi represents a cutting-edge blockchain platform that harmoniously merges blockchain technology with reliable product labels, thereby assuring authenticity and safety within supply chains. By empowering consumers with a user-friendly mobile app, Wabi allows them to effortlessly verify the origin and legitimacy of products through the scanning of unique labels. The primary objective of Wabi's platform is to actively combat the proliferation of counterfeit goods and cultivate a foundation of trust between discerning consumers and reputable brands (C. Zhang et al., 2023). Chronicled stands as a prominent blockchain platform with a keen emphasis on optimizing supply chains and establishing product provenance. Catering to diverse industries such as pharmaceuticals, luxury goods, and agriculture, Chronicled offers tailored solutions. By harnessing the potential of blockchain technology, Chronicled's platform enables secure tracking and tracing of products, thereby guaranteeing compliance, authenticity, and ethical sourcing throughout the entire supply chain journey (Srinivas et al., 2023).A

Figure 10. Secure decentralized IoT using consortium blockchain
(R. Zhang et al., 2022)

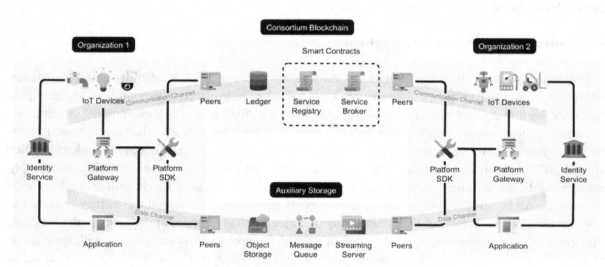

Collaborative Networks and Consortia Leveraging Blockchain Technology

Collaborative networks and consortia have garnered considerable interest in recent years, particularly with the utilization of blockchain technology. The decentralized and transparent nature of blockchain offers a multitude of benefits, particularly in terms of establishing trust and enabling seamless collaboration among various entities. This section provides an outline of how collaborative networks and consortia leverage blockchain technology.

The implementation of blockchain technology furnishes a shared infrastructure that facilitates direct interaction and transactions among multiple participants, eliminating the reliance on intermediaries. By creating a distributed ledger, blockchain ensures that all transactions are recorded and verified by participants within the network, thereby ensuring transparency and obviating the need for a central governing authority (Setyowati et al., 2023). In the realm of collaborative networks and consortia, smart contracts play a pivotal role as they operate as self-executing agreements, encoded directly on the blockchain. These intelligent contracts automatically enforce predefined rules and conditions, thus eliminating the necessity for intermediaries or manual enforcement. By leveraging smart contracts, collaborative networks and consortia ensure automated and secure collaboration by ensuring that all participants adhere to the predetermined terms (Ullah & Al-Turjman, 2021). One significant application of blockchain technology in collaborative networks and consortia is observed in supply chain management. In this context, blockchain enhances visibility, traceability, and efficiency within the supply chain. By recording every transaction and movement of goods on the blockchain, stakeholders can gain real-time insights into the entire supply chain, thus reducing the occurrence of fraudulent activities, streamlining documentation processes, and augmenting overall transparency and integrity within the supply chain (Srivastava et al., 2021). Blockchain technology facilitates secure and auditable data sharing among organizations, ensuring that the shared data remains tamper-proof and establishing a dependable and transparent source of truth. This capability proves particularly valuable in sectors like healthcare, finance, and logistics, wherein multiple organizations require access to and the ability to update sensitive data while upholding privacy and security protocols (Gupta et al., 2023).

Decentralized identity management is an area where collaborative networks can effectively harness blockchain technology. By utilizing blockchain-based identity solutions, individuals gain the ability to retain control over their data and selectively share it with trusted entities. This approach not only enhances security but also mitigates the risk of data breaches, while simultaneously streamlining identity verification processes (Das et al., 2023). Consensus mechanisms play a crucial role in blockchain networks, serving as the foundation for participants to collectively validate and reach an agreement on the state of the blockchain. By employing a decentralized governance model, this approach ensures that decision-making authority is distributed among network participants, thereby promoting transparency and diminishing the concentration of power (Mehta et al., 2023). When it comes to collaborative networks and consortia, consortium blockchains are often favoured. These blockchains involve a specific group of pre-selected participants who jointly maintain the blockchain network. Consortium blockchains offer several advantages over public blockchains, including increased scalability, privacy, and efficiency. Despite these advantages, consortium blockchains still uphold a distributed and trustless environment, ensuring the reliability and integrity of the network (Juma et al., 2023).

Case Studies of Successful Blockchain Implementations in Supply Chains

- **Walmart and IBM (Food Traceability)**

In a collaborative effort, Walmart partnered with IBM to develop a blockchain-based food traceability system. The primary objective of this solution was to augment transparency and traceability within the food supply chain. By harnessing the capabilities of blockchain technology, customers gained the ability to track the complete journey of products, starting from the farm to the store. The implementation of blockchain technology significantly reduced the time needed to trace the origin of contaminated food items, decreasing the timeframe from several days to mere minutes. Consequently, this innovative solution not only enhanced food safety but also contributed to the reduction of waste within the supply chain. In a pilot project focused on tracking mangos, Walmart successfully implemented a blockchain solution. This system enabled the company to meticulously trace the origin of every mango, capturing crucial details such as farm information, harvest dates, processing data, and other relevant information. The high level of traceability facilitated swift issue identification and resolution, thereby mitigating the spread of foodborne illnesses. This application exemplifies the effectiveness of blockchain technology in enhancing the transparency and safety of the food supply chain (Supply Chain Insight: Inside IBM's Food Trust Blockchain System, 2020).

- **Maersk and IBM (Shipping Industry)**

Maersk, a prominent global shipping company, collaborated with IBM to create TradeLens, a blockchain solution aimed at revolutionizing the global supply chain ecosystem. TradeLens leverages blockchain technology to digitize and provide comprehensive visibility across the entire supply chain, encompassing shipping documents and container tracking. By utilizing blockchain, TradeLens significantly reduces paperwork, fosters transparency, and streamlines processes, ultimately leading to enhanced efficiency and reduced costs. This innovative solution has been successfully implemented in numerous ports and terminals worldwide, empowering participants to access real-time data regarding container movement, shipment statuses, customs documents, and other pertinent information. TradeLens, the blockchain solution developed by Maersk and IBM, facilitates secure and efficient information sharing among diverse stakeholders involved in the supply chain. This includes shipping carriers, freight forwarders, customs officials, and port authorities. By enabling seamless collaboration and effective communication, TradeLens minimizes delays and optimizes operational efficiency within the supply chain (Trueman, 2022).

- **De Beers (Diamond Industry)**

De Beers, a prominent diamond company, has successfully implemented Tracr, a blockchain platform designed to track the entire journey of diamonds from mining operations to the hands of retailers. Tracr allows participants within the diamond supply chain to securely record and verify transactions, thereby minimizing the risk of fraudulent activities and guaranteeing the authenticity and ethical sourcing of diamonds. The platform also contributes to operational efficiency by streamlining the verification process for diamond certifications and enhancing inventory management practices. Through the implementation of Tracr, De Beers has leveraged blockchain technology to enhance transparency, trust, and efficiency within the diamond industry. Tracr, the blockchain platform, was developed through a collaborative effort involving industry leaders such as diamond manufacturers and retailers. Its primary purpose is to utilize blockchain technology to establish a comprehensive digital trail for each diamond, capturing essential data points like origin, cut, clarity, and certification details. By securely recording this information on the blockchain, Tracr ensures that consumers have confidence in the authenticity and ethical sourcing of their diamond purchases. Additionally, the platform assists participants within the diamond industry in streamlining processes and mitigating the risk of counterfeit diamonds infiltrating the market. Through its transparent and efficient approach, Tracr fosters trust and integrity within the diamond industry (Tracr, n.d.).

BHP and Mitsubishi (Mining Industry)

BHP, a renowned global mining company, joined forces with Mitsubishi Development to implement a blockchain-based supply chain solution specifically tailored for the mining industry. This collaborative project focused on improving the transparency and traceability of minerals and metals, commencing with the tracking of raw cobalt sourced from BHP's Nickel West mine in Australia. The blockchain solution plays a pivotal role by facilitating the secure and unalterable recording of transactions, thereby ensuring adherence to responsible sourcing standards and mitigating the risks associated with unethical practices. Through this innovative approach, the mining industry can achieve enhanced transparency and integrity within its supply chains. The blockchain platform implemented by BHP and Mitsubishi offers an immutable and auditable record of cobalt movements and transactions, ensuring its tamper-proof nature. It captures crucial data at various stages of the supply chain, encompassing mining, processing, and distribution. This high level of transparency enables verification of responsible sourcing practices and aids in the identification of potential issues, such as the presence of conflict minerals or unethical practices. By harnessing the power of blockchain technology, BHP and Mitsubishi strive to establish a more sustainable and ethical supply chain for minerals and metals (BHP, 2019).

- **Everledger (Luxury Goods)**

Everledger is a notable blockchain platform that specializes in verifying the authenticity and provenance of luxury goods, spanning from diamonds and gemstones to high-end wines. Through the utilization of blockchain technology, Everledger establishes a digital record for each item, capturing crucial information regarding its origin, ownership history, and unique characteristics. This innovative solution plays a pivotal role in combating counterfeiting, facilitating efficient supply chain management, and instilling consumer confidence by assuring the authenticity of their luxury purchases. By leveraging blockchain technology, Everledger aims to enhance trust, transparency, and integrity within the luxury goods industry. Everledger's platform harnesses the power of blockchain to create a secure and reliable storage and sharing system for information about luxury goods. In the diamond industry, for instance, the platform records crucial data encompassing the diamond's cut, colour, clarity, certification, and entire journey through the supply chain. By utilizing blockchain technology, Everledger effectively combats the circulation of counterfeit goods, streamlines supply chain operations, and empowers consumers to authenticate the genuineness of their purchases. Through these mechanisms, Everledger enhances trust and transparency within the luxury goods market (Everledger, 2022).

Figure 11. Limitation of blockchain

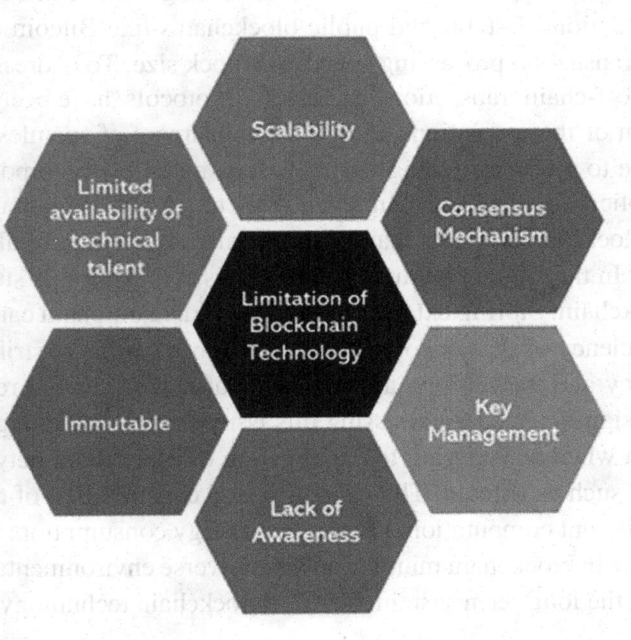

CHALLENGES AND LIMITATIONS OF BLOCKCHAIN IN SUPPLY CHAIN MANAGEMENT

Scalability and Performance Issues

The emergence of blockchain technology has garnered considerable interest within the domain of supply chain management owing to its inherent capacity to augment transparency, traceability, and security.

Nevertheless, akin to any technological innovation, blockchain faces certain impediments to its scalability and performance. One of the primary concerns regarding the utilization of blockchain in supply chain management revolves around the challenges associated with scalability and performance. Notably, transaction throughput emerges as a key issue in this context. Conventional blockchain systems, like Bitcoin and Ethereum, exhibit constrained capabilities when it comes to processing transactions. Consequently, in a supply chain environment characterized by a multitude of participants and a high volume of transactions, the blockchain network may encounter difficulties in effectively handling the necessary transaction throughput. Consequently, this can lead to undesirable outcomes such as delays, escalated transaction costs, and a suboptimal user experience, as highlighted by Krishnan et al. (2023). Another significant issue related to scalability and performance in the application of blockchain technology in supply chain management pertains to network congestion. As the number of participants within a blockchain network grows and the transaction volume surges, the network can experience congestion. This congestion results in prolonged transaction confirmation times, elevated fees, and the potential for bottlenecks to occur. In the context of supply chain management, where real-time visibility and swift transaction processing are of paramount importance, network congestion can significantly impede the efficiency of the system, as emphasized by Rožman et al. (2023). The limitations associated with scalability pose a significant obstacle for blockchain networks aiming to accommodate an expanding number of participants and transactions. Established public blockchains like Bitcoin and Ethereum encounter restrictions in terms of transaction processing speed and block size. To address this issue, various scaling solutions, including off-chain transactions and layer-2 protocols, have been proposed. However, the effective implementation of these solutions and the establishment of seamless interoperability across diverse systems continue to present ongoing challenges, as noted by Taghipour (2021). An important consideration in the application of blockchain technology to supply chain management is the requirement for data storage. Blockchain systems maintain an unalterable ledger of all transactions conducted by network participants. In the context of supply chains, this can result in a substantial volume of data being stored on the blockchain. Storing extensive amounts of data on-chain can lead to elevated storage costs and hinder the efficiency of the network. Thus, it becomes crucial to strike a balance between the necessity for transparency and traceability, and the associated data storage requirements. Meisami et al. (2023) highlight the significance of addressing this issue effectively. Energy consumption emerges as a noteworthy concern when considering the application of blockchain networks, particularly those based on proof-of-work, such as Bitcoin. The validation and confirmation of transactions within these systems necessitate significant computational power and energy consumption. The considerable energy consumption associated with blockchain mining can have adverse environmental ramifications and raise apprehensions regarding the long-term sustainability of blockchain technology, as highlighted by Abed et al. (2023).

Interoperability and Standardization Challenges

One of the notable challenges in the realm of blockchain technology is the absence of common standards. This lack of standardized protocols, consensus mechanisms, data structures, and smart contract languages across various platforms creates difficulties in seamlessly integrating and exchanging data between different blockchain systems. In the context of supply chain management, where stakeholders may utilize different blockchain networks, the absence of common standards presents a hurdle in achieving interoperability. Basu et al. (2023) emphasize the significance of addressing this challenge to enhance the effectiveness and efficiency of blockchain integration in supply chains. In the realm of supply chain management, ensuring data privacy and confidentiality is paramount, even as blockchain technology promotes transparency and immutability. Participants within the supply chain frequently deal with sensitive information, including pricing details, contracts, and customer data. Striking a delicate balance between the transparent nature of blockchain and the need for selective data sharing with robust privacy controls presents a notable challenge. It becomes essential to address this challenge effectively to safeguard sensitive information while harnessing the benefits of blockchain technology. Wenhua et al. (2023) underscore the significance of finding appropriate solutions in this regard. The integration of blockchain technology with existing systems poses a complex task within supply chain networks that already rely on established legacy systems and databases. Achieving smooth data flow and interoperability between blockchain and these existing systems necessitates meticulous planning and integration endeavours. The challenge lies in seamlessly connecting blockchain with pre-existing systems without causing disruptions to the current processes. Huynh-The et al. (2023a) emphasize the need for careful consideration and strategic implementation to address this challenge effectively. The implementation of blockchain technology in supply chain management is subject to regulatory and legal considerations, especially in the context of cross-border transactions. Various jurisdictions possess distinct regulations and legal frameworks that might not align seamlessly with blockchain technology. Ensuring compliance and harmonizing these regulations becomes imperative for the successful adoption and implementation of blockchain in supply chains. Guntara et al. (2023) highlight the significance of addressing these regulatory and legal challenges for a smooth integration of blockchain technology in the supply chain domain.

Figure 12. Challenges in blockchain
(Feldman, 2019)

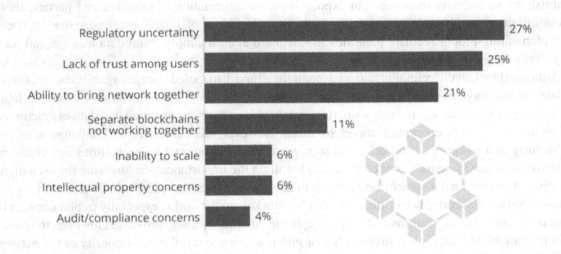

Data Privacy and Security Concerns

Within the realm of blockchain technology, a distinction exists between pseudonymity and anonymity. Blockchain offers pseudonymity, wherein participants are identified by their public keys instead of their actual identities. However, if someone's public key becomes linked to their real-world identity, their activities on the blockchain can be traced back to them. This linkage raises privacy concerns, particularly when sensitive business information or personal data is stored on the blockchain. It is crucial to managing the connection between public keys and real-world identities meticulously to safeguard privacy. Zieglmeier et al. (2023) underscore the importance of carefully addressing this issue to uphold privacy protections effectively. The immutable nature of data in blockchain technology serves to maintain data integrity and prevent unauthorized modifications. However, this characteristic can present a conflict with regulations such as the General Data Protection Regulation (GDPR), which grants individuals the right to have their data erased or modified. On a public blockchain, achieving complete data erasure becomes exceedingly challenging as the data is replicated across multiple nodes. Consequently, ensuring compliance with regulations that necessitate data deletion or modification can pose significant challenges when utilizing blockchain technology. Marthews and Tucker (2022) highlight the importance of addressing these challenges to navigate the intersection between blockchain and regulatory requirements effectively.

Smart contracts, integral components of blockchain-based supply chain systems, are self-executing agreements governed by predefined rules. Despite their advantages, smart contracts are not immune to coding errors or security vulnerabilities that could be exploited by malicious actors. Such vulnerabilities may result in unauthorized access to sensitive data or manipulation of supply chain transactions. To mitigate these risks, thorough testing and auditing of smart contracts are essential. By conducting comprehensive assessments, potential vulnerabilities can be identified and addressed, thus minimizing the associated risks. Vidal (2023) emphasizes the importance of rigorous testing and auditing procedures to enhance the security and reliability of smart contracts in supply chain applications. In blockchain-based supply chain systems, the sharing of data among multiple participants, such as suppliers, manufacturers, distributors, and customers, is a fundamental aspect. However, to prevent unauthorized access or data leakage, it is vital to implement robust access controls and encryption mechanisms. Neglecting to establish strong security measures can expose sensitive information to unauthorized parties, thereby increasing the risk of breaches and privacy violations. Panghal et al. (2022) emphasize the significance of implementing proper security measures to safeguard against supply chain data leakage and protect the privacy of sensitive information.

Although blockchain technology offers decentralized and distributed storage capabilities, certain types of data, such as large or confidential files, may not be well-suited for on-chain storage due to scalability and privacy considerations. In such scenarios, organizations may opt to store such data off-chain using traditional databases or encrypted storage solutions. However, this introduces the challenge of ensuring the security and integrity of the off-chain storage, as well as potential vulnerabilities associated with centralized storage systems. Goint et al. (2023) highlight the importance of addressing these challenges effectively to maintain the security and privacy of data stored off-chain in blockchain-based supply chain systems. Network security is a critical concern for blockchain networks, especially public ones, as they depend on consensus algorithms and cryptographic techniques to safeguard data. However, they are not entirely immune to attacks. If a single entity or group acquires control of the majority of the network's computing power, commonly referred to as a 51% attack, they could manipulate the blockchain's history or disrupt its operations, thereby compromising the privacy and integrity of the data. To mitigate these risks, robust network security measures must be implemented, including distributed consensus mechanisms and frequent monitoring. Wenhua et al. (2023) emphasize the importance of maintaining strong network security to protect blockchain-based supply chain systems from potential vulnerabilities and attacks.

To address the various concerns associated with implementing blockchain in supply chain management, organizations should consider implementing the following measures:

1. Conduct comprehensive risk assessments and privacy impact assessments before implementing blockchain solutions to identify potential risks and privacy implications.
2. Evaluate the use of private or permissioned blockchains that offer greater control over access and governance compared to public blockchains.
3. Implement strong access controls, encryption mechanisms, and robust key management practices to safeguard sensitive data stored on the blockchain.
4. Ensure compliance with relevant data protection regulations, such as the GDPR, by exploring techniques like data minimization or off-chain storage for personal data.
5. Regularly audit and test smart contracts and the overall blockchain infrastructure to identify and address security vulnerabilities.
6. Monitor network activity and employ robust cybersecurity measures to protect against attacks and unauthorized access.

By implementing these precautions, organizations can effectively leverage the benefits of blockchain technology while mitigating potential data privacy and security risks in supply chain management.

Adoption Barriers and Resistance to Change

A significant challenge in implementing blockchain technology in the supply chain industry is the lack of awareness and understanding among businesses. Many stakeholders may not have a clear grasp of blockchain's fundamentals or its potential benefits. This lack of awareness can result in scepticism and resistance to change within the industry. To address this challenge, it becomes essential to educate stakeholders about the fundamentals of blockchain, its advantages, and how it can effectively address specific pain points in the supply chain. Prabhakar et al. (2023) emphasize the importance of proactive education and communication efforts to foster a better understanding and acceptance of blockchain technology within the supply chain industry. One of the major challenges of implementing blockchain solutions in the supply chain is the cost and complexity involved. It is a significant investment that requires financial resources for infrastructure, development, and training. This can pose difficulties, particularly for small and medium-sized businesses that may have limited budgets and resources. Additionally, integrating blockchain with existing systems and processes can be a complex task, necessitating careful planning and implementation to ensure seamless integration. Dylag and Smith (2021) highlight the importance of addressing these cost and complexity challenges and finding practical solutions to facilitate the adoption of blockchain technology in the supply chain industry.

Achieving interoperability within the supply chain, which encompasses various entities such as manufacturers, suppliers, distributors, retailers, and logistics providers, poses a significant challenge in the adoption of blockchain technology. Integrating different blockchain platforms or integrating blockchain with existing legacy systems requires overcoming interoperability hurdles. To address this challenge, the establishment of standards and protocols becomes crucial to enable seamless communication and data exchange across diverse blockchain networks. Alshudukhi et al. (2023) emphasize the importance of developing and implementing standardized approaches to ensure interoperability in the supply chain domain, enabling efficient collaboration and data sharing among stakeholders.

The dynamic regulatory landscape surrounding blockchain technology presents challenges and uncertainties for businesses considering its adoption in the supply chain. Compliance with existing regulations, data privacy laws, and legal implications related to the use of blockchain can pose barriers to implementation. To address these concerns, collaborative efforts between industry participants and regulators are essential. Such efforts can facilitate the establishment of clear guidelines and frameworks that address the regulatory and legal considerations associated with blockchain implementation in the supply chain. Karisma and Tehrani (2023) emphasize the importance of dialogue and cooperation between stakeholders to navigate the regulatory landscape and ensure compliant and successful integration of blockchain technology in the supply chain industry. The introduction of blockchain technology in the supply chain can be met with resistance from existing stakeholders, particularly intermediaries or middlemen who may perceive it as a disruptive force that could diminish their role or potentially render them obsolete. To overcome this resistance, effective communication and engagement with all stakeholders are crucial. It is important to address their concerns, clarify misconceptions, and demonstrate the benefits that blockchain can bring to the supply chain ecosystem. By highlighting the potential efficiencies, transparency, and cost savings that blockchain technology offers, organizations can foster support and cooperation from existing stakeholders. Jang et al. (2023) stress the significance of open and transparent communication to overcome resistance and gain the necessary buy-in for the successful adoption of blockchain in the supply chain.

The scalability and performance limitations of blockchain networks, particularly public blockchains, can pose challenges in high-volume supply chains that require real-time processing and swift transaction settlements. The processing capacity of traditional blockchain systems may not be sufficient to handle a large number of transactions effectively. To address these limitations, it is essential to explore scalable solutions and alternative blockchain architectures. This may involve the development of new technologies or the adoption of private or consortium blockchains that offer enhanced scalability and performance. By leveraging these approaches, supply chain participants can ensure that the blockchain network can handle the transaction volume and meet the performance requirements of their operations. Pabitha et al. (2023) highlight the importance of considering scalability solutions to optimize the application of blockchain in supply chain management. Building trust among supply chain participants and establishing effective governance models are critical aspects of implementing blockchain technology. While blockchain is designed to provide decentralized consensus and cryptographic security, trust in the system and its participants needs to be established. Mechanisms should be developed to verify the authenticity and credibility of participants in the supply chain network. Additionally, frameworks for addressing disputes and establishing rules for consensus and decision-making should be in place to ensure smooth operations and effective governance. These mechanisms play a vital role in creating a trusted and secure environment for all participants involved. Chen et al. (2022) emphasize the significance of trust-building and robust governance structures to maximize the benefits of blockchain technology in the supply chain.

Figure 13. Future approach of blockchain
(Awan et al., 2021)

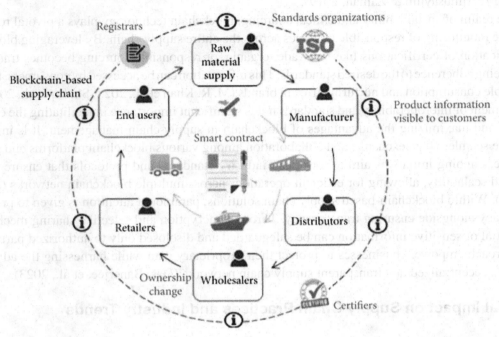

FUTURE TRENDS AND IMPLICATIONS

Emerging Developments and Advancements in Blockchain for Supply Chain Management

Blockchain technology provides enhanced traceability in the supply chain by recording all transactions and movements on a distributed ledger. This end-to-end traceability allows participants to have a transparent view of the product's journey, from raw materials to the end consumer. The ability to verify authenticity, identify bottlenecks or delays, and address recalls or quality issues quickly are facilitated through this feature. By leveraging blockchain technology, supply chain participants can improve visibility and accountability throughout the supply chain (Tao et al., 2023). Additionally, blockchain-based supply chain financing platforms are emerging, offering more efficient financing options for businesses. Leveraging the immutability and transparency of blockchain, these platforms enable lenders to validate transactions, track goods, and manage risk more effectively. By providing a secure and transparent platform for financial transactions, blockchain facilitates smoother and more efficient supply chain financing processes (Tao et al., 2023).

The application of this technology contributes to the enhancement of liquidity, mitigation of fraudulent activities, and reduction of expenses associated with conventional financing methods (Xiao et al., 2023). Integration of the IoT: The amalgamation of blockchain and IoT devices holds the potential to amplify supply chain transparency and automation. By leveraging IoT devices such as sensors and RFID tags, real-time data regarding the status, location, and quality of goods can be gathered. This data can be securely stored on the blockchain, establishing an immutable record and empowering stakeholders to make well-informed decisions based on precise and current information (Xue et al., 2022; Alshammari et al., 2017; Almusaylim & Zaman, 2019).

In the realm of sustainability and ethical sourcing, blockchain technology plays a pivotal role in enabling the monitoring of responsible practices across the entire supply chain. By leveraging blockchain, the verification of certifications like fair trade, organic, or responsible sourcing becomes transparent, guaranteeing adherence to the desired standards. This information can be accessed by consumers, fostering responsible consumption and nurturing trust in brands (M. R. Khan et al., 2023; Shafiq et al., 2019). The establishment of interoperability and standards holds significant importance in facilitating the extensive adoption and maximizing the advantages of blockchain in supply chain management. It is imperative to achieve seamless data exchange and collaboration among various blockchain platforms and systems. Therefore, ongoing initiatives aim to formulate industry standards and protocols that ensure compatibility and scalability, allowing for efficient operations across multiple blockchain networks (Kotey et al., 2023). Within blockchain-based supply chain solutions, paramount attention is given to preserving data privacy alongside ensuring transparency. Through encryption and selective sharing mechanisms, confidential or sensitive information can be safeguarded and disclosed only to authorized participants. This approach empowers businesses to protect their proprietary data while harnessing the advantages offered by decentralized and transparent supply chain networks (Das, Banerjee, et al., 2023).

Potential Impact on Supply Chain Practices and Industry Trends

In this section, we explore the potential influence of blockchain technology on supply chain practices and industry trends. Blockchain, as a decentralized and unalterable digital ledger, holds the promise of revolutionizing supply chains by augmenting transparency, traceability, efficiency, and security. This report delves into the crucial applications of blockchain in supply chains, delves into its potential advantages and challenges, and scrutinizes emerging industry trends that can be shaped by this transformative technology.

Enhanced transparency and traceability represent notable advantages brought about by blockchain technology. Through the establishment of a decentralized and unalterable ledger, transactions and data can be securely recorded. Consequently, the supply chain benefits from heightened transparency and traceability. Each transaction or event, such as the movement of goods, changes in ownership, and quality inspections, can be diligently recorded on the blockchain. This transparency aids in identifying bottlenecks, pinpointing inefficiencies, and mitigating risks associated with counterfeit products or unauthorized alterations (R. Gupta & Shankar, 2023). Blockchain technology contributes to improved efficiency within the supply chain by offering real-time visibility into the movement of goods. This facilitates the streamlining of supply chain operations by reducing the reliance on manual record-keeping, paperwork, and data reconciliation among various stakeholders. Through the implementation of automated smart contracts on the blockchain, predefined actions can be automatically executed when specific conditions are met. This automation expedites processes such as payment settlements, order fulfilment, and inventory management (X. Chen et al., 2022). Blockchain technology fosters improved trust and security within supply chain transactions through its decentralized nature and cryptographic techniques. The immutability of blockchain records mitigates the risk of data manipulation or tampering. Smart contracts play a pivotal role in establishing trust between parties by automating the enforcement of agreements based on predetermined rules. Moreover, blockchain can verify the authenticity and provenance of products, effectively reducing counterfeiting and bolstering consumer confidence (Han et al., 2023).

Figure 14. Blockchain supply chain network
(Hader et al., 2020)

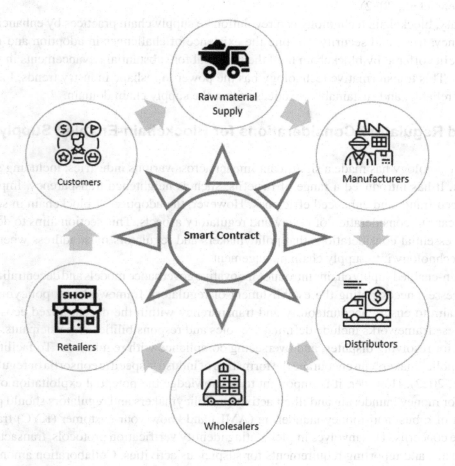

Blockchain technology enables efficient inventory management through real-time tracking and monitoring. With each product transition or change in location, the corresponding transaction can be recorded on the blockchain, ensuring instantaneous updates to inventory data. This real-time visibility facilitates improved demand forecasting, optimized inventory levels, and minimizes occurrences of stockouts or overstocks. Furthermore, smart contracts can automate inventory replenishment based on predefined triggers, ensuring timely restocking and minimizing disruptions within the supply chain (X. Li, 2023c). Blockchain technology simplifies supplier onboarding and management processes by streamlining the storage of supplier information, certifications, and compliance records. These crucial details can be securely stored on the blockchain, offering a transparent and auditable view. Consequently, supplier qualification procedures can be expedited, paperwork can be minimized, and compliance with regulatory requirements and sustainability standards can be ensured (Lee et al., 2023). Blockchain-based systems contribute to supply chain finance and payment optimization by enabling faster and more secure cross-border transactions, thereby minimizing the reliance on intermediaries and associated fees. Through the implementation of smart contracts, payment processes can be automated, with payments triggered once predetermined conditions, such as successful delivery or quality inspection, are met. This automation helps to reduce payment disputes, enhance cash flow, and foster improved financial liquidity for businesses (L. Deng et al., 2022).

In summary, blockchain technology can revolutionize supply chain practices by enhancing transparency, efficiency, trust, and security. Despite the existence of challenges in adoption and implementation, the benefits offered by blockchain hold the potential for substantial advancements in supply chain management. This transformative technology has the power to reshape industry trends, fostering more streamlined, reliable, and sustainable practices within the supply chain domain.

Policy and Regulatory Considerations for Blockchain-Enabled Supply Chains

Blockchain technology has made a significant impact across various industries, including supply chain management. It has introduced a range of benefits, such as heightened transparency, improved traceability, reduced fraud, and enhanced efficiency. However, the adoption of blockchain in supply chains necessitates careful consideration of policy and regulatory aspects. This section aims to delve into and examine the essential considerations that policymakers and regulators must address when integrating blockchain technology into supply chain management.

Blockchain-enabled supply chains introduce innovative governance models and decentralized decision-making processes, necessitating the establishment of regulatory frameworks by policymakers. These frameworks aim to ensure accountability and transparency within the decentralized ecosystems. Key aspects of these frameworks include defining the roles and responsibilities of participants, establishing mechanisms for resolving disputes, and overseeing compliance with regulations. To facilitate effective governance, policymakers can encourage the formation of industry-specific consortia or regulatory bodies (Y. Liu et al., 2022). However, it is important to acknowledge the potential exploitation of blockchain technology for money laundering and illicit activities. Policymakers and regulators should prioritize the development of robust anti-money laundering (AML) and know-your-customer (KYC) frameworks to address these concerns. This involves implementing identity verification protocols, transaction monitoring mechanisms, and reporting requirements for suspicious activities. Collaboration among regulatory authorities, financial institutions, and blockchain solution providers is crucial for the development and implementation of effective AML and KYC measures (Van Vliet, 2023).

Within blockchain-enabled supply chains, the sharing and transfer of intellectual property (IP)-related information is integral. To safeguard IP rights within these decentralized systems, policymakers must establish unambiguous regulations. Implementing measures such as digital rights management, patent protection, and licensing frameworks becomes crucial to guarantee that innovators and creators receive fair recognition and rewards for their contributions (Okunade et al., 2023). The computational power required by blockchain technology, particularly in energy-intensive consensus mechanisms like proof-of-work, has notable environmental consequences. Policymakers should actively promote the adoption of energy-efficient consensus mechanisms or explore alternative approaches to mitigate the environmental impact of blockchain-enabled supply chains. This could involve incentivizing the adoption of greener practices and developing regulatory frameworks that encourage sustainable behaviour within the blockchain industry (Quayson et al., 2023). The integration of blockchain technology into supply chain management presents substantial advantages, but it necessitates thoughtful deliberation of policy and regulatory elements. Policymakers and regulators hold a pivotal position in creating an advantageous ecosystem that fosters innovation, safeguards stakeholders' interests, ensures adherence to legal frameworks, and tackles emerging issues. By addressing the essential considerations delineated in this report, policymakers can effectively unleash the complete potential of blockchain-enabled supply chains. Simultaneously, they can mitigate risks and cultivate trust in these transformative systems.

CONCLUSION

In summary, blockchain technology can bring about a transformative shift in supply chain management, effectively tackling the significant challenges and inefficiencies encountered in traditional systems. This paper has thoroughly examined the diverse applications, advantages, and characteristics of blockchain in the context of supply chains, while also acknowledging the obstacles and limitations that must be addressed. The importance of blockchain technology in supply chain management cannot be emphasized enough. By harnessing the decentralized and transparent nature of blockchain, organizations can attain unparalleled levels of transparency and traceability in their supply chains. The immutable nature of blockchain records plays a crucial role in guaranteeing the authenticity and origin of products, effectively minimizing the occurrences of counterfeiting and fraudulent activities. Moreover, the incorporation of smart contracts brings about streamlined transaction and settlement procedures, eliminating the need for intermediaries and resulting in cost reduction. An essential benefit of implementing blockchain in supply chains is the heightened visibility and accountability it offers. By leveraging real-time tracking and monitoring capabilities, organizations can gain comprehensive insights into their inventory management, supplier partnerships, and quality control procedures. This not only enhances operational efficiency but also facilitates proactive decision-making and expedites problem resolution. Current blockchain-enabled supply chain platforms and collaborative networks have effectively showcased the practicality and achievements of integrating blockchain in real-world settings. Through various case studies, the favourable outcomes of blockchain implementation in domains such as product provenance, inventory management, supplier verification, and compliance have been highlighted. These examples serve as inspiration and benchmarks for organizations seeking to adopt blockchain technology within their supply chains. Nevertheless, it is crucial to recognize the hurdles and limitations associated with blockchain implementation. Challenges encompass scalability and performance issues, interoperability and standardization obstacles, as well as concerns regarding data privacy and security. Addressing these challenges requires meticulous deliberation and the development of innovative solutions.

In addition, the resistance to change and barriers to adoption from stakeholders present substantial challenges that must be addressed to facilitate the widespread adoption of blockchain in supply chains. However, the future outlook for blockchain in supply chain management is highly promising. Ongoing advancements and innovations in blockchain technology, including the integration of IoT devices and artificial intelligence, hold great potential for further enhancing supply chain practices (A. Khan et al., 2020; Humayun, Zaman, & Alamri, 2020). These developments are expected to bring about improved efficiency, increased automation, and enhanced decision-making capabilities within supply chain operationsFurthermore, these advancements have the potential to optimize processes, facilitate real-time data sharing, and enable predictive analytics, resulting in more efficient and responsive supply chains. However, it is essential to recognize that policy and regulatory considerations play a vital role in the successful integration of blockchain-enabled supply chains. Governments and industry bodies must collaborate to establish frameworks that effectively address legal and compliance issues, promote standardization across the industry, and protect data privacy. By establishing clear guidelines and regulations, policymakers can provide a conducive environment for the adoption and implementation of blockchain technology in supply chain management while safeguarding the interests of stakeholders. In conclusion, blockchain technology presents a transformative solution to address the challenges encountered in supply chain management. By harnessing the inherent features of blockchain, organizations can attain heightened levels of transparency, traceability, trust, and efficiency within their supply chains. Although there are hurdles to overcome, the potential benefits are too substantial to overlook. It is imperative for organizations to actively explore and embrace blockchain technology as they strive for more resilient, secure, and efficient supply chains in the future. Through proactive adoption, organizations can position themselves at the forefront of innovation and gain a competitive edge in the evolving landscape of supply chain management.

REFERENCES

Abed, S., Jaffal, R., & Mohd, B. J. (2023). A Review on Blockchain and IoT Integration from Energy, Security and Hardware Perspectives. *Wireless Personal Communications*, *129*(3), 2079–2122. doi:10.1007/s11277-023-10226-5

Agrawal, T. K., Angelis, J., Khilji, W. A., Kalaiarasan, R., & Wiktorsson, M. (2022). Demonstration of a blockchain-based framework using smart contracts for supply chain collaboration. *International Journal of Production Research*, *61*(5), 1497–1516. doi:10.1080/00207543.2022.2039413

Akella, G. K., Wibowo, S., Grandhi, S., & Mubarak, S. (2023). A Systematic Review of Blockchain Technology Adoption Barriers and Enablers for Smart and Sustainable Agriculture. *Big Data and Cognitive Computing*, *7*(2), 86. doi:10.3390/bdcc7020086

Al-Khatib, A. W. (2022). Internet of things, big data analytics and operational performance: The mediating effect of supply chain visibility. *Journal of Manufacturing Technology Management*, *34*(1), 1–24. doi:10.1108/JMTM-08-2022-0310

Al-Sumaidaee, G., Alkhudary, R., Zilic, Z., & Swidan, A. (2023). Performance analysis of a private blockchain network built on Hyperledger Fabric for healthcare. *Information Processing & Management*, *60*(2), 103160. doi:10.1016/j.ipm.2022.103160

Alamsyah, A., Widiyanesti, S., Wulansari, P., Nurhazizah, E., Dewi, A. S., Rahadian, D., Ramadhani, D. P., Hakim, M. N., & Tyasamesi, P. (2023). Blockchain traceability model in the coffee industry. *Journal of Open Innovation*, *9*(1), 100008. doi:10.1016/j.joitmc.2023.100008

Ali, I., Zaman, N., Amsaad, F., & Razaque, A. (2022). The Role of Cutting-Edge Technologies in Industry 4.0. Chapman and Hall/CRC eBooks. doi:10.1201/9781003203087-4

Alkhodair, A., Mohanty, S. P., & Kougianos, E. (2023). FlexiChain 3.0: Distributed Ledger Technology-Based Intelligent Transportation for Vehicular Digital Asset Exchange in Smart Cities. *Sensors (Basel)*, *23*(8), 4114. doi:10.3390/s23084114 PMID:37112453

Allenbrand, C. (2023). Smart contract-enabled consortium blockchains for the control of supply chain information distortion. *Blockchain: Research and Applications*, *100134*(3), 100134. doi:10.1016/j.bcra.2023.100134

Almusaylim, Z. A., & Zaman, N. (2019). A review on smart home present state and challenges: Linked to context-awareness internet of things (IoT). *Wireless Networks*, 25(6), 3193–3204. doi:10.1007/s11276-018-1712-5

Alqarni, M. A., Alkatheiri, M. S., Chauhdary, S. H., & Saleem, S. (2023). Use of Blockchain-Based Smart Contracts in Logistics and Supply Chains. *Electronics (Basel)*, 12(6), 1340. doi:10.3390/electronics12061340

Alshammari, M. O., Almulhem, A. A., & Zaman, N. (2017). Internet of Things (IoT) : Charity Automation. *International Journal of Advanced Computer Science and Applications*, 8(2). Advance online publication. doi:10.14569/IJACSA.2017.080222

Alshudukhi, K. S., Khemakhem, M., Eassa, F. E., & Jambi, K. M. (2023). An Interoperable Blockchain Security Frameworks Based on Microservices and Smart Contract in IoT Environment. *Electronics (Basel)*, 12(3), 776. doi:10.3390/electronics12030776

Ashraf, H., Hanif, M., Ihsan, U., Al-Quayed, F., Humayun, M., & Jhanjhi, N. (2023). *A Secure and Reliable Supply chain management approach integrated with IoT and Blockchain*. doi:10.1109/ICBATS57792.2023.10111371

Assiri, M., & Humayun, M. (2023). A Blockchain-Enabled Framework for Improving the Software Audit Process. *Applied Sciences (Basel, Switzerland)*, 13(6), 3437. doi:10.3390/app13063437

Aste, T., Tasca, P., & Di Matteo, T. (2017). Blockchain Technologies: The Foreseeable Impact on Society and Industry. *Computer*, 50(9), 18–28. doi:10.1109/MC.2017.3571064

Awan, S. H., Ahmed, S., Ullah, F., Nawaz, A., Khan, A. J., Uddin, M. N., Alharbi, A. G., Alosaimi, W., & Alyami, H. (2021). IoT with BlockChain: A Futuristic Approach in Agriculture and Food Supply Chain. *Wireless Communications and Mobile Computing*, 2021, 1–14. doi:10.1155/2021/5580179

Baniata, H., & Kertesz, A. (2023). Approaches to Overpower Proof-of-Work Blockchains Despite Minority. *IEEE Access : Practical Innovations, Open Solutions*, 11, 2952–2967. doi:10.1109/ACCESS.2023.3234322

Basu, P., Deb, P., & Singh, A. (2023). Blockchain and the carbon credit ecosystem: Sustainable management of the supply chain. *The Journal of Business Strategy*. doi:10.1108/JBS-09-2022-0157

BelMannoubi, S., Touati, H., Hadded, M., Toumi, K., Shagdar, O., & Kamoun, F. (2023). A Comprehensive Survey on Blockchain-Based C-ITS Applications: Classification, Challenges, and Open Issues. *Vehicular Communications*, 100607, 100607. doi:10.1016/j.vehcom.2023.100607

Bhardwaj, A., Akhil, K., Tripathi, A., & Srivastava, S. (2021). Blockchain-based solutions for supply chain management: A comprehensive review. *Computers & Industrial Engineering*, 164, 107249.

Bhatt, J. (2023a). *Use of Blockchain in Medical Supply and Pharmacy*. www.onlineengineeringeducation.com. https://doi.org/ doi:10.52783/joee.v14i1s.79

BHP. (2019). *BHP and Mitsubishi Development Pty Ltd enter into a new partnership for the future of nickel*. BHP. https://www.bhp.com/media-and-insights/news-releases/2019/07/bhp-and-mitsubishi-development-pty-ltd-enter-into-a-new-partnership-for-the-future-of-nickel/

Casino, F., Dasaklis, T. K., & Patsakis, C. (2019). A systematic literature review of blockchain-based applications: Current status, classification and open issues. *Telematics and Informatics*, *36*, 55–81. doi:10.1016/j.tele.2018.11.006

Chandan, A., Rosano, M., & Potdar, V. (2023). Achieving UN SDGs in Food Supply Chain Using Blockchain Technology. *Sustainability (Basel)*, *15*(3), 2109. doi:10.3390/su15032109

Chen, R. R., Chen, K., & Ou, C. X. (2022). Facilitating interorganizational trust in strategic alliances by leveraging blockchain-based systems: Case studies of two eastern banks. *International Journal of Information Management*, *68*, 102521. doi:10.1016/j.ijinfomgt.2022.102521

Chen, X., He, C., Chen, Y., & Xie, Z. (2022). Internet of Things (IoT)—Blockchain-enabled pharmaceutical supply chain resilience in the post-pandemic era. *Frontiers of Engineering Management*, *10*(1), 82–95. doi:10.1007/s42524-022-0233-1

Chen, Y. (2023). How blockchain adoption affects supply chain sustainability in the fashion industry: A systematic review and case studies. *International Transactions in Operational Research*, itor.13273. doi:10.1111/itor.13273

Chopra, S., & Meindl, P. (2000). *Supply Chain Management: Strategy, Planning and Operations*. NII. http://ci.nii.ac.jp/ncid/BB10149318

Choudhary, A. S. (2023). Concept of Blockchain Technology. *Analytics Vidhya*. https://www.analyticsvidhya.com/blog/2022/09/concept-of-blockchain-technology/

Christopher, M. (2016). *Logistics & Supply Chain Management*. NII. https://ci.nii.ac.jp/ncid/BB05643450

Christopher, M., & Peck, H. (2012). Building the Resilient Supply Chain. *International Journal of Logistics Management*, *15*(2), 1–14. doi:10.1108/09574090410700275

Council of Supply Chain Management Professionals (CSCMP). (2021). Supply chain management definitions. *CSCMP's Supply Chain Quarterly*. https://www.supplychainquarterly.com/topics/Strategy/20211210-supply-chain-management-definitions/

Crosby, M., Pattanayak, P., Verma, S., & Kalyanaraman, V. (2016). Blockchain technology: Beyond bitcoin. *Applied Innovation*, *2*(6-10), 71–81.

Cyrus, R. (2023). Custody, Provenance, and Reporting of Blockchain and Cryptoassets. Emerald Publishing Limited. doi:10.1108/978-1-80455-320-620221016

Dai, H., Zheng, Z., & Zhang, Y. (2019). Blockchain for Internet of Things: A Survey. *IEEE Internet of Things Journal*, *6*(5), 8076–8094. doi:10.1109/JIOT.2019.2920987

Das, D., Banerjee, S., Chatterjee, P., Ghosh, U., & Biswas, U. (2023). *Blockchain for Intelligent Transportation Systems: Applications, Challenges, and Opportunities*. IEEE. doi:10.1109/JIOT.2023.3277923

Das, D., Dasgupta, K., & Biswas, U. (2023). *A secure blockchain-enabled vehicle identity management framework for intelligent transportation systems*. Elsevier. doi:10.1016/j.compeleceng.2022.108535

David, R., Goel, P. K., & Abujamra, R. (2017). Blockchain Applications and Use Cases in Health Information Technology. *Journal of Health & Medical Informatics*, *08*(03). doi:10.4172/2157-7420.1000276

Deng, L., Li, Y., Wang, S., & Luo, J. (2022). The impact of blockchain on optimal incentive contracts for online supply chain finance. *Environmental Science and Pollution Research International*, *30*(5), 12466–12494. doi:10.1007/s11356-022-22498-8 PMID:36112286

Deng, W., Huang, T., & Wang, H. (2022). A Review of the Key Technology in a Blockchain Building Decentralized Trust Platform. *Mathematics*, *11*(1), 101. doi:10.3390/math11010101

Dias, H., & Meratnia, N. (2023). BlockLearning: A Modular Framework for Blockchain-Based Vertical Federated Learning. In Communications in computer and information science (pp. 319–333). Springer Science+Business Media. doi:10.1007/978-981-99-0272-9_22

Dietrich, F., Louw, L., & Palm, D. (2023). Blockchain-Based Traceability Architecture for Mapping Object-Related Supply Chain Events. *Sensors (Basel)*, *23*(3), 1410. doi:10.3390/s23031410 PMID:36772452

Do, T. (2023). *SoK on Blockchain Evolution and a Taxonomy for Public Blockchain Generations*. Hong Kong University of Science & Technology. doi:10.2139/ssrn.4377849

Dorri, A., Kanhere, S. S., Jurdak, R., & Gauravaram, P. (2017). *Blockchain for IoT security and privacy: The case study of a smart home*. IEEE. doi:10.1109/PERCOMW.2017.7917634

Drescher, D. (2017). *Blockchain Basics: A Non-Technical Introduction in 25 Steps*. Booktopia. https://www.booktopia.com.au/blockchain-basics-daniel-drescher/book/9781484226032.html?gclid=CjwKCAjwpayjBhAnEiwA-7ena_-4H32E_N3AOxW0nA1rhovh-VvxnfELAnk2ZF-UjQErY9kGdO1oBxoCcI0QAvD_BwE

Dyer, J. H., Singh, H., & Hesterly, W. S. (2018). The relational view revisited: A dynamic perspective on value creation and value capture. *Strategic Management Journal*, *39*(12), 3140–3162. doi:10.1002/smj.2785

Dylag, M., & Smith, H. (2021). From cryptocurrencies to cryptocourts: Blockchain and the financialization of dispute resolution platforms. *Information Communication and Society*, *26*(2), 372–387. doi:10.1080/1369118X.2021.1942958

Escobar, F., Santos, H., & Pereira, T. (2023). Blockchain in the Public Sector: An Umbrella Review of Literature. In Lecture notes in networks and systems (pp. 142–152). Springer International Publishing. doi:10.1007/978-3-031-21229-1_14

Everledger. (2022, October 12). *Main Home - Everledger*. https://everledger.io/

Fawcett, S. E., Ellram, L. M., & Ogden, J. A. (2007). *Supply chain management : from vision to implementation*. Pearson Prentice Hall eBooks. http://ci.nii.ac.jp/ncid/BA88237110

Feldman, S. (2019, May 9). *Infographic: What's Blocking Blockchain?* Statista Infographics. https://www.statista.com/chart/17948/worlwide-barriers-to-blockchain-adoption/

Fernie, J., & Sparks, L. (2014). *Logistics and Retail Management: Emerging Issues and New Challenges in the Retail Supply Chain*. NII. http://ci.nii.ac.jp/ncid/BA89825001

Gazzola, P., Pavione, E., Barge, A., & Fassio, F. (2023). Using the Transparency of Supply Chain Powered by Blockchain to Improve Sustainability Relationships with Stakeholders in the Food Sector: The Case Study of Lavazza. *Sustainability (Basel)*, *15*(10), 7884. doi:10.3390/su15107884

GEP. (n.d.). *Blockchain in Procurement & Supply Chain.* GEP. https://www.gep.com/blockchain-procurement-supply-chain

Goint, M., Bertelle, C., & Duvallet, C. (2023). Secure Access Control to Data in Off-Chain Storage in Blockchain-Based Consent Systems. *Mathematics*, *11*(7), 1592. doi:10.3390/math11071592

Guntara, N. R. G., Nurfirmansyah, N. M. N., & Ferdiansyah, N. (2023). Blockchain Implementation in E-Commerce to Improve The Security Online Transactions. *Journal of Scientific Research. Educational Technology*, *2*(1), 328–338. doi:10.58526/jsret.v2i1.85

Gupta, C., Gupta, V., & Fernandez-Crehuet, J. M. (2023). A blockchain-enabled solution to improve intra-inter organizational innovation processes in software small medium enterprises. *Engineering Reports*, *5*(7), e12674. doi:10.1002/eng2.12674

Gupta, R., & Shankar, R. (2023). Managing food security using blockchain-enabled traceability system. *Benchmarking*. doi:10.1108/BIJ-01-2022-0029

Hader, M., Elmhamedi, A., & Abouabdellah, A. (2020). *Blockchain technology in supply chain management and loyalty programs: toward blockchain implementation in retail market.* doi:10.1109/LOGISTIQUA49782.2020.9353879

Han, H., Shiwakoti, R. K., Jarvis, R., Mordi, C., & Botchie, D. (2023). Accounting and auditing with blockchain technology and artificial Intelligence: A literature review. *International Journal of Accounting Information Systems*, *48*, 100598. doi:10.1016/j.accinf.2022.100598

Hastig, G. M., & Sodhi, M. S. (2020). Blockchain for Supply Chain Traceability: Business Requirements and Critical Success Factors. *Production and Operations Management*, *29*(4), 935–954. doi:10.1111/poms.13147

HossainM. Z. (2023). Transforming Financial Reporting Practices in Bangladesh: The Benefits and Challenges of Implementing Blockchain Technology. *Social Science Research Network*. doi:10.2139/ssrn.4428469

Hu, H., Xu, J., Liu, M., & Lim, M. K. (2023). Vaccine supply chain management: An intelligent system utilizing blockchain, IoT and machine learning. *Journal of Business Research*, *156*, 113480. doi:10.1016/j.jbusres.2022.113480 PMID:36506475

Humayun, M. (2021). Industry 4.0 and Cyber Security Issues and Challenges. [TURCOMAT]. *Turkish Journal of Computer and Mathematics Education*, *12*(10), 2957–2971. doi:10.17762/turcomat.v12i10.4946

Humayun, M., Zaman, N., & Alamri, M. Z. (2020). IoT-based Secure and Energy Efficient scheme for E-health applications. *Indian Journal of Science and Technology*, *13*(28), 2833–2848. doi:10.17485/IJST/v13i28.861

Humayun, M., Zaman, N., Hamid, B., & Ahmed, G. (2020). Emerging Smart Logistics and Transportation Using IoT and Blockchain. *IEEE, 3*(2), 58–62. doi:10.1109/IOTM.0001.1900097

Humayun, M., Zaman, N., Niazi, M., Amsaad, F., & Masood, I. (2022). Securing Drug Distribution Systems from Tampering Using Blockchain. *Electronics (Basel)*, *11*(8), 1195. doi:10.3390/electronics11081195

Huynh-The, T., Gadekallu, T. R., Wang, W., Yenduri, G., Ranaweera, P., Pham, Q., Da Costa, D. B., & Liyanage, M. (2023). Blockchain for the metaverse: A Review. *Future Generation Computer Systems*, *143*, 401–419. doi:10.1016/j.future.2023.02.008

Iansiti, M., & Lakhani, K. R. (2017). The Truth about Blockchain. *Harvard Business Review*, *95*(1), 118–127. https://www.hbs.edu/faculty/Pages/item.aspx?num=52100

Iansiti, M., & Lakhani, K. R. (2017). The Truth about Blockchain. *Harvard Business Review*. https://www.hbs.edu/faculty/Pages/item.aspx?num=52100

IBM. (n.d.). *Blockchain - Enterprise Blockchain Solutions and Services*. IBM. https://www.ibm.com/blockchain

Igbekele, E. O., Aideloje, J., Adebiyi, A. A., & Adebiyi, A. (2023). Product Verification using Blockchain Technology. *Systematic Reviews*, 1–8. doi:10.1109/SEB-SDG57117.2023.10124602

Iredale, G. (2023). Public Vs Private Blockchain: Key Differences. *101 Blockchains*. https://101blockchains.com/public-vs-private-blockchain/

Islam, M. M., & In, H. P. (2023). Decentralized Global Copyright System Based on Consortium Blockchain with Proof of Authority. *IEEE Access : Practical Innovations, Open Solutions*, *1*, 43101–43115. doi:10.1109/ACCESS.2023.3270627

Jabbar, S., Lloyd, H., Hammoudeh, M., Adebisi, B., & Raza, U. (2021). Blockchain-enabled supply chain: Analysis, challenges, and future directions. *Multimedia Systems*, *27*(4), 787–806. doi:10.1007/s00530-020-00687-0

Jang, H., Yoo, J. J., & Cho, M. (2023). Resistance to blockchain adoption in the foodservice industry: Moderating roles of public pressures and climate change awareness. *International Journal of Contemporary Hospitality Management*. doi:10.1108/IJCHM-09-2022-1127

Jebamikyous, H., Li, M., Suhas, Y., & Kashef, R. (2023). Leveraging machine learning and blockchain in E-commerce and beyond: Benefits, models, and application. *Discover Artificial Intelligence*, *3*(1), 3. doi:10.1007/s44163-022-00046-0

Joo, M., Kim, S. U., Ghose, A., & Wilbur, K. C. (2022). Designing Distributed Ledger technologies, like Blockchain, for advertising markets. *International Journal of Research in Marketing*, *40*(1), 12–21. doi:10.1016/j.ijresmar.2022.08.004

Julie, E. G., Nayahi, J. J. V., & Jhanjhi, N. Z. (2020). *Blockchain Technology: Fundamentals, Applications, and Case Studies*. CRC Press.

Jum'a, L. (2023). The role of blockchain-enabled supply chain applications in improving supply chain performance: The case of Jordanian manufacturing sector. *Management Research Review*, *46*(10), 1315–1333. doi:10.1108/MRR-04-2022-0298

Juma, M., AlAttar, F., & Touqan, B. (2023). Securing Big Data Integrity for Industrial IoT in Smart Manufacturing Based on the Trusted Consortium Blockchain (TCB). *Iot*, *4*(1), 27–55. doi:10.3390/iot4010002

Karisma, K., & Tehrani, P. M. (2023). Blockchain Adoption in the Energy Sector: A Comprehensive Regulatory Readiness Assessment Framework to Assess the Regulatory Readiness Levels of Countries. In Lecture notes in networks and systems (pp. 454–460). Springer International Publishing. doi:10.1007/978-3-031-21229-1_42

Kashem, M. A., Shamsuddoha, M., Nasir, T., & Chowdhury, A. A. (2023). Supply Chain Disruption versus Optimization: A Review on Artificial Intelligence and Blockchain. *Knowledge (Beverly Hills, Calif.)*, *3*(1), 80–96. doi:10.3390/knowledge3010007

Khan, A., Zaman, N., Humayun, M., & Ahmad, M. (2020). The Role of IoT in Digital Governance. In IGI Global eBooks (pp. 128–150). IGI Global. doi:10.4018/978-1-7998-1851-9.ch007

Khan, A. A., Bourouis, S., Kamruzzaman, M. M., Hadjouni, M., Shaikh, Z. A., Laghari, A. A., Elmannai, H., & Dhahbi, S. (2023). Data Security in Healthcare Industrial Internet of Things with Blockchain. *IEEE Sensors Journal*, *1*(20), 25144–25151. doi:10.1109/JSEN.2023.3273851

Khan, M. I., Zaman, S. A., & Khan, S. A. (2023). Relationship and Impact of Block Chain Technology and Supply Chain Management on Inventory Management. In *Management for professionals* (pp. 53–74). Springer Nature., doi:10.1007/978-981-99-0699-4_4

Khan, M. R., Khan, M. R., & Nallaluthan, K. (2023). Blockchain Supply Chain Management and Supply Chain Sustainability. In *Management for professionals* (pp. 155–180). Springer Nature., doi:10.1007/978-981-99-0699-4_10

Khan, A., Jhanjh, N. Z., & R, S. (2022). *Emerging Industry Revolution IR 4.0 Issues and Challenge* (1st ed.). Taylor & Francis. https://www.taylorfrancis.com/chapters/edit/10.1201/9781003203087-7/emerging-industry-revolution-ir-4-0-issues-challenges-azeem-khan-noor-zaman-jhanjhi-sujatha

Khedekar, V. B., Hiremath, S. R., Sonawane, P. D., & Rajput, D. S. (2022). Protection to Personal Data Using Decentralizing Privacy of Blockchain. In IGI Global eBooks (pp. 570–587). doi:10.4018/978-1-6684-7132-6.ch032

Kordestani, A., Oghazi, P., & Mostaghel, R. (2023). Smart contract diffusion in the pharmaceutical blockchain: The battle of counterfeit drugs. *Journal of Business Research*, *158*, 113646. doi:10.1016/j.jbusres.2023.113646

Kosba, A., Miller, A., Shi, E., Wen, Z., & Papamanthou, C. (2016). Hawk: The Blockchain Model of Cryptography and Privacy-Preserving Smart Contracts. *Proceedings of the 2016 ACM SIGSAC Conference on Computer and Communications Security,* (pp. 839-851). ACM. 10.1109/SP.2016.55

Kotey, S. D., Tchao, E. T., Ahmed, A., Agbemenu, A. S., Nunoo-Mensah, H., Sikora, A., Welte, D., & Keelson, E. (2023). Blockchain interoperability: The state of heterogenous blockchain-to-blockchain communication. *IET Communications*, *17*(8), 891–914. doi:10.1049/cmu2.12594

Kouhizadeh, M., & Sarkis, J. (2018). Blockchain Practices, Potentials, and Perspectives in Greening Supply Chains. *Sustainability (Basel)*, *10*(10), 3652. doi:10.3390/su10103652

Krishnan, L. P., Vakilinia, I., Reddivari, S., & Ahuja, S. (2023). Scams and Solutions in Cryptocurrencies—A Survey Analyzing Existing Machine Learning Models. *Information (Basel)*, *14*(3), 171. doi:10.3390/info14030171

Kumar, A. (n.d.). *Blockchain in Supply Chain*. LinkedIn. https://www.linkedin.com/pulse/blockchain-supply-chain-aditya-kumar/

Kumar, M. S., Vimal, S., Zaman, N., Sundar, D. S., & Alhumyani, H. (2021). Blockchain based peer to peer communication in autonomous drone operation. *Energy Reports*, *7*, 7925–7939. doi:10.1016/j. egyr.2021.08.073

Lacity, M. C., Yan, A., & Willcocks, L. P. (2022). Robotic process automation and smart contracts: A comparison of design characteristics. *Journal of Management Information Systems*, *39*(1), 292–331.

Lambert, D. M. (2010). Supply Chain Management – Processes, Partnerships, Performance. In Gabler eBooks (pp. 553–572). doi:10.1007/978-3-8349-6515-8_29

Lee, D., Wen, L., Choi, J. O., & Lee, S. (2023). Sensor-Integrated Hybrid Blockchain System for Supply Chain Coordination in Volumetric Modular Construction. *Journal of Construction Engineering and Management*, *149*(1), 04022147. doi:10.1061/(ASCE)CO.1943-7862.0002427

Li, C., Wang, L. S., & Yang, H. (2022). The optimal asset trading settlement based on Proof-of-Stake blockchains. *Decision Support Systems*, *166*, 113909. doi:10.1016/j.dss.2022.113909

Li, D., Han, D., Crespi, N., Minerva, R., & Li, K. (2022). A blockchain-based secure storage and access control scheme for supply chain finance. *The Journal of Supercomputing*, *79*(1), 109–138. doi:10.1007/s11227-022-04655-5

Li, L., Wang, Z., Chen, L., Zhao, X., & Yang, S. (2023). Supply chain collaboration and supply chain finance adoption: The moderating role of information transparency and transaction dependence. *Supply Chain Management*, *28*(4), 710–723. doi:10.1108/SCM-04-2022-0169

Li, X. (2023). Inventory management and information sharing based on blockchain technology. *Computers & Industrial Engineering*, *179*, 109196. doi:10.1016/j.cie.2023.109196

Li, X. (2023c). Inventory management and information sharing based on blockchain technology. *Computers & Industrial Engineering*, *179*, 109196. doi:10.1016/j.cie.2023.109196

Liu, H., Han, S., & Zhu, Z. (2023). Blockchain Technology toward Smart Construction: Review and Future Directions. *Journal of Construction Engineering and Management*, *149*(3), 03123002. doi:10.1061/JCEMD4.COENG-11929

Liu, Y., Lu, Q., Zhu, L., Paik, H., & Staples, M. (2022). A systematic literature review on blockchain governance. *Journal of Systems and Software*, *197*, 111576. doi:10.1016/j.jss.2022.111576

Marthews, A., & Tucker, C. (2022). What blockchain can and can't do: Applications to marketing and privacy. *International Journal of Research in Marketing*, *40*(1), 49–53. doi:10.1016/j.ijresmar.2022.09.001

Mehta, M., Khurana, A., & Kumar, V. R. (2023). *Leveraging Blockchain Technology for Improving the Quality of Corporate Governance*. IEEE. doi:10.1109/ISCON57294.2023.10112178

Meisami, S., Meisami, S., Yousefi, M., & Aref, M. R. (2023). Combining Blockchain and IoT for Decentralized Healthcare Data Management. *International Journal of Cryptography and Information Security*, *13*(1), 35–50. doi:10.5121/ijcis.2023.13102

Mentzer, J. T., Moon, M. A., & Dwyer, F. R. (2016). Creating a sustainable competitive advantage through sales and operations planning. *Journal of Business Logistics*, *37*(1), 6–18. doi:10.1111/jbl.12117

Mentzer, J. T., Stank, T. P., & Esper, T. L. (2015). Supply chain management and its relationship to logistics, marketing, production, and operations management. *Journal of Business Logistics*, *36*(1), 1–7. doi:10.1002/j.2158-1592.2008.tb00067.x

Modak, S. K. S. (2023). Application of Blockchain in Supply Chain Management. *International Journal for Multidisciplinary Research*, *5*(2), 2216. doi:10.36948/ijfmr.2023.v05i02.2216

Munasinghe, U. J., & Halgamuge, M. N. (2023). Supply chain traceability and counterfeit detection of COVID-19 vaccines using novel blockchain-based Vacledger system. *Expert Systems with Applications*, *228*, 120293. doi:10.1016/j.eswa.2023.120293 PMID:37197005

Murray-Rust, D., Elsden, C., Nissen, B., Tallyn, E., Pschetz, L., & Speed, C. (2022). Blockchain and Beyond: Understanding Blockchains Through Prototypes and Public Engagement. *ACM Transactions on Computer-Human Interaction*, *29*(5), 1–73. doi:10.1145/3503462

Namasudra, S., & Akkaya, K. (2023). Introduction to Blockchain Technology. In *Studies in big data* (pp. 1–28). Springer International Publishing. doi:10.1007/978-981-19-8730-4_1

Naoum-Sawaya, J., Elhedhli, S., & De Carvalho, P. (2023). Strategic Blockchain Adoption to Deter Deceptive Counterfeiters. *European Journal of Operational Research*, *311*(1), 373–386. doi:10.1016/j.ejor.2023.04.031

Naraindath, N. R., Bansal, R. C., & Naidoo, R. (2023). The Uprising of Blockchain Technology in the Energy Market Industry. In Lecture notes in electrical engineering (pp. 497–509). Springer Science+Business Media. doi:10.1007/978-981-19-7993-4_41

Nawab, F., & Sadoghi, M. (2023). Consensus in Data Management: From Distributed Commit to Blockchain. *Foundations and Trends in Databases*, *12*(4), 221–364. doi:10.1561/1900000075

Negi, S. (2022). Improving Supply Chain Management Performance with Blockchain Technology. In Springer eBooks (pp. 327–344). doi:10.1007/978-3-031-10507-4_14

Ohood, M. A., Mohammed, A. A., Mehedi, M., & Jhanjhi, N. (2021). A Survey of Blockchain and E-governance applications: Security and Privacy. *ProQuest, 12*(1), 3126–3134. https://www.proquest.com/openview/79c4f3046c069f6c83d1acb8f32ef91a/1?pq-origsite=gscholar&cbl=2045096

Okunade, S. O., Alimi, A. S., & Olayiwola, A. S. (2023). Intellectual property rights protection and prospect of industrial development in Nigeria. *International Journal of Intellectual Property Management*, *13*(1), 78. doi:10.1504/IJIPM.2023.129079

Pabitha, P., Jayabal, C. P., Ramalingam, P., & Jagatheswari, S. (2023). ModChain: A hybridized secure and scaling blockchain framework for IoT environment. *International Journal of Information Technology : an Official Journal of Bharati Vidyapeeth's Institute of Computer Applications and Management*, *15*(3), 1741–1754. doi:10.1007/s41870-023-01218-6

Pacheco, M., Oliva, G. A., Rajbahadur, G. K., & Hassan, A. E. (2023). What makes Ethereum blockchain transactions be processed fast or slow? An empirical study. *Empirical Software Engineering*, *28*(2), 39. doi:10.1007/s10664-022-10283-7 PMID:36776918

Panghal, A., Manoram, S., Mor, R. S., & Vern, P. (2022). Adoption challenges of blockchain technology for reverse logistics in the food processing industry. *Supply Chain Forum: An International Journal*, *24*(1), 7–16. 10.1080/16258312.2022.2090852

Peregrina-Pérez, M. J., Lagares-Galán, J., & Boubeta-Puig, J. (2023). Hyperledger Fabric blockchain platform. In Elsevier eBooks (pp. 283–295). Elesvier. doi:10.1016/B978-0-323-96146-2.00014-0

Prabhakar, V. V., Xavier, C. B., & Abubeker, K. (2023). A Review on Challenges and Solutions in the Implementation of Ai, IoT and Blockchain in Construction Industry. *Materials Today: Proceedings*. doi:10.1016/j.matpr.2023.03.535

Quayson, M., Bai, C., Sun, L., & Sarkis, J. (2023). Building blockchain-driven dynamic capabilities for developing circular supply chain: Rethinking the role of sensing, seizing, and reconfiguring. *Business Strategy and the Environment*, *32*(7), 4821–4840. doi:10.1002/bse.3395

RamzanM. S.AsgharA.UllahA.JhanjiN. Z.AlsolamiF.AhmadI. (2022). Enhanced Artificial Bee Colony Based Optimization for Mitigating Replication in Large Data for Internet of Things (Iot). SSRN. doi:10.2139/ssrn.4281666

Ravi, N., & Verma, S. (1979). Kavita, Zaman, N., & Talib, M. N. (2021). Securing VANET Using Blockchain Technology. *Journal of Physics*, *012035*(1). doi:10.1088/1742-6596/1979/1/012035

Raza, S. A. (2021). A systematic literature review of RFID in supply chain management. *Journal of Enterprise Information Management*, *35*(2), 617–649. doi:10.1108/JEIM-08-2020-0322

Review, H. B., Tapscott, D., Iansiti, M., & Lakhani, K. R. (2019). *Blockchain: The Insights You Need from Harvard Business Review*. Harvard Business Press.

Riadi, M. (2021, September 14). Supply Chain Management (SCM). *Literature review*. https://www.kajianpustaka.com/2017/08/supply-chain-management-scm.html

Rožman, N., Corn, M., Škulj, G., Berlec, T., Diaci, J., & Podržaj, P. (2023). Exploring the Effects of Blockchain Scalability Limitations on Performance and User Behavior in Blockchain-Based Shared Manufacturing Systems: An Experimental Approach. *Applied Sciences (Basel, Switzerland)*, *13*(7), 4251. doi:10.3390/app13074251

Saeed, S., Almuhaideb, A. M., Kumar, N., Zaman, N., & Zikria, Y. B. (2022). *Handbook of Research on Cybersecurity Issues and Challenges for Business and FinTech Applications*. IGI Global. doi:10.4018/978-1-6684-5284-4

Sarfaraz, A., Chakrabortty, R. K., & Essam, D. (2022). The implications of blockchain-coordinated information sharing within a supply chain: A simulation study. *Blockchain: Research and Applications*, *4*(1), 100110. doi:10.1016/j.bcra.2022.100110

Sargent, C. S., & Breese, J. L. (2023). Blockchain Barriers in Supply Chain: A Literature Review. *Journal of Computer Information Systems*, 1–12. doi:10.1080/08874417.2023.2175338

Schäfer, N. (2022). Making transparency transparent: a systematic literature review to define and frame supply chain transparency in the context of sustainability. *Management Review Quarterly*. doi:10.1007/s11301-021-00252-7

Seth, S. (2022). Public, Private, Permissioned Blockchains Compared. *Investopedia*. https://www.investopedia.com/news/public-private-permissioned-blockchains-compared/

Setyowati, M. S., Utami, N. W., Saragih, A. H., & Hendrawan, A. (2023). Strategic factors in implementing blockchain technology in Indonesia's value-added tax system. *Technology in Society*, *72*, 102169. doi:10.1016/j.techsoc.2022.102169

Shafiq, D. A., Zaman, N., & Abdullah, A. (2019). Proposing A Load Balancing Algorithm For The Optimization Of Cloud. *Computer Applications (Nottingham)*, 1–6. doi:10.1109/MACS48846.2019.9024785

Sharma, H. (2023, March 30). *Towards A Sustainable and Ethical Supply Chain Management: The Potential of IoT Solutions*. arXiv.org. https://arxiv.org/abs/2303.18135

Silva, F. J. F. (2023, February 23). *A volatilidade das criptomoedas: Os casos da Polygon, Solana, Bit-Torrent Token e VeChain*. https://repositorio.uac.pt/handle/10400.3/6715

Simchi-Levi, D., Kaminsky, P., & Simchi-Levi, E. (2017). *Designing and managing the supply chain : concepts, strategies, and case studies*. McGraw-Hill eBooks. http://perpustakaan.ithb.ac.id/index.php?p=show_detail&id=7926

Singh, A. P., Pradhan, N. R., Luhach, A. K., Agnihotri, S., Zaman, N., & Verma, S. (2021). A Novel Patient-Centric Architectural Framework for Blockchain-Enabled Healthcare Applications. *IEEE Transactions on Industrial Informatics*, *17*(8), 5779–5789. doi:10.1109/TII.2020.3037889

Singh, O. (2022, November 26). *How blockchain technology is used in supply chain management?* Cointelegraph. https://cointelegraph.com/explained/how-blockchain-technology-is-used-in-supply-chain-management

Solistica. (n.d.). *Blockchain in supply chain [Infographics]*. Solistica. https://blog.solistica.com/en/blockchain-in-supply-chain-infographics

Soria, J., Moya, J., & Mohazab, A. (2022). Optimal mining in proof-of-work blockchain protocols. *Finance Research Letters*, *103610*. doi:10.1016/j.frl.2022.103610

SquarepantsS. (2008). Bitcoin: A Peer-to-Peer Electronic Cash System. *Social Science Research Network*. doi:10.2139/ssrn.3977007

Srinivas, N. T. S., Donald, N. D., Srihith, N. I. D., Anjali, N. D., & Chandana, N. A. (2023). The Rise of Secure IoT: How Blockchain is Enhancing IoT Security. *International Journal of Advanced Research in Science. Tongxin Jishu*, 32–40. doi:10.48175/IJARSCT-9006

Srinivasan, K., & Mukhopadhyay, S. K. (2019). Performance analysis of a JIT-based two-echelon inventory system with correlated demands. *International Journal of Production Research*, 57(6), 1766–1783.

Srivastava, P. R., Zhang, Z., & Eachempati, P. (2021). Blockchain technology and its applications in agriculture and supply chain management: A retrospective overview and analysis. *Enterprise Information Systems*, 17(5), 1995783. doi:10.1080/17517575.2021.1995783

Sujatha, R., Prakash, G., & Jhanjhi, N. Z. (2022). *Cyber Security Applications for Industry 4.0*. CRC Press. doi:10.1201/9781003203087

Suliyanti, W. N. (2023). *Blockchain-Based Double-Layer Byzantine Fault Tolerance for Scalability Enhancement for Building Information Modeling Information Exchange*. MDPI. doi:10.3390/bdcc7020090

Supply chain insight: Inside IBM's Food Trust Blockchain system. (2020, May 17). Supply Chain Magazine. https://supplychaindigital.com/technology/supply-chain-insight-inside-ibms-food-trust-blockchain-system

Swan, M. (2015). *Blockchain: Blueprint for a New Economy*. CDS. http://cds.cern.ch/record/2000805

Swan, M. (2015). *Blockchain: Blueprint for a New Economy*. CDS. http://cds.cern.ch/record/2000805

Swan, M. (2015). *Blockchain: Blueprint for a New Economy*. O'Reilly Media.

Taghipour, A. (2021). *Digitalization of Decentralized Supply Chains During Global Crises*. IGI Global.

Taherdoost, H. (2023). Smart Contracts in Blockchain Technology: A Critical Review. *Information (Basel)*, 14(2), 117. doi:10.3390/info14020117

Tan, C. L., Tei, Z., Yeo, S. F., Lai, K., Kumar, A., & Chung, L. (2022). Nexus among blockchain visibility, supply chain integration and supply chain performance in the digital transformation era. *Industrial Management & Data Systems*, 123(1), 229–252. doi:10.1108/IMDS-12-2021-0784

Tanvir, D. H., Amin, R., Islam, A., Islam, M. S., & Rashid, M. M. (2023). Blockchain Interoperability for A Reputation-Based Drug. *Supply Chain Management*, 1–6. doi:10.1109/ISCON57294.2023.10112196

Tao, Q., Chen, X., & Cui, X. (2022). A technological quality control system for rice supply chain. *Food and Energy Security*. doi:10.1002/fes3.382

Tao, X., Das, M., Zheng, C., Liu, Y., Wong, P. K., Xu, Y., Liu, H., Gong, X., & Cheng, J. C. (2023). Enhancing BIM security in emergency construction projects using lightweight blockchain-as-a-service. *Automation in Construction*, 150, 104846. doi:10.1016/j.autcon.2023.104846 PMID:37035753

Tapscott, D., & Tapscott, A. (2016). *Blockchain Revolution: How the Technology Behind Bitcoin Is Changing Money, Business, and the World*. Open Library. https://openlibrary.org/books/OL27212411M/Blockchain_revolution

Tapscott, D., & Tapscott, A. (2016). *Blockchain revolution: How the technology behind bitcoin is changing money, business, and the world*. Penguin.

Tavana, M., Nasr, A. K., Ahmadabadi, A. B., Amiri, A. S., & Mina, H. (2023). An interval multi-criteria decision-making model for evaluating blockchain-IoT technology in supply chain networks. *Internet of Things : Engineering Cyber Physical Human Systems*, *22*, 100786. doi:10.1016/j.iot.2023.100786

Thakur, A. (2023). Market trends and analysis of blockchain technology in supply chain. *Frontiers in Blockchain*, *6*, 1142599. doi:10.3389/fbloc.2023.1142599

Thangamayan, S., Pradhan, K., Loganathan, G. B., Sitender, S., Sivamani, S., & Tesema, M. (2023). Blockchain-Based Secure Traceable Scheme for Food Supply Chain. *Journal of Food Quality*, *2023*, 1–11. doi:10.1155/2023/4728840

Theeraworawit, M., Suriyankietkaew, S., & Hallinger, P. (2022). Sustainable Supply Chain Management in a Circular Economy: A Bibliometric Review. *Sustainability (Basel)*, *14*(15), 9304. doi:10.3390/su14159304

Tokkozhina, U., Martins, A. L., & Ferreira, J. C. (2023). Multi-tier supply chain behavior with blockchain technology: evidence from a frozen fish supply chain. *Operations Management Research*. doi:10.1007/s12063-023-00377-w

Trueman, C. (2022, November 30). *IBM, Maersk scuttle blockchain-based TradeLens supply chain platform*. Computerworld. https://www.computerworld.com/article/3681098/ibm-maersk-scuttle-blockchain-based-tradelens-supply-chain-platform.html

Turki, M., Cheikhrouhou, S., Dammak, B., Baklouti, M., Mars, R., & Dhahbi, A. (2023). NFT-IoT Pharma Chain : IoT Drug traceability system based on Blockchain and Non Fungible Tokens (NFTs). *Journal of King Saud University. Computer and Information Sciences*, *35*(2), 527–543. doi:10.1016/j.jksuci.2022.12.016

Ullah, F., & Al-Turjman, F. (2021). A conceptual framework for blockchain smart contract adoption to manage real estate deals in smart cities. *Neural Computing & Applications*, *35*(7), 5033–5054. doi:10.1007/s00521-021-05800-6

Uma, S. (2023). Blockchain and AI: Disruptive Digital Technologies in Designing the Potential Growth of Healthcare Industries. In Advanced technologies and societal change (pp. 137–150). Springer Nature. doi:10.1007/978-981-99-0377-1_9

Valdivia, A. D. (2023). Between decentralization and reintermediation: Blockchain platforms and the governance of 'commons-led' and 'business-led' energy transitions. *Energy Research & Social Science*, *98*, 103034. doi:10.1016/j.erss.2023.103034

Van VlietB. (2023). Cryptocurrency Anti-Money Laundering (AML) and Know-Your-Customer (KYC) Management System Standard—Requirements. *Social Science Research Network*. doi:10.2139/ssrn.4403529

Vidal, F. R. (2023, March 25). *OpenSCV: An Open Hierarchical Taxonomy for Smart Contract Vulnerabilities*. arXiv.org. https://arxiv.org/abs/2303.14523

Viswanadham, Y. V. R. S., & Jayavel, K. (2023). A Framework for Data Privacy Preserving in Supply Chain Management Using Hybrid Meta-Heuristic Algorithm with Ethereum Blockchain Technology. *Electronics (Basel)*, *12*(6), 1404. doi:10.3390/electronics12061404

Wang, M., Zhu, T., Zuo, X., Yang, M., Yu, S., & Zhou, W. (2023). Differentially private crowdsourcing with the public and private blockchain. *IEEE Internet of Things Journal*, *10*(10), 8918–8930. doi:10.1109/JIOT.2022.3233360

WangZ.LiuS.WangP.ZhangL. (2023). BW-PBFT: Practical Byzantine Fault Tolerance Consensus Algorithm Based on Credit Bidirectionally Waning. Research Square *(Research Square)*. doi:10.21203/rs.3.rs-2900100/v1

Wang, Z., Ren, Y., Cao, Z., & Zhang, L. (2023). LRBFT: Improvement of practical Byzantine fault tolerance consensus protocol for blockchains based on Lagrange interpolation. *Peer-to-Peer Networking and Applications*, *16*(2), 690–708. doi:10.1007/s12083-022-01431-3

Wendl, M., Doan, M. H., & Sassen, R. (2023). The environmental impact of cryptocurrencies using proof of work and proof of stake consensus algorithms: A systematic review. *Journal of Environmental Management*, *326*, 116530. doi:10.1016/j.jenvman.2022.116530 PMID:36372031

Wenhua, Z., Qamar, F., Abdali, T. N., Hassan, R., Jafri, S. T. A., & Nguyen, Q. N. (2023). Blockchain Technology: Security Issues, Healthcare Applications, Challenges and Future Trends. *Electronics (Basel)*, *12*(3), 546. doi:10.3390/electronics12030546

Wenhua, Z., Qamar, F., Abdali, T. N., Hassan, R., Jafri, S. T. A., & Nguyen, Q. N. (2023). Blockchain Technology: Security Issues, Healthcare Applications, Challenges and Future Trends. *Electronics (Basel)*, *12*(3), 546. doi:10.3390/electronics12030546

Wieland, A., & Wallenburg, C. M. (2012). Dealing with supply chain risks. *International Journal of Physical Distribution & Logistics Management*, *42*(10), 887–905. doi:10.1108/09600031211281411

Wu, H., Jiang, S., & Cao, J. (2023). High-Efficiency Blockchain-Based Supply Chain Traceability. *IEEE Transactions on Intelligent Transportation Systems*, *24*(4), 3748–3758. doi:10.1109/TITS.2022.3205445

Xiao, P., Salleh, M. I., Zaidan, B., & Xuelan, Y. (2023). Research on risk assessment of blockchain-driven supply chain finance: A systematic review. *Computers & Industrial Engineering*, *176*, 108990. doi:10.1016/j.cie.2023.108990

Xu, J., Lou, J., Lu, W., Wu, L., & Chen, C. (2023). Ensuring construction material provenance using Internet of Things and blockchain: Learning from the food industry. *Journal of Industrial Information Integration*, *33*, 100455. doi:10.1016/j.jii.2023.100455

Xu, J., Wang, C., & Jia, X. (2023). A Survey of Blockchain Consensus Protocols. *ACM Computing Surveys*, *55*(13s), 1–35. doi:10.1145/3579845

Xu, X., Tian, N., Gao, H., Lei, H., Liu, Z., & Liu, Z. (2023). *A Survey on Application of Blockchain Technology in Drug Supply Chain Management*. doi:10.1109/ICBDA57405.2023.10104779

Xue, H., Chen, D., Zhang, N., Dai, H., & Yu, K. (2022). Integration of blockchain and edge computing in internet of things: A survey. *Future Generation Computer Systems*, *144*, 307–326. doi:10.1016/j.future.2022.10.029

Yadav, A. K., Singh, K., Amin, A., Almutairi, L., Alsenani, T. R., & Ahmadian, A. (2023). A comparative study on consensus mechanism with security threats and future scopes: Blockchain. *Computer Communications*, *201*, 102–115. doi:10.1016/j.comcom.2023.01.018

Yli-Huumo, J., Ko, D., Choi, S., Park, S., & Smolander, K. (2016). Where Is Current Research on Blockchain Technology?—A Systematic Review. *PLoS One*, *11*(10), e0163477. doi:10.1371/journal.pone.0163477 PMID:27695049

Zhang, C., Gong, Y., & Brown, S. (2023). *Blockchain Applications in Food Supply Chain Management: Case Studies and Implications*. Springer Nature.

Zhang, M., & Chen, W. (2021). Blockchain technology for improving the transparency and traceability of supply chain management. *Computers & Industrial Engineering*, *155*, 107222. doi:10.1016/j.cie.2021.107222

Zhang, P., Schmidt, D. C., White, J., & Lenz, G. (2019). Blockchain Technology Use Cases in Healthcare. In *Advances in Computers* (pp. 1–41). Elsevier BV. doi:10.1016/bs.adcom.2018.03.006

Zhang, R., Xu, C., & Xie, M. (2022). Secure Decentralized IoT Service Platform Using Consortium Blockchain. *Sensors (Basel)*, *22*(21), 8186. doi:10.3390/s22218186 PMID:36365884

Zhang, Y., Xu, C., Lin, X., & Shen, X. (2021). Blockchain-Based Public Integrity Verification for Cloud Storage against Procrastinating Auditors. *IEEE Transactions on Cloud Computing*, *9*(3), 923–937. doi:10.1109/TCC.2019.2908400

Zhao, M. (2023, January 1). Safe and Efficient Delegated Proof of Stake Consensus Mechanism Based on Dynamic Credit in Electronic Transaction. *Journal of Internet Technology*. https://jit.ndhu.edu.tw/article/view/2845

Zheng, Z., Xie, S., Dai, H., Chen, X., & Wang, H. (2017). *An Overview of Blockchain Technology: Architecture*. Consensus, and Future Trends., doi:10.1109/BigDataCongress.2017.85

Zieglmeier, V., Daiqui, G. L., & Pretschner, A. (2023). *Decentralized Inverse Transparency With Blockchain*. Digital Library. doi:10.1145/3592624

Chapter 10
The Internet of Things (IoT) Applications in Inventory Management Through Supply Chain

Yesim Deniz Ozkan-Ozen
Yasar University, Turkey

ABSTRACT

Supply chains are affected by globalization and digitalization, and organizations face a great challenge in order to stay up-to date and competitive. As a very significant element of the supply chains, inventory management plays a crucial role in supply chain success. Therefore, traditional approaches in inventory management should be altered according to new trends. From this point of view, this study focuses on Internet of Things (IoT) applications in inventory management with a scope of supply chains. The aim of this chapter is to analyze the current studies related to IoT impacts in inventory management by conducting a literature review and a bibliometric analysis, and propose the future research directions that are interrelated with the current trends.

1. INTRODUCTION

Globalization and digitalization through the supply chains affect all the stakeholders and processes, and organizations face a great challenge in order to stay up-to date and competitive. As a very important element of the supply chains, inventory management plays a critical role in terms enterprises success. Inventory management is an important part of the supply chains in terms of planning, implementing, and controlling both forward and reverse flow of any kind of inventory (i.e. raw materials, work in process products, finished goods, spare parts etc.) between stakeholders and processes (Singh and Verma, 2017). Although, high amount of inventory holding is considered as waste, and organizations aim to minimize it; inventory management has a crucial role for increasing predictability in production scheduling and capacity planning, it helps to deal with unexpected changes in demand, it is useful for price protection, it

DOI: 10.4018/978-1-6684-7625-3.ch010

may provide quantity discounts or lower ordering costs, and it can be served as a protection mechanism against unreliable supplies (Muller, 2019).

Inventory accuracy and process management are essential to achieve smooth inbound and outbound logistics, which are directly related with inventory management (Lee et al., 2018). However, traditional inventory management approaches are not sufficient to deal with the complexity of the current markets, high product diversity, and customer-centric approaches. Therefore, current inventory management practices should be altered according to the new requirements and expectations caused by digitalization. Businesses are leveraging past data related to demand and sales to apply smart inventory management systems as data has become more abundant and data processing tools have improved (Zohra et al., 2021). As a result of digitalization and information technology, demand and inventory data can now be shared quickly and easily across firms in the supply chain inventory management process.

Internet of Things (IoT) is one of a technology that is highly associate with the current digital trends, and refers to "interconnection of computing devices embedded in physical objects to gather and save information without the requirement for human interaction" (Birkel and Hartmann, 2020, p.537). However, it has a longer history, and firstly introduced in 1999 by Kevin Ashton (Li et al., 2015). Ashton (2009) stated defined IoT as: "we need to empower computers with their own means of gathering information, so they can see, hear and smell the world for themselves. RFID and sensor technology enable computers to observe, identify and understand the world—without the limitations of human-entered data" (Evtodive et al., 2019, p. 397). Different technologies such as wireless sensor networks, RFID, barcodes, intelligent sensors, low energy wireless communications are involved in IoT, therefore, it defines the next generation of the internet technologies (Li et al., 2015).

IoT applications play a crucial role in today's supply chains in terms of achieving operational efficiency as well as integrated supply chain structures. IoT enables supply chain management to make machine-enabled decision making without human interaction, which also integrates ICT technologies such as RFID, machine-to machine systems and wireless sensor networks to improve the operational processes (Zhou et al., 2015). Furthermore, IoT empowers supply chains to deal with uncertainties caused by global competition and adoptability problems by providing continuous monitoring, remote control of equipment and processes, minimizing any kind of wastes by processes and stakeholder integrations (Manavalan and Jayakrishna, 2019)

Under the supply chain processes, Ben-Daya et al. (2019) summarized the impacts of IoT on inventory management as providing inventory accuracy, enabling real-time visibility in inventory levels, avoiding inventory misplacement by using RFID tags. Furthermore, employing IoT increases the responsiveness in terms of changing inventory levels according to changes in demand, and avoids shortages in production lines by increasing the traceability of inventory (Mashayekhy et al., 2022). Explicitly, IoT can decrease inventory costs as well as the bullwhip effect crosswise the supply chain (Mostafa et al., 2019).

The proposed book chapter aims to analyze the current studies related to IoT impacts in inventory management with a special focus on supply chains by conducting a literature review and a bibliometric analysis, and propose the future research directions that are interrelated with the current trends. With this chapter, the author wishes to contribute the production, supply chain, and logistics fields by presenting a detailed review related to IoT and inventory management.

This chapter is organized as follows; after the introduction section a literature review related to IoT in inventory management is presented under the supply chain perspective. In the third section, survey methodology is presented. Fourth section includes the bibliometric analysis for the selected field and discussions related to results. Fifth section includes conclusion part.

2. LITERATURE REVIEW ON INTERNET OF THINGS IN INVENTORY MANAGEMENT THROUGH SUPPLY CHAIN

As the initial step of this chapter, a general literature review is conducted without database restriction to reveal the studies that are directly related to IoT in inventory management. Various studies have been reached, however the ones who solely connected to this chapter are selected and analyzed deeply. To summarize the studies that are focused in this chapter, Table 1 is created.

Table 1. Summary of the literature review

Author(s)	Subject Area/Sector	Methodology	Type of Paper	Findings/ Aim
Liu and Sun (2011)	Vendor-managed inventory management	Review	Conference Paper	Analyzing information flow model of vendor-managed inventory in IoT environment.
Fan et al. (2015)	Supply chains	Case study	Journal Article	Investigating effects of RFID technology on supply chain decisions with inventory inaccuracies.
Zhang et al. (2016)	Warehousing companies	Decision support system proposal	Conference Paper	Proposing an inventory management system for warehousing companies
Wang et al. (2018)	Supply chains	Immune genetic algorithm.	Journal Article	investigating multi-echelon inventory cost control of IoT based supply chains
Paul et al. (2019)	Customer service	Inventory optimization	Journal Article	Presenting IoT based intelligent inventory management system
Wang et al. (2019)	Supply chain finance business	Peak Over Threshold model	Conference Paper	Measuring the operational risk of the inventory pledge financing model based IoT
Ekren et al. (2021)	E-grocery networks	Simulation optimization	Journal Article	Investigating lateral inventory share-based business models for e-grocery network in IoT environment
Maheshwari et al. (2021)	Micro, Small, and Medium Enterprises and perishable inventory management	Fractional program method	Journal Article	Optimizing IoT implementation in MSMEs' inventory management systems
Ran (2021)	Supply chain	Genetic Algorithm	Journal Article	Optimizing supply chains by increasing the efficiency of inventory management
Bose et al. (2022)	Construction sector	Computer based architecture proposal	Journal Article	Designing an IoT based smart inventory system for construction sector
El Jaouhari et al. (2022)	Green warehouse	Fuzzy Inference System	Journal Article	Investigating the applications of IoT in green warehouse management systems
Mashayekhy et al. (2022)	Supply chains	Literature Review	Journal Article	Presenting the impact of IoT on inventory management in supply chains
Papanagnou (2022)	Closed-loop supply chains	Stochastic state-space model	Journal Article	Analyzing impact of the IoT on inventory variance and the bullwhip effect in closed loop supply chains
Smitha and Aslekar (2022)	Retail sector	Literature Review	Conference Paper	Presenting a review on IoT in inventory management
Bader et al. (2023)	Pharmaceutical Inventory Management	Structural equation modeling	Journal Article	Investigating impacts of IoT on pharmaceutical inventory management

To start with one of an early study, Liu and Sun (2011) published a paper related to information management in in vendor managed inventory, with a special focus on IoT. This study especially has significant output in terms of analyzing information flow control of vendor managed inventory in IoT environment. Another relatively early study was conducted by Fan et al. (2015). Under inventory management, they paid attention to inventory accuracies in supply chain decisions, and investigated the impact of RFID technologies, which is a key element of IoT.

Zhang et al. (2016) proposed system for inventory management, which integrates self-adaptive distribution support model and RFID technology. They also validated their model with a simulation experiment, and concluded that their proposed model has the ability to increase efficiency by 10%, when it is compared to current procedures. Furthermore, Wang et al. (2018) considered the topic from a different angle and focused on inventory costs in an IoT based supply chains that includes multiple distributes, manufacturers and suppliers. They used immune genetic algorithm to minimize the inventory costs, and their results showed the decrease in the costs.

Another different area was selected by Paul et al. (2019), and they focused on customer service stage in the supply chains. An IoT based supply chain simulation platform, which includes warehouse management systems related to customer service items such as smart shopping charts or smart shelves was built by the authors. At the end of the study, they suggested that the proposed model supplies a cost reduction, when it is compared to current systems in the marketplaces. Wang et al. (2019) approached the subject from supply chain financial risks perspectives. They designed an inventory pledged financing model based on IoT to measure the operational risks, and concluded that their model decreased the operational risks.

Ran (2021) presented a study related to supply chain competitiveness in terms of managing inventory in an efficient way in the IoT environment. Multiple analysis related to supply and demand relationships with a scope of inventory management were made by the author. At the end of the study, an inventory management system that includes cloud edge collaborative computing is constructed. On the other hand, Papanagnou (2022) proposed an IoT based model to measure and eliminate the bullwhip effect in closed loop supply chains. The result of the study showed that IoT is able to decrease costs related to inventory variations and overcome bullwhip effect in closed loop supply chains.

When it is moved to more sectoral studies, Ekren et al. (2021) worked on IoT enabled e-commerce for sustainable food supply chains with a special attention on lateral inventory share. They aimed to minimize food wastes and back orders in food supply chains by the application of lateral inventory share policies in strategic alliances. The result of their simulation approach in e-groceries showed an improvement in efficiency compared to traditional systems. Similarly, Maheshwari et al. (2021) studied on perishable inventory management systems and conducted and implementation in micro, small and medium enterprises in food retailing sector. They aimed to optimize IoT applications in inventory management for micro, small and medium enterprises, and proposed a model which was tested in two case studies. They concluded that there is a positive correlation between reduced inventory costs, improved perishability performance and IoT adoption.

In addition to sectoral studies, Bose et al. (2022) made a research for construction sector, and designed an IoT based smart inventory management system. They also integrated cloud computing to their model that aims to manage inventory of necessary form work shuttering products. Furthermore, El Jaouhari et al. (2022) focused on IoT applications in green warehouse inventory management system. They conducted a case study in automotive semi-conductor firm, where integration of IoT to achieve green and sustainable inventory management in warehousing is presented. Smitha and Aslekar (2022) also conducted a sectoral study, and investigated IoT impacts on inventory management practices in retail industry.

A similar research to this chapter was conducted by Mashayekhy et al. (2022), which made a literature review on impacts of IoT on inventory management. They reviewed 55 articles from Springer, Science Direct and Emerald, and made sectoral analysis as well as general structure of the studies. They also provided research ideas for future studies.

A very recent research was published by Bader et al. in 2023, which focuses on impacts of IoT on pharmaceutical inventory management. They conducted a survey in Jordan, and applied structural equation modelling, and concluded that all aspects of IoT has an impact on inventory management, however employee training is essential for successful applications.

This part of the chapter aimed to present a brief review related to the subject area. In the following section details of the methodology is explained.

3. METHODOLOGY

This part of the chapter explains the methodology of the research. Literature review and bibliometric analysis is combined as the research methodology. An approach, which has 6 stages, is followed by the researcher, which is presented in Figure 1.

Figure 1. Research methodology

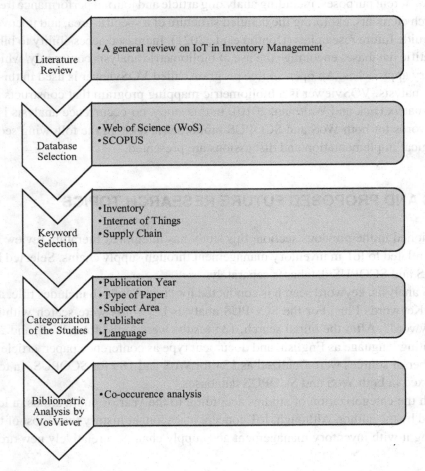

The research flow starts with a detailed literature review related to IoT in inventory management. At this stage, author has not limited the databases and aimed to focus on studies that directly reflect the area. A summary of the review is presented as a table that includes the sectoral information (if applicable), method of the study, type of the study and main aim.

The second stage includes the database selection for bibliometric analysis. Availability of the scientific databases is increasing rapidly, which results in high volumes of bibliometric data. In this study, two well-known and highly accepted databases, SCOPUS and Web of Science (WoS) are selected. Separate analysis is conducted in order to reveal the similarities and differences, also mutual studies are also identified.

The third stage of the methodology is the keyword selection. To avoid missing important studies, and to be as much inclusive as possible keywords are selected as: *internet of things*, *inventory* and *supply chain*. With these keywords, concepts including inventory management, inventory control, supply chain management, supply chain design, industrial internet of things etc., and abbreviations such as IoT, SCM etc. are included.

The following stage is the categorization of the selected studies. This categorization is made based on publication year, type of the paper subject are and the publisher. Separate analysis is conducted for WoS and SCOPUS results.

Finally, this study uses bibliometric analysis for analyzing current trends in the field of IoT applications in inventory management with a scope of supply chains. Bibliographic analysis is used by researchers for different purposes, including analyzing article and journal performance trends, associated patterns, research elements, exploring the detailed structure of a specific area, and uncovering emerging approaches to guide future researches (Donthu et al., 2021). Increased accessibility to bibliometric software, and scientific databases encourage the use of bibliometric analysis commonly, which also enables inter-disciplinary approaches. An open source program called VOSviewer is used in this study to make co-occurrence analysis. VOSviewer is a bibliometric mapping program that constructs maps based on co-occurrence matrix (Eck and Waltman, 2010). In this study, co-occurrence analysis is conducted for the author keywords for both WoS and SCOPUS bibliometric data. In the following section, results of the methodological implementation and discussions are presented.

4. RESULTS AND PROPOSED FUTURE RESEARCH TOPICS

As it was mentioned in the previous section, this study has integrated literature review and the bibliometric analysis related to IoT in inventory management through supply chains. Selected keywords were searched in WoS and SCOPUS databases separately.

For the WoS analysis, keyword search is conducted for "topic", which includes title, abstract, author keywords, and Keywords Plus. For the SCOPUS analysis keywords were search within "article title, abstract and keyword". After the initial search, 135 results were found from WoS, and 201 from SCOPUS. After limiting language as English, and document type as conference paper, article, book chapter, and book; number of sources were finalized as 134 for WoS and 189 for SCOPUS. In total 84 of these studies are indexed in both WoS and SCOPUS databases.

To start with the categorization of studies according to the year of publications, a lower range has not been defined by the author. Although, IoT concept has a longer history than most of the digital concepts, integrating it with inventory management and supply chain is a relatively new area. In Figure 2, distribution of studies between 2006 to February 2023 is presented. As it can be seen from the graph, number of studies started climbing dramatically after 2011, which is the year of introducing Industry 4.0 or Fourth Industrial Revolution officially. IoT became an indispensable technology for Industry 4.0 and application areas are not limited to computer science or manufacturing, but extended to different sectors. The number of studies reflect this popularity as well. However, a decrease in the number of studies is appeared for both databases in 2020, which can ben the result of COVID-19 impact.

*Figure 2. Yearly Publications in Wos and Scopus (*time range for 2023 is limited to 15th of February, 2023)*

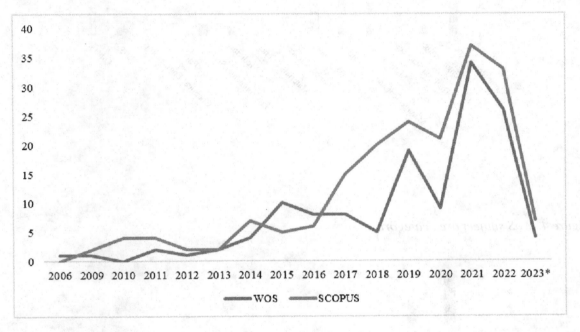

Another categorization for studies was made for the subject areas. Both databases use different names for subject categorization. SCOPUS subject area categorization (Figure 3), and WoS Subject are categorization (Figure 4) in the below figures. The key difference between databases subject categorization is reveal as the order of computer science and engineering areas. Furthermore, in WoS categorization, operation research management science appears as an individual area and locates in the third place. On the other hand, in SCOPUS categorization mathematics field is in the third place. For both of the databases, "other" topics include the areas that has 5 or less then studies.

Figure 3. SCOPUS subject area categorization

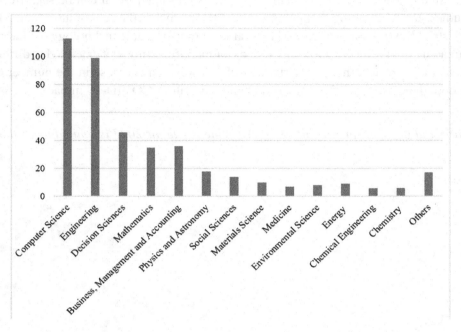

Figure 4. WoS subject area categorization

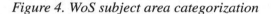

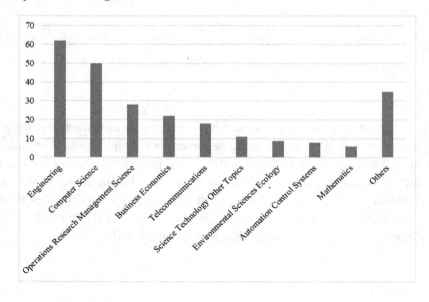

Results of the subject area categorization reveals the gap in the fields of especially social sciences, including business administration and finance. Majority of the current studies are under computers science and engineering, which shows the attention of technical aspects of IoT in inventory management and supply chains. On the other hand, focusing on managerial approaches and the social aspects of IoT in inventory management in supply chains can be suggested as future research ideas. Furthermore, topics including sustainability, circular economy, reverse logistics as well as environmental issues regarding inventory management are also promising fields. The social, environmental and economic impacts of inventory management in supply chains might be affected positively by IoT applications.

Another categorization is made for type of studies for this chapter. Only articles, proceeding papers/conference papers, book chapters and books were considered. Results of the analysis is presented in Figure 5.

Figure 5. Type of studies for WoS and SCOPUS

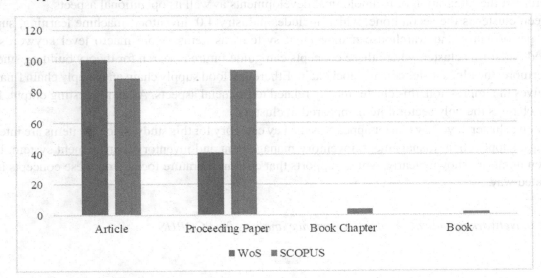

Results showed that majority of the studies were articles and proceeding papers, and under SCOPUS only 4 book chapters and 2 books appeared. In terms of type of studies, the current literature can be diversified by publishing more books or book chapters on IoT in inventory management.

As it was mentioned in the methodology section, a bibliometric analysis is conducted by using VOSviewer software. VOSviewer is an open source software that provides graphical representations of the bibliometric data. VOSviewer analyses data from bibliometric database files, where both WoS and SCOPUS databases provides these datasets with different formats (i.e. txt files for WoS, csv for SCOPUS). Although, there are 84 studies that are indexed in both WoS and SCOPUS, separate analysis was conducted in VOSviewer to represent the cluster and item similarities and differences in co-occurrence maps.

Network visualization is used in this chapter to present co-occurrence analysis of the keywords. In network visualization, items are represented by labels and frames. And size of the labels and frames varies according to weight of the item, and they are connected to each other to show the links between item. Furthermore, each color represents a cluster, and these clusters can be used as themes or groups, which is useful for categorization.

In this study, co-occurrence analysis is conducted by focusing on keywords for WoS and SCOPUS datasets. Minimum number of occurrences for items is limited to 2 in order to reveal maximum amount of links and keywords in the field. Also, bibliographic coupling for sources is conducted for SCOPUS. Due to limited number of studies, other analysis including co-authorship, citation and co-citations were not includes, since they did not give useful outputs.

Results of the co-occurrence analysis of SCOPUS studies is presented in Figure 6. In total 22 items are revealed under 4 clusters after necessary eliminations. Clusters are limited to at least 4 items under them. Each of the cluster has different color, and as it can be seen from the figure, internet of things has the biggest size. When the clusters are analyzed separately, red cluster is created as cluster 1, and includes big data, cloud computing, logistics, RFID, security, sensors and smart manufacturing. These items reflect the integration of technological developments as well as operational aspects.

Green cluster is the second one, which includes industry 4.0, inventory, machine learning, supply chain, performance and warehouse management systems as items. More macro level keywords are grouped under this cluster, where these concepts can guide future research for theory building studies. Furthermore, the blue cluster consist blockchain, Ethereum, food supply chain and supply chain finance. As it gives the impression, this cluster mostly related to financial aspects. As an interesting output, food supply chain is the only sectoral item appeared in clusters.

Finally, cluster 4, yellow cluster appears as the key category for this study, since the items are internet of things, supply chain management, inventory management and inventory management system. Link between items are shown clearly, which supports that current literature focuses on these concepts in an integrated way.

Figure 6. Network visualization of co-occurrence analysis for SCOPUS

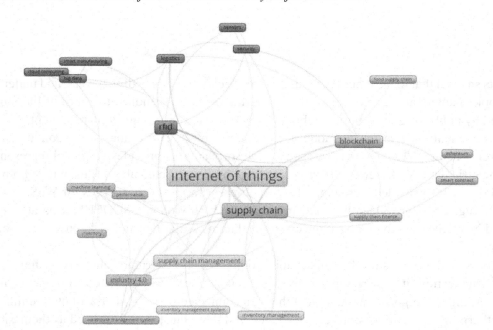

Although the number of studies in WoS is lower than the SCOPUS, co-occurrence analysis for WoS includes more items. In total 40 items are grouped under 5 clusters for WoS analysis. Network visualization of co-occurrence analysis of WoS is presented in Figure 7.

Figure 7. Network visualization of co-occurrence analysis for WoS

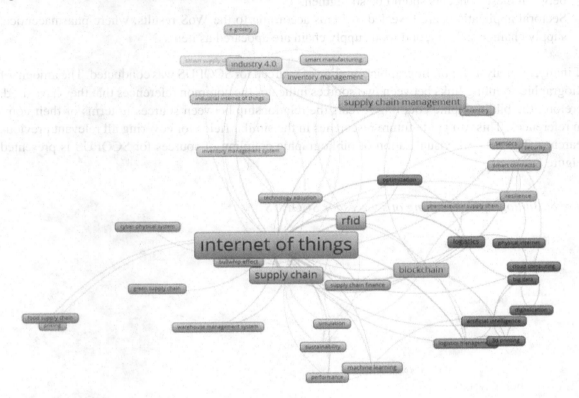

According to the results of the analysis red cluster includes 3D printing, artificial intelligence, big data, cloud computing, digitalization, logistics, logistics management, optimization and physical internet. This cluster is similar to the red cluster of SCOPUSs. Including 3D printing and artificial intelligence is critical for this analysis since they were neglected in the previous one. On the other hand, green cluster includes blockchain, pharmaceutical supply chain, privacy, resilience, security, sensors, smart contracts and supply chain management. Blue cluster includes machine learning, bullwhip effect, performance, RFID, simulation, supply chain, sustainability, technology adoption and warehouse management system. Moreover, yellow cluster covered e-grocery, industrial internet of things, inventory management, inventory management system, smart manufacturing and smart supply chain. Finally, purple cluster has cyber physical system, food supply chain, green supply chain, internet of things, pricing and supply chain finance.

The main differences in WoS and SCOPUS analysis can be summarized as follows:

- Clusters and items in SCOPUS analysis are mainly based on digital technologies, on the other hand WoS results includes approaches such as technology adoption, resilience, optimization2, bullwhip effect etc.
- WoS results includes key items as sustainability and green logistics. The gap in knowledge related to sustainability integration to IoT in inventory management was revealed previously and the link between these concepts should be strengthen.
- Sectoral applications are revealed as items according to the WoS results, where pharmaceutical supply chain, e-grocery, and food supply chain are appeared as items.

Finally, an analysis for bibliographic coupling of sourced for SCOPUS was conducted. The amount of bibliographic coupling links between two sources indicates the common references that they have used. Therefore, the bibliographic coupling reveals the relationship between sources in terms of their common references. This can guide future researches in the similar fields for covering all relevant previous researches. The network visualization of bibliographic coupling of sources for SCOPUS is presented in Figure 8.

Figure 8. Bibliographic coupling of sources for SCOPUS

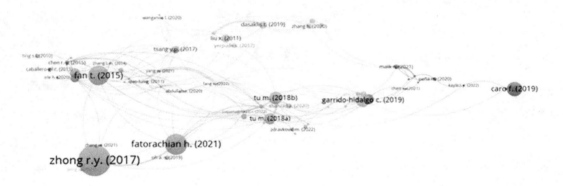

According to the results of the bibliometric analysis, although there are valuable studies in the field, some areas are still promising. With this view, five different themes are proposed in this study for future research ideas. Proposed research themes are visualized in Figure 9.

Figure 9. Proposed research themes for IoT in inventory management

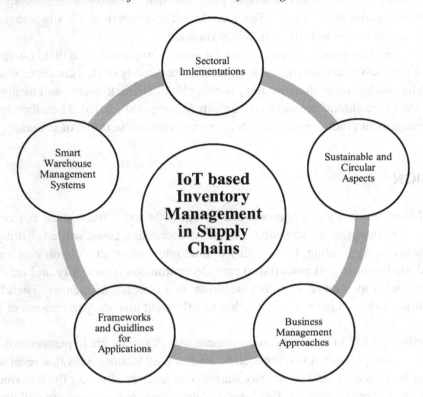

According to the figure, the first research theme is presented as *sectoral implementations*. Mashayekhy et al. (2022) summarized some of the sectoral implementation of IoT in inventory management by presenting different industries, namely, spare parts, agricultural products, food industry, pharmaceutical industry, retailing and people with disabilities. However, current studies are limited in terms of sectoral implementations, which is supported by the results of the bibliometric analysis. Therefore, to extend the applications of IoT in inventory management, sectoral comparisons can be conducted to achieve best practices as well as know-how transfers.

The second research theme is suggested as *sustainable and circular aspects* of IoT in inventory management. IoT rises as a capable technology for green, sustainable and circular approaches (Jauhari et al., 2022). Future studies can be focused on revealing the potentials of IoT in inventory management to achieve sustainable and circular supply chain practices. Continuous monitoring and tracing capability of IoT can be useful for eliminating wastes and preventing unnecessary inventories, and greening the supply chains.

As it was revealed previously, managerial implementations and social science perspective studies are limited in the current literature. Therefore, business management approaches are presented as another research theme. Operation management perspective that covers the entire organization and stakeholders is essential to sustain applications of IoT in inventory management activities. Therefore, future studies can focus on managerial side of the transitions as well as issues related to workforce.

Clear guidelines and frameworks are essential for the adoption of IoT through the supply chains, and all stakeholders and participants should be considered (Ben-Daya et al., 2019). As in line with this view, results show that there is a shortage in framework proposals that can assist organizations in IoT applications in inventory management practices. Therefore, fourth research theme is suggested as *frameworks and guidelines for applications* to fulfil gap in this knowledge.

Finally, *smart warehouse management systems* are another important area that is suggested as future research theme. Warehousing and inventory management are directly related concepts, since warehouses can be defined as the storage areas that inventory is being hold. To track, secure and manage costs related to inventories, warehouses should be managed carefully (Zhang et al., 2016). Therefore, IoT applications in warehouse management practices should receive more attention in terms of inventory management.

5. CONCLUSION

The benefits of IoT in inventory management are indisputable and it has a great potential to improve supply chain processes in terms of increasing efficiency, decreasing costs, while fulfilling the demands without excessive inventory holding. IoT's ability to integrate with other technologies including RFID, sensors, artificial intelligence, and potential to provide continuous traceability and real-time monitoring of the systems helps to achieve inventory accuracy in a continuous manner. Therefore, transition from traditional inventory management approaches to IoT based inventory management is essential for organizations.

This study focuses on IoT in inventory management from a supply chain perspective. Although IoT is a relatively older concept when it is compared to other digital technologies that received attention in these days, the application areas and popularity started to extend rapidly after the introduction of fourth industrial revolution. Therefore, specific fields such as inventory management are still promising. From this point of view, this chapter aimed to conduct a literature review and a bibliometric analysis to reveal the current trends in the IoT applications in inventory management.

To do so, a multi-stage research methodology is followed. After a general literature review, the author focused on WoS and SCOPUS databases to conduct bibliometric analysis. Mutual studies are identified, and similarities and differences are revealed. For the co-occurrence analysis, VOSviewer software is used. Results showed that, especially computer science and engineering areas put a lot of effort on the field. On the other hand, studies on business and management areas are limited. Moreover, more sectoral implementations, and frameworks and guidelines for solid applications are needed. In addition, sustainable and circular aspects can be integrated to the system, and smart warehouse systems can be enhanced with a special focus on IoT in inventory management.

The main limitation of this study is to keep the information up-to date. Due to the march of time, new studies are publishing in a continuous way, and therefore results will vary in timely manner. However, current results are expected to contribute to the future researches, and expand the research field.

REFERENCES

Bader, D., Innab, N., Atoum, I., & Alathamneh, F. (2023). The influence of the Internet of things on pharmaceutical inventory management. *International Journal of Data and Network Science*, 7(1), 381–390. doi:10.5267/j.ijdns.2022.9.009

Ben-Daya, M., Hassini, E., & Bahroun, Z. (2019). Internet of things and supply chain management: A literature review. *International Journal of Production Research*, *57*(15-16), 4719–4742. doi:10.1080/00207543.2017.1402140

Birkel, H. S., & Hartmann, E. (2020). Internet of Things–the future of managing supply chain risks. *Supply Chain Management*, *25*(5), 535–548. doi:10.1108/SCM-09-2019-0356

Bose, R., Mondal, H., Sarkar, I., & Roy, S. (2022). Design of smart inventory management system for construction sector based on IoT and cloud computing. *e-Prime-Advances in Electrical Engineering. Electronics and Energy*, *2*, 100051.

Donthu, N., Kumar, S., Mukherjee, D., Pandey, N., & Lim, W. M. (2021). How to conduct a bibliometric analysis: An overview and guidelines. *Journal of Business Research*, *133*, 285–296. doi:10.1016/j.jbusres.2021.04.070

Ekren, B. Y., Mangla, S. K., Turhanlar, E. E., Kazancoglu, Y., & Li, G. (2021). Lateral inventory share-based models for IoT-enabled E-commerce sustainable food supply networks. *Computers & Operations Research*, *130*, 105237. doi:10.1016/j.cor.2021.105237

El Jaouhari, A., El Bhilat, E. M., & Arif, J. (2022). Scrutinizing IoT applicability in green warehouse inventory management system based on Mamdani fuzzy inference system: a case study of an automotive semiconductors industrial firm. *Journal of Industrial and Production Engineering*, 1-15.

Evtodieva, T. E., Chernova, D. V., Ivanova, N. V., & Wirth, J. (2019). The internet of things: possibilities of application in intelligent supply chain management. *Digital transformation of the economy: Challenges, trends and new opportunities*, 395-403.

Fan, T., Tao, F., Deng, S., & Li, S. (2015). Impact of RFID technology on supply chain decisions with inventory inaccuracies. *International Journal of Production Economics*, *159*, 117–125. doi:10.1016/j.ijpe.2014.10.004

Lee, C. K., Lv, Y., Ng, K. K. H., Ho, W., & Choy, K. L. (2018). Design and application of Internet of things-based warehouse management system for smart logistics. *International Journal of Production Research*, *56*(8), 2753–2768. doi:10.1080/00207543.2017.1394592

Li, S., Xu, L. D., & Zhao, S. (2015). The internet of things: A survey. *Information Systems Frontiers*, *17*(2), 243–259. doi:10.1007/s10796-014-9492-7

Li, S., Xu, L. D., & Zhao, S. (2015). The internet of things: A survey. *Information Systems Frontiers*, *17*(2), 243–259. doi:10.1007/s10796-014-9492-7

Liu, X., & Sun, Y. (2011). Information flow control of vendor-managed inventory based on internet of things. In *Advanced Research on Computer Science and Information Engineering: International Conference, CSIE 2011,* (pp. 448-454). Springer Berlin Heidelberg. 10.1007/978-3-642-21402-8_71

Maheshwari, P., Kamble, S., Pundir, A., Belhadi, A., Ndubisi, N. O., & Tiwari, S. (2021). Internet of things for perishable inventory management systems: An application and managerial insights for micro, small and medium enterprises. *Annals of Operations Research*, 1–29. doi:10.1007/s10479-021-04277-9 PMID:34642526

Manavalan, E., & Jayakrishna, K. (2019). A review of Internet of Things (IoT) embedded sustainable supply chain for industry 4.0 requirements. *Computers & Industrial Engineering*, *127*, 925–953. doi:10.1016/j.cie.2018.11.030

Mashayekhy, Y., Babaei, A., Yuan, X. M., & Xue, A. (2022). Impact of Internet of Things (IoT) on Inventory Management: A Literature Survey. *Logistics*, *6*(2), 33. doi:10.3390/logistics6020033

Mostafa, N., Hamdy, W., & Alawady, H. (2019). Impacts of internet of things on supply chains: A framework for warehousing. *Social Sciences (Basel, Switzerland)*, *8*(3), 84. doi:10.3390/socsci8030084

Muller, M. (2019). *Essentials of inventory management*. HarperCollins Leadership.

Papanagnou, C. I. (2022). Measuring and eliminating the bullwhip in closed loop supply chains using control theory and Internet of Things. *Annals of Operations Research*, *310*(1), 153–170. doi:10.1007/s10479-021-04136-7

Paul, S., Chatterjee, A., & Guha, D. (2019). Study of smart inventory management system based on the internet of things (IOT). [IJRTBT]. *International Journal on Recent Trends in Business and Tourism*, *3*(3), 27–34.

Ran, H. (2021). Construction and optimization of inventory management system via cloud-edge collaborative computing in supply chain environment in the Internet of Things era. *PLoS One*, *16*(11), e0259284. doi:10.1371/journal.pone.0259284 PMID:34731183

Singh, D., & Verma, A. (2018). Inventory management in supply chain. *Materials Today: Proceedings*, *5*(2), 3867–3872. doi:10.1016/j.matpr.2017.11.641

Smitha & Aslekar., A. (2022, March). IoT in Inventory Management. In *2022 International Conference on Decision Aid Sciences and Applications (DASA)* (pp. 1045-1050). IEEE.

Van Eck, N., & Waltman, L. (2010). Software survey: VOSviewer, a computer program for bibliometric mapping. *scientometrics, 84*(2), 523-538.

Wang, D., Zhao, D., Wang, B., & Wu, J. (2019, December). Design of inventory pledge financing model based on internet of things technology and operational risk management. In *2019 IEEE International Conference on Industrial Engineering and Engineering Management (IEEM)* (pp. 990-996). IEEE. 10.1109/IEEM44572.2019.8978839

Wang, Y., Geng, X., Zhang, F., & Ruan, J. (2018). An immune genetic algorithm for multi-echelon inventory cost control of IOT based supply chains. *IEEE Access : Practical Innovations, Open Solutions*, *6*, 8547–8555. doi:10.1109/ACCESS.2018.2799306

Zhang, L., Alharbe, N., & Atkins, A. S. (2016, December). An IoT application for inventory management with a self-adaptive decision model. In *2016 IEEE International Conference on Internet of Things (iThings) and IEEE Green Computing and Communications (GreenCom) and IEEE Cyber, Physical and Social Computing (CPSCom) and IEEE Smart Data (SmartData)* (pp. 317-322). IEEE. 10.1109/iThings-GreenCom-CPSCom-SmartData.2016.77

Zhou, L., Chong, A. Y., & Ngai, E. W. (2015). Supply chain management in the era of the internet of things. *International Journal of Production Economics*, *159*, 1–3. doi:10.1016/j.ijpe.2014.11.014

Zohra Benhamida, F., Kaddouri, O., Ouhrouche, T., Benaichouche, M., Casado-Mansilla, D., & López-de-Ipina, D. (2021). Demand forecasting tool for inventory control smart systems. *Journal of Communications Software and Systems*, *17*(2), 185–196. doi:10.24138/jcomss-2021-0068

Chapter 11
QR Multilevel Codes to Reduce Cybersecurity Risks in the Logistics of Freight Transport in Ports

Gerardo Reyes Ruiz

iD https://orcid.org/0000-0003-0212-2952

Center for Higher Naval Studies (CESNAV), Mexico

ABSTRACT

A country's national security depends on many combined and constantly changing factors. However, one of the most preponderant aspects is the access control of goods and people entering and leaving the country through its customs, as a result of mobility and international trade currently taking place. Throughout the territory of a country, the entry and exit of both merchandise and people of different natures or nationalities, respectively, are carried out by different means of transport. Therefore, it is necessary to establish more efficient control points that manage, supervise, and, where appropriate, tax this activity, because otherwise products, materials, or people that pose a risk to human health may enter the country. In this context, this chapter shows a practical tool, based on multilevel QR codes, to improve the identification and supervision of goods entering a country through its port customs to show a technology that reduces cybersecurity risks in freight transport logistics.

INTRODUCTION

The concepts of security, peace, identity, and other terminologies contextualized in the scenario of international political theory have been the object of many interpretations (most of them with an evident ideological bias). However, due to its apparent lack of conceptual limits, security, as a concept, is used to attract and stimulate the sponsorship of multiple political projects at the federal and international levels of politics. In this sense, Williams (2008) argued that "security is, therefore, a powerful political tool to draw attention to priority elements in the competition for government attention." On the other

DOI: 10.4018/978-1-6684-7625-3.ch011

hand, Makinda (1998) defined security as "the preservation of society's norms, rules, institutions, and values". In addition, he also assured that all institutions, principles, and structures associated with society, including its population, must be protected from "military and non-military threats." The term "preservation", as an important component of this definition, presupposes conscious, deliberate, and well-defined actions. Thus, the perception of a society's leadership determines its actions and guides its efforts, which becomes evident in the breadth and depth of that society's security agenda.

Now let's see another very interesting concept which refers to National Security. The modern concept of National Security emerged in the 17th century during the Thirty Years' War in Europe and the Civil War in England. In 1648, the Peace of Westphalia established the idea that the relationship between State and Nation had sovereign control not only of the internal affairs of a country or religion but also of external security. The definition of National Security is complex, since it encompasses, in turn, different concepts such as Power (which can be better understood as the possession of a nation's control over its sovereignty and destiny); Military strength (refers to the military capacity and capabilities of the armed forces); Force (refers to the use of a military or police capacity to achieve some objective) and National Defense (refers, strictly, to the capacity of the armed forces to defend both the sovereignty of a nation and the lives of its people) (Holmes, 2015).

On the other hand, there are currently non-military concepts associated with National Security. Even though in 1947 the United States created the National Security Council to "advise the President regarding the integration of domestic, foreign, and military policies related to national security…" and that for much of the 20th century, the conception of National Security was oriented to topics oriented to the military environment, the concept of National Security expanded, gradually, beyond the powers that could be made to the armed forces. Consequently, the days when National Security was defined solely in terms of the military were a thing of the past. Since then, Homeland Security has come to mean different things to different people knowledgeable about the subject. Currently, there are all kinds of definitions for this concept, which include economic security; energy security; environmental security, food security, sanitary and health security, women's security, maritime security, and port security, among others. In addition, today there are the following terms associated with the concept of National Security: Political security (refers to protecting the sovereignty of the government and its political system and the security of society against illegal internal attacks); Economic security (recently, this term has been contextualized in an environment of human security from the perspective of eradicating poverty and eliminating income inequality); Energy and natural resources security (refers to the degree to which a country or region has access to energy resources such as oil, gas, water and various minerals); Homeland security (refers to the security of airports, ports, border security, transportation security, immigration control and other related matters); Cybersecurity (refers to the protection of the computer infrastructure, data processing, operating systems of a country or region against harmful interference, whether carried out from outside or inside the country or region); Human security (this term was developed by the United Nations at the end of the Cold War and refers to the security and protection of people from hunger, disease and repression, including harmful disturbances of daily life (The White House, 2021-2022a-2022b; Holmes, 2015).

Over time, and as already mentioned, the term National Security was expanded to include other terms such as economic security, environmental security, food security, health security, personal security, community security, political security. and the protection of women and minorities and, finally, environmental security (refers, roughly, to conflicts caused by problems such as water scarcity, power interruptions or severe climate change; these problems are supposed to be "transnational" and therefore can cause conflicts between nations). That is, the abstract concepts referred to as "environment" and "climate" must be protected as an end in themselves. Therefore, National Security must be understood as the safeguarding of a nation as a whole and, very probably, at its most important level is the protection of all its territory and people against attacks, internal or external, and other dangers through the maintenance of the armed forces and the protection of state secrets (Holmes, 2015).

In this context, the conceptualization of National Security is increasingly infiltrating world economic affairs. The global economic order and the concept of National Security are today deeply intertwined and are increasingly difficult to differentiate. Furthermore, major geopolitical disputes now take place within the trade and investment institutions themselves rather than outside of them. The new National Security presents a sensitive challenge for international economic institutions. Simply because contemporary security policy provides a wealth of possible justifications for departing from the ordinary rules of trade and investment. In addition to this, the current dynamic of trade policy, which presents constant changes, also provides incentives for the State to make use of these new National Security justifications (Heath, 2020). Consequently, current global Homeland Security policies increasingly threaten the rules governing trade and investment flows. This problem runs deeper and much more difficult than recent controversies between some countries suggest (for example, the disputes over steel and aluminum tariffs under President Trump's administration). Therefore, governments around the world have gradually adopted Homeland Security policies that address an increasingly broad range of risks and vulnerabilities, including climate change, disease pandemics, cybercrime or cybersecurity, terrorism, threats to infrastructure, attacks on industry and the media (The White House, 2022a).

In these scenarios, the issue of cybersecurity is extremely relevant and, in particular, that which is carried out to reduce the risks in the logistics of freight transport in ports. The CISA (Cybersecurity & Infrastructure Security Agency, 2022) defines cybersecurity as the art of protecting networks, devices, and data from unauthorized access or criminal use and the practice of guaranteeing the confidentiality, integrity, and availability of information (see Figure 1). This dependence also ensures that now everything depends on computers and the internet because currently communications (email, smartphones, tablets), entertainment (interactive video games, social networks, applications), transportation (navigation systems), shopping (made online through e-commerce), credit card purchases, medicines (medical equipment, medical records) and, of course, goods transiting port customs are vulnerable targets.

Figure 1. Cyber security concept
Source: Internet

For this reason, the new technologies that show information on the goods that are moved around the world, more than being a fad, are increasingly necessary tools to guarantee the safety of both the goods themselves and the country or region where they are moved (Figure 2). These technologies, in turn, have served as a platform for many companies that want to move their products more securely and, with this, increase their sales through more efficient logistics by reducing cybersecurity risks that could be triggered at all customs. ports of the world. Of course, the new technologies seek, through more innovative and efficient strategies or technological tools, to present the information associated with a finished product or merchandise in a safe manner and with simple, economical, but interesting multimedia, capable of generating the movement of merchandise, throughout the world, the assurance that the information and/ or characteristics associated with a product/merchandise is trustworthy, truthful and, above all, that it does not represent a risk when introduced into a country or region (Cheung, Bell and Bhattacharjya, 2021; Cempírek, Nachtigall and Široký, 2016).

Figure 2. New technologies in cybersecurity
Source: Internet

BACKGROUND

Trade is one of the oldest economic activities since it began with the man himself. Trade has been considered as the exchange, between two or more individuals, of products and services that are necessary to satisfy their primary needs. To satisfy their human needs, the causes that motivated trade was, among others, the inequality in the natural resources of their environment and the specialization in production. The first trade was by land, later by the river, and later by sea. It is in this last means of transporting goods, throughout the world, where the vast majority of foreign trade activities are currently focused (OECD, 2022).

The origin of the ports goes back to antiquity itself, man as a society, since he established the different modes of government, has sought to regulate trade through the transport of merchandise, either for the protection of internal producers or for security owned by the state. Over the years, this exclusive function of the government has been perfected, adding protocols, signing international agreements, and releasing or restricting the access or exit of merchandise; all this to facilitate international trade. Of course, the concept of a port has also changed over time. The classic concept of a port is conceived as a place on the coast, natural or artificial, whose main function is to shelter ships to carry out multiple tasks related to the loading or unloading of various merchandise (Figure 3). In other words, the port was a business center and also a place where ships were loaded and unloaded, the merchandise was deposited, ships were built and repaired, and where the crew, shipowners, merchants, sailors, stevedores, etc., met. that, little by little, they were building a population around the ports that would later become port cities (Palmer, 2020).

Figure 3. The classic concept of a port
Source: Claudio de Lorena "Puesta de sol en un Puerto (1639)"

Likewise, the European Union defines a port as "an area of land and water equipped with works and equipment that mainly allow the reception of ships, their loading and unloading, and the storage, reception, and delivery of merchandise, as well as the shipment and disembarkation of passengers. This area of land and water includes the necessary infrastructure (shelter works, docks, dry docks, etc.) as well as the superstructure (fixed constructions located on top of the infrastructure such as warehouses, silos, sheds, etc.) and fixed equipment and necessary for its correct operation (transport pipes, cranes, hoppers, etc.) (Rúa Costa, 2006). To access the port, the presence of maritime access infrastructures (entry channels, navigation aids) as well as land infrastructures (roads, railways, etc.) is necessary.

For its part, the United Nations Conference on Trade and Development (UNCTAD, 2022) defines ports as interfaces between the different modes of transport and are typically centers of combined transport. Thus, they are considered commercial and industrial multifunctional areas where goods are not only in transit but are also handled, manufactured, and distributed. Therefore, ports are multifunctional systems, which, to function properly, must be integrated into the global logistics chain. Consequently, an efficient port is not only in infrastructure, superstructure, and adequate equipment, but also in good communications and, especially, having a dedicated, qualified management team, with a motivated and trained workforce to offer better security in the transfer of goods (Figure 4).

Figure 4. A modern port (Shanghai, China)
Source: Internet

The port as a transport node is not only important for the fluidity of cargo movements but also irreplaceable for regional economic development due to its motivating function to encourage these movements. The globalization of the economy has changed the focus of ports from being a public infrastructure with little competition to being nodes with multiple responsibilities to provide a competitive and secure environment (Brooks and Cullinane, 2006). In this way, and like large ships, ports are currently the main element, worldwide, related to the movement of goods. However, the ports are the ones that are setting the trends worldwide for the transport of merchandise (Figure 5).

Figure 5. Main ports in the world in the transport of TEUs
Source: World Shiping Council

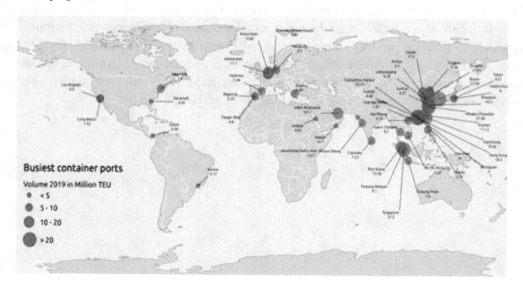

On the other hand, the dynamics of the transport of merchandise in international trade, through the sea, has grown considerably: In the year 2010, 544,870,578 containers were mobilized throughout the world (TEU: units equivalent to 20 feet), while in the year 2020, 758,734,020 containers (TEU: 20-foot equivalent units) were mobilized worldwide (World Bank, 2022). This increase represented a variation of 39.25% from 2010 to 2020. That is, in a decade the transport of containers, with merchandise, increased by more than a third about 2010. Therefore, the transport of merchandise using the Maritime is the main means, globally, for the transfer of goods. Undoubtedly, this increase related to the movement of goods around the world deserves special attention in terms of the National Security of a country or region. It is precisely here where all the technological tools that guarantee and ensure that the goods introduced into a country are carried out first, in the best legal way and, second, in the safest possible way, make sense (World Trade Organization et al, 2019; World Trade Organization, 2018; UNCTAD, 2021). For the latter to be carried out, in all the ports of the world there is an area designated to ensure both good traffic and good protection of the merchandise that is introduced in an area subject to the payment of rights for a certain merchandise that is introduced in a country or region: These enclosures are known as customs, and port customs are of particular interest. This is due, and as we have already seen, to the fact that the largest number of goods in the world are transferred to these port areas. In this sense, the European Postgraduate Center (CEUPE, 2022) defines a customs office as a public agency that is under the mandate of the State; They are physical spaces that are strategically located on the most important borders of a country or region and with the aim of organizing, reviewing and, above all, setting taxes, when this is the case, on all merchandise that enters or leaves the country. Furthermore, the Revised Kyoto Convention (RKC) defines a customs office as the government service responsible for the administration of customs legislation and the collection of duties and taxes, which also has responsibility for enforcing other related laws and regulations. to the import, export, movement, or storage of merchandise (World Customs Organization, 2008).

Figure 6. Importance of customs in international trade
Source: AMG Guide

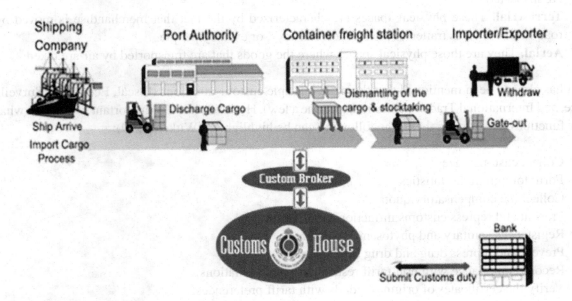

Of course, a customs office has multiple purposes (missions), however, one of its main objectives is to efficiently manage the transit of all material resources that are imported/exported through the inspection and correct application of tariffs, which will be paid by private/public companies or a group of them. It is important to mention that there are also customs offices whose objective is to guarantee the correct transit of people (non-material resources), however, these premises will not be the subject of study for this work, since these non-material resources (that is, people) they do not have customs control. In this scenario, the World Customs Organization (2022b) mentions that the most common mission of a customs office, and accepted worldwide, is to develop and implement an integrated set of policies and procedures that guarantee greater security and protection, as well as effective trade facilitation and revenue collection. Undoubtedly, this can only be achieved through the efficient and effective use of both technological tools and information related to the international movement of goods, means of transport, and people associated with those goods. Therefore, a customs office plays a very important role in the so-called supply chain (Pourakbar and Zuidwijk, 2018; Mikuriya, 2007; Chen and Ma, 2015). For his part, Rohde Ponce (2005) argued that customs activity is carried out exclusively by the State and consists of establishing authorized places that allow merchandise, means of transport, and people to enter or exit the national territory; execute and verify the acts and formalities, that are carried out before the customs, that all those people that intervene in those activities of entry, transit, or exit of a territory; demand and verify compliance with the obligations and requirements established by the laws and other regulations that allow these entries and exits through the borders of their territory; establish and execute acts of control over merchandise and means of transport during the duration of their stay, whether in the national territory or abroad.

The classification or types of customs will depend on the country or region, however, it can be mentioned that the types of customs are classified as follows (in all these customs the control and supervision of the transit of people can also be carried out) (World Customs Organization, 2022; CEUPE, 2022; Chamber of Deputies of Mexico, 2021):

- **Maritime.** They are those physical spaces where the goods that are transported by ships or boats are inspected.
- **Terrestrial.** These physical spaces are characterized by the fact that merchandise is moved by road means such as trailers, automobiles, railways, or even by people.
- **Aerial.** They are those physical spaces where the goods that are transported by air are taxed.

It has already been mentioned that there are multiple customs missions (Fiscal, Economic, Surveillance, and International Trade Facilitation, to name a few). However, it is also important to mention what their functions are. Among these, the following can be highlighted (Witker, 1999):

- Collect customs taxes.
- Form foreign trade statistics.
- Collect the compensatory quotas.
- Prevent and repress customs infractions and crimes.
- Register the sanitary and phytosanitary controls.
- Prevent and repress drug and drug trafficking.
- Record compliance with non-tariff restrictions and regulations.
- Verify the certificates of origin of goods with tariff preferences.

- Control the use of goods in the customs suspension regimes of taxes on foreign trade (customs taxes).
- Prevent the traffic of waste and toxic residues in compliance with national and international ecological legislation.

Among the functions of a customs office, and as the main objective to avoid fraud, the one that refers to capital evasion (taxes through tariffs applied to merchandise) or the smuggling of prohibited merchandise stands out. To do this, CEUPE (2022) proposes three transcendental phases that are carried out in the processes involved during the transit of merchandise through customs:

1. **Customs declaration.** At that point, the destination, definition of the content, and all the characteristics of the issuer, receiver, and merchandise are placed.
2. **Inspection of the goods.** This phase is carried out by the customs authorities both for validation and confirmation.
3. **Payment of tariffs.** It refers to the correct payment of taxes, when this is the case, by the entity responsible for the merchandise.

At this point, it makes sense to ask the following question: Why are customs important? In the first instance, it is important to highlight that customs are one of the three basic indicators measured by the World Bank (World Bank, 2022) to establish the competitiveness of International Logistics (the other two indicators are infrastructure and quality of logistics services). On the other hand, customs comply with monitoring the logistics of the goods, that is, the entry or exit of these goods but, above all, those goods considered prohibited or that can seriously harm the country's economy, the health of the flora and fauna and, of course, human beings, historical heritage or any other legal asset that is under the protection of the State and that is considered very valuable by that country or region.

A customs malfunction hurts the economic development of a country or region, since, in addition to increasing transaction costs and lengthening clearance times, it can put the National Security of that country or region at risk (OECD, 2013). This malfunction may be due, among other things, to an administration that only uses paper documents, which significantly slows down all the procedures carried out in customs facilities. However, a poor administration and operation of customs, in general, is the result, in turn, of a malfunction of the government of that country or region. In this scenario, the World Customs Organization's 21st Century Customs Strategy (2022a) is created with a 'vision statement' that was formulated by world customs leaders and is aimed at meeting the requirements of governments, citizens, and all those interested in this topic. The strategy expresses the need for customs administrations to respond, as soon as possible, to the needs and demands that the globalization process entails, the dynamics of international trade, and the technicalities of the trade supply chain (national or international), the new directions that policies are taking, and, above all, the complexities and challenges of the global panorama.

MAIN FOCUS OF THE CHAPTER

Issues, Controversies, Problems

Maritime transport and ports are not isolated entities and follow the same patterns by which they are governed in the global socio-economic context, in such a way that the globalization of the economy and the considerable increase in international trade lead to growing inter-port competition. This competition allows to generation, in turn, new mechanisms for the transport of goods that are not ignored by the main shipping companies in the world. One consequence of this international competition has been the gradual reduction in the number of ports where large interoceanic ships call. This action has generated, among other things, that a large number of capital investments are selective and, therefore, favor some ports in particular and not others. However, these investments not only boost ports but also positively and directly affect the territories where these port areas are located and the economic activity that takes place there.

The territorial limits of a country or region are well-defined. However, throughout its territory, the entry and exit of both people and goods of different nationalities or natures, respectively, are carried out through different means of transport. Therefore, it is necessary to establish control points that manage, supervise, and, when this is the case, tax this activity, because if this is not the case, then it can facilitate the entry into the country of people and/or materials that are a risk to the health (both human and for the endemic species of that country), threats to internal security, dangers to the environment, among others. Undoubtedly, the National Security of a country depends on multiple factors that are combined and constantly changing. However, one of the most preponderant aspects is the control of merchandise, through customs, that enter and leave the country, as a result of mobility and international trade that the country or region carries out. At first glance, it would seem like a simple job, however, in reality, it is much more complex than it seems. However, the current situation of these tax facilities shows that, even when there are already digital means of control (for example, identification badges and unique identification badges with two-dimensional barcodes and QR codes), security devices can be easily falsified and violated, thus presenting the risk that they are misused and, consequently, put the security of any country or region at risk.

The facilities occupied by customs are strategic areas, particularly port customs, since they are responsible for multiple actions that are derived, in turn, from activities related to foreign trade, a situation that can make them a clear target of crime to alter the stability of a country or region or be the most common means to introduce goods that are a risk to National Security, health, the environment, animal life, or simply seek tax evasion, damaging, mainly, tax collection seriously and, more generally, the economy of a country or region. Therefore, it is of the utmost importance that access to customs is strictly controlled and supervised, not only by the Customs Administrator but also by a whole trained team that has at its disposal the necessary tools to meet all its objectives (Figure 7). In particular, ensure the rapid transit of goods with functional technologies and tools and thus reduces, to a minimum, cybersecurity risks in logistics related to the movement of goods in a country or region.

Figure 7. Customs control as a team effort
Source: https://www.teamnet.com.mx

Port customs are government entities in charge of registering and controlling the entry and exit of goods and carrying out the assessment of this activity. The latter refers to the payments or costs that the importer or exporter must make to the State to allow the exit or entry of the goods. These tariffs represent an important income for the nation and, of course, it is to protect the country's internal market, its production, and the establishment of balanced bases for local trade. Customs is located at the borders, international airports, high-altitude ports, and railway terminals where the clearance of merchandise from international trade is carried out.

A very important stage and perhaps the most transcendental, in the transfer of merchandise is customs clearance because it is at this stage that the review (both physical and documentary) of the merchandise introduced into the country or region where it is shipped begins. They shipped those goods. The concept related to customs control has been defined in the Glossary of Customs Terms of the World Customs Organization as those measures applied to ensure compliance with the laws and regulations for whose application customs is responsible (OMA, 2022a). Customs control is classified into the following categories (Garavito Castillo, 2007):

1. According to the time of control.
   1.1. Previous check. It is the one exercised by the customs administration before the admission of the customs declaration of goods.
   1.2. Control during dispatch. It is the one exercised from the precise moment in which the declaration of the admission of merchandise is received by customs until the moment of the removal of the merchandise.
   1.3. Backcheck. It is the one exercised from the lifting of the goods dispatched through a certain customs regime.
2. According to the customs regime. The customs regimes are the provisions established in the customs legislation of each country, regarding the legal treatment that corresponds to the merchandise. The

Kyoto Convention (2022) on the simplification and harmonization of customs procedures is an important document and one of the usual considerations for the definition of the customs regimes of the countries.

3. According to the type of obligation.
    3.1. Control of tax obligations. They refer to the control of the correct payment of tax obligations in imports. This control is extremely important in countries where taxes on imports have high participation in total tax revenue.
    3.2. Control of obligations for taxpayers. They refer to the control of the customs administration on non-tax obligations, such as verifying the obligation to present certificates or sanitary records, licenses, and other procedures that are required through customs clearance.

At present, the paradigms of commercial globalization are referred to through concepts such as electronic commerce, electronic customs facilitation and control, customs simplification and harmonization, commercial logistics, and security in the supply chain, among many others. However, its conceptualization goes beyond its simple reference, since these concepts have serious implications in the transformation of world trade operations, in such a way that they affect not only the trade and customs policies of the countries, but also because they also affect the commercial transactions of foreign trade companies, especially multinationals. These paradigms that have arisen in contemporary international trade have also had a multifunctional interpretation, since in addition to serving as objectives of international organizations (for example, the World Trade Organization, the Organization for Economic Cooperation and Development, and the World Customs Organization), also function as integrated principles within their regulatory frameworks that regulate the international exchange of goods. Of these contemporary paradigms, "commercial logistics" and "security in the supply chain" stand out due to the importance they currently have in foreign trade and logistics companies (Saldanha et al., 2015). In this way, the concept of logistics, applied to foreign trade, is understood as the set of operations carried out in support of the exchange or flow of merchandise or services in world markets, which include the procurement, maintenance, security, and transportation of goods. with the sole purpose of efficiently satisfying customers or consumers with the least possible cost, effort, and time. In a few words, commercial logistics translates into being competitive in a globalized world trade environment and providing quality customer services. In the same way, the security paradigm in the supply chain is here to stay and coexist with logistics. Thus, security in the supply chain aims for organizations to establish and document reasonable levels of security within international supply chains and their components, also allowing better risk-based decisions to be made (Customs Strategy, 2019). Derived from these paradigms, the following most common problems in logistics and documentation have been detected:

1. Not informing the logistics operator on time that the dispatch of the merchandise arrived at the port.
2. Not carrying out the previous review of the rigorous documents, by the customs brokerage companies.
3. Send the goods to other destinations.
4. Delays of the container in the Port.
5. Failure of carriers.
6. Storage.
7. Theft of merchandise in storage warehouses.
8. The inaccuracy of the inventories of the stored merchandise.

9. The storage of useless material.
10. The lack of planning.

As can be seen, the vast majority of these problems can be solved with the implementation of new technologies and in particular with the use of multilevel QR codes (Figure 8). This type of technological tool helps to minimize the following vulnerabilities in port customs: a) Identification of physical vulnerabilities and; b) Identification of electronic vulnerabilities. Therefore, the implementation of electronic identification devices, through multilevel QR codes, is an innovative and efficient strategy that allows for strengthening access control and increasing the security of a country, region, institution, or company. In this way, the present work proposes to show a new technological tool, in particular the multilevel QR codes, which serves to reduce the cybersecurity risks associated with the logistics of freight transport in port customs. In other words, the main objective of this work is to establish some criteria to be considered by port customs to strengthen the security of merchandise that is introduced into a country or region, for which a relatively new technological tool is presented for its application in the access control of merchandise at port customs and, with this, can foresee against potential threats and prompt response in the event of a state of emergency.

Figure 8. Multilevel QR code
Source: Own elaboration based on Badawi et al (2019)

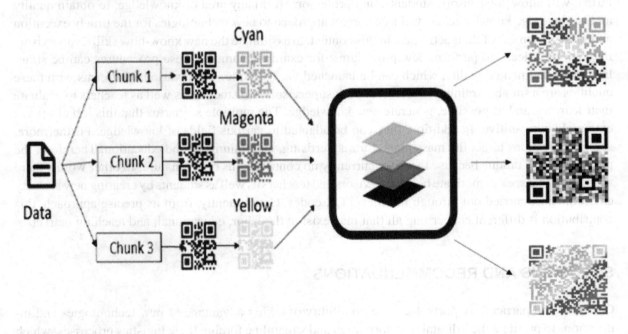

Quick Response multilevel codes, known as multilevel QR (Hill and Whitty, 2021; Denso Wave Incorporated, 2021), are a reliable and fully adaptable tool that allows you to add any type of information, even encrypted, associated with the merchandise that is displayed through a web page, which makes it an innovative technology to discover new uses, forms and consumption habits but, above all, it allows all the information associated with that merchandise to be displayed in an interesting, innovative and simple way (Pantano and Servidio, 2012). These multi-level QR codes contain multiple layers of information, which can independently function as a single QR code (Figure 8). Through the information shown using a QR code, which is easily identifiable, using a marker, if it is presented on the side of the merchandise, it is intended to configure complete and independent databases (although related) to obtain a perspective of all those details of the goods (Mostafa, 2015). Of course, the main objective of the supervision of merchandise when making use of this type of new technology is to ensure that those merchandise introduced into a country or region do so in the safest way, even this review can be carried out, alternatively, through an App, usually through a mobile phone (Ozkaya et al., 2015). This approach, without a doubt, originates a new security strategy that currently very few port customs use (Sen et al., 2019). Perhaps the latter is because port customs assume that its cost is high, however, this type of technology is highly affordable and has great potential to guarantee the security of merchandise that is introduced through port customs (Hossain et al., 2018). In other words, and through the multilevel QR codes, seeks to present all the information that is important to the supervisor and is of complete interest: Another way of presenting the information is currently being developed, known as Inbound (generally used in Marketing), which is intended to discard all information that is not important to the supervisor (Patrutiu-Baltes. 2016; Halligan and Shah, 2014). However, this concept focuses on the type of information presented and not on the form and clarity that information will be presented to the supervisor.

The creation of new security platforms/tools, through multilevel QR codes (Thompson and Lee, 2013), will allow supervisors, students, and professors, from any area of knowledge, to obtain quality and cutting-edge knowledge, as well as a correct approach to new technologies for the timely execution and/or development of their activities. In this context, to assimilate the new know-how skills, supervisors must, in turn, learn to perform new procedures: for example, some of these procedures can be simulated with augmented reality, which can be launched via QR code. Thus, various platforms with these qualities are a suitable training medium for both supervisors and students as well as teachers to evaluate their learning and, if possible, generate new knowledge. The multiple scenarios that this job offers are extremely competitive. In addition, they can be adapted to various fields of knowledge. Furthermore, some applications target the mass market for advertising, entertainment, and education. Therefore, the present work is unique because there are currently no contributions of this nature. In other words, there are no jobs that seek to motivate both supervisors and teachers as well as students by creating new security environments, carried out through multilevel QR codes. Consequently, from its precise approach, this contribution is different concerning all that may exist in the labor, educational, and teaching markets.

SOLUTIONS AND RECOMMENDATIONS

Customs, and particularly ports, have the possibility of taking advantage of new technologies and innovations to promote their digital transformation and streamline foreign trade logistics processes, which can contribute to improving the competitiveness and growth of their country's economies. The pandemic enhanced the importance of trade and the logistics of foreign trade. COVID-19 globally suspended daily life since the beginning of 2020, commercial activity, even with the well-known disruptions caused by international transport restrictions and social isolation policies, led to considerable increases in trade electronic and digital. In particular, the pandemic put customs response capabilities to the test, highlighting the opportunities presented by digital transformation processes. A good part of the acceleration in digital adoption in customs was caused by the urgency in the clearance of critical merchandise to attend to the emergency and maintain the flow of regular trade. Therefore, the economic reactivation of port customs depends, to a large extent, on the logistics performance of its foreign trade (Technologies to innovate and transform customs management), backed by an adequate infrastructure (Use of new technologies for Coordinated Border Management both physical and digital) and associated transport services (Inter-American Development Bank, 2022).

Technology has played an important role in these global changes by being able to send and receive information in near real-time. The evolution of the means of transport has made governments agree on how to carry out the procedures required to facilitate the exchange of goods between countries that sign free trade agreements in the most standardized way possible. The actions of port customs have been adapting to the great technological changes, allowing their activities to be carried out more transparently and efficiently, allowing the growth of international trade, better performance of tariff quotas, and, finally, coordination and collaboration of governments globally. The implementation of technological tools allows customs authorities to carry out verifications and risk analysis in a faster and more timely manner, as well as implement security policies such as electronic audits for taxpayers, importers, exporters, customs agents, carriers, and courier providers. and operators involved in foreign trade activities that will help detect inconsistencies in commercial activities and even potential risks such as illegal merchandise, health risks, or dual-use merchandise.

An automated system that contains digital authentication in the access controls of merchandise in a country or region, guarantees greater security, modernity, convenience, and speed both for companies that export/import these merchandise and for users who have to carry out various procedures. at those access points. By supervising physical control, without the need for the intervention of authority, considerable savings can be obtained in the review phase, which will undoubtedly strengthen specialization in control and/or surveillance areas that are more critical and where there are higher incidences of robberies, contraband, arms, money, and drug trafficking, among others. These automated systems are intended to minimize and simplify the work of those in charge of guaranteeing security at the access points, thus speeding up and facilitating the passage of both goods and users through these access points. These systems must be designed so that they automatically manage the goods to declare, take pictures, and process the data of the credentials and the fingerprints of a person, through the use of biometrics, and identification card readers, guaranteeing, with it, the safety of users and facilitate the detection of a possible threat to the corresponding authorities. In this way, it will be possible to transmit an image to the agency that is in charge of security and access control to a country or region as a fast, secure, modern, and reliable authority. Therefore, the implementation of electronic identification devices, such as multilevel QR codes (Yu, Fu and Liu, 2019), is the strategy that will strengthen the access control of merchandise to a country or region and, without a doubt, will increase the security at the port customs of that country or region. Due to all of the above, the electronic customs system must be accompanied by a robust cybersecurity system, which will give greater certainty to the operation of electronic systems and programs, becoming a preventive shield against any cyberattack that threatens foreign trade. and that can have serious consequences for National Security (Figure 9). Therefore, the different vulnerabilities, both physical and electronic, that customs access presents can and should be mitigated in such a way that they present an acceptable risk that can be eliminated quickly and effectively, in the event of a critical situation. supposes an attack on the security/cybersecurity of the facilities, the personnel, or the processes that are carried out in the customs.

Figure 9. Activity diagram of a cybersecurity system based on QR codes
Source: Own elaboration

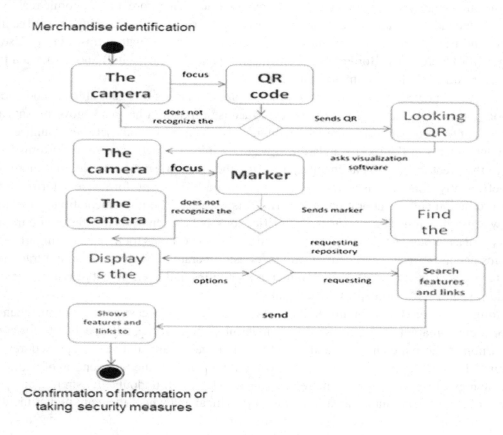

The recent evolution of hardware has allowed multilevel QR codes to be the "triggers" to reproduce multiple applications and tools in physically small units such as smartphones or tablets. These devices contain all the necessary components to present all kinds of information about merchandise, such as high-resolution cameras and screens, accelerometers, GPS, wireless connectivity via WLAN, and radio links (Honkamaa et al., 2007). For the execution of this security system, through QR codes (Wahsheh and Luccio, 2020; NPO, 2022), a camera is used, which produces a point of view to show all the information linked to merchandise and that will be superimposed on it. a marker (see Figure 10). In addition, information display events such as price, quantity, stock, composition, origin, destination, buyer data, seller data, port of origin and destination, ship information, tax calculation data, and information display events can be "triggered". etc. which will be useful for port customs, because they will be able to compare all this information, even encrypted (Song and Chu, 2021; Mandal and Deepti, 2019), with their databases and, if necessary, take all security measures /cybersecurity possible to guarantee the correct introduction to the country or region of these merchandise In addition, through the multilevel QR codes, you can direct to the official site of the product, social networks such as Facebook, Twitter and you could even make the purchase through these means (Yang et al., 2016). If desired, the physical supervision of the merchandise can be done with a mobile device and through buttons with superimposed icons, the objects or links associated with the merchandise are shown (Figure 10) (Liu, Yang and Liu, 2008).

Figure 10. Reading a QR code
Source: Own elaboration

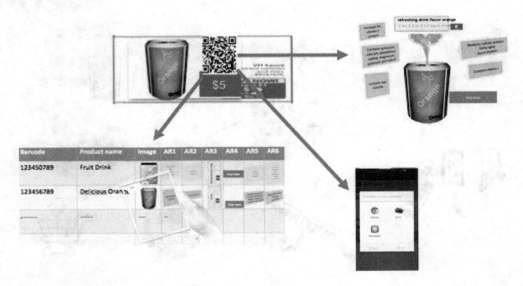

Agrebi and Jallais (2015) point out that the greater the perception of information through multilevel QR codes, regarding the ease of use, the greater the intention of people to use the new technologies associated with this tool, such as augmented or virtual reality, and have another perspective of the goods that are being monitored. Based on this, it can be indicated that when the supervisor uses new technology, such as those mentioned above, to visualize more details of merchandise (through a web page, in 2D, 3D, video, augmented reality, reality, virtual, mixed reality) (Yuan et al., 2019; Dcouth and Jaichandran, 2019; AlNajdi, 2022), then such supervision will be more interesting and novel to you. After creating the marker, we proceed to generate all the information that will be added to the merchandise when that marker is focused on by the device's camera to review and validate that information. This information, which can also be generated through a 3D virtual object, is designed with a wide variety of specialized software, which can be used to create innovative content for all the information associated with the merchandise (Figure 11).

Figure 11. Apps associated with merchandise through multilevel QR codes
Source: Own elaboration

All the information that is added to the goods, through a multilevel QR code, can be very specific, even encrypted, that is downloaded from a website (text, images, sound, video or multimedia files, augmented or virtual reality, etc. .) and/or content from a 3D presentation of the product for its correct use (Google, yellow pages, the cloud, etc.), its construction through a manual or video, the location of sale, stock in the store (such as the reception of discounts, coupons in a local store, taxis, etc.), the email of the contact, a purchase button, put the product away, follow up on the purchase or shipment, support services, emergency services, entertainment, among others. All these aspects can be carried out in real-time, which will logically depend only on the speed at which the data is transmitted. On the other hand, this type of new technology allows the connection with others that, jointly, can achieve a new supervision experience. In this context, all the information associated with the merchandise, through a multilevel QR code, can be an important component to guarantee security/cybersecurity throughout the supply chain (Krombholz et al., 2014), since when making Using these codes would mean using a technological tool as an interaction and security/cybersecurity device in each of the stages involved in the logistics of freight transport and which are reviewed at a port customs. Therefore, and through this simple mechanism, the supervisor will be able to view with a device (computer, mobile device such as a tablet, smartphone, etc.) all the information found on the internet and that is associated with the goods displayed or by Supervise. In other words, with this dynamic, it is intended that all the information associated with the goods can be reviewed or supervised in all the stages concerning transport logistics and, with this, deduce as much as possible all the security/cybersecurity risks implemented in a company. port customs (Figure 12).

Figure 12. Apps associated with a product using QR codes
Source: Own elaboration

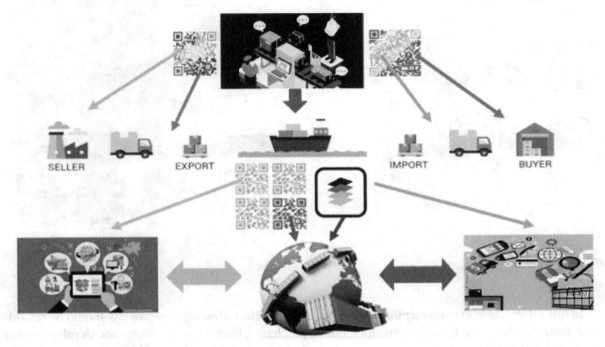

FUTURE RESEARCH DIRECTIONS

The tool presented in this work can be scaled to a computer system. This is to share all the information associated with the goods at each stage of the logistics of freight transport. In this sense, the first action that begins with the system design is the determination of the system architecture, which is the hierarchical structure of the program modules, the way its components interact, and the data structure used. by its modules (Bass et al., 2012). There are several software architectural styles (Erickson and Siau, 2008), however, due to the nature of the proposed system, the one that should be modeled is the Service Oriented Architecture (SOA) type (Josuttis, 2007; Fajar, Nurcahyo and Sriratnasari, 2018), which is an architectural paradigm for designing and developing distributed systems and has been created to provide ease and flexibility of integration with linked systems, as well as to establish direct alignment with information management processes, thus reducing costs. of implementation. Other advantages of this system are: 1) it implements service innovation for consumers and; 2) has an agile adaptation to changes, including an early reaction to competitiveness (Bianco et al., 2007). The main characteristic of SOA is that information systems are built on a set of computer standards and with the sole objective that all of them, even those made with different technologies, can operate in an integrated manner and without any dependencies between them. An SOA system represents a model where a logical unit is decomposed into several smaller units; in this architecture, the services can be used by other services or other programs (Niknejad et al., 2020; Erl, 2017). The architecture of the system for the management/administration of the information associated with the goods, through multilevel QR codes, is shown in Figure 14.

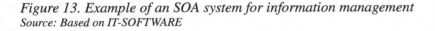

Figure 13. Example of an SOA system for information management
Source: Based on IT-SOFTWARE

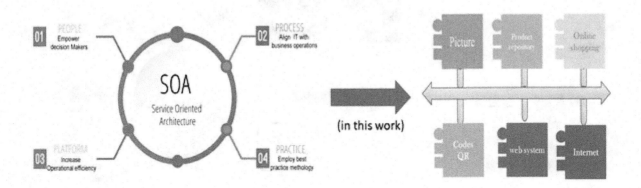

In this information management/administration system, the following components should be considered: image design, merchandise repository, online purchases, internet, web system, and development of multilevel QR codes and their respective markers (Uchiyama and Marchand, 2012). The programming paradigms for this type of architecture require a structure that integrates different modules to be interconnected and, simultaneously, can operate individually; this characteristic is called "loosely coupled services". To graphically show the architecture of this system, it is necessary to build a diagram to show its operation from the precise moment the supervisor views information until he finishes using the system: a technique that can be used is known as an "activity diagram" (see Figure 9).

Taking into account that computer systems have evolved from the moment factors such as the mobile platform, the growing use of big data for business and the enormous use of Cloud Computing have been added (Laundon and Laudon, 2019), it is necessary to look for tools and technologies that make more effective use of the Internet and devices that are up to the requirements of the supervisors of a port customs. To be at the forefront of these security issues, this choice must be improved by using information resources that are, to a large extent, the invention and improvement of information and communication technologies, that is, of those systems that involve new technologies with characteristics and capabilities in information management.

Information systems are codes built to help people make decisions in an easy, accessible, and fast way. These decisions would be aimed at different areas that are directly involved in the logistics of freight transport, and that goes through port customs, in a newer and more innovative way. Currently, there are few examples of these systems that provide this type of ease to port customs supervisors, simply because there is no standardization in the way of offering the inspection of merchandise. This could be seen during COVID-19, that is, e-commerce sales considerably increased the movement of merchandise around the world: The COVID-19 pandemic evidenced a more innovative and efficient way, the transaction of purchases/sales of products and services through the Internet of what was daily offered through catalogs, magazines or simply on the shelf. Of course, these international changes also deserve adequate supervision but, above all, stricter supervision of those goods that are introduced into a country or region to avoid possible violations of the security/cybersecurity protocols implemented in port customs.

The strategy of supervision and validation of the information, through a system based on multilevel QR codes, that is proposed in this work offers a very accessible format to interact with the supervisor. In addition, this strategy can be acquired by all those companies interested in supervising their merchandise that is transported to port customs. Undoubtedly, one of the advantages of this system is its adaptability, since it can be quickly adapted to all types of merchandise: this new supervision and management strategy can be offered with the inclusion of a software update service and an extra service oriented to technical support. Multilevel QR codes allow this supervision strategy to be related to other new technologies, social networks, and multiple apps for mobile devices that serve, in turn, to generate more innovative environments (such as augmented reality, virtual reality, or mixed reality)(Lin, Wu and Yang, 2021). This novel supervision approach allows the information associated with all types of merchandise to be displayed in an original and novel way. Undoubtedly, this supervision strategy will favor and position any company that decides to use a technological tool of this nature to show/manage its supervision strategy from a differentiated perspective. There is much to be done with multilevel QR codes, however, the priority is to bring this new technology closer to companies that bet on a strategy of supervision, validation, and management of cutting-edge information, since currently, very few companies risk using this technological tool because it is considered expensive and susceptible to the issue of cybersecurity.

CONCLUSION

With the present work it has been shown that even when there are already digital control means (such as barcodes, and two-dimensional QR codes) for merchandise that is introduced into a country or region, through port customs, these can be easily forged, which can increase the risk of misuse and breach the security/cybersecurity of port customs. The logistics involved in moving goods from one country to another seem to be a fairly simple task, however, it is not as simple as it seems. This is because currently, the transport of merchandise through the sea is the main means used to export/import merchandise. Undoubtedly, this is because in Maritime Commerce, the greater the volume of merchandise transported, then the freight cost is lower. Furthermore, the COVID-19 pandemic considerably increased purchases/sales through electronic commerce (e-commerce), which implied a greater movement of large quantities of merchandise around the world. In this dynamic, the information that is currently handled on all these merchandises is quite considerable. Therefore, large shipping companies must stop using paper for the support and movement of these goods, which are generally transported by container.

The use of simple and cheap tools, such as multilevel QR codes, allows all this world of information to be administered and managed in a more orderly and efficient way. From the precise moment in which the import/export of some merchandise between different countries or regions begins, information begins to be created, generally on paper, which can generate errors, precisely from its creation. Unfortunately, these errors cannot be detected until the documentation of the goods is delivered at the destination, then we proceed to make the corrections and adjustments to the documentation so that the goods can be introduced in the best way to the country or region of destiny. In addition, a poor capture/reading of the information associated with the goods can end with the violation of the security/cybersecurity codes implemented at any stage of the logistics for the transport of those goods. All these errors can be minimized if multilevel QR codes are used because: 1) this tool allows large amounts of information associated with merchandise to be related, even in encrypted form; 2) these codes can efficiently replace paper; 3) the information associated with each QR code can be validated at any stage associated with transport logistics; 4) errors associated with documentation are considerably reduced; 5) the mobility of the merchandise in the port customs is carried out in a faster way; 6) consequently, the waiting time at port customs is reduced; 7) the supervisory staff is considerably reduced; 8) other new technologies can be used, fully associated with multilevel QR codes, such as augmented reality, virtual reality or mixed reality; 9) the physical revisions of the goods can be reduced; 10) customs costs can be considerably reduced because this tool, based on multilevel QR codes, does not require large financial investments; 11) a correct, and more efficient, collection of taxes associated with each merchandise is promoted. Therefore, it can be determined that the access control of merchandise in a port custom must be automated, which does not require great technological or cutting-edge innovations.

In addition, and with a view to the short term, this tool, based on multilevel QR codes, can be the basis for creating a computer system that relates all the information generated for all the goods transported by ship. This system must be shared by all those responsible for the transfer of these goods, even each person responsible for a stage of the logistics of the transport of the goods must have access to validate and correct, when this is the case, the information related to some transported goods. on the ship. On the other hand, world experience shows that more and more countries are inclined to promote training initiatives and the development of port clusters. The cluster idea is part of the well-known concept of agglomeration economies, it is a new way of looking at the economy, and it is better aligned with the nature of competitiveness and the sources of competitive advantages. Therefore, the cluster offers great advantages and allows substantial improvements in the equipment, processes, and organization of companies, in addition to encouraging innovation and the implementation of simple and economical, but efficient, and innovative technological tools, such as the one presented in this work.

REFERENCES

Aaker, D. (1996). *Building Strong Brands*. The Free Press.

Abdoli-Sejzi, A. (2015). Augmented reality and virtual learning environment. *Journal of Applied Sciences Research*, *11*(8), 1–5. https://www.researchgate.net/profile/Abbas-Abdoli-Sejzi/publication/277137476_Augmented_Reality_and_Virtual_Learning_Environment/links/5562ccbe08ae8c0cab3338f3/Augmented-Reality-and-Virtual-Learning-Environment.pdf

Aghekyan-Simonian, M., Forsythe, S., Kwon, W. S., & Chattaraman, V. (2012). The role of product brand image and online store image on perceived risks and online purchase intentions for apparel. *Journal of Retailing and Consumer Services*, *19*(3), 325–331. doi:10.1016/j.jretconser.2012.03.006

Agrebi, S., & Jallais, J. (2015). Explain the intention to use smartphones for mobile shopping. *Journal of Retailing and Consumer Services*, *22*, 16–23. doi:10.1016/j.jretconser.2014.09.003

Ailawadi, K. L., Neslin, S., & Gedenk, K. (2001). Pursing the value-conscious consumer: Store brands versus national brand promotions. *Journal of Marketing*, *65*(1), 71–89. doi:10.1509/jmkg.65.1.71.18132

AlNajdi, S. M. (2022). The effectiveness of using augmented reality (AR) to enhance student performance: Using quick response (QR) codes in student textbooks in the Saudi education system. *Educational Technology Research and Development*, *70*(3), 1105–1124. doi:10.1007/s11423-022-10100-4 PMID:35400977

Badawi, B. (2019). A smart fuzzy auto suggestion system for a multilayer QR code generator. *Journal of Theoretical and Applied Information Technology*, *19*(13), 3585–3603. https://iaeme.com/MasterAdmin/Journal_uploads/IJARET/VOLUME_11_ISSUE_12/IJARET_11_12_122.pdf

Bass, L., Clements, P., & Kazman, R. (2012). *Software Architecture in Practice* (3rd ed.). Addison-Wesley Professional.

Bianco, P., Kotermanski, R., & Merson, P. (2007). *Evaluating a Service-Oriented Architecture* (Report number CMU/SEI-2007-TR-015). CMU. https://resources.sei.cmu.edu/library/asset-view.cfm?AssetID=8443

Brooks, M. R., & Cullinane, K. (2006). Chapter 1 Introduction. *Research in Transportation Economics*, *17*, 3–28. doi:10.1016/S0739-8859(06)17001-8

Cámara de Diputados de México. (2021). *Ley aduanera de México*. Diputados. https://www.diputados.gob.mx/LeyesBiblio/pdf/LAdua.pdf

Cempírek, V., Nachtigall, P., & Široký, J. (2016). Security in Logistics. *Open Engineering*, *6*(1), 637–641. doi:10.1515/eng-2016-0082

Chen, L., & Ma, Y. (2015). A Study of the Role of Customs in Global Supply Chain Management and Trade Security Based on the Authorized Economic Operator System. *Journal of Risk Analysis and Crisis Response*, *5*(2), 87–92. doi:10.2991/jrarc.2015.5.2.2

Cheung, K. F., Bell, M. G. H., & Bhattacharjya, J. (2021). Cybersecurity in logistics and supply chain management: An overview and future research directions. *Transportation Research Part E, Logistics and Transportation Review*, *146*(C), 102217. Advance online publication. doi:10.1016/j.tre.2020.102217

Convention, K. (2022). *Directives of the General Annex*. Directives on Customs Control., https://www.wcoomd.org/en/topics/facilitation/instrument-and-tools/conventions/pf_revised_kyoto_conv/kyoto_new/gach6.aspx

Dcouth, J. R., & Jaichandran, R. (2019). An Adaptive Secret QR Code Message Passing Method Using Video Steganography. *International Journal of Innovative Technology and Exploring Engineering*, *9*(1), 1510–1514. doi:10.35940/ijitee.A4331.119119

Erickson, J., & Siau, K. (2008). Web Services, Service-Oriented Computing, and Service-Oriented Architecture: Separating Hype from Reality. *Journal of Database Management*, *19*(3), 42–54. doi:10.4018/jdm.2008070103

Erl, T. (2017). *SOA design patterns*. Pearson.

Fajar, A. N., Nurcahyo, A., & Sriratnasari, S. R. (2018). SOA system architecture for interconected modern higher education in Indonesia. *Procedia Computer Science*, *135*, 354–360. doi:10.1016/j.procs.2018.08.184

Garavito Castillo, J. A. (2007). *Secretaría General de la Comunidad Andina*. Proyecto de Cooperación UE-CAN, Asistencia Relativa al Comercio I. Perú: Bellido Ediciones E.I.R.L. https://www.comunidad-andina.org/StaticFiles/201165195749libro_atrc_control.pdf

Halligan, B., & Shah, D. (2014). *Inbound Marketing: Attract, Engage, and Delight Customers Online*. Wiley.

Heath, J. B. (2020). The New National Security Challenge to the Economic Order. *The Yale Law Journal*, *129*(1020), 1022–1098. https://www.yalelawjournal.org/pdf/HeathArticle_jx8mdn4b.pdf

Hill, G. N., & Whitty, M. A. (2021). Embedding metadata in images at time of capture using physical Quick Response (QR) codes. *Information Processing & Management*, *58*(3), 102504. Advance online publication. doi:10.1016/j.ipm.2021.102504

Holmes, K. R. (2015). What Is National Security? *Index of U.S. Military Strength,* 17-26. The Heritage Foundation. https://www.heritage.org/sites/default/files/2019-10/2015_IndexOfUSMilitaryStrength_ What%20Is%20National%20Security.pdf

Honkamaa, P., Jäppinen, J., & Woodward, C. (2007). A Lightweight Approach for Augmented Reality on Camera Phones using 2D Images to Simulate in 3D. VTT. *MUM '07: Proceedings of the 6th international conference on Mobile and ubiquitous multimedia.* ACM. 10.1145/1329469.1329490

Hossain, M., Zhou, X., & Rahman, M. F. (2018). Examining the impact of QR codes on purchase intention and customer satisfaction on the basis of perceived flow. *International Journal of Engineering Business Management*, *10*, 1–11. doi:10.1177/1847979018812323

Josuttis, N. M. (2007). *SOA in Practice: The Art of Distributed System Design* (Theory in Practice) 1st Edición. USA: O'Reilly Media.

Krombholz, K., Frühwirt, P., Kieseberg, P., Kapsalis, I., Huber, M., & Weippl, E. (2014). QR Code Security: A Survey of Attacks and Challenges for Usable Security. In: Tryfonas, T., Askoxylakis, I. (Eds.) Human Aspects of Information Security, Privacy, and Trust. Springer, Cham. doi:10.1007/978-3-319-07620-1_8

Lin, P. Y., Wu, W. C., & Yang, J. H. (2021). A QR Code-Based Approach to Differentiating the Display of Augmented Reality Content. *Applied Sciences (Basel, Switzerland)*, *11*(24), 11801. doi:10.3390/app112411801

Liu, Y., Yang, J., & Liu, M. (2008). *Recognition of QR Code with mobile phones*. *2008 Chinese Control and Decision Conference*, Yantai, Shandong. 10.1109/CCDC.2008.4597299

Makinda, S. M. (1998). Sovereignty and Global Security. *Security Dialogue*, *29*(3), 281–292. doi:10.1177/0967010698029003003

Mandal, S. K., & Deepti, A. R. (2019). A Review Paper on Encryption Techniques. *International Journal of Research and Analytical Reviews*, *6*(2), 70–75. https://www.ijrar.org/papers/IJRAR1ANP010.pdf

Mikuriya, K. (2007). Supply Chain Security: The Customs Community's Response. *World Customs Journal*, *1*(2), 51–60.

Moïsé, E., & Sorescu, S. (2013). *Trade Facilitation Indicators: The Potential Impact of Trade Facilitation on Developing Countries' Trade. OECD Trade Policy Papers, No. 144.* OECD Publishing. doi:10.1787/5k4bw6kg6ws2-

Mostafa, A. A. (2015). The effectiveness of product podes in marketing. *Procedia: Social and Behavioral Sciences, 175,* 12–15. doi:10.1016/j.sbspro.2015.01.1168

Niknejad, N., Ismail, W., Ghani, I., Nazari, B., Bahari, M., & Hussin, A. R. B. C. (2020). Understanding Service-Oriented Architecture (SOA): A systematic literature review and directions for further investigation. *Information Systems, 91,* 101491. doi:10.1016/j.is.2020.101491

NPO. (2022). *FY2008 Investigation Report on In-formation Security Incidents* (Ver.1.3). Japan Network Security Association. https://www.jnsa.org/en/reports/incident.html

OECD. (2022). *Freight transport.* OECD. https://data.oecd.org/transport/freight-transport.htm

Ozkaya, E., Ozkaya, H. E., Roxas, J., Bryant, F., & Whitson, D. (2015). Factors affecting consumer usage of QR codes. *Journal of Direct, Data and Digital Marketing Practice, 16*(3), 209–224. doi:10.1057/dddmp.2015.18

Palmer, S. (2020). History of the Ports. *International Journal of Maritime History, 32*(2), 426–433. doi:10.1177/0843871420921266

Pantano, E., & Servidio, R. (2012). Modeling innovative points of sales through virtual and immersive technologies. *Journal of Retailing and Consumer Services, 19*(3), 279–286. doi:10.1016/j.jretconser.2012.02.002

Patrutiu-Baltes, L. (2016). Inbound Marketing-the most important digital marketing strategy. *Bulletin of the Transilvania University of Braşov. Series V: Economic Sciences 9*(58/2), 61-68. https://webbut.unitbv.ro/BU2016/Series%20V/Contents_V_MK.html

Pourakbar, M., & Zuidwijk, R. A. (2018). The role of customs in securing containerized global supply chains. *European Journal of Operational Research, 271*(1), 331–340. doi:10.1016/j.ejor.2018.05.012

Rohde Ponce, A. (2005). *Derecho aduanero mexicano, fundamentos y regulaciones de la actividad aduanera (4ª reimpresión)* (Vol. I). ISEF.

Rúa Costa, C. (2006). *Los puertos en el transporte marítino.* Universitat Politécnica de Catalunya. https://upcommons.upc.edu/bitstream/handle/2117/289/8.%20Rua.pdf

Saldanha, J. P., Mello, J. E., Knemeyer, A. M., & Vijayaraghavan, T. A. S. (2015). Implementing supply chain technologies in emerging markets: An institutional theory perspective. *The Journal of Supply Chain Management, 51*(1), 5–26. doi:10.1111/jscm.12065

Sen, S., Rocco, R. A., Ranganathan, S., & Brooks, J. R. (2019). Revisiting quick response code technology: Corporate perspectives. *International Journal of Mobile Communications, 17*(6), 703–726. doi:10.1504/IJMC.2019.102722

Song, Y., & Chu, M. (2021). Research on the Application of Data Encryption Technology in Computer Network Security Based on Machine Learning, *2021 IEEE 4th International Conference on Information Systems and Computer Aided Education (ICISCAE),* (pp. 399-403), Dalian, China. 10.1109/ICISCAE52414.2021.9590794

The White House. (2021). *Interim National Security Atrategic Guidance.* The White House. https://www.whitehouse.gov/wp-content/uploads/2021/03/NSC-1v2.pdf

The White House. (2022a). *National Security Strategic.* The White House. https://www.whitehouse.gov/wp-content/uploads/2022/10/Biden-Harris-Administrations-National-Security-Strategy-10.2022.pdf

Thompson, N., & Lee, K. (2013). Information Security Challenge of QR Codes. *Journal of Digital Forensics, Security and Law, 8(2)*, 2. https://commons.erau.edu/jdfsl/vol8/iss2/2

Uchiyama, H., & Marchand, E. (2012). *Object Detection and Pose Tracking for Augmented Reality: Recent Approaches.* 18th Korea-Japan Joint Workshop on Frontiers of Computer Vision (FCV), Kawasaki, Japan. https://hal.inria.fr/hal-00751704

UNCTAD. (2021). *Technology and Innovation Report 2021.* UNCTAD. https://unctad.org/system/files/official-document/tir2020_en.pdf

Wahsheh, H. A. M., & Luccio, F. L. (2020). Security and Privacy of QR Code Applications: A Comprehensive Study, General Guidelines and Solutions. *Information (Basel)*, *11*(4), 217. doi:10.3390/info11040217

Williams, P. D. (2008). *Security Studies: An Introduction.* Routledge. doi:10.4324/9780203926604

Witker, V. J. A. (1999). *Derecho tributario aduanero.* México: UNAM. http://ru.juridicas.unam.mx/xmlui/handle/123456789/9192

World Bank. (2022). Website. https://www.worldbank.org/en/home

World Bank. (2022). *Historical Container Data Series.* World Bank. https://data.worldbank.org/indicator/IS.SHP.GOOD.TU?end=2020&start=2000&view=chart

World Customs Organization. (2022a). *Home.* WCO. https://www.wcoomd.org

World Customs Organization. (2022b). *What is customs.* WCO. https://www.wcoomd.org/en/search.aspx?keyword=what+is+a+customs

World Trade Organization. (2018). *The future of world trade: How digital technologies are transforming global commerce.* WTO. https://www.wto.org/english/res_e/publications_e/world_trade_report18_e.pdf

World Trade Organization et al. (2019). *Technological innovation, supply chain trade, and workers in a globalized world.* WTO. https://www.wto.org/english/res_e/booksp_e/gvc_dev_report_2019_e.pdf

Yang, Z., Cheng, Z., Loy, C. C., Lau, W. C., Li, C. M., & Li, G. (2016). Towards robust color recovery for high-capacity color QR codes. *2016 IEEE International Conference on Image Processing (ICIP),* (pp. 2866-2870). IEEE. . doi:10.1109/ICIP.2016.7532883

Yu, B., Fu, Z., & Liu, S. (2019). A Novel Three-Layer QR Code Based on Secret Sharing Scheme and Liner Code. *Security and Communication Networks*. https://doi.org/ doi:10.1155/2019/7937816

Yuan, T., Wang, Y., Xu, K., Martin, R. R., & Hu, S. (2019). Two-Layer QR Codes. *IEEE Transactions on Image Processing*, 28(9), 4413–4428. doi:10.1109/TIP.2019.2908490 PMID:31071029

KEY TERMS AND DEFINITIONS

Carrier: It is the company dedicated to the transfer of merchandise from a point of origin to its final destination, using different means of transport.

Client: It is the physical or legal person who will make final use of the merchandise.

Customs Agent: It is the natural person authorized before the Tax Administration Service to carry out the necessary administrative procedures in customs matters for the clearance of merchandise. He is responsible for verifying the veracity of the data provided by the Importer/Exporter, establishing the necessary customs regimes according to the law and their tariff classification, and managing the documentation required for the customs clearance of the goods.

Customs Clearance: Customs clearance is the set of acts and formalities related to the entry of merchandise into a territory and its exit from it, which, by the different traffic and established customs regimes, must be carried out before customs, customs authorities, and those who introduce or Goods are extracted from a territory, either by consignees, recipients, owners, possessors or holders in imports and senders in exports, as well as customs agents, using an electronic customs system.

Customs: They are physical spaces that are strategically located on the most important borders of a country or region and with the objective of organizing, reviewing and, above all, setting taxes, when this is the case, on all merchandise that enters or leaves. from the country.

Foreign Trade: It is the exchange of products and services between two or more different countries.

Importer/Exporter: It is the physical or moral person who is duly authorized to carry out international trade, enter, or extract merchandise from the national territory temporarily or permanently, depending on the customs regime in question. To carry out this activity, it is necessary to be part of the Register of Importers.

International Trade: It is the set of commercial and financial movements, and in general, all those operations, whatever their nature, that are carried out between nations; It is therefore a universal phenomenon in which the various human communities participate.

Logistics: Logistics are all the activities that allow raw material to become merchandise, leave its point of production, and reach the consumer. These logistics activities consist of planning flows, as well as control, storage, transport, and distribution of the product at strategic points.

Marker: It is a 2D image that, thanks to its predefined color and shape characteristics, allows the information associated with it to be easily extracted.

New Technologies: New technologies today comprise the study and application of digital technologies and telecommunication systems, that is, multimedia computers and peripherals such as scanners, printers, digital cameras, etc., and computer networks, whose maximum exponent is the network known as the internet.

Tariff: A tariff is a tax or levy that applies only to goods that are imported or exported. The most common is the one charged on imports.

Compilation of References

(1758–1761). R, S. T., & T, S. K. (2023). A Review on Major Cyber Threats and Recommended Counter Measures. *International Journal for Research in Applied Science and Engineering Technology, 11*(3). Advance online publication. doi:10.22214/ijraset.2023.49764

Aadil, F., Mehmood, B., Hasan, N. U., Lim, S., Ejaz, S., & Zaman, N. (2021). Remote health monitoring using IoT-based smart wireless body area network. *Computers, Materials & Continua, 68*(2), 2499–2513. doi:10.32604/cmc.2021.014647

Aaker, D. (1996). *Building Strong Brands*. The Free Press.

Abbasi, M., Plaza-Hernández, M., Prieto, J., & Corchado, J. M. (2022). Security in the Internet of Things Application Layer: Requirements, Threats, and Solutions. *IEEE Access : Practical Innovations, Open Solutions, 10*, 97197–97216. doi:10.1109/ACCESS.2022.3205351

Abdoli-Sejzi, A. (2015). Augmented reality and virtual learning environment. *Journal of Applied Sciences Research, 11*(8), 1–5. https://www.researchgate.net/profile/Abbas-Abdoli-Sejzi/publication/277137476_Augmented_Reality_and_Virtual_Learning_Environment/links/5562ccbe08ae8c0cab3338f3/Augmented-Reality-and-Virtual-Learning-Environment.pdf

Abdulqadder, I. H., Zhou, S., Zou, D., Aziz, I. T., & Akber, S. M. A. (2020). Multi-layered intrusion detection and prevention in the SDN/NFV enabled cloud of 5G networks using AI-based defense mechanisms. *Computer Networks, 179*, 107364. doi:10.1016/j.comnet.2020.107364

Abed, A. K., & Anupam, A. (2022). Review of security issues in Internet of Things and artificial intelligence-driven solutions. *Security and Privacy, 285.*

Abed, S., Jaffal, R., & Mohd, B. J. (2023). A Review on Blockchain and IoT Integration from Energy, Security and Hardware Perspectives. *Wireless Personal Communications, 129*(3), 2079–2122. doi:10.1007/s11277-023-10226-5

Abomhara, M., & Køien, G. M. (2014, May). Security and privacy in the Internet of Things: Current status and open issues. In 2014 international conference on privacy and security in mobile systems (PRISMS) (pp. 1-8). IEEE.

Abusitta, A., De Carvalho, G. H., Wahab, O. A., Halabi, T., Fung, B. C., & Mamoori, S. A. (2023). Deep learning-enabled anomaly detection for IoT systems. *Internet of Things : Engineering Cyber Physical Human Systems, 21*, 100656. doi:10.1016/j.iot.2022.100656

Adeyemo, V. E., Abdullah, A., Jhanjhi, N. Z., Supramaniam, M., & Balogun, A. O. (2019). Ensemble and Deep-Learning Methods for Two-Class and Multi-Attack Anomaly Intrusion Detection: An Empirical study. *International Journal of Advanced Computer Science and Applications, 10*(9). doi:10.14569/IJACSA.2019.0100969

Adnan, A., Muhammed, A., Abd Ghani, A. A., Abdullah, A., & Hakim, F. (2021). 2021, 'An Intrusion Detection System for the Internet of Things Based on Machine Learning: Review and Challenges'. *Symmetry, 13*(6), 1011. doi:10.3390/sym13061011

Afenyo, M., & Caesar, L. D. (2023). Maritime cybersecurity threats: Gaps and directions for future research. *Ocean and Coastal Management, 236*, 106493. doi:10.1016/j.ocecoaman.2023.106493

Agbede, O. M. (2023). *Incident Handling and Response Process in Security Operations*. Theseus. https://www.theseus.fi/handle/10024/795764

Aghekyan-Simonian, M., Forsythe, S., Kwon, W. S., & Chattaraman, V. (2012). The role of product brand image and online store image on perceived risks and online purchase intentions for apparel. *Journal of Retailing and Consumer Services, 19*(3), 325–331. doi:10.1016/j.jretconser.2012.03.006

Agrafiotis, I., Nurse, J. R., Goldsmith, M., Creese, S., & Upton, D. (2018). A taxonomy of cyber-harms: Defining the impacts of cyber-attacks and understanding how they propagate. *Journal of Cybersecurity, 4*(1), tyy006. doi:10.1093/cybsec/tyy006

Agrawal, T. K., Angelis, J., Khilji, W. A., Kalaiarasan, R., & Wiktorsson, M. (2022). Demonstration of a blockchain-based framework using smart contracts for supply chain collaboration. *International Journal of Production Research, 61*(5), 1497–1516. doi:10.1080/00207543.2022.2039413

Agrebi, S., & Jallais, J. (2015). Explain the intention to use smartphones for mobile shopping. *Journal of Retailing and Consumer Services, 22*, 16–23. doi:10.1016/j.jretconser.2014.09.003

Ahmad, Z., Shahid Khan, A., Wai Shiang, C., Abdullah, J., & Ahmad, F. (2020). Network intrusion detection system: A systematic study of machine learning and deep learning approaches. *Transactions on Emerging Telecommunications Technologies, 32*(1), e4150. doi:10.1002/ett.4150

Ahmed, W., Khan, M. A., Najmi, A., & Khan, S. A. (2023). Strategizing risk information sharing framework among supply chain partners for financial performance. *Supply Chain Forum*, 1–18. Taylor & Francis. 10.1080/16258312.2022.2162321

Ahmed, A. A., & Ahmed, W. A. (2019). An effective multifactor authentication mechanism based on combiners of hash function over internet of things. *Sensors (Basel), 19*(17), 3663. doi:10.3390/s19173663 PMID:31443608

Ahmed, J., Nguyen, T. N., Ali, B., Javed, M. A., & Mirza, J. (2022). On the physical layer security of federated learning based IoMT networks. *IEEE Journal of Biomedical and Health Informatics, 27*(2), 691–697. doi:10.1109/JBHI.2022.3173947 PMID:35536821

AhmedM. R.IslamS.ShatabdaS.IslamA. K. M. M.RobinM. T. I. (2022). Intrusion Detection System in Software-Defined Networks Using Machine Learning and Deep Learning Techniques –A Comprehensive Survey. *Tech Rxiv*. doi:10.36227/techrxiv.17153213.v2

Ahmed, T., Karmaker, C. L., Nasir, S. B., Moktadir, M. A., & Paul, S. K. (2023). Modeling the artificial intelligence-based imperatives of industry 5.0 towards resilient supply chains: A post-COVID-19 pandemic perspective. *Computers & Industrial Engineering, 177*, 109055. doi:10.1016/j.cie.2023.109055 PMID:36741206

Ahmim, A., Maazouzi, F., Ahmim, M., Namane, S., & Dhaou, I. B. (2023). Distributed denial of service attack detection for the Internet of Things using hybrid deep learning model. *IEEE Access : Practical Innovations, Open Solutions, 11*, 119862–119875. doi:10.1109/ACCESS.2023.3327620

Ailawadi, K. L., Neslin, S., & Gedenk, K. (2001). Pursing the value-conscious consumer: Store brands versus national brand promotions. *Journal of Marketing, 65*(1), 71–89. doi:10.1509/jmkg.65.1.71.18132

Akanmu, M. D., Hassan, M. G., Mohamad, B., & Nordin, N. (2021). Sustainability through TQM practices in the food and beverages industry. *International Journal of Quality & Reliability Management, 40*(2), 335–364. doi:10.1108/IJQRM-05-2021-0143

Akella, G. K., Wibowo, S., Grandhi, S., & Mubarak, S. (2023). A Systematic Review of Blockchain Technology Adoption Barriers and Enablers for Smart and Sustainable Agriculture. *Big Data and Cognitive Computing*, 7(2), 86. doi:10.3390/bdcc7020086

Akhtar, N. (2020). Security in the internet of Things: a systematic Mapping Study. *Foundation University Journal of Engineering and Applied Sciences (HEC Recognized Y Category, ISSN 2706-7351), 1*(2), 31-42.

Akoglu, L., Tong, H. and Koutra, D. (2014). Graph based anomaly detection and description: a survey. *Data Mining and Knowledge Discovery*, 29(3), 626–688. . doi:10.1007/s10618-014-0365-y

Al Lail, M., Garcia, A. and Olivo, S. (2023). Machine Learning for Network Intrusion Detection—A Comparative Study. *Future Internet*, 15(7), p.243. . doi:10.3390/fi15070243

Alamri, M., Jhanjhi, N. Z., & Humayun, M. (2019). Blockchain for Internet of Things (IoT) Research Issues Challenges \& Future Directions: A Review. *Int. J. Comput. Sci. Netw. Secur*, 19, 244–258.

Al-Amri, R., Murugesan, R. K., Man, M., Abdulateef, A. F., Al-Sharafi, M. A., & Alkahtani, A. A. (2021). A review of machine learning and deep learning techniques for anomaly detection in iot data. *Applied Sciences (Basel, Switzerland)*, 11(12), 5320. doi:10.3390/app11125320

Alam, S. (2021). A Blockchain-based framework for secure Educational Credentials. [TURCOMAT]. *Turkish Journal of Computer and Mathematics Education*, 12(10), 5157–5167. doi:10.17762/turcomat.v12i10.5298

Alamsyah, A., Widiyanesti, S., Wulansari, P., Nurhazizah, E., Dewi, A. S., Rahadian, D., Ramadhani, D. P., Hakim, M. N., & Tyasamesi, P. (2023). Blockchain traceability model in the coffee industry. *Journal of Open Innovation*, 9(1), 100008. doi:10.1016/j.joitmc.2023.100008

Alani, M. M. (2021). Big data in cybersecurity: A survey of applications and future trends. *Journal of Reliable Intelligent Environments*, 7(2), 85–114. doi:10.1007/s40860-020-00120-3

Al-Banna, A., Yaqot, M., & Menezes, B. C. (2023). Roadmap to digital supply chain resilience under investment constraints. *Production & Manufacturing Research*, 11(1), 2194943. doi:10.1080/21693277.2023.2194943

Albasheer, H., Md Siraj, M., Mubarakali, A., Elsier Tayfour, O., Salih, S., Hamdan, M., Khan, S., Zainal, A., & Kamarudeen, S. (2022). Cyber-Attack Prediction Based on Network Intrusion Detection Systems for Alert Correlation Techniques: A Survey. *Sensors (Basel)*, 22(4), 1494. doi:10.3390/s22041494 PMID:35214394

Albazar, H., Abdel-Wahab, A., Alshar'e, M., & Abualkishik, A. (2023). An Adaptive Two-Factor Authentication Scheme Based on the Usage of Schnorr Signcryption Algorithm. *Informatica (Vilnius)*, 47(5). doi:10.31449/inf.v47i5.4627

Aldowah, H., Ul Rehman, S., & Umar, I. (2019). Security in internet of things: issues, challenges and solutions. In *Recent Trends in Data Science and Soft Computing: Proceedings of the 3rd International Conference of Reliable Information and Communication Technology (IRICT 2018)* (pp. 396-405). Springer International Publishing. 10.1007/978-3-319-99007-1_38

Aledhari, M., Razzak, R., Parizi, R. M., & Saeed, F. (2020). Federated learning: A survey on enabling technologies, protocols, and applications. *IEEE Access : Practical Innovations, Open Solutions*, 8, 140699–140725. doi:10.1109/ACCESS.2020.3013541 PMID:32999795

Alferidah, D. K., & Jhanjhi, N. (2020). Cybersecurity impact over bigdata and iot growth. *Paper presented at the 2020 International Conference on Computational Intelligence (ICCI)*. IEEE. 10.1109/ICCI51257.2020.9247722

Alferidah, D. K., & Jhanjhi, N. Z. (2020). A Review on Security and Privacy Issues and Challenges in Internet of Things, 20(4), 263–285.

Alferidah, D. K., & Jhanjhi, N. Z. (2020). A Review on Security and Privacy Issues and Challenges. *Internet of Things,* *20*(4), 263–285.

Alhajri, M. I., Ali, N. T., & Shubair, R. M. (2018). Classification of Indoor Environments for IoT Applications: A Machine Learning Approach. *IEEE Antennas and Wireless Propagation Letters, 17*(12), 2164–2168. doi:10.1109/LAWP.2018.2869548

Al-Harrasi, A. S., Shaikh, A. R., & Al-Badi, A. H. (2021). Towards protecting organisations' data by preventing data theft by malicious insiders. *The International Journal of Organizational Analysis.* Advance online publication. doi:10.1108/IJOA-01-2021-2598

Ali, A. M., Mahfouz, A., & Arisha, A. (2017). Analysing supply chain resilience: Integrating the constructs in a concept mapping framework via a systematic literature review. *Supply Chain Management, 22*(1), 16–39. doi:10.1108/SCM-06-2016-0197

Ali, S. E., Tariq, N., Khan, F. A., Ashraf, M., Abdul, W., & Saleem, K. (2023). BFT-IoMT: A Blockchain-Based Trust Mechanism to Mitigate Sybil Attack Using Fuzzy Logic in the Internet of Medical Things. *Sensors (Basel), 23*(9), 4265. doi:10.3390/s23094265 PMID:37177468

Ali, S., Li, Q., & Yousafzai, A. (2024). Blockchain and federated learning-based intrusion Detection Approaches for edge-enabled industrial IoT networks: A survey. *Ad Hoc Networks, 152,* 103320. doi:10.1016/j.adhoc.2023.103320

Aljabhan, B., & Obaidat, M. A. (2023). Privacy-Preserving Blockchain Framework for Supply Chain Management: Perceptive Craving Game Search Optimization (PCGSO). *Sustainability (Basel), 15*(8), 6905. doi:10.3390/su15086905

Aljanabi, M., Ismail, M. A., & Ali, A. (2021). Intrusion Detection Systems, Issues, Challenges, and Needs. *International Journal of Computational Intelligence Systems., 14*(1), 560. doi:10.2991/ijcis.d.210105.001

Aljemy, K., Alanazi, M., Alsofiry, M., & Baig, A. (2019). Improving IoT security using blockchain. *Paper presented at the 2019 IEEE 10th GCC Conference and Exhibition, GCC 2019.* IEEE. 10.1109/GCC45510.2019.1570521015

Al-Jumeily, D., Arshad, D., Tariq, N., Baker, T., Tawfik, H., & Asim, M. (2022). A Lightweight Trust-enabled Routing in RPL-based IoT Networks Against Sybil Attack. *PLoS One, 17*(7). PMID:35901074

Al-Khatib, A. W. (2022). Internet of things, big data analytics and operational performance: The mediating effect of supply chain visibility. *Journal of Manufacturing Technology Management, 34*(1), 1–24. doi:10.1108/JMTM-08-2022-0310

Alkhodair, A., Mohanty, S. P., & Kougianos, E. (2023). FlexiChain 3.0: Distributed Ledger Technology-Based Intelligent Transportation for Vehicular Digital Asset Exchange in Smart Cities. *Sensors (Basel), 23*(8), 4114. doi:10.3390/s23084114 PMID:37112453

Alkinani, M. H., Almazroi, A. A., Jhanjhi, N. Z., & Khan, N. A. (2021). 5G and IoT Based Reporting and Accident Detection (RAD) System to Deliver First Aid Box Using Unmanned Aerial Vehicle. *Sensors (Basel), 21*(20), 6905. doi:10.3390/s21206905 PMID:34696118

Allenbrand, C. (2023). Smart contract-enabled consortium blockchains for the control of supply chain information distortion. *Blockchain: Research and Applications, 100134*(3), 100134. doi:10.1016/j.bcra.2023.100134

Alloghani, M., Alani, M. M., Al-Jumeily, D., Baker, T., Mustafina, J., Hussain, A., & Aljaaf, A. J. (2019). A systematic review on the status and progress of homomorphic encryption technologies. *Journal of Information Security and Applications, 48,* 102362. doi:10.1016/j.jisa.2019.102362

Al-mashhadi, S., Anbar, M., Hasbullah, I., & Alamiedy, T. A. (2021). Hybrid rule-based botnet detection approach using machine learning for analysing DNS traffic. *PeerJ. Computer Science, 7,* 1–34. doi:10.7717/peerj-cs.640 PMID:34458571

Almeida, T., & Hidalgo, J. (2012). *UCI Machine Learning Repository.* [online] UC Irvine Machine Learning Repository. https://archive.ics.uci.edu/dataset/228/sms+spam+collection

Almusaylim, Z. A., & Jhanjhi, N. Z. (2018). A review on smart home present state and challenges: Linked to context-awareness internet of things (IoT). *Wireless Networks*, *25*(6), 3193–3204. doi:10.1007/s11276-018-1712-5

Almusaylim, Z. A., Jhanjhi, N. Z., & Jung, L. T. (2018). Proposing A Data Privacy Aware Protocol for Roadside Accident Video Reporting Service Using 5G. In *Vehicular Cloud Networks Environment.* IEEE. doi:10.1109/ICCOINS.2018.8510588

AlNajdi, S. M. (2022). The effectiveness of using augmented reality (AR) to enhance student performance: Using quick response (QR) codes in student textbooks in the Saudi education system. *Educational Technology Research and Development*, *70*(3), 1105–1124. doi:10.1007/s11423-022-10100-4 PMID:35400977

Alqarni, M. A., Alkatheiri, M. S., Chauhdary, S. H., & Saleem, S. (2023). Use of Blockchain-Based Smart Contracts in Logistics and Supply Chains. *Electronics (Basel)*, *12*(6), 1340. doi:10.3390/electronics12061340

Alrashdi, I., Alqazzaz, A., Aloufi, E., Alharthi, R., Zohdy, M., & Ming, H. (2019). AD-IoT: Anomaly detection of IoT cyberattacks in smart city using machine learning. *2019 IEEE 9th Annual Computing and Communication Workshop and Conference, CCWC 2019*, (pp. 305–310). IEEE. 10.1109/CCWC.2019.8666450

Alrefaei, F., Alzahrani, A., Song, H., & Alrefaei, S. (2022, June). A Survey on the Jamming and Spoofing attacks on the Unmanned Aerial Vehicle Networks. In *2022 IEEE International IOT, Electronics and Mechatronics Conference (IEMTRONICS)* (pp. 1-7). IEEE. 10.1109/IEMTRONICS55184.2022.9795809

Alsboui, T., Qin, Y., Hill, R., & Al-Aqrabi, H. (2021). Distributed Intelligence in the Internet of Things: Challenges and Opportunities. *SN Computer Science*, *2*(4), 277. doi:10.1007/s42979-021-00677-7

Alshehri, M. (2023). Blockchain-assisted internet of things framework in smart livestock farming. *Internet of Things : Engineering Cyber Physical Human Systems*, *22*, 100739. doi:10.1016/j.iot.2023.100739

Alshudukhi, K. S., Khemakhem, M., Eassa, F. E., & Jambi, K. M. (2023). An Interoperable Blockchain Security Frameworks Based on Microservices and Smart Contract in IoT Environment. *Electronics (Basel)*, *12*(3), 776. doi:10.3390/electronics12030776

Alsmadi, I. (2023). *The NICE cyber security framework: Cyber security intelligence and analytics.* Springer Nature. doi:10.1007/978-3-031-21651-0

Al-Sumaidaee, G., Alkhudary, R., Zilic, Z., & Swidan, A. (2023). Performance analysis of a private blockchain network built on Hyperledger Fabric for healthcare. *Information Processing & Management*, *60*(2), 103160. doi:10.1016/j.ipm.2022.103160

Al-Zahrani, A. (2022). Assessing and Proposing Countermeasures for Cyber-Security Attacks. *International Journal of Advanced Computer Science and Applications*, *13*(1), 885–895. doi:10.14569/IJACSA.2022.01301102

Amro, A., & Gkioulos, V. (2023). Cyber risk management for autonomous passenger ships using threat-informed defense-in-depth. *International Journal of Information Security*, *22*(1), 249–288. doi:10.1007/s10207-022-00638-y

Anandan, R., Gopalakrishnan, S., Pal, S., & Zaman, N. (2022). *Industrial Internet of Things (IIoT): Intelligent Analytics for Predictive Maintenance.* John Wiley & Sons. doi:10.1002/9781119769026

Ananna, F. F., Nowreen, R., Jahwari, S. S. R. A., Costa, E., Angeline, L., & Sindiramutty, S. R. (2023). Analysing Influential factors in student academic achievement: Prediction modelling and insight. *International Journal of Emerging Multidisciplinaries Computer Science & Artificial Intelligence*, *2*(1). doi:10.54938/ijemdcsai.2023.02.1.254

Anderson, T. (2018). Evaluating Third-Party Vendors and Suppliers. *Security Magazine, 62*(9), 52–56.

Andersson, K., You, I., & Palmieri, F. (2018). Security and Privacy for Smart, Connected, and Mobile IoT Devices and Platforms. *Security and Communication Networks, 2018*, 2018. doi:10.1155/2018/5346596

Ang, K. L. M., Seng, J. K. P., & Ngharamike, E. (2022). Towards crowdsourcing internet of things (crowd-iot): Architectures, security and applications. *Future Internet, 14*(2), 49. doi:10.3390/fi14020049

Anjum, N., Latif, Z., Lee, C., Shoukat, I. A., & Iqbal, U. (2021). MIND: A Multi-Source Data Fusion Scheme for Intrusion Detection in Networks. *Sensors (Basel), 21*(14), 4941. doi:10.3390/s21144941 PMID:34300681

Annadurai, C., Nelson, I., Devi, K. N., Ramachandran, M., Jhanjhi, N. Z., Masud, M., & Sheikh, A. M. (2022). Biometric Authentication-Based Intrusion Detection using Artificial intelligence internet of things in smart city. *Energies, 15*(19), 7430. doi:10.3390/en15197430

Anthi, E., Williams, L., Javed, A., & Burnap, P. (2021). Hardening machine learning denial of service (DoS) defences against adversarial attacks in IoT smart home networks. *Computers & Security, 108*, 102352. doi:10.1016/j.cose.2021.102352

Anuradha Samarakoon, S. (2022). Bypassing Content-based internet packages with an SSL/TLS Tunnel, SNI Spoofing, and DNS spoofing. *arXiv e-prints*, arXiv-2212.

Aqeel, M., Ali, F., Iqbal, M. W., Rana, T. A., Arif, M., & Auwul, M. R. (2022). A Review of Security and Privacy Concerns in the Internet of Things (IoT). *Journal of Sensors, 2022*, 2022. doi:10.1155/2022/5724168

Arass, M. E., & Souissi, N. (2019). *Smart SIEM: From Big Data logs and events to Smart Data alerts.* ResearchGate. https://www.researchgate.net/publication/333752299_Smart_SIEM_From_Big_Data_logs_and_events_to_Smart_Data_alerts

Ar, I. M., Erol, I., Peker, I., Ozdemir, A. I., Medeni, T. D., & Medeni, I. T. (2020). Evaluating the feasibility of blockchain in logistics operations: A decision framework. *Expert Systems with Applications, 158*, 113543. doi:10.1016/j.eswa.2020.113543

Arshad, D., Asim, M., Tariq, N., Baker, T., Tawfik, H., & Al-Jumeily, O. B. E. (2022). THC-RPL: A lightweight Trust-enabled routing in RPL-based IoT networks against Sybil attack. *PLoS One, 17*(7), e0271277. doi:10.1371/journal.pone.0271277 PMID:35901074

Aruna, S., Priya, S. M., Reshmeetha, K., Sudhayini, E. S., & Narayanan, A. A. (2023). *Blockchain Integration with Artificial Intelligence and Internet of Things Technologies.* IEEE. doi:10.1109/ICICCS56967.2023.10142527

Ashraf, H., Hanif, M., Ihsan, U., Al-Quayed, F., Humayun, M., & Jhanjhi, N. (2023*).* A Secure and Reliable Supply chain management approach integrated with IoT and Blockchain. *Paper presented at the 2023 International Conference on Business Analytics for Technology and Security (ICBATS).* IEEE.10.1109/ICBATS57792.2023.10111371

Aslan, Ö., Aktuğ, S. S., Ozkan-Okay, M., Yılmaz, A. A., & Akin, E. (2023). A comprehensive review of cyber security vulnerabilities, threats, attacks, and solutions. *Electronics (Basel), 12*(6), 1333. doi:10.3390/electronics12061333

Assibi, A. T. (2023). Literature Review on Building Cyber Resilience Capabilities to Counter Future Cyber Threats: The Role of Enterprise Risk Management (ERM) and Business Continuity (BC). *OAlib, 10*(04), 1–15. doi:10.4236/oalib.1109882

Assiri, M., & Humayun, M. (2023). A Blockchain-Enabled Framework for Improving the Software Audit Process. *Applied Sciences (Basel, Switzerland), 13*(6), 3437. doi:10.3390/app13063437

Aste, T., Tasca, P., & Di Matteo, T. (2017). Blockchain Technologies: The Foreseeable Impact on Society and Industry. *Computer, 50*(9), 18–28. doi:10.1109/MC.2017.3571064

Ates, C., Ozdel, S., & Anarim, E. (2019). Clustering Based DDoS Attack Detection Using the Relationship between Packet Headers. *Proceedings - 2019 Innovations in Intelligent Systems and Applications Conference, ASYU 2019*. IEEE. 10.1109/ASYU48272.2019.8946331

Atlam, H. F., & Oluwatimilehin, O. (2022). Business Email Compromise Phishing Detection Based on Machine Learning: A Systematic Literature Review. *Electronics (Basel)*, *12*(1), 42. doi:10.3390/electronics12010042

Attou, H., Mohy-Eddine, M., Guezzaz, A., Benkirane, S., Azrour, M., Alabdulatif, A., & Almusallam, N. (2023). Towards an intelligent intrusion detection system to detect malicious activities in cloud computing. *Applied Sciences (Basel, Switzerland)*, *13*(17), 9588. doi:10.3390/app13179588

Augello, W. J. (2001). *Transportation, logistics and the law.*

Awan, S. H., Ahmed, S., Ullah, F., Nawaz, A., Khan, A. J., Uddin, M. N., Alharbi, A. G., Alosaimi, W., & Alyami, H. (2021). IoT with BlockChain: A Futuristic Approach in Agriculture and Food Supply Chain. *Wireless Communications and Mobile Computing*, *2021*, 1–14. doi:10.1155/2021/5580179

Ayoub, I., Balakrichenan, S., Khawam, K., & Ampeau, B. (2023). DNS for IoT: A Survey. *Sensors (Basel)*, *23*(9), 4473. doi:10.3390/s23094473 PMID:37177679

Azam, H., Dulloo, M. I., Majeed, M. H., Wan, J. P. H., Xin, L. T., & Sindiramutty, S. R. (2023). Cybercrime Unmasked: Investigating cases and digital evidence. *International Journal of Emerging Multidisciplinaries Computer Science & Artificial Intelligence*, *2*(1). doi:10.54938/ijemdcsai.2023.02.1.255

Azam, H., Dulloo, M. I., Majeed, M. H., Wan, J. P. H., Xin, L. T., Tajwar, M. A., & Sindiramutty, S. R. (2023). Defending the digital Frontier: IDPS and the battle against Cyber threat. *International Journal of Emerging Multidisciplinaries Computer Science & Artificial Intelligence*, *2*(1). doi:10.54938/ijemdcsai.2023.02.1.253

Azam, H., Tajwar, M. A., Mayhialagan, S., Davis, A. J., Yik, C. J., Ali, D., & Sindiramutty, S. R. (2023). Innovations in Security: A study of cloud Computing and IoT. *International Journal of Emerging Multidisciplinaries Computer Science & Artificial Intelligence*, *2*(1). doi:10.54938/ijemdcsai.2023.02.1.252

AzamH.TanM.PinL. T.SyahmiM. A.QianA. L. W.JingyanH.UddinH.SindiramuttyS. R. (2023). Wireless Technology Security and Privacy: A Comprehensive Study. *Preprint*. doi:10.20944/preprints202311.0664.v1

Aziz, F. (2023). *Beyond the Ledger: Enhancing Global Sustainability through Data-Driven Accounting Frameworks.* Farooq Aziz.

BadaM.HameedF. (2019). Report on cybersecurity maturity level in Albania. *Social Science Research Network*. doi:10.2139/ssrn.3658345

Badawi, B. (2019). A smart fuzzy auto suggestion system for a multilayer QR code generator. *Journal of Theoretical and Applied Information Technology*, *19*(13), 3585–3603. https://iaeme.com/MasterAdmin/Journal_uploads/IJARET/VOLUME_11_ISSUE_12/IJARET_11_12_122.pdf

Bader, D., Innab, N., Atoum, I., & Alathamneh, F. (2023). The influence of the Internet of things on pharmaceutical inventory management. *International Journal of Data and Network Science*, *7*(1), 381–390. doi:10.5267/j.ijdns.2022.9.009

Bajpai, S., Sharma, K., & Chaurasia, B. K. (2023). Intrusion Detection Framework in IoT Networks. *SN Computer Science*, *4*(4), 1–17. doi:10.1007/s42979-023-01770-9

Bakhsh, S. A., Khan, M. A., Ahmed, F., Alshehri, M., Ali, H., & Ahmad, J. (2023). Enhancing IoT network security through deep learning-powered Intrusion Detection System. *Internet of Things : Engineering Cyber Physical Human Systems*, *24*, 100936. doi:10.1016/j.iot.2023.100936

Bakshi, G. (2021). IoT Architecture Vulnerabilities and Security Measures. *Security Incidents & Response Against Cyber Attacks*, 199-215.

Bandari, V. (2023, January 20). *Enterprise Data Security Measures: A Comparative Review of Effectiveness and Risks Across Different Industries and Organization Types*. Tensor Gate. https://research.tensorgate.org/index.php/IJBIBDA/article/view/3

Baniata, H., & Kertesz, A. (2023). Approaches to Overpower Proof-of-Work Blockchains Despite Minority. *IEEE Access : Practical Innovations, Open Solutions*, *11*, 2952–2967. doi:10.1109/ACCESS.2023.3234322

Barbaschow, A. (2020, February 3). Toll Group shuts down IT systems in response to "cybersecurity incident." *ZDNET*. https://www.zdnet.com/article/toll-group-shuts-down-it-systems-in-response-to-cybersecurity-incident/

Barnett, M., Samori, I., Griffin, B., Palmer, X., & Potter, L. (2023). A Commentary and Exploration of Maritime Applications of Biosecurity and Cybersecurity Intersections. *Proceedings of the 22nd European Conference on Cyber Warfare and Security, 22*(1), 65–72. 10.34190/eccws.22.1.1283

Basati, A., & Faghih, M. M. (2023). APAE: An IoT intrusion detection system using asymmetric parallel auto-encoder. *Neural Computing & Applications*, *35*(7), 4813–4833. doi:10.1007/s00521-021-06011-9

Bass, L., Clements, P., & Kazman, R. (2012). *Software Architecture in Practice* (3rd ed.). Addison-Wesley Professional.

Basu, P., Deb, P., & Singh, A. (2023). Blockchain and the carbon credit ecosystem: Sustainable management of the supply chain. *The Journal of Business Strategy*. doi:10.1108/JBS-09-2022-0157

Battaglioni, M., Rafaiani, G., Chiaraluce, F., & Baldi, M. (2022). MAGIC: A Method for Assessing Cyber Incidents Occurrence. *IEEE Access : Practical Innovations, Open Solutions*, *10*, 73458–73473. doi:10.1109/ACCESS.2022.3189777

Bavoria, R. K. (2023, May 1). *A Study On Enablers And Barriers Of Additive Manufacturing Adoption In Industry 4.0: An Ahp Approach*. D-Space. http://www.dspace.dtu.ac.in:8080/jspui/handle/repository/19859

Baz, J. E., Cherrafi, A., Benabdellah, A. C., Zekhnini, K., Nguema, J. B. B., & Derrouiche, R. (2023). Environmental Supply Chain Risk Management for Industry 4.0: A Data Mining Framework and Research Agenda. *Systems*, *11*(1), 46. doi:10.3390/systems11010046

Behie, S. W., Pasman, H. J., Khan, F. I., Shell, K., Alarfaj, A., El-Kady, A. H., & Hernandez, M. (2023). Leadership 4.0: The changing landscape of industry management in the smart digital era. *Process Safety and Environmental Protection*, *172*, 317–328. doi:10.1016/j.psep.2023.02.014

Belenguer, A., Navaridas, J., & Pascual, J. A. (2022). *A review of Federated Learning in Intrusion Detection Systems for IoT*, 1–13.

Belenguer, A., Navaridas, J., & Pascual, J. A. (2022). A review of federated learning in intrusion detection systems for iot. arXiv preprint arXiv:2204.12443.

BelMannoubi, S., Touati, H., Hadded, M., Toumi, K., Shagdar, O., & Kamoun, F. (2023). A Comprehensive Survey on Blockchain-Based C-ITS Applications: Classification, Challenges, and Open Issues. *Vehicular Communications*, *100607*, 100607. doi:10.1016/j.vehcom.2023.100607

Ben-Daya, M., Hassini, E., & Bahroun, Z. (2019). Internet of things and supply chain management: A literature review. *International Journal of Production Research*, *57*(15-16), 4719–4742. doi:10.1080/00207543.2017.1402140

Ben-Itzhak, Y., Möllering, H., Pinkas, B., Schneider, T., Suresh, A., Tkachenko, O., & Yanai, A. (2022). *ScionFL: Secure Quantized Aggregation for Federated Learning*. arXiv preprint arXiv:2210.07376.

Benkhelifa, E., Welsh, T., & Hamouda, W. (2018). A critical review of practices and challenges in intrusion detection systems for IoT: Toward universal and resilient systems. *IEEE Communications Surveys and Tutorials*, 20(4), 3496–3509. doi:10.1109/COMST.2018.2844742

Benyahya, M., Collen, A., Kechagia, S., & Nijdam, N. A. (2022). Automated city shuttles: Mapping the key challenges in cybersecurity, privacy and standards to future developments. *Computers & Security*, 122, 102904. doi:10.1016/j.cose.2022.102904

Berry, H. S. (2023). *The Importance of Cybersecurity in Supply Chain.* IEEE. doi:10.1109/ISDFS58141.2023.10131834

Besiekierska, A. (2022). Legal Aspects of the Supply Chain Cybersecurity in the Context of 5G Technology. *Rev. Eur. & Comp. L.*, 51(4), 129–147. doi:10.31743/recl.14623

Bhardwaj, A., Akhil, K., Tripathi, A., & Srivastava, S. (2021). Blockchain-based solutions for supply chain management: A comprehensive review. *Computers & Industrial Engineering*, 164, 107249.

Bhatt, J. (2023a). *Use of Blockchain in Medical Supply and Pharmacy.* www.onlineengineeringeducation.com. https://doi.org/ doi:10.52783/joee.v14i1s.79

Bhattacharya, S., Maurya, B., Talukdar, D., Asokan, A., & N, M. (2023). Challenges Faced in Countering Cyber Crimes in Political Science and Management: a Critical Study. *EcB, 12*(7).

Bhoi, S. K., Panda, S. K., Jena, K. K., Sahoo, K. S., Jhanjhi, N., Masud, M., & Aljahdali, S. (2022). IoT-EMS: An Internet of Things Based Environment Monitoring System in Volunteer Computing Environment. *Intelligent Automation & Soft Computing*, 32(3).

BHP. (2019). *BHP and Mitsubishi Development Pty Ltd enter into a new partnership for the future of nickel.* BHP. https://www.bhp.com/media-and-insights/news-releases/2019/07/bhp-and-mitsubishi-development-pty-ltd-enter-into-a-new-partnership-for-the-future-of-nickel/

Bhuvana, J., Hashmi, H., Adhvaryu, R., Kashyap, S., Kumari, S., & Wadhwa, D. (2023). Intelligent analytics algorithms in breach detection systems for securing VANETs and data for smart transportation management. *Soft Computing*. doi:10.1007/s00500-023-08399-z

Bianchi, V., Bassoli, M., Lombardo, G., Fornacciari, P., Mordonini, M., & De Munari, I. (2019). IoT Wearable Sensor and Deep Learning: An Integrated Approach for Personalized Human Activity Recognition in a Smart Home Environment. *IEEE Internet of Things Journal*, 6(5), 8553–8562. doi:10.1109/JIOT.2019.2920283

Bianco, P., Kotermanski, R., & Merson, P. (2007). *Evaluating a Service-Oriented Architecture* (Report number CMU/SEI-2007-TR-015). CMU. https://resources.sei.cmu.edu/library/asset-view.cfm?AssetID=8443

Bilali, V., Kosyvas, D., Theodoropoulos, T., Ouzounoglou, E., Karagiannidis, L., & Amditis, A. (2022). IRIS Advanced Threat Intelligence Orchestrator- a way to manage cybersecurity challenges of IoT ecosystems in smart cities. In Lecture Notes in Computer Science (pp. 315–325). doi:10.1007/978-3-031-20936-9_25

Birkel, H. S., & Hartmann, E. (2020). Internet of Things–the future of managing supply chain risks. *Supply Chain Management*, 25(5), 535–548. doi:10.1108/SCM-09-2019-0356

Bi, Y., Fan, K., Zhang, K., Yuhan, B., Li, H., & Yang, Y. (2023). A secure and efficient two-party protocol enabling ownership transfer of RFID objects. *IEEE Internet of Things Journal*, 1(18), 16225–16237. doi:10.1109/JIOT.2023.3267501

Bloch, F., Jackson, M., & Tebaldi, P. (2016). *Centrality measures in networks.* [online] Social Choice and Welfare. Available at: https://www.semanticscholar.org/paper/Centrality-measures-in-networks-Bloch-Jackson/6bf5a02cd5c9ace5c275416bec0b72a645ce7299.

Bocquet-AppelN.NoyelleM.CattaneoA. (2023). Graph-based Intrusion Detection: A Modern Approach. figshare.*com.* [online] doi:10.6084/m9.figshare.22216987.v1

Bø, E., Hovi, I. B., & Pinchasik, D. R. (2023). COVID-19 disruptions and Norwegian food and pharmaceutical supply chains: Insights into supply chain risk management, resilience, and reliability. *Sustainable Futures : An Applied Journal of Technology, Environment and Society, 5*, 100102. doi:10.1016/j.sftr.2022.100102 PMID:36530767

Bonawitz, K., Eichner, H., Grieskamp, W., Huba, D., Ingerman, A., Ivanov, V., & Roselander, J. (2019). Towards federated learning at scale: System design. *Proceedings of machine learning and systems, 1*, 374-388.

Borghesi, A., Molan, M., Milano, M., & Bartolini, A. (2022). Anomaly Detection and Anticipation in High Performance Computing Systems. *IEEE Transactions on Parallel and Distributed Systems, 33*(4), 739–750. doi:10.1109/TPDS.2021.3082802

BorwankarJ.PanditS.PatelV.NirmalJ. (2023). IOT-Based Smart Warehouse Monitoring System. *Available at* SSRN 4461490.

Bose, R., Mondal, H., Sarkar, I., & Roy, S. (2022). Design of smart inventory management system for construction sector based on IoT and cloud computing. *e-Prime-Advances in Electrical Engineering. Electronics and Energy, 2*, 100051.

Botari, T., Izbicki, R., & de Carvalho, A. C. P. L. F. (2020). Local interpretation methods to machine learning using the domain of the feature space. *Paper presented at the Communications in Computer and Information Science.* Springer. 10.1007/978-3-030-43823-4_21

BrohiS. N.JhanjhiN. Z.BrohiN. N.BrohiM. N. (2020). Key Applications of State-of-the-Art Technologies to Mitigate and Eliminate COVID-19.pdf. Authorea Preprints. doi:10.36227/techrxiv.12115596.v1

Brooks, M. R., & Cullinane, K. (2006). Chapter 1 Introduction. *Research in Transportation Economics, 17*, 3–28. doi:10.1016/S0739-8859(06)17001-8

Buettner, R., & Schunter, M. (2019, October). Efficient machine learning based detection of heart disease. In *2019 IEEE international conference on E-health networking, application & services (HealthCom)* (pp. 1-6). IEEE.

Buntak, K., Kovačić, M., & Mutavdžija, M. (2019). Internet of things and smart warehouses as the future of logistics. *Tehnički glasnik, 13*(3), 248-253.

Cámara de Diputados de México. (2021). *Ley aduanera de México.* Diputados. https://www.diputados.gob.mx/Leyes-Biblio/pdf/LAdua.pdf

Capano, D. E. (2022). Throwback Attack: How NotPetya accidentally took down global shipping giant Maersk. *Industrial Cybersecurity Pulse.* https://www.industrialcybersecuritypulse.com/threats-vulnerabilities/throwback-attack-how-notpetya-accidentally-took-down-global-shipping-giant-maersk/

Carmi, L., Zohar, M., & Riva, G. M. (2022). The European General Data Protection Regulation (GDPR) in mHealth: Theoretical and practical aspects for practitioners' use. *Medicine, Science, and the Law, 63*(1), 61–68. doi:10.1177/00258024221118411 PMID:35950240

Carnley, P. R., & Kettani, H. (2019). Identity and access management for the internet of things. *International Journal of Future Computer and Communication, 8*(4), 129–133. doi:10.18178/ijfcc.2019.8.4.554

Casino, F., Dasaklis, T. K., & Patsakis, C. (2019). A systematic literature review of blockchain-based applications: Current status, classification and open issues. *Telematics and Informatics, 36*, 55–81. doi:10.1016/j.tele.2018.11.006

Çelik, Y., Petri, I., & Rezgui, Y. (2023). Integrating BIM and Blockchain across construction lifecycle and supply chains. *Computers in Industry, 148*, 103886. doi:10.1016/j.compind.2023.103886

Cempírek, V., Nachtigall, P., & Široký, J. (2016). Security in Logistics. *Open Engineering, 6*(1), 637–641. doi:10.1515/eng-2016-0082

Chaabouni, N., Mosbah, M., Zemmari, A., Sauvignac, C., & Faruki, P. (2019). Network intrusion detection for IoT security based on learning techniques. *IEEE Communications Surveys and Tutorials, 21*(3), 2671–2701. doi:10.1109/COMST.2019.2896380

Chai, A., Le, J. P., Lee, A. S., & Lo, S. M. (2019). Applying Graph Theory to Examine the Dynamics of Student Discussions in Small-Group Learning. *CBE Life Sciences Education, 18*(2), ar29. doi:10.1187/cbe.18-11-0222 PMID:31150318

Chaiban, A., Sovilj, D., Soliman, H., Salmon, G., & Lin, X. (2022). Investigating the Influence of Feature Sources for Malicious Website Detection. *Applied Sciences (Basel, Switzerland), 12*(6), 2806. doi:10.3390/app12062806

Chai, T. U., Goh, H. G., Liew, S. Y., & Ponnusamy, V. (2023). Protection Schemes for DDoS, ARP Spoofing, and IP Fragmentation Attacks in Smart Factory. *Systems, 11*(4), 211. doi:10.3390/systems11040211

Chaithanya, B. N., & Brahmananda, S. H. (2022). AI-enhanced Defense Against Ransomware Within the Organization's Architecture. *Journal of Cyber Security and Mobility*, 621-654.

Chan, N. W. X., & Teah, N. Y. F. (2023). *Spam Detection using Naïve Bayes*. CoLab. https://colab.research.google.com/drive/1q3P-3g9SDE5BRIVab1eqFzJyM4hr6IDC?usp=sharing

Chandan, A., Rosano, M., & Potdar, V. (2023). Achieving UN SDGs in Food Supply Chain Using Blockchain Technology. *Sustainability (Basel), 15*(3), 2109. doi:10.3390/su15032109

Chatterjee, A., & Ahmed, B. S. (2022). IoT anomaly detection methods and applications: A survey. *Internet of Things : Engineering Cyber Physical Human Systems, 19*, 100568. doi:10.1016/j.iot.2022.100568

Chatziamanetoglou, D., & Rantos, K. (2023). Blockchain-Based Security Configuration Management for ICT Systems. *Electronics (Basel), 12*(8), 1879. doi:10.3390/electronics12081879

Chaurasiya, S. K., Biswas, A., Nayyar, A., Jhanjhi, N. Z., & Banerjee, R. (2023). DEICA: A differential evolution-based improved clustering algorithm for IoT-based heterogeneous wireless sensor networks. *International Journal of Communication Systems, 36*(5), e5420. Advance online publication. doi:10.1002/dac.5420

Chen, L., & Ma, Y. (2015). A Study of the Role of Customs in Global Supply Chain Management and Trade Security Based on the Authorized Economic Operator System. *Journal of Risk Analysis and Crisis Response, 5*(2), 87–92. doi:10.2991/jrarc.2015.5.2.2

Chen, M., & Yan, M. (2023). How to protect smart and autonomous vehicles from stealth viruses and worms. *ISA Transactions, 141*, 52–58. doi:10.1016/j.isatra.2023.04.019 PMID:37217376

Chen, R. R., Chen, K., & Ou, C. X. (2022). Facilitating interorganizational trust in strategic alliances by leveraging blockchain-based systems: Case studies of two eastern banks. *International Journal of Information Management, 68*, 102521. doi:10.1016/j.ijinfomgt.2022.102521

Chen, X., He, C., Chen, Y., & Xie, Z. (2022). Internet of Things (IoT)—Blockchain-enabled pharmaceutical supply chain resilience in the post-pandemic era. *Frontiers of Engineering Management, 10*(1), 82–95. doi:10.1007/s42524-022-0233-1

Chen, Y. (2023). How blockchain adoption affects supply chain sustainability in the fashion industry: A systematic review and case studies. *International Transactions in Operational Research*, itor.13273. doi:10.1111/itor.13273

Chesti, I. A., Humayun, M., Sama, N. U., & Jhanjhi, N. Z. (2020). Evolution, Mitigation, and Prevention of Ransomware. *2020 2nd International Conference on Computer and Information Sciences (ICCIS)*. IEEE. 10.1109/ICCIS49240.2020.9257708

Cheung, K. F., Bell, M. G. H., & Bhattacharjya, J. (2021). Cybersecurity in logistics and supply chain management: An overview and future research directions. *Transportation Research Part E, Logistics and Transportation Review*, *146*(C), 102217. Advance online publication. doi:10.1016/j.tre.2020.102217

Chicco, D., & Jurman, G. (2020). The advantages of the Matthews correlation coefficient (MCC) over F1 score and accuracy in binary classification evaluation. *BMC Genomics*, *21*(1), 1–13. doi:10.1186/s12864-019-6413-7 PMID:31898477

Chimuco, F. T., Sequeiros, J. B. F., Lopes, C. G., Simões, T. M. C., Freire, M. M., & Inácio, P. R. M. (2023). Secure cloud-based mobile apps: Attack taxonomy, requirements, mechanisms, tests and automation. *International Journal of Information Security*, *22*(4), 833–867. Advance online publication. doi:10.1007/s10207-023-00669-z

Chin, H., Marasini, D. P., & Lee, D. (2023). Digital transformation trends in service industries. *Service Business*, *17*(1), 11–36. doi:10.1007/s11628-022-00516-6

Chopra, S., & Meindl, P. (2000). *Supply Chain Management: Strategy, Planning and Operations*. NII. http://ci.nii.ac.jp/ncid/BB10149318

Choudhary, A. S. (2023). Concept of Blockchain Technology. *Analytics Vidhya*. https://www.analyticsvidhya.com/blog/2022/09/concept-of-blockchain-technology/

Chow, J. K., Su, Z., Wu, J., Tan, P. S., Mao, X., & Wang, Y. H. (2020). Anomaly detection of defects on concrete structures with the convolutional autoencoder. *Advanced Engineering Informatics*, *45*(December 2019). doi:10.1016/j.aei.2020.101105

Chowdhury, S., & Zhu, J. (2023). Investigation of critical factors for future-proofed transportation infrastructure planning using topic modeling and association rule mining. *Journal of Computing in Civil Engineering*, *37*(1), 04022044. doi:10.1061/(ASCE)CP.1943-5487.0001059

Christopher, M. (2016). *Logistics & Supply Chain Management*. NII. https://ci.nii.ac.jp/ncid/BB05643450

Christopher, M., & Peck, H. (2012). Building the Resilient Supply Chain. *International Journal of Logistics Management*, *15*(2), 1–14. doi:10.1108/09574090410700275

Churcher, A., Ullah, R., Ahmad, J., Ur Rehman, S., Masood, F., Gogate, M., Alqahtani, F., Nour, B., & Buchanan, W. J. (2021). An experimental analysis of attack classification using machine learning in IoT networks. *Sensors (Basel)*, *21*(2), 446. doi:10.3390/s21020446 PMID:33435202

Cisco. (n.d.). *Firepower Management Center Configuration Guide, Version 6.0 - External Alerting with Alert Responses [Cisco ASA 5500-X Series Firewalls]*. Cisco. https://www.cisco.com/c/en/us/td/docs/security/firepower/60/configuration/guide/fpmc-config-guide-v60/Configuring_External_Alerting.html

Clark, C. (2018) 1. What is Sagan? *Sagan User Guide 1.2.2 documentation*. Sagan. https://sagan.readthedocs.io/en/latest/what-is-sagan.html?highlight=data+collection

Cohen, A., & Shaheen, S. (2023). *Future of Aviation: Advancing Aerial Mobility through Technology*. Sustainability, and On-Demand Flight.

Convention, K. (2022). *Directives of the General Annex*. Directives on Customs Control., https://www.wcoomd.org/en/topics/facilitation/instrument-and-tools/conventions/pf_revised_kyoto_conv/kyoto_new/gach6.aspx

Corallo, A., Lazoi, M., Lezzi, M., & Luperto, A. (2022). Cybersecurity awareness in the context of the Industrial Internet of Things: A systematic literature review. *Computers in Industry*, *137*, 103614. doi:10.1016/j.compind.2022.103614

Council of Supply Chain Management Professionals (CSCMP). (2021). Supply chain management definitions. *CSCMP's Supply Chain Quarterly*. https://www.supplychainquarterly.com/topics/Strategy/20211210-supply-chain-management-definitions/

Coutinho, B., Ferreira, J. C., Yevseyeva, I., & Basto-Fernandes, V. (2023). Integrated cybersecurity methodology and supporting tools for healthcare operational information systems. *Elsevier, 129*, 103189. doi:10.1016/j.cose.2023.103189

Cowan, A. (2021). Coming off the tracks: The cyberthreats facing rail operators. *Network Security, 2021*(11), 12–14. doi:10.1016/S1353-4858(21)00131-8

Cox, D. (2019). Five Characteristics That MakeIoTVulnerable To Cyber Attacks.' *Forbes.*

Crosby, M., Pattanayak, P., Verma, S., & Kalyanaraman, V. (2016). Blockchain technology: Beyond bitcoin. *Applied Innovation, 2*(6-10), 71–81.

Crosignani, M., Macchiavelli, M., & Silva, A. F. (2023). Pirates without borders: The propagation of cyberattacks through firms' supply chains. *Journal of Financial Economics, 147*(2), 432–448. doi:10.1016/j.jfineco.2022.12.002

Cui, J., Xiao, J., & Wang, Q. (2023). *Research on Data Protection Scheme for Road Maintenance System Based on Hybrid Encryption*. European Union Digital Library. doi:10.4108/eai.24-2-2023.2330677

Cvahte Ojsteršek, T., Šinko, S., & Gajšek, B. (2023). Determining Learning Outcomes Relevant for Logistics Higher Education on Sustainability and Industry 4.0. *Tehnički glasnik, 17*(3), 447-454.

Cvitić, I., Peraković, D., Periša, M., & Gupta, B. (2021). Ensemble machine learning approach for classification of IoT devices in smart home. *International Journal of Machine Learning and Cybernetics, 12*(11), 3179–3202. doi:10.1007/s13042-020-01241-0

Cyrus, R. (2023). Custody, Provenance, and Reporting of Blockchain and Cryptoassets. Emerald Publishing Limited. doi:10.1108/978-1-80455-320-620221016

D., Kumar, R. & Tomkins, A. (2006). *Evolutionary clustering*. ResearchGate. https://www.researchgate.net/publication/221654105_Evolutionary_clustering

Dai, H., Zheng, Z., & Zhang, Y. (2019). Blockchain for Internet of Things: A Survey. *IEEE Internet of Things Journal, 6*(5), 8076–8094. doi:10.1109/JIOT.2019.2920987

Das, D., Banerjee, S., Chatterjee, P., Ghosh, U., & Biswas, U. (2023). *Blockchain for Intelligent Transportation Systems: Applications, Challenges, and Opportunities*. IEEE. doi:10.1109/JIOT.2023.3277923

Das, D., Dasgupta, K., & Biswas, U. (2023). *A secure blockchain-enabled vehicle identity management framework for intelligent transportation systems*. Elsevier. doi:10.1016/j.compeleceng.2022.108535

Das, P., Singh, M., & Roy, D. G. (2021, December). A secure softwarized blockchain-based federated health alliance for next generation IoT networks. In *2021 IEEE Globecom Workshops (GC Wkshps)* (pp. 1-6). IEEE.

DasS. (2023). Digital Twin Technology: Enhancing Efficiency and Decision-Making in Industry 4.0. *Social Science Research Network*. doi:10.2139/ssrn.4459204

Das, V., Cherukuri, A. K., Hu, Q., Kamalov, F., & Jonnalagadda, A. (2023). Proactive AI Enhanced Consensus Algorithm with Fraud Detection in Blockchain. In *Blockchain for Cybersecurity in Cyber-Physical Systems* (pp. 259–274). Springer International Publishing. doi:10.1007/978-3-031-25506-9_13

David, R., Goel, P. K., & Abujamra, R. (2017). Blockchain Applications and Use Cases in Health Information Technology. *Journal of Health & Medical Informatics, 08*(03). doi:10.4172/2157-7420.1000276

Day, B. (n.d.). *Real-Time Alerting with Snort*. LinuxSecurity. https://linuxsecurity.com/features/real-time-alerting-with-snort

Dcouth, J. R., & Jaichandran, R. (2019). An Adaptive Secret QR Code Message Passing Method Using Video Steganography. *International Journal of Innovative Technology and Exploring Engineering, 9*(1), 1510–1514. doi:10.35940/ijitee.A4331.119119

Debbarma, R. (2023, September 10). *The changing landscape of privacy laws in the age of big data and surveillance.* Rifanalitica. https://www.rifanalitica.it/index.php/journal/article/view/470

Decker, L., & Zoghi, B. (2023). The Case for RFID-Enabled Traceability in Cash Movements. *FinTech, 2*(2), 344–373. doi:10.3390/fintech2020020

Deng, L., Li, Y., Wang, S., & Luo, J. (2022). The impact of blockchain on optimal incentive contracts for online supply chain finance. *Environmental Science and Pollution Research International, 30*(5), 12466–12494. doi:10.1007/s11356-022-22498-8 PMID:36112286

Deng, W., Huang, T., & Wang, H. (2022). A Review of the Key Technology in a Blockchain Building Decentralized Trust Platform. *Mathematics, 11*(1), 101. doi:10.3390/math11010101

Dhasarathan, C., Hasan, M. K., Islam, S., Abdullah, S., Khapre, S., Singh, D., Alsulami, A. A., & Alqahtani, A. (2023). User privacy prevention model using supervised federated learning-based block chain approach for internet of Medical Things. *CAAI Transactions on Intelligence Technology*, cit2.12218. Advance online publication. doi:10.1049/cit2.12218

Dias, H., & Meratnia, N. (2023). BlockLearning: A Modular Framework for Blockchain-Based Vertical Federated Learning. In Communications in computer and information science (pp. 319–333). Springer Science+Business Media. doi:10.1007/978-981-99-0272-9_22

Dietrich, F., Louw, L., & Palm, D. (2023). Blockchain-Based Traceability Architecture for Mapping Object-Related Supply Chain Events. *Sensors (Basel), 23*(3), 1410. doi:10.3390/s23031410 PMID:36772452

Dixit, S., & Hussain, G. (2023). An effective intrusion detection system in cloud computing environment. In Lecture notes in networks and systems (pp. 671–680). Springer. doi:10.1007/978-981-19-7982-8_56

Djenouri, Y., Belhadi, A., Djenouri, D., Srivastava, G., & Lin, J. C.-W. (2023). A Secure Intelligent System for Internet of Vehicles: Case Study on Traffic Forecasting. *IEEE Transactions on Intelligent Transportation Systems, 24*(11), 13218–13227. doi:10.1109/TITS.2023.3243542

Dobilas, R. (2023). *Improving Supply Chain Performance by Means of Information Sharing: The Case of a Logistics Service Company* [MA Thesis, Kaunas University of Technology].

Doğdu, E. (2023, May 1). *Virtual networking cybersecurity and vulnerabilities in cloud computing applications: a systematic review*. TDL. https://asu-ir.tdl.org/handle/2346.1/39593

Dogra, V., Singh, A., & Verma, S., Kavita, Jhanjhi, N., & Talib, M. (2021). Analyzing DistilBERT for sentiment classification of banking financial news. *Paper presented at the Intelligent Computing and Innovation on Data Science: Proceedings of ICTIDS 2021*. Springer. 10.1007/978-981-16-3153-5_53

Donthu, N., Kumar, S., Mukherjee, D., Pandey, N., & Lim, W. M. (2021). How to conduct a bibliometric analysis: An overview and guidelines. *Journal of Business Research, 133*, 285–296. doi:10.1016/j.jbusres.2021.04.070

Dorri, A., Kanhere, S. S., Jurdak, R., & Gauravaram, P. (2017). *Blockchain for IoT security and privacy: The case study of a smart home*. IEEE. doi:10.1109/PERCOMW.2017.7917634

Do, T. (2023). *SoK on Blockchain Evolution and a Taxonomy for Public Blockchain Generations*. Hong Kong University of Science & Technology. doi:10.2139/ssrn.4377849

Douch, S., Abid, M. R., Zine-Dine, K., Bouzidi, D., & Benhaddou, D. (2022). Edge Computing Technology Enablers: A Systematic Lecture Study. *IEEE Access : Practical Innovations, Open Solutions*, 10, 69264–69302. doi:10.1109/ACCESS.2022.3183634

Doyle, D. (2020). CyberScotland Bulletin November 2020 — CyberScotland Week. *CyberScotland Week*. https://cyberscotlandweek.com/news-database/bulletinnovember2020

Drescher, D. (2017). *Blockchain Basics: A Non-Technical Introduction in 25 Steps*. Booktopia. https://www.booktopia.com.au/blockchain-basics-daniel-drescher/book/9781484226032.html?gclid=CjwKCAjwpayjBhAnEiwA-7ena_-4H32E_N3AOxW0nA1rhovh-VvxnfELAnk2ZF-UjQErY9kGdO1oBxoCcI0QAvD_BwE

Drissi Elbouzidi, A., Ait El Cadi, A., Pellerin, R., Lamouri, S., Tobon Valencia, E., & Bélanger, M.-J. (2023). The Role of AI in Warehouse Digital Twins: Literature Review. *Applied Sciences (Basel, Switzerland)*, 13(11), 6746. doi:10.3390/app13116746

Driss, M., Almomani, I., Huma, Z., & Ahmad, J. (2022). A federated learning framework for cyberattack detection in vehicular sensor networks. *Complex & Intelligent Systems*, 8(5), 4221–4235. doi:10.1007/s40747-022-00705-w

Druehl, C., Carrillo, J., & Hsuan, J. (2018) Technological innovations: Impacts on supply chains. In. *Contributions to Management Science* (pp. 259-281).

Dubey, R., Bryde, D. J., Dwivedi, Y. K., Graham, G., Foropon, C., & Papadopoulos, T. (2023). Dynamic digital capabilities and supply chain resilience: The role of government effectiveness. *International Journal of Production Economics*, 258, 108790. doi:10.1016/j.ijpe.2023.108790

Duman, Ş. A., Hayran, R., & Sogukpınar, İ. (2023). *Impact Analysis and Performance Model of Social Engineering Techniques*. IEEE. doi:10.1109/ISDFS58141.2023.10131771

Dwivedi, Y. K., Hughes, L., Wang, Y., Alalwan, A. A., Ahn, S. J., Balakrishnan, J., Barta, S., Belk, R. W., Buhalis, D., Dutot, V., Felix, R., Filieri, R., Flavián, C., Gustafsson, A., Hinsch, C., Hollensen, S., Jain, V., Kim, J., Krishen, A. S., & Wirtz, J. (2022). Metaverse marketing: How the metaverse will shape the future of consumer research and practice. *Psychology and Marketing*, 40(4), 750–776. doi:10.1002/mar.21767

Dyer, J. H., Singh, H., & Hesterly, W. S. (2018). The relational view revisited: A dynamic perspective on value creation and value capture. *Strategic Management Journal*, 39(12), 3140–3162. doi:10.1002/smj.2785

Dylag, M., & Smith, H. (2021). From cryptocurrencies to cryptocourts: Blockchain and the financialization of dispute resolution platforms. *Information Communication and Society*, 26(2), 372–387. doi:10.1080/1369118X.2021.1942958

Dzemydienė, D., Burinskienė, A., Čižiūnienė, K., & Miliauskas, A. (2023). Development of E-Service Provision System Architecture Based on IoT and WSNs for Monitoring and Management of Freight Intermodal Transportation. *Sensors (Basel)*, 23(5), 2831. doi:10.3390/s23052831 PMID:36905034

Ebert, J., Newton, O., O'rear, J., Riley, S., Park, J., & Gupta, M. (2021). Leveraging aviation risk models to combat cybersecurity threats in vehicular networks. *Information (Basel)*, 12(10), 390. doi:10.3390/info12100390

Edirisinghe, E. (2023). *Warehouse Management System*. Research Gate.

Ekren, B. Y., Mangla, S. K., Turhanlar, E. E., Kazancoglu, Y., & Li, G. (2021). Lateral inventory share-based models for IoT-enabled E-commerce sustainable food supply networks. *Computers & Operations Research*, 130, 105237. doi:10.1016/j.cor.2021.105237

El Jaouhari, A., El Bhilat, E. M., & Arif, J. (2022). Scrutinizing IoT applicability in green warehouse inventory management system based on Mamdani fuzzy inference system: a case study of an automotive semiconductors industrial firm. *Journal of Industrial and Production Engineering*, 1-15.

El Jaouhari, A., El Bhilat, E. M., & Arif, J. (2023). Scrutinizing IoT applicability in green warehouse inventory management system based on Mamdani fuzzy inference system: A case study of an automotive semiconductors industrial firm. *Journal of Industrial and Production Engineering*, *40*(2), 87–101. doi:10.1080/21681015.2022.2142303

Elrawy, M., Awad, A., & Hamed, H. (2018). Intrusion detection systems for IoT-based smart environments: A survey. *Journal of Cloud Computing (Heidelberg, Germany)*, *7*(1), 21. doi:10.1186/s13677-018-0123-6

Enache, G. I. (2023). Logistics Security in the Era of Big Data, Cloud Computing and IoT. Paper presented at the *Proceedings of the International Conference on Business Excellence*. Sciendo. 10.2478/picbe-2023-0021

Erickson, J., & Siau, K. (2008). Web Services, Service-Oriented Computing, and Service-Oriented Architecture: Separating Hype from Reality. *Journal of Database Management*, *19*(3), 42–54. doi:10.4018/jdm.2008070103

Erl, T. (2017). *SOA design patterns*. Pearson.

Erola, A., Agrafiotis, I., Goldsmith, M., & Creese, S. (2022). Insider-threat detection: Lessons from deploying the CITD tool in three multinational organisations. *Journal of Information Security and Applications*, *67*, 103167. doi:10.1016/j.jisa.2022.103167

Escobar, F., Santos, H., & Pereira, T. (2023). Blockchain in the Public Sector: An Umbrella Review of Literature. In Lecture notes in networks and systems (pp. 142–152). Springer International Publishing. doi:10.1007/978-3-031-21229-1_14

Everledger. (2022, October 12). *Main Home - Everledger*. https://everledger.io/

Evtodieva, T. E., Chernova, D. V., Ivanova, N. V., & Wirth, J. (2019). The internet of things: possibilities of application in intelligent supply chain management. *Digital transformation of the economy: Challenges, trends and new opportunities*, 395-403.

Fadhil. S. M.NizarN. B. M.RostamR. J. (2023). Security and Privacy Issues in Cloud Computing. *Tech Riv*. doi:10.36227/techrxiv.23506905.v1

Faisal, S. M., & Zaidi, T. (2020). Timestamp Based Detection of Sybil Attack in VANET. *International Journal of Network Security*, *22*(3), 397–408.

Fajar, A. N., Nurcahyo, A., & Sriratnasari, S. R. (2018). SOA system architecture for interconected modern higher education in Indonesia. *Procedia Computer Science*, *135*, 354–360. doi:10.1016/j.procs.2018.08.184

Fan, T., Tao, F., Deng, S., & Li, S. (2015). Impact of RFID technology on supply chain decisions with inventory inaccuracies. *International Journal of Production Economics*, *159*, 117–125. doi:10.1016/j.ijpe.2014.10.004

Farid, G., Warraich, N. F., & Iftikhar, S. (2023). Digital information security management policy in academic libraries: A systematic review (2010–2022). *Journal of Information Science*, *016555152311600*. doi:10.1177/01655515231160026

Farooq, S., Altaf, A., Iqbal, F., Thompson, E. B., Vargas, D. L. R., De La Torre Díez, I., & Ashraf, I. (2023). Resilience Optimization of Post-Quantum Cryptography Key Encapsulation Algorithms. *Sensors (Basel)*, *23*(12), 5379. doi:10.3390/s23125379 PMID:37420546

Farooq, U., Tariq, N., Asim, M., Baker, T., & Al-Shamma'a, A. (2022). Machine learning and the Internet of Things security: Solutions and open challenges. *Journal of Parallel and Distributed Computing*, *162*, 89–104. doi:10.1016/j.jpdc.2022.01.015

Farrukh, Y. A., Khan, I., Wali, S., Bierbrauer, D., Pavlik, J., & Bastian, N. (2022). Payload-Byte: A Tool for Extracting and Labeling Packet Capture Files of Modern Network Intrusion Detection Datasets (Version 2). TechRxiv. doi:10.1109/BDCAT56447.2022.00015

Fatima, A., Khan, T. A., Abdellatif, T. M., Zulfiqar, S., Asif, M., Safi, W., Hamadi, H. A., & Al-Kassem, A. H. (2023). *Impact and Research Challenges of Penetrating Testing and Vulnerability Assessment on Network Threat*. doi:10.1109/ICBATS57792.2023.10111168

Fatima-Tuz-Zahra. Jhanjhi, N. Z., Brohi, S. N., Malik, N. A., & Humayun, M. (2020). Proposing a Hybrid RPL Protocol for Rank and Wormhole Attack Mitigation using Machine Learning. *2020 2nd International Conference on Computer and Information Sciences (ICCIS)*. IEEE. 10.1109/ICCIS49240.2020.9257607

Fawcett, S. E., Ellram, L. M., & Ogden, J. A. (2007). *Supply chain management : from vision to implementation*. Pearson Prentice Hall eBooks. http://ci.nii.ac.jp/ncid/BA88237110

Feldman, S. (2019, May 9). *Infographic: What's Blocking Blockchain?* Statista Infographics. https://www.statista.com/chart/17948/worlwide-barriers-to-blockchain-adoption/

Fernandez, E. B., Washizaki, H., Yoshioka, N., & Okubo, T. (2021). The design of secure IoT applications using patterns: State of the art and directions for research. *Internet of Things : Engineering Cyber Physical Human Systems, 15*, 100408. doi:10.1016/j.iot.2021.100408

Fernando, Y., Suhaini, A., Tseng, M.-L., Abideen, A. Z., & Shaharudin, M. S. (2023). A smart warehouse framework, architecture and system aspects under industry 4.0: a bibliometric networks visualisation and analysis. *International Journal of Logistics Research and Applications*, 1-24.

Fernando, Y., Tseng, M., Wahyuni-Td, I. S., De Sousa Jabbour, A. B. L., Jabbour, C. J. C., & Foropon, C. (2022). Cyber supply chain risk management and performance in industry 4.0 era: Information system security practices in Malaysia. *Journal of Industrial and Production Engineering, 40*(2), 102–116. doi:10.1080/21681015.2022.2116495

Fernie, J., & Sparks, L. (2014). *Logistics and Retail Management: Emerging Issues and New Challenges in the Retail Supply Chain*. NII. http://ci.nii.ac.jp/ncid/BA89825001

Ferrag, M. A., Shu, L., Yang, X., Derhab, A., & Maglaras, L. (2020). Security and privacy for green IoT-based agriculture: Review, blockchain solutions, and challenges. *IEEE Access : Practical Innovations, Open Solutions, 8*, 32031–32053. doi:10.1109/ACCESS.2020.2973178

Filippova, T., & Voronina, S. (2021). Organizational and Legal Aspects of Transport Logistics as a Factor of Sustainable Development. Paper presented at the *IOP Conference Series: Earth and Environmental Science*. IOP. 10.1088/1755-1315/670/1/012048

Fonseca, O., Cunha, Í., Fazzion, E., Meira, W., da Silva, B. A., Ferreira, R. A., & Katz-Bassett, E. (2021). Identifying networks vulnerable to IP spoofing. *IEEE Transactions on Network and Service Management, 18*(3), 3170–3183. doi:10.1109/TNSM.2021.3061486

Ford, N. (2023). *List of Data Breaches and Cyber Attacks in 2023*. IT Governance UK. https://www.itgovernance.co.uk/blog/list-of-data-breaches-and-cyber-attacks-in-2023

Fourné, M. (2023, May 1). *It's like flossing your teeth: On the Importance and Challenges of Reproducible Builds for Software Supply Chain Security*. TeamUSEC. https://teamusec.de/publications/conf-oakland-fourne23/

Freeman, L. (2017). *Centrality in social networks conceptual clarification.* Social Networks. https://www.semantic-scholar.org/paper/Centrality-in-social-networks-conceptual-Freeman/5d61ef638fd684facc1e68e654053e9bc065b36f [Accessed 23 Oct. 2023].

Friday, D., Ryan, S., Melnyk, S. A., & Proulx, D. (2023). Supply Chain Deep Uncertainties and Risks: The 'New Normal.' In *Flexible systems management* (pp. 51–72). Springer Nature. doi:10.1007/978-981-99-2629-9_3

Fung, C., Yoon, C. J., & Beschastnikh, I. (2020, October). The Limitations of Federated Learning in Sybil Settings. In RAID (pp. 301-316).

Gao, D., Wang, S., Liu, Y., Jiang, W., Li, Z., & He, T. (2021). Spoofing-jamming attack based on cross-technology communication for wireless networks. *Computer Communications, 177*, 86–95. doi:10.1016/j.comcom.2021.06.017

Gao, Z., Cao, J., Wang, W., Zhang, H., & Xu, Z. (2021). Online-Semisupervised Neural Anomaly Detector to Identify MQTT-Based Attacks in Real Time. *Security and Communication Networks, 2021*, 1–11. doi:10.1155/2021/4587862

Garavito Castillo, J. A. (2007). *Secretaría General de la Comunidad Andina.* Proyecto de Cooperación UE-CAN, Asistencia Relativa al Comercio I. Perú: Bellido Ediciones E.I.R.L. https://www.comunidadandina.org/StaticFiles/201165195749libro_atrc_control.pdf

Garay-Rondero, C. L., Martínez-Flores, J., Smith, N., Morales, S. C., & Aldrette-Malacara, A. (2019). Digital supply chain model in Industry 4.0. *Journal of Manufacturing Technology Management, 31*(5), 887–933. doi:10.1108/JMTM-08-2018-0280

Gartner. (2022). *Top 8 Supply Chain Technology Trends for 2023.* Gartner. https://www.gartner.com/en/documents/4117858/top-8-supply-chain-technology-trends-for-2023

Gaur, L., Zaman, N., Bakshi, S., & Gupta, P. (2022). Analyzing Consequences of Artificial Intelligence on Jobs using Topic Modeling and Keyword Extraction. In *2022 2nd International Conference on Innovative Practices in Technology and Management (ICIPTM)*. IEEE. 10.1109/ICIPTM54933.2022.9754064

Gazzola, P., Pavione, E., Barge, A., & Fassio, F. (2023). Using the Transparency of Supply Chain Powered by Blockchain to Improve Sustainability Relationships with Stakeholders in the Food Sector: The Case Study of Lavazza. *Sustainability (Basel), 15*(10), 7884. doi:10.3390/su15107884

Gelman, B., Taoufiq, S., Vörös, T., & Berlin, K. (2023). *That Escalated Quickly: An ML Framework for Alert Prioritisation.* [online] arXiv.org. doi:https://doi.org//arXiv.2302.06648. doi:10.48550

George, D., & George, A. (2023). Revolutionizing Manufacturing: Exploring the Promises and Challenges of Industry 5.0. Zenodo *(CERN European Organization for Nuclear Research)*. doi:10.5281/zenodo.7852124

GEP. (n.d.). *Blockchain in Procurement & Supply Chain.* GEP. https://www.gep.com/blockchain-procurement-supply-chain

Gerodimos, A., Maglaras, L., Ferrag, M. A., Ayres, N., & Kantzavelou, I. (2023). IOT: Communication protocols and security threats. *Internet of Things and Cyber-Physical Systems.*

Ghazal, T. M., Afifi, M. A. M., & Kalra, D. (2020). Security vulnerabilities, attacks, threats and the proposed counter-measures for the Internet of Things applications. *Solid State Technology, 63*(1s).

Ghobakhloo, M., Iranmanesh, M., Tseng, M., Grybauskas, A., Stefanini, A., & Amran, A. (2023). Behind the definition of Industry 5.0: a systematic review of technologies, principles, components, and values. *Journal of Industrial and Production Engineering*, 1–16. doi:10.1080/21681015.2023.2216701

Ghosh, G., Kavita, Verma, S., Jhanjhi, N. Z., & Talib, M. (2020). Secure surveillance system using chaotic image encryption technique. *IOP Conference Series, 993*(1), 012062. 10.1088/1757-899X/993/1/012062

Ghosh, G., & Bhandari, P. (2023). Supply Chain Related Cyber Attacks. *International Conference on Industrial Engineering and Operations Management Manila.*

Giorgi, G., Saracino, A., & Martinelli, F. (2020). Email Spoofing Attack Detection through an End to End Authorship Attribution System. In ICISSP (pp. 64-74). ScitePress. doi:10.5220/0008954600640074

Girdler, T., & Vassilakis, V. G. (2021). Implementing an intrusion detection and prevention system using Software-Defined Networking: Defending against ARP spoofing attacks and Blacklisted MAC Addresses. *Computers & Electrical Engineering, 90*, 106990. doi:10.1016/j.compeleceng.2021.106990

Goint, M., Bertelle, C., & Duvallet, C. (2023). Secure Access Control to Data in Off-Chain Storage in Blockchain-Based Consent Systems. *Mathematics, 11*(7), 1592. doi:10.3390/math11071592

Gondron, S., & Mödersheim, S. (2021, June). Vertical Composition and Sound Payload Abstraction for Stateful Protocols. In *2021 IEEE 34th Computer Security Foundations Symposium (CSF)* (pp. 1-16). IEEE. 10.1109/CSF51468.2021.00038

Gong, H., Li, J., Ni, R., Xiao, P., Ouyang, H., Mu, Y., & Tyasi, T. L. (2021). The Data Acquisition and Control System Based on IoT-CAN Bus. *Intelligent Automation & Soft Computing, 30*(3), 1049–1062. doi:10.32604/iasc.2021.019730

Goodfellow, I., Bengio, Y., & Courville, A. (2016). *Deep learning.* MIT press.

Gopi, R., Sathiyamoorthi, V., Selvakumar, S., Ramesh, M., Chatterjee, P., Jhanjhi, N. Z., & Luhach, A. K. (2021). Enhanced method of ANN based model for detection of DDoS attacks on multimedia internet of things. *Multimedia Tools and Applications, 81*(19), 26739–26757. doi:10.1007/s11042-021-10640-6

Grover, A. K., & Ashraf, M. H. (2023). *Autonomous and IoT-driven intra-logistics for Industry 4.0 warehouses: A Thematic Analysis of the Literature.* Research Gate.

Gruchmann, T., Elgazzar, S., & Ali, A. H. (2023). Blockchain technology in pharmaceutical supply chains: a transaction cost perspective. *Modern Supply Chain Research and Applications.* doi:10.1108/MSCRA-10-2022-0023

Gugueoth, V., Safavat, S., & Shetty, S. (2023). *Security of Internet of Things (IoT) using federated learning and deep learning-Recent advancements, issues and prospects.* ICT Express. doi:10.1016/j.icte.2023.03.006

Guntara, N. R. G., Nurfirmansyah, N. M. N., & Ferdiansyah, N. (2023). Blockchain Implementation in E-Commerce to Improve The Security Online Transactions. *Journal of Scientific Research. Educational Technology, 2*(1), 328–338. doi:10.58526/jsret.v2i1.85

Gupta, D., Kayode, O., Bhatt, S., Gupta, M., & Tosun, A. S. (2021). Hierarchical Federated Learning based Anomaly Detection using Digital Twins for Smart Healthcare. *Proceedings - 2021 IEEE 7th International Conference on Collaboration and Internet Computing, CIC 2021,* (pp. 16–25). IEEE. 10.1109/CIC52973.2021.00013

Gupta, K., Jiwani, N., & Afreen, N. (2022). Blood Pressure Detection Using CNN-LSTM Model. *Proceedings - 2022 IEEE 11th International Conference on Communication Systems and Network Technologies, CSNT 2022,* (April), (pp. 262–366). IEEE. 10.1109/CSNT54456.2022.9787648

Gupta, C., Gupta, V., & Fernandez-Crehuet, J. M. (2023). A blockchain-enabled solution to improve intra-inter organizational innovation processes in software small medium enterprises. *Engineering Reports, 5*(7), e12674. doi:10.1002/eng2.12674

Gupta, M. K., & Seetharaman, A. (2019). Reputation Risk Management: A New Framework and Its Application in Cybersecurity. *Journal of Risk and Financial Management, 12*(2), 102.

Gupta, M., Akiri, C., Aryal, K., Parker, E., & Praharaj, L. (2023). From ChatGPT to ThreatGPT: Impact of Generative AI in Cybersecurity and Privacy. *IEEE Access : Practical Innovations, Open Solutions, 11*, 80218–80245. doi:10.1109/ACCESS.2023.3300381

Gupta, N., Soni, G., Mittal, S., Mukherjee, I., Ramtiyal, B., & Kumar, D. (2023). Evaluating Traceability Technology Adoption in Food Supply Chain: A Game Theoretic Approach. *Sustainability (Basel), 15*(2), 898. doi:10.3390/su15020898

Gupta, R., & Shankar, R. (2023). Managing food security using blockchain-enabled traceability system. *Benchmarking.* doi:10.1108/BIJ-01-2022-0029

Gu, Y., Li, K., Guo, Z., & Wang, Y. (2019). Semi-supervised K-means DDoS detection method using hybrid feature selection algorithm. *IEEE Access : Practical Innovations, Open Solutions, 7*, 64351–64365. doi:10.1109/ACCESS.2019.2917532

Gyamfi, E. and Jurcut, A. (2022). Intrusion Detection in Internet of Things Systems: A Review on Design Approaches Leveraging Multi-Access Edge Computing, Machine Learning, and Datasets. *Sensors, 22*(10), 3744. . doi:10.3390/s22103744

Gyamfi, E., Ansere, J. A., Kamal, M., Tariq, M., & Jurcut, A. (2023). An Adaptive Network Security System for IoT-Enabled Maritime Transportation. *IEEE Transactions on Intelligent Transportation Systems, 24*(2), 2538–2547. doi:10.1109/TITS.2022.3159450

Hader, M., Elmhamedi, A., & Abouabdellah, A. (2020). *Blockchain technology in supply chain management and loyalty programs: toward blockchain implementation in retail market.* doi:10.1109/LOGISTIQUA49782.2020.9353879

Halbouni, A. H., Gunawan, T. S., Habaebi, M. H., Halbouni, M., Kartiwi, M., & Ahmad, R. (2022). CNN-LSTM: Hybrid Deep Neural Network for Network Intrusion Detection System. *IEEE Access : Practical Innovations, Open Solutions, 10*, 99837–99849. doi:10.1109/ACCESS.2022.3206425

Halligan, B., & Shah, D. (2014). *Inbound Marketing: Attract, Engage, and Delight Customers Online.* Wiley.

Hamdy, W., Al-Awamry, A., & Mostafa, N. (2022). Warehousing 4.0: A proposed system of using node-red for applying internet of things in warehousing. *Sustainable Futures : An Applied Journal of Technology, Environment and Society, 4*, 100069. doi:10.1016/j.sftr.2022.100069

Hameed, S., Khan, F. I., & Hameed, B. (2019). Understanding Security Requirements and Challenges in Internet of Things (IoT): A Review. *Journal of Computer Networks and Communications, 2019*, 1–14. doi:10.1155/2019/9629381

Hamid, B., Jhanjhi, N. Z., Humayun, M., Khan, A., & Alsayat, A. (2019, December). Cyber security issues and challenges for smart cities: A survey. In *2019 13th International Conference on Mathematics, Actuarial Science, Computer Science and Statistics (MACS)* (pp. 1-7). IEEE. 10.1109/MACS48846.2019.9024768

Hamid, B. (2023). A Hybrid Model for Botnet Detection using. *Machine Learning.*

Hammi, B., Zeadally, S., & Nebhen, J. (2023). Security threats, countermeasures, and challenges of digital supply chains. *ACM Computing Surveys, 55*(14s), 1–40. doi:10.1145/3588999

Handfield, R., & Finkenstadt, D. J. (2022). Major Supply Chain Events of 2020 Beyond COVID. In Springer eBooks (pp. 87–102). doi:10.1007/978-3-031-19344-6_8

Han, H., Kim, H., & Kim, Y. (2022). An efficient hyperparameter control method for a network intrusion detection system based on proximal policy optimization. *Symmetry, 14*(1), 161. doi:10.3390/sym14010161

Han, H., Shiwakoti, R. K., Jarvis, R., Mordi, C., & Botchie, D. (2023). Accounting and auditing with blockchain technology and artificial Intelligence: A literature review. *International Journal of Accounting Information Systems*, *48*, 100598. doi:10.1016/j.accinf.2022.100598

Han, J., & Pak, W. (2023). High Performance Network Intrusion Detection System Using Two-Stage LSTM and Incremental Created Hybrid Features. *Electronics (Basel)*, *12*(4), 956. doi:10.3390/electronics12040956

Harb, E., & Mangino, A. (2019). *ZEEK (BRO) INTRUSION DETECTION SYSTEM (IDS) Training Workshop for Network Engineers and Educators on Tools and Protocols for High-Speed Networks NSF Award 1829698 CyberTraining CIP: Cyberinfrastructure Expertise on High-throughput Networks for Big Science Data Transfers*. CESC. https://ce.sc.edu/cyberinfra/docs/workshop/Bro%20Intrusion%20Detection%20System%20(IDS).pdf

Hasan, I. (2023, February 16). *Blockchain Database and IoT: A Technology driven Agri-Food Supply Chain*. https://isctj.com/index.php/isctj/article/view/269

Hasan, I., Habib, M., Mohamed, Z., & Tewari, V. (2023). Integrated Agri-Food Supply Chain Model: An Application of IoT and Blockchain. *American Journal of Industrial and Business Management*, *13*(02), 29–45. doi:10.4236/ajibm.2023.132003

Hasan, M. K., Shafiq, M., Islam, S., Pandey, B., Baker El-Ebiary, Y. A., Nafi, N. S., Ciro Rodriguez, R., & Vargas, D. E. (2021). Lightweight cryptographic algorithms for guessing attack protection in complex internet of things applications. *Complexity*, *2021*, 1–13. doi:10.1155/2021/5540296

Hashmi, M. A., & Tariq, N. (2023). An Efficient Substitution Box design with a chaotic logistic map and Linear Congruential Generator for secure communication in Smart cities. *EAI Endorsed Transactions on Smart Cities, 7*(1).

Hastig, G. M., & Sodhi, M. S. (2020). Blockchain for Supply Chain Traceability: Business Requirements and Critical Success Factors. *Production and Operations Management*, *29*(4), 935–954. doi:10.1111/poms.13147

Hazra, A., Alkhayyat, A., & Adhikari, M. (2022). Blockchain-aided Integrated Edge Framework of Cybersecurity for Internet of Things. *IEEE Consumer Electronics Magazine*. doi:10.1109/MCE.2022.3141068

Heath, J. B. (2020). The New National Security Challenge to the Economic Order. *The Yale Law Journal*, *129*(1020), 1022–1098. https://www.yalelawjournal.org/pdf/HeathArticle_jx8mdn4b.pdf

Heluany, J. B., & Galvão, R. (2023). IEC 62443 Standard for Hydro Power Plants. *Energies*, *16*(3), 1452. doi:10.3390/en16031452

Henriques, J., Caldeira, F., Cruz, T., & Simões, P. (2023). A forensics and compliance auditing framework for critical infrastructure protection. *International Journal of Critical Infrastructure Protection*, *42*, 100613. doi:10.1016/j.ijcip.2023.100613

Herrera, M. (2022, August 25). *Never Break the Chain: Supply Chain Risk Management*. BCMMETRICS. https://bcmmetrics.com/supply-chain-risk-management/

He, W., Zhang, Z., & Li, W. (2021). Information technology solutions, challenges, and suggestions for tackling the COVID-19 pandemic. *International Journal of Information Management*, *57*, 102287. doi:10.1016/j.ijinfomgt.2020.102287 PMID:33318721

He, X., Hu, W., Li, W., & Hu, R. (2023). Digital transformation, technological innovation, and operational resilience of port firms in case of supply chain disruption. *Marine Pollution Bulletin*, *190*, 114811. doi:10.1016/j.marpolbul.2023.114811 PMID:36963261

Hill, G. N., & Whitty, M. A. (2021). Embedding metadata in images at time of capture using physical Quick Response (QR) codes. *Information Processing & Management, 58*(3), 102504. Advance online publication. doi:10.1016/j.ipm.2021.102504

Hippold, S. (2020). *6 Strategies for a More Resilient Supply Chain*. Gartner. https://www.gartner.com/smarterwithgartner/6-strategies-for-a-more-resilient-supply-chain

Hitachi, Ltd. (2020). Digital Supply Chain: Reimagining the Supply Chain of Tomorrow. *Social Innovation.* https://social-innovation.hitachi/en-in/knowledge-hub/collaborate/digital-supply-chain

Hoang, K. (2023). *Post Quantum Cryptography for Public Key Infrastructure*. Theseus. https://www.theseus.fi/handle/10024/802390

Hoffmann, T., & Prause, G. (2018). On the regulatory framework for last-mile delivery robots. *Machines, 6*(3), 33. doi:10.3390/machines6030033

Holmes, K. R. (2015). What Is National Security? *Index of U.S. Military Strength,* 17-26. The Heritage Foundation. https://www.heritage.org/sites/default/files/2019-10/2015_IndexOfUSMilitaryStrength_What%20Is%20National%20Security.pdf

Honkamaa, P., Jäppinen, J., & Woodward, C. (2007). A Lightweight Approach for Augmented Reality on Camera Phones using 2D Images to Simulate in 3D. VTT. *MUM '07: Proceedings of the 6th international conference on Mobile and ubiquitous multimedia.* ACM. 10.1145/1329469.1329490

Hossain, M. A., Hossain, M. S., & Karim, R. (2023). Comprehensive architectural network design based on intrusion detection system. *International Journal of Communication and Information Technology, 4*(2), 12–19. doi:10.33545/2707661X.2023.v4.i2a.66

HossainM. Z. (2023). Transforming Financial Reporting Practices in Bangladesh: The Benefits and Challenges of Implementing Blockchain Technology. *Social Science Research Network.* doi:10.2139/ssrn.4428469

Hossain, M., Zhou, X., & Rahman, M. F. (2018). Examining the impact of QR codes on purchase intention and customer satisfaction on the basis of perceived flow. *International Journal of Engineering Business Management, 10,* 1–11. doi:10.1177/1847979018812323

Hubballi, N., & Suryanarayanan, V. (2014). False alarm minimization techniques in signature-based intrusion detection systems: A survey. *Computer Communications, 49,* 1–17. doi:10.1016/j.comcom.2014.04.012

Hu, H., Xu, J., Liu, M., & Lim, M. K. (2023). Vaccine supply chain management: An intelligent system utilizing blockchain, IoT and machine learning. *Journal of Business Research, 156,* 113480. doi:10.1016/j.jbusres.2022.113480 PMID:36506475

Humayun, M., Afsar, S., Almufareh, M. F., Jhanjhi, N., & AlSuwailem, M. (2022). Smart Traffic Management System for Metropolitan Cities of Kingdom Using Cutting Edge Technologies. *Journal of Advanced Transportation.*

Humayun, M., Hamid, B., Jhanjhi, N., Suseendran, G., & Talib, M. (2021). 5G network security issues, challenges, opportunities and future directions: A survey. *Paper presented at the Journal of Physics: Conference Series.* IOP Science. 10.1088/1742-6596/1979/1/012037

Humayun, M., Jhanjhi, N. Z., Hamid, B., & Ahmed, G. (2020). *Emerging mart Logistics and Transportation Using IoT and Blockchain,* 58–62. Research Gate.

Humayun, M., Jhanjhi, N., Talib, M., Shah, M. H., & Suseendran, G. (2021). Cybersecurity for Data Science: Issues, Opportunities, and Challenges. *Intelligent Computing and Innovation on Data Science: Proceedings of ICTIDS 2021,* (pp. 435-444). Research Gate.

Humayun, M., Sujatha, R., Almuayqil, S. N., & Jhanjhi, N. Z. (2022, June). A transfer learning approach with a convolutional neural network for the classification of lung carcinoma. In Healthcare (Vol. 10, No. 6, p. 1058). MDPI. doi:10.3390/healthcare10061058

Humayun, M., Zaman, N., Talib, M. N., Shah, M. H., & Suseendran, G. (2021). Cybersecurity for Data Science: Issues, Opportunities, and Challenges. In Lecture notes in networks and systems (pp. 435–444). Springer International Publishing. doi:10.1007/978-981-16-3153-5_46

Humayun, M. (2020). IoT-based Secure and Energy Efficient scheme for E-health applications. *Indian Journal of Science and Technology*, 13(28), 2833–2848. doi:10.17485/IJST/v13i28.861

Humayun, M. (2020). Role of emerging IoT big data and cloud computing for real time application. [IJACSA]. *International Journal of Advanced Computer Science and Applications*, 11(4). doi:10.14569/IJACSA.2020.0110466

Humayun, M. (2021). Industry 4.0 and Cyber Security Issues and Challenges. [TURCOMAT]. *Turkish Journal of Computer and Mathematics Education*, 12(10), 2957–2971. doi:10.17762/turcomat.v12i10.4946

Humayun, M., Jhanjhi, N. Z., Alamri, M. Z., & Khan, A. (2020). Smart cities and digital governance. In *Employing Recent Technologies for Improved Digital Governance* (pp. 87–106). IGI Global. doi:10.4018/978-1-7998-1851-9.ch005

Humayun, M., Jhanjhi, N. Z., & Almotilag, A. (2022). Real-Time Security Health and Privacy Monitoring for Saudi Highways Using Cutting-Edge Technologies. *Applied Sciences (Basel, Switzerland)*, 12(4), 2177. doi:10.3390/app12042177

Humayun, M., Jhanjhi, N. Z., Alsayat, A., & Ponnusamy, V. (2021). Internet of things and ransomware: Evolution, mitigation and prevention. *Egyptian Informatics Journal*, 22(1), 105–117. doi:10.1016/j.eij.2020.05.003

Humayun, M., Jhanjhi, N. Z., Hamid, B., & Ahmed, G. (2020). Emerging smart logistics and transportation using IoT and blockchain. *IEEE Internet of Things Magazine*, 3(2), 58–62. doi:10.1109/IOTM.0001.1900097

Humayun, M., Jhanjhi, N., Alruwaili, M., Amalathas, S. S., Balasubramanian, V., & Selvaraj, B. (2020). Privacy protection and energy optimization for 5G-aided industrial Internet of Things. *IEEE Access : Practical Innovations, Open Solutions*, 8, 183665–183677. doi:10.1109/ACCESS.2020.3028764

Humayun, M., Niazi, M., Jhanjhi, N. Z., Alshayeb, M., & Mahmood, S. (2020). Cyber Security Threats and Vulnerabilities: A Systematic Mapping study. *Arabian Journal for Science and Engineering*, 45(4), 3171–3189. doi:10.1007/s13369-019-04319-2

Humayun, M., Zaman, N., Niazi, M., Amsaad, F., & Masood, I. (2022). Securing Drug Distribution Systems from Tampering Using Blockchain. *Electronics (Basel)*, 11(8), 1195. doi:10.3390/electronics11081195

Huong, T. T., Bac, T. P., Ha, K. N., Hoang, N. V., Hoang, N. X., Hung, N. T., & Tran, K. P. (2022). Federated Learning-Based Explainable Anomaly Detection for Industrial Control Systems. *IEEE Access : Practical Innovations, Open Solutions*, 10, 53854–53872. doi:10.1109/ACCESS.2022.3173288

Hussain Naqvi, S. K., & Batool, K. (2023). A comparative analysis between General Data Protection Regulations and California Consumer Privacy Act. *Journal of Computer Science. Information Technology and Telecommunication Engineering*, 4(1). doi:10.30596/jcositte.v4i1.13330

Hussain, F., Hussain, R., Hassan, S. A., & Hossain, E. (2020). Machine learning in IoT security: Current solutions and future challenges. *IEEE Communications Surveys \& Tutorials, 22*(3), 1686–1721.

Hussain, M. N. (2023). Evaluating the impact of air transportation, railway transportation, and trade openness on inbound and outbound tourism in BRI countries.[[industrialcybersecuritypulse. cyber security attack. Retrieved from]. *Journal of Air Transport Management, 106*, 102307. https://www.industrialcybersecuritypulse.com/threats-vulnerabilities/throwback-attack-how-notpetya-accidentally-took-down-global-shipping-giant-maersk/. doi:10.1016/j.jairtraman.2022.102307

Hussain, S. J., Ahmed, U., Liaquat, H., Mir, S., Jhanjhi, N. Z., & Humayun, M. (2019). *IMIAD: Intelligent Malware Identification for Android Platform*. IEEE. doi:10.1109/ICCISci.2019.8716471

Hussain, S. J., Irfan, M., Jhanjhi, N. Z., Hussain, K., & Humayun, M. (2021). Performance Enhancement in Wireless Body Area Networks with Secure Communication. *Wireless Personal Communications, 116*(1), 1–22. doi:10.1007/s11277-020-07702-7 PMID:33558792

Huynh-The, T., Gadekallu, T. R., Wang, W., Yenduri, G., Ranaweera, P., Pham, Q., Da Costa, D. B., & Liyanage, M. (2023). Blockchain for the metaverse: A Review. *Future Generation Computer Systems, 143*, 401–419. doi:10.1016/j.future.2023.02.008

Iansiti, M., & Lakhani, K. R. (2017). The Truth about Blockchain. *Harvard Business Review*. https://www.hbs.edu/faculty/Pages/item.aspx?num=52100

Iansiti, M., & Lakhani, K. R. (2017). The Truth about Blockchain. *Harvard Business Review, 95*(1), 118–127. https://www.hbs.edu/faculty/Pages/item.aspx?num=52100

IBM. (n.d.). *Blockchain - Enterprise Blockchain Solutions and Services*. IBM. https://www.ibm.com/blockchain

Igbekele, E. O., Aideloje, J., Adebiyi, A. A., & Adebiyi, A. (2023). Product Verification using Blockchain Technology. *Systematic Reviews*, 1–8. doi:10.1109/SEB-SDG57117.2023.10124602

Iglesias Perez, S., & Criado, R. (2022). Increasing the Effectiveness of Network Intrusion Detection Systems (NIDSs) by Using Multiplex Networks and Visibility Graphs. *Mathematics, 11*(1), 107. doi:10.3390/math11010107

IMB. (2022). *Cost of a Data Breach Report 2022*. IBM. https://www.ibm.com/downloads/cas/3R8N1DZJ

Inayat, U., Zia, M. F., Mahmood, S., Khalid, H. M., & Benbouzid, M. (2022). Learning-based methods for cyber attacks detection in IoT systems: A survey on methods, analysis, and future prospects. *Electronics (Basel), 11*(9), 1502. doi:10.3390/electronics11091502

Ioulianou, P., Vassilakis, V., Moscholios, I., & Logothetis, M. (2018). *A Signature-based Intrusion Detection System for the Internet of Things. A Signature-based Intrusion Detection System for the Internet of Things*. White Rose Research Online. https://eprints.whiterose.ac.uk/133312/1/ictf_2018_IoT.pdf

Iranmanesh, M., Maroufkhani, P., Asadi, S., Ghobakhloo, M., Dwivedi, P. K., & Tseng, M. (2023). Effects of supply chain transparency, alignment, adaptability, and agility on blockchain adoption in supply chain among SMEs. *Computers & Industrial Engineering, 176*, 108931. doi:10.1016/j.cie.2022.108931

Iredale, G. (2023). Public Vs Private Blockchain: Key Differences. *101 Blockchains*. https://101blockchains.com/public-vs-private-blockchain/

Islam, M. D. (2023). A survey on the use of blockchains to achieve supply chain security. *Information Systems, 117*, 102232. doi:10.1016/j.is.2023.102232

Islam, M. M., & In, H. P. (2023). Decentralized Global Copyright System Based on Consortium Blockchain with Proof of Authority. *IEEE Access : Practical Innovations, Open Solutions, 1*, 43101–43115. doi:10.1109/ACCESS.2023.3270627

Ivanov, D., & Dolgui, A. (2021). A digital supply chain twin for managing the disruption risks and resilience in the era of Industry 4.0. *Production Planning and Control*, 32(9), 775–788. doi:10.1080/09537287.2020.1768450

Jabbar, S., Lloyd, H., Hammoudeh, M., Adebisi, B., & Raza, U. (2021). Blockchain-enabled supply chain: Analysis, challenges, and future directions. *Multimedia Systems*, 27(4), 787–806. doi:10.1007/s00530-020-00687-0

Jabeen, T., Jabeen, I., Ashraf, H., Jhanjhi, N., Yassine, A., & Hossain, M. S. (2023). An Intelligent Healthcare System Using IoT in Wireless Sensor Network. *Sensors (Basel)*, 23(11), 5055. doi:10.3390/s23115055 PMID:37299782

Jacob, S., Alagirisamy, M., Xi, C., Balasubramanian, V., Srinivasan, R., Parvathi, R., & Islam, S. M. (2021). AI and IoT-enabled smart exoskeleton system for rehabilitation of paralyzed people in connected communities. *IEEE Access : Practical Innovations, Open Solutions*, 9, 80340–80350. doi:10.1109/ACCESS.2021.3083093

Jahani, H., Jain, R., & Ivanov, D. (2023). Data science and big data analytics: A systematic review of methodologies used in the supply chain and logistics research. *Annals of Operations Research*, 1–58. doi:10.1007/s10479-023-05390-7

Jaime, F., Muñoz, A., Rodríguez-Gómez, F., & Jeréz-Calero, A. (2023). Strengthening privacy and data security in biomedical microelectromechanical systems by IoT communication security and protection in smart healthcare. *Sensors (Basel)*, 23(21), 8944. doi:10.3390/s23218944 PMID:37960646

Jain, G., & Anubha. (2021). Application of SNORT and Wireshark in Network Traffic Analysis. *IOP Conference Series. Materials Science and Engineering*, 1119(1), 012007. doi:10.1088/1757-899X/1119/1/012007

Jain, N., Chaudhary, A., & Kumar, A. (2022). *Credit Card Fraud Detection using Machine Learning Techniques*. IEEE., doi:10.1109/SMART55829.2022.10047360

Jalali, A. (2023). *Password Management : A Study about Current Challenges with Password Management*. DIVA. https://www.diva-portal.org/smash/record.jsf?pid=diva2%3A1765652&dswid=-2613

James, E. (2023, January 9). *Fortifying the IoT landscape: Strategies to Counter security Risks in Connected systems*. Tensor Gate. https://research.tensorgate.org/index.php/tjstidc/article/view/42

Jang, H., Yoo, J. J., & Cho, M. (2023). Resistance to blockchain adoption in the foodservice industry: Moderating roles of public pressures and climate change awareness. *International Journal of Contemporary Hospitality Management*. doi:10.1108/IJCHM-09-2022-1127

Javaid, M., Haleem, A., Singh, R. P., & Suman, R. (2023). Towards insighting Cybersecurity for Healthcare domains: A comprehensive review of recent practices and trends. *Science Direct*, 1, 100016. doi:10.1016/j.csa.2023.100016

Javed, A. R., Fahad, L. G., Farhan, A. A., Abbas, S., Srivastava, G., Parizi, R. M., & Khan, M. S. (2021). Automated cognitive health assessment in smart homes using machine learning. *Sustainable Cities and Society*, 65(April 2020), 102572. doi:10.1016/j.scs.2020.102572

JayakumarP.BrohiS. N.ZamanN. (2021). Artificial Intelligence and Military Applications: Innovations, Cybersecurity Challenges & Open Research Areas. *Preprint.org*. doi:10.20944/preprints202108.0047.v1

Jayanthi, E., Ramesh, T., Kharat, R. S., Veeramanickam, M. R. M., Bharathiraja, N., Venkatesan, R., & Marappan, R. (2023). Cybersecurity enhancement to detect credit card frauds in health care using new machine learning strategies. *Soft Computing*, 27(11), 7555–7565. doi:10.1007/s00500-023-07954-y

Jebamikyous, H., Li, M., Suhas, Y., & Kashef, R. (2023). Leveraging machine learning and blockchain in E-commerce and beyond: Benefits, models, and application. *Discover Artificial Intelligence*, 3(1), 3. doi:10.1007/s44163-022-00046-0

Jeldi, S. B., & Kumar, A. (2022). Data Acquisition And Pre-Processing Using Kf Model For An Intrusion Detection System In Web Mining. *ECB*. https://www.eurchembull.com/uploads/paper/1239d617b696cf0c069cc81a23fa5e72.pdf

Jenkins, A. (2022). Digital Supply Chain Explained. *Oracle NetSuite*. https://www.netsuite.com/portal/resource/articles/erp/digital-supply-chain.shtml

Jerbi, D. (2023). Beyond Firewalls: Navigating the Jungle of Emerging Cybersecurity Trends. *J Curr Trends Comp Sci Res*, 2(2), 191–195.

Jhanjhi, N., Khan, M. A., Ahmad, M., & Hussain, M. (2022). The Impact of Cyber Attacks on E-Governance During the COVID-19 Pandemic. *Cybersecurity Measures for E-Government Frameworks*, 123.

Jhanjhi, N. (2021). A design of IoT-based medicine case for the multi-user medication management using drone in elderly centre. *Journal of Engineering Science and Technology*, 16(2), 1145–1166.

Jhanjhi, N. Z., Humayun, M., & Almuayqil, S. N. (2021). Cyber security and privacy issues in industrial internet of things. *Computer Systems Science and Engineering*, 37(3), 361–380. doi:10.32604/csse.2021.015206

Jiang, X., Zhou, X., & Grossklags, J. (2022). Comprehensive Analysis of Privacy Leakage in Vertical Federated Learning During Prediction. *Proceedings on Privacy Enhancing Technologies. Privacy Enhancing Technologies Symposium*, 2022(2), 263–281. doi:10.2478/popets-2022-0045

Jin, D., Lu, Y., Qin, J., Cheng, Z., & Mao, Z. (2020). SwiftIDS: Real-time intrusion detection system based on Light-GBM and parallel intrusion detection mechanism. *Computers & Security*, 97, 101984. doi:10.1016/j.cose.2020.101984

Jmal, R., Ghabri, W., Guesmi, R., Alshammari, B. M., Alshammari, A. S., & Alsaif, H. (2023). Distributed Blockchain-SDN Secure IoT System Based on ANN to Mitigate DDoS Attacks. *Applied Sciences (Basel, Switzerland)*, 13(8), 4953. doi:10.3390/app13084953

Jmila, H., & Khedher, M. I. (2022). Adversarial machine learning for network intrusion detection: A comparative study. *Computer Networks*, 214, 109073. doi:10.1016/j.comnet.2022.109073

Johnson, R. (2020). Evaluating the Security Practices of Potential Vendors. *Journal of Information Privacy & Security*, 16(3), 98–104.

Joo Fong, T., Abdullah, A., Jhanjhi, N., & Supramaniam, M. (2019). The coin passcode: A shoulder-surfing proof graphical password authentication model for mobile devices. *International Journal of Advanced Computer Science and Applications, 10*(1).

Joo, M., Kim, S. U., Ghose, A., & Wilbur, K. C. (2022). Designing Distributed Ledger technologies, like Blockchain, for advertising markets. *International Journal of Research in Marketing*, 40(1), 12–21. doi:10.1016/j.ijresmar.2022.08.004

Josuttis, N. M. (2007). *SOA in Practice: The Art of Distributed System Design* (Theory in Practice) 1st Edición. USA: O'Reilly Media.

Julie, E. G., Nayahi, J. J. V., & Jhanjhi, N. Z. (2020). *Blockchain Technology: Fundamentals, Applications, and Case Studies*. CRC Press.

Jum'a, L. (2023). The role of blockchain-enabled supply chain applications in improving supply chain performance: The case of Jordanian manufacturing sector. *Management Research Review*, 46(10), 1315–1333. doi:10.1108/MRR-04-2022-0298

Juma, M., AlAttar, F., & Touqan, B. (2023). Securing Big Data Integrity for Industrial IoT in Smart Manufacturing Based on the Trusted Consortium Blockchain (TCB). *Iot*, 4(1), 27–55. doi:10.3390/iot4010002

Kähkönen, A., Marttinen, K., Kontio, A., & Lintukangas, K. (2023). Practices and strategies for sustainability-related risk management in multi-tier supply chains. *Journal of Purchasing and Supply Management, 29*(3), 100848. doi:10.1016/j.pursup.2023.100848

Kalogeraki, E., Papastergiou, S., Mouratidis, H., & Polemi, N. (2018). A Novel Risk Assessment Methodology for SCADA Maritime Logistics Environments. *Applied Sciences (Basel, Switzerland), 8*(9), 1477. doi:10.3390/app8091477

Kalubanga, M., & Mbekeka, W. (2023). Compliance with government and firm's own policy, reverse logistics practices and firm environmental performance. *International Journal of Productivity and Performance Management*. doi:10.1108/IJPPM-09-2022-0463

Kang, Y. (2023). Development of Large-Scale Farming Based on Explainable Machine Learning for a Sustainable Rural Economy: The Case of Cyber Risk Analysis to Prevent Costly Data Breaches. *Applied Artificial Intelligence, 37*(1), 2223862. doi:10.1080/08839514.2023.2223862

Kanyepe, J. (2023). Transport management practices and performance of diamond mining companies in Zimbabwe. *Cogent Business & Management, 10*(2), 2216429. doi:10.1080/23311975.2023.2216429

Kao, C.-Y., & Chueh, H.-E. (2022). A Vendor-Managed Inventory Mechanism Based on SCADA of Internet of Things Framework. *Electronics (Basel), 11*(6), 881. doi:10.3390/electronics11060881

Karim, A. (2022). Development of secure Internet of Vehicle Things (IoVT) for smart transportation system. *Computers & Electrical Engineering, 102*, 108101. doi:10.1016/j.compeleceng.2022.108101

Karim, M. S. (2022). Maritime cybersecurity and the IMO legal instruments: Sluggish response to an escalating threat? *Marine Policy, 143*, 105138. doi:10.1016/j.marpol.2022.105138

Karisma, K., & Tehrani, P. M. (2023). Blockchain Adoption in the Energy Sector: A Comprehensive Regulatory Readiness Assessment Framework to Assess the Regulatory Readiness Levels of Countries. In Lecture notes in networks and systems (pp. 454–460). Springer International Publishing. doi:10.1007/978-3-031-21229-1_42

Kashem, M. A., Shamsuddoha, M., Nasir, T., & Chowdhury, A. A. (2023). Supply Chain Disruption versus Optimization: A Review on Artificial Intelligence and Blockchain. *Knowledge (Beverly Hills, Calif.), 3*(1), 80–96. doi:10.3390/knowledge3010007

Kaur, M., Kaur, H., & Singh, A. (2020). Smart transportation system using Internet of Things (IoT): A review. *Int. J. Adv. Sci. Technol., 29*, 2293–2298.

Kaur, R., Gabrijelčič, D., & Klobučar, T. (2023). Artificial intelligence for cybersecurity: Literature review and future research directions. *Information Fusion, 97*, 101804. doi:10.1016/j.inffus.2023.101804

Kaushik, A., & Pillai, A. S. (2021). Blockchain and IoT based inventory monitoring system. Paper presented at the *Proceedings of the 2nd International Conference on Electronics and Sustainable Communication Systems, ICESC 2021*. IEEE. 10.1109/ICESC51422.2021.9532876

Kayode-Ajala, O. (2023, August 4). *Applications of Cyber Threat intelligence (CTI) in financial institutions and challenges in its adoption*. Research Blog. https://researchberg.com/index.php/araic/article/view/159

Kepli, M. Y. Z. (2023). *Shipping and Logistics in Malaysia: Maritime Institute of Malaysia*. MIMA.

Kerner, S. M. (2022). Colonial Pipeline hack explained: Everything you need to know. *WhatIs.com*. https://www.techtarget.com/whatis/feature/Colonial-Pipeline-hack-explained-Everything-you-need-to-know

Kerner, S. O. S. M. (2022). SolarWinds hack explained: Everything you need to know. *WhatIs.com*. https://www.techtarget.com/whatis/feature/SolarWinds-hack-explained-Everything-you-need-to-know

Khaleefah, A. D., & Al-Mashhadi, H. M. (2023). Methodologies, Requirements and Challenges of Cybersecurity Frameworks: A Review. *Int. J. Wirel. Microw. Technol*, 13, 1–13. doi:10.5815/ijwmt.2023.01.01

Khan, A., Jhanjh, N. Z., & R, S. (2022). *Emerging Industry Revolution IR 4.0 Issues and Challenge* (1st ed.). Taylor & Francis. https://www.taylorfrancis.com/chapters/edit/10.1201/9781003203087-7/emerging-industry-revolution-ir-4-0-issues-challenges-azeem-khan-noor-zaman-jhanjhi-sujatha

Khan, A., Jhanjhi, N. Z., & Sujatha, R. (2022a). Emerging Industry Revolution IR 4.0 Issues and Challenges. In Cyber Security Applications for Industry 4.0 (pp. 151-169). Chapman and Hall/CRC.

Khan, A. A., Bourouis, S., Kamruzzaman, M. M., Hadjouni, M., Shaikh, Z. A., Laghari, A. A., Elmannai, H., & Dhahbi, S. (2023). Data Security in Healthcare Industrial Internet of Things with Blockchain. *IEEE Sensors Journal*, 1(20), 25144–25151. doi:10.1109/JSEN.2023.3273851

Khan, A. A., Laghari, A. A., Shaikh, Z. A., & Dacko-Pikiewicz, Z., & Kot, S. (2022). Internet of Things (IoT) security with blockchain technology: A state-of-the-art review. *IEEE Access : Practical Innovations, Open Solutions*.

Khan, A., Jhanjhi, N. Z., & Humayun, M. (2022). The Role of Cybersecurity in Smart Cities. In *Cyber Security Applications for Industry 4.0* (pp. 195–208). Chapman and Hall/CRC. doi:10.1201/9781003203087-9

Khan, A., Jhanjhi, N. Z., Humayun, M., & Ahmad, M. (2020). The role of IoT in digital governance. In *Employing Recent Technologies for Improved Digital Governance* (pp. 128–150). IGI Global. doi:10.4018/978-1-7998-1851-9.ch007

Khan, K., Mehmood, A., Khan, S., Khan, M. A., Iqbal, Z., & Mashwani, W. K. (2020). A survey on intrusion detection and prevention in wireless ad-hoc networks. *Journal of Systems Architecture*, 105, 101701. doi:10.1016/j.sysarc.2019.101701

Khan, M. I., Zaman, S. A., & Khan, S. A. (2023). Relationship and Impact of Block Chain Technology and Supply Chain Management on Inventory Management. In *Management for professionals* (pp. 53–74). Springer Nature., doi:10.1007/978-981-99-0699-4_4

Khan, M. R., Khan, M. R., & Nallaluthan, K. (2023). Blockchain Supply Chain Management and Supply Chain Sustainability. In *Management for professionals* (pp. 155–180). Springer Nature., doi:10.1007/978-981-99-0699-4_10

Khan, N. A., Jhanjhi, N. Z., Brohi, S. N., Usmani, R. S. A., & Nayyar, A. (2020). Smart traffic monitoring system using unmanned aerial vehicles (UAVs). *Computer Communications*, 157, 434–443. doi:10.1016/j.comcom.2020.04.049

Khanna, T., Nand, P., & Bali, V. (2023). FruitBlock: A layered approach to implement blockchain-based traceability system for agri-supply chain. *International Journal of Business Information Systems*, 43(1), 107. doi:10.1504/IJBIS.2023.131088

Khan, S., Amin, M. B., Azar, A. T., & Aslam, S. (2021). Towards interoperable blockchains: A survey on the role of smart contracts in blockchain interoperability. *IEEE Access : Practical Innovations, Open Solutions*, 9, 116672–116691. doi:10.1109/ACCESS.2021.3106384

Khan, Y., Su'ud, M. B. M., Alam, M. M., Ahmad, S. F., Salim, N. A., & Khan, N. (2022). Architectural Threats to Security and Privacy: A Challenge for Internet of Things (IoT) Applications. *Electronics (Basel)*, 12(1), 88. doi:10.3390/electronics12010088

Khedekar, V. B., Hiremath, S. R., Sonawane, P. D., & Rajput, D. S. (2022). Protection to Personal Data Using Decentralizing Privacy of Blockchain. In IGI Global eBooks (pp. 570–587). doi:10.4018/978-1-6684-7132-6.ch032

Kiac, M., Sikora, P., Malina, L., Lokaj, Z., & Srivastava, G. (2023). ADEROS: Artificial Intelligence-Based Detection System of Critical Events for Road Security. *IEEE Systems Journal*, *17*(4), 1–12. doi:10.1109/JSYST.2023.3276644

Kimmy. (2022). *What Is Supply Chain Risk Management?* Kyin Bridges. https://www.kyinbridges.com/what-is-supply-chain-risk-management-2/

Kioskli, K., Fotis, T., Mavrogiorgou, A., & Mouratidis, H. (2023). The Importance of Conceptualising the Human-Centric Approach in Maintaining and Promoting Cybersecurity-Hygiene in Healthcare 4.0. *Applied Sciences (Basel, Switzerland)*, *13*(6), 3410. doi:10.3390/app13063410

Kirmani, S., Mazid, A., Khan, I. A., & Abid, M. (2023). A Survey on IoT-Enabled Smart Grids: Technologies, Architectures, Applications, and Challenges. *Sustainability (Basel)*, *15*(1), 717. doi:10.3390/su15010717

Kishore Kumar, K. (2021). IoT-based smart agriculture. Handbook of Research on Innovations and Applications of AI, IoT, and Cognitive Technologies, *5*(6), 63–77. doi:10.4018/978-1-7998-6870-5.ch004

Kishor, K. (2022). Communication-efficient federated learning. In *Federated Learning for IoT Applications* (pp. 135–156). Springer International Publishing. doi:10.1007/978-3-030-85559-8_9

Kitsios, F., Chatzidimitriou, E., & Kamariotou, M. (2023). The ISO/IEC 27001 Information Security Management Standard: How to Extract Value from Data in the IT Sector. *Sustainability (Basel)*, *15*(7), 5828. doi:10.3390/su15075828

Kocabasoglu-Hillmer, C., Roden, S., Vanpoucke, E., Son, B., & Lewis, M. W. (2023). Radical innovations as supply chain disruptions? A paradox between change and stability. *The Journal of Supply Chain Management*, *59*(3), 3–19. doi:10.1111/jscm.12299

Koduru, S. S., Machina, V. S. P., & Madichetty, S. (2023). Cyber Attacks in Cyber-Physical Microgrid Systems: A Comprehensive Review. *Energies*, *16*(12), 4573. doi:10.3390/en16124573

Kordestani, A., Oghazi, P., & Mostaghel, R. (2023). Smart contract diffusion in the pharmaceutical blockchain: The battle of counterfeit drugs. *Journal of Business Research*, *158*, 113646. doi:10.1016/j.jbusres.2023.113646

Korpela, K., Hallikas, J., & Dahlberg, T. (2017). Digital Supply Chain Transformation toward Blockchain Integration. In *Proceedings of the . . . Annual Hawaii International Conference on System Sciences*. IEEE. 10.24251/HICSS.2017.506

Kosba, A., Miller, A., Shi, E., Wen, Z., & Papamanthou, C. (2016). Hawk: The Blockchain Model of Cryptography and Privacy-Preserving Smart Contracts. *Proceedings of the 2016 ACM SIGSAC Conference on Computer and Communications Security*, (pp. 839-851). ACM. 10.1109/SP.2016.55

Kotey, S. D., Tchao, E. T., Ahmed, A., Agbemenu, A. S., Nunoo-Mensah, H., Sikora, A., Welte, D., & Keelson, E. (2023). Blockchain interoperability: The state of heterogenous blockchain-to-blockchain communication. *IET Communications*, *17*(8), 891–914. doi:10.1049/cmu2.12594

Kotsias, J., Ahmad, A., & Scheepers, R. (2023). Adopting and integrating cyber-threat intelligence in a commercial organisation. *European Journal of Information Systems*, *32*(1), 35–51. doi:10.1080/0960085X.2022.2088414

Kouhizadeh, M., & Sarkis, J. (2018). Blockchain Practices, Potentials, and Perspectives in Greening Supply Chains. *Sustainability (Basel)*, *10*(10), 3652. doi:10.3390/su10103652

Koukiadaki, A. (2023). Global Supply Chains and Labour Standards: From a Patchwork of Rules to a Web of Rules? In Emerald Publishing Limited eBooks (pp. 127–140). doi:10.1108/978-1-80071-248-520221016

Ko, W. H., Satchidanandan, B., & Kumar, P. R. (2019). Dynamic watermarking-based defense of transportation cyber-physical systems. *ACM Transactions on Cyber-Physical Systems*, *4*(1), 1–21. Advance online publication. doi:10.1145/3361700

Kozlenko, M., & Tkachuk, V. (2019). *Deep learning based detection of DNS spoofing attack.*

Krishnan, L. P., Vakilinia, I., Reddivari, S., & Ahuja, S. (2023). Scams and Solutions in Cryptocurrencies—A Survey Analyzing Existing Machine Learning Models. *Information (Basel)*, *14*(3), 171. doi:10.3390/info14030171

Krishnan, S., Thangaveloo, R., Rahman, S. B. A., & Sindiramutty, S. R. (2021). Smart Ambulance Traffic Control system. *Trends in Undergraduate Research*, *4*(1), c28–c34. doi:10.33736/tur.2831.2021

Krombholz, K., Frühwirt, P., Kieseberg, P., Kapsalis, I., Huber, M., & Weippl, E. (2014). QR Code Security: A Survey of Attacks and Challenges for Usable Security. In: Tryfonas, T., Askoxylakis, I. (Eds.) Human Aspects of Information Security, Privacy, and Trust. Springer, Cham. doi:10.1007/978-3-319-07620-1_8

Kshetri, N. (2022). Supply chain management. Edward Elgar Publishing eBooks. doi:10.4337/9781802208177.00013

Kulkarni, V., Kulkarni, M., & Pant, A. (2020, July). Survey of personalization techniques for federated learning. In *2020 Fourth World Conference on Smart Trends in Systems, Security and Sustainability (WorldS4)* (pp. 794-797). IEEE. 10.1109/WorldS450073.2020.9210355

Kumar, A. (n.d.). *Blockchain in Supply Chain.* LinkedIn. https://www.linkedin.com/pulse/blockchain-supply-chain-aditya-kumar/

Kumar, D., Singh, R. K., Mishra, R., & Wamba, S. F. (2022). Applications of the internet of things for optimizing warehousing and logistics operations: A systematic literature review and future research directions. *Computers & Industrial Engineering*, *171*, 108455. doi:10.1016/j.cie.2022.108455

Kumar, M. S., Vimal, S., Zaman, N., Sundar, D. S., & Alhumyani, H. (2021). Blockchain based peer to peer communication in autonomous drone operation. *Energy Reports*, *7*, 7925–7939. doi:10.1016/j.egyr.2021.08.073

Kumar, P. M., Konstantinou, C., Basheer, S., Manogaran, G., Rawal, B. S., & Babu, G. C. (2023). Agreement-Induced Data Verification Model for Securing Vehicular Communication in Intelligent Transportation Systems. *IEEE Transactions on Intelligent Transportation Systems*, *24*(1), 980–989. doi:10.1109/TITS.2022.3191757

Kumar, P., Bagga, H., Netam, B. S., & Uduthalapally, V. (2022). Sad-iot: Security analysis of ddos attacks in iot networks. *Wireless Personal Communications*, *122*(1), 87–108. doi:10.1007/s11277-021-08890-6

Kumar, S., Gupta, S., & Arora, S. (2021). Research Trends in Network-Based Intrusion Detection Systems: A Review. *IEEE Access : Practical Innovations, Open Solutions*, *9*, 157761–157779. doi:10.1109/ACCESS.2021.3129775

KumarU. V.ReddyE. (2023). Preventing Unauthorized Users from Accessing Cloud Data. *Social Science Research Network*. doi:10.2139/ssrn.4448543

Kumar, V., Malik, N., Singla, J., Zaman, N., Amsaad, F., & Razaque, A. (2022). Light Weight Authentication Scheme for Smart Home IoT Devices. *Cryptography*, *6*(3), 37. doi:10.3390/cryptography6030037

Kunduru, A. R. (2023). Cloud Appian BPM (Business Process Management) Usage In health care Industry. *International Journal of Advanced Research in Computer and Communication Engineering*, *12*(6). doi:10.17148/IJARCCE.2023.12658

Kwon, H. Y., Kim, T., & Lee, M. K. (2022). Advanced intrusion detection combining signature-based and behavior-based detection methods. *Electronics (Basel)*, *11*(6), 867. doi:10.3390/electronics11060867

L'Esteve, R. C. (2023). Designing a Secure Data Lake. In The Cloud Leader's Handbook: Strategically Innovate, Transform, and Scale Organizations (pp. 183-201): Springer. doi:10.1007/978-1-4842-9526-7_11

Lacity, M. C., Yan, A., & Willcocks, L. P. (2022). Robotic process automation and smart contracts: A comparison of design characteristics. *Journal of Management Information Systems*, *39*(1), 292–331.

Lambert, D. M. (2010). Supply Chain Management – Processes, Partnerships, Performance. In Gabler eBooks (pp. 553–572). doi:10.1007/978-3-8349-6515-8_29

Lazăra, A. (2023, January 1). *Security Testing for E-Commerce Applications*. Questa Soft. https://www.ceeol.com/search/chapter-detail?id=1123486

Leal, M., & Musgrave, P. (2023). Backwards from zero: How the U.S. public evaluates the use of zero-day vulnerabilities in cybersecurity. *Contemporary Security Policy*, *44*(3), 437–461. doi:10.1080/13523260.2023.2216112

Lee, C. K., Lv, Y., Ng, K. K. H., Ho, W., & Choy, K. L. (2018). Design and application of Internet of things-based warehouse management system for smart logistics. *International Journal of Production Research*, *56*(8), 2753–2768. doi:10.1080/00207543.2017.1394592

Lee, D., Wen, L., Choi, J. O., & Lee, S. (2023). Sensor-Integrated Hybrid Blockchain System for Supply Chain Coordination in Volumetric Modular Construction. *Journal of Construction Engineering and Management*, *149*(1), 04022147. doi:10.1061/(ASCE)CO.1943-7862.0002427

Lee, S. H., Shiue, Y. L., Cheng, C. H., Li, Y. H., & Huang, Y. F. (2022). Detection and Prevention of DDoS Attacks on the IoT. *Applied Sciences (Basel, Switzerland)*, *12*(23), 12407. doi:10.3390/app122312407

Lee, S., Abdullah, A., Jhanjhi, N., & Kok, S. (2021). Classification of botnet attacks in IoT smart factory using honeypot combined with machine learning. *PeerJ. Computer Science*, *7*, e350. doi:10.7717/peerj-cs.350 PMID:33817000

Lehto, M., & Pöyhönen, J. (2023). Comprehensive cyber security for port and harbor ecosystems. *Frontiers of Computer Science*, *5*, 1154069.

Lele, A., & Lele, A. (2019). Artificial intelligence (AI). *Disruptive technologies for the militaries and security*, 139-154.

Leonel, M., & Prado, M. (2022). *Anomaly detection in IoT: Federated Learning approach on the IoT-23 Dataset*. [Thesis, University of Twente].

Lepiane, C. D., Pereira, F. L., Pieri, G., Martins, D., Martina, J. E., & Rabelo, M. L. (2019, September). Digital degree certificates for higher education in brazil: A technical policy specification. In *Proceedings of the ACM Symposium on Document Engineering 2019* (pp. 1-10). ACM. 10.1145/3342558.3345398

Lessambo, F. I. (2023). AML/CFT and Cybersecurity Laws in the European Union (pp. 79–90). Springer. doi:10.1007/978-3-031-23484-2_6

Liang, H., Sun, X., Sun, Y., & Gao, Y. (2017). Text feature extraction based on deep learning: A review. *EURASIP Journal on Wireless Communications and Networking*, *2017*(1), 1–12. doi:10.1186/s13638-017-0993-1 PMID:29263717

Liang, T., Zeng, B., Liu, J., Ye, L., & Zou, C. (2018). An unsupervised user behavior prediction algorithm based on machine learning and neural network for smart home. *IEEE Access : Practical Innovations, Open Solutions*, *6*, 49237–49247. doi:10.1109/ACCESS.2018.2868984

Liang, W., Li, K.-C., Long, J., Kui, X., & Zomaya, A. Y. (2019). An industrial network intrusion detection algorithm based on multifeature data clustering optimization model. *IEEE Transactions on Industrial Informatics*, *16*(3), 2063–2071. doi:10.1109/TII.2019.2946791

Li, C., Wang, L. S., & Yang, H. (2022). The optimal asset trading settlement based on Proof-of-Stake blockchains. *Decision Support Systems*, *166*, 113909. doi:10.1016/j.dss.2022.113909

Li, C., Zheng, P., Yin, Y., Wang, B., & Wang, L. (2023). Deep reinforcement learning in smart manufacturing: A review and prospects. *CIRP Journal of Manufacturing Science and Technology*, *40*, 75–101. doi:10.1016/j.cirpj.2022.11.003

Li, D., Han, D., Crespi, N., Minerva, R., & Li, K. (2022). A blockchain-based secure storage and access control scheme for supply chain finance. *The Journal of Supercomputing*, *79*(1), 109–138. doi:10.1007/s11227-022-04655-5

Li, G., Shen, Y., Zhao, P., Lu, X., Liu, J., Liu, Y., & Hoi, S. C. H. (2019). Detecting cyberattacks in industrial control systems using online learning algorithms. *Neurocomputing*, *364*, 338–348. doi:10.1016/j.neucom.2019.07.031

Li, J., Xiao, W., & Zhang, C. (2023). Data security crisis in universities: Identification of key factors affecting data breach incidents. *Humanities & Social Sciences Communications*, *10*(1), 270. doi:10.1057/s41599-023-01757-0 PMID:37273415

Li, J., Zhang, W., Zhang, Z., Li, X., & Yang, X. (2022). Predictive control based on event-triggering mechanism of cyber-physical systems under denial-of-service attacks. *Information Sciences*, *586*, 294–309. doi:10.1016/j.ins.2021.11.082

Li, L., Gong, Y., Wang, Z., & Liu, S. (2023). Big data and big disaster: A mechanism of supply chain risk management in global logistics industry. *International Journal of Operations & Production Management*, *43*(2), 274–307. doi:10.1108/IJOPM-04-2022-0266

Li, L., Wang, Z., Chen, L., Zhao, X., & Yang, S. (2023). Supply chain collaboration and supply chain finance adoption: The moderating role of information transparency and transaction dependence. *Supply Chain Management*, *28*(4), 710–723. doi:10.1108/SCM-04-2022-0169

Lim, M., Abdullah, A., & Jhanjhi, N. Z. (2021). Performance optimization of criminal network hidden link prediction model with deep reinforcement learning. *Journal of King Saud University. Computer and Information Sciences*, *33*(10), 1202–1210. doi:10.1016/j.jksuci.2019.07.010

Lin, P. Y., Wu, W. C., & Yang, J. H. (2021). A QR Code-Based Approach to Differentiating the Display of Augmented Reality Content. *Applied Sciences (Basel, Switzerland)*, *11*(24), 11801. doi:10.3390/app112411801

Li, S., Hao, Z., Ding, L., & Xu, X. (2019). Research on the application of information technology of Big Data in Chinese digital library. *Library Management*, *40*(8/9), 518–531. doi:10.1108/LM-04-2019-0021

Li, S., Xu, L. D., & Zhao, S. (2015). The internet of things: A survey. *Information Systems Frontiers*, *17*(2), 243–259. doi:10.1007/s10796-014-9492-7

Liu, X., & Sun, Y. (2011). Information flow control of vendor-managed inventory based on internet of things. In *Advanced Research on Computer Science and Information Engineering: International Conference, CSIE 2011*, (pp. 448–454). Springer Berlin Heidelberg. 10.1007/978-3-642-21402-8_71

Liu, Y., Kumar, N., Xiong, Z., Lim, W. Y. B., Kang, J., & Niyato, D. (2020). Communication-Efficient Federated Learning for Anomaly Detection in Industrial Internet of Things. *2020 IEEE Global Communications Conference, GLOBECOM 2020 - Proceedings, 2020-Janua*(July). IEEE. 10.1109/GLOBECOM42002.2020.9348249

Liu, H., Han, S., & Zhu, Z. (2023). Blockchain Technology toward Smart Construction: Review and Future Directions. *Journal of Construction Engineering and Management*, *149*(3), 03123002. doi:10.1061/JCEMD4.COENG-11929

Liu, J., Huang, J., Zhou, Y., Li, X., Ji, S., Xiong, H., & Dou, D. (2022). From distributed machine learning to federated learning: A survey. *Knowledge and Information Systems*, *64*(4), 885–917. doi:10.1007/s10115-022-01664-x

Liu, J., Liu, B., Zhang, R., & Wang, C. (2019). Multi-step Attack Scenarios Mining Based on Neural Network and Bayesian Network Attack Graph. *Lecture Notes in Computer Science*, *11633*, 62–74. doi:10.1007/978-3-030-24265-7_6

Liu, J., Wu, J., & Gong, Y. (2023). A Resilient Maritime Supply Chain in the Post COVID-19 Era. *Computers & Industrial Engineering*, *109366*. doi:10.1016/j.cie.2023.109366

Liu, M., Zhang, Z., Chen, Y., Ge, J., & Zhao, N. (2023). Adversarial attack and defense on deep learning for air transportation communication jamming. *IEEE Transactions on Intelligent Transportation Systems*.

Liu, Q., Zhou, J., & Liang, H. (2021). Security and privacy in cloud computing. In *Handbook of Research on Cloud Computing and Big Data Applications in IoT* (pp. 174–192). IGI Global.

Liu, W., Liu, Y., & Bucknall, R. (2023). Filtering based multi-sensor data fusion algorithm for a reliable unmanned surface vehicle navigation. *Journal of Marine Engineering & Technology*, *22*(2), 67–83. doi:10.1080/20464177.2022.2031558

Liu, W., Xu, X., Wu, L., Qi, L., Jolfaei, A., Ding, W., & Khosravi, M. R. (2022). Intrusion detection for maritime transportation systems with batch federated aggregation. *IEEE Transactions on Intelligent Transportation Systems*, 1–12. doi:10.1109/TITS.2022.3181436

Liu, Y., Garg, S., Nie, J., Zhang, Y., Xiong, Z., Kang, J., & Hossain, M. S. (2021). Deep Anomaly Detection for Time-Series Data in Industrial IoT: A Communication-Efficient On-Device Federated Learning Approach. *IEEE Internet of Things Journal*, *8*(8), 6348–6358. doi:10.1109/JIOT.2020.3011726

Liu, Y., Lu, Q., Zhu, L., Paik, H., & Staples, M. (2022). A systematic literature review on blockchain governance. *Journal of Systems and Software*, *197*, 111576. doi:10.1016/j.jss.2022.111576

Liu, Y., Yang, J., & Liu, M. (2008). *Recognition of QR Code with mobile phones. 2008 Chinese Control and Decision Conference*, Yantai, Shandong. 10.1109/CCDC.2008.4597299

Li, X. (2023). Inventory management and information sharing based on blockchain technology. *Computers & Industrial Engineering*, *179*, 109196. doi:10.1016/j.cie.2023.109196

Li, Z., Liang, F., & Hu, H. (2023). Blockchain-Based and Value-Driven Enterprise Data Governance: A Collaborative Framework. *Sustainability (Basel)*, *15*(11), 8578. doi:10.3390/su15118578

Lo Piano, S. (2020). Ethical principles in machine learning and artificial intelligence: Cases from the field and possible ways forward. *Humanities & Social Sciences Communications*, *7*(1), 1–7. doi:10.1057/s41599-020-0501-9

Locicero, G. (2020). *Suricata review and attack sceneries*. [online] ResearchGate. https://www.researchgate.net/publication/344292913_Suricata_review_and_attack_sceneries

Logeshwaran, J. (2023, February 8). *A Secured Database Monitoring Method to Improve Data Backup and Recovery Operations in Cloud Computing*. Bohrpub. https://journals.bohrpub.com/index.php/bijcs/article/view/131

Lombard, C. (2023). Expanding and enhancing incident command system communications support. *Journal of Business Continuity & Emergency Planning*, *16*(4), 304–312. PMID:37170453

LukicK.MillerK. M.SkieraB. (2023). The Impact of the General Data Protection Regulation (GDPR) on Online Tracking. *Available at* SSRN. doi:10.2139/ssrn.4399388

Luo, Y., & Zhou, Q. (2021). Optimization Strategy of Cross-Border E-commerce Logistics Chain from the Perspective of Supply Chain. Paper presented at the *Cyber Security Intelligence and Analytics: 2021 International Conference on Cyber Security Intelligence and Analytics (CSIA2021)*, (Volume 2). Springer. 10.1007/978-3-030-69999-4_62

Luoma-Aho, M. (2023). *Analysis of Modern Malware: obfuscation techniques*. Theseus. https://www.theseus.fi/handle/10024/798038

Ma, J. (2023). *Full Steam Ahead: Enhancing Maritime Cybersecurity*.

Maharana, M., & Lathabhavan, R. (2023). Industry 4.0 and its impact on supply chain management: An overview. *International Journal of Services. Economics and Management*, *14*(2), 224–248.

Maheshwari, P., Kamble, S., Pundir, A., Belhadi, A., Ndubisi, N. O., & Tiwari, S. (2021). Internet of things for perishable inventory management systems: An application and managerial insights for micro, small and medium enterprises. *Annals of Operations Research*, 1–29. doi:10.1007/s10479-021-04277-9 PMID:34642526

Mahmood, Y., Afrin, T., Huang, Y., & Yodo, N. (2023). Sustainable Development for Oil and Gas Infrastructure from Risk, Reliability, and Resilience Perspectives. *Sustainability (Basel)*, 15(6), 4953. doi:10.3390/su15064953

Majeed, A., & Rauf, I. (2020). Graph Theory: A Comprehensive Survey about Graph Theory Applications in Computer Science and Social Networks. *Inventions (Basel, Switzerland)*, 5(1), 10. doi:10.3390/inventions5010010

Mak, W. J., Aziz, M. L. A., Hamid, M. R., & Hashim, M. M. H. M. (2023). *Improving Accessibility of Technical Drilling Applications via Wells on Cloud-based Platform*. IEEE. doi:10.2118/214541-MS

Makinda, S. M. (1998). Sovereignty and Global Security. *Security Dialogue*, 29(3), 281–292. doi:10.1177/0967010698029003003

Mallah, R. A., Lopez, D., & Farooq, B. (2021). Cyber-Security Risk Assessment Framework for Blockchains in Smart Mobility. *IEEE Open Journal of Intelligent Transportation Systems*, 2, 294–311. doi:10.1109/OJITS.2021.3106863

Manavalan, E., & Jayakrishna, K. (2019). A review of Internet of Things (IoT) embedded sustainable supply chain for industry 4.0 requirements. *Computers & Industrial Engineering*, 127, 925–953. doi:10.1016/j.cie.2018.11.030

Mandal, S. K., & Deepti, A. R. (2019). A Review Paper on Encryption Techniques. *International Journal of Research and Analytical Reviews*, 6(2), 70–75. https://www.ijrar.org/papers/IJRAR1ANP010.pdf

Manna, P., & Das, R. K. (2021). Scalability in Internet of Things: Techniques, Challenges and Solutions. *International Journal for Research in Engineering Application & Management (IJREAM)*, 259-261.

Mantravadi, S., & Srai, J. S. (2023). How Important are Digital Technologies for Urban Food Security? A Framework for Supply Chain Integration using IoT. *Procedia Computer Science*, 217, 1678–1687. doi:10.1016/j.procs.2022.12.368

Manzoor, U. (2023, May 16). *Blockchain Technology in Marketing: Potential Applications and Implications*. ASMARA Publications. http://asmarapublications.com/journals/index.php/PMS/article/view/8

Marbut, A. R., & Harms, P. D. (2023). Fiends and Fools: A Narrative Review and Neo-socioanalytic Perspective on Personality and Insider Threats. *Journal of Business and Psychology*. doi:10.1007/s10869-023-09885-9

Marquez-Tejon, J., Partearroyo, M. J., & Benito-Osorio, D. (2023). Integrated security management model: A proposal applied to organisational resilience. *Security Journal*. doi:10.1057/s41284-023-00381-6

Marthews, A., & Tucker, C. (2022). What blockchain can and can't do: Applications to marketing and privacy. *International Journal of Research in Marketing*, 40(1), 49–53. doi:10.1016/j.ijresmar.2022.09.001

Maseer, Z. K., Yusof, R., Bahaman, N., Mostafa, S. A., & Foozy, C. F. M. (2021). Benchmarking of machine learning for anomaly based intrusion detection systems in the CICIDS2017 dataset. *IEEE Access : Practical Innovations, Open Solutions*, 9, 22351–22370. doi:10.1109/ACCESS.2021.3056614

Mashayekhy, Y., Babaei, A., Yuan, X.-M., & Xue, A. (2022). Impact of Internet of Things (IoT) on Inventory Management: A Literature Survey. *Logistics*, 6(2), 33. doi:10.3390/logistics6020033

Mebawondu, J. O., Alowolodu, O. D., Mebawondu, J. O., & Adetunmbi, A. O. (2020). Network intrusion detection system using supervised learning paradigm. *Scientific African*, 9, e00497. doi:10.1016/j.sciaf.2020.e00497

Meftah, A., Do, T. N., Kaddoum, G., Talhi, C., & Singh, S. (2023). Federated Learning-Enabled Jamming Detection and Waveform Classification for Distributed Tactical Wireless Networks. *IEEE Transactions on Network and Service Management*, 20(4), 5053–5072. doi:10.1109/TNSM.2023.3271578

Mehdi Rizvi, Q., & Kushwaha, R. S. (2023). EXPLORING MODERN CRYPTOGRAPHY: A COMPREHENSIVE GUIDE TO TECHNIQUES AND APPLICATIONS. *International Research Journal of Modernization in Engineering Technology and Science*, 05(05), 2582–5208. doi:10.56726/IRJMETS40247

Mehmood, M. T., Amin, R., Muslam, M. M. A., Xie, J., & Aldabbas, H. (2023). Privilege escalation attack detection and mitigation in cloud using machine learning. *IEEE Access : Practical Innovations, Open Solutions*, 11, 46561–46576. doi:10.1109/ACCESS.2023.3273895

Mehta, M., Khurana, A., & Kumar, V. R. (2023). *Leveraging Blockchain Technology for Improving the Quality of Corporate Governance*. IEEE. doi:10.1109/ISCON57294.2023.10112178

Meidan, Y., Bohadana, M., Shabtai, A., Guarnizo, J. D., Ochoa, M., Tippenhauer, N. O., & Elovici, Y. (2017). ProfilIoT: A machine learning approach for IoT device identification based on network traffic analysis. *Proceedings of the ACM Symposium on Applied Computing, Part F1280*, (pp. 506–509). ACM. 10.1145/3019612.3019878

Meisami, S., Meisami, S., Yousefi, M., & Aref, M. R. (2023). Combining Blockchain and IoT for Decentralized Healthcare Data Management. *International Journal of Cryptography and Information Security*, 13(1), 35–50. doi:10.5121/ijcis.2023.13102

Menon, S., Anand, D., Kavita, Verma, S., Kaur, M., Jhanjhi, N. Z., Ghoniem, R. M., & Ray, S. K. (2023). Blockchain and Machine Learning Inspired Secure Smart Home Communication Network. *Sensors (Basel)*, 23(13), 6132. doi:10.3390/s23136132 PMID:37447981

Mentzer, J. T., Moon, M. A., & Dwyer, F. R. (2016). Creating a sustainable competitive advantage through sales and operations planning. *Journal of Business Logistics*, 37(1), 6–18. doi:10.1111/jbl.12117

Mentzer, J. T., Stank, T. P., & Esper, T. L. (2015). Supply chain management and its relationship to logistics, marketing, production, and operations management. *Journal of Business Logistics*, 36(1), 1–7. doi:10.1002/j.2158-1592.2008.tb00067.x

Miao, Y., Li, F., Li, X., Liu, Z., Ning, J., Li, H., Choo, K. R., & Deng, R. H. (2023). Time-Controllable Keyword Search Scheme with Efficient Revocation in Mobile E-health Cloud. *IEEE Transactions on Mobile Computing*, 1–15. doi:10.1109/TMC.2023.3277702

Microcosm. (n.d.). *User Access Control | Prevent Unauthorized Access to Systems and Applications*. Microcosm. https://www.microcosm.com/solutions/user-access-control

Midha, S., Verma, S., Mittal, M., Jhanjhi, N., Masud, M., & AlZain, M. A. (2023). A Secure Multi-factor Authentication Protocol for Healthcare Services Using Cloud-based SDN. *Computers, Materials & Continua*, 74(2). doi:10.32604/cmc.2023.027992

Mijalkovic, J., & Spognardi, A. (2022). Reducing the false negative rate in deep learning based network intrusion detection systems. *Algorithms*, 15(8), 258. doi:10.3390/a15080258

Mijwil, M., Salem, I. E., & M. Ismaeel, M. (2023). The Significance of Machine Learning and Deep Learning Techniques in Cybersecurity: A Comprehensive Review. *Iraqi Journal for Computer Science and Mathematics*, 87–101. doi:10.52866/ijcsm.2023.01.01.008

Mikuriya, K. (2007). Supply Chain Security: The Customs Community's Response. *World Customs Journal*, 1(2), 51–60.

Mishra, A., & Mohapatro, M. (2020). Real-time RFID-based item tracking using IoT efficient inventory management using Machine Learning. Paper presented at the *4th IEEE Conference on Information and Communication Technology, CICT 2020*. IEEE. 10.1109/CICT51604.2020.9312074

Mishra, N., & Keshri, A. K. (2021) Smart Racking and Retailing Using IOT. Lecture Notes in Electrical Engineering (pp. 645-653). doi:10.1007/978-981-15-5546-6_54

Mishra, S. (2023). Blockchain and Machine Learning-Based hybrid IDS to protect smart networks and preserve privacy. *Electronics (Basel)*, *12*(16), 3524. doi:10.3390/electronics12163524

Mishra, S. K., Mishra, S., Alsayat, A., Jhanjhi, N. Z., Humayun, M., Sahoo, K. S., & Luhach, A. K. (2020). Energy-aware task allocation for multi-cloud networks. *IEEE Access : Practical Innovations, Open Solutions*, *8*, 178825–178834. doi:10.1109/ACCESS.2020.3026875

Mishra, S., Albarakati, A., & Sharma, S. K. (2022). Cyber Threat Intelligence for IoT Using Machine Learning. *Processes (Basel, Switzerland)*, *10*(12), 2673. doi:10.3390/pr10122673

Modak, S. K. S. (2023). Application of Blockchain in Supply Chain Management. *International Journal for Multidisciplinary Research*, *5*(2), 2216. doi:10.36948/ijfmr.2023.v05i02.2216

Mohamed, S. K., Haddad, S., Barakat, M., & Rosi, B. (2023). Blockchain Technology Adoption for Improved Environmental Supply Chain Performance: The Mediation Effect of Supply Chain Resilience, Customer Integration, and Green Customer Information Sharing. *Sustainability (Basel)*, *15*(10), 7909. doi:10.3390/su15107909

Mohezar, S., Mohamad, M. N., & Nor, M. N. M. (2023). Supply chain risk and SME business continuity strategies in the food industry during COVID-19 pandemic. *Continuity & Resilience Review*. doi:10.1108/CRR-09-2022-0021

Moïsé, E., & Sorescu, S. (2013). *Trade Facilitation Indicators: The Potential Impact of Trade Facilitation on Developing Countries' Trade. OECD Trade Policy Papers, No. 144*. OECD Publishing. doi:10.1787/5k4bw6kg6ws2-

Molina-Coronado, B., Mori, U., Mendiburu, A., & Miguel-Alonso, J. (2021). *Survey of Network Intrusion Detection Methods from the Perspective of the Knowledge Discovery in Databases Process*. https://arxiv.org/ftp/arxiv/papers/2001/2001.09697.pdf

Mollah, M. B., Azad, M. A. K., & Vasilakos, A. (2017). Secure data sharing and searching at the edge of cloud-assisted internet of things. *IEEE Cloud Computing*, *4*(1), 34–42. doi:10.1109/MCC.2017.9

Möller, D. P. (2023). NIST Cybersecurity Framework and MITRE Cybersecurity Criteria. In Guide to Cybersecurity in Digital Transformation: Trends, Methods, Technologies, Applications and Best Practices (pp. 231-271). Springer. doi:10.1007/978-3-031-26845-8_5

Möller, D. P. F. (2023). Intrusion Detection and Prevention. Springer. doi:10.1007/978-3-031-26845-8_3

Möller, D. P. F. (2023). Ransomware Attacks and Scenarios: Cost Factors and Loss of Reputation. Springer. doi:10.1007/978-3-031-26845-8_6

Moore, S. J., Nugent, C. D., Zhang, S., & Cleland, I. (2020). IoT reliability: A review leading to 5 key research directions. *CCF Transactions on Pervasive Computing and Interaction*, *2*(3), 147–163. doi:10.1007/s42486-020-00037-z

Morsy, S. M., & Nashat, D. (2022). D-ARP: An Efficient Scheme to Detect and Prevent ARP Spoofing. *IEEE Access : Practical Innovations, Open Solutions*, *10*, 49142–49153. doi:10.1109/ACCESS.2022.3172329

Mostafa, A. A. (2015). The effectiveness of product podes in marketing. *Procedia: Social and Behavioral Sciences*, *175*, 12–15. doi:10.1016/j.sbspro.2015.01.1168

Mostafa, N., Hamdy, W., & Alawady, H. (2019). Impacts of internet of things on supply chains: A framework for warehousing. *Social Sciences (Basel, Switzerland)*, *8*(3), 84. doi:10.3390/socsci8030084

Mothukuri, V., Khare, P., Parizi, R. M., Pouriyeh, S., Dehghantanha, A., & Srivastava, G. (2022). Federated-Learning-Based Anomaly Detection for IoT Security Attacks. *IEEE Internet of Things Journal*, *9*(4), 2545–2554. doi:10.1109/JIOT.2021.3077803

Mothukuri, V., Parizi, R. M., Pouriyeh, S., Huang, Y., Dehghantanha, A., & Srivastava, G. (2021). A survey on security and privacy of federated learning. *Future Generation Computer Systems*, *115*, 619–640. doi:10.1016/j.future.2020.10.007

Mpatziakas, A., Drosou, A., Papadopoulos, S., & Tzovaras, D. (2022). IoT threat mitigation engine empowered by artificial intelligence multi-objective optimization. *Journal of Network and Computer Applications*, *203*, 103398. doi:10.1016/j.jnca.2022.103398

Mubarik, M. S., Khan, S. A., Kusi-Sarpong, S., & Mubarik, M. (2023). Supply chain sustainability in VUCA: Role of BCT-driven SC mapping and 'Visiceability.'. *International Journal of Logistics*, 1–19. doi:10.1080/13675567.2023.2222660

Muhammad, Z., Anwar, Z., Javed, A. R., Saleem, B., Abbas, S., & Gadekallu, T. R. (2023). Smartphone Security and Privacy: A Survey on APTs, Sensor-Based Attacks, Side-Channel Attacks, Google Play Attacks, and Defenses. *Technologies*, *11*(3), 76. doi:10.3390/technologies11030076

Mukherjee, D., Ghosh, S., Pal, S., Akila, D., Jhanjhi, N., Masud, M., & AlZain, M. A. *Optimized energy efficient strategy for data reduction between edge devices in cloud-iot.*

Mukherjee, D., Ghosh, S., Pal, S., Akila, D., Jhanjhi, N., Masud, M., & AlZain, M. A. (2022). Optimized Energy Efficient Strategy for Data Reduction Between Edge Devices in Cloud-IoT. *Computers, Materials & Continua*, *72*(1). doi:10.32604/cmc.2022.023611

Muller, M. (2019). *Essentials of inventory management*. HarperCollins Leadership.

Munasinghe, U. J., & Halgamuge, M. N. (2023). Supply chain traceability and counterfeit detection of COVID-19 vaccines using novel blockchain-based Vacledger system. *Expert Systems with Applications*, *228*, 120293. doi:10.1016/j.eswa.2023.120293 PMID:37197005

Murimi, R., Bell, G., Rasheed, A. A., & Beldona, S. (2023). Blockchains: A Review and Research Agenda for International Business. *Research in International Business and Finance*, *66*, 102018. doi:10.1016/j.ribaf.2023.102018

Murray-Rust, D., Elsden, C., Nissen, B., Tallyn, E., Pschetz, L., & Speed, C. (2022). Blockchain and Beyond: Understanding Blockchains Through Prototypes and Public Engagement. *ACM Transactions on Computer-Human Interaction*, *29*(5), 1–73. doi:10.1145/3503462

Murshed, M. S., Murphy, C., Hou, D., Khan, N., Ananthanarayanan, G., & Hussain, F. (2021). Machine learning at the network edge: A survey. *ACM Computing Surveys*, *54*(8), 1–37. doi:10.1145/3469029

Muzafar, S., Jhanjhi, N. Z., Khan, N. A., & Ashfaq, F. (2022). DDOS attack detection approaches in on software defined network. *2022 14th International Conference on Mathematics, Actuarial Science, Computer Science and Statistics (MACS)*. IEEE. 10.1109/MACS56771.2022.10022653

Muzafar, S., & Jhanjhi, N. Z. (2022). DDoS attacks on software defined Network: Challenges and issues. *2022 International Conference on Business Analytics for Technology and Security (ICBATS)*. IEEE. 10.1109/ICBATS54253.2022.9780662

Muzammal, S. M., Murugesan, R. K., Jhanjhi, N. Z., & Jung, L. T. (2020). SMTrust: Proposing Trust-Based Secure Routing Protocol for RPL Attacks for IoT Applications. *2020 International Conference on Computational Intelligence (ICCI)*. IEEE. 10.1109/ICCI51257.2020.9247818

N, S., Vivekananda, B. K., Rajarajan, M., & Das, A. K. (2023). A New Scalable and Secure Access Control Scheme using Blockchain Technology for IoT. *IEEE Transactions on Network and Service Management*, 1. IEEE. doi:10.1109/TNSM.2023.3246120

N. (2019). *Exploring Information Centrality for Intrusion Detection in Large Networks*. ResearchGate. https://www.researchgate.net/publication/332750935_Exploring_Information_Centrality_for_Intrusion_Detection_in_Large_Networks [.

Nadeem, R., Amir Latif, R. M., Hussain, K., Jhanjhi, N., & Humayun, M. (2022). A flexible framework for requirement management (FFRM) from software architecture toward distributed agile framework. *Open Computer Science*, *12*(1), 364–377. doi:10.1515/comp-2022-0239

Najmi, K. Y., AlZain, M. A., Masud, M., Jhanjhi, N., Al-Amri, J., & Baz, M. (2021). A survey on security threats and countermeasures in IoT to achieve users confidentiality and reliability. *Materials Today: Proceedings*.

Namasudra, S., & Akkaya, K. (2023). Introduction to Blockchain Technology. In *Studies in big data* (pp. 1–28). Springer International Publishing. doi:10.1007/978-981-19-8730-4_1

Nanda, S. K., Panda, S. K., & Dash, M. (2023). Medical supply chain integrated with blockchain and IoT to track the logistics of medical products. *Multimedia Tools and Applications*, *82*(21), 32917–32939. doi:10.1007/s11042-023-14846-8 PMID:37362711

Naoum-Sawaya, J., Elhedhli, S., & De Carvalho, P. (2023). Strategic Blockchain Adoption to Deter Deceptive Counterfeiters. *European Journal of Operational Research*, *311*(1), 373–386. doi:10.1016/j.ejor.2023.04.031

Naraindath, N. R., Bansal, R. C., & Naidoo, R. (2023). The Uprising of Blockchain Technology in the Energy Market Industry. In Lecture notes in electrical engineering (pp. 497–509). Springer Science+Business Media. doi:10.1007/978-981-19-7993-4_41

Nardi, M., Valerio, L., & Passarella, A. (2022). *Anomaly Detection through Unsupervised Federated Learning*. IEEE. doi:10.1109/MSN57253.2022.00085

Nasser, Y., & Nassar, M. (2023). Toward Hardware-Assisted Malware Detection Utilizing Explainable Machine Learning: A survey. *IEEE Access : Practical Innovations, Open Solutions*, *11*, 131273–131288. doi:10.1109/ACCESS.2023.3335187

National Institute of Standards and Technology (NIST). (2021). *Computer Security Incident Handling Guide* (NIST Special Publication 800-61 Revision 2). NIST. doi:10.6028/NIST.SP.800-61r2

Navone, E. C. (2020). *Dijkstra's Shortest Path Algorithm - A Detailed and Visual Introduction*. Free Code Camp. https://www.freecodecamp.org/news/dijkstras-shortest-path-algorithm-visual-introduction/

Nawab, F., & Sadoghi, M. (2023). Consensus in Data Management: From Distributed Commit to Blockchain. *Foundations and Trends in Databases*, *12*(4), 221–364. doi:10.1561/1900000075

Nayak, P., & Swapna, G. (2023). Security issues in IoT applications using certificateless aggregate signcryption schemes: An overview. *Internet of Things : Engineering Cyber Physical Human Systems*, *21*, 100641. doi:10.1016/j.iot.2022.100641

Negar, J. J. (2023, January 1). *Evaluating the Effect of Supply Chain Management Practice on Implementation of Halal Agroindustry and Competitive Advantage for Small and Medium Enterprises*. SSRN. https://papers.ssrn.com/sol3/papers.cfm?abstract_id=4348136

Negi, S. (2022). Improving Supply Chain Management Performance with Blockchain Technology. In Springer eBooks (pp. 327–344). doi:10.1007/978-3-031-10507-4_14

Nelligere, L., Swamy, T., & Mubashir Ahmed, A. (n.d.). Vulnerability Assessment and Analysis of SCADA and Foundation Fieldbus on Industrial Control System (ICS) Networks: A Literature Revie. *Journal of Computer Sciences, 17*(2), 34–65. https://search.ebscohost.com/login.aspx?direct=true&profile=ehost&scope=site&authtype=crawler&jrnl=097 39904&AN=163472952&h=RIfIAHCsUQBAX7WEHsAZJ2psL9s%2FaeGPwAn6wgfCB7jHTDV216xabNXSyiX7S yekzAsXaiiUoSNh0yHd56IzXg%3D%3D&crl=c&casa_token=vQeuhcveouAAAAAA:2nRq7od2LEIedxhtbARWgHI iIowH_-NVZA1aGE0dnJ4RZLijyvOOC-T8uUIydu-s8f10b6n_PO_Qa6Ip

Nguyen, T. D., Marchal, S., Miettinen, M., Fereidooni, H., Asokan, N., & Sadeghi, A. R. (2019). DÏoT: A federated self-learning anomaly detection system for IoT. *Proceedings - International Conference on Distributed Computing Systems, 2019-July*(Icdcs), (pp. 756–767). IEEE. 10.1109/ICDCS.2019.00080

Nguyen, D. C., Ding, M., Pathirana, P. N., Seneviratne, A., Li, J., & Poor, H. V. (2021). Federated learning for internet of things: A comprehensive survey. *IEEE Communications Surveys and Tutorials, 23*(3), 1622–1658. doi:10.1109/COMST.2021.3075439

Niknejad, N., Ismail, W., Ghani, I., Nazari, B., Bahari, M., & Hussin, A. R. B. C. (2020). Understanding Service-Oriented Architecture (SOA): A systematic literature review and directions for further investigation. *Information Systems, 91*, 101491. doi:10.1016/j.is.2020.101491

Nour, B., Pourzandi, M., & Debbabi, M. (2023). A survey on threat hunting in enterprise networks. *IEEE Communications Surveys and Tutorials, 25*(4), 2299–2324. doi:10.1109/COMST.2023.3299519

Nozari, H., & Edalatpanah, S. A. (2023). Smart Systems Risk Management in IoT-Based Supply Chain. In *Industrial and applied mathematics* (pp. 251–268). Springer Nature. doi:10.1007/978-981-19-9909-3_11

NPO. (2022). *FY2008 Investigation Report on In-formation Security Incidents* (Ver.1.3). Japan Network Security Association. https://www.jnsa.org/en/reports/incident.html

Nweke, L. O. (2023). National identification Systems as enablers of Online Identity. In IntechOpen eBooks. doi:10.5772/intechopen.1002294

Odeh, A., & Taleb, A. A. (2023). Ensemble-Based Deep learning models for enhancing IoT intrusion detection. *Applied Sciences (Basel, Switzerland), 13*(21), 11985. doi:10.3390/app132111985

OECD. (2022). *Freight transport*. OECD. https://data.oecd.org/transport/freight-transport.htm

Ohood, M. A., Mohammed, A. A., Mehedi, M., & Jhanjhi, N. (2021). A Survey of Blockchain and E-governance applications: Security and Privacy. *ProQuest, 12*(1), 3126–3134. https://www.proquest.com/openview/79c4f3046c069f6c 83d1acb8f32ef91a/1?pq-origsite=gscholar&cbl=2045096

Ojha, T., Misra, S., & Raghuwanshi, N. S. (2021). Internet of Things for Agricultural Applications: The State of the Art. *IEEE Internet of Things Journal, 8*(14), 10973–10997. doi:10.1109/JIOT.2021.3051418

Okunade, S. O., Alimi, A. S., & Olayiwola, A. S. (2023). Intellectual property rights protection and prospect of industrial development in Nigeria. *International Journal of Intellectual Property Management, 13*(1), 78. doi:10.1504/IJIPM.2023.129079

Okuno, I. (2023). Introduction of business continuity plan for small and medium-sized local construction companies and restoration activities in Japan in the event of natural disasters. *Paper presented at the IOP Conference Series: Earth and Environmental Science*. IOP Science. 10.1088/1755-1315/1195/1/012047

Omar, M. A. A., & Zaman, N. (2017). Internet of Things (IoT) : Charity Automation. *International Journal of Advanced Computer Science and Applications, 8*(2), 166–170. doi:10.14569/IJACSA.2017.080222

Ozkaya, E., Ozkaya, H. E., Roxas, J., Bryant, F., & Whitson, D. (2015). Factors affecting consumer usage of QR codes. *Journal of Direct, Data and Digital Marketing Practice, 16*(3), 209–224. doi:10.1057/dddmp.2015.18

Pabitha, P., Jayabal, C. P., Ramalingam, P., & Jagatheswari, S. (2023). ModChain: A hybridized secure and scaling block-chain framework for IoT environment. *International Journal of Information Technology : an Official Journal of Bharati Vidyapeeth's Institute of Computer Applications and Management, 15*(3), 1741–1754. doi:10.1007/s41870-023-01218-6

Pacheco, M., Oliva, G. A., Rajbahadur, G. K., & Hassan, A. E. (2023). What makes Ethereum blockchain transactions be processed fast or slow? An empirical study. *Empirical Software Engineering, 28*(2), 39. doi:10.1007/s10664-022-10283-7 PMID:36776918

Padovan, P. A., Martins, C., & Reed, C. (2022). Black is the new orange: How to determine AI liability. *Artificial Intelligence and Law, 31*(1), 133–167. doi:10.1007/s10506-022-09308-9

Palmer, S. (2020). History of the Ports. *International Journal of Maritime History, 32*(2), 426–433. doi:10.1177/0843871420921266

Pal, S., Hitchens, M., Rabehaja, T., & Mukhopadhyay, S. (2020). Security requirements for the internet of things: A systematic approach. *Sensors (Basel), 20*(20), 5897. doi:10.3390/s20205897 PMID:33086542

Pal, S., Jhanjhi, N., Abdulbaqi, A. S., Akila, D., Alsubaei, F. S., & Almazroi, A. A. (2023). An Intelligent Task Scheduling Model for Hybrid Internet of Things and Cloud Environment for Big Data Applications. *Sustainability (Basel), 15*(6), 5104. doi:10.3390/su15065104

Pandey, S., & Munjal, D. (2023). E-Commerce Website In The Pandemic Situation. *International Research Journal, 20*(5).

Pandian, D. A. P. (2019). Artificial intelligence application in smart warehousing environment for automated logistics. *Journal of Artificial Intelligence and Capsule Networks, 1*(2), 63–72. doi:10.36548/jaicn.2019.2.002

Panghal, A., Manoram, S., Mor, R. S., & Vern, P. (2022). Adoption challenges of blockchain technology for reverse logistics in the food processing industry. *Supply Chain Forum: An International Journal, 24*(1), 7–16. 10.1080/16258312.2022.2090852

Pantano, E., & Servidio, R. (2012). Modeling innovative points of sales through virtual and immersive technologies. *Journal of Retailing and Consumer Services, 19*(3), 279–286. doi:10.1016/j.jretconser.2012.02.002

Papanagnou, C. I. (2022). Measuring and eliminating the bullwhip in closed loop supply chains using control theory and Internet of Things. *Annals of Operations Research, 310*(1), 153–170. doi:10.1007/s10479-021-04136-7

Papastergiou, S., Mouratidis, H., & Kalogeraki, E. M. (2021). Handling of advanced persistent threats and complex incidents in healthcare, transportation and energy ICT infrastructures. *Evolving Systems, 12*(1), 91–108. doi:10.1007/s12530-020-09335-4

Pargoo, N. S., & Ilbeigi, M. (2023). A Scoping Review for Cybersecurity in the Construction Industry. *Journal of Management Engineering, 39*(2), 03122003. doi:10.1061/JMENEA.MEENG-5034

Park, W. Y., Kim, S. H., Vu, D., Song, C. H., Jung, H., & Jo, H. (2022). Intrusion Detection System for industrial network. In Lecture notes in networks and systems (pp. 646–658). Springer. doi:10.1007/978-3-031-16075-2_48

Parker, A., Nithyanand, R., & Juarez, M. (2021). Federated Learning for Private Intrusion Detection. Proceedings of the 2021 Conference on Detection of Intrusions and Malware, and Vulnerability Assessment, (pp. 497-500). Springer. doi: 10.1007/978-3-030-85891-5_24

Parker, S., Wu, Z., & Christofides, P. D. (2023). *Cybersecurity in process control, operations, and supply chain.* Elsevier. doi:10.1016/j.compchemeng.2023.108169

Patel, K. K., Patel, S. M., & Scholar, P. (2016). Internet of things-IOT: definition, characteristics, architecture, enabling technologies, application & future challenges. *International journal of engineering science and computing, 6*(5).

Patrutiu-Baltes, L. (2016). Inbound Marketing-the most important digital marketing strategy. *Bulletin of the Transilvania University of Braşov. Series V: Economic Sciences 9*(58/2), 61-68. https://webbut.unitbv.ro/BU2016/Series%20V/Contents_V_MK.html

Paul, S., Chatterjee, A., & Guha, D. (2019). Study of smart inventory management system based on the internet of things (IOT). [IJRTBT]. *International Journal on Recent Trends in Business and Tourism, 3*(3), 27–34.

Pawlicki, M., Pawlicka, A., Kozik, R., & Choraś, M. (2023). The survey and meta-analysis of the attacks, transgressions, countermeasures and security aspects common to the Cloud, Edge and IoT. *Neurocomputing, 551*, 126533. doi:10.1016/j.neucom.2023.126533

Peng, Y., Welden, N. A., & Renaud, F. G. (2023). A framework for integrating ecosystem services indicators into vulnerability and risk assessments of deltaic social-ecological systems. *Journal of Environmental Management, 326*, 116682. doi:10.1016/j.jenvman.2022.116682 PMID:36375428

Peregrina-Pérez, M. J., Lagares-Galán, J., & Boubeta-Puig, J. (2023). Hyperledger Fabric blockchain platform. In Elsevier eBooks (pp. 283–295). Elesvier. doi:10.1016/B978-0-323-96146-2.00014-0

Peter, O., Pradhan, A., & Mbohwa, C. (2023). Industrial internet of things (IIoT): Opportunities, challenges, and requirements in manufacturing businesses in emerging economies. *Procedia Computer Science, 217*, 856–865. doi:10.1016/j.procs.2022.12.282

Peterson, E. (2021). Achieving Visibility and Control in OT Systems: Remote Maintenance, Securing Remote Access, and the Zero-Trust Approach. *Idaho National Library*. https://www.cisa.gov/sites/default/files/2023-05/Achieving%20Visibility%20and%20Control%20in%20OT%20Systems%20Remote%20Maintenace%2C%20Securing%20Remote%20Access%2C%20and%20the%20Zero-Trust%20Approach_508c.pdf

Petrosyan, A. (2023). *Daily number of spam emails sent worldwide as of January 2023, by country*. Statista. https://www.statista.com/statistics/1270488/spam-emails-sent-daily-by-country/

Pey, J. N. A., Nze, G. D. A., & de Oliveira Albuquerque, R. (2022, June). Analysis of jamming and spoofing cyber-attacks on drones. In *2022 17th Iberian Conference on Information Systems and Technologies (CISTI)* (pp. 1-4). IEEE.

Piccialli, F., Cuomo, S., Cola, V. S., & Casolla, G. (2019). A machine learning approach for IoT cultural data. *Journal of Ambient Intelligence and Humanized Computing*, (0123456789). doi:10.1007/s12652-019-01452-6

Piramuthu, S. (2022). Drone-Based Warehouse Inventory Management with IoT for Perishables. In Smart Services Summit: Smart Services Supporting the New Normal (pp. 13-21): Springer. doi:10.1007/978-3-030-97042-0_2

PissanidisD. L.DemertzisK. (2023). Integrating AI/ML in Cybersecurity: An Analysis of Open XDR Technology and its Application in Intrusion Detection and System Log Management. *Preprints2023*. doi:10.20944/preprints202312.0205.v1

Ponnusamy, V., Aun, Y., Jhanjhi, N. Z., Humayun, M., & Almufareh, M. F. (2022). IoT wireless intrusion detection and network Traffic Analysis. *Computer Systems Science and Engineering, 40*(3), 865–879. doi:10.32604/csse.2022.018801

Ponnusamy, V., Humayun, M., Jhanjhi, N., Yichiet, A., & Almufareh, M. F. (2022). Intrusion Detection Systems in Internet of Things and Mobile Ad-Hoc Networks. *Computer Systems Science and Engineering, 40*(3). doi:10.32604/csse.2022.018518

Ponnusamy, V., Zaman, N., & Humayun, M. (2020). Fostering Public-Private Partnership. In *Advances in electronic government, digital divide, and regional development book series* (pp. 237–255). IGI Global. doi:10.4018/978-1-7998-1851-9.ch012

Pourakbar, M., & Zuidwijk, R. A. (2018). The role of customs in securing containerized global supply chains. *European Journal of Operational Research*, *271*(1), 331–340. doi:10.1016/j.ejor.2018.05.012

Pournader, M., Shi, Y., Seuring, S., & Koh, S. L. (2019). Blockchain applications in supply chains, transport and logistics: A systematic review of the literature. *International Journal of Production Research*, *58*(7), 2063–2081. doi:10.1080/00207543.2019.1650976

Pöyhönen, J., Simola, J., & Lehto, M. (2023). Basic Elements of Cyber Security for a Smart Terminal Process. *Paper presented at the The Proceedings of the... International Conference on Cyber Warfare and Security*. IOP Science.

Prabakar, D., Sundarrajan, M., Manikandan, R., Jhanjhi, N., Masud, M., & Alqhatani, A. (2023). Energy Analysis-Based Cyber Attack Detection by IoT with Artificial Intelligence in a Sustainable Smart City. *Sustainability (Basel)*, *15*(7), 6031. doi:10.3390/su15076031

Prabhakar, V. V., Xavier, C. B., & Abubeker, K. (2023). A Review on Challenges and Solutions in the Implementation of Ai, IoT and Blockchain in Construction Industry. *Materials Today: Proceedings*. doi:10.1016/j.matpr.2023.03.535

Prabowo, W. A., Fauziah, K., Nahrowi, A. S., Faiz, M. N., & Muhammad, A. W. (2023). Strengthening Network Security: Evaluation of intrusion detection and prevention systems tools in networking systems. *International Journal of Advanced Computer Science and Applications*, *14*(9). doi:10.14569/IJACSA.2023.0140934

PrabuckiR. (2023). The Analysis of the NIS 2 Directive, Preamble 54 in Terms of Sectors Related to Manufacturing. *Social Science Research Network*. doi:10.2139/ssrn.4408587

Praptodiyono, S., Firmansyah, T., Anwar, M. N. B., Wicaksana, C. A., Pramudyo, A. S., & Khudher, A. A. (2023). Development of hybrid intrusion detection system based on Suricata with pfSense method for high reduction of DDoS attacks on IPv6 networks. *Eastern-European Journal of Enterprise Technologies*, *5*(9 (125)), 75–84. doi:10.15587/1729-4061.2023.285275

Pravdiuk, A. (2022). The state and current issues of legal regulation of cyber security in Ukraine. *European Political and Law Discourse.*, *9*(3), 19–28. doi:10.46340/eppd.2022.9.3.3

Pritika, N., Shanmugam, B., & Azam, S. (2023). Risk Assessment of Heterogeneous IoMT Devices: A Review. *Technologies*, *11*(1), 31. doi:10.3390/technologies11010031

Priyadarshini, I., Chatterjee, J. M., Sujatha, R., Zaman, N., Karime, A., & Masud, M. (2021). Exploring Internet Meme Activity during COVID-19 Lockdown Using Artificial Intelligence Techniques. *Applied Artificial Intelligence*, *36*(1), 2014218. doi:10.1080/08839514.2021.2014218

Priyadarshini, I., Sahu, S., Kumar, R., & Taniar, D. (2022). A machine-learning ensemble model for predicting energy consumption in smart homes. *Internet of Things : Engineering Cyber Physical Human Systems*, *20*(November), 100636. doi:10.1016/j.iot.2022.100636

Priyantha. (2023). *Logistic Conference*. Naval and Maritime Academy. https://nma.navy.lk/wp-content/uploads/2023/04/E-Journal-LLMC.pdf#page=98

Progoulakis, I., Nikitakos, N., Dalaklis, D., Christodoulou, A., Dalaklis, A., & Yaacob, R. (2023). Digitalization and cyber physical security aspects in maritime transportation and port infrastructure. In Smart Ports and Robotic Systems: Navigating the Waves of Techno-Regulation and Governance (pp. 227-248): Springer. doi:10.1007/978-3-031-25296-9_12

Puica, E. (2023). Improving Supply Chain Management by Integrating RFID with IoT Shared Database: Proposing a System Architecture. In IFIP advances in information and communication technology (pp. 159–170). Springer Science+Business Media. doi:10.1007/978-3-031-34107-6_13

Quayson, M., Bai, C., Sun, L., & Sarkis, J. (2023). Building blockchain-driven dynamic capabilities for developing circular supply chain: Rethinking the role of sensing, seizing, and reconfiguring. *Business Strategy and the Environment*, *32*(7), 4821–4840. doi:10.1002/bse.3395

Queiroz, M. M., Wamba, S. F., Pereira, S. C. F., & Jabbour, C. J. C. (2023). The metaverse as a breakthrough for operations and supply chain management: Implications and call for action. *International Journal of Operations & Production Management*, *43*(10), 1539–1553. doi:10.1108/IJOPM-01-2023-0006

R, S. (2023). Immutable Secure Online Electoral Voting System Using Blockchain Technology. SSRN. doi:10.2139/ssrn.4456808

Ragab, M., & Altalbe, A. (2022). A Blockchain-Based Architecture for Enabling Cybersecurity in the Internet-of-Critical Infrastructures. *Computers, Materials & Continua*, *72*(1), 1579–1592. doi:10.32604/cmc.2022.025828

Rahaman, M. S., Tisha, S. N., Song, E., & Cerny, T. (2023). Access Control Design Practice and Solutions in Cloud-Native Architecture: A Systematic Mapping Study. *Sensors (Basel)*, *23*(7), 3413. doi:10.3390/s23073413 PMID:37050474

Rahardja, U. (2023). Implementation of Enterprise Resource Planning (ERP) in Indonesia to Increase the Significant Impact of Management Control Systems. *APTISI Transaction on Management*, *7*(2), 152–159. Advance online publication. doi:10.33050/atm.v7i2.1881

Rahman, M. A., Hossain, M. S., Islam, M. S., Alrajeh, N. A., & Muhammad, G. (2020). Secure and provenance enhanced internet of health things framework: A blockchain managed federated learning approach. *IEEE Access : Practical Innovations, Open Solutions*, *8*, 205071–205087. doi:10.1109/ACCESS.2020.3037474 PMID:34192116

Raj, A., Sharma, V., Shukla, D. M., & Sharma, P. (2023). Advancing supply chain management from agility to hyperagility: A dynamic capability view. *Annals of Operations Research*. doi:10.1007/s10479-022-05158-5 PMID:36619697

Rajakrishnan, M. (2023). *Effectiveness Of Modern Warehousing Technology*. Research Gate.

Rajapaksha, S., Kalutarage, H., Al-Kadri, M. O., Petrovski, A., Madzudzo, G., & Cheah, M. (2023). AI-Based Intrusion Detection Systems for In-Vehicle Networks: A survey. *ACM Computing Surveys*, *55*(11), 1–40. doi:10.1145/3570954

Ramachandran, V., Ramalakshmi, R., Kavin, B. P., Hussain, I., Almaliki, A. H., Almaliki, A. A., Elnaggar, A., & Hussein, E. E. (2022). Exploiting IoT and Its Enabled Technologies for Irrigation Needs in Agriculture. *Water (Basel)*, *14*(5), 719. doi:10.3390/w14050719

Ramgovind, S., Eloff, M. M., & Smith, E. J. (2010). *The management of security in Cloud computing*. IEEE. doi:10.1109/ISSA.2010.5588290

RamzanM. S.AsgharA.UllahA.JhanjiN. Z.AlsolamiF.AhmadI. (2022). Enhanced Artificial Bee Colony Based Optimization for Mitigating Replication in Large Data for Internet of Things (Iot). SSRN. doi:10.2139/ssrn.4281666

Ran, H. (2021). Construction and optimization of inventory management system via cloud-edge collaborative computing in supply chain environment in the Internet of Things era. *PLoS One*, *16*(11), e0259284. doi:10.1371/journal.pone.0259284 PMID:34731183

Rani, S., Bhambri, P., Kataria, A., Khang, A., & Sivaraman, A. K. (2023). *Big Data, Cloud Computing and IoT: Tools and Applications*. CRC Press. doi:10.1201/9781003298335

Rathore, B. (2023, January 19). Digital Transformation 4.0: Integration of Artificial Intelligence & Metaverse in Marketing. *EduZone Journal.* https://www.eduzonejournal.com/index.php/eiprmj/article/view/248

Rathore, B. (2023b, January 30). *Integration of Artificial Intelligence & It's Practices in Apparel Industry.* IJNMS. https://ijnms.com/index.php/ijnms/article/view/40

Ravi, N., & Verma, S. (1979). Kavita, Zaman, N., & Talib, M. N. (2021). Securing VANET Using Blockchain Technology. *Journal of Physics, 012035*(1). doi:10.1088/1742-6596/1979/1/012035

Rawat, A. (2023, May 15). *Smart Contract Based Approach for Fixed Deposit in Blockchain Networks with Remix IDE.* SSRN. https://papers.ssrn.com/sol3/papers.cfm?abstract_id=4451822

Rawat, R., Rimal, Y. N., William, P., Dahima, S., Gupta, S., & Sakthidasan Sankaran, K. (2022). Malware Threat Affecting Financial Organization Analysis Using Machine Learning Approach. *International Journal of Information Technology and Web Engineering, 17*(1), 1–20. doi:10.4018/IJITWE.304051

Raza, S. A. (2021). A systematic literature review of RFID in supply chain management. *Journal of Enterprise Information Management, 35*(2), 617–649. doi:10.1108/JEIM-08-2020-0322

Razzaq, A., Altamimi, A. B., Alreshidi, A., Ghayyur, S. A. K., Khan, W., & Alsaffar, M. (2023). IoT Data Sharing Platform in Web 3.0 Using Blockchain Technology. *Electronics (Basel), 12*(5), 1233. doi:10.3390/electronics12051233

Read, T. (2023, February 4). *What Is Supply Chain 4.0 and Where Does It Drive Value?* Blog - Agistix. https://www.agistix.com/blog/what-is-supply-chain-4-0-and-where-does-it-drive-value/

Rejeb, A., Rejeb, K., Simske, S. J., & Treiblmaier, H. (2023). Drones for supply chain management and logistics: A review and research agenda. *International Journal of Logistics, 26*(6), 708–731. doi:10.1080/13675567.2021.1981273

Review, H. B., Tapscott, D., Iansiti, M., & Lakhani, K. R. (2019). *Blockchain: The Insights You Need from Harvard Business Review.* Harvard Business Press.

Riadi, M. (2021, September 14). Supply Chain Management (SCM). *Literature review.* https://www.kajianpustaka.com/2017/08/supply-chain-management-scm.html

Riaz, S., Latif, S., Usman, S. M., Ullah, S. S., Algarni, A. D., Yasin, A., Anwar, A., Elmannai, H., & Hussain, S. (2022). Malware Detection in Internet of Things (IoT) Devices Using Deep Learning. *Sensors (Basel), 22*(23), 9305. doi:10.3390/s22239305 PMID:36502007

Ribeiro, R. C., de Almeida, M. G., & Canedo, E. D. (2021). A digital signature model using XAdES standard as a rest service. *Information (Basel), 12*(8), 289. doi:10.3390/info12080289

Riggs, H., Tufail, S., Parvez, I., Tariq, M., Khan, M. A., Amir, A., Vuda, K. V., & Sarwat, A. I. (2023). Impact, Vulnerabilities, and Mitigation Strategies for Cyber-Secure Critical Infrastructure. *Sensors (Basel), 23*(8), 4060. doi:10.3390/s23084060 PMID:37112400

Roberts, L. (2023). *Countermeasures for Preventing Malicious Infiltration on the Information Technology Supply Chain* [Doctor of Technology]. Purdue Polytechnic Institute.

Rohde Ponce, A. (2005). *Derecho aduanero mexicano, fundamentos y regulaciones de la actividad aduanera (4ª reimpresión)* (Vol. I). ISEF.

Romadhona, P. F., Ismail, M. L., & Ruldeviyani, Y. (2023). Evaluation of information security management in crisis response using KAMI index: The case of company XYZ. In AIP Conference Proceedings. American Institute of Physics. doi:10.1063/5.0115555

Rose, S. H., & Jayasree, T. (2019). Detection of jamming attack using timestamp for WSN. *Ad Hoc Networks, 91*, 101874. doi:10.1016/j.adhoc.2019.101874

Rožman, N., Corn, M., Škulj, G., Berlec, T., Diaci, J., & Podržaj, P. (2023). Exploring the Effects of Blockchain Scalability Limitations on Performance and User Behavior in Blockchain-Based Shared Manufacturing Systems: An Experimental Approach. *Applied Sciences (Basel, Switzerland), 13*(7), 4251. doi:10.3390/app13074251

Rúa Costa, C. (2006). *Los puertos en el transporte marítino.* Universitat Politécnica de Catalunya. https://upcommons. upc.edu/bitstream/handle/2117/289/8.%20Rua.pdf

Russo, N., Reis, L., Silveira, C., & Mamede, J. H. P. S. (2023). Towards a Comprehensive Framework for the Multidisciplinary Evaluation of Organizational Maturity on Business Continuity Program Management: A Systematic Literature Review. *Information Security Journal: A Global Perspective*, 1–19. doi:10.1080/19393555.2023.2195577

Sabokrou, M., Fayyaz, M., Fathy, M., Moayed, Z., & Klette, R. (2018). Deep-anomaly: Fully convolutional neural network for fast anomaly detection in crowded scenes. *Computer Vision and Image Understanding, 172*(October 2017), 88–97. doi:10.1016/j.cviu.2018.02.006

Sabrina, F., Li, N., & Sohail, S. (2022). A Blockchain Based Secure IoT System Using Device Identity Management. *Sensors (Basel), 22*(19), 7535. doi:10.3390/s22197535 PMID:36236634

Sadhu, P. K., Yanambaka, V. P., & Abdelgawad, A. (2022). Internet of Things: Security and Solutions Survey. *Sensors (Basel), 22*(19), 7433. doi:10.3390/s22197433 PMID:36236531

Saeed, S., Jhanjhi, N., Naqvi, S. M. R., & Khan, A. (2022). Analytical Approach for Security of Sensitive Business Cloud. *Deep Learning in Data Analytics: Recent Techniques, Practices and Applications*, 257-266.

Saeed, A., & Shoukat, R. (2023). Lean, Green, and Agile Supply Chain Practices. In *Emerging Trends in Sustainable Supply Chain Management and Green Logistics* (pp. 121–142). IGI Global. doi:10.4018/978-1-6684-6663-6.ch006

Saeed, S., Almuhaideb, A. M., Kumar, N., Zaman, N., & Zikria, Y. B. (2022). *Handbook of Research on Cybersecurity Issues and Challenges for Business and FinTech Applications.* IGI Global. doi:10.4018/978-1-6684-5284-4

Sáez-de-Cámara, X., Flores, J. L., Arellano, C., Urbieta, A., & Zurutuza, U. (2023). *Clustered Federated Learning Architecture for Network Anomaly Detection in Large Scale Heterogeneous IoT Networks.* Elesvier. doi:10.1016/j. cose.2023.103299

Sahu, P., & Balfour, D. (2022). *Smart Manufacturing with Augmented Reality.* Paper presented at the SAE Technical Papers. SAE. 10.4271/2022-26-0026

Said, D., Elloumi, M., & Khoukhi, L. (2022). Cyber-Attack on P2P Energy Transaction between Connected Electric Vehicles: A False Data Injection Detection Based Machine Learning Model. *IEEE Access : Practical Innovations, Open Solutions, 10*, 63640–63647. doi:10.1109/ACCESS.2022.3182689

Saldanha, J. P., Mello, J. E., Knemeyer, A. M., & Vijayaraghavan, T. A. S. (2015). Implementing supply chain technologies in emerging markets: An institutional theory perspective. *The Journal of Supply Chain Management, 51*(1), 5–26. doi:10.1111/jscm.12065

Saleh, M., Abdullah, A., & Saher, R. (2022). Message security level integration with iotes: A design dependent encryption selection model for iot devices. *IJCSNS, 22*(8), 328.

Salikhov, J., Hayrutdinov, S., & Muminov, T. K. (2023). Blockchain-Enabled Sustainable Supply Chain under Information Sharing and Recovery Quality Efforts. *Sustainability (Basel), 15*(5), 3929. doi:10.3390/su15053929

Sánchez, J. M. G., Jörgensen, N., Törngren, M., Inam, R., Berezovskyi, A., Feng, L., Fersman, E., Ramli, M. R., & Tan, K. (2022). Edge Computing for Cyber-physical Systems: A Systematic Mapping Study Emphasizing Trustworthiness. *ACM Transactions on Cyber-Physical Systems*, 6(3), 1–28. doi:10.1145/3539662

Sánchez, M. A., & De Batista, M. (2023). Business continuity for times of vulnerability: Empirical evidence. *Journal of Contingencies and Crisis Management*, 31(3), 431–440. doi:10.1111/1468-5973.12449

Sankar, S., Ramasubbareddy, S., Luhach, A. K., Deverajan, G. G., Alnumay, W. S., Jhanjhi, N. Z., Ghosh, U., & Sharma, P. K. (2020). Energy efficient optimal parent selection based routing protocol for Internet of Things using firefly optimization algorithm. *Transactions on Emerging Telecommunications Technologies*, 32(8), e4171. doi:10.1002/ett.4171

Santhosh Kumar, S. V. N., Selvi, M., & Kannan, A. (2023). A comprehensive survey on machine learning-based intrusion detection systems for secure communication in internet of things. *Computational Intelligence and Neuroscience*, *2023*, 2023. doi:10.1155/2023/8981988

Saqr, M., Elmoazen, R., Tedre, M., López-Pernas, S., & Hirsto, L. (2022). How well centrality measures capture student achievement in computer-supported collaborative learning? – A systematic review and meta-analysis. *Educational Research Review*, 35, 100437. doi:10.1016/j.edurev.2022.100437

Saranya, P., & Maheswari, R. (2023). Proof of Transaction (PoTx) Based Traceability System for an Agriculture Supply Chain. *IEEE Access : Practical Innovations, Open Solutions*, 11, 10623–10638. doi:10.1109/ACCESS.2023.3240772

Sarfaraz, A., Chakrabortty, R. K., & Essam, D. (2022). The implications of blockchain-coordinated information sharing within a supply chain: A simulation study. *Blockchain: Research and Applications*, 4(1), 100110. doi:10.1016/j.bcra.2022.100110

Sargent, C. S., & Breese, J. L. (2023). Blockchain Barriers in Supply Chain: A Literature Review. *Journal of Computer Information Systems*, 1–12. doi:10.1080/08874417.2023.2175338

Sarhan, M., Layeghy, S., Moustafa, N., & Portmann, M. (2022). Cyber Threat Intelligence Sharing Scheme Based on Federated Learning for Network Intrusion Detection. *Journal of Network and Systems Management*, 31(1), 3. doi:10.1007/s10922-022-09691-3

Sarker, I. H. (2021). CyberLearning: Effectiveness analysis of machine learning security modeling to detect cyber-anomalies and multi-attacks. *Internet of Things : Engineering Cyber Physical Human Systems*, 14, 100393. doi:10.1016/j.iot.2021.100393

Sathyamoorthy, D., Fitry, Z., Selamat, E., Hassan, S., Firdaus, A., & Zaimy, Z. (2020). Evaluation of the vulnerabilities of unmanned aerial vehicles (uavs) to global positioning system (GPS) jamming and spoofing. *Defence and Technical Bulletin, 13*, 333-343.

Satriawan, N. (2023). *Proposed Customer Knowledge Management (CKM) in the Truku Logistics Application Feature PT Biru Samudera Selatan*. research.e-siber.org. https://doi.org/ doi:10.31935/sjtl.v1i1.39

Saura, J. R., Ribeiro-Soriano, D., & Palacios-Marqués, D. (2021). Setting privacy "by default" in social IoT: Theorizing the challenges and directions in Big Data Research. *Big Data Research*, 25, 100245. doi:10.1016/j.bdr.2021.100245

Sawal, A. B., Ahmad, M., Muralitharan, M. A., Loganathan, V., & Jhanjhi, N. (2022). Machine Intelligence in Customer Relationship Management in Small and Large Companies. In *Empowering Sustainable Industrial 4.0 Systems With Machine Intelligence* (pp. 132–153). IGI Global. doi:10.4018/978-1-7998-9201-4.ch007

Schäfer, N. (2022). Making transparency transparent: a systematic literature review to define and frame supply chain transparency in the context of sustainability. *Management Review Quarterly*. doi:10.1007/s11301-021-00252-7

Schniederjans, D. G., Curado, C., & Khalajhedayati, M. (2020). Supply chain digitisation trends: An integration of knowledge management. *International Journal of Production Economics*, *220*, 107439. doi:10.1016/j.ijpe.2019.07.012

Sen, S., Rocco, R. A., Ranganathan, S., & Brooks, J. R. (2019). Revisiting quick response code technology: Corporate perspectives. *International Journal of Mobile Communications*, *17*(6), 703–726. doi:10.1504/IJMC.2019.102722

Seong, T. B., Ponnusamy, V., Jhanjhi, N. Z., Annur, R., & Talib, M. (2021). A comparative analysis on traditional wired datasets and the need for wireless datasets for IoT wireless intrusion detection. *Indonesian Journal of Electrical Engineering and Computer Science*, *22*(2), 1165. doi:10.11591/ijeecs.v22.i2.pp1165-1176

Seseli, E. M. I., Risakotta, K. A., & Bawono, A. (2023). The Role of Accounting Digitization in Entrepreneurial Success in West Java : Quantitative Study of Efficiency, Accuracy, Cost Reduction, Customer Satisfaction, and Data Security. *The Es Accounting and Finance*, *1*(02), 82–94. doi:10.58812/esaf.v1i02.65

Seth, S. (2022). Public, Private, Permissioned Blockchains Compared. *Investopedia*. https://www.investopedia.com/news/public-private-permissioned-blockchains-compared/

Setyowati, M. S., Utami, N. W., Saragih, A. H., & Hendrawan, A. (2023). Strategic factors in implementing blockchain technology in Indonesia's value-added tax system. *Technology in Society*, *72*, 102169. doi:10.1016/j.techsoc.2022.102169

Shafik, W. (2023). A Comprehensive Cybersecurity Framework for Present and Future Global Information Technology Organizations. In *Effective Cybersecurity Operations for Enterprise-Wide Systems* (pp. 56–79). IGI Global. doi:10.4018/978-1-6684-9018-1.ch002

Shafi, M., Jha, R. K., & Jain, S. (2022). LGTBIDS: Layer-wise Graph Theory Based Intrusion Detection System in Beyond 5G. *IEEE Transactions on Network and Service Management*, 1–1. doi:10.1109/TNSM.2022.3197921

Shafiq, D. A., Jhanjhi, N., & Abdullah, A. (2021). Machine learning approaches for load balancing in cloud computing services. *Paper presented at the 2021 National Computing Colleges Conference (NCCC)*. IEEE. 10.1109/NCCC49330.2021.9428825

Shafiq, D. A., Zaman, N., & Abdullah, A. (2019). Proposing A Load Balancing Algorithm For The Optimization Of Cloud. *Computer Applications (Nottingham)*, 1–6. doi:10.1109/MACS48846.2019.9024785

Shafiq, M., Ashraf, H., Ullah, A., Masud, M., Azeem, M., Jhanjhi, N., & Humayun, M. (2021). Robust cluster-based routing protocol for IoT-assisted smart devices in WSN. *Computers, Materials & Continua*, *67*(3), 3505–3521. doi:10.32604/cmc.2021.015533

Shafiq, M., Gu, Z., Cheikhrouhou, O., Alhakami, W., & Hamam, H. (2022). The rise of "Internet of Things":review and open research issues related to detection and prevention of IoT-based security attacks. *Wireless Communications and Mobile Computing*, *2022*, 1–12. doi:10.1155/2022/8669348

Shah, I. A., Jhanjhi, N., & Laraib, A. (2023). Cybersecurity and Blockchain Usage in Contemporary Business. In Handbook of Research on Cybersecurity Issues and Challenges for Business and FinTech Applications (pp. 49-64): IGI Global.

Shahadat, M. M. H., Chowdhury, A. H. M. Y., Nathan, R. J., & Fekete-Farkas, M. (2023). Digital Technologies for Firms' Competitive Advantage and Improved Supply Chain Performance. *Journal of Risk and Financial Management*, *16*(2), 94. doi:10.3390/jrfm16020094

Shah, I. A., Jhanjhi, N. Z., Amsaad, F., & Razaque, A. (2022). The Role of Cutting-Edge Technologies in Industry 4.0. In *Cyber Security Applications for Industry 4.0* (pp. 97–109). Chapman and Hall/CRC. doi:10.1201/9781003203087-4

Shah, I. A., Jhanjhi, N., & Laraib, A. (2023). Cybersecurity and Blockchain Usage in Contemporary Business. In *Handbook of Research on Cybersecurity Issues and Challenges for Business and FinTech Applications* (pp. 49–64). IGI Global.

Shah, I. A., Zaman, N., & Laraib, A. (2022a). Cybersecurity and Blockchain Usage in Contemporary Business. In *Advances in information security, privacy, and ethics book series* (pp. 49–64). IGI Global. doi:10.4018/978-1-6684-5284-4.ch003

Shahid, H., Ashraf, H., Javed, H., Humayun, M., Jhanjhi, N. Z., & AlZain, M. A. (2021). Energy optimised security against wormhole attack in iot-based wireless sensor networks. *Computers, Materials & Continua, 68*(2), 1967–1981. doi:10.32604/cmc.2021.015259

Shahriar, H. (2020). Ransomware: Evaluation of Mitigation and Prevention Techniques. *Symposium of Student Scholar.* https://digitalcommons.kennesaw.edu/undergradsymposiumksu/spring2023/presentations/301/

Shahzad, K. (2023). *The Role of Marketing Ethics in Ensuring Clients' Satisfaction.* doi:10.54183/jssr.v3i2.325

Shajek, A., & Hartmann, E. A. (2023). *New Digital Work: Digital Sovereignty at the Workplace.* Springer Nature. doi:10.1007/978-3-031-26490-0

Shamshirband, S., Fathi, M., Chronopoulos, A. T., Montieri, A., Palumbo, F., & Pescapè, A. (2020). Computational intelligence intrusion detection techniques in mobile cloud computing environments: Review, taxonomy, and open research issues. *Journal of Information Security and Applications, 55*, 102582. doi:10.1016/j.jisa.2020.102582

Shankar, A. and Shankar, A. (2021). Network Intrusion Detection and Prevention. *International Journal of Applied Engineering Research, 16*(4), 267–270. doi:https://doi.org/. doi:10.37622/IJAER/16.4.2021.267-270

Shao, K. (2023). Design and implementation of network security management system based on K-means algorithm. *Paper presented at the Second International Symposium on Computer Applications and Information Systems (ISCAIS 2023).* SPIE. 10.1117/12.2683547

Sharma, H. (2023, March 30). *Towards A Sustainable and Ethical Supply Chain Management: The Potential of IoT Solutions.* arXiv.org. https://arxiv.org/abs/2303.18135

Sharma, A., Gupta, B. B., Singh, A. K., & Saraswat, V. K. (2023). Advanced Persistent Threats (APT): Evolution, anatomy, attribution and countermeasures. *Journal of Ambient Intelligence and Humanized Computing, 14*(7), 9355–9381. doi:10.1007/s12652-023-04603-y

Sharma, M., & Joshi, S. (2020). Digital supplier selection reinforcing supply chain quality management systems to enhance firm's performance. *The TQM Journal, 35*(1), 102–130. doi:10.1108/TQM-07-2020-0160

Sharma, V., & Meena, K. K. (2023). Dentistry in the Digital Age: Embracing Blockchain Technology. *Cureus.* doi:10.7759/cureus.39710 PMID:37398809

Sheehan, J. (2023). 4 Beyond lip-service: Content clouds, 10-K filings, cyber risk and the electric grid. In De Gruyter eBooks (pp. 51–72). doi:10.1515/9783110731217-004

Shen, J., Ji, B., Zhang, C., & Feng, H. (2020, October). Federated Learning-based Spoofing and Jamming Detection for Wireless Networks. *IEEE Transactions on Vehicular Technology, 69*(10), 11611–11622. doi:10.1109/TVT.2020.3018239

Shi, S., He, D., Li, L., Kumar, N., Khan, M. K., & Choo, K.-K. R. (2020). Applications of blockchain in ensuring the security and privacy of electronic health record systems: A survey. *Computers & Security, 97*, 101966.

Shiau, W., Wang, X., & Zheng, F. (2023). What are the trend and core knowledge of information security? A citation and co-citation analysis. *Elsevier, 60*(3), 103774. doi:10.1016/j.im.2023.103774

Shimeall, T. J. (2018). *Four Valuable Data Sources for Network Security Analytics.* Carnegie Mellon University. https://insights.sei.cmu.edu/library/four-valuable-data-sources-for-network-security-analytics-2/

Shimels, T., & Lessa, L. (2023). Maturity of information systems' security in Ethiopian banks: Case of selected private banks. *International Journal of Industrial Engineering and Operations Management*, 5(2), 86–103. doi:10.1108/IJIEOM-10-2021-0014

Shojae Chaeikar, S., Jolfaei, A., & Mohammad, N. (2023). AI-Enabled Cryptographic Key Management Model for Secure Communications in the Internet of Vehicles. *IEEE Transactions on Intelligent Transportation Systems*, 24(4), 4589–4598. doi:10.1109/TITS.2022.3200250

Shu, J., & Tang, D. (2019). Recent advances in photoelectrochemical sensing: From engineered photoactive materials to sensing devices and detection modes. *Analytical Chemistry*, 92(1), 363–377. doi:10.1021/acs.analchem.9b04199 PMID:31738852

Siampondo, G., & Sumbwanyambe, M. (2023). A Review of the Role of Risk Management in Online Transactions: The Growing Issues of Network and System Security among Zambia's Financial Institutions. *American Journal of Finance*, 8(2), 1–12. doi:10.47672/ajf.1510

Sicato, J. C. S., Singh, S. K., Rathore, S., & Park, J. H. (2020). A comprehensive analyses of intrusion detection system for IoT environment. *Journal of Information Processing Systems*, 16(4), 975–990.

Silva, F. J. F. (2023, February 23). *A volatilidade das criptomoedas: Os casos da Polygon, Solana, BitTorrent Token e VeChain*. https://repositorio.uac.pt/handle/10400.3/6715

Simchi-Levi, D., Kaminsky, P., & Simchi-Levi, E. (2017). *Designing and managing the supply chain : concepts, strategies, and case studies*. McGraw-Hill eBooks. http://perpustakaan.ithb.ac.id/index.php?p=show_detail&id=7926

Simon, C. G. K., Jhanjhi, N. Z., Goh, W. W., & Sukumaran, S. (2022). Applications of Machine Learning in Knowledge Management System: A Comprehensive Review. *Journal of Information & Knowledge Management*, 21(02), 2250017. doi:10.1142/S0219649222500174

Sindiramutty, S. R., Jhanjhi, N. Z., Ray, S. K., Jazri, H., Khan, N. A., & Gaur, L. (2024). Metaverse: Virtual Meditation. In Metaverse Applications for Intelligent Healthcare (pp. 93–158). IGI Global. doi:10.4018/978-1-6684-9823-1.ch003

Singh, O. (2022, November 26). *How blockchain technology is used in supply chain management?* Cointelegraph. https://cointelegraph.com/explained/how-blockchain-technology-is-used-in-supply-chain-management

Singh, A. P., Pradhan, N. R., Luhach, A. K., Agnihotri, S., Zaman, N., & Verma, S. (2021). A Novel Patient-Centric Architectural Framework for Blockchain-Enabled Healthcare Applications. *IEEE Transactions on Industrial Informatics*, 17(8), 5779–5789. doi:10.1109/TII.2020.3037889

Singhal, V., Jain, S. P., Anand, D., Singh, A., Verma, S., Kavita, Rodrigues, J. J. P. C., Jhanjhi, N. Z., Ghosh, U., Jo, O., & Iwendi, C. (2020). Artificial Intelligence Enabled Road Vehicle-Train Collision Risk Assessment Framework for Unmanned railway level crossings. *IEEE Access : Practical Innovations, Open Solutions*, 8, 113790–113806. doi:10.1109/ACCESS.2020.3002416

Singh, D., & Verma, A. (2018). Inventory management in supply chain. *Materials Today: Proceedings*, 5(2), 3867–3872. doi:10.1016/j.matpr.2017.11.641

Sing, R., Bhoi, S. K., Panigrahi, N., Sahoo, K. S., Jhanjhi, N., & AlZain, M. A. (2022). A Whale Optimization Algorithm Based Resource Allocation Scheme for Cloud-Fog Based IoT Applications. *Electronics (Basel)*, 11(19), 3207. doi:10.3390/electronics11193207

Siraj, M. T., Debnath, B., Kumar, A., Bari, A. M., Samadhiya, A., & Payel, S. B. (2023). Evaluating barriers to sustainable boiler operation in the apparel manufacturing industry: Implications for mitigating operational hazards in the emerging economies. *PLoS One*, *18*(4), e0284423. doi:10.1371/journal.pone.0284423 PMID:37058513

Sirisomboonsuk, P., & Burns, J. (2023). Sustainability in Supply Chains through Rapid Capacity Increases and Minimized Disruptions. *Sustainability (Basel)*, *15*(7), 5629. doi:10.3390/su15075629

Siris, V. A., Fotiou, N., Mertzianis, A., & Polyzos, G. C. (2019). Smart application-aware IoT data collection. *Journal of Reliable Intelligent Environments*, *5*(1), 17–28. doi:10.1007/s40860-019-00077-y

Slesman, L., & Hoon, C.-Y. (2023). Brunei Darussalam in 2022: Towards Post-COVID-19 Economic Recovery, Diversification and Sustainability. *Southeast Asian Affairs*, *2023*(1), 52–68.

Smitha & Aslekar., A. (2022, March). IoT in Inventory Management. In *2022 International Conference on Decision Aid Sciences and Applications (DASA)* (pp. 1045-1050). IEEE.

Smitha, & Aslekar, A. (2022). *IoT in Inventory Management.* Paper presented at the 2022 International Conference on Decision Aid Sciences and Applications, DASA.

Smith, A. D. (2012). Green supply chain management and consumer sensitivity to greener and leaner options in the automotive industry. *International Journal of Logistics Systems and Management*, *12*(1), 1–31. doi:10.1504/IJLSM.2012.047056

Snort. (2023). *Network Intrusion Detection & Prevention System.* Snort. https://www.snort.org/

Soares, L. (2023). The evolution of cyber threats and its future landscape. *ResearchGate*. https://www.researchgate.net/publication/369010694_The_evolution_of_cyber_threats_and_its_future_landscape

Soe, Y. N., Feng, Y., Santosa, P. I., Hartanto, R., & Sakurai, K. (2019). Rule generation for signature based detection systems of cyber attacks in iot environments. Bulletin of Networking, Computing. *Systems & Software*, *8*(2), 93–97.

Soe, Y. N., Feng, Y., Santosa, P. I., Hartanto, R., & Sakurai, K. (2020). Machine learning-based IoT-botnet attack detection with sequential architecture. *Sensors (Basel)*, *20*(16), 4372. doi:10.3390/s20164372 PMID:32764394

SolarWinds. (n.d.) Security event manager - view event logs remotely. SolarWinds. https://www.solarwinds.com/security-event-manager

Solistica. (n.d.). *Blockchain in supply chain [Infographics]*. Solistica. https://blog.solistica.com/en/blockchain-in-supply-chain-infographics

Song, Y., & Chu, M. (2021). Research on the Application of Data Encryption Technology in Computer Network Security Based on Machine Learning, *2021 IEEE 4th International Conference on Information Systems and Computer Aided Education (ICISCAE)*, (pp. 399-403), Dalian, China. 10.1109/ICISCAE52414.2021.9590794

Song, Y., Yu, F. R., Zhou, L., Yang, X., & He, Z. (2020). Applications of the Internet of Things (IoT) in smart logistics: A comprehensive survey. *IEEE Internet of Things Journal*, *8*(6), 4250–4274. doi:10.1109/JIOT.2020.3034385

Soori, M., Arezoo, B., & Dastres, R. (2023). Internet of things for smart factories in industry 4.0, a review. *Science Direct*, *3*, 192–204. doi:10.1016/j.iotcps.2023.04.006

Soria, J., Moya, J., & Mohazab, A. (2022). Optimal mining in proof-of-work blockchain protocols. *Finance Research Letters*, *103610*. doi:10.1016/j.frl.2022.103610

Sovacool, B. K., & Del Rio, D. D. F. (2020). Smart home technologies in Europe: A critical review of concepts, benefits, risks and policies. *Renewable & Sustainable Energy Reviews*, *120*, 109663. doi:10.1016/j.rser.2019.109663

Spanos, G., Giannoutakis, K. M., Votis, K., & Tzovaras, D. (2019). Combining statistical and machine learning techniques in IoT anomaly detection for smart homes. *IEEE International Workshop on Computer Aided Modeling and Design of Communication Links and Networks, CAMAD, 2019-Septe*, (pp. 1–6). IEEE. 10.1109/CAMAD.2019.8858490

Spens, N., Lee, D. K., Nedelkov, F., & Akos, D. (2022). Detecting GNSS Jamming and Spoofing on Android Devices. NAVIGATION. *Journal of the Institute of Navigation, 69*(3).

SquarepantsS. (2008). Bitcoin: A Peer-to-Peer Electronic Cash System. *Social Science Research Network*. doi:10.2139/ssrn.3977007

Sreedevi, A. G., Nitya Harshitha, T., Sugumaran, V., & Shankar, P. (2022). Application of cognitive computing in healthcare, cybersecurity, big data and IoT: A literature review. *Information Processing & Management, 59*(2), 102888. Advance online publication. doi:10.1016/j.ipm.2022.102888

Srihith, N. I. D., Donald, N. D., Srinivas, N. T. S., Anjali, N. D., & Chandana, N. A. (2023). Firmware Attacks: The Silent Threat to Your IoT Connected Devices. *International Journal of Advanced Research in Science. Tongxin Jishu*, 145–154. doi:10.48175/IJARSCT-9104

Srikanth, G. U., Geetha, R., & Prabhu, S. (2023). An efficient Key Agreement and Authentication Scheme (KAAS) with enhanced security control for IIoT systems. *International Journal of Information Technology : an Official Journal of Bharati Vidyapeeth's Institute of Computer Applications and Management, 15*(3), 1221–1230. doi:10.1007/s41870-023-01173-2

Srinivasan, K., & Mukhopadhyay, S. K. (2019). Performance analysis of a JIT-based two-echelon inventory system with correlated demands. *International Journal of Production Research, 57*(6), 1766–1783.

Srinivas, N. T. S., Donald, N. D., Srihith, N. I. D., Anjali, N. D., & Chandana, N. A. (2023). The Rise of Secure IoT: How Blockchain is Enhancing IoT Security. *International Journal of Advanced Research in Science. Tongxin Jishu*, 32–40. doi:10.48175/IJARSCT-9006

Srivastava, P. R., Zhang, Z., & Eachempati, P. (2021). Blockchain technology and its applications in agriculture and supply chain management: A retrospective overview and analysis. *Enterprise Information Systems, 17*(5), 1995783. doi:10.1080/17517575.2021.1995783

Srivatsa, S. G., Bharadwaj, K. R. M., Alamuri, S. L., Shanif, M. M. C., & Shreenidhi, H. S. (2021). Smart Cold Storage and Inventory Monitoring System. *Paper presented at the 2021 6th International Conference on Recent Trends on Electronics, Information, Communication and Technology, RTEICT 2021*. Statista. https://www.statista.com/statistics/1183457/iot-connected-devices-worldwide/

Ssa, W., Moustafa, N., Turnbull, B., & Sohrabi, N. (2023). Blockchain-based federated learning for securing internet of things: A comprehensive survey. *ACM Computing Surveys, 55*(9), 1–43. doi:10.1145/3560816

Stellios, I., Kotzanikolaou, P., & Grigoriadis, C. (2021). Assessing IoT enabled cyber-physical attack paths against critical systems. *Computers & Security, 107*, 102316. doi:10.1016/j.cose.2021.102316

Stormshield. (2023). *Maritime security and port infrastructure: reconciling modern operational practices and cybersecurity*. Stormshield. https://www.stormshield.com/news/maritime-security-and-port-infrastructure-reconciling-modern-operational-practices-and-cybersecurity/

Strengers, Y., Kennedy, J., Arcari, P., Nicholls, L., & Gregg, M. (2019). Protection, productivity and pleasure in the smart home: Emerging expectations and gendered insights from Australian early adopters. In *Proceedings of the 2019 CHI conference on human factors in computing systems* (pp. 1–13). ACM. 10.1145/3290605.3300875

Suganya, M., & Sasipraba, T. (2023). Stochastic Gradient Descent long short-term memory based secure encryption algorithm for cloud data storage and retrieval in cloud computing environment. *Journal of Cloud Computing (Heidelberg, Germany)*, *12*(1), 74. doi:10.1186/s13677-023-00442-6

Sugumaran, D., John, Y. M. M., C, J. S. M., Joshi, K., Manikandan, G., & Jakka, G. (2023). *Cyber Defence Based on Artificial Intelligence and Neural Network Model in Cybersecurity*. IEEE. doi:10.1109/ICONSTEM56934.2023.10142590

Sujatha, R., & Prakash, G. (2022). Cyber Security Applications for Industry 4.0, Chapman and Hall/CRC Cyber-Physical Systems Series. CRC Press.

Sujatha, R., Prakash, G., & Jhanjhi, N. Z. (2022). *Cyber Security Applications for Industry 4.0*. CRC Press. doi:10.1201/9781003203087

Sulaiman, N. S., Nasir, A., Othman, W. R. W., Abdul Wahab, S. F., Aziz, N. S., Yacob, A., & Samsudin, N. (2021). Intrusion Detection System Techniques: A Review. *Journal of Physics: Conference Series*, *1874*(1), 012042. doi:10.1088/1742-6596/1874/1/012042

Suliyanti, W. N. (2023). *Blockchain-Based Double-Layer Byzantine Fault Tolerance for Scalability Enhancement for Building Information Modeling Information Exchange*. MDPI. doi:10.3390/bdcc7020090

Sunitha, T., Vijayashanthi, V., Navaneethakrishan, M., Mohanaprakash, T. A., Ashwin, S., Harish, T. R., & Stanes, E. A. (2023). Key Observation to Prevent IP Spoofing in DDoS Attack on Cloud Environment. In *Soft Computing: Theories and Applications* [Singapore: Springer Nature Singapore.]. *Proceedings of SoCTA, 2022*, 493–505.

Sun, J., Tekleab, A. G., Cheung, M. F., & Wu, W. (2022). The contingent roles of market turbulence and organizational innovativeness on the relationships among interfirm trust, formal contracts, interfirm knowledge sharing and firm performance. *Journal of Knowledge Management*, *27*(5), 1436–1457. doi:10.1108/JKM-04-2022-0289

Sun, Z., An, G., Yang, Y., & Liu, Y. (2024). Optimized machine learning enabled Intrusion Detection 2 System for Internet of Medical Things. *Franklin Open*, *6*, 100056. doi:10.1016/j.fraope.2023.100056

Supply chain insight: Inside IBM's Food Trust Blockchain system. (2020, May 17). Supply Chain Magazine. https://supplychaindigital.com/technology/supply-chain-insight-inside-ibms-food-trust-blockchain-system

supplychain247. (2021). *Using Technology to Protect Against Supply Chain Risk*. SupplyChain247. https://www.supplychain247.com/article/using_technology_to_protect_against_supply_chain_risk

Suren, E., Heiding, F., Olegård, J., & Lagerström, R. (2022). PatrIoT: Practical and agile threat research for IoT. *International Journal of Information Security*, *22*(1), 213–233. doi:10.1007/s10207-022-00633-3

Suricata. (2019). *9.2. Packet Capture - Suricata 6.0.1 documentation*. Suricata. https://docs.suricata.io/en/suricata-6.0.1/performance/packet-capture.html

Suryavanshi, A., G, A., N, M. B. T., M, R., & N, A. H. (2023). *The integration of Blockchain and AI for Web 3.0: A security Perspective*. IEEE. doi:10.1109/ICITIIT57246.2023.10068672

Suwannalai, E., & Polprasert, C. (2020, November). Network intrusion detection systems using adversarial reinforcement learning with deep Q-network. In *2020 18th International Conference on ICT and Knowledge Engineering (ICT&KE)* (pp. 1-7). IEEE.

Swan, M. (2015). *Blockchain: Blueprint for a New Economy*. CDS. http://cds.cern.ch/record/2000805

Swan, M. (2015). *Blockchain: Blueprint for a New Economy*. O'Reilly Media.

Syed. (2023). Evaluating the Effectiveness of Cyber Security Regulations. All Student Theses. 138.

Taghipour, A. (2021). *Digitalization of Decentralized Supply Chains During Global Crises*. IGI Global.

Ta, H., Esper, T. L., Hofer, A. R., & Sodero, A. C. (2023). Crowdsourced delivery and customer assessments of e-Logistics Service Quality: An appraisal theory perspective. *Journal of Business Logistics*, *44*(3), 345–368. doi:10.1111/jbl.12327

Taherdoost, H. (2023). Security and Internet of Things: Benefits, Challenges, and Future Perspectives. *Electronics (Basel)*, *12*(8), 1901. doi:10.3390/electronics12081901

Taherdoost, H. (2023). Smart Contracts in Blockchain Technology: A Critical Review. *Information (Basel)*, *14*(2), 117. doi:10.3390/info14020117

Tahir, S., Hafeez, Y., Abbas, M. A., Nawaz, A., & Hamid, B. (2022). Smart Learning Objects Retrieval for E-Learning with Contextual Recommendation based on Collaborative Filtering. *Education and Information Technologies*, *27*(6), 1–38. doi:10.1007/s10639-022-10966-0

Taj, I., & Zaman, N. (2022). Towards Industrial Revolution 5.0 and Explainable Artificial Intelligence: Challenges and Opportunities. *International Journal of Computing and Digital Systems*, *12*(1), 285–310. doi:10.12785/ijcds/120124

Talwadker, A., Olabiyi, O., Kosba, A., & Kim, Y. (2021, February). Detecting Jamming Attacks on IoT Devices Using Sequential Federated Learning. *IEEE Internet of Things Journal*, *8*(3), 1409–1418. doi:10.1109/JIOT.2020.3048914

Tan, C. L., Tei, Z., Yeo, S. F., Lai, K., Kumar, A., & Chung, L. (2022). Nexus among blockchain visibility, supply chain integration and supply chain performance in the digital transformation era. *Industrial Management & Data Systems*, *123*(1), 229–252. doi:10.1108/IMDS-12-2021-0784

Tang, M., Chen, W., & Yang, W. (2022). Anomaly detection of industrial state quantity time-Series data based on correlation and long short-term memory. *Connection Science*, *34*(1), 2048–2065. doi:10.1080/09540091.2022.2092594

Tang, Y. M., Chau, K. Y., Lau, Y., & Zheng, Z. (2023). Data-Intensive Inventory Forecasting with Artificial Intelligence Models for Cross-Border E-Commerce Service Automation. *Applied Sciences (Basel, Switzerland)*, *13*(5), 3051. doi:10.3390/app13053051

Tanvir, D. H., Amin, R., Islam, A., Islam, M. S., & Rashid, M. M. (2023). Blockchain Interoperability for A Reputation-Based Drug. *Supply Chain Management*, 1–6. doi:10.1109/ISCON57294.2023.10112196

Tan, W. C., & Sidhu, M. S. (2022). Review of RFID and IoT integration in supply chain management. *Operations Research Perspectives*, *9*, 100229. doi:10.1016/j.orp.2022.100229

Tao, Q., Chen, X., & Cui, X. (2022). A technological quality control system for rice supply chain. *Food and Energy Security*. doi:10.1002/fes3.382

Tao, X., Das, M., Zheng, C., Liu, Y., Wong, P. K., Xu, Y., Liu, H., Gong, X., & Cheng, J. C. (2023). Enhancing BIM security in emergency construction projects using lightweight blockchain-as-a-service. *Automation in Construction*, *150*, 104846. doi:10.1016/j.autcon.2023.104846 PMID:37035753

Tapscott, D., & Tapscott, A. (2016). *Blockchain Revolution: How the Technology Behind Bitcoin Is Changing Money, Business, and the World*. Open Library. https://openlibrary.org/books/OL27212411M/Blockchain_revolution

Tapscott, D., & Tapscott, A. (2016). *Blockchain revolution: How the technology behind bitcoin is changing money, business, and the world*. Penguin.

Tariq, N., & Khan, F. A. (2018). Match-the-sound captcha. In *Information Technology-New Generations: 14th International Conference on Information Technology* (pp. 803-808). Springer International Publishing.

Tariq, N., Asim, M., Al-Obeidat, F., Zubair Farooqi, M., Baker, T., Hammoudeh, M., & Ghafir, I. (2019). The security of big data in fog-enabled IoT applications including blockchain: A survey. *Sensors (Basel)*, *19*(8), 1788. doi:10.3390/s19081788 PMID:31013993

Tashtoush, Y. M., Darweesh, D. A., Husari, G., Darwish, O. A., Darwish, Y., Issa, L. B., & Ashqar, H. I. (2022). Agile Approaches for Cybersecurity Systems, IoT and Intelligent Transportation. *IEEE Access : Practical Innovations, Open Solutions*, *10*, 1360–1375. doi:10.1109/ACCESS.2021.3136861

Tasneem, A. Kumar, A. & Sharma, S. (2018). *Intrusion Detection Prevention System using SNORT*. ResearchGate. https://www.researchgate.net/publication/329716671_Intrusion_Detection_Prevention_System_using_SNORT

Tavana, M., Nasr, A. K., Ahmadabadi, A. B., Amiri, A. S., & Mina, H. (2023). An interval multi-criteria decision-making model for evaluating blockchain-IoT technology in supply chain networks. *Internet of Things : Engineering Cyber Physical Human Systems*, *22*, 100786. doi:10.1016/j.iot.2023.100786

Tawalbeh, L. A., Muheidat, F., Tawalbeh, M., & Quwaider, M. (2020). IoT Privacy and security: Challenges and solutions. *Applied Sciences (Basel, Switzerland)*, *10*(12), 4102. doi:10.3390/app10124102

Taylor, P. J., Dargahi, T., Dehghantanha, A., Parizi, R. M., & Choo, K. K. R. (2020). A systematic literature review of blockchain cyber security. *Digital Communications and Networks*, *6*(2), 147–156. doi:10.1016/j.dcan.2019.01.005

Team, X. (2023, June 22). *Maintaining an integrated Supply Chain : Key Solutions*. Xcelpros. https://xcelpros.com/maintaining-an-integrated-supply-chain-key-solutions/

Telo, J. (2023, February 27). *Smart City Security Threats and Countermeasures in the Context of Emerging Technologies*. https://research.tensorgate.org/index.php/IJIAC/article/view/18

Thakkar, A., & Lohiya, R. (2023). Fusion of statistical importance for feature selection in Deep Neural Network-based Intrusion Detection System. *Information Fusion*, *90*, 353–363. doi:10.1016/j.inffus.2022.09.026

Thakur, A. (2023). Market trends and analysis of blockchain technology in supply chain. *Frontiers in Blockchain*, *6*, 1142599. doi:10.3389/fbloc.2023.1142599

Thangamayan, S., Pradhan, K., Loganathan, G. B., Sitender, S., Sivamani, S., & Tesema, M. (2023). Blockchain-Based Secure Traceable Scheme for Food Supply Chain. *Journal of Food Quality*, *2023*, 1–11. doi:10.1155/2023/4728840

Thantilage, R. D., Le-Khac, N.-A., & Kechadi, M.-T. (2023). Healthcare data security and privacy in Data Warehouse architectures. *Informatics in Medicine Unlocked*, *39*, 101270. doi:10.1016/j.imu.2023.101270

The White House. (2021). *Interim National Security Atrategic Guidance*. The White House. https://www.whitehouse.gov/wp-content/uploads/2021/03/NSC-1v2.pdf

The White House. (2022a). *National Security Strategic*. The White House. https://www.whitehouse.gov/wp-content/uploads/2022/10/Biden-Harris-Administrations-National-Security-Strategy-10.2022.pdf

The Zeek. (2023). *Monitoring With Zeek - Book of Zeek (git/master)*. Zeek. https://docs.zeek.org/en/master/monitoring.html#instrumentation-and-collection

Theeraworawit, M., Suriyankietkaew, S., & Hallinger, P. (2022). Sustainable Supply Chain Management in a Circular Economy: A Bibliometric Review. *Sustainability (Basel)*, *14*(15), 9304. doi:10.3390/su14159304

Thi, T. T. T., Luong, D. T., Nguyen, H. D., & Hoang, T. M. (2023). A Study on Heuristic Algorithms Combined With LR on a DNN-Based IDS Model to Detect IoT Attacks. *Mendel*, *29*(1), 62–70. doi:10.13164/mendel.2023.1.062

Thompson, N., & Lee, K. (2013). Information Security Challenge of QR Codes. *Journal of Digital Forensics, Security and Law, 8(2)*, 2. https://commons.erau.edu/jdfsl/vol8/iss2/2

Tiwari, K., Patil, N., Gupta, A., Sabale, A., & Lomte, V. (n.d.). Fake Product Detection Using Blockchain Technology. *International Research Journal of Modernization in Engineering Technology and Science, 05*(05), 2582–5208. https://www.irjmets.com/uploadedfiles/paper/issue_5_may_2023/41058/final/fin_irjmets1685631927.pdf

Tiwari, S., Sharma, P., Choi, T.-M., & Lim, A. (2023). Blockchain and third-party logistics for global supply chain operations: Stakeholders' perspectives and decision roadmap. *Transportation Research Part E, Logistics and Transportation Review, 170*, 103012. doi:10.1016/j.tre.2022.103012

Tokkozhina, U., Martins, A. L., & Ferreira, J. C. (2023). Multi-tier supply chain behavior with blockchain technology: evidence from a frozen fish supply chain. *Operations Management Research*. doi:10.1007/s12063-023-00377-w

Toldinas, J., Venčkauskas, A., Liutkevičius, A., & Morkevičius, N. (2022). Framing Network Flow for Anomaly Detection Using Image Recognition and Federated Learning. *Electronics (Basel), 11*(19), 3138. doi:10.3390/electronics11193138

Tombe, R., & Smuts, H. (2023). Society 5.0-Inspired Digitalization Framework for Resilient and Sustainable Agriculture. In EPiC series in computing. doi:10.29007/xc5q

Topcu, A. E., Alzoubi, Y. I., Elbaşi, E., & Çamalan, E. (2023). Social media Zero-Day attack detection using TensorFlow. *Electronics (Basel), 12*(17), 3554. doi:10.3390/electronics12173554

Tripathi, S. (2021). Secure Architecture For IoTSystems To Counter CyberspaceThreats And Mitigate IntrusionRisk — A Survey Paper. *International Journal Of IntegratedEngineering, 13*(1), 167 -177. availableathttps//ijiedu org accessed 21stMarch 2021

Tripathi, P. K., Deshmukh, A. K., & Nath, T. (2023). Emergent Technologies for Supply Chain Risk and Disruption Management. In *Flexible systems management* (pp. 73–94). Springer Nature., doi:10.1007/978-981-99-2629-9_4

Trueman, C. (2022, November 30). *IBM, Maersk scuttle blockchain-based TradeLens supply chain platform*. Computerworld. https://www.computerworld.com/article/3681098/ibm-maersk-scuttle-blockchain-based-tradelens-supply-chain-platform.html

Truong, D. (2014). *Cloud-based solutions for supply chain management: a post-adoption study*. Semantic Scholar. https://www.semanticscholar.org/paper/CLOUD-BASED-SOLUTIONS-FOR-SUPPLY-CHAIN-MANAGEMENT%3A-Truong/716e4240a4f5733464bfee9b0c3a43ab08938479

Truong, V. T., Le, L. B., & Niyato, D. (2023). Blockchain meets metaverse and digital asset management: A comprehensive survey. *IEEE Access : Practical Innovations, Open Solutions, 11*, 26258–26288. doi:10.1109/ACCESS.2023.3257029

Tsai, C. (2022). Supply chain financing scheme based on blockchain technology from a business application perspective. *Annals of Operations Research, 320*(1), 441–472. doi:10.1007/s10479-022-05033-3 PMID:34092839

Tukade, T. M., & Banakar, R. (2018). Data transfer protocols in IoT—An overview. *International Journal of Pure and Applied Mathematics, 118*(16), 121–138.

Turki, M., Cheikhrouhou, S., Dammak, B., Baklouti, M., Mars, R., & Dhahbi, A. (2023). NFT-IoT Pharma Chain : IoT Drug traceability system based on Blockchain and Non Fungible Tokens (NFTs). *Journal of King Saud University. Computer and Information Sciences, 35*(2), 527–543. doi:10.1016/j.jksuci.2022.12.016

Uchiyama, H., & Marchand, E. (2012). *Object Detection and Pose Tracking for Augmented Reality: Recent Approaches*. 18th Korea-Japan Joint Workshop on Frontiers of Computer Vision (FCV), Kawasaki, Japan. https://hal.inria.fr/hal-00751704

Ullah, A., Azeem, M., Ashraf, H., Alaboudi, A. A., Humayun, M., & Jhanjhi, N. Z. (2021). Secure Healthcare Data Aggregation and Transmission in IoT - A Survey. *IEEE Access : Practical Innovations, Open Solutions, 9*, 16849–16865. doi:10.1109/ACCESS.2021.3052850

Ullah, A., Ishaq, N., Azeem, M., Ashraf, H., Jhanjhi, N., Humayun, M., Tabbakh, T. A., & Almusaylim, Z. A. (2021). A survey on continuous object tracking and boundary detection schemes in IoT assisted wireless sensor networks. *IEEE Access : Practical Innovations, Open Solutions, 9*, 126324–126336. doi:10.1109/ACCESS.2021.3110203

Ullah, F., & Al-Turjman, F. (2021). A conceptual framework for blockchain smart contract adoption to manage real estate deals in smart cities. *Neural Computing & Applications, 35*(7), 5033–5054. doi:10.1007/s00521-021-05800-6

Ullah, I., & Mahmoud, Q. H. (2020). A scheme for generating a dataset for anomalous activity detection in iot networks. In *Advances in Artificial Intelligence: 33rd Canadian Conference on Artificial Intelligence, Canadian AI 2020, Ottawa, ON, Canada, May 13–15, 2020. Proceedings, 33*, 508–520.

Ullah, I., & Mahmoud, Q. H. (2021). A Framework for Anomaly Detection in IoT Networks Using Conditional Generative Adversarial Networks. *IEEE Access : Practical Innovations, Open Solutions, 9*, 165907–165931. doi:10.1109/ACCESS.2021.3132127

Uma, S. (2023). Blockchain and AI: Disruptive Digital Technologies in Designing the Potential Growth of Healthcare Industries. In Advanced technologies and societal change (pp. 137–150). Springer Nature. doi:10.1007/978-981-99-0377-1_9

UNCTAD. (2021). *Technology and Innovation Report 2021*. UNCTAD. https://unctad.org/system/files/official-document/tir2020_en.pdf

United Nations. (2020). *The Impact of Digital Technologies*. UN. https://www.un.org/en/un75/impact-digital-technologies

University of Texas at San Antonio. (2020). *Zeek Intrusion Detection Series*. [online] Available at: https://ce.sc.edu/cyberinfra/docs/workshop/Zeek_Lab_Series.pdf

Vaishnavi, K. N., Khorvi, S. D., Kishore, R., & Gurugopinath, S. (2021, June). A survey on jamming techniques in physical layer security and anti-jamming strategies for 6G. In *2021 28th International Conference on Telecommunications (ICT)* (pp. 174-179). IEEE.

Valdivia, A. D. (2023). Between decentralization and reintermediation: Blockchain platforms and the governance of 'commons-led' and 'business-led' energy transitions. *Energy Research & Social Science, 98*, 103034. doi:10.1016/j.erss.2023.103034

Van Eck, N., & Waltman, L. (2010). Software survey: VOSviewer, a computer program for bibliometric mapping. *scientometrics, 84*(2), 523-538.

Van VlietB. (2023). Cryptocurrency Anti-Money Laundering (AML) and Know-Your-Customer (KYC) Management System Standard—Requirements. *Social Science Research Network*. doi:10.2139/ssrn.4403529

Vanichchinchai, A. (2023). Links between components of business continuity management: An implementation perspective. *Business Process Management Journal, 29*(2), 339–351. doi:10.1108/BPMJ-07-2022-0309

Vanin, P., Newe, T., Dhirani, L.L., O'Connell, E., O'Shea, D., Lee, B. and Rao, M. (2022). A Study of Network Intrusion Detection Systems Using Artificial Intelligence/Machine Learning. *Applied Sciences, 12*(22), 11752. . doi:10.3390/app122211752

Veeraraghavan, P., Hanna, D., & Pardede, E. (2020). NAT++: An efficient micro-nat architecture for solving ip-spoofing attacks in a corporate network. *Electronics (Basel), 9*(9), 1510. doi:10.3390/electronics9091510

Verbraeken, J., Wolting, M., Katzy, J., Kloppenburg, J., Verbelen, T., & Rellermeyer, J. S. (2020). A survey on distributed machine learning. [csur]. *ACM Computing Surveys*, *53*(2), 1–33. doi:10.1145/3377454

Verma, J., Bhandari, A., & Singh, G. (2022). iNIDS: SWOT Analysis and TOWS Inferences of State-of-the-Art NIDS solutions for the development of Intelligent Network Intrusion Detection System. *Computer Communications*, *195*, 227–247. doi:10.1016/j.comcom.2022.08.022

Verma, P., Ahluwalia, P., & Sharma, V. (2022). Cyber Supply Chain Risk Management Framework for the Internet of Things. *Computers & Electrical Engineering*, *97*, 107491.

Vice, J., & Khan, M. M. (2022). Toward Accountable and Explainable Artificial Intelligence Part Two: The Framework Implementation. *IEEE Access : Practical Innovations, Open Solutions*, *10*, 36091–36105. doi:10.1109/ACCESS.2022.3163523

Vidal, F. R. (2023, March 25). *OpenSCV: An Open Hierarchical Taxonomy for Smart Contract Vulnerabilities*. arXiv. org. https://arxiv.org/abs/2303.14523

Vimal, V., Muruganantham, R., Prabha, R., Arularasan, A. N., Nandal, P., Chanthirasekaran, K., & Reddy Ranabothu, G. (2022). Enhance Software-Defined Network Security with IoT for Strengthen the Encryption of Information Access Control. *Computational Intelligence and Neuroscience*, *2022*, 2022. doi:10.1155/2022/4437507 PMID:36225550

Vishwakarma, A., Dangayach, G. S., Meena, M. L., Gupta, S., & Luthra, S. (2022). Adoption of blockchain technology enabled healthcare sustainable supply chain to improve healthcare supply chain performance. *Management of Environmental Quality*, *34*(4), 1111–1128. doi:10.1108/MEQ-02-2022-0025

Viswanadham, Y. V. R. S., & Jayavel, K. (2023). A Framework for Data Privacy Preserving in Supply Chain Management Using Hybrid Meta-Heuristic Algorithm with Ethereum Blockchain Technology. *Electronics (Basel)*, *12*(6), 1404. doi:10.3390/electronics12061404

Wahsheh, H. A. M., & Luccio, F. L. (2020). Security and Privacy of QR Code Applications: A Comprehensive Study, General Guidelines and Solutions. *Information (Basel)*, *11*(4), 217. doi:10.3390/info11040217

Wallarm. (2023, April 17). *Cyber Attacks*. Wallarm. https://www.wallarm.com/what/what-is-a-cyber-attack

Wallis, T., & Dorey, P. (2023). Implementing Partnerships in Energy Supply Chain Cybersecurity Resilience. *Energies*, *16*(4), 1868. doi:10.3390/en16041868

Wang, C., & Zhu, H. (2022). Wrongdoing Monitor: A Graph-Based Behavioral Anomaly Detection in Cyber Security. *IEEE Transactions on Information Forensics and Security*, *17*, 2703–2718. doi:10.1109/TIFS.2022.3191493

Wang, D., Zhao, D., Wang, B., & Wu, J. (2019, December). Design of inventory pledge financing model based on internet of things technology and operational risk management. In *2019 IEEE International Conference on Industrial Engineering and Engineering Management (IEEM)* (pp. 990-996). IEEE. 10.1109/IEEM44572.2019.8978839

Wang, G., Wang, X., & Zhao, C. (2020). An iterative hybrid harmonics detection method based on discrete wavelet transform and bartlett–hann window. *Applied Sciences (Basel, Switzerland)*, *10*(11), 3922. doi:10.3390/app10113922

Wang, G., Wang, Z., Jiang, G., & McLaughlin, K. (2021). Intrusion Detection in Computer Networks: A Review. *IEEE Communications Surveys and Tutorials*, *23*(2), 1277–1310.

Wang, M., Zhu, T., Zuo, X., Yang, M., Yu, S., & Zhou, W. (2023). Differentially private crowdsourcing with the public and private blockchain. *IEEE Internet of Things Journal*, *10*(10), 8918–8930. doi:10.1109/JIOT.2022.3233360

Wang, S., Luo, X., Qian, Y., Zhu, Y., Chen, K., Chen, Q., Xin, B., & Yang, W. (2023). Shuffle differential private data aggregation for random population. *IEEE Transactions on Parallel and Distributed Systems, 34*(5), 1667–1681. doi:10.1109/TPDS.2023.3247541

Wang, S., Wan, J., Li, D. M., & Zhang, C. (2016). Implementing Smart Factory of Industrie 4.0: An Outlook. *International Journal of Distributed Sensor Networks, 12*(1), 3159805. doi:10.1155/2016/3159805

Wang, W., Aguilar Sanchez, I., Caparra, G., McKeown, A., Whitworth, T., & Lohan, E. S. (2021). A survey of spoofer detection techniques via radio frequency fingerprinting with focus on the gnss pre-correlation sampled data. *Sensors (Basel), 21*(9), 3012. doi:10.3390/s21093012 PMID:33923015

Wang, Y., Geng, X., Zhang, F., & Ruan, J. (2018). An immune genetic algorithm for multi-echelon inventory cost control of IOT based supply chains. *IEEE Access : Practical Innovations, Open Solutions, 6*, 8547–8555. doi:10.1109/ACCESS.2018.2799306

WangZ.LiuS.WangP.ZhangL. (2023). BW-PBFT: Practical Byzantine Fault Tolerance Consensus Algorithm Based on Credit Bidirectionally Waning. Research Square (Research Square). doi:10.21203/rs.3.rs-2900100/v1

Wang, Z., Ren, Y., Cao, Z., & Zhang, L. (2023). LRBFT: Improvement of practical Byzantine fault tolerance consensus protocol for blockchains based on Lagrange interpolation. *Peer-to-Peer Networking and Applications, 16*(2), 690–708. doi:10.1007/s12083-022-01431-3

Wani, A., & Revathi, S. (2020). Ransomware protection in IoT using software defined networking. *Iranian Journal of Electrical and Computer Engineering, 10*(3), 3166–3175.

Wei, G. (2023). The Impact of Blockchain Technology on Integrated Green Supply Chain Management in China: A Conceptual Study. *Dream Journal, 2*(02), 58–65. doi:10.56982/dream.v2i02.112

Weinger, B., Kim, J., Sim, A., Nakashima, M., Moustafa, N., & Wu, K. J. (2022). Enhancing IoT anomaly detection performance for federated learning. *Digital Communications and Networks, 8*(3), 314–323. doi:10.1016/j.dcan.2022.02.007

Wendl, M., Doan, M. H., & Sassen, R. (2023). The environmental impact of cryptocurrencies using proof of work and proof of stake consensus algorithms: A systematic review. *Journal of Environmental Management, 326*, 116530. doi:10.1016/j.jenvman.2022.116530 PMID:36372031

Wenhua, Z., Qamar, F., Abdali, T. N., Hassan, R., Jafri, S. T. A., & Nguyen, Q. N. (2023). Blockchain Technology: Security Issues, Healthcare Applications, Challenges and Future Trends. *Electronics (Basel), 12*(3), 546. doi:10.3390/electronics12030546

Widerholm, A., & Zickerman, A. (2023). *Exploring Supply Chain Risk Management & Business Continuity Practices During Disruptive Times: A Case Study on Swedish Firms.* DiVA.

Wieland, A., & Wallenburg, C. M. (2012). Dealing with supply chain risks. *International Journal of Physical Distribution & Logistics Management, 42*(10), 887–905. doi:10.1108/09600031211281411

Williams, P. D. (2008). *Security Studies: An Introduction.* Routledge. doi:10.4324/9780203926604

Williams, P., Dutta, I. K., Daoud, H., & Bayoumi, M. (2022). A survey on security in internet of things with a focus on the impact of emerging technologies. *Internet of Things : Engineering Cyber Physical Human Systems, 19*, 100564. doi:10.1016/j.iot.2022.100564

Witker, V. J. A. (1999). *Derecho tributario aduanero.* México: UNAM. http://ru.juridicas.unam.mx/xmlui/handle/123456789/9192

Wong, C. M. V., Chan, R. Y. Y., Yum, Y. N., & Wang, K. (2021). Internet of Things (IoT)-Enhanced Applied Behavior Analysis (ABA) for Special Education Needs. *Sensors (Basel)*, *21*(19), 6693. doi:10.3390/s21196693 PMID:34641011

Wong, L., Lee, V., Tan, G. W., Ooi, K., & Sohal, A. S. (2022). The role of cybersecurity and policy awareness in shifting employee compliance attitudes: Building supply chain capabilities. *International Journal of Information Management*, *66*, 102520. doi:10.1016/j.ijinfomgt.2022.102520

World Bank. (2022). *Historical Container Data Series*. World Bank. https://data.worldbank.org/indicator/IS.SHP.GOOD. TU?end=2020&start=2000&view=chart

World Bank. (2022). Website. https://www.worldbank.org/en/home

World Customs Organization. (2022a). *Home*. WCO. https://www.wcoomd.org

World Customs Organization. (2022b). *What is customs*. WCO. https://www.wcoomd.org/en/search. aspx?keyword=what+is+a+customs

World Trade Organization et al. (2019). *Technological innovation, supply chain trade, and workers in a globalized world*. WTO. https://www.wto.org/english/res_e/booksp_e/gvc_dev_report_2019_e.pdf

World Trade Organization. (2018). *The future of world trade: How digital technologies are transforming global commerce*. WTO. https://www.wto.org/english/res_e/publications_e/world_trade_report18_e.pdf

Wu, H., Jiang, S., & Cao, J. (2023). High-Efficiency Blockchain-Based Supply Chain Traceability. *IEEE Transactions on Intelligent Transportation Systems*, *24*(4), 3748–3758. doi:10.1109/TITS.2022.3205445

Wu, X., Wang, Q., Wang, L., & Zhao, X. (2023). Customer integration and the performance of third-party logistics firms: A moderated mediation model. *International Journal of Logistics*, *26*(6), 615–632. doi:10.1080/13675567.2021.1969349

Xia, J., Li, H., & He, Z. (2023). The Effect of Blockchain Technology on Supply Chain Collaboration: A Case Study of Lenovo. *Systems*, *11*(6), 299. doi:10.3390/systems11060299

Xiao, L., Wan, X., Lu, X., Zhang, Y., & Wu, D. (2018). IoT security techniques based on machine learning: How do IoT devices use AI to enhance security? *IEEE Signal Processing Magazine*, *35*(5), 41–49. doi:10.1109/MSP.2018.2825478

Xiao, P., Salleh, M. I., Zaidan, B., & Xuelan, Y. (2023). Research on risk assessment of blockchain-driven supply chain finance: A systematic review. *Computers & Industrial Engineering*, *176*, 108990. doi:10.1016/j.cie.2023.108990

Xu, X., Tian, N., Gao, H., Lei, H., Liu, Z., & Liu, Z. (2023). *A Survey on Application of Blockchain Technology in Drug Supply Chain Management*. doi:10.1109/ICBDA57405.2023.10104779

Xue, H., Chen, D., Zhang, N., Dai, H., & Yu, K. (2022). Integration of blockchain and edge computing in internet of things: A survey. *Future Generation Computer Systems*, *144*, 307–326. doi:10.1016/j.future.2022.10.029

Xue, Y., & Lai, K. (2023). Responsible shipping for sustainable development: Adoption and performance value. *Transport Policy*, *130*, 89–99. doi:10.1016/j.tranpol.2022.11.007

Xu, J., Lou, J., Lu, W., Wu, L., & Chen, C. (2023). Ensuring construction material provenance using Internet of Things and blockchain: Learning from the food industry. *Journal of Industrial Information Integration*, *33*, 100455. doi:10.1016/j.jii.2023.100455

Xu, J., Wang, C., & Jia, X. (2023). A Survey of Blockchain Consensus Protocols. *ACM Computing Surveys*, *55*(13s), 1–35. doi:10.1145/3579845

Yaacoub, J. P. A., Noura, H. N., Salman, O., & Chehab, A. (2023). Ethical hacking for IoT: Security issues, challenges, solutions and recommendations. *Internet of Things and Cyber-Physical Systems*.

Yadav, A. K., Singh, K., Amin, A., Almutairi, L., Alsenani, T. R., & Ahmadian, A. (2023). A comparative study on consensus mechanism with security threats and future scopes: Blockchain. *Computer Communications*, *201*, 102–115. doi:10.1016/j.comcom.2023.01.018

Yadav, N., Pande, S., Khamparia, A., & Gupta, D. (2022). Intrusion detection system on IoT with 5G network using deep learning. *Wireless Communications and Mobile Computing*, *2022*, 1–13. doi:10.1155/2022/9304689

Yaman, O., Ayav, T., & Erten, Y. M.YAMAN. (2023). A Lightweight Self-Organized Friendly Jamming. *International Journal of Information Security Science*, *12*(1), 13–20. doi:10.55859/ijiss.1194643

Yang, M., Chen, X., Tan, L., Lan, X., & Luo, Y. (2023). Listen carefully to experts when you classify data: A generic data classification ontology encoded from regulations. *Elsevier*, *60*(2), 103186. doi:10.1016/j.ipm.2022.103186

Yang, Z., Cheng, Z., Loy, C. C., Lau, W. C., Li, C. M., & Li, G. (2016). Towards robust color recovery for high-capacity color QR codes. *2016 IEEE International Conference on Image Processing (ICIP)*, (pp. 2866-2870). IEEE. . doi:10.1109/ICIP.2016.7532883

Yang, R., He, H., Xu, Y., Xin, B., Wang, Y., Qu, Y., & Zhang, W. (2023). Efficient intrusion detection toward IoT networks using cloud–edge collaboration. *Computer Networks*, *228*, 109724. doi:10.1016/j.comnet.2023.109724

Yang, S., Tan, J., Lei, T., & Linares-Barranco, B. (2023). Smart traffic navigation system for fault-tolerant edge computing of internet of vehicle in intelligent transportation gateway. *IEEE Transactions on Intelligent Transportation Systems*, *24*(11), 13011–13022. doi:10.1109/TITS.2022.3232231

Yang, X., Liu, H., Liu, X., & Mao, J. (2020, December). The Detection for Spoofing and Jamming Attacks via Federated Learning in Wireless Networks. *IEEE Transactions on Computational Social Systems*, *7*(6), 1484–1495. doi:10.1109/TCSS.2020.302116

Yazdinejad, A., Rabieinejad, E., Hasani, T., & Srivastava, G. (2023). A BERT-based recommender system for secure blockchain-based cyber physical drug supply chain management. *Cluster Computing*, *26*(6), 3389–3403. doi:10.1007/s10586-023-04088-6

Yeboah-Ofori, A., Islam, S., Lee, S. W., Shamszaman, Z. U., Muhammad, K., Altaf, M., & Al-Rakhami, M. S. (2021). Cyber Threat Predictive Analytics for Improving Cyber Supply Chain Security. *IEEE Access : Practical Innovations, Open Solutions*, *9*, 94318–94337. doi:10.1109/ACCESS.2021.3087109

Yeboah-Ofori, A., & Opoku-Boateng, F. A. (2023). *Mitigating cybercrimes in an evolving organizational landscape*. Continuity & Resilience Review. doi:10.1108/CRR-09-2022-0017

Yenugula, M., Sahoo, S. K., & Goswami, S. S. (2023). Cloud computing in supply chain management: Exploring the relationship. *Management Science Letters*, *13*(3), 193–210. doi:10.5267/j.msl.2023.4.003

Yerpude S., e. a. (2018). *SMART Warehouse with Internet of Things supported Inventory Management System*. Research Gate.

Yin, F., Lin, Z., Kong, Q., Xu, Y., Li, D., Theodoridis, S., & Cui, S. R. (2020). FedLoc: Federated learning framework for data-driven cooperative localization and location data processing. *IEEE Open Journal of Signal Processing*, *1*, 187–215. doi:10.1109/OJSP.2020.3036276

Yin, X., Zhu, Y., & Hu, J. (2021). A comprehensive survey of privacy-preserving federated learning: A taxonomy, review, and future directions. *ACM Computing Surveys*, *54*(6), 1–36. doi:10.1145/3460427

Yli-Huumo, J., Ko, D., Choi, S., Park, S., & Smolander, K. (2016). Where Is Current Research on Blockchain Technology?—A Systematic Review. *PLoS One*, *11*(10), e0163477. doi:10.1371/journal.pone.0163477 PMID:27695049

Yontar, E. (2023). The role of blockchain technology in the sustainability of supply chain management: Gray based dematel implementation. *Cleaner Logistics and Supply Chain*, 8, 100113. doi:10.1016/j.clscn.2023.100113

You, J., Liu, B., Wang, Y., & Jiang, L. (2023). Tracking the prevalence of compromised passwords using long-term honeypot data. *Proc. SPIE 12700, International Conference on Electronic Information Engineering and Data Processing.* Spie. https://www.spiedigitallibrary.org/conference-proceedings-of-spie/12700/127000K/Tracking-the-prevalence-of-compromised-passwords-using-long-term-honeypot/10.1117/12.2682267.short?SSO=1

Young, C., Zambreno, J., Olufowobi, H., & Bloom, G. (2019). Survey of automotive controller area network intrusion detection systems. *IEEE Design & Test*, *36*(6), 48–55. doi:10.1109/MDAT.2019.2899062

Yousef, W. A., Traore, I., & Briguglio, W. (2023). Classifier Calibration: With Application to Threat Scores in Cybersecurity. *IEEE Transactions on Dependable and Secure Computing*, *20*(3), 1994–2010. doi:10.1109/TDSC.2022.3170011

Yu, B., Fu, Z., & Liu, S. (2019). A Novel Three-Layer QR Code Based on Secret Sharing Scheme and Liner Code. *Security and Communication Networks*. https://doi.org/ doi:10.1155/2019/7937816

Yuan, T., Wang, Y., Xu, K., Martin, R. R., & Hu, S. (2019). Two-Layer QR Codes. *IEEE Transactions on Image Processing*, *28*(9), 4413–4428. doi:10.1109/TIP.2019.2908490 PMID:31071029

Yuan, X.-M., & Xue, A. (2023). Supply Chain 4.0: New Generation of Supply Chain Management. *Logistics*, *7*(1), 9. doi:10.3390/logistics7010009

Yu, D., & Frincke, D. (2007). Improving the quality of alerts and predicting intruder's next goal with Hidden Colored Petri-Net. *Computer Networks*, *51*(3), 632–654. doi:10.1016/j.comnet.2006.05.008

Yu, Z., Qin, Y., Li, X., Zhao, C., Lei, Z., & Zhao, G. (2022). Deep learning for face anti-spoofing: A survey. *IEEE Transactions on Pattern Analysis and Machine Intelligence*, *45*(5), 5609–5631. doi:10.1109/TPAMI.2022.3215850 PMID:36260579

Zaheer, A., Tahir, S., Almufareh, M. F., & Hamid, B. (2023). A Hybrid Model for Botnet Detection using Machine Learning. In *2023 International Conference on Business Analytics for Technology and Security (ICBATS)* (pp. 1–8). IEEE. 10.1109/ICBATS57792.2023.10111161

Zaib, M. H. (2018). *NSL-KDD Dataset*. Kaggle. https://www.kaggle.com/datasets/hassan06/nslkdd

Zaidan, A. A., & Zaidan, B. B. (2020). A review on intelligent process for smart home applications based on IoT: Coherent taxonomy, motivation, open challenges, and recommendations. *Artificial Intelligence Review*, *53*(1), 141–165. doi:10.1007/s10462-018-9648-9

Zakzouk, A., El-Sayed, A., & Hemdan, E. E. (2023). A blockchain-based electronic medical records management framework in smart healthcare infrastructure. *Multimedia Tools and Applications*, *82*(23), 35419–35437. doi:10.1007/s11042-023-15152-z

Zankl, A., Seuschek, H., Irazoqui, G., & Gulmezoglu, B. (2021). Side-channel attacks in the Internet of Things: threats and challenges. In *Research Anthology on Artificial Intelligence Applications in Security* (pp. 2058–2090). IGI Global.

Zhamshid, V., Nusratilloevich, Y. A., Shahida, K., & Azamat, K. (2023). Rise of the Machines: The Legal Implications of Robotics and Automation for the Digital Workforce. *International Journal of Cyber Law*, *1*(4).

Zhang, C., Gong, Y., & Brown, S. (2023). *Blockchain Applications in Food Supply Chain Management: Case Studies and Implications*. Springer Nature.

Zhang, T., He, C., Ma, T., Gao, L., Ma, M., & Avestimehr, S. (2021). Federated Learning for Internet of Things. *SenSys 2021 - Proceedings of the 2021 19th ACM Conference on Embedded Networked Sensor Systems*, (pp. 413–419). ACM. 10.1145/3485730.3493444

Zhang, B., Ji, D., Liu, S., Zhu, X., & Xu, W. (2023). Autonomous underwater vehicle navigation: A review. *Ocean Engineering*, *273*, 113861. doi:10.1016/j.oceaneng.2023.113861

Zhang, C., Xie, Y., Bai, H., Yu, B., Li, W., & Gao, Y. (2021). A survey on federated learning. *Knowledge-Based Systems*, *216*, 106775. doi:10.1016/j.knosys.2021.106775 PMID:34909232

Zhang, D., & Wang, S. (2019). Optimization of traditional Snort intrusion detection system. *IOP Conference Series. Materials Science and Engineering*, *569*(4), 042041. doi:10.1088/1757-899X/569/4/042041

Zhang, J., Li, S., & Wang, Y. (2023). Shaping a smart transportation system for sustainable value co-creation. *Information Systems Frontiers*, *25*(1), 365–380. doi:10.1007/s10796-021-10139-3

Zhang, L., Alharbe, N., & Atkins, A. S. (2016, December). An IoT application for inventory management with a self-adaptive decision model. In *2016 IEEE International Conference on Internet of Things (iThings) and IEEE Green Computing and Communications (GreenCom) and IEEE Cyber, Physical and Social Computing (CPSCom) and IEEE Smart Data (SmartData)* (pp. 317-322). IEEE. 10.1109/iThings-GreenCom-CPSCom-SmartData.2016.77

Zhang, M., & Chen, W. (2021). Blockchain technology for improving the transparency and traceability of supply chain management. *Computers & Industrial Engineering*, *155*, 107222. doi:10.1016/j.cie.2021.107222

Zhang, P., Schmidt, D. C., White, J., & Lenz, G. (2019). Blockchain Technology Use Cases in Healthcare. In *Advances in Computers* (pp. 1–41). Elsevier BV. doi:10.1016/bs.adcom.2018.03.006

Zhang, R., Xu, C., & Xie, M. (2022). Secure Decentralized IoT Service Platform Using Consortium Blockchain. *Sensors (Basel)*, *22*(21), 8186. doi:10.3390/s22218186 PMID:36365884

Zhang, Y., Liao, Q. V., & Bellamy, R. K. E. (2020). Effect of confidence and explanation on accuracy and trust calibration in AI-assisted decision making. In *Proceedings of the 2020 conference on fairness, accountability, and transparency* (pp. 295–305). IEEE. 10.1145/3351095.3372852

Zhang, Y., Xu, C., Lin, X., & Shen, X. (2021). Blockchain-Based Public Integrity Verification for Cloud Storage against Procrastinating Auditors. *IEEE Transactions on Cloud Computing*, *9*(3), 923–937. doi:10.1109/TCC.2019.2908400

Zhan, Y., Zhang, J., Hong, Z., Wu, L., Li, P., & Guo, S. (2021). A survey of incentive mechanism design for federated learning. *IEEE Transactions on Emerging Topics in Computing*, *10*(2), 1035–1044. doi:10.1109/TETC.2021.3063517

Zhao, L. (2023, June 7). *A Study on the Protection of Consumer Rights and Interests in Online Shopping*. Pioneer Publisher. https://www.pioneerpublisher.com/slj/article/view/329

Zhao, M. (2023, January 1). Safe and Efficient Delegated Proof of Stake Consensus Mechanism Based on Dynamic Credit in Electronic Transaction. *Journal of Internet Technology*. https://jit.ndhu.edu.tw/article/view/2845

Zhao, N., Hong, J., & Lau, K. H. (2023). Impact of supply chain digitalization on supply chain resilience and performance: A multi-mediation model. *International Journal of Production Economics*, *259*, 108817. doi:10.1016/j.ijpe.2023.108817 PMID:36852136

Zhao, X., Abdo, A., Liao, X., Barth, M. J., & Wu, G. (2022). Evaluating Cybersecurity Risks of Cooperative Ramp Merging in Mixed Traffic Environments. *IEEE Intelligent Transportation Systems Magazine, 14*(6), 52–65. doi:10.1109/MITS.2022.3151097

Zheng, Y., Pal, A., Abuadbba, S., Pokhrel, S. R., Nepal, S., & Janicke, H. (2020, October). Towards IoT security automation and orchestration. In *2020 Second IEEE International Conference on Trust, Privacy and Security in Intelligent Systems and Applications (TPS-ISA)* (pp. 55-63). IEEE.

Zheng, Z., Xie, S., Dai, H., Chen, X., & Wang, H. (2017). *An Overview of Blockchain Technology: Architecture.* Consensus, and Future Trends., doi:10.1109/BigDataCongress.2017.85

Zhi, Y., Fu, Z., Sun, X., & Yu, J. (2020). Security and privacy issues of UAV: A survey. *Mobile Networks and Applications, 25*(1), 95–101. doi:10.1007/s11036-018-1193-x

Zhou, D., Yan, Z., Fu, Y. and Yao, Z. (2018). A survey on network data collection. *Journal of Network and Computer Applications, 116*, 9–23. . doi:10.1016/j.jnca.2018.05.004

Zhou, L., Chong, A. Y., & Ngai, E. W. (2015). Supply chain management in the era of the internet of things. *International Journal of Production Economics, 159*, 1–3. doi:10.1016/j.ijpe.2014.11.014

Zhu, Q. (2023, February 26). *The Doctrine of Cyber Effect: An Ethics Framework for Defensive Cyber Deception.* arXiv.org. https://arxiv.org/abs/2302.13362

Zhu, X., Lu, Z., Hua, T., Yang, F., Tu, G., & Chen, X. (2022). A Novel GPS Meaconing Spoofing Detection Technique Based on Improved Ratio Combined with Carrier-to-Noise Moving Variance. *Electronics (Basel), 11*(5), 738. doi:10.3390/electronics11050738

Zieglmeier, V., Daiqui, G. L., & Pretschner, A. (2023). *Decentralized Inverse Transparency With Blockchain.* Digital Library. doi:10.1145/3592624

Zohra Benhamida, F., Kaddouri, O., Ouhrouche, T., Benaichouche, M., Casado-Mansilla, D., & López-de-Ipina, D. (2021). Demand forecasting tool for inventory control smart systems. *Journal of Communications Software and Systems, 17*(2), 185–196. doi:10.24138/jcomss-2021-0068

Zunarelli, S. (2023). The logistics industry in the digital era: problems and opportunities for the SMEs of the transport sector. *SMEs in the Digital Era: Opportunities and Challenges of the Digital Single Market*, 208. Elger.

About the Contributors

Noor Zaman Jhanjhi (NZ Jhanjhi) is currently working as Associate Professor, Director Center for Smart society 5.0 [CSS5], & Cluster Head for Cybersecurity, at the School of Computer Science and Engineering, Taylor's University, Malaysia. He is supervising a great number of Postgraduate students, mainly in cybersecurity for Data Science. Dr Jhanjhi serves as Associate Editor and Editorial Assistant Board for several reputable journals, received Outstanding Associate Editor Award for IEEE ACCESS for 2020, PC member for several conferences, guest editor for the reputed journals. He is awarded globally as a top 1% reviewer by Publons (WoS). His collective research Impact factor is 400 plus. He has Patents on his account, edited/authored 35 plus research books published by world-class publishers. He is an external Ph.D./Master thesis examiner/evaluator globally, completed more than 22 internationally funded research grants. Served as a keynote speaker for several conferences, presented Webinars, chaired conference sessions, provided Consultancy internationally. His research areas include Cybersecurity, IoT security, Wireless security, Data Science, Software Engineering, UAVs.

***

Muhammad Ashraf received his Bachelor's degree in Avionics Engineering from College of Aeronautical Engineering, Risalpur, National University of Sciences and Technology (NUST), Pakistan. He received his M.S. Information Security Degree from NUST, Pakistan, and PhD (Cryptography) from Middle East Technical University, Ankara Turkiye, in 2013. He is working as the Chair Avionics Engineering Department at Air University Islamabad. He also works as the Director General for the Institute of Avionics and Aeronautics at Air University, Islamabad, Pakistan. His research interests include but are not limited to Public Key Cryptography, Efficient Computation over Finite Fields, Stream Ciphers, Elliptic Cure-based Cryptography, Random Number Generation, and Information Security.

Loveleen Gaur, Program Director (Artificial Intelligence and Data Analytics), Senior IEEE member, and Series Editor. For over 18 years she served in India and abroad in different capacities. Prof. Gaur has significantly contributed to enhancing scientific understanding by participating in over three hundred scientific conferences, symposia, and seminars, by chairing technical sessions and delivering plenary and invited talks. She has specialized in the fields of Artificial Intelligence, Machine Learning, Information Sciences, IoT, Data Analytics. Prof. Gaur pursued research in truly inter-disciplinary areas and authored and co-authored many books with renowned International and National publishers like Elsevier, Springer, Taylor and Francis. She has been invited as Guest Editor for reputed Q1, ABDC, SCI journals. She has also published various research papers in SCI and Q1 Journals. She is actively involved in various professional activities and has chaired various positions in International Conferences of repute and is a reviewer with IEEE, SCI, and ABDC Journals. She is currently involved in various projects of the Government of India and abroad.

Abdalla Hassan Gharib earned his Ph.D. and M.Sc. in Computer Science from Universiti Malaysia Sarawak, Malaysia. Currently, he serves as a lecturer and Quality Assurance Coordinator within the Faculty of Engineering at Zanzibar University, located in Zanzibar, Tanzania. In 2022, he was honored to be appointed as a council member of the Karume Institute of Science and Technology (KIST) by the Minister of Education and Vocational Training, Zanzibar, Tanzania. With numerous research articles to his name and supervision of eight Master's degree students by the end of 2023, Dr. Abdalla Gharib has emerged as a dedicated scholar in the realm of Mobile Communication Networks. His research specialization lies in communication protocols and information dissemination within Opportunistic Networks, addressing scenarios where traditional network infrastructures may be limited or absent. Beyond his core focus, he displays versatility and a wide array of interests, encompassing Artificial Intelligence (AI), Internet of Things (IoT), Quality Assurance, Digital Transformation, Cybersecurity and Graphic Design.. Driven by a profound passion for innovation and technology, his ultimate goal is to assist organizations and communities in harnessing technology ethically for competitive advantage and sustainable societal progress.

Mamoona Humayun has completed her PhD in Computer Sciences from Harbin Institute of Technology, China. She has 15 years of teaching and administrative experience internationally. She has an extensive teaching, research supervision, and administrative work background. She is the guest Editor and reviewer for several reputable journals and conferences around the globe. She has authored several research papers, supervised many postgraduate students, and has an external thesis examiner to her credit. She has strong analytical, problem-solving, interpersonal, and communication skills. Her areas of interest include Cyber Security, Wireless Sensor Networks (WSN), the Internet of Things (IoT), Requirement Engineering, Global Software Development, and Knowledge Management.

Khor Jia Yun has a Bachelor of Science in Computer Science with Campbell University. Masters of Science in Information Technology with Universiti Utara Malaysia (UUM). The title of my Master's Thesis was Pattern Extraction and Rule Generation of Forest Fire using Sliding Window Technique (completed in 2008).

Sidra Tahir is a PhD Scholar (Computer Science) in PMAS Arid Agriculture University, Pakistan. She is working as Lecturer Computer Science at UIIT, PMAS Arid Agriculture University, Rawalpindi. Her research interests are Data Mining, Information Retrieval Systems, Machine Learning, Automation of Business Processes etc.

Chong Eng Tan, an Associate Professor at Universiti Malaysia Sarawak (UNIMAS), has been a dedicated member of the Faculty of Computer Science and Information Technology since 1999. He earned his Ph.D. from the University of Cambridge in 2004, specializing in wireless networks and broadband access technology. With over 25 years of research experience, Dr. Tan has focused his research on connecting remote areas to the internet. Notably, he designed the pilot long-range wireless system in 2010 in Bario and played a pivotal role in establishing Telecentres in remote locations in Malaysia. Dr. Tan is a senior member of the IEEE and a graduate member of IEM, and he currently leads the 5G& Connectivity Keylab, contributing significantly to technology advancements in connectivity and rural ICT solutions. His notable research achievements include the development of the Virtual Telecentre concept and innovative solar power solutions for ICT systems.

Noshina Tariq is an accomplished researcher in Computer Science and Cybersecurity. She completed her Ph.D. and M.S. in Computer Science from FAST - National University of Computer and Emerging Sciences in Islamabad, Pakistan. Her research interests include various aspects of Cybersecurity, such as Network Security, the Internet of Things (IoT), Wireless Sensor Networks (WSN), Fog and Cloud Computing, Blockchain, and Artificial Intelligence. She is an Assistant Professor in the Department of Avionics Engineering and Information Security at Air University, Islamabad, Pakistan. She is also an active research community member, serving as a peer reviewer for many high-repute research journals. With her passion for research and dedication to the field, Dr. Noshina Tariq is poised to contribute further to advancing Cybersecurity and Computer Science.

Anam Zaheer is a research scholar at department of computer science in University of Arid Agriculture University. She is currently doing MS degree in Computer Science from University. Her research interests include machine learning, computer security and information security.

Index

T

W

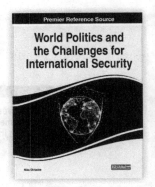

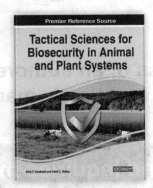

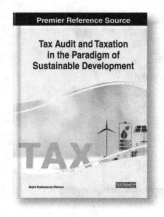

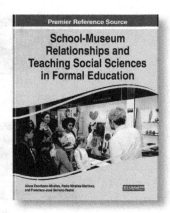
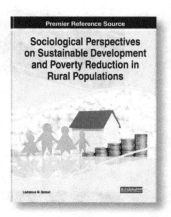

Printed in the United States
by Baker & Taylor Publisher Services